Stephen Oppenheimer qualified in medicine from Oxford University in 1971. After qualifying, he followed a career in tropical paediatrics, and has spent most of the last twenty years working and travelling in the Far East and Pacific region. From 1990 to 1994 he was Professor of Paediatrics at the Chinese University of Hong Kong. Much of his research interest has been in malaria and the unique genetic mutations that protect against it. These mutations acting as markers hold some of the best evidence for the Indo-Pacific migrations that followed the flood at the end of the last ice age – and it was this kind of evidence that first persuaded him to seriously investigate the possibility of 'founder cultures' in Southeast Asia.

Stephen Oppenheimer is the author of many articles in medical and scientific journals, but *Eden in the East* is his first book for the general reader. He is married with two children and now lives in Oxford.

EDEN IN THE EAST

The Drowned Continent of Southeast Asia

STEPHEN OPPENHEIMER

PHŒNIX

FOR MY WIFE FREDA

A Phoenix paperback
First published in Great Britain by Weidenfeld & Nicolson in 1998
This paperback edition published in 1999 by Phoenix,
a division of Orion Books Ltd,
Orion House, 5 Upper St Martin's Lane, London WC2H 9EA

A CIP catalogue record for this book is
available from the British Library.

ISBN: 0 75380 679 7

Printed and bound in Great Britain by
The Guernsey Press Co. Ltd, Guernsey, C.I.

CONTENTS

PART II: CHINESE WHISPERS

ILLUSTRATIONS

PREFACE

The origins of this book go back to 1972, when as a newly qualified doctor I moved out to the Far East and worked in a variety of hospitals scattered around Southeast Asia. This culminated in a flying-doctor job in Borneo. In my time off, I took all possible opportunities to travel around Thailand, Malaysia and Indonesia; the brightly coloured pictures of these varied cultures that flooded my mind were more intense than anything I had experienced travelling in Europe, Morocco and the Middle East. Clearly the Southeast Asian peoples had borrowed much, in terms of religions and ideas, from their Indian and Chinese neighbours on the mainland and also from the West. But I was not so stunned by these diverse images to miss the common cultural base underlying the Hindu, Buddhist, Muslim, Christian and animist societies of Southeast Asia. I began to wonder, then, about the sort of civilisation that had existed before the arrival of Chinese and Indian cultures. Only much later did I begin to appreciate where the balance of cultural debt lay.

A second nudge to my unanswered question came when I was working in Papua New Guinea in the 1980s. After taking higher degrees, I followed a career in tropical paediatrics. In 1978, after a two-year contract as a government paediatrician in Papua New Guinea, my career took an academic turn. I spent the next six years based in the Liverpool School of Tropical Medicine, but working mainly on secondment back in Papua New Guinea. While in New Guinea on my first visit I had developed an interest in origin stories – tales like those found in Genesis, that try to explain where we started. This interest bore unexpected fruit when I returned in 1979 to carry out research on iron-deficiency anaemia in children of the north coast of New Guinea.

I was talking to a village elder about the preliminary results of my field research. I told him about genetic difference in the blood of children from certain villages along the northern coastline. He looked at me curiously and said that those children were the descendants of Kulabob. I discovered later that he was referring to an ancient migration myth 'Kulabob and Manup', well known to the north coastal people. It seemed that this myth was indeed later recognised by anthropologists as a migration myth and that the villagers who were descendants of the itinerant 'Kulabob' spoke languages similar to those of people in Southeast Asia and Polynesia. The genetic mutation in 'the Children of Kulabob' along the north coast of New Guinea protects against malaria and turned out to be a key marker that shadows the migration trail of the Polynesians into the Pacific. The descendants of Manup are thought to be the indigenous Papuans who had migrated to New Guinea much earlier, during the last Ice Age, and mainly by land bridges (the study of that genetic trail still goes on today, and I have also continued with research into the genetic mechanism that protects people from malaria).

So I began to wonder what had led the ancient peoples of Southeast Asia to leave their lush and fertile homeland and sail out into the watery vastness of the Pacific, leaving a genetic, cultural and linguistic 'fingerprint' along the north coast of New Guinea in their passage east.

After Liverpool I moved my base to the University of Oxford and then back out to the East. By this time my own roots lay as much in the East as the West, because I had married a Malaysian research assistant I met in Liverpool. I spent two and a half years as a clinical academic in a Malaysian medical school before moving to a professorial chair in paediatrics in Hong Kong. After four years in this post, I decided to move in 1994 to Borneo.

The third and decisive nudge to my longstanding speculation on Southeast Asia and the Pacific came in 1993, nine months before leaving Hong Kong. I had flown to Manila in the Philippines to give a series of lectures in a medical school, and took time off to visit the National Museum. I stayed until closing time, fascinated by a new display on maritime archaeology. One of the prize exhibits was a long boat, preserved like some Viking boat burial. It so happened there was an opening ceremony that evening for a new exhibition of treasure trove from a sunken galleon. The last stragglers leaving the museum, myself among them, were invited to the cocktail party and ceremony. I met the curator of the museum, Professor Jesus Peralta. I shared my New Guinea obsession with him and he, in return, told me about the numerous flood stories held by different tribes in the Philippines. That evening, and on the flight back over the South China Sea next morning, I speculated about what these stories meant.

As the aircraft climbed, I could see flooded paddy fields, then fish ponds, then, finally, bamboo platforms and large fish traps further out to sea, planted over the shallow water. There was little to tell where the flooded land ended and the sea started. Fishing folk were living both sides of the margin. Almost unconsciously I began to connect the amphibious fishermen, the flood myths and the shallow continental shelf lying under the South China Sea. Then the daydream evaporated. I suddenly realised the real possibility that a flooding of the vast Southeast Asian continental shelf at the end of the Ice Age could have been precisely the stimulus that sent coastal dwellers scattering out to the Pacific, thousands of years ago. In their flight, they would also have carried their legends and concepts of religion, astronomy, magic and social hierarchy. And these ideas and traditions could have been the seeds that fertilised the great civilisations of India, Mesopotamia, Egypt and the Mediterranean.

The improbability of this theory soon re-asserted itself in my mind. The dates were wrong, for a start. According to conventional wisdom, the Polynesians did not start their first migrations until well *after* the sea-level had reached today's point. And, in any case, how could a gradual rising of the sea have been noticed as a flood, or have caused more than a minor irritation?

Over the following months, the idea of the flood myths kept coming back and I began to read widely around the subject. At first, my reading had no more purpose than satisfying my curiosity about Asian flood myths. The more I read, however, the more evidence I found not only for common flood myths around the Asia-Pacific region, but also of astonishing links between a whole range of origin stories right out in the Pacific, and the folklore treasury of the Mediterranean and the Ancient Near East. My reading extended to genetics and historical linguistics, both of which I had touched on in my medical research in Papua New Guinea. Now I turned to oceanography and archaeology as well. I quickly realised that merely trawling for evidence to support my theory might be self-fulfilling but would certainly be unscientific. I had to test the hypothesis using hard evidence from as many disciplines as possible.

In this book I describe my own exploration and analysis of the evidence for the peoples of the lost continent who fertilised the great cultures not only of the Far East but the Middle and Near East as well over 7000 years ago, and provided Eurasia with its library of folklore. I came to believe that all but a few archaeological traces of those founder cultures, located in Southeast Asia, were destroyed by a catastrophic flood at the end of the last Ice Age.

While researching and writing this book, I found I was building on the ideas of others. Several geologists and oceanographers, such as the Americans Bill Ryan and Walt Pitman, regard the flood myths as prehistoric realities and have begun to appreciate the power and rapidity of the rises in sea-level after the Ice Age in, for example, the Black Sea region and elsewhere. Archaeologists in Hong Kong and the United States such as William Meacham and Wilhelm Solheim have recently promoted the idea that the ancestors of today's Polynesians and Indonesians once lived on the submerged continent of Southeast Asia and did not, after all, come from China – as many historical linguists still believe. Several scholars writing over the last hundred years have argued for Polynesian homelands further south and east of China. And the famous Scottish anthropologist and folklorist Sir James Frazer pointed out hundreds of connections between myths of Europe and Asia in the early 1900s; I draw on many of these myths in the second half of this book.

I do, however, claim some new ideas. I believe that I am the first to argue for Southeast Asia as the source of the elements of Western civilisation. Second, the new genetic evidence I shall present shows that Polynesian-speaking people began their great Pacific dispersal from Southeast Asia, not China. And, third, my analysis of folklore links – building on Frazer's pioneering work – confirms a prehistoric East-West connection and provides a logical basis for the original meaning of much Western myth and folklore.

Stephen Oppenheimer
Oxford, February 1998

Postscript

Last week – two weeks before my manuscript was due with the printer – I saw an article in the Sunday Times (26 April 1998) entitled 'Divers Find the World's Oldest Building'. With some reservation, I read on to find that the 'building' in question was of comparable size to the Great Pyramid of Khufu at Giza. Lying 25 metres beneath the ocean just east of Taiwan, it bore some resemblance to the stepped ziggurats of Mesopotamia, although it was made of stone rather than mud bricks. The article claimed antiquity for the structure back beyond 8000 years ago – before the time of the last rise in sea-level.

So far I have been unable to locate any scientific publication describing this stone structure which, along with other similar ones, was found ten years ago by Japanese divers. A number of startling photographs are available on the Internet, one of which is reproduced at the end of this book. Opinion among geologists is divided as to whether the structures are man-made, man-modified or entirely natural phenomena, like the Giant's Causeway in Ireland.

May 1998

ACKNOWLEDGEMENTS

A number of people have helped or given advice in the preparation of *Eden in the East*. Robert Campbell, a school friend now in publishing, advised, over a beer, that I should write up my ideas in a book and introduced me to Felicity Bryan, an excellent agent. My nephew Oli Hein assisted in the literature search for a number of months, taking particular care with the referencing. Michael Rogers introduced me to Sarah Bunney, scientific editor, who gave valuable help and advice in reorganisation of the text. Benjamin Buchan, Emma Baxter and Myrna Blumberg gave expert and tolerant editorial support. John Gilkes did magic with my diagram sketches. Martin Richards, Ian Lilley, Beatrice Clayre, Adrian Clynes, Nicholas Luker, Waruno Mahdi and Aone Van Engelenhoven all kindly read parts of the manuscript and gave useful advice and criticism. Roger Moorey was a mine of useful references on Mesopotamia. Peter Bellwood, while disagreeing with my model of Polynesian origins, was open and generous with his assistance and advice. Michael Pietrusewsky, Robert Blust, Tjeerd H. van Andel, Kurt Lambeck, Richard Huggett, Stephen Jett, Peter Becker, Surin Pookajorn, Somsonge Burusphat, Robert Barnes, Ryk Ward, Chris Gosden, Jean-Michel Chazine, Rosalind Harding, Alexander Adelaar, Jeff Marck, Chris Tyler-Smith, Susanne Schröter, William Meacham, Adrian Johnson and Fr. John Z'Graggen, to name a few, all gave their time, knowledge and insight. Finally and posthumously, Sir James Frazer, still in print after 100 years, remains a source of wonder to all those who read his timeless books.

Acknowledgement of those listed above does not necessarily indicate their agreement with the ideas or arguments expressed in this book.

PROLOGUE

Southeast Asia encompasses one of the richest, most ancient and most diverse cultural regions on Earth. Yet historians have assumed, by default, that Southeast Asian cultures are simply secondary offshoots from the mainland Asian civilisations of India and China. Such a dismissive view is undeserved and ignores abundant evidence of antiquity and unique sophistication.

The region holds some of the most popular tourist destinations in the world. Spread out like a handnet thrown into water by a fisherman, the whole region, islands and all, forms one huge continental platform – the so-called Sunda shelf – approaching the size of North America. Given that most of the area is now sea, it supports a surprisingly large human population. Politically and geographically, there are two distinct regions – mainland and island (see Figure 10). The Asian mainland part has two peninsulas: the large blunt one includes Burma (also known as Myanmar) to the northeast, Thailand in the middle and Laos, Cambodia and Vietnam squeezed like sausages to the east and southeast; the long thin one, the Malay Peninsula, snakes down from Thailand and Burma. Thailand, like an elephant's head on its side, covers the upper two-thirds of this trunk. Today, you can take a train ride from cool upland subtropical Chiang Mai in northern Thailand, through the capital Bangkok, on down the thin peninsula, past limestone mountains with vertical sides, to Penang in Malaysia. The train then goes on through the capital Kuala Lumpur and on to hot, humid Singapore near the equator. I can recommend it as one of the great train rides of Asia (with wonderful food laid on).

Burma is the northernmost country of mainland Southeast Asia, with teak forests and mountains, extraordinary pagodas in Rangoon, carved palaces in Mandalay and the stately ruins of Pagan. Where Burma gives way through Karen country on its eastern side to the uplands of Thailand, you can follow the route of the Buddhist faith down through the older northern capitals of Chiang Rai, Chiang Mai, Muang Lamphun and on through the fine ruins of Sukhothai to Ayutthaya in the south. On the eastern side of the Indo-Chinese peninsula, the north–south coast journey can be taken by rail as well. If anything, the images of endless rice fields backed by mountains are more green and vivid in Vietnam than Thailand. In the far north, beautiful sculpted limestone outcrops stand out in the shallow sea of the Ha Long Bay, which would have been surrounded by dry land less than 10,000 years ago. About halfway down Vietnam, two neighbouring areas, Hue and Danang, show the contrast between Chinese and Indian influence. The Chinese-influenced Imperial city of Hue, although older than Danang, has the younger buildings. Danang is famous for the remains of the Indian-influenced civilisation of the Chams. These brilliant people are linguistically related to the peoples of Borneo and Sumatra. The adventurer will want to visit East Asia's crumbling jewel, the ruins of Angkor Wat, inland in Cambodia with its promise of even older cultures under mounds deep in the jungle.

Nine main islands of Southeast Asia form a semi-circle outside the two central landmasses of Borneo and Sulawesi, and these together are known as 'island Southeast Asia'. Also called the Malay Archipelago, this region has a greater diversity of culture than anywhere else in Asia. (See Figure 10.)

If, after travelling round Thailand and west Malaysia, you were expecting more of the same in island Southeast Asia, you would be surprised. The only features that remain the same are the fruits, and the core, imported religious traditions – Islam, Hinduism, Christianity and Buddhism. Even these have subtle local flavours.

Burma and Thailand are mainly Buddhist, whereas Malaya and the Greater Sunda islands of Sumatra and Java are mainly Muslim. The Philippines, by contrast, are mainly Catholic except in the south, which has a large Muslim population. Other parts of the islands have a variety of religions, both traditional and imported. The influence of Indian cultures over the past 2000 years has been mainly in the Greater Sundas of the west, although it reached as far as East Kalimantan (Indonesian Borneo).

For those who have not had the fortune to visit Southeast Asia, descriptions are inadequate. The combination of fine food, lush scenery, graceful and colourful arts, seas, islands, mountains and crumbling monuments hinting at past splendour is a bounty to the travel courier. Tourists who visit the famous ruins in Indo-China and Java might find it surprising that they are young, when compared, say, with Knossos in Crete and similar ancient sites in the Mediterranean, Europe and the Middle East. Considering their age some Asian ruins are in rather poor repair as a result of war, climate and vegetation.

The famous monumental site at the former Thai capital of Ayutthaya was sacked by the Burmese in 1767. In that year cast-iron tracks were first made for trams in the West, and it was also shortly before the mutiny on the *Bounty*. Polynesians were making their late great push from Samoa to the eastern Pacific by AD 500, several hundred years before the founding of the most famous early monumental sites, such as Angkor in Cambodia, Prambanan and Borobudur in Java, and Chiang Mai in northern Thailand. Angkor Wat, along with the magnificent temple city of Pagan, on the Irawaddy River in Burma, were not built until after the Norman invasion of England, and Sukhothai, the last Thai capital before Ayutthaya, was founded in the twelfth century AD. Of the earliest accessible great monumental sites, the Champa towers in Vietnam are well worth seeing. What remains of them after the war is found scattered around Danang on the east coast. Some of these date to the time of the Roman Empire. Vietnam also has the earliest Southeast Asian urban sites. Those at Co Loa inland in the north date to the third century BC.

One characteristic unites the famous monumental sites in Southeast Asia that I have mentioned: they were all built by locally based, but Indianised, societies. They feature both Buddhist and Hindu religious images. Chinese culture also had an enormous effect on Vietnam particularly in the north, starting from around 200 BC, although we have less in the way of architectural remains from that period. Influence from these big neighbours was much more by trade than invasion. Three different groups of maritime traders plied the coast of the Indian Ocean from 2000 years ago – Arab, Indian and Southeast Asian. The latter started at a much earlier date. The moulding influence of Indian and Chinese culture on the arts and religion of Southeast Asia over this period is reflected in the name of the mainland region: Indo-China.

Southeast Asia: a lost prehistory

Given the extraordinary cultural diversity in Southeast Asia I find the lack of curiosity about the origins of these unique civilisations puzzling. A Western example of this cultural bias lies in the story of the discovery of language families. Two hundred years ago it was realised that most Indian and European languages belonged to a single family, now called the Indo-European language group. This insight has been called one of the great intellectual achievements of the time. The cultural self-discovery that it engendered was even said to have contributed significantly to the Romantic movement. In contrast, the discovery of the Austronesian language group a few years earlier stimulated no such curiosity until the 1970s. The languages that have spread as far as Madagascar, Easter Island, Taiwan, Hawai'i and New Zealand all form one family with those in Southeast Asia. They had spread across the Pacific and probably round the Indian Ocean before Buddha was born.

Books on the origins of world civilisations leave out Southeast Asia completely. Histories of specific countries in the region usually skip the prehistoric period in a few lines and concentrate on the Indian and Chinese-influenced cultures of the last 2000 years and the later colonial periods. Until recently, the Bronze Age Dong Son culture, and its forerunners in Vietnam of the first millennium BC, was virtually the only early complex civilisation to be given credence as indigenous to the region. Ethnographers often find ancient religious, magical and mythological beliefs among Pacific islanders that have close parallels with European and Near Eastern cultures. They usually make the assumption of a West-to-East influence. Yet there is no evidence of such a cultural flow before the relatively recent period of European exploration.

There are more reasons than cultural arrogance for this blinkered view of Southeast Asian prehistory. One is that, apart from in Thailand and Vietnam, archaeologists have scratched only the surface of known Neolithic and Bronze Age sites in Southeast Asia. Another reason is lack of decipherable written records of the pre-Indian period. A third – probably important – reason may be that most of the relevant sites in the region are now under water.

Several recent archaeological finds have cast doubt on the accepted view that this area was first civilised from China and the West. Systematic agriculture in Indonesia long antedated parallel achievements in the traditional Old World cradles of the Neolithic Revolution in the Near East. Evidence of wild yam and taro cultivation has been found in Indonesia dating between 15,000 and 10,000 BC. Furthermore, rice cultivation may have been practised as far back as the sixth to seventh millennium BC in peninsula Thailand – significantly earlier than the Chinese discovered it.

Astonishingly early Bronze Age artefacts have been found in grave sites in Ban Chiang, in southern Thailand and Phung Nguyen in northern Vietnam. The dating of these sites has aroused much controversy, but, recently, impeccable carbon dates taken from rice chaff within pots has given confidence for a Bronze Age date of the early second millennium BC in Ban Chiang. Two of these dates went back much further – one to nearly 5000 years ago and the other to nearly 6000 years ago. These latter dates, if valid, would straddle the earliest Near Eastern Bronze Age sites, and would be before the Chinese achieved this stage of development.

These developments in Southeast Asia are generally thought to have been independent of the same events happening far to the west, and were in any case thousands of years before the advent of Indian influence in Southeast Asia during the early Christian era. Parts of Southeast Asia thus mastered skills that were achieved during the graduation of the Sumerian, Egyptian and Indus Valley civilisations, but apparently at the same time, if not earlier. If Southeast Asians learnt their skills of civilisation from Indians, who taught them farming and metallurgical technology thousands of years before? And what were they doing during the gap? Such gaps in the timeline of East Asian archaeology are a feature going back over 10,000 years.

When breakthroughs like cereal farming, pottery and bronze-making occur at the same time in widely separated regions, the usual explanation is that the discoveries were independent. This may seem a weak argument, but for academics it is much safer to say this, rather than risk ridicule by having to prove how the inventions were transmitted over a great distance. Theoretically, however, both points of view have an obligation of proof. The alternative hypothesis for the Neolithic Revolution – and one which seems more plausible than the independent origins implied by the archaeological record – is that the farming technology was invented in one cultural region over a long period; knowledge of the innovations then spread to other continents by sea and land routes. To have escaped the archaeologists' attention, such a culture would need to have been permanently flooded or have suffered the volcanic fate of the island of Thera (Santorini) in the Eastern Mediterranean. The Sunda continental shelf of Southeast Asia and the east coast of China are prime candidate sites where such catastrophic obliteration occurred.

Three great revolutions occurred in the development of human societies, during the sea-level rise after the Ice Age. After farming and metallurgy, the last was the simultaneous flowering of sophisticated civilisations in the Near East from 3200 to 2500 BC. These dates coincide with the plateau of post-glacial sea-level rise. The new civilisations included Sumer, Elam, Upper Egypt, Crete, Syria, Palestine and the Indus Valley. They were different from each other in many respects, but shared cultural features that distinguished them from the Neolithic agricultural societies from which they had all sprung. Among their characteristics were the formation of city states with monumental building, hierarchical societies, priest rulers, similar theogonies and creation myths. Common technological developments included the inventions of pictographic writing and metallurgy. Above all, there was a flourishing of fine arts. It should be stressed that although the innovation was shared, the expression was unique in each civilisation. For instance, the original pictographic scripts of Sumer, Elam and Egypt appeared within generations of each other around 3000 BC, but were all different in style and function.

Lost continents and civilisations

Other authors have suggested a lost founder-civilisation. In his 1995 bestseller *Fingerprints of the Gods*, investigative journalist Graham Hancock uses many ancient intercontinental religious and technological links to argue for a lost founder-civilisation in the Antarctic. A key to his argument is the analysis by Charles Hapgood (1966) of the well-authenticated 'Piri Re'is' map, thought to have been copied by Arab scholars from lost originals in the great Library of Alexandria. This map, drawn on gazelle hide by a Turkish admiral in 1513, shows, with an appropriate projection, a reasonably accurate representation of the Atlantic coast of the Antarctic *beneath* the present ice cap. The other features shown with equal accuracy on the map are the east coast of South America and the west coast of Africa and Europe. Several other maps of the time, discovered by Hapgood, show similar features. Since the last time the Antarctic continent was free of ice was around 4000 BC, Hancock's hypothesis, made previously by other authors, is that someone living at least 6000 years ago had the seafaring and mathematical ability to survey coastlines and calculate global projections. The Europeans could not even do this in 1513. The other implication is that an advanced civilisation travelled round the Atlantic a very long time ago. There is in fact other evidence, not mentioned in his book, that advanced seafaring populations colonised both sides of the North Atlantic at least 7000 years ago.

To back his theory of older civilisations, Hancock also cites John West, a self-taught American tour guide in Egypt. West has developed an exotic view of Egyptian prehistory that has upset conventional archaeologists. What has annoyed the establishment most is that he has converted some academics to his view that the Sphinx is much older than supposed. His evidence of ancient water-erosion lines at the base of this monument, suggesting an ancient and long-lasting flood, has had geological support.

Much of the rest of *Fingerprints of the Gods* deals with artefacts of the Ancient Near East and of South and Central America, but Hancock places the site of his lost civilisation in the Antarctic. His main argument for this choice is that Antarctica is the only continent now inaccessible to archaeologists that could hide the evidence, thus fulfilling a requirement of anonymity.

I am, to a certain extent, using a similar argument for a different continent – the drowned Sunda shelf of Southeast Asia. But for the following reasons, I think my choice of continent is more plausible: it is likely that the Antarctic coast was briefly free of ice when sea-levels were high around 7000 years ago, and also possible that an advanced maritime civilisation could have mapped it at the time. Most of the continent, however, would still have been under an ice cap and the window of time that any civilisation would have had to develop in Antarctica was much shorter than that postulated by Hancock. In contrast, Southeast Asia theoretically had the whole Ice Age to nurture its first civilisation. What is more, there clearly appears to be surviving local evidence for that civilisation.

As mentioned above, stories of a civilisation-destroying catastrophe are older than writing. The commonest event described in these myths was a flood preceded by a deluge. Sea-level rise was also mentioned, as were seismic disturbances. Besides the earthly causes, which include melting ice caps, several writers have suggested cosmic events to account for the dramatic nature of the legendary disaster and to explain the extinction of so many mammals at the end of the Ice Age. The most famous and controversial of these catastrophists was Immanuel Velikovsky. This distinguished Russian-born polymath published a book called *Worlds in Collision* in 1950 that caused immediate furore. He produced detailed evidence to support his theory that Venus repeatedly approached the Earth more than 4000 years ago, causing widespread natural disasters because of gravitational effects, overheating and flooding. The intensity of the hate campaign directed at him by the establishment might tempt us to suspect that he was not merely a crank but had germs of plausibility in his predictions, many of which incidentally turned out later to be correct.

Although such a dramatic cosmic event could have accelerated the sea-level rise that I think was the source of the flood myths, it is not essential for my hypothesis. There is already ample oceanographic evidence of the three massive and rapid ice-melts that accounted for the bulk of the 120–130 metre rise in the world sea-levels after the last Ice Age. I am also not the first to suggest a rise in sea-level as the origin of the flood myth (although at present it is not the most fashionable explanation). It has the additional advantage of providing a motive for the prehistoric colonisation of the Southwest Pacific.

Several authors from the nineteenth century onwards have claimed connections between megalithic (big stones) cultures around the world. Some examples have survived until recent times in Southeast Asia and the Pacific, and others have left their mark in Europe, Asia and the New World. The idea of antiquity and unity between such cultures was increasingly popular at the turn of the century. In his *Outline of History* published in 1920 the English novelist and historian H. G. Wells reviewed evidence for the worldwide distribution of the so-called 'Heliolithic' cultures and 'Brunet' races among whom he included the Polynesians. The Heliolithic theory, which had sun-worshipping megalithic cultures radiating out of Egypt, was championed by English anatomist Sir Grafton Elliot Smith in the 1920s, but due to lack of evidence later fell into disrepute. This example has often been used as a cautionary tale for those venturing too far into cultural diffusionism. In spite of a blanket of academic disapproval, these sorts of ideas have never quite left popular imagination and resurface from time to time outside the academic establishment. More recently, Norwegian adventurer Thor Heyerdahl has published five popular books since the Second World War suggesting various prehistoric cultural links between the continents. Heyerdahl captured popular imagination not only with his idea of the colonisation of Polynesia from Peru, but with his courage in personally putting his theory to the test. His 'Kon Tiki' expedition from Peru to Easter Island by balsa-wood raft was one of the epics of twentieth-century exploration.

Footprints on the beach: did East come West?

The idea of teachers from the East is not new. As I argue in greater detail in the second half of this book (Chapters 8–16), there is evidence for an ancient unknown civilisation that fertilised the northwest coast of the Indian Ocean in the written, artistic and archaeological record of the Near East, as well as in the incomplete prehistory of Southeast Asia. Both of the two main contenders for the first civilisation – Egypt and Sumer – have stories and evidence of Eastern influence at their beginnings.

Several archaeologists have argued for an early Eastern input in Pre-dynastic Egypt before 3000 BC. Evidence for this includes artistic styles in bas reliefs, architecture and paintings on pottery of large timber-built ships with high masts. It has usually been assumed, for lack of any other likely site, that this Eastern influence was Mesopotamian. The parallels between the two civilisations, however, suggest cousinship rather than paternity. The Egyptian *Book of the Dead*, which is thought to contain much Pre-dynastic material, mentions the East sixteen times, mainly in a tone of fear. It is described as a place of slaughter across the seas from which the soul has to be protected. This ancient book also mentions several times 'the domain of Manu across the water ... where Ra returns to'. Curiously, Manu in Hindu mythology is the progenitor of humanity, one of whose incarnations was 'Manu the fisherman'. This Manu, incidentally, was also the Indian equivalent of Noah.

In Mesopotamia, the statements of Eastern influence were more direct. The biblical version, based on earlier Sumerian texts, is the best known. Eden is placed in the East in Genesis 2. Genesis 11 relates that: 'as men migrated from the east, they found a plain ... of Shinar [Sumer] and settled there.' They subsequently built the tower (or ziggurat) of Babel, and further suffered a confusion of languages.

Linguistically the Sumerians were odd ones out in the region. They spoke a so-called 'agglutinative' language unrelated to those of either their Indo-European or Semitic neighbours. The other agglutinative language spoken in the region, Elamite, was also an orphan. Most authorities agree that Sumerians came from somewhere east, and had also mastered the art of sailing, but the precise location of their eastern origin remains speculative. There is now evidence from several sources that the arrival of the Sumerians in Mesopotamia was preceded by a major rise in sea-level; this will be discussed in detail in Chapters 1–3. As newcomers to the shores of the Arabian Gulf, the Sumerians had an electrifying effect on the Neolithic culture of the early indigenous 'Ubaidian population. These followers of Ea the sea god supposedly taught the Mesopotamians all their skills, thus also suggesting a seafaring origin of the newcomers. The archaeology of the Near East takes on a new dimension when put in the context of ancient sea-levels.

These selections from Westerners' earliest written attempts to describe where their cultural roots came from hold two common themes: the concept of an original catastrophe and a dispersal from the East. Other early written accounts that combine the elements of a lost civilisation and a catastrophe include the legends of Atlantis, a Lost Eden and the flood myths. The common underlying theme of an original civilisation or Golden Age destroyed in a great disaster has spawned thousands of articles and commentaries over the millennia. I have mentioned but a few.

With the hindsight of twentieth-century oceanographers, who tell us of a huge continent that really did sink below the waves just before the time of the first Western civilisations, we may now be able to make more sense of those stories of cataclysm, death, dispersal and a new start.

The flood in Southeast Asia and the Asian dispersal

After the Ice Age, the worst effects of the flood were in those areas with coastal cultures and flat continental shelves, such as Southeast Asia and China. The geological story reveals that the flood was not gradual – three sudden ice-melts between 14,000 and 7000 years ago resulted in three episodes of rapid flooding as water ran off the polar ice caps of both hemispheres to the oceans. The sudden shift of water from land to sea also caused deep cracks in the Earth's crust, which set off huge tidal waves.

At the height of the Ice Age around 20,000–18,000 years ago, Southeast Asia formed a continent twice the size of India, and included what we now call Indo-China, Malaysia, and Indonesia. The South China Sea, the Gulf of Thailand and the Java Sea, which were then all dry, formed the connecting parts of the continent. Geologically, this half-sunken continent is termed the Sunda shelf, or Sundaland. The flat land area lost by Sundaland after the Ice Age was as large as India. Eventually only the scattered mountainous islands of the Malay archipelago were left. A similar and vast swathe of land was also lost from the Pacific coast of Asia. Land that formerly stretched between Korea, Japan, China and Taiwan is now called the Yellow Sea and the East China Sea. Today's ports along the present south coastline of China, such as Hong Kong, were hundreds of miles inland during the Ice Age.

This book discusses the possibility that when the final dramatic rise in water-level occurred between about 8000 and 7500 years ago, the last of a series of emigrations from the sinking Sunda shelf began. Migration routes went south towards Australia, east towards the Pacific, west into the Indian Ocean and north into the Asian Mainland. Today's descendants of the eastern refugees in the Pacific, inhabiting the many islands of Melanesia, Polynesia and Micronesia, speak languages of the Austronesian family, which they share with island Southeast Asians. In their flight they carried their domestic animals and food plants with them in large ocean-going canoes. Some of those who fled west took rice-growing into India. Those in northern Sundaland fled north into Indo-China and Asia and founded sophisticated cultures in Southwest China, Burma and Tibet. Some of the splendid artefacts of these early civilisations are only now being unearthed.

The northern migrants from the flooded lands of Indo-China may have spoken tongues of the other great Southeast Asian language families Austro-Asiatic, Tibeto-Burman and Tai-Kadai. Above all, the initial flood-forced dispersals established communication and trade routes throughout Eurasia and the South Pacific that ensured the subsequent rapid and continuous flow of ideas, knowledge and skills during the following millennia.

Of all the postulated different dispersals, the refugees who may have retained their original culture with least dilution are those who went east into the Pacific. From the time of their diaspora until the arrival of European explorers, these closely related groups remained in a relative cultural isolation, separated from the rest of Asia by New Guinea and island Melanesia and a large expanse of ocean. The Polynesians who spread the furthest east finally arrived in Fiji and Samoa only around 3500 years ago and then went on to colonise eastern Polynesia 1500 years ago, but their ancestors had started moving through island Southeast Asia long before then, certainly before there was any significant Indian or Chinese influence in that region. In many ways, therefore, these argonauts of the Pacific may carry the nearest image to the original Southeast Asian emigrants. Early visitors such as Captain Cook in the eighteenth century recorded their complex stratified societies and remarkable navigation skills. While the latter were essential for their success, the former seems to hark back to a grander past.

The Polynesians' spiritual life was rich with large pantheons. In all groups the Sun God was paramount and in some he was called Ra, as in Ancient Egypt. Almost without exception their myths recalled a lost earthly paradise to the west or northwest, called variously Avaiki and Bolutu. A story similar to Adam and Eve was widespread, with most languages using *ivi* as the word for a bone. Furthermore, a story of two brothers of different cultures having a fight was prevalent. The ancestors of these people, and their Austro-Asiatic-speaking neighbours now on the Asian mainland, founded the first complex societies in Southeast Asia. While cereal agriculture was a mainland development, hierarchical societies, the concept of kingship, magic, religion and astronomy were features of the maritime coastal Austronesian peoples. What I suggest here is that these developments *preceded* similar changes in western Asia, and that in their dispersals the Southeast Asian explorers fertilised the Neolithic cultures of China, India, Mesopotamia, Egypt and Crete.

Because I propose a revision of conventional views of prehistory and the origins of early civilisations, all potential sources of that prehistory need critical appraisal. It is in human nature to wonder about our ancestors. The study of history and archaeology is a self-conscious and objective extension of this interest in the past. From the time of

Herodotus histories have been written in abundance. Archaeologists have further unearthed tablets in Mesopotamia (modern Iraq) that stretch the written record sketchily back to the protoliterate period (circa 3200–2800 BC). Even history of the third millennium BC, however, still relies heavily on the archaeological record to verify the written one. The dating of the rulers of the earliest Western civilisation of Sumer in Mesopotamia remains problematic: anything before this time is 'prehistory', for which archaeology provides the only recognised record.

For countries where writing developed late, the prehistoric record is generally supplied by archaeology. In Southeast Asia and the Pacific, where early written historical records are absent, even archaeology fails to furnish a continuous picture of the earliest developments in farming. Prehistorians have resorted to studying the family trees of languages to trace population movements. They have then tried to marry the linguistic 'history' with the incomplete archaeological record. There are many problems and pitfalls with this 'archaeolinguistic' approach, not the least of which are the gaps in the archaeological record and the lack of accuracy in dating the linguistic record. In spite of the appearance of a united front in some schools, there is also no agreement among linguists as to the relationship of the main East Asian language families, or where they originated in Asia.

Because of the gaps in the prehistory of the Far East and Southeast, we have to look at other sources to illuminate the past. Genetics has advanced our knowledge of ancient migrations over great time periods, and of population movements in more recent times. So far, however, it has helped more in testing theories derived from the linguists and archaeologists than in suggesting its own models. Recent discoveries described in Chapters 6 and 7 will help change this, and put Southeast Asia at the centre of migrations after the Ice Age.

History in myth

There is another, more controversial source of ancient history, that may have a greater time depth than language. This is folklore in secular and religious traditions. Folk-tales – bizarre echoes of the past – started me on an unlikely trail of Asian prehistory. The folk-tales (legends, myths and fairy-tales), creation stories, sagas and epics composed over the millennia are the oldest expression of people's interest in their forebears. In addition, sacred texts largely consist of chronicles, genealogies and creation myths. In their search for other windows on the past, scholars have increasingly turned to such texts as potential sources of information. For example, study of the Bible as a historical source is an established discipline, with an increasingly secular approach. Archaeological findings of contemporary texts in Syria and Mesopotamia have tended to reinforce and corroborate the historical basis of the Old Testament.

Although many of the later Old Testament books are clearly historiographic – written as history and containing verifiable detail – the reader may wonder if the Genesis stories of creation, the Garden of Eden and Cain and Abel, could ever have historical relevance. I found, to my surprise, that they *do* act as prehistoric allegories. For example, the biblical Cain and Abel are clearly not brothers but competing cultures. The biblical and Sumerian versions portray Cain as a farmer and Abel as a herder. The Pacific versions of this story have one brother as a dark-skinned hunter-gatherer, whereas the other is a paler-skinned coastal fisherman who invaded from the sea. Much information can be obtained by objectively comparing the content of such stories. The approach is analogous to historical linguistics. Like our languages and our genes, traditional stories are related to each other in a measurable way. Consequently, we can construct family trees.

In contrast to biblical study, the use of folk-tales, origin myths and epics for clarifying events in ancient history and prehistory have not been generally recommended by scholars. There are obvious reasons for this caution. As a class, these stories are imaginative, rich in supernatural events and appear to lack useful context. To most readers they are incredible and fantastic. Academic reserve has not, however, stopped some eminent archaeologists from chasing these tales. The most famous successes in this line were the discovery and excavations of legendary Troy and Mycenae by Heinrich Schliemann and of Minoan Knossos by Sir Arthur Evans. Notable past failures have been the search for the 'lost' continent of Atlantis and for evidence of Noah's Ark. In spite of the continuing lack of convincing evidence the last two legends, however, have been the most persistent of all. Between them they have launched more than two thousand books.

Apart from their quasi-historical and allegorical content, there is a recognised academic aspect to the study of folk-tales. The collection and comparison of folk-tales, myths and legends in their own right have a respectable pedigree. Starting in the nineteenth century with the Grimm brothers, Hans Christian Andersen, Andrew Lang and Sir James Frazer, research has emphasised the similarities between stories from different parts of the world. These similarities have been much more widespread than cultural and linguistic affinities would predict. A famous example is *The Golden Bough*, first published in 1914. In this ethnological odyssey, Sir James Frazer traced an obscure custom of priestly succession, first described in the Temple of Diana at Nemi in Italy. He found echoes of the rite in every continent of the Old and New Worlds. But although Frazer's work had an enormous impact, his approach to the study of folklore sadly went out of fashion with academics in the first part of the twentieth century. Because the archaeological record of prehistory in Southeast Asia and the Far East is as yet incomplete, I have chosen to look more critically at such tales as additional sources of prehistory in the second half of this book, as they may hold some of the best clues we are ever likely to have.

PART I

STONES, BONES, GENES AND TONES

INTRODUCTION TO PART I

The theory that I present in this book places Southeast Asia for the first time at the centre of the origins of culture and civilisation. I argue that many people were driven out of their coastal homes in the East by flooding. These refugees then fertilised the great civilisations in the West. In this first half of the book, I look at the evidence supporting the story of dispersal using four conventional tools of the prehistorian: geology, archaeology, linguistics and genetics. In my synthesis, some elements are not in doubt, others are recent but established discoveries, while still others contain a degree of speculation and need to be argued.

To simplify things, I would like to start with the established facts of the floods. It is beyond doubt that during the Ice Age, Southeast Asia was a single huge continent – a land mass which included Indo-China, Malaysia and Indonesia. After the Ice Age ended there was a dramatic rise in sea-level that split up the continent into the archipelago of islands we see today. The same process flooded the Arabian Gulf and swamped the coast of China. The land-bridge between North America and Asia also disappeared. Many other coasts were affected. In the last two decades evidence has accumulated showing that the rise in sea-level after the last Ice Age was not gradual; three sudden ice-melts, the last of which was only 8000 years ago, had a catastrophic effect on tropical coasts with flat continental shelves. Rapid land loss was compounded by great earthquakes, caused by cracks in the earth's crust as the weight of ice shifted to the seas. It is fairly certain that these quakes set off superwaves in the world's great oceans. I will present this evidence in Chapter 1. What is not clearly established is how these world-shaking events affected the people inhabiting Southeast Asia and the coasts of the Indo-Pacific region.

To answer these questions, we should naturally ask archaeologists. In contrast to the historic and protohistoric periods, which have ancient texts to illuminate them, the prehistoric period is completely dependent for hard information on archaeological remains. Archaeologists are good at reconstructing and dating ancient sites, but the main danger of this dependence lies in the missing record. Certain Neolithic skills – such as the cultivation of domestic rice – may have taken a long time to develop. Without archaeological evidence of the early stages, archaeologists might call the first appearance of the fully fledged skill an 'agricultural revolution'. Furthermore, if archaeological evidence of such early agricultural breakthroughs – or, for instance, of bronze-casting – was unavailable in one region, but accessible elsewhere, a later date in the first area would imply that it had lagged behind, and was learnt from the other region. This seems to have been the case in East and Southeast Asia.

Although there is some element of chance in finding good archaeological sites, it would be bad luck to miss them all over such a large region as Southeast Asia. We would require a major catastrophe, which left little evidence of its passing, to produce such a regional void in the archaeological record. Three such catastrophes *did* happen, and affected the western rim of the Pacific more than anywhere else in the world. These, as has already been mentioned, were the rapid episodic ice-melts at the end of the Ice Age that led to three rises in sea-level over low-lying continental shelves. Each was followed by apparent revolutions or cultural milestones.

The oceanographic record shows that the sea rose at least 120 metres (500 feet) during three floods, which started approximately 14,000, 11,500 and 8000 years ago, respectively. This accelerated period of sea-level rise had three effects on the evidence of human activities. First, in Southeast Asia and China, where there is a flat continental shelf, any evidence of coastal and lowland settlements and technology before 8000 years ago was drowned for ever (see Chapters 1 and 2). Second, during the third and final rise in sea-level, water spread out widely on flat continental shelves, and did not start retreating until about 5500 years ago. Those coastal settlements dating from between 7500 to 5500 years ago that still remain above water are therefore now covered with a thick layer of silt. Archaeologists have peered beneath this layer in Mesopotamia, south China, Southeast Asia and Melanesia to find evidence of the last dispersal caused by the floods. Third, the inhabitants of the flooded coastal settlements would have been forced to move, carrying any skills they had elsewhere (see Chapters 2 and 3).

These predictions are borne out in the strange chronology of the Neolithic Revolution in Eurasia. The Pacific Rim countries seemed to start their revolution well before the West, but then apparently stopped. Around 12,500 years ago, not long after the first flood, pottery appeared for the first time in southern Japan. Some 1500 years later there is evidence of pots being made in China and Indo-China. These examples of pottery making antedate any from Mesopotamia, India or the Mediterranean region by 2500–3500 years. Stones for grinding wild cereal grains appeared in the Solomon Islands of the Southwest Pacific as early as 26,000 years ago, whereas they were not apparently used in Upper Egypt and Nubia until about 14,000 years ago, and in Palestine some 12,000 years ago.

Around 11,000 years ago about the same time as the Chinese started making pots, sheep were first domesticated in northern Mesopotamia and einkorn wheat was harvested in Syria. Within a thousand years, fully domesticated wheat, barley and pulses were being cultivated in Jericho, and the fertile crescent of the Ancient Near East moved into an agricultural revolution that eventually spread the new domesticated crops and animals from Asia Minor (Turkey) to Iraq and on to Pakistan by 9000 years ago. Also around that time, the first farming village was built in Asia Minor and, finally, the first pots were made in the Near East, 3500 years later than in Japan. By 9000 years ago therefore, the Ancient Near East was well into its Neolithic Revolution.

In other scattered parts of the world people had also begun cultivating crops by 9000 years ago. Barley cultivation was developed in the Indus Valley, and root crops such as taro were grown in the Highlands of New Guinea. Incredibly for such an early date, the New Guinean Highlanders were already using ditches to drain swamps for crop-growing. By 9000 years ago, crop cultivation had also started in North, Central and South America.

The explanations for the rapidity of this extraordinary worldwide revolution are meagre. Some authorities quote the improvement in environmental conditions after the Ice Age. In the subtropical and temperate areas, however, where much evidence of the Neolithic Revolution has been found, the climate had been temperate-to-warm throughout the Ice Age. The picture of a clement, stable environment after the Ice Age is also unconvincing; coastal conditions were, if anything, unstable and deteriorating.

There are two notable absentee regions to that first Eurasian flowering of agricultural skills – the east coast of Asia and Southeast Asia. If the fertile crescent of the Near East is, for the sake of argument, taken as a model fast-track developer, the first records of making a pot – that durable artefact so loved by archaeologists – come just 1000 years after farming in the Near East. It is puzzling, then, that although the first pots were made in Japan, China and Indo-China thousands of years before, rice was apparently not grown as a domestic crop anywhere in Asia until about 8000 years ago. Why is there this gap? There is certainly fragmentary evidence of a Neolithic lifestyle in East Asia, with a wide range of tools such as choppers, scrapers, awls and grinding stones, as well as pots, hearths and kitchen waste going back to a much earlier period. This Neolithic debris, however, tends to be scattered in inland caves.

Caves in both China and Southeast Asia have been the best, and often the only, sources of early remains. Was this the preferred place of habitation? Surely not all the Asians were troglodytes? What is missing in the early Neolithic record in East Asia is what past travellers saw and what we still see today – a thriving coastal culture with rice and other crops and intensive marine exploitation. This is absent, as is any other evidence of human activity. There is an almost total absence of open Neolithic sites in lowland areas dating from 10,000 to 5000 BC.

The situation in island Southeast Asia is even more bizarre. A decade ago, there was no archaeological evidence of rice-growing in Indonesia or East Malaysia older than 1500 years. This date is a thousand years after estimated dates for the introduction of bronze and iron artefacts to the same region. Prehistorians thus described island Southeast Asia, south of the Philippines, as moving into the Bronze and Iron Ages from the Stone Age before there was any local evidence of rice-growing. As I describe in Chapters 2 and 4, however, there is exciting new evidence from Sakai Cave in southern Thailand suggesting that rice-growing started in Indo-China even before the last flood, and the skill could have been carried west to India. The present archaeological evidence of early agriculture in China and Southeast Asia may, therefore, give an incomplete story of its development. Because of coastal inundation, evidence of earlier agriculture in the coastal areas is now likely to be deep under water. Supporting this is the observation that the earliest sites with evidence of agriculture in Asia are generally in inland and upland parts.

The result of this nearly blank sheet in Southeast Asian Neolithic prehistory is that archaeological views have polarised. One side – the majority – sees the island Southeast Asian Neolithic period as starting only perhaps 4000 years ago, with migrants coming down from China through Taiwan and the Philippines. The other group, with whom I agree, argue that the ancestors of the people in Southeast Asia today were living there at the end of the Ice Age and not only developed their sailing and agricultural skills much earlier than people in the Near East, but started long-distance sailing round Asia and the Pacific more than 7000 years ago. The archaeological and linguistic arguments for the second view form the bulk of Chapters 3 and 5 respectively.

The final, and perhaps most compelling technical evidence – that the present inhabitants of Southeast Asia have been there since the Ice

Age, and started moving in all directions at the time of the floods – comes from the genes they carry (see Chapters 6 and 7). Gene markers reveal Aboriginals of Southeast Asia at the root of Asian family trees and spreading to all points of the compass as far as America and the Middle East. One particular marker – called the 'Polynesian motif' because such a high proportion of Polynesians carry it – originated in the people of Maluku (the Moluccas) in eastern Indonesia during the Ice Age. The fact that this marker has not so far been found in China, Taiwan or the Philippines contradicts the conventional theory and allows a much older view of Southeast Asian prehistory.

1

AN ICE AGE AND THREE FLOODS

The image of teams of fundamentalist investigators solemnly marching up Mount Ararat to search for the remaining timbers of the Ark arouses amusement in all but those of a similar persuasion. Any discussion of the historicity of Noah's flood and other flood myths had a similar reaction in geological circles until recently. The history of people's attempts to explain the flood stories helps to understand why the topic still arouses such antagonism in scientific circles. We need only go back to the late eighteenth century to find the origin of this prejudice. We will see that any concept of the historicity of Noah's flood went out with the bathwater of indignant anti-clerical feeling among nineteenth-century uniformitarians.

From the earliest records until 200 years ago, Noah's flood was regarded as a historical fact. In 1785, however, a Scottish geologist called James Hutton introduced the concept of uniformitarianism according to which the history of the Earth could be interpreted solely on the basis of gradual geological processes working at a uniform rate.[1] Because he envisaged millions of years for these processes to take place, he created much antagonism from scientifically inclined Christian believers. This was because the current theological view of the day held that the Earth was only about 4000 years old. Hutton's first most notable antagonist was a French naturalist, Georges Cuvier, who argued that the geological features around us were caused by a series of abrupt natural disasters such as floods and earthquakes. Cuvier's view came to be known as catastrophism. The stage was set for a battle between uniformitarianism and catastrophism that has oscillated to and fro up to this day.

Hutton was initially ignored because his views were anathema to Christians of the time. The first victory for the uniformitarian camp in geological circles came in the 1830s with Charles Lyell's championing of uniformitarianism in his *Principles of Geology*. An apparent reverse to the uniformitarian cause then came in 1837, when Louis Agassiz in his *Discourse of Neuchâtel* lucidly presented a catastrophic glacial theory. Although Agassiz was not the first to have the idea of past ice ages, his contribution to the debate was the most significant in terms of impact. Uniformitarian Charles Lyell at first naturally denounced Agassiz's catastrophic ideas, but he later came to accept them and became one of their most enthusiastic proponents.

Thus the glacial theory came to be adopted into the uniformitarian camp as being sufficiently gradualist, and in any case very attractive. With the loss of the powerful, essentially catastrophic idea as an arguing point, catastrophist geologists, who believed, among other things, in the doctrine of Noah's flood, became a defensive and dying minority led by the Scottish scientist Roderick Impey Murchison. It was the demise of the flood doctrine that led Sir James Frazer, the distinguished British ethnologist and folklorist, to state confidently in his analysis of flood stories early in the twentieth century that there had been no Noah's flood: '... for, if the best accredited testimony of modern geology can be trusted, no such cataclysm has befallen the earth during the period of man's abode on it'.[2]

In retrospect it can also be seen that the idea of the historicity of the great flood suffered particularly from its association with religious orthodoxy. Lyell, after all, rubbed shoulders with Charles Darwin and was particularly vigorous in rejecting what he saw as the influence of theological prejudice on the new science of geology. After its rout, catastrophism really reared its head again only in the middle of the twentieth century with the writings of Immanuel Velikovsky.[3] Then the latent fury and venom of the scientific establishment was unleashed on him like a Jehad.

In this chapter, I will describe three great world floods. These happened within the context of the only type of catastrophe that the nineteenth-century uniformitarians recognised – namely, the gradual forming and melting of the great ice caps. The three floods were, respectively, around 14,000, 11,500, and 8000 years ago (see Figure 1). The rapidity of these three hikes in sea-level would have surprised those frock-coated gentlemen geologists, and the use of the term 'flood' might have further annoyed them. Modern establishment views as to the heavenly movements that influenced the timing of these floods, are, however, still influenced by astronomical theories pioneered by the nineteenth-century glaciologists. These theories have been collected in the twentieth century under one eponym, the 'Milankovitch hypothesis' of ice ages.

The genius of Milankovitch: out of place, out of time

Milutin Milankovitch was a Serb. Like another seminal Eastern European thinker, the anthropologist Bronislaw Malinowsky, he was caught in the wrong country at the outbreak of the First World War in 1914 and interned. Luckily a friendly Hungarian professor had him parolled and moved from his cell to Budapest where he had access to the library of the Hungarian Academy of Sciences. Oblivious to the war, he continued his calculations and finally published his first set of predictions in 1920. The Milankovitch astronomical theory was not an original approach. His model was preceded by two others published by Alphonse Adhémar (1842) and James Croll (1864). The genius of Milankovitch lay in the correct combination of variables and meticulous calculation. When he died in 1958, the theory was falling out of vogue partly because of various discrepancies between his predictions and geologists' findings. Since then, the older techniques of geologists, particularly the accuracy of carbon-dating, have been found wanting and the Milankovitch model has emerged triumphant, thus standing the test of time.

I will not give a detailed description of the theory here; that can be found elsewhere.[4] But I do wish to show that frequent, apparently random, episodes of warming and cooling of the Earth can be explained to a great extent by the interplay of at least three celestial cycles, all running at different speeds. These cycles affect the warmth transmitted by the Sun to various parts of the Earth in a complex way. Of particular importance for glaciation is a decline in heat transmitted to northern temperate latitudes during summer. The three important heavenly cycles can be called the 100,000-year stretch, the 41,000-year tilt and the 23,000-year wobble.

Every year when the Earth circles the Sun, it moves alternately nearer and farther at different points of the circuit. This motion is called elliptical and the Sun lies to one end of the ellipse rather than in the middle. Over a period of approximately 100,000 years this ellipse stretches, and then shortens and fattens until it is nearly circular. The process is rather like taking a child's hula-hoop and distorting it intermittently with two hands to make an ellipse. Over the cycle, the distance between the Earth and the Sun varies by as much as 18·26 million kilometres (11·35 million miles). Although the change in heat delivery over this cycle is relatively small, the effect on the Earth's climate is, for some reason, greater than with the other two mechanisms. At present the Sun's circuit does not particularly favour an ice age. As with many natural cycles there is more than one note being played at the same time; there are often additional harmonics. For the 100,000-year stretch this manifests as a much slower and less important stretch cycle of 400,000 years. Apart from changing the settings a little, these harmonics do not affect the validity of the model.[5]

As we know, the Earth's axis of rotation is tilted at an angle to the Sun. The situation is rather like a top that will not spin upright. This is the reason for summer and winter, as the globe presents first its northern then its southern face to the Sun during one circuit. At present the tilt is about 23·5 degrees, but it varies between 21·5 and 24·5 degrees over a cycle of roughly 41,000 years. The greater the tilt, the more the seasonal imbalance in heat delivery from the Sun and the less the chance of ice remaining through the summer in temperate climates. At present we are near a neutral point between the extremes of this oscillation of tilt, thus neither favouring nor promoting an ice age. There is an additional minor cycle of variation of 54,000 years.

The Earth is very like a child's top in some ways. Not only does it spin at an angle of about 23 degrees to the Sun, but it also performs a slow pirouette as the sloped axis gyrates round itself. If you were a god accompanying the Earth on its orbit round the Sun but perched up high looking down on the North Pole from directly above, you would see the pole performing a slow circle every 22,000 to 23,000 years. If you could see right through an imaginary glass globe to the South Pole you would see it performing the same circle 180 degrees out of phase. This spinning of the axis on itself is called axial precession, and all spinning tops can do it.

The effect of this precession is that the Earth slowly changes the face it presents to the Sun at different parts of the elliptical orbit. Precession does not change the angle of tilt, merely the direction of tilt. As a result, in the next 11,000 years or so, 21 June will become mid-winter in Europe and North America, and mid-summer in Australia. A fancy term for this ballet is the 'precession of the equinoxes'. Again there is an additional less important cycle of 19,000 years superimposed on the 22,000-year wobble.[6] Recently geologists have detected further minor harmonics of precession with much shorter cycles. As we shall see, these may partly explain the jerky nature of de-glaciation.

At present, the Earth presents the Northern Hemisphere to the Sun (that is, during summer) when it is at its furthest away from the Sun. Conversely, the Southern Hemisphere has its summer when it is nearest to the Sun. Today's position of axial precession actually favours glaciation in the Northern Hemisphere. There was a similar situation about 20,000 years ago at the height of the last great Ice Age, but then the position of the other two cycles happened to tip the balance towards glaciation. About 11,000 years ago the summers were warmer in the Northern Hemisphere which should have favoured melting of the polar ice caps.

The Milankovitch cycles are thus three elegant and stately celestial dances completely out of time with each other. They play out infinite yet predictable variations of heat stress on our planetary climate. In the last twenty years geologists and oceanographers have developed methods that enable them to measure indirectly the past course and variations in the melting and freezing of the ice caps. The more refined these measurements have become, the better they fit Milankovitch's model predictions of the waxing and waning of the ice ages of the past two million years.

Milankovitch and the floods

Milankovitch's theoretical model anticipated and out-performed the laborious practical geological measurements of the real world. But all good models have limits and are open to modification. Even the theory of relativity, which worked well for the very large, was modified and joined by quantum theory for the very small. Although the Milankovitch model works well for broad changes over periods from tens to hundreds of thousands of years, it did not predict the three big floods of the last 15,000 years that I describe below. Rather, it predicted a smooth 'S'-shaped uniformitarian curve of melting ice caps over the past 20,000 years.

Geologists now wrestle with mathematical/geophysical models in an attempt to explain why the melting of the ice sheets appeared to take place in a jerky 'binge and purge' fashion. One approach is to look at regional geophysical reasons and triggers why melting ice caps should intrinsically melt in a jerky unstable way. For that is what happens at all scales of melting ice, down to the snow falling off a roof in lumps. Another approach is to look for new external cycles of warming and/or cooling that affect the whole planet more frequently than the main Milankovitch curves. A particularly fruitful field of research here are the minor harmonics of precession that I mentioned earlier. A third approach is to look for some externally induced unknown catastrophe, such as an asteroid strike or a visiting planet which caused the Earth to tilt rapidly.

The flood trigger – an inside job?

Later on, we will look at the most promising local trigger of massive ice release – that is, the sudden superfloods of glacial lakes, championed by the Canadian geologist Paul Blanchon and others.[7] These superfloods could have their effects, both locally by 'greasing the runnels' under the ice, and supra-regionally by suddenly raising sea-levels. The latter effect, which would work by rafting out more icebergs, could have a catastrophic positive feedback effect as more ice was released and raised sea-levels still further.

The second trigger of local floods may come from the sea. As the sea-levels rise, salt sea water seeps in under the ice plates. Those of us who experience cold winters know that salt is used to melt ice on frozen roads. On a larger scale, therefore, salt accelerates glacial melting by lowering the melting point. This melting effect of sea water under the northern ice sheets is further enhanced by the conveyor-belt supply of warm tropical water to the North Atlantic coming up from the Gulf of Mexico along the western boundary current. This is somewhat similar to the Gulf Stream, only more westerly. The strength, direction and temperature of this western warm current varies seasonally, and from one long period to the next, so it might act as a trigger for a cascade of melting events.[8]

A wobble on the conveyor belt

A key corollary of heat transfer from the tropics to the sub-polar regions by warm currents is that any tropical cyclic behaviour, whether it is seasonal or wobbling over thousands of years, gets itself transmitted to the north on a warm-current conveyor belt. Add to this the observation that the tropical precessional heat cycles occur twice as frequently (that is, every 11,500 years) as those in temperate and polar regions and then there may be additional Milankovitch cyclic glacial effects. A crude explanation of this complicated observation is that the tropical regions benefit from heat coming from both sides of the equator. Several minor precessional and other wobbles affecting climate have been proposed, some as short as 1450 years.[9] Even the Sun's cycle of varying intensity has been introduced.

One key recent report seems to link the fast equatorial precessional cycles and the warm-current conveyor belt, with at least two out of the three big floods of the last 15,000 years.[10] Researchers Andrew McIntyre and Barbara Molfino of Columbia University, New York, using ancient sea-floor records, showed cyclical changes in the south equatorial current below Sierra Leone. This current is a long way away from the northern ice plates and its cycles should therefore be independent of any local factors in the north. These cycles, which repeated about every 8400 calendar years, coincided with and shadowed the regular iceberg armadas that have been released from the ice caps into the North Atlantic over the last 80,000 years. The ice armadas were reported ten years ago[11] by Hartmut Heinrich and were first characterised by the layers of Canadian continental gravel dropped on the Atlantic Ocean floor by the passing processions of melting icebergs. The last-recorded such Heinrich event certainly coincided 14,000 years ago with the first of the three floods I will describe next. The sea-floor record of the south equatorial current predicts that there should also have been another Heinrich event peaking at around 7500 years ago.[12] Recently, as we shall see, good evidence has been found around the world for a huge and sudden world flood at that date.

Not one, but three floods

It would be too simplistic to explain the flood myths away simply on the basis that the sea rose as the last Ice Age came to an end and that Stone Age people recorded the events in their folk stories. Sea-levels are certainly 120–130 metres higher than they were 20,000 years ago at the height of the last Ice Age, but 20,000 years is a long time for such an event to take place. If the inundation had happened gradually and smoothly over that time, then no one would have noticed. But it did not happen that way, and people did notice. As we have just seen, the ice melted in a jerky way. Much of the ice of the polar caps thawed in three great gushes of meltwater into the North Atlantic. All three of the resulting floods were preceded by short, intense and dry cold snaps. In this chapter I concentrate on these three catastrophic cycles – why they happened and when, and how they affected our ancestors. In Chapter 3, I describe what action people took when confronted by the third great flood of 7500–8000 years ago.

The sea-level curve I use to illustrate the flood cycles is adapted from the work of Canadian oceanographer Paul Blanchon and his colleagues.[13] It refers mainly to studies in Barbados in the Caribbean but it is the best available that shows all three floods. The curve pinpoints the flood events, but is not a detailed record, being rather an envelope of the results from several studies. For instance, falls in sea-level that may have occurred before each flood are not shown. Also, as we shall see, the coast of Barbados is different in several key aspects from the coastlines of Southeast Asia and the Arabian Gulf.

The cold snaps initiating the first two cycles are well known and received their sibling names of the Older Dryas and the Younger Dryas events some time ago. These two cold periods occurred well after the beginning of the general world warm-up that started at the end of the last Ice Age around 20,000 years ago. They were so named because they were marked in Europe by the resurgence of the polar wildflower *Dryas octopetala*, which flourished in the cold spells.

The Older Dryas event and the first flood

The first or Older Dryas cold event had two components, the Older and the Oldest, separated by a warmer, so-called Bølling phase.[14] The Oldest Dryas freeze started more than 15,000 years ago and grumbled on for several thousand years to the extent that the sea-level, which had been rising, may have briefly fallen again by up to 10 metres.[15]

At the end of the Older Dryas episode just over 14,000 years ago,[16]

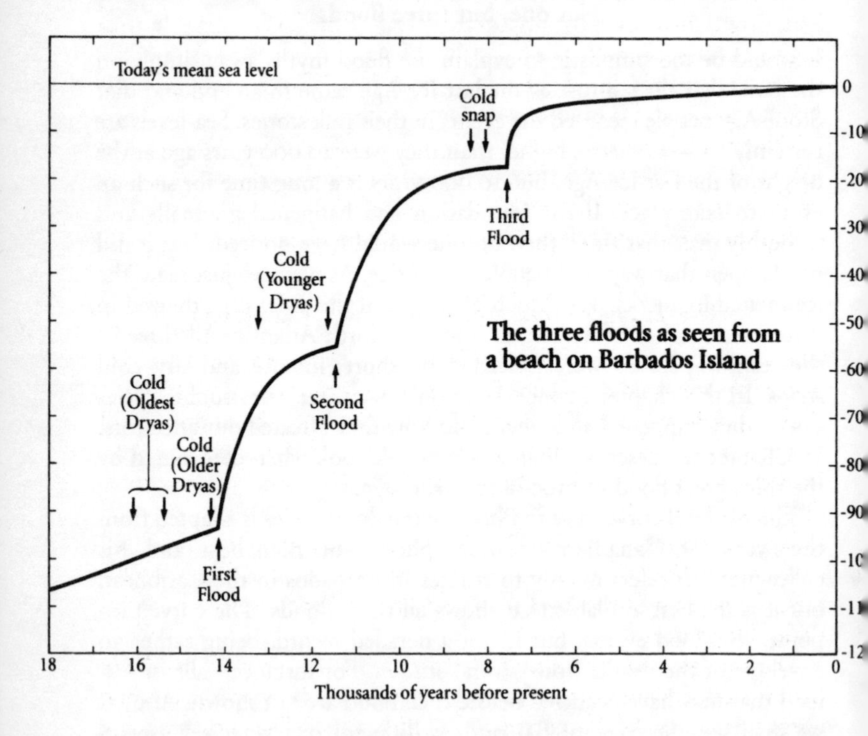

Figure 1. **Three floods.** After the end of the last Ice Age, three dramatic ice-melts were each preceded by a cold spell lasting from 400 to 1200 years. A smoothed record of post-glacial sea-level rise is shown here for the shoreline of Barbados Island in the Caribbean. Effects such as the fall in sea-level during cold spells, and the overshoot of sea-levels observed on continental shelves, are not shown. (Curve adapted from Blanchon and Shaw (1995; fig. 3).[13])

ice melting started in earnest again. The rate of melt was, however, much greater than before. Icebergs drifted into the North Atlantic like endless carpets of fallen petals as the vast European ice sheet collapsed. On cue, at the same time as the ice armadas began their journeys (that is just over 14,000 years ago) the sea-level started to rise again dramatically.[17] Part of this rise was contributed by the sudden collapse of glacial Lake Livingstone in North America, which resulted in 84,000 cubic kilometres of fresh water suddenly flowing into the North Atlantic. This mega-flood instantaneously raised the world sea-level some 23 centimetres. There were other side-effects, such as wide-spread seismic disturbances and super waves, as the great pressure of water shifted off the Canadian crustal plate to the North Atlantic. Some argue that the most important effect of the lake collapse was to trigger further ice-melts as a huge area of the grounded ice plate of the north was literally lifted off its rocky bed and floated out into the Atlantic as hundreds of icebergs and ice islands.

Whatever happened, in less than 300 years, during the so-called Allerød phase, the sea had risen some 13·5 metres to 80 metres below its present level. At the peak discharge of icebergs and meltwater, global sea-levels were rising more than 7 centimetres a year.[18]

The Younger Dryas event and the second flood

The catastrophic haemorrhage of the European and American ice plates that followed the Older Dryas event soon slowed down. Then, about 13,000 years ago,[19] the world went crackling into another cold dry snap. This was the Younger Dryas, a period reputed to be colder than the Ice Age itself. Recent estimates put Greenland temperatures during the Younger Dryas 20 degrees centigrade lower than they are today.[20] During the Younger Dryas period, discharge of meltwater fell to a trickle. The rise in sea-levels may have been as little as 2 milli-metres a year[21] and the level may even have fallen as in the previous Older Dryas freeze.

The Younger Dryas cold snap ended 11,500 years ago more suddenly than it started, with a return to very warm times. Most of the ensuing warming in Greenland occurred within fifty years.[22] The rate of this rise has been traced by measuring trapped methane (marsh gas) in deep layers of the central Greenland ice cap (world production of methane is very sensitive to climate changes). At the same time as the warming, armadas of icebergs started reappearing in their hundreds over the North Atlantic. This time it was the great Laurentide ice sheet over Northeast Canada that shuddered, partially collapsed and contributed most of the ice and water. Sea-levels rose rapidly, soon reaching rates over 7 centimetres annually. Paul Blanchon and John Shaw estimate that they rose 7·5 metres to less than 50 metres below the present sea-level in under 160 years.

Geologists have again identified several catastrophic collapses of glacial lakes which caused superfloods at the beginning of this surge and may even have precipitated it. One of these prehistoric lakes, called by geologists the 'Baltic ice lake', breached and collapsed about 12,000 years ago, discharging 30,000 cubic kilometres of fresh water from Scandinavia into the North Sea. Lake Agassiz, a Canadian glacial lake sited in present-day Saskatchewan, discharged similar volumes into the Gulf of Mexico at least twice – 11,500 and 11,400 years ago.[23] The total volume of these three superfloods was 81,000 cubic kilometres. After each discharge, huge areas of previously drowned lake floor suddenly emerged on the southwest margins of the Laurentide ice sheet.

Another cold dry snap and the third flood

Following the cathartic partial discharge of the Canadian Laurentide ice sheet, times continued to be mostly warm. The rise in ocean levels also continued, but from 10,000 years ago they slowed to a more modest pace of less than a centimetre a year.[24] There may even have been a period of relative stability in sea-levels around 10,000 years ago, reflected by a coral terrace at 30 metres below present-day sea-level in Hawai'i and other Pacific Islands.[25] Over the period 9500–8000 years ago river deltas formed throughout the world as a response to the slow-down in sea-level rise over continental shelves.[26] These deltas included and constituted the bases of the fertile alluvial plains of Mesopotamia. Similar deltas were formed by the Ganges in India, the Chao Phraya in Thailand, the Mahakam in Borneo and the Chiang Jiang (Yangtze) in China, to name but a few of over forty that have been dated throughout the world. These alluvial plains were the reason for the great agricultural success of those regions, both before and well after the third great flood that struck about 8000 years ago. However the flat nature of the plains laid down and sculpted so gently by the rivers also held the key to their recurrent vulnerability to floods.

The initially rapid then slower rise of the sea after the Younger Dryas event, resulted 8400 years ago in equatorial sea-levels from 19 to 24 metres below the present-day shoreline.[27] The cold snap that then followed brought the rising sea to a halt again.[28] Although the two previous cold episodes, named after the hardy polar flower *Dryas*, were well known, this cold event has only recently been recognised. The main reason for this gap in knowledge was that the period of cold was too short, lasting only about 400 years. The stratal markers on the ocean floor and in the ice caps that geologists and others had been using to define the Dryas events were, until recently, too blunt to detect the outline of this cold snap. The change has, however, been detected recently, again by analysing trapped methane at different levels in the central Greenland ice cap. Starting 8400 years ago methane levels that had been high since the end of the Younger Dryas freeze, suddenly fell sharply to low levels for 400 years.[29] Measurements from Moroccan lake-floor sediments also indicate that this was a time when the world was again plunged into a very dry period.[30] Some researchers working on the Great Barrier Reef off Australia have detected a fall of 6 metres in sea-level between 8400 and 8000 years ago during the cold snap.[31]

The third dry cold period was interrupted suddenly around 8000 years ago by an event which, although only discovered in the last decade, has been described as 'possibly the single largest flood of the [past two million years]'.[32] The melting Laurentide ice cap had dammed up vast volumes of fresh water in glacial lakes occupying a third of the land area of eastern Canada. The melting ice plates were complex entities but it might help to liken the Laurentide ice cap to a bowl (the Hudson Bay) of frozen water gradually warming. Around the edge, meltwater collected leaving the block in the centre. This meltwater was periodically siphoned off, causing flooding elsewhere (usually down the Mississippi and St Lawrence rivers) and leaving the remaining ice block sitting on the base of the bowl rather than floating. On a short section of the side of the bowl there was a gap in the porcelain that went right down to the base. This was the Hudson Strait. The backed-up water could not get through this gap for a long time, because the ice block was wedged right up against it, plugging the hole.

Geologists have calculated that the combined surface area of these glacial lakes, circled around the Laurentide ice sheet, at this point exceeded 700,000 square kilometres. The largest was a complex of two lakes, Agassiz and Ojibway, which stretched over 4800 kilometres across the continent and around the ice sheet, and sat at an altitude of 450–600 metres above sea-level. When this great cistern in the hills flushed 8000 years ago, it did not trickle and splash south into the Mississippi or St Lawrence rivers as on previous occasions. Instead it ran north and east straight into the Hudson Basin and out through the Hudson Strait, carrying more than half of the rest of the Laurentide ice sheet with it. The ice had been loosened and lifted both by invading

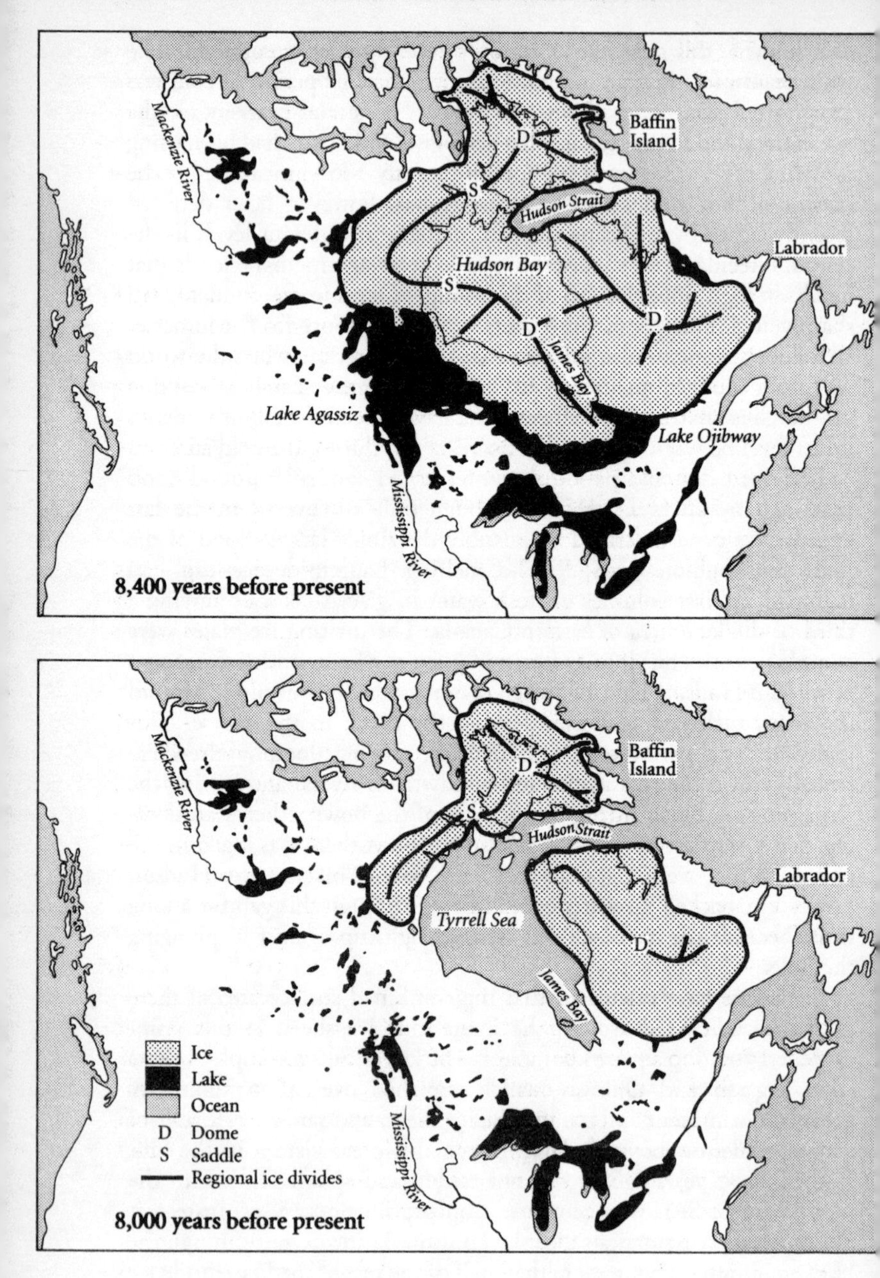

Mackenzie River
Baffin Island
Hudson Strait
Hudson Bay
Labrador
James Bay
Lake Agassiz
Lake Ojibway
Mississippi River
D
S
8,400 years before present
Mackenzie River
Baffin Island
Hudson Strait
Labrador
Tyrrell Sea
James Bay
Mississippi River
D
S
Ice
Lake
Ocean
D Dome
S Saddle
Regional ice divides
8,000 years before present

Figure 2. **The collapse of the Laurentide ice sheet and the great flood.** The last of three dramatic ice-melts was the most cataclysmic. Around 8400 years ago a huge complex ice dome still covered northeast Canada, damming vast volumes of water in the peri-glacial lakes (black). When these discharged around 8000 years ago, they carried most of the ice sheet through the Hudson Strait. (Adapted from Dyke and Prest (1987).)[82 (chap. 2)]

sea coming through under the Hudson Strait and by the lake water tunnelling underneath the other way. Calculations of the total unfrozen water volume discharged instantly vary between 75,000 and 150,000 cubic kilometres – enough to raise the global sea-level by 20–40 centimetres instantaneously. The centre of the ice cap that was also flushed out through the Hudson Strait, however, would have rapidly added another 5–10 metres to the sea-level as the ice plate, 1·6 kilometres thick and a third the size of Canada, broke up.[33] The rapid rise in sea-levels would also have rafted ice off from other plates.

A sudden increase in global sea-levels by 5–10 metres, 8000 years ago, should be enough to satisfy some catastrophists that here was a real candidate for the great flood. Reports now appearing in geological journals, however, seem to be saying that this event was, if anything, even more catastrophic and more complicated. Instead of 5–10 metres, the rise could have been as much as 25 metres. Further, this rise could have been a rise followed by a similar fall, just as the legends said. At a meeting of the American Association for the Advancement of Science in 1995 on sea-level changes in the recent geological past, several participants working in places as widely separated as Greenland, the North Atlantic and Denmark reported a major event roughly 8000 years ago. The Danish work suggested: 'A rapid sea-level rise (25 m), then a similar drop centered at 8000 B.P. at 8–15 cm/yr.'[34]

Northwest England also had a period of rapid rise between 3·4 and 4·4 centimetres a year around 7800 years ago. Dramatic coastline loss was reported in Germany for the same time.[35] The sea-level change at a rate of 8–15 centimetres per year sustained, for instance, in Denmark over a range of 25 metres is outside anything recorded in the previous two world floods. It means that much of the cycle of rise and fall that could have done so much damage to the plains of Mesopotamia would have been completed in a few generations or maybe less.

The question is whether these dramatic oscillations of relative sea-level recorded in formerly glacial regions had their counterparts further south: it seems they did. China's coastal sea level rose 2·0–7·5 centimetres a year 7800 years ago, as it did for the previous two floods.[36]

The ripples were felt as far south as the Great Barrier Reef of Australia. Recently researchers in Townsville analysed hundreds of dates and depths from the Barrier Reef and concluded that there was a dramatic oscillation of sea-level between 8400 and 7800 years ago (see Figure 3). The first point in the cycle was around 8500 years ago when sea-levels peaked at about 11 metres below its present level. This was followed by a fall of 6 metres over 300 years to a trough, 8200 years ago, that was 17 metres below today's level. The next phase was the most rapid. Over 400 years, the sea-level rose by 12 metres from 17 to 5 metres below today's level.[37]

The last surge of sea over the Great Barrier Reef achieved an average rate of rise of 3 centimetres a year which, although dramatic, is less than that recorded in Denmark at around the same time.[38] We should remember when comparing these figures that very fast and very large events would be lost or blurred by the lack of definition of the methods. If we consider that the 'minus 17 metres' level at the Barrier Reef might have been caused by a freeze-up in Greenland, whereas the last rise in level followed the sudden collapse and discharge of a whole ice sheet, then the latter may have taken much less than 400 years.

On equatorial continental shelves, sea flooding may have been even worse than the 10 metres estimated above. There is clearly some difference in opinion about the sea-level at which the last rapid flood-rise started. Take-off levels, for the start of the rapid rise, vary from 17 to 24 metres below present relative sea-levels. There is also some disagreement exactly when the third flood happened, how far it rose and when it slowed down. Although there are several estimates of 8000 years ago for the start of this flood as described above,[39] some put it as recently as around 7600 years ago.[40] In geological terms, however, the disagreement is surprisingly small.

For reasons I will discuss shortly, the rate of rise of the sea was not the same everywhere, so a graph of sea-level rise around the world produces curves that can look very different (see Figure 3). In Barbados, for example, the sea did not reach its present level until recently. But on the continental shelf of Southeast Asia, by contrast, the sea crossed present-day shorelines 7600–7500 years ago and continued rising.[41] Depending on the actual date of the flood, this might have produced anything from an instantanous elevation of sea-levels by 24 metres to a less terrifying but still amazing similar rise over 400–1000 years. In the Arabian Gulf sea-levels rose rapidly by 7·5 metres in less than 100 years around 7600 years ago, and by a total of 24 metres in 1000 years.[42]

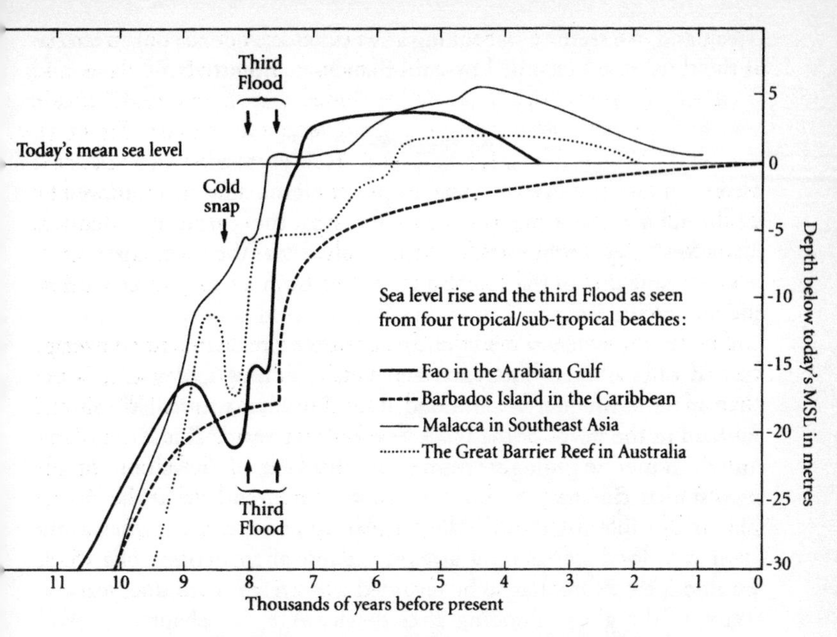

Figure 3. **The final rise in sea-levels as seen from four tropical and sub-tropical beaches around the world.** A short cold spell 8400 years ago slowed the rise and even reversed it; then about 8000 years ago a rapid rise, the 'Third Flood', occurred on all beaches. The sea did not, however, reach today's levels in Barbados and over the Great Barrier Reef until later. (Curves adapted from Zarins (1992)[42], Blanchon and Shaw (1995),[13] Geyh *et al.* (1979)[41] and Larcombe *et al.* (1995; fig. 5)[31]; timescale: corrected calendar years BP.)

At first glance these sea-level curves from four different tropical beaches round the world – the Straits of Malacca, Fao in the Persian Gulf, the Great Barrier Reef and Barbados – may look no more informative than spaghetti being eaten by an Englishman. On closer inspection of the period between 8400 and 7600 years ago, however, some similarities emerge. Around 8400 years ago, the time of the cold snap, the rate of rise in all curves slows down; in two curves – from the Great Barrier Reef and Fao in the Arabian Gulf – there is even a marked fall in level. Then, after the fall, all the curves show sharp upturns of sea-level, most of which are complete by 7500 years ago. Allowing for the error inherent in dating, these sudden upturns are nearly synchronous. Along with records from Denmark and

Greenland, we seem to be looking at worldwide evidence of the effects of the third flood recorded by Paul Blanchon and others.[43]

The Black Sea flood

This last rapid rise in global sea-levels was presumably also responsible for breaching the Hellespont and flooding the partially desiccated Black Sea.[44] Before the last flood the level of the Black Sea was tens of metres below that of the neighbouring Mediterranean Sea. The narrow channel of the Bosporus silted up. But as world sea-levels rose, there came a point when the silt plug was overtopped and then rapidly flushed out. About 7250 years ago with the flow and roar of 200 Niagaras, the Mediterranean flooded in. Flooding was worst over the flat land in the north of the Black Sea. Bill Ryan and Walt Pitman, the American marine geologists from New York who discovered this flood, suggest that this may have given rise to the legend of Noah's flood. This is possible for the Middle East, but it does not explain all the other 500 flood stories from around the rest of the world. The Black Sea flood, therefore, has to be regarded as merely one of the dramatic events of the global flooding after the Ice Age. In Chapter 3, I will describe who was affected, where, and how badly.

Land-raisers after the flood

In Chapter 8, I shall suggest that the North American flood stories of Algonquian Indians with their sudden lake floods and land-raisers may have had some basis in what happened locally in Canada after the Ice Age. At the beginning of the story there was a period of cold, drought and famine, followed by a rapidly rising lake flood. The cold, drought and famine would fit any of the lead-up periods to the three great floods I have outlined. The sudden and rapid lake rise was a feature of the partially connected ring of lakes round the Laurentide ice cap. As the cap melted, periodically one lake would rise sufficiently to breach a temporary obstruction of flow into a neighbouring lake. The sudden release of pent-up water would cause the second lake to rise rapidly. The same process might be repeated into the next lake in the chain until the flood finally made its way out of the ring and down as a long gush to the Mississippi, or through the 'Great Lakes' to the St Lawrence. In this context, the 'Great Lakes' that we know of today were of quite modest size beside the giants of Lake Agassiz and Lake Ojibway. The greatest inter-lake floods of this nature occurred just before the third world flood of 8000 years ago. As we saw above, these were the largest floods of man's time on Earth. Within the confines of the region they may also have been truly mountain-topping.

The last of these great lake floods was the largest and may have triggered the final collapse and meltdown of the Laurentide ice dome. In this case the released water did not flow south as before but north into the basin under the ice cap that we now know as Hudson Bay. As the lake water rushed on under the ice towards the Hudson Strait, the ice cap was riven in two and its heart and western flank were flushed on out to the North Atlantic. Invading salt water would have accelerated the melting underneath and assisted the flow. What was left at the end of this vast flushing of the cistern were two ice caps, one in the north and one in the south divided by a rather larger Hudson Bay, known to geologists as the Tyrrell Sea.

The Tyrrell Sea, which was now filled with salt water, had a much larger surface area and depth than its smaller descendant, the Hudson Bay. This was because the whole continental plate below the ice dome had been pushed down by as much as 300 metres.[45] Some of the greatest land depression was around the southern shore and 'James Bay'. The rapidity of the clearing ice and water left little time for the Earth's crust to rise back again after the load was removed. The floor of the Tyrrell Sea did lift afterwards, however, at first rapidly enough for observers to see the land of the southern shore literally rising out of the sea, as in the land-raiser or land-diver stories (see Chapter 11). A famous picture of the Great Bear Lake shows the ladder of multiple natural terraces formed by the receding lake shoreline (see illustration 1). It is therefore perhaps not entirely surprising that the Algonquian land-raiser motif is shared by peoples from the Great Lakes on the east in a broad swathe across lands formerly occupied by glacial lakes to the Athapascans in the northwest. Significantly the lake-flood motif is found only in the eastern wing of the story in the areas formerly covered, or threatened by, the great glacial lakes of Agassiz and Ojibway.

It was everything they said it was

The events surrounding the break-up of the great Laurentide ice cap were truly cataclysmic. At this point we are looking at a flood, which, apart from satisfying catastrophists, could have matched up to some of the fantastical stories told around the world. The rapidity of water release was greatest in this, the most recent of the floods. The sudden sea rise was large. The sudden change of pressure from the North American and European continents to the world's ocean basins would have caused great earthquakes and increased volcanism throughout the world. There would thus have been seismic superwaves (tsunamis) across the Atlantic and Pacific oceans (see Chapter 8).

One piece of evidence of the strains and energy unleashed on the Earth's brittle crust by melting ice caps at this time, comes not from Canada but Sweden. As Arch Johnston of the Earthquake Center at the University of Memphis has vividly described, the massive and sudden oscillatory movements of the Earth's brittle crust, as the remains of the Finno-scandian ice plate melted in the period 8500–8000 years ago,[46] caused waves in the ground. These waves, or post-glacial faults, are now seen as frozen 'rock tsunami' in Scandinavia (see also Chapter 8). One of the largest of these is 150 kilometres long and 10 metres high and is called the pärvie, a Lappish word meaning literally 'wave in the ground'. It can be seen in northern Sweden. The faults are not minor surface curiosities. They plunge, to 40 kilometres, down into the Earth's crust. Arch Johnston's calculations of the energy required to cause these fresh faults reveals that they were associated with earthquakes of unbelievable magnitude. If these earthquakes occurred at the continental edges of all the main retreating ice caps, then it is likely that mountain-topping super waves would have radiated out into the oceans of the Northern Hemisphere on three fronts at the same time as the three floods. The North Atlantic would have suffered super waves from both sides – Canada and Europe. The North Pacific would have suffered in the same way, as the Cordilleran ice plate over the Rockies melted. The location of the maximum energy release in this instance would have been along the Canadian coastal faultline of the Pacific seismic ring of fire. This drama in the Rockies, however, was over earlier than the last two of the three floods. Several massive collapses of the western glacial Lake Missoula happened before the Younger Dryas event.[47]

The periodic rapid freezing and de-glaciation that I have described for the northern ice plates has not yet been well described for Antarctica. It is increasingly recognised, however, that the accompanying climatic changes were worldwide, not local, events and rapid melts were not confined to the ice caps on either side of the North Atlantic.[48] Super waves emanating from earthquakes in Antarctica would have threatened the whole of South and East Asia, Australia and South America.

In summary, the most recent of the three great post-glacial 'freeze and melt' episodes was different from the other two. First, the preceding freeze was almost too short to be detected. Second, the following melt-flood and sea rise was much more sudden and catastrophic than the other two, with rises in relative sea-level anything from 12 to 25 metres. The cataclysmic nature of this disaster would not have given the Earth's flexible but brittle crust time to readjust to the new weight distribution of ice and water in different regions. Apart from the dramatic nature of the sea-level rise, there would also have been more giant earthquakes and super waves.

A soft, springy, plastic and liquid Earth

The fact that sea-levels in different parts of the world did not each rise at the same rate as the ice caps melted is one of the most difficult concepts for anyone, including geologists, to grasp. At first sight this seems nonsensical, given that the oceans are all connected with each other. It makes sense, however, when movements of the Earth's crust underneath the sea and coast are taken into account. The change in relative sea-levels is how the sea-level looks to someone living on or near the coast compared to how it was before. For instance, the north-east coast of Canada is rising, as it has done for over 10,000 years since the great weight of ice came off at the end of the Ice Age. The relative sea-level hence appears to be falling.

Local changes are obviously more important to individuals than changes occurring elsewhere in the ocean. A grasp of these effects helps to understand the timescale and local quirks of the flooding of Southeast Asia and the Arabian Gulf. They therefore need to be explained. Before I do this, there are some horrid-sounding terms which have to be disposed of, such as isostasy, hydro-isostasy, eustasy, tectono-eustasy, glacial eustasy and geoidal eustasy, which are used by geophysicists to describe the Earth's behaviour when the ice sheets melted. Because they are all 'New Greek', however, I will not use them here.

The first idea to grasp is that the Earth is mostly hot and liquid. Imagine you are a weightless astronaut orbiting the Earth who tries to pour a cup of hot cocoa. Let us assume you have overcome the problems of getting the liquid out of the pot but then miss the cup. By some chance the glob of hot liquid does not hit the wall of the cabin but remains suspended. After a time the cocoa rounds off into a wobbly spinning ball. Because it is spinning, the poles of the ball tend to flatten a bit while the equator bulges a little. How flat the poles and how bulgy the equator are depends on the rate of spin. Because you made the cocoa with rich full milk, a crinkly skin forms on the surface. It is more solid than the underlying liquid, and is also flexible but rather brittle. The bits of chocolate that would have settled in a cup, gravitate to the centre of the ball and become solid. Now imagine playing gently with this spinning ball of liquid. If you try to push in the two poles of the ball with your forefingers they dent, but at the same time you set off changes elsewhere in the ball. Ripples run through and around it, and it changes shape. Even when you take your fingers away the disturbance that you started continues. The dents you made take some time to recover, and so on. Now let us think of the Earth as this spinning ball of hot matter.

A cool, springy, broken crust

The outer crust of the Earth is less than 50 kilometres thick, cool, stiff and brittle yet elastic. It can bend, but if it is pushed too hard or fast it cracks. There are some permanent cracks or faults already in the crust called 'seismic belts', which form part of the crazy-paving of our continents and seas. So any unusual vertical strain on one of the paving stones will usually be released at the nearest permanent crack causing an earthquake. In some cases during the last 10,000 years this controlled release of energy could not happen because no crack was near enough.

One of the best examples of this is seen in the case of the pärvie fault in Sweden. When the Finno-scandian ice plate finally melted 8000 years ago during the last flood, the dented underlying Earth's crust strained to recover its shape. Unfortunately there was just no permanent seismic crack near enough to release the strain and dissipate the energy. So, instead, the whole continental plate developed a new crack through the full thickness of the Earth's crust. The super tidal waves caused by these earth-cracking events would have travelled round the world. This sort of crack in the Earth's crust can happen with quite small changes in load as well. Pocket-sized Glen Roy in Scotland suddenly discharged its pennyworth of 5 cubic kilometres of glacial meltwater 10,500 years ago (at the end of the Younger Dryas freeze-up).[49] This relatively tiny excretion caused widespread faulting (cracks) and landslides. The discharge of Glen Roy is dwarfed by the lake collapse of the most recent flood around 8000 years ago when up to 36,000 times more water was suddenly released.

The well-studied example of Glen Roy also shows that the initial response of the Earth's crust after a load has been suddenly and completely removed is a rapid elastic or springy recoil. The rapid *unrestrained* recoil incidentally also enhances the catastrophic effects of ice-sheet collapse. The initial elastic upward recoil of the floor of the Baltic and Hudson Bay basins just after they had finally flushed out their respective ice caps could have disgorged additional immense volumes of water to the world's oceans. Unrestrained rebound only happened when lakes burst or when the ice sheets finally lost their caps, as in the last of the three floods at the end of the Ice Age. For most of the period of post-glacial melting there was still some ice cap left on top of the depressed areas, which restrained the rebound.

The outer mantle: hot, weak and plastic

From 50 to 100 kilometres below the thin crust, the Earth's viscosity changes rapidly. From a rigid shell we pass to the hot outer mantle which has a much lower viscosity. Although it has many properties of a liquid and contains molten material, the outer mantle (Asthenosphere) also has much suspended solid matter – it behaves a little like toothpaste under pressure. The outer mantle has a depth of about 350 kilometres,[50] and is far below the surface when compared to the depth of the dents made by the ice sheets. Because it is semi-fluid, however, it has some role in redistributing the volume displaced by such depressions. How much of the redistribution of hot toothpaste is global, and how much is purely local is not clear. A local example of redistribution is the forebulge found as a rim about 300 kilometres away from the edge of an ice sheet. The Isle of Wight off the English south coast was never covered by ice. It was instead raised up as the forebulge to the edge of an ice sheet further up in England. Because there is no ice left now, the Isle of Wight is sinking, as residents have found to their cost over generations. London, which was nearer the ice sheet, is also sinking in the same way by 16 centimetres every century.[51]

Because of the huge volumes and relative viscosities of the crust and mantle, correction of ice dents after the initial rapid phase continued at a declining rate over more than 10,000 years. Today, the floor of the Gulf of Bothnia in the Baltic Sea which was under the Finno-scandian sheet, is still rising by a metre every century, recovering from the load of the last Ice Age. The evidence of the deep change left in the mantle can be seen in a negative gravity defect centred on the Gulf of Bothnia.[52]

The loading of the ocean floors

When the ice caps returned their locked-up water to the world's oceans the result was in effect a redistribution of the crustal load from the polar land masses to the ocean basins. These new vessels, of course, were obliged to take the strain. The initial 'give' would have been elastic downward recoil of the stiff but springy ocean plates. This was followed by a slower phase, all in reverse to what was happening to the polar land masses.

The depression of basins caused by the rise in sea-level was not the same in all areas of the sea: in many places they even rose. The oceanic crustal plates, although thinner than continental plates, have the same general properties of brittle springiness that I mentioned earlier. But the distribution of the meltwater weight over two-thirds of the world's surface could cause a general depression of the ocean basins only if there was some compensatory rise of the continental plates. Because the continents were not being loaded by more water, and may even have been rising a little as the ocean floor sank, we can see a conflict on the coastlines, where oceans meet land. The edge of a continent is also thicker than the neighbouring oceanic plate, so will tend to resist being dragged under. This difference between the coast and the deep sea gives rise to unexpected and interesting effects when the apparent or relative sea-level rise is considered.

In this book I am dealing particularly with sub-tropical and tropical coasts, where there was never any ice; in general, relative sea-level has risen there. Let me take two extreme tropical situations. The first is a tiny sub-tropical island in the Caribbean, now called Barbados, lived on by an immortal Carib/Arawak fisherman. The island has steep sides all round, which plunge down to ocean depths of more than 2000 metres. As sea-levels rose around the world, the ocean floor sank slowly, carrying the island down with it. The island's base was not too much affected by the neighbouring continent and the drop in the sea floor reflected what was happening over many equatorial deep ocean basins. The apparent change in sea-level on the island coast could thus be said to reflect the maximum real change in sea-levels of around 127 metres around the world at those latitudes (see Figures 1 and 3). There are many qualifications to this statement, but they can be ignored for the purpose of this argument. Because the ocean basin is still slowly sinking there, the sea-level on the coast of Barbados has continued to rise slowly to this day. The sea has never been above today's level in Barbados since the last Ice Age.

Our second situation might be seen by an immortal fisherman 'Adad' living on the coast of a continent with 1000 kilometres of continental shelf to sail over before he got to the deep ocean. Such places do exist. One example might be Fao near Kuwait in the Arabian Gulf, another could be Malacca near Singapore. The gulf was largely dry 12,000 years ago. Moreover, Fao was also nestling 1000 kilometres into a solid continental plate. As a result, the 127 metres of meltwater that eventually loaded the Earth's crust under the Indian Ocean would have had little denting effect on the gulf crust when measured at Fao right inside the gulf. The continental plate was thus a sort of splint.

There were three results of this 'splinting' effect of the continental shelf on relative sea-levels – namely, more rapid rise during recent melts, overshoot above today's levels and lower net rise of sea-levels. First the rising sea had already reached the level of Fao's present beachline about 7500 years ago, just after the last rapid melt. When this is compared with the Barbados curve, the rate of rise in sea-levels in the Arabian Gulf after 8000 years ago was very rapid. Second the gulf sea-level continued to rise until it was 3 metres above the present-day Fao beach 6500–5000 years ago. Thereafter the sea receded to the swamped Fao beach in a wobbly oscillating fashion, and has settled back at around today's beach only in the last 3000 years. The recent decline resulted from the continued sinking of the great ocean basins that drained some water back off the continental shelves. In spite of the earlier peak, the total net rise in sea-level, seen by our immortal fisherman Adad in Fao, was only 106 metres, not the 127 metres seen in Barbados.[53] Further evidence of the splinting effect of the wide continental shelf is seen at Muscat in Oman just outside the Arabian Gulf, where the continental shelf is narrow. In Muscat the sea-level curve during the past 10,000 years was intermediate between Fao and Barbados. The rise to near present sea-levels was rapid as at Fao, but there was no overshoot, and the sea-level remained 1 metre below today's levels for a long time, only gradually creeping up.

The curious behaviour of the sea at the Fao beach had profound social and archaeological implications and was repeated on many

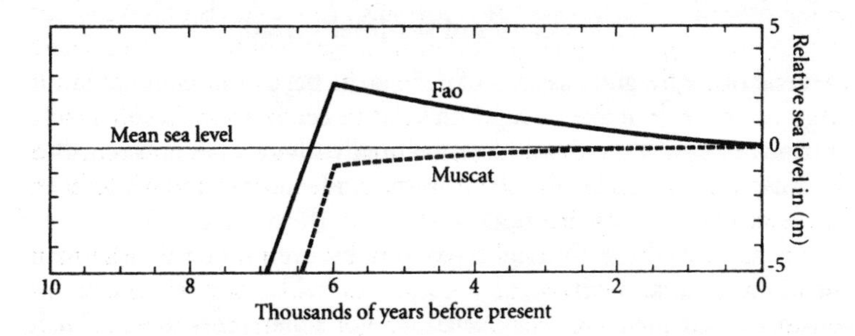

Figure 4. **The effect of the continental shelf on relative sea-levels at two sites of the Arabian Gulf 6000 years ago.** At Fao, in the northern Gulf, the sea peaked around 3 metres above the present beach (upper curve), while at Muscat (lower curve), outside the Gulf on the edge of the continental shelf, the level never crossed today's beach. (Computer-modelled curves adapted from Lambeck (1996; fig. 4)[53]; timescale uncorrected.)

tropical and sub-tropical continental shelves, those of the Arabian Gulf, the Far East and India being the most important for my argument here. First, the overshoot of around 3 metres was enough to take the invading sea 150–180 kilometres further inland than today's Fao beach. Such an incursion, which is technically termed the Flandrian transgression, took the sea up to lap the shores of the ancient Sumerian city of Ur and to within 25 kilometres of the even more ancient city of Eridu (see next chapter). The cities of the State of Lagash were also along this raised shoreline 6500–5000 years ago.[54] (See Figure 9.)

This geography fits with the concept of the Sumerians as coastal seafarers, but it also suggests that the sharp timeline for the start of urban centres in Mesopotamia in the fourth millennium BC may be an illusion. Eridu may have been the oldest coastal city *not* destroyed by the invading sea. In other words, it could have been the last old city to be built at the post-glacial highwater point. The 'Ubaid people who made the oldest pottery ('Ubaid 1) recovered in Eridu also seem to have given the cities of Ur and Eridu their non-Sumerian names.[55] These pre-Sumerian agriculturalists may have built coastal settlements more than 8000 years ago in parts of the Arabian Gulf now flooded by 15 metres of sea water.[56] Although the idea of drowned 'Ubaid prehistoric settlements is speculative, the destructive effect of the Flandrian transgression in wiping out coastal archaeological sites up to about 5500 years ago is now well recognised for other parts of Asia, including Thailand and the China coast.[57]

Other causes of sea-level variation

Several other irregular aspects of the Earth's behaviour after the last Ice Age conspire to make changes in relative sea-levels look different in various places, which I will describe briefly. In general, however, these change only the details on tropical and sub-tropical continental shelves. For example, the peak sea-level on the Southeast Asian Sunda shelf may have been 5 metres above today's levels rather than 3 metres as in the Arabian Gulf.

One consequence of de-glaciation was a net movement of water from the poles, mainly the North Pole, towards the equator. At the same time the unequal release of the load on the polar continental crusts led to complex compensation of the mantle and crust nearer the equator. These factors among others changed the shape and properties of the flattened spinning ball. Depression of ocean floors, for instance, tended to be greater at the equator although this effect was patchy.[58]

Another maverick cause of variability in relative sea-level rise is the fact that the ocean does not adopt the smooth contours of the ideal flattened spinning ball. Instead, when orbiting satellites measure the height of the ocean surface, there are broad humps here, and broad dents there. The highest equatorial hump, over 70 metres high, centres on the seas around Papua New Guinea. The deepest dents are on two sites. One is the Maldive Islands south of India where the depth of the dent exceeds 100 metres. The other is near Barbados in the Caribbean and exceeds 50 metres. These humps and dents reflect gravitational anomalies of the underlying crust and mantle. The reason they are maverick is that no one knows what they have done in the past, and what they are going to do. They may have moved, and that not necessarily in time with the glacial cycle. If they have stayed in the same place since the last Ice Age, then relative sea-levels may not have been affected too much. On the other hand, if they have moved there could have been large changes in relative sea-level near them. This might also be a big problem for geologists working on Barbados and the north coast of New Guinea, where some of the most important ideas of sea-level change have come from.

Another problem affecting sea-levels in post-glacial times is vertical movements of the Earth's crust due to factors other than ice melting. These 'tectonic' movements have, in the past, been blamed for many of the unexplained differences in sea-level curves around the world.[59] They are still important – for instance in New Zealand, Tonga and the Mediterranean – and serve to perpetuate uncertainty in analysis.

The last potential sources of variation I want to mention are minor degrees of pole shift. In 1978, Edward Weyer suggested that the change in centrifugal force resulting from melting ice caps could be associated with cyclical 'slippage' of the geographic pole.[60] (The geographic pole is the point where lines of longitude meet.) Even if this slippage was as little as half a degree, there would be profound unequal compensatory changes in sea-levels, maximally around the meridian of slippage. Weyer calculated that changes in sea-level caused in this way could vary by as much as 300 metres every 5600 years. The meridian (line of longitude) of slippage that best fitted his figures exactly split the northern ice caps and went through Beijing, Hong Kong, Borneo and Perth (Australia) in the East, and the Hudson Strait, Bermuda and Tierra Del Fuego in the West. I can find no further follow-up studies to confirm this idea. Whether such geographic polar slippage occurs or not, the magnetic pole also passes through a nearby but asymmetrical meridian near Hudson Bay, and there is definite evidence that this slips. The magnetic pole is definitely known to wander and even to reverse polarity periodically.

Evidence for the third flood

In this chapter, I have described the three great post-glacial floods. Any or all of these could have been the model for the myths. The last of the three had the most rapid rise just before arriving at today's sea-level, and was accompanied by world-shaking quakes. This strengthens the case for the last flood being the one that was remembered in Southeast Asia.

The three floods had varying effects in different parts of the world. The variations in relative sea-level change continue to confound experts' predictions and the search for a 'true' curve of post-glacial sea rise. In the past these studies of sea-level rise produced such wildly varying curves with such bizarre oscillations that scientists could not believe their eyes, at least not those of their colleagues. More accurate complete local curves have shown that oscillations due to the three floods affected widely separated coasts at the same time, as I have shown, and also that minor oscillations have continued for the last 6000 years.[61] In the end, the final gold standard for knowing what went on at a particular beach or continental shelf still lies in the direct study of that location. This means analysing dates of beaches, the layers of sediment underneath them, the underwater terraces in the sea below them that were once beaches and so on.

Over the next two chapters I will use local sea-level curves to map the loss of coastal land since the last Ice Age in two areas, the Far East and South Asia. From there, we will look with a more archaeological eye at three of the drowning coastlines I have discussed here. The flood of the fifth millennium BC had profoundly disturbing effects on people living on flat continental shelves at the time. In addition, the elevation of the sea above present-day levels in these areas also had important effects. This overshoot started approximately 5500 BC and peaked at varying times generally around 3500 BC. The effect this had on the archaeological records of people such as Mesopotamians living on flat plains was to obliterate or smudge evidence of settlement before 3500 BC. In many cases this has given a false prehistoric horizon.

2
THE SILT CURTAIN

This chapter is about the great Flood – the last in my sequence of three – and how it wiped out the evidence of its own role in shaping the birth of agriculture. So effectively did the Flood erase its own traces on every shoreline, however, that we still call it a myth.

On 16 March 1929 Sir Leonard Woolley, a famous English archaeologist working in Mesopotamia, shook his colleagues by a letter in *The Times*. This announced that he had found the silt deposit made by the flood of Utnapishtim (the Babylonian Noah) underlying the Royal Cemetery of Ur, and 40 feet (12 metres) below the present desert. He also stated that in his view this flood was identical with that of Noah in the Bible. His claim, although frequently attacked and finally passed over by default, has not been convincingly debunked to date. It now appears that the significance of Woolley's find lay less in its local association with the myth, although he was probably right about this, than in the evidence it yields – that the flood of Utnapishtim came from the sea. The story also tells us, on the way, much about academics and about how archaeologists arrive at their reconstructions of prehistory.

The last flushing of glacial meltwater finally slowed to a trickle as the rise in sea-level peaked on continental shelves around 5500 years ago. It was as if a curtain of water had been drawn across the remains of previous coastal settlements. Pots and implements that allow archaeologists to define prehistoric cultures were inaccessible; they lay under silt and under the sea, miles from the shoreline. But there was a window. Over the next few thousand years the sea-level settled back by up to 5 metres, and the coastline emerged again, to a distance over 100 kilometres.[1] This partial drawing back of the curtain allowed Woolley to peer under the silt layer, at the few hundred years after the main force of the flood of Utnapishtim struck. Because the marine inundation persisted from around 7500 to 5500 years ago on many of these sites, there was a big gap between the archaeological remains under the silt layer and those above it. Woolley's extended example bridged the transition from the Neolithic to the Metal Age.

In the next two chapters I explore examples of flooded continental shelves from three different regions to show the effect of the third flood on coastal Neolithic cultures over 7000 years ago. Additionally, I discuss the speculation of archaeologists who try to piece together the history of the time in terms of archaeological 'horizons'. The first of these regional examples, as I have mentioned, is Woolley's flood from Ur in the Arabian Gulf; the second is from Southeast Asia and Oceania, and the third from Australia. I will also present evidence that the first Austronesian dispersal may have started more than 7000 years ago reaching the North Coast of New Guinea within a very short time. To the west, around the same time, ancestors of the Austro-Asiatic speakers may have taken rice growing to India.

Noah's flood re-examined

Archaeologists have told us much about the prehistoric and protohistoric periods in Mesopotamia. They have been helped in this by a study of the cuneiform texts of later times.[2] It is perhaps surprising that such a devastating event, as the third flood was recounted to be, has produced so little agreement among academics as to its reality, let alone its date. Part of the reason for this may be that archaeologists were looking for the wrong sort of flood, a seasonal riverine flood rather than a sea flood. The other reason may be that the geological and oceanographic knowledge and tools were not available when the questions were still fresh and being asked.

Woolley's layer of silt at Ur separated much of the pre-Sumerian 'Ubaidian period beneath from the Sumerian periods of Uruk and Jemdat-Nasr above. Below the 3–4-metre layer at Ur, Woolley found no evidence of metallurgy, but immediately above it and dug into the top layer were fragments of copper and evidence of the last artefacts of the ancient 'Ubaidian people. Thus in Woolley's view this stratigraphic timing of the silt layer corresponded to the chronology given in the Sumerian King Lists inscribed on cuneiform tablets.[3] These ancient chronicles marked the great flood as the major event preceding the dynastic periods of Kish, Erech and Ur. Thus, according to both the cuneiform record and the archaeological one, this flood appeared to mark the collapse of the old 'Ubaidian Neolithic order and to herald the first Sumerian urban-age civilisation of the Ancient Near East. His archaeological conclusion – that the silt divided the Neolithic period from the Age of Metal – was a major feature of Woolley's claim that caught the imagination of the time.[4]

Controversy was quick to follow. A colleague of Woolley's, Langdon, announced two days after Woolley's revelations that evidence of a similar flood of a later date (*c.* 2600 BC) had been found at Kish the previous year.[5] Doubts were also expressed by Woolley's colleagues as to the nature of the silt deposit. In response, Woolley rejected the rival Kish flood as being that of Utnapishtim for several chronological reasons. He also took steps to have his silt deposit analysed. The mud of claim and counterclaim, thus stirred up, never resolved the issue.

At the time, the most convincing of Woolley's objections to the candidacy of Langdon's flood was chronological. Woolley used a reference to the Gilgamesh[6] cycle in seals excavated from The Royal Cemetery of Ur to establish the antiquity of the legendary Flood. Gilgamesh was the first of all epics to be put in writing. It is also the source of the story of Utnapishtim's flood, upon which the biblical version is thought by many to be based. The Royal Cemetery of Ur, where the seals were found, antedated Langdon's Kish flood. This logically ruled out the latter as a candidate for Utnapishtim's flood. Because Noah's flood story also contains many elements found in Gilgamesh, this would have put the biblical event earlier as well.

Other archaeologists have challenged Woolley's claim to have found Noah's flood. One of the better known was Agatha Christie's husband, Max Mallowan. Present during all the early Ur excavations, he returned to the old question thirty-five years later – after Woolley's death – in a review, 'Noah's Flood Reconsidered'.[7] Mallowan agreed with Woolley that there had to be a historical counterpart to the Mesopotamian flood story. He also felt that the Gilgamesh epic was the key to its date, but for different reasons. Gilgamesh, King of Uruk, had visited the elderly King Utnapishtim to consult him on immortality. The latter told Gilgamesh the story of a world-drowning flood which he had survived, after which ordeal he had been granted immortality and a retirement home in the East. Using the epic account and a large dose of licence Mallowan placed Gilgamesh as a historical character around 2600 BC, and Utnapishtim's flood at 2900 BC. Traces of riverine floods corresponding with this timing were present both at Kish and at Fara but not in Ur. These floods were, however, much less severe than either Woolley's or Langdon's candidate floods.

Mallowan also agreed with Woolley's reason for rejecting Langdon's Kish flood as being too late to have been described by Utnapishtim. Based on his own literary interpretation of the dates of Gilgamesh's life, however, Mallowan in turn rejected Woolley's Ur flood as being far too early for the same semi-mythical person. From an evidential standpoint Mallowan's reasoning seems to be on softer ground than Woolley's. Woolley used the stratigraphy to date the events in the story; Mallowan did it the other way round using literary evidence to

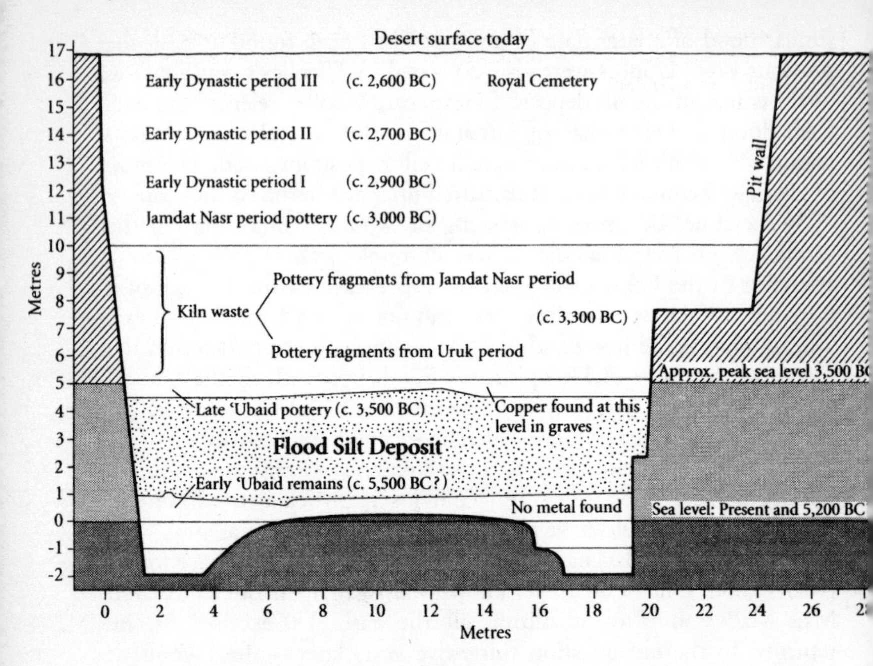

Figure 5. **Sir Leonard Woolley's flood.** This vertical section of Sir Leonard Woolley's famous 'Pit F' at Ur in Mesopotamia spans maybe three thousand years of human occupation from early 'Ubaid times to the great dynasties of the early third millennium BC. The Flood silt deposit at the base which divides the 'Ubaidian period is bounded above by the peak post-glacial sea-level, and at the bottom by today's sea-level, suggesting that it was laid down by the sea. (Adapted, by permission of the British Museum, from the original.[3])

try and identify the correct flood stratum. In choosing the lesser of the floods, Mallowan admitted that the catastrophic, 'civilisation-destroying' element would be lost from the historic event. His approach thus seems to ignore the most common feature of the Near Eastern family of flood myths. In any case, it reduces the relevance of the whole question.

Missing strata

Although he made a strong case for his silt layer marking the demise of the 'Ubaid Neolithic period, Woolley did acknowledge an unanswered question. This was implicit in the overall paucity of 'Ubaid

C	Woolley's 'F' Pit at Ur stratigraphy	Woolley's chronology	Sumerian King list	Suggested chronology	Pottery periods
00	Early Dynastic period III Early Dynastic period II Early Dynastic period I	Early Dynastic III Early Dynastic II	First Dynasty of Ur	First Dynasty of Ur	
00	Jamdat-Nasr pottery Uruk pottery Late 'Ubaid	Early Dynastic I Jamdat-Nasr Uruk period 'Ubaid late			Jamdat-Nasr
00	Upper limit of silt	— Short Flood — 'Ubaid early			Uruk
00			First Dynasty of Erech	First Dynasty of Uruk ?Kish	
00	Sea covered 'F' site during this period		First Dynasty of Kish	'Ubaid Neolithic in Eridu and on parts of Gulf now submerged	'Ubaid
00	Sea crosses present mean level				
00	Early 'Ubaid remains Rapid sea level rise		**The Flood** Long period of ante-deluvian kings	**The Flood** Ante-diluvian kings Eridu	
00					
00					

Figure 6. **Stretching the timeline.** Different views of the Mesopotamian timeline and the Flood are revealed in Sir Leonard Woolley's 'Pit F'. From 3500 to 2500 BC there is no conflict. Woolley's assumed short duration of the Flood does not, however, allow sufficient time for the long post-diluvian dynasties of Erech and Kish. A prolonged flood covering the F site throughout most of the 'Ubaid period (left column) resolves the problem and pushes the start of the flood back 2000 years.

remains in the famous pit F of his Ur dig, which contained the important silt layer. (The 'Ubaid pottery period lasted for some 1500–2000 years and pre-dated the so-called Uruk, Jemdat Nasr and Early Dynastic ceramic periods of Sumer.)

The archaeology of the 'Ubaid period indicates a sophisticated Neolithic culture characterised by fine painted pottery with distinct styles. Nineteen phases of this period have been described from the earliest settlement in Eridu. The depth and the numbers of 'Ubaid strata at the nearby site of Eridu were simply not apparent in the F-pit remains of Ur. The sequence of the lowest strata in Woolley's F pit from Ur shows less than 2 metres of early 'Ubaid remains at the base. They are sandwiched between virgin soil and the water-laid silt deposit

3–4 metres thick. The artefacts in the layer beneath the silt were mostly broken early 'Ubaid sherds lying flat. Woolley commented that these had probably been thrown out of windows into a shallow marsh. Immediately above the silt layer was, in Woolley's words, an apparently 'short-lived survival of the 'Ubaid culture in a degenerate form … underlying the Uruk period'.[8]

If there were early 'Ubaid remains beneath the silt, and late 'Ubaid remains above it, the silt layer must either have been there throughout the rest of the 'Ubaid period, or the flood must have washed away the intervening layers.

A sea flood?

This anomalous gap in the Ur record is now easy to explain on the basis of the silt layer. Rather than scouring 'Ubaid remains away, the flood had covered the site of the F pit for many years during the 'Ubaid period. It thus physically prevented occupation. For this model, however, we would have to recognise that either the river changed course or an incursion of the sea covered the site during this period rather than a short-lived riverine flood. The latter is not a new idea. In fact, Woolley himself mentions contemporary texts referring to Ur and Eridu 'by the sea'. Mallowan also suggested that Woolley's layer was marine or estuarine silt.[9] He felt that this disqualified Woolley's hypothesis even further because in his (Mallowan's) view Genesis made no mention of a sea flood. As we shall see later, most legendary or mythological floods were marine, so this argument is actually supportive of Woolley's case.[10]

As described in Chapter 1, geologists and archaeologists have found evidence of just such an incursion of sea water in the Arabian Gulf,[11] supporting the notion that the flowering of the Sumerian civilisation in Mesopotamia was preceded by a major rise in sea-level. Combining data from six sources, American archaeologist Juris Zarins plotted the Flandrian (or Hammar) sea transgression in the gulf region. This rose to peak at 3 metres above present-day mean sea-level (MSL) around 5500 years ago at the end of the 'Ubaid period, and eventually returned to present-day sea-levels between 2000 and 1000 BC. This Flandrian transgression was in fact the final overshoot of the 120–150 metre rise in sea-level that converted the Arabian Gulf from dry land after the Ice Age to the large expanse of water we see today.

At the height of the last Ice Age 20,000 years ago, the Arabian Gulf was dry, except for three small lakes that did not communicate with the sea. After the first of the three post-glacial floods abated around

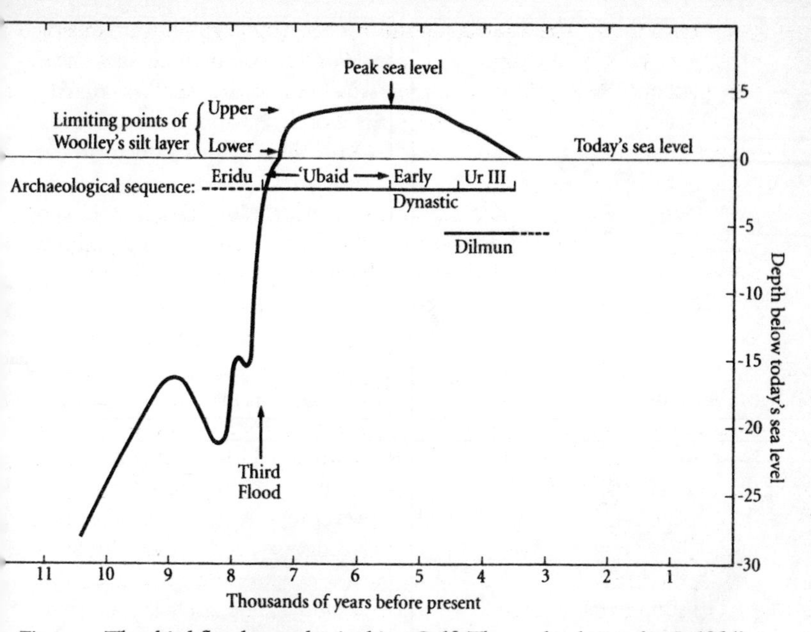

Figure 7. **The third flood over the Arabian Gulf.** The sea-level over the Gulf fell briefly in the seventh millennium BC and then rose rapidly to cross present-day mean sea-level (MSL) in the middle of the sixth millennium BC. Thereafter it continued to rise more slowly, peaking about three metres above MSL around 3500 BC during the 'Ubaid period, and eventually returned to present-day sea-levels between 2000–1000 BC. Archaeological sequences are as shown in Figures 5 and 6. (Curve adapted from Zarins (1992);[11] timescale corrected to absolute calendar years.)

13,500 years ago, two of these lakes had joined up with each other for half the length of the gulf, and through the Straits of Hormuz to the sea. The Gulf was still mostly dry land with a few disconnected lakes. There was some further flooding of land up to the start of the second flood 11,500 years ago. Nevertheless, the Gulf was at that time merely a narrow channel and more than half of the basin was still dry.

The second surge of the sea, starting 11,500 years ago, inundated much of the gulf coastline. Consequently, when sea-levels stabilised before the last of the three floods more than three-quarters of the present gulf outline was sea.

The final and third flood, which struck sometime after 8000 years

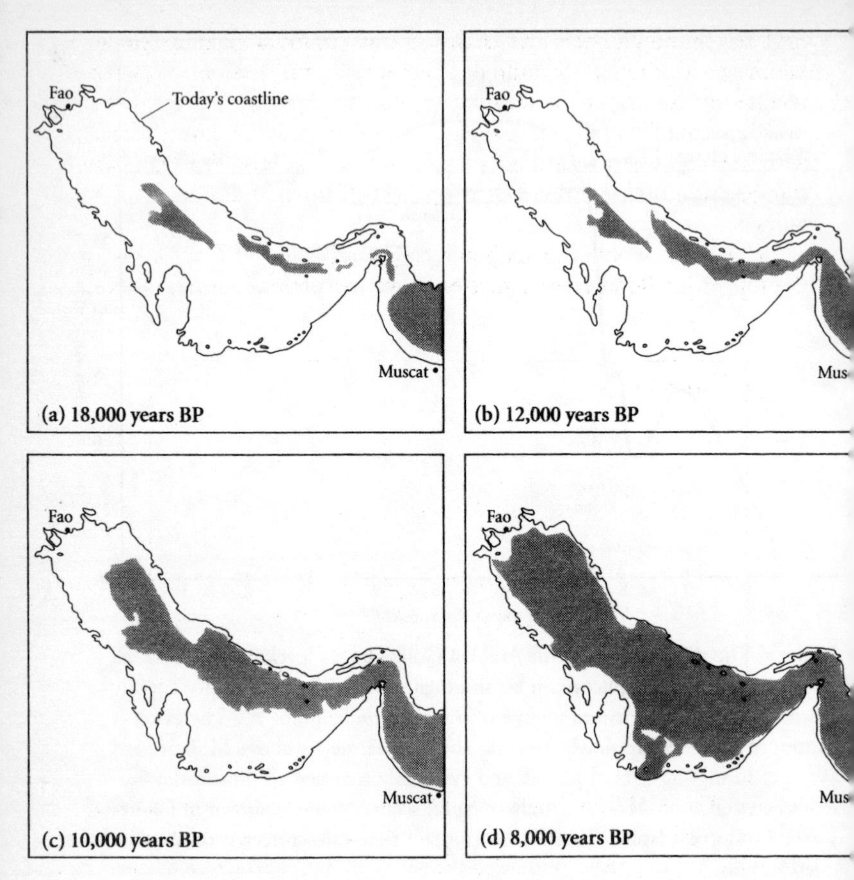

Figure 8. **The flooding of the Arabian Gulf.** To get an idea of the rapidity and scale of land loss in the Gulf we are fortunate to have computerized maps of the Gulf basin, as it changed with postglacial flooding. (Maps adapted with permission from Lambeck (1996; fig. 7);[11] timescale: uncorrected radiocarbon years before present.)

ago, resulted, as we have seen, mainly from the spectacular collapse of the Canadian Laurentide ice plate. During this inundation less land was probably lost in the Gulf than in the previous flood but it disappeared over a much shorter timescale. By the time the sea reached present-day levels, the waves had raced in over 200 kilometres of coastline during a few years or less. The flood did not stop there. Over the next few hundred years the coastline was eroded a further 150–180 kilometres during the Flandrian (Hammar) transgression. This represented a rise of 3–5 metres over present-day levels.[12] Curiously, but probably coincidentally, such a sea-level overshoot agrees not too badly with the high-water record of 15 cubits in Genesis 7:20. The Flandrian transgression took the flood right up to Ur, Lagash and other cities of Sumer.

Sir Leonard Woolley's stratigraphical record from pit F at Ur places the top of his flood layer 4 metres above the present mean sea-level.

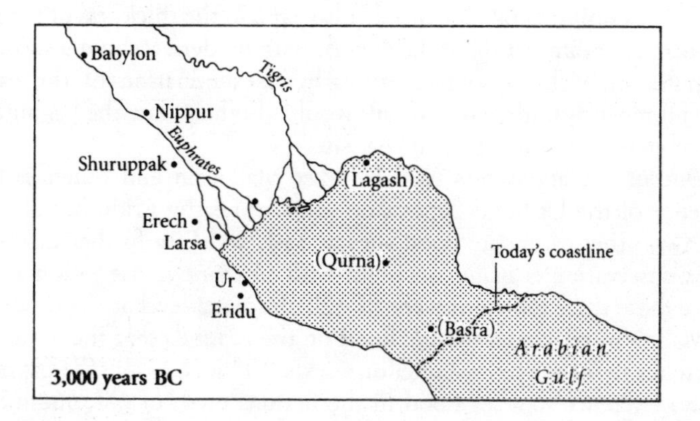

Figure 9. **The third flood in the Arabian Gulf.** Sometime after 8000 years ago the third flood struck, crossing today's coastline between 7500 and 7000 years ago. It did not stop there, invading a further 170 km up to the ancient cities of Ur, Eridu and Lagash by 3000 BC. Present-day sites such as the city of Basra were at that time inundated.

This is remarkably close to the maximum height of the Flandrian transgression estimated by other means. The coincidence is extraordinary and, unless one of the original measurements was wrong, the only explanation that fits is that the silt layer was laid below sea- or estuarine-level (see Figures 5–7). That means Woolley's flood must have been marine. As to whether the whole of the Ur site was inundated at the time of that flood even Woolley reserved judgement because the centre of the old city appeared to be raised on a knoll or island. Equivalent pits that would have answered this question, however, were not dug in the centre. A map of the Gulf reconstructed to 5000–2500 BC (Figure 9) places Ur on the edge of, but not inundated by, the marine transgression.[13]

In the discussions of the nature and origin of the silt layer in the Ur pits most authorities describe it as of fluvial origin. This does not contradict a marine transgression. Ur was close to the Euphrates and in a region of active delta formation. Hence any silt deposited in this area as the sea-level rose from the southeast would therefore be more likely to be estuarine than marine. Silt deposition in an estuary would actually be enhanced by a rising sea due to the slowing of the current. This effect could indeed have shortened the time that the site as a whole was uninhabitable. It would also explain the thickness of the silt deposit. Re-examination of the deposit with modern techniques would help to establish its source. Similarly, re-examination of the early 'Ubaid remains underlying the silt would also help date the beginning of the marine transgression at that site.

One of the arguments used by Max Mallowan and others is the absence of the Ur flood deposit not only in nearby Eridu but also in the two other candidate flood sites at Kish and Fara further inland.[14] This observation is again consistent with a marine transgression at Ur since these three locations were all well above sea-level at the time.

Mallowan rejected a marine flood on the grounds that there was no reference to the sea in the cuneiform texts.[15] This is curious. There may be no reference to a sea flood in the famous myth of Gilgamesh but the Sumerian dragon-slaying myth of Ninurta and Kur[16] refers specifically to a lasting marine transgression over the Tigris delta. Surprisingly Mallowan also refers to the following key Genesis verses to support his argument:

> were all the fountains of the great deep broken up, and the windows of heaven were opened (Genesis 7:11)

> The fountains also of the deep and the windows of heaven were stopped, and the rain from heaven was restrained (Genesis 8:2)

Having introduced this evidence in context Mallowan then goes on to say, illogically in my view, that it would be stretching the imagination to infer a marine inundation from these verses. To the untutored reader the words 'great deep' seem to refer to the sea. Having said this, it also seems highly likely that frequent seasonal river floods would have exacerbated the effects of the marine transgression. The period 8000–7000 years ago was approaching the period of 'climatic optimum' of the interglacial.[17] Not only were the northern glaciers discharging huge volumes of water into the Atlantic, the mean global temperature was 4 degrees centigrade higher than today, and global annual precipitation was much higher. Areas such as the Indus Valley and Mesopotamia, which are arid today, were enjoying a particularly high rainfall. In his recent book on the archaeology of the Arabian Gulf, archaeologist Michael Rice refers to the time 7000–4000 BC as the 'Neolithic Moist Phase'.[18]

In identifying the Fara flood as the most likely candidate for Utnapishtim's (and thus in his view Noah's) flood, Mallowan discounted the biblical emphasis on a world-destroying catastrophe because this quite clearly did not fit the archaeological record of the Fara flood. This problem of a short-lived fluvial flood, however, does not apply to a prolonged sea-level rise. According to Juris Zarins, the Flandrian marine transgression would have inundated all the 'Ubaid I settlements southeast of a line from Ur through Lagash to Amara.[19] Many early 'Ubaid ruins may still lie under the waters of the Gulf. If this transgression was the same as Woolley's flood it would thus have a strong claim to be catastrophic.

Was Noah's flood the same as Utnapishtim's?

What seems to be wrong in the literary arguments made by Max Mallowan and Leonard Woolley is the assumption that, because of the other similarities between the Gilgamesh epic and the Noachian flood story, both were intended by their bards to refer to the same flood. The Gilgamesh epic was crafted for dynastic rulers. One well-recognised tendency of epic authors is to add modern context to ancient stories, perhaps to make them more interesting, credible or flattering to their audience. Thomas Malory's re-setting and transposition of the *Morte d'Arthur*, from Celtic legends of the Dark Ages forward into the Age of Chivalry is one such example.[20] It is possible that the writer(s) of Gilgamesh used the same device to personalise an older prehistoric flood still present in folk memory to more recent well-known dynastic heroes (Gilgamesh and Utnapishtim) and a known contemporary historic flood (Fara). The Genesis authors would have had no such obligation to the Sumerian royal dynasties although their original folk source may have been the same. It is possible that the Gilgamesh epic was not available to the patriarch Abraham and his family before they left Ur carrying with them their own ancient oral tradition.

Apart from Mallowan's anachronistic dating of the flood based on Gilgamesh, the other main ancient source, the Sumerian King Lists, place that flood firmly before the first dynasties of Kish, Erech and Ur.

This is chronologically more or less where Woolley placed it in 1928. There is, however, a major problem with Woolley's chronology. Woolley, like most diluvial commentators, assumed that the flood was a short-lived event. Mallowan dated this event, as defined by the top of the silt layer, to 3500 BC. Even if this was an underestimate, it would have left only 500 years for the first dynasties of Kish and Erech to have evolved before that of Ur. The Sumerian King Lists record these three dynasties sequentially with some very long-lived kings. Five hundred years would have been quite a squeeze for three dynasties, even with kings living a normal life-span. The usual solution to this chronology problem has been to argue that the three dynasties were really contemporaneous rather than sequential. If the start of that flood was 2000 years before (that is, 7500 years ago) as shown in the geological record, this overcomes the problem (see Figure 6).

A curious consequence of identifying Woolley's silt layer as a result of prolonged inflooding of sea water, the same flood of the Sumerian King Lists, is that it could make most of the long 'Ubaid period effectively post-diluvian. This follows logically if we date the legendary flood to the rapid first incursion, which occurred at least 7500 years ago. The flood would then have hit at the same time, or before the beginning of, the 'Ubaid pottery styles. The pre-Sumerian 'Ubaidians also lived in the cities of Kish, Erech and Ur. They could thus, on this model, be regarded in the context of the Sumerian King Lists as co-citizens of the respective first post-diluvian dynasty, namely Kish. The King Lists record the dynasty of Kish being established immediately following the subsidence of the flood.[21] Depending on interpretation of the onset of subsidence, and on the accuracy of the sea-level curves, this named marine retreat could have been any time between 7000 and 5500 years ago.

If the 'Ubaidians were mainly post-diluvian then certain other opaque historiographic records take on a different light. The god Ea, whose first temple was in the ancient city of Eridu, was credited with bringing in the seven amphibian sages from the East to teach crafts to man.[22] Whatever form this importation of expatriate skills took, it could have started as early as 7000 years ago. Eridu holds the most complete and ancient record of the development of 'Ubaidian pottery and could have been the first city of southeast Mesopotamia. Whoever the 'Ubaidians were, the continuity of their pottery in the same locations as the succeeding cruder Uruk style, dating from 6000 years ago, suggests a continuous joint development of civilisation in the region over a long period from 5500 BC. The plain and red-slipped Uruk pottery, which appears on the Ur site 6000 years ago, may well define the arrival of the new Sumerians.[23] Little is known of the origin of the earlier 'Ubaidian people, or of their language. They are not generally regarded as Sumerian. One suggestion, based on the non-Sumerian names of the main Sumerian cities, is that the 'Ubaidians were Semitic.[24]

The Sumerians were by contrast regarded as migrants from the East. Archaeologist Henri Frankfort, in discussing the ethnic affinities of the Sumerians, states: 'Regarding the people who appeared in the south at the beginning of the Uruk period ... they were brachycephalic ...'[25] While several different shapes of skull have been attributed to Sumerians, brachycephalic skulls, (literally broad-headed) are a distinct feature of people from the Far East.[26] Brachycephaly was also a feature noted in the mysterious 'Beaker People' who appeared all over the coasts and up the rivers of western Europe during the third millennium BC. The issue of prehistoric invasions of broad-headed people from the East into Europe has a long and controversial history. At present it is definitely out of favour and is in any case beyond the scope of this book.[27]

If the Sumerians came from the East, the real antediluvian Kings may not even have all lived in coastal Mesopotamia, because there is no archaeological evidence for habitation of these cities before the appearance of the finely painted 'Ubaid pottery. We have the curious story of one of the kings recounted in Gilgamesh.[28] This was none other than Utnapishtim, the Sumerian Noah, who survived the flood only to retire and live his immortal life far across the sea to the east. We may wonder from Gilgamesh's epic sea journey to visit Utnapishtim, just how far east this was. One of the most famous archaeological commentators on the origins of the Sumerians, Benno Landsberger, argued that they sailed from the East across the sea, and that stories such as Divine Creation, Paradise and Noah's flood came with them:[29]

> the urban culture of Mesopotamia was already developed to a high degree before the immigration of the Sumerians; but it was the Sumerians who created the intellectual and artistic values of this culture. The date of the Sumerian immigration cannot yet be fixed. It can also not be determined that they produced these intellectual accomplishments only in Mesopotamia itself, or whether they already brought the seeds of them from their eastern home. The legend of the Seven Sages who, emerging from the sea, imparted all technical skills and all knowledge to the Babylonians may quite possibly have some historical basis.[30]

I move next to the sea flood those sages may have been fleeing in the East.

The drowning of Southeast Asia and the Austronesian dispersal

I have discussed the false archaeological horizon in the Arabian Gulf – represented by the silt layer at Ur – and the controversy about it. Archaeologists throughout the Far East are now beginning to take stock of a similar effect on their extensive continental shelves. Island Southeast Asia has the highest concentration of flood myths in the world. It is an area with few large river deltas and no recent reputation for flooding, but it lost more than 50 per cent of its landmass after the Ice Age. Again, as in the case of the Gulf, the effect of the rise in sea-level was to obliterate evidence of older coastal Neolithic cultures and to give archaeologists a false horizon. The resulting gaps have given rise to widely differing views of East Asian prehistory. China's flat coastline suffered vast losses as well, and it is from here that some of the best evidence of the effects of the flooding comes.

Geologists have now shown that the last great flood hit the Chinese coast in the eighth millennium before our time. One of the first archaeologists to recognise the effect of this flooding on the appearance and chronology of Far Eastern coastal Neolithic sites was William Meacham. Working from Hong Kong since 1970 and with mainland colleagues, Meacham has opened a window on many Neolithic sites of the South China coast. He has stressed the importance of the drowned coastal strip 'Nanhailand' that once spread up to 160 kilometres out into the South China Sea in interpretations of the region's prehistory. He argues that the early Neolithic coastal dwellers would have made a rich marine harvest from the tidal mud flats and mangrove swamps before the flooding. He believes that these coastal people were from diverse backgrounds, but were not directly linked culturally or linguistically with the Neolithic cultures on the Yangtze (Chiang Jiang) River further north. (See Figure 13, top map).[31]

During the first half of the post-glacial period (10,000–5000 years ago), sea-level along the South China coast and Vietnam went through very much the same pattern of rise, plateau and fall as in the Arabian Gulf. The final rise and fall of the sea probably obliterated much of the early Neolithic on the Chinese coast. Meacham noted in 1985: 'The most important gap in the Neolithic record now is the total absence of open sites in lowland areas dating from 10,000 to 5000 BC.'[32] The last period of rapid rise crossed present-day sea-levels around 7000 years ago. Levels then peaked around 5 metres above today's, and declined later. Although there clearly was an overshoot, researchers cannot agree about the date and height of the highest water level, and some geologists believe the peaks oscillated a great deal before sea-levels finally fell.[33] After the decline from 6000 years onwards, pot-making maritime settlements appeared all the way down from Taiwan to central Vietnam.[34]

Charles Higham, a New Zealand archaeologist working mainly in Thailand, argues that these settlements were simply relocations of maritime people who had always lived in this area but who had been flooded out. These hypothetical coastal cultures would have been continuously rebuilding during and after the flood. Higham's argument is based on the lack of evidence of people moving from anywhere else, and certain cultural resemblances with the pre-existing, much older pre-Neolithic 'Hoabinhian' cultures further inland in Vietnam.[35] Recently, however, archaeologists have found exciting and more direct evidence of the effect of this flood on coastal settlements that throws a different light on human settlement along the south China coast. The story that the finds reveal has an uncanny resemblance to the saga of Sir Leonard Woolley's silt layer described earlier. Some ninety Neolithic settlements on coastal sand bars dating back over 7000 years have been found in the Hainan Island and Pearl River estuary regions near Hong Kong.

Many of the pots and other artefacts from these settlements are similar, and this has led to attempts to construct a unified prehistoric sequence of cultural development on the south China coast. At one extreme, four phases or layers of development have been discerned.[36] A more simple view is expressed by Li Guo from Zhongshan University of Guangzhou. He recognises only two main cultural phases among these numerous Neolithic sites. The first phase coincided with the period immediately after the rapid rise of the sea, when levels were just crossing the present-day mark; this phase lasted from about 7000 to 5750 years ago. The second phase began after the decline of sea-level, and lasted from about 4850 to 3550 years ago. These two phases are separated by a silt layer up to 150 centimetres thick, which Li Guo describes thus:

> Between the first and the second phases in many major sites there is a sterile layer which might be caused by changes in sea-level. This sterile layer suggests a cultural discontinuity, especially when taking into account the material culture of the two phases ... in the first phase painted pottery was most common ... The second phase contains soft geometric pottery.[37]

Artefacts and the painted and incised pottery of the first phase are also found elsewhere along the south China coast, and are described as Middle Neolithic.[38] The plain and geometric wares of Li Guo's second phase similarly occur elsewhere in south China and constitute the Late Neolithic. Li Guo points out that this widespread cultural and chronological hiatus on sand bars may be more apparent than real in terms of the real continuity of coastal cultures. In spite of the apparent desertion of these sites for over 700 years, other archaeological sites in the Pearl River area show well-dated, continuous habitation and cultural development over the same period. This contrast between flooded and unflooded settlements is analogous to that of the 'Ubaid people who lived on over a thousand years in Eridu during the flood that submerged part of Ur during the same period. Again, as for the Arabian Gulf, the Middle Neolithic stratum from 7000 to 5750 years ago discovered on the south China coast represents a short archaeological window when the rising sea was crossing present-day levels. Earlier coastal Neolithic sites which could well go back thousands of years further into the past will now be inaccessible far out on the tidal flats and under the South China Sea. Many of the artefacts found on the south China coast in Middle Neolithic deposits under the silt[39] even have functional counterparts in those found in Ur beneath Woolley's silt. These include perforated clay discs or net sinkers, clay spindle whorls, painted bowls, shell beads and imported semi-precious stones, quadrangular polished stone adzes and stone hoes.[40]

Although covering long periods of occupation, the Pearl River sand-bar settlements appear to be temporary fishing habitations, and were often paired with more permanent settlements characterised by shell deposits further inland. This kind of 'long-term temporary' settlement is like the stilted fishing platforms with small huts found on coastal tidal flats throughout Austronesian-speaking island Southeast Asia and the Pacific (see illustration 2).

A maritime trading network in Southeast Asia and the Pacific

In contrast to Meacham's and Higham's view of the essentially local nature of the Middle Neolithic development in coastal southern China, American archaeologist Wilhelm Solheim has argued that these sand-bar settlements were occupied by migrant people who were part of an extended coastal and island maritime trading network throughout the Pacific rim and into island Southeast Asia from around 7000 years ago to the present day. Most of the people of this network would have spoken Austronesian tongues, a language family spoken throughout island Southeast Asia and today also from Madagascar in the Indian Ocean to most of the small islands of the Pacific (see Chapter 5). Solheim calls the culture of this network 'Nusantao'. Solheim regards the rapidly flooding Sunda shelf of island Southeast Asia at the end of the Ice Age as the original homeland of the Nusantao maritime culture:

> My hypothesis of the origin and development of the Nusantao maritime trading network is as follows. The origin of the Nusantao as a sailing and navigating people was in eastern Indonesia and the nearby southern Philippines. Improvement in their sailing abilities was forced upon them by the rising sea-levels ... which required movement across gradually longer stretches of open sea to maintain contact with relatives and homeland. Outrigger canoes were probably necessary for the expansion of the Nusantao and the origin and center of innovation of all Austronesian boat traits probably lies in the islands surrounding Sulawesi.[41]

In taking the view of a homeland in island Southeast Asia for Austronesians, Wilhelm Solheim is in broad agreement with fellow archaeologist William Meacham but in complete disagreement with Australia-based archaeologist Peter Bellwood and most Austronesian linguists (see Figure 12). Solheim sees the Pearl River sand-bar settlements as an amalgam of Nusantao culture and the Middle Neolithic of southern China. He also believes that this hybrid may have spread locally to Taiwan to produce similar Austronesian-speaking settlements, which archaeologists call the Ta-p'en-k'eng culture.[42]

The alternative idea – that one of the Middle Neolithic cultures from the mouth of the Yangtze River further north in China could be ancestral to an Austronesian-speaking dispersal to the Pacific through Taiwan and the Philippines – has been championed by Peter Bellwood. Taiwan, as we shall see, is also the favoured linguistic launching ground for such a dispersal in the view of Robert Blust, Austronesian linguist from Hawai'i. Blust developed his hypothesis of a Taiwanese homeland for Austronesian tongues during the 1970s and 1980s primarily on linguistic evidence. The theory refined with archaeological suggestions over the years (from Bellwood) has expanded to include an Asian mainland home as well as a comprehensive reconstruction of Southeast Asian and Oceanic prehistory. This China-Taiwan theory of Austronesian origins is presently the most widely accepted model. Bellwood and Blust present a comprehensive and tantalising picture, because today there is no other candidate site with Austronesian tongues nearer China than Taiwan. Taiwan's own Austronesian tongues are very different from each other and from those in the rest of the dispersed language family, thus giving the Taiwanese Aboriginal cultures an authentic antiquity.

There are, however, no clear antecedents to Austronesian tongues in mainland Asia today, and a mainland origin of Austronesian languages has yet to be established, let alone locating a site for it. Because pots cannot identify their makers' speech and language splits are difficult to place and date, much of the argument relating to Austronesian origins depends on mutual underpinning by linguistics and archaeology. It is very important, therefore, that each piece of evidence in the structure be independent and not reciprocally linked to the other discipline as Blust himself has pointed out.[43]

William Meacham with his long experience of Chinese archaeology notes that there is no direct linguistic evidence for a mainland Austronesian homeland, and has refuted Bellwood's archaeological evidence as well. Like Wilhelm Solheim, Tsang and others, Meacham sees Taiwan as an isolated backwater on the periphery of Austronesian prehistory, protected through the Neolithic from much linguistic and cultural change.[44]

This is not a minor academic difference of opinion. The whole prehistory of Southeast Asia and the Pacific takes on a radically different look depending on which side is taken. It is important to establish the reliability, or otherwise, of the Bellwood and Blust hypothesis from the start. This is because in their model, the dates of the whole Austronesian dispersal are very closely determined by the initial archaeological sequence in Taiwan and the Philippines. These are: (1) Arrival in Taiwan from China 4500 BC; (2) Arrival in the Philippines from Taiwan 3000 BC; (3) South Philippines 2000 BC.[45] The rest of Southeast Asian and Oceanic prehistory, then, has to follow a tightly imposed breakneck geographic and chronological schedule, ending in a rapid dispersal to the Pacific 3500 years ago, over a period of maybe less than 200 years. Many aspects of Oceanic and Southeast Asian archaeology, however, simply do not support this tight schedule. Clearly several other routes and origins of the Austronesian dispersal are possible. For instance, Austronesian languages could have arisen in Oceania or in island Southeast Asia, allowing a potentially much longer time for the migration. Finally, if Austronesians did originate on the Asian mainland, they could have migrated several times from the coast, not just once through Taiwan, which, again, would allow a deeper timescale than a single spread through Taiwan.

What I will show here is first, that Bellwood's model based on food and material culture of the south China coastal peoples is insecure; second, arguments based on archaeological remains in Taiwan and the Philippines could theoretically apply in reverse to direct migrations from any part of the south China coast or from Southeast Asia, thus avoiding Taiwan;[46] and third, I will quote other evidence that there were maritime dispersals from Southeast Asia much earlier than supposed in the Bellwood and Blust 'China-Taiwan-Philippines' hypothesis.

In addition to plotting an archaeological sequence of possible sites that early Austronesian speakers could have occupied, Bellwood puts forward a speculative model of the cultural development of the early Austronesians basing it on linguistic reconstructions of an Austronesian proto-language and specific terms for foodstuffs and other everyday items. The content of this proto-language depends however on the pre-conceived shape of the language tree used for the reconstruction. If the shape or sub-grouping of the tree is wrong, so is the proto-tongue. For Bellwood, the most important skill or cultural marker of the first Austronesians was growing rice. But as I shall show, this conviction is based more on a perceived need to explain why the Austronesians migrated than on any linguistic argument.

The diet of the first Austronesians

Bellwood lists three skills or habits that he feels are the backbone of his archaeolinguistic reconstruction of an Austronesian dispersal from China to Taiwan and then to the Philippines – chewing of betel-nuts, rice farming and pottery styles. The second of these is a puzzling choice. Archaeological and ethnological evidence suggests that sago and root crops such as taro and yams were the prehistoric staples, not rice, throughout most of the Austronesian dispersal. The importance Bellwood attaches to rice may be seen from the following passage relating to the origins of Austronesian tongues:

> in the case of the oldest Taiwanese Neolithic assemblages I think the possibility of an expansion of rice cultivation and its associated technology from the Yangtze region through Zhejiang and Fujian must be accepted. This is simply because I regard rice cultivation as an important component of the economy behind early Austronesian expansion, and because the Yangtze sites do have an impressive chronological priority for rice cultivation in terms of present knowledge. Should evidence for rice cultivation prior to 3500 BC eventually be found in Vietnam, Hong Kong and Guangdong then I would perhaps change this view.[47]

Figure 10. **Neolithic fragments from Southeast Asia.** Distribution of Southeast Asian early Neolithic archaeological sites (in italics) referred to in Chapters 2 and 3. Note the predominance of protected cave sites, reflecting probable destruction of other early Neolithic remains over the Sunda shelf. Shaded area indicates continental shelf to 100m.

Bellwood may have to change his view if some new findings are confirmed. Thai archaeologist Surin Pookajorn has found rice grains associated with pottery and other Neolithic artefacts such as polished stone adzes in Sakai Cave way south of China, down the Malay Peninsula (see Figure 10). These settlements date to between 9260 and 7620 years ago. The artefacts in this archaeological level are comparable in style to other early Indo-Chinese Neolithic sites in Ban Kao

(Thailand) and in Gua Cha further down the peninsula. Immediately beneath the Neolithic layer was a typical pre-Neolithic, pre-flood Hoabinhian culture, thus indicating continuity of occupation.[48] While he wisely takes care to qualify the risk of generalising from a few dates, Pookajorn concludes that, 'the Neolithic period in Southeast Asia must be reconsidered'.[49]

This is an understatement. Pookajorn's finding, if confirmed, could turn at least two pre-conceptions in East Asian prehistory on their heads. The so-called Hoabinhians, the pre-Neolithic inhabitants of Indo-China from at least 10,000 years ago, are usually thought to have been ancestors of Austro-Asiatic speakers and are presumed to have learnt their agricultural skills thousands of years later by diffusion from Early Neolithic cultures further north in China. Pookajorn's finding may reverse the direction of the learning process. His finding is not a lone one. Wilhelm Solheim has argued that the Hoabinhians may not have been as backward as is thought, and may have begun growing tubers at a very early date.[50] American archaeologist Joyce White has also pushed the date base of the Ban Chiang, a fully agricultural society of peninsula Thailand, as far back as the sixth to seventh millennium BC.[51] In other words, Indo-China may well prove able to match the earliest Chinese agricultural dates. The earliest archaeological site in China with clear evidence of large-scale rice growing is Hemudu just below the mouth of the Yangtze River. This Middle Neolithic site, occupied between 7000 and 5900 year ago[52] is where Bellwood believes the Austronesian cultures originated. The earliest sign of rice in China is further up the Yangtze at Pengtoushan dated to 6500–5800 BC, but it is not clear if the grains were from wild or domesticated plants. Charles Higham has said that, 'identifying the transition to rice cultivation is a central issue in the prehistory of Southeast Asia'.[53] As yet it is still a Holy Grail.

Several Neolithic sites in Indo-China, often where Austro-Asiatic languages are still spoken, have revealed tantalising artefactual evidence of early rice-growing and other agriculture, such as small ground-edged slate knives for rice-cutting and hoes, but no actual rice or identifiable plants were found until recently. These sites range from the famous Spirit Cave near the Burmese border to coastal sedentary settlements in the Bay of Bangkok and in Vietnam.[54] All of them date back to the fifth millennium BC, and show continuity with the previous Hoabinhian cultures. The Vietnamese sites yield pottery with characteristic cord markings and incised decorations and polished stone adzes familiar from the Middle Neolithic of Hong Kong. As I have mentioned, the Thai site of Sakai contains similar artefacts and is of comparable date, but it also has rice, suggesting primacy over the Chinese claim to have discovered rice first. This conclusion is biologically the most likely. As Peter Bellwood has pointed out, the prime 'home' sites for the culture of rice – where, climatically, the least manipulation is required to grow it – are in tropical Indo-China down to the Malay border, Burma, Bangladesh and the extreme south coast of China. Most of the Yangtze River and all of the Yellow River (Huang He) – China's riverine heartlands of Neolithic development – are outside these areas. An early Southeast Asian origin of rice culture could also have profound implications for the prehistoric spread of rice-growing further west to India, as I shall show.

To return to Taiwan, Bellwood, having invested his stake in the importance of rice to early Austronesian expansion out of the Philippines, surprisingly then shows rice only appearing in Taiwan 5000 years ago. This was 1500 years *after* the Austronesians were supposed to have arrived from China according to his model, and at the same time that he has them moving on to the Philippines.[55]

Rice was certainly grown before AD 1000 in the northern Philippines and in the Mariana islands 2500 kilometres to the east, and the cereal may well have been locally important in these isolated sites after the initial dispersal. But its presence or otherwise in these outposts does not seem to do anything to help the 'China-Taiwan' leg of Bellwood's hypothesis of early Austronesian expansion. In fact, rice seems to be a later aspect in Taiwanese Austronesian prehistory.[56]

More recently Bellwood has reported an early date of 2334 BC for rice temper found in pottery in Gua Sireh, a cave in Sarawak (Borneo). Wilhelm Solheim has pointed out, however, that this finding, far from showing a route of transmission of rice-growing through Taiwan and the Philippines to Borneo, suggests exactly the opposite route – namely from southwest to northeast.[57] New archaeological dates in the region also support this reverse sequence. The earliest site with evidence for agriculture is 5150 years old from Gua Sireh (Borneo), followed by Ulu Leang in Sulawesi 5100 years ago. This is followed by Rabel cave in Luzon, Philippines 4850 years ago and Uai Bobo in Timor 4100 years ago.[58] As we have seen, Bellwood regards rice cultivation as a crucial motive force to the hypothetical expansion of Austronesians south out of the Philippines, but it spoils rather than supports the case.

If the hypothetical founder proto-Austronesians on Taiwan were not rice growers, then the other barrel of the Bellwood and Blust linguistic/culinary reconstruction backfires as well. Bellwood argues that the acquisition of the foodstuffs that are most clearly identified with the subsequent Austronesian dispersal happened only after they arrived in the Philippines. He mentions chickens, breadfruit, taro, yams, banana, betel-nuts, sago and coconuts as being characteristic of the dispersed Austronesian speakers. Significantly, however, none of these appears in the reconstructed hypothetical proto-Austronesian vocabulary of Taiwan although they are in Blust's reconstructed hypothetical ancient proto-Malayo-Polynesian language of the Philippines.[59] Many of these items – except possibly bananas and coconuts – were also eaten by the prehistoric people of mainland Indo-China.

If they were not eating rice either, what staple did the proto-Austronesian Taiwanese eat, and where did all the delicious new Filipino foods come from 5000 years ago? Presuming for sake of argument that the Austronesian-speakers did originate somewhere on the Chinese mainland, it is much more likely that they would have taken their staple cultivars and animals with them rather than chancing what they might pick up in the Philippines. Although bananas may have originated in New Guinea or Maluku, taro still grows wild in Burma and Assam and is eaten widely by peoples of southern China and Indo-China. If proto-Austronesians had taken their food crops with them, then their terms for those plants should be similar in Taiwanese and Filipino tongues. But they are not. Thus, as with rice, the reverse direction of diffusion seems just as likely for root crops. Because growing of root crops started in New Guinea 9000 years ago, there is no reason to suppose that horticulture was not already established in island Southeast Asia long before the date of Bellwood's hypothetical Austronesian migration from China to Taiwan – if, that is, there ever was such a movement.

To summarise: rice-growing may not have been a feature of early Taiwanese life after all and the dates are wrong for it to have spread south from there to Borneo. Although rice may have been important later in the Austronesian settlements, other forms of agriculture in island Southeast Asia date back much earlier into the seventh millennium before present.

Rice, though, was clearly pivotal to the Neolithic stay-at-home mainland Indo-Chinese – from a very early stage, that is, if the Sakai Cave findings are confirmed. We now have a strange new image: instead of the sinocentric model with the Chinese inventing rice cultivation, we have Austro-Asiatic-speaking 'Southern Barbarians' from Indo-China teaching the know-how about rice to the Chinese. This view of a south-north spread of rice-growing has recently received support from Wilhelm Solheim on the basis of rice varieties.[60] For rice, the dates of first cultivation seem to be much earlier than suspected in mainland Southeast Asia, possibly even pre-flood. Other aspects of early farmers in the Far East also do not fit the notion of a late dispersal of Austronesians from China. While the notion of rice agriculture driving the hypothetical expansion of Austronesians from China to Taiwan is not supported by the evidence, the archaeological links also seem to be non-specific as we find next.

Incised, cord-marked and ring-footed pottery

To Peter Bellwood, characteristic pottery and other durable artefacts in the earliest Neolithic culture of western Taiwan, which include the site of Ta-p'en-k'eng (about 4000–2500 BC), suggest the route of the hypothetical early proto-Austronesian culture from Hemudu in China.[61] Among these cultural objects are cord-marked pots (made with a cord-wrapped paddle), pots with incised, stamped circular and puntate decorations, and pots with perforated ring-feet. Other items include stone adzes with a quadrangular cross-section, stone net weights, flaked hoes and bark-cloth beaters.[62] All these items are, however, also found in the pre-flood, first or Early Neolithic layer of the Pearl River delta near Hong Kong that I mentioned earlier. Archaeologists Kwang-Chi Chang from Harvard University and Ward Goodenough from the University of Pennsylvania, have pointed out that such groups of artefacts spread all the way down to Vietnam in the fifth millennium BC.[63]

This does not necessarily mean that the Taiwanese Early Neolithic came from Hong Kong in the south rather than from Hemudu further north in China, rather, more simply, that the whole tradition seems to have had a wider Southeast Asian distribution. French archaeologist Jean-Michel Chazine, for instance, has found cord-marked pottery dated to 5500 years ago in eastern Borneo.[64] There may be more potential links, for instance between Taiwan and the mainland coast to its southwest, than Bellwood accepted when he wrote in 1985: 'More information on southern Chinese developments has been excavated in recent years in Hong Kong, ... I believe this area to be rather too far south to be directly connected with Taiwanese prehistory.'[65]

The dates Bellwood cites for the earliest nearby mainland origin of the Ta-p'en-k'eng culture vary from about 11,000–7500 years ago on one site, to 7200–6200 years ago at another. On these dates, the Early Neolithic remains of the Pearl River and South China coast exposed at sights where the sea-level crossed present-day levels were clearly in the same cultural phase at the same time. Chang and Goodenough suggest that as there is no evidence for the non-Taiwanese Austronesian languages (that is, all the others) arising directly from Taiwan, it is equally possible, presuming a China origin, that they spread to island Southeast Asia separately and directly from the Chinese coast.[66] If an early and specific Hemudu-Taiwan-Philippines dispersal route is so vague archaeologically and linguistically, the link seems to fade into multiple possible tracks.

Blowpipes, bark-cloth, and megaliths

In his 1985 review *The Prehistory of the Indo-Malaysian Archipelago*, Peter Bellwood makes a comprehensive reconstruction of Austronesian societies of the region, before they were exposed to Indian cultural influences from the end of the first millennium BC onwards.[67] He acknowledges several characteristic non-food cultural features of Austronesians that cannot be traced archaeologically or linguistically in the supposed Taiwan homeland. Others, although found in Taiwan, have a variable representation on the Asian mainland. One characteristic hunting tool he mentions, the blowpipe, could make a hole in Bellwood's 'China-Taiwan-Philippines' model of Austronesian prehistory.

The historic use of blowpipes for hunting in Eurasia has been well defined by Stephen Jett, an American geographer.[68] His analysis of some related design features of blowpipes suggests that they were invented in prehistoric times around Borneo, with later regional elaboration. Today, there is a clear linguistic distribution of blowpipe use among two major language groups – the Austronesians and Austro-Asiatics. Among the latter group, blowpipe use stretches in an intermittent fashion from Austro-Asiatic Aboriginals in Malaya to Mundaics in India. It is also characteristic of some other Indian Aboriginals in the south and in Sri Lanka. With few exceptions, the region of continuous use of blowpipes in island Southeast Asia almost exactly describes the large western half of the distribution of Austronesian languages (see Chapters 4 and 5). Blowpipes are thus even found among the Chams of South Vietnam, Madagascar and one tiny Austronesian-speaking Micronesian island thousands of kilometres into the Pacific. Jett reasonably suggests that this joint Austronesian and Austro-Asiatic distribution points to the blowpipe being a marker for the original 'Austric' speakers.[69] Jett's hypothesis for the prehistoric origin of the blowpipe in Asia is very plausible; the exceptions in blowpipe distribution in Southeast Asia near Oceania also tell us much about the prehistory of Austronesians.

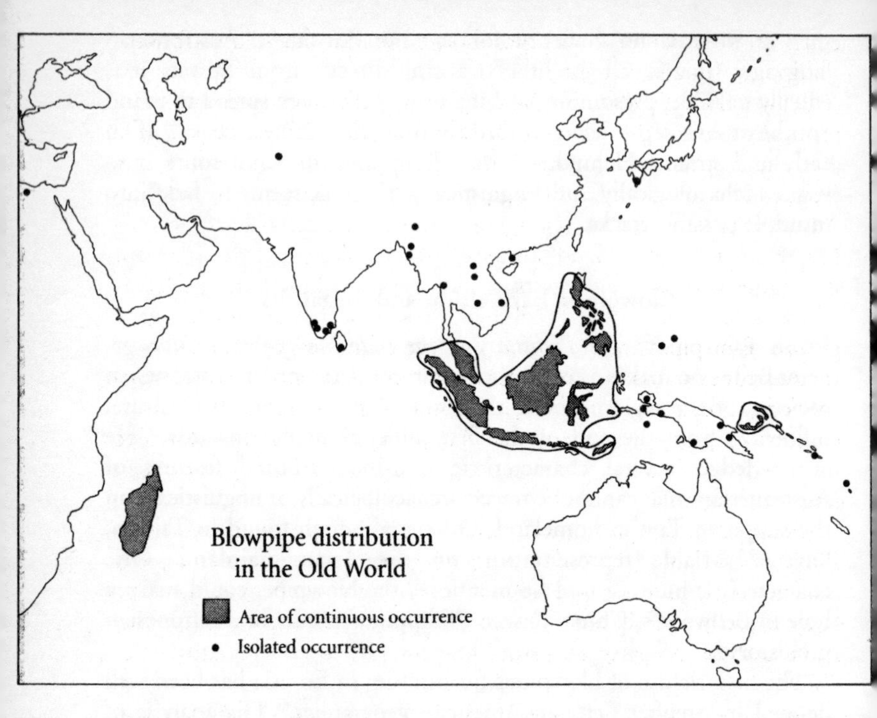

Figure 11. **Blowpipe distribution in the Old World.** Analysis of the technology and distribution of this prehistoric weapon indicates its origin in the Island of Borneo by people speaking languages still spoken in that region. The areas of continuous occurrence are nearly exclusively those of the 'Western Austronesian' language groups. Its spread into Indo-China supports the 'Austric' language link. Spread round the Indian Ocean is consistent with Austronesian colonisation. (Adapted, with permission, from Jett (1991).[68])

The most important exceptions to blowpipe distribution in the western region of Austronesian languages are northern Luzon in the Philippines and the whole of Taiwan. This gap clearly concerned Peter Bellwood because these were the key early corridor-sites in his and Robert Blust's archaeolinguistic model for a single Austronesian dispersal out of Taiwan (see Chapter 5). Bellwood argued that because blowpipes were absent from Taiwan and from a word list in the hypothetical reconstructed proto-Austronesian language, it followed that they could not have been in the original inventory of Austronesian crafts. In other words, blowpipes did not fit into the 'China-Taiwan-Philippines' linguistic model.

Bellwood localised the problem by using Jett's suggestion that blowpipes were invented in Borneo. Bellwood implied that blowpipes were a recent invention in Borneo,[70] but 'recent' was not what Jett wrote. Jett saw the invention of blowpipes as ancient, either 'Austric' (pre-Austronesian), or at least belonging to the earliest Neolithic or 'proto-Malay' migrants into island Southeast Asia. If blowpipes were a recent invention, as Bellwood suggests, then it is unclear how complex details of the skill came to be distributed so widely in the two language groups. Blowpipes are not found in most of the rest of the islands of the Austronesian diaspora in Oceania nor in the isolated Austronesian-speaking islands of Enngano and Mentawai a few miles off the west coast of Sumatra. This very specific linguistic distribution of blowpipe use needs to be taken into account in any model of Austronesian linguistic dispersal.

Although blowpipes are not used in Taiwan nor in the northern Philippines, they are recorded in isolated parts of southern Japan and also in southern mainland China, in the Leizhou peninsula.[71] The latter is a strip of land that once connected the mainland of China with its most southerly extension, tropical Hainan Island, way southwest of Taiwan.

Jett's conclusion, that the blowpipe was invented in ancient times somewhere in North Borneo where the greatest technical diversity and development is found, seems to fit the facts best. If that is the case its language-defined distribution would support the proposal that Austronesian languages originated in island Southeast Asia and dispersed from there, rather than from the mainland. The isolated occurrences in south China and Japan would then follow on by diffusion from the Nusantao maritime trading network along the east coast of Asia proposed by Wilhelm Solheim.

Another characteristic sign of Austronesian culture seen in the earlier Middle Neolithic phase around Hong Kong was the bark-cloth beaters. Bark-cloth beaters are thin paddles with parallel scores rather like a butter paddle. Austronesian-speakers throughout their dispersal, including Taiwan, traditionally made cloth from bark, particularly that of the paper mulberry tree. The bark is soaked to soften it and then beaten repeatedly by a flat club to macerate and separate the fibres.[72] By contrast, Hemudu further north significantly lacked bark-cloth beaters.

Bellwood lists megaliths (large boulders arranged or shaped in a distinctive way) as an important feature of many Austronesian speaking societies. Discussion of megaliths as cultural markers is presently out of favour with many prehistorians. Where dolmens (a tomb made from a flat boulder laid on upright boulders), menhirs (tall upright stones), and slab or cist graves are found among Austronesian speakers, however, it is reasonable to assume a cultural connection. In this context William Meacham has pointed out that the ancient megalithic Chihlin and Peinan cultures, found on the southeast and east coasts of Taiwan, and dating from the early second millennium BC, show every sign of diffusion from similar cultures in the Philippines to the south rather than the other way round.[73] These megalithic traits significantly do not feature in the much earlier Ta-p'en-k'eng culture on the west coast which is held up by Bellwood as the first Austronesian settlement of Taiwan. Again the evidence fails to support the fully developed Austronesian cultural trail out of China.

Out of Taiwan?

Peter Bellwood makes a good case for Austronesian colonisation of the Philippines by 5000 years ago.[74] Rice could even have been brought into northern Luzon at this time from Taiwan. But early Neolithic sites in Taiwan, and Robert Blust's linguistic reconstructions, paint a picture of Taiwan's proto-Austronesians lacking much of the culture, skills and tropical foodstuffs that characterised their subsequent success in the Philippines and elsewhere. The simplest answer to the prehistoric puzzle presented by these different cultural distributions is the view of William Meacham and Wilhelm Solheim that the Austronesian homeland was in island Southeast Asia. Subsequently Austronesian-speaking maritime traders influenced the Pacific coast of China and Korea and offshore islands such as Taiwan and Japan through trade.

Cultural links between East Asia and Ur

I have already mentioned the concordance of the same classes of Neolithic artefacts found under the silt layer of southern coastal China to those Woolley found under his silt layer in Mesopotamian Ur.[75] These included painted pottery, perforated clay discs or net sinkers, clay spindle whorls, shell beads and imported semi-precious stones, quadrangular polished adzes and stone hoes.[76] There is in addition one distinctly Austronesian trait that appears in the early 'Ubaid ceramics found under, and in graves let deep into, the silt layer at Ur. This is the tattooing of the female figurines. Among the most bizarre of all the early Mesopotamian finds, these figurines are of slim naked women with exaggerated genitalia, sometimes carrying children. Although the bodies are attractive, their heads are broad-headed, have black bitumen wigs and the slanted eyes have exaggerated folds under the eyelids (see illustration 3). There are paint marks and implants of clay pellets around the shoulders, suggestive of tattooing[77] and skin scarification. A few naked men with the same slanted eyes, broad shoulders and tapered waists were also found in Eridu. Whether these figures were some attempt of the local 'Ubaidian potter to represent, in caricature, the strange-looking visitors from the Far East is unclear.

Another specúlation comes from André Parrot, a French archaeologist, who found the figurines' faces so grotesque that he suggested an allusion to snake women.[78] Eerily similar grotesque figurines are still carved in wood along the north coast to New Guinea. Woolley noted with surprise the nature of the graves in which these figurines were found. Rectangular in shape, the base of the grave was carpeted in deliberately shattered pottery. The bodies were extended, unlike later burials, and were also powdered in red haematite (iron ore). One body had an extra lump of red haematite and another statuette had its face painted bright red. A bracelet of shell beads was found around one wrist. The custom of painting extended bodies with haematite is also seen in wooden box burials from Niah Cave in Borneo. The earliest date for these box burials is 3800 BC.[79]

Tattooing is a widespread Austronesian practice,[80] but skin scarification has a more limited distribution in Oceania. The inhabitants of the Middle Sepik area on the north coast of New Guinea still practise this custom. Although these people do not speak an Austronesian tongue, they have extensive cultural borrowings. In some villages patterned scarification of the shoulders and torso is performed as an initiation rite and imitates the teeth marks of crocodiles. The resulting raised, patterned oval keloid scars resemble those of the 'Ubaid figurines.[81]

Returning to the other artefacts of the post-flood settlements, although the exact pottery styles may not match East and West, it is inexplicable that the Far East and West Asian peoples should have remained in the same Neolithic phase of development throughout the dramatic changes of the last flood and yet did not communicate. If Solheim is correct, the Indian Ocean and Pacific Rim cultures were kept in continual communication to the present day by the trading network of the Nusantao boat people. Were these the amphibious educators or sages from the East who travelled to Ur?

3

WET FEET

We have seen how the flood fragmented and distorted the timeline of early coastal settlements and agriculture on the Eurasian mainland and in Southeast Asia. In this chapter we examine more closely the evidence for an early Neolithic in Southeast Asia and for flood-driven dispersals from there starting long before the Polynesian expansion.

The feats of discovery of the early Austronesians, which culminated in the colonisation of the Pacific by the Polynesians 3500 years ago, have always amazed and puzzled Westerners. The idea promoted by archaeologist Peter Bellwood that the first Austronesian-speaking people originated in China around 6000 years ago and migrated from there to the Philippines from Taiwan, is the most widely accepted and respected of all theories of Austronesian origins today, and is supported by the Hawai'ian linguist Professor Robert Blust.[1] I believe, however, that this theory is wrong.

Apart from the points discussed in the last chapter, my main objection to the Bellwood model is that his China-Taiwan-Philippine route to the Pacific makes the dates of the first Austronesian dispersal from the southern Philippines too late for a cascade of other events in the region. In other words, according to the model, when Austronesian sailors spread out from the southern Philippines 4000 years ago, they took agriculture, long-distance sailing and other skills, as brand-new technology which had never been seen before in the other islands of Southeast Asia and the Pacific.

This conclusion conflicts with the views of several other respected prehistorians.[2] Recent archaeological reports suggest a picture of earlier agricultural settlements in island Southeast Asia, and therefore an earlier spread to island and coastal Melanesia, than Bellwood proposes. Solheim has suggested that Southeast Asian maritime Neolithic cultures go back to the flooding of Southeast Asia over 7000 years ago, and that the homeland of Austronesian languages and sailing skills was in the region of Sulawesi. He proposes that they spread out from eastern Indonesia, starting before 5000 BC, north through the Philippines to Taiwan and then the China coast.[3] As we will see, there

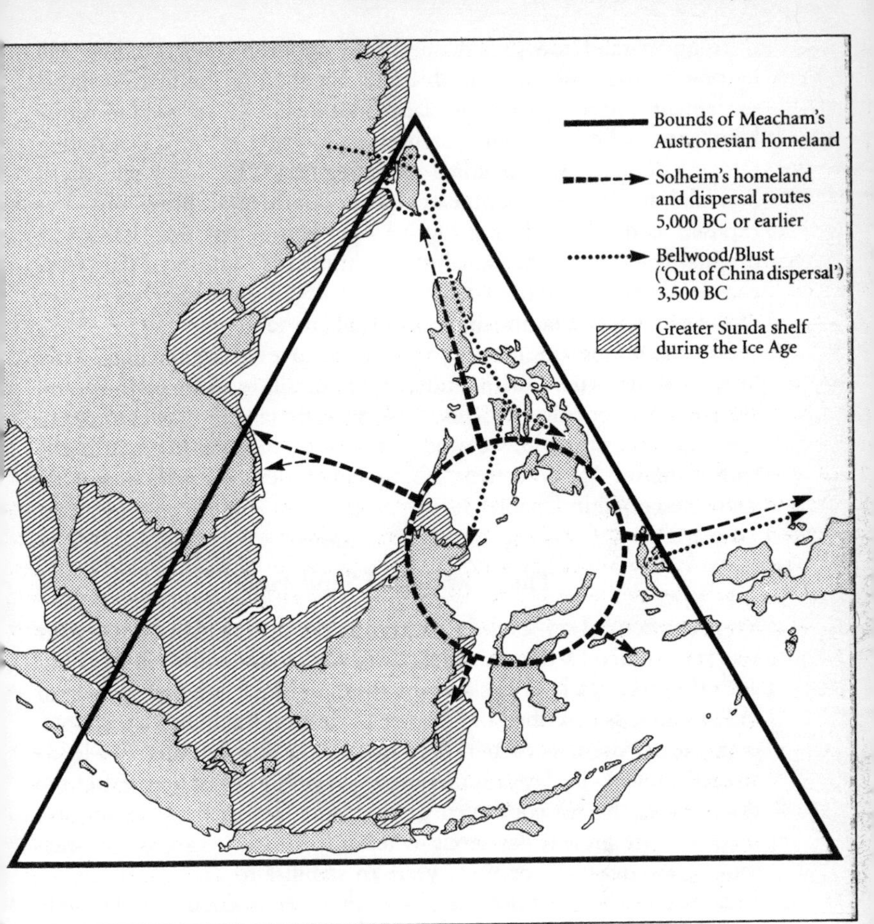

Figure 12. **Three archaeological views of the Austronesian Homeland.** An Asian Mainland origin is here represented by the Bellwood/Blust model, with the Pacific argonauts emerging from China through Taiwan some 5500 years ago. In the models of William Meacham (triangle) and Wilhelm Solheim (circle), the genesis of Austronesian culture is placed where it is found today, but over 7000 years ago, as the Sunda continent was drowning. (Adapted from Bellwood (1995), Meacham (1985), Solheim (1996): see Chapter 2, notes 45, 32 and 50.)

is evidence that they were also moving east and west around the same time.

To understand how such diametrically opposite views could be held by prehistorians on the timetable and direction of the first Neolithic settlement in the huge area of island Southeast Asia, we need to realise how few useful prehistoric archaeological sites of any description remain, and have been explored in the region.[4] What today remains of Sundaland, the vast Southeast Asian continental plate that was exposed as dry land during the Ice Age, is now less than half of its original land area. What was lost was hundreds of miles of flat fertile coastland with a high rainfall, in other words all evidence of the homes of the original coastal inhabitants of Sundaland.

Some clues remain, mostly in protected caves above the high-water line, in settlements buried under layers of silt, and in early upland clearance for agriculture. Before looking at these, and to get an idea of the scale of destruction, we need to return to the great floods after the end of the Ice Age with their subsequent sea-level rise and final overshoot described in Chapter 1.

The drowning of Sundaland

The behaviour of sea-levels in Southeast Asia over the last 14,000 years was very similar to that in the Arabian Gulf and on the China coast, with the jerky sea-level rise and the third and final surge of the eighth millennium, as described in Chapter 1. Here on the Sunda shelf, however, the sea drew its curtain over an area the size of India. Sea-levels crossed present-day levels sometime around 7500 years ago.[5] After the third flood, the sea continued to rise more slowly, peaking out at 5 metres above present-day levels as recently as 4500 years ago. It then took a few thousand or more years to stabilise to present-day levels. Because of the flatness and size of the Sunda continental shelf, far more coastal settlements were obliterated than in the Arabian Gulf. Also because of the delayed peak and fall, there is a falsely recent horizon on coastal remains (see Figures 3 and 13).

The scale of land loss in Southeast Asia comes home only when we translate the sea-level curves to the huge Sunda continental shelf and imagine that great Asian continent which has shrivelled to the Malay Peninsula on our maps today. Around 14,000 years ago, just before the first of the three great floods, Taiwan and Hainan islands were both part of the Chinese mainland and Victoria Peak in Hong Kong was part of a mountain range far inland. The South China Sea, the Gulf of Bangkok and the Java Sea were all dry plains connecting Indo-China, Borneo, Sumatra and Java into one continent, shaped like a crocodile's foot, which dwarfed India. In those days, Singapore was the watch on the crocodile's wrist, situated 1000 kilometres from the sea. The extent of Sundaland is clear from the shape of the 100-metre contour.

Just before the second flood 11,500 years ago, the sea was 50 metres below today's levels. The Sunda continent still had a recognisable foot, and all the main landmasses were still well attached to each other, but cracks were appearing in the east between Indo-China and Borneo and between Borneo and Java. Taiwan had already all but separated.

On the eve of the last flood the sea-level may still have been 20 metres below present-day levels. The 20-metre depth contour is revealing of the coastlines that suffered the most and the least in the third flood. The regions with the flattest shelves and hinterland lost most land. The most striking of these were off the Malay Peninsula, the east coasts of Java and Sumatra, and the south and west coasts of Borneo and Indo-China. The shelf around Singapore and Malacca would have been the last major area to flood.

Flooding of the Strait of Malacca

The Malacca Strait probably opened up as a long treacherous narrow channel right at the beginning of the flood sometime in the ninth millennium before present. Before then the only access to the Indian Ocean would have been a small gap between Sumatra and Java that had opened in the previous flood (the second in my story). It is important to recognise how recent were these constraints to contact between the Far East and the West. Before the second flood, the only route for exchange of agricultural and other secrets between South China and South Asia was through a narrow trail, now used by the opium trade, between Yunnan and Burma.

Although the foot of the Malay Peninsula is still physically part of the Asian continent, geographically and culturally it has always been closer to island Southeast Asia. In the previous chapter, I mentioned Surin Pookajorn's finding of an unsuspected early Neolithic rice-growing culture on the Malay Peninsula, dated from the tenth to the early eighth millennium, thousands of years before (see Figure 10). Apart from the surprise of such early rice cultivation, these and other findings suggest a much earlier agricultural revolution in Southeast Asia than previously suspected. Pookajorn's contention is that the main stimulus to changes in food-seeking habits, such as rice-growing and exploitation of sea foods 10,000–5000 years ago, were the fluctuations in sea-level rather than climatic, faunal or vegetational change.[6] A good reason why the Sakai cave sites in southern Thailand survived whereas other clues were lost lies in their location. Even at the highest point of

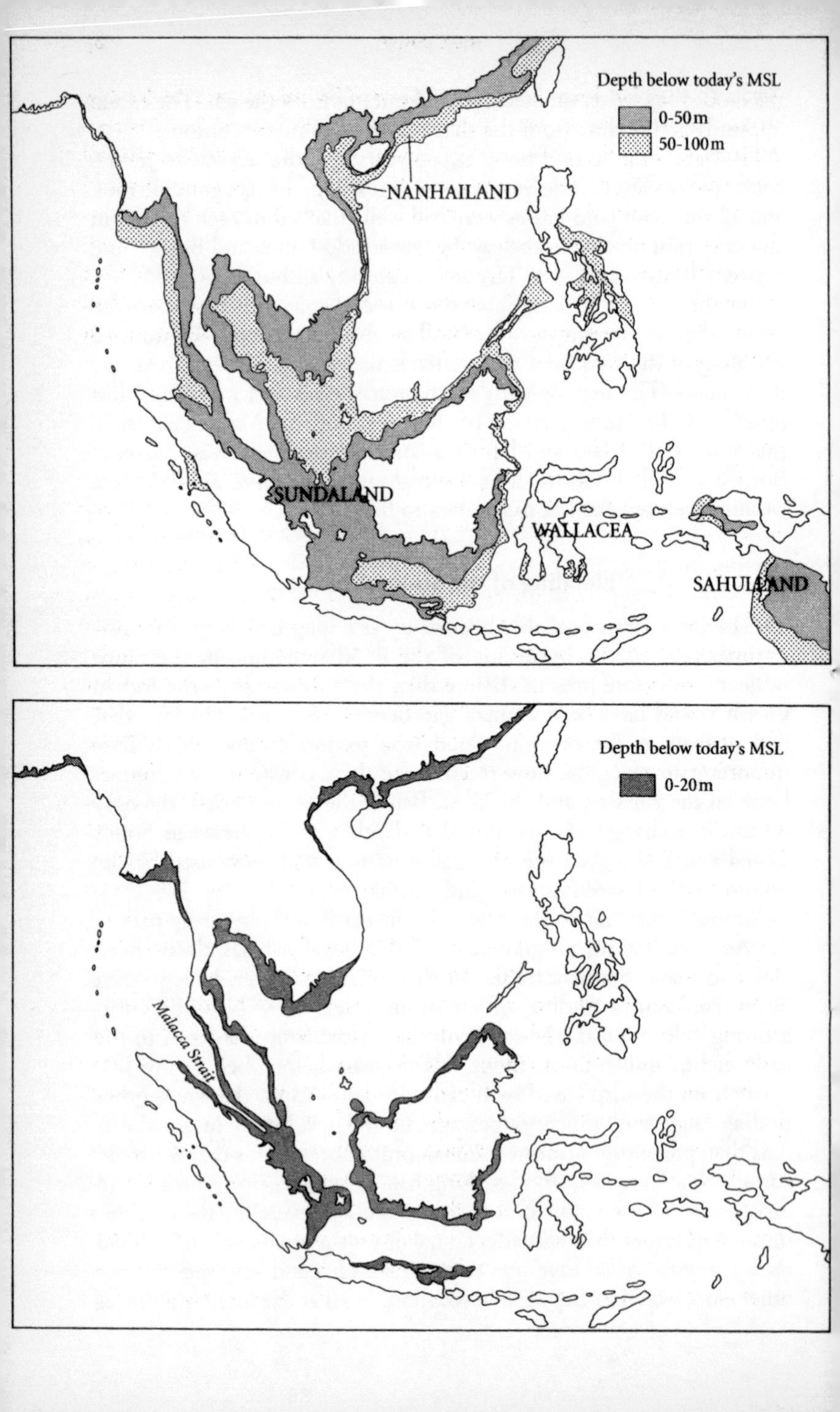
Depth below today's MSL
0-50m
50-100m
NANHAILAND
SUNDALAND
WALLACEA
SAHULLAND
Depth below today's MSL
0-20m
Malacca Strait

Figure 13. **Land lost from the Asian continent of Sundaland since the Ice Age.** At the height of the Ice Age, Sundaland spread from Indo-China to Bali. Nanhailand along the south coast of China and the Sahul shelf (Australia and New Guinea) also extended hundreds of kilometres. The greatest post-glacial land loss occurred to the west and south of Borneo, resulting in the South China Sea and the Java Sea. The 100m, 50m (top map) and 20m contours (lower map) correspond approximately with 14,000, 11,000 and 8500 years ago. The land lost in the third flood (lower map) was less than in the preceding two, but most dramatically the flood freed the passage to the west between Singapore and Sumatra and on through the Strait of Malacca.

the sea, 5 metres above today's level, they were still not threatened by the flood although close enough to the ocean to exploit it for food.

Recent results from Sakon Nakon inland in northeastern Thailand have shown extensive land clearance in the seventh millennium before present. In this report American archaeologist Joyce White argues that the 'Ban Chiang Tradition' started between 8000 and 7500 years ago in Thailand. She points out that Ban Chiang could thus have been first settled two millennia before the previous estimate for agriculture in the area.[7] Although White's important find lends support to early dates for rice-growing, it also allows that the Sakai Cave site in the Malay Peninsula further south, which pre-dates the third flood, may still have preceded the main agricultural revolution in Thailand.

Who were these early, pre-flood rice growers? The only available candidates are among the present-day speakers of Austro-Asiatic languages in the southern Malay Peninsula. These are the Aboriginal so-called Aslian groups in the jungles and coasts of Malaya. They are a physically and culturally separate group from the Mon-Khmer speakers further north in Thailand, Burma and Vietnam (see Chapter 7). Bellwood notes from the evidence of skeletal remains that one group of Aboriginals, the Senoi, may be descended from the Neolithic folk of the southern Malay Peninsula. Other early agricultural dates have been found in the region. Another cave, Gua Kechil, this time further south in Malaya, had remains of the same culture dated to the fourth millennium BC, overlying the older Hoabinhian levels.[8]

If Surin Pookajorn's dates for Sakai Cave are confirmed, rice growers on the coast of the Malay Peninsula exploiting the sea were around between the seventh and fifth millennia BC when the sea route to India opened up via the Malacca Strait. This date raises an important question. Did the presumed Austro-Asiatic-speakers (post-Hoabinhians) originating in the south of the peninsula not only colonise Thailand but also then take the idea of rice west to India by sea, 8000 years ago? Several pieces of evidence could support this idea.

Early Neolithic people on the western side of India started agriculture as early as the seventh millennium BC,[9] planting six-row barley, and herding cattle, sheep and goats. This could have been the precursor to the early Indus Valley civilisations. Farming started a little later in the *central* and *eastern* areas of India, as a separate development, with rice the staple rather than wheat and barley. The earliest remains of this development come from central India in the Vindhya Hills, possibly as long ago as the fifth to sixth millennia BC. Megalithic remains abound in this particular region, as they do further east in Burma. Pots with cord markings and paddle impressions provide a ceramic link with Southeast Asia. The latter, which date from the early Neolithic periods, suggest a prolonged contact between India and the maritime sand-bar cultures of Southeast Asia.[10] Moreover, the sites of early rice cultivation in India have the same general distribution as the present-day Austro-Asiatic-speaking Mundaic tribes in the north-central and northeastern areas.

Although the Mundaic languages come from the root branches of the Austro-Asiatic tree, they still share cognates (words of the same origin) connected with rice growing with the Mon-Khmer branch of Austro-Asiatic tongues in Indo-China. Such words include husked rice, bamboo and bamboo shoots, pestle and mortar, to get drunk, the dog, cow and chicken and, most intriguingly, copper bronze. Charles Higham has suggested that the ancestors of these Austro-Asiatic Mundaic-speaking people: 'who grew rice and knew of metallurgy, ... may well have expanded in a westerly direction from the Austro-Asiatic heartland in Southeast Asia (to India) deep in the prehistoric past'.[11]

Incidentally when Higham says 'deep in the prehistoric past' he does not specify, or mean, the fifth and sixth millennia BC.[12] But this is what could be implied by the record of early rice growing in central India and the dates from the Sakai Cave in southern Thailand. If the linguistic argument and the Sakai Cave rice evidence stand up to scrutiny, however, then there is a problem with the existence of cognates for bronze and copper. If the Mundaic speakers split off 7000 years ago from other Austro-Asiatic tongues, how did they come to carry the words for copper bronze at that time?

The most recent confirmed dates for bronze artefacts, from Ban Chiang in Thailand, are around 3500 years ago,[13] which might put a damper on the hypothesis. Two older dates of 5805 years ago and 4810 years ago were, however, also obtained for the Ban Chiang artefacts but

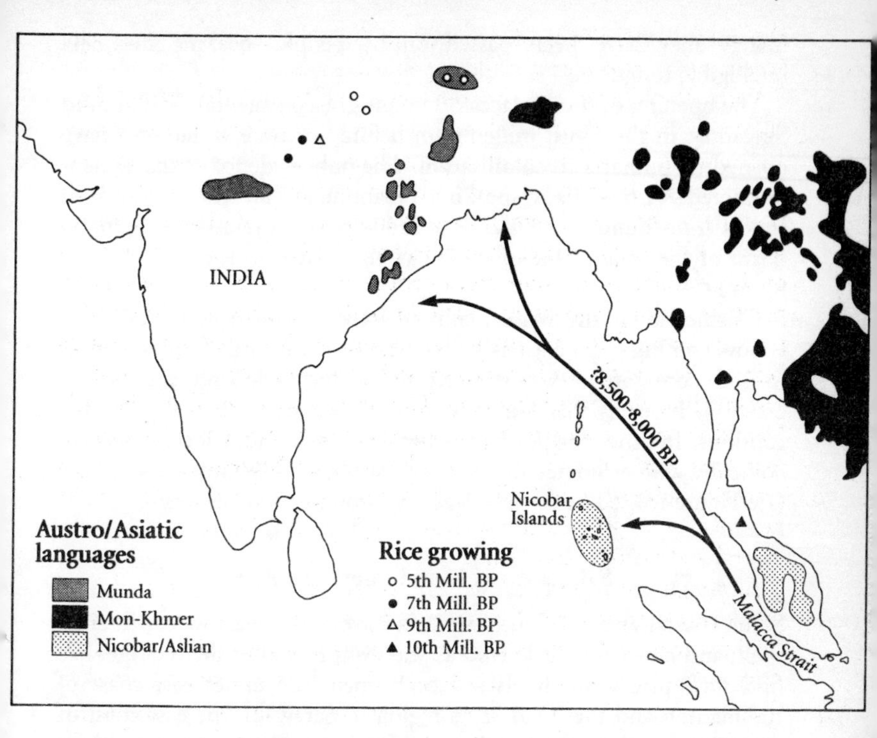

Figure 14. **The spread of rice growing from Southeast Asia to India.** The opening of the passage to the west through the Strait of Malacca over 8000 years ago created a potential East-West route for seaborne trade and interchange of ideas. This may have been a route for rice growing to reach India. The distribution of early rice-farming sites in India matches the spread of Austro-Asiatic languages. (Language map adapted from Higham (1996);[12] rice-growing dates.[5,9])

were rejected by Joyce White, an American archaeologist, as not being 'archaeologically meaningful'.[14] Although the date of nearly 6000 years ago for the appearance of bronze or copper in the Far East may be hard to swallow, it is still within the time-frame that White established for the Ban Chiang colonial culture as a whole. The fourth millennium BC is also about the time that a copper blade appeared in a grave set into Leonard Woolley's flood layer at Ur. In any case, if the first migration of Mundaic-speakers from Indo-China to India used the Nusantao shipping line of coast-hugging boats, trade would have continued for some time after. If bronze manufacture was discovered later, the technology may have been passed on by people speaking mutually intelligible tongues.

The opening of the Malacca Strait and the continental shelf around Singapore in the ninth millennium before our time would also have opened up Sumatra to colonisation. The only evidence of the ancient presumed Austro-Asiatic-speaking Hoabinhian cultures of mainland Indo-China found in the islands of Indonesia lies in northeast Sumatra north of the Strait. One of these has been dated to the sixth millennium BC.[15]

Clarification of the first agricultural activity in the region of Sumatra is now coming from experts who study pollen records (pollen counts in soil cores are a sensitive record of forest-clearing agricultural activity). It seems that Sumatra suffered two separate ecological disruptions after the Ice Age. The earliest of these, around 8000 years ago, coincides with estimated dates of the last of the three great flood events (see Figure 10).[16] The second peak was around 3000 years ago.

Safe caves of island Southeast Asia

Some coastal areas of Southeast Asia have only a narrow continental shelf, and hence lost little land as sea-levels rose after the Ice Age. We find such places on the Island of Borneo (the upper east coast of Kalimantan and the Niah caves region in Sarawak), the east coast of Vietnam, the Philippines, Sulawesi, Maluku, the Lesser Sundas, the far west coast of Indonesia and, last but not least, the east and south coast of Taiwan. With the exception of the inaccessible west coasts of Java and Sumatra, these are where the oldest Neolithic remains are found. We might think that these coasts with little continental shelf and a steep hinterland could have been let off rather lightly during the third flood, but this may not be so. They were particularly vulnerable to the local effects of the giant Pacific tsunamis that almost certainly rolled in from the other side of the sea when the Canadian ice plate collapsed. Curiously this is just the phenomenon complained of in the flood stories of the ancient coastal Aboriginal populations on the east of Taiwan and the Philippines (see Chapters 1 and 10).

Other effects of the third great flood may still be seen in otherwise inexplicable discontinuities of occupation in the seventh millennium before present on the steeper coasts of Sundaland. One of these comes from Madai Cave on the east coast of Sabah, which was abandoned inexplicably 7000 years ago.[17] But the most famous of the ancient cave sites is the complex of limestone caverns at Niah in Sarawak on the north coast of Borneo (see Figure 10). This has yielded some of the early dates in island Southeast Asia that are problematic for Peter Bellwood's 'Out of Taiwan' theory. Some apparently Neolithic burials in Niah, for instance, may date back to the early sixth millennium BP. The problem is acknowledged by Bellwood in a reference to Niah:

> The Niah evidence thus presents some very major problems. On the one hand there is a very large series of radiocarbon dates, but mainly on collagen or apatite [bone samples] and of uncertain reliability. On the other hand there are large numbers of artefacts, but it is almost impossible to associate the vast majority of them in any convincing way with the dated bones.[18]

Bellwood solves the problems firstly by doubting the stratigraphy of the original excavator, Tom Harrison, in Niah and then by judicious assignment of 'acceptable' and 'unacceptable' dates (the latter, though, could be regarded as even more subjective than Harrison's stratigraphy). There are many reasons why certain radiocarbon dates may be inaccurate or even consistently biased, but there are also standard methods for dealing with these problems and rejecting dubious dates.[19]

I recently paid a visit to Niah. Now a national park and popular tourist destination, the vast Niah Cave complex hollows out a mountainous limestone outcrop that is also still worked by collectors of birds' nests. The expedition starts with a walk for miles along a raised plank-way above a dark forest swamp set back some way from the sea. On finally reaching the cliffs, the path passes through a great fissure and starts climbing. When I got to this point, almost immediately I became aware of a deep notch a few metres in width, cut into and all around the base of the cliff. The notch, which could have been cut into the limestone by the high sea-level over 6000 years ago, is parallel to the ground a few metres above the level of the swamp. The path passes into the notch, which becomes like a half tunnel. Soon the tunnel opens out into the great 'Dragon Mouth' of the Niah cave complex. Tom Harrison's famous[20] archaeological dig was in the right corner of this mouth near the notch.

I was lucky. The Penan guide whose sick child I had examined on the previous day took us on through the cave complex and out again through a high locked steel fence into a green chasm crossed by a wooden bridge. On the other side of the chasm the notch appears again as the path leads up the cliff to the 'Painted Cave'. There, set just above the flood notch on the cave wall, are numerous paintings of high-prowed open boats loaded with up to twenty people (see illustration 4). Some people are depicted out of the boats. There are also geometric patterns, concentric spirals, a representation of the sun and some animals, including fish. Abstract web-shaped patterns around the boats possibly represent waves or nets. Against the wall of this cave I saw some crumbling, short and unseaworthy dugout canoes, which had acted as coffins. These had been excavated recently. The contents of the coffins are now in Kuching, the capital of Sarawak. Corrected radiocarbon dates for coffins from the painted cave and their contents put them in the metal age around 2500–2800 years ago.[21]

The coffins emphasise the function of the Niah Caverns as a mortuary through the ages; the paintings are also of great interest because Borneo had been thought to lack these kind of messages from the past. French archaeologist Jean-Michel Chazine has found similar cave paintings in the eastern part of Indonesian Borneo (Kalimantan) (see Figure 10).[22] In addition to the well-known Austronesian 'boats of the dead' motif seen in Niah, the Kalimantan caves also feature hand prints. The association between the boats of the dead and the notch at high sea-level on the Niah limestone seems more than a coincidence. The images were presumably painted after the peak sea-level of the third flood 5500 years ago. Preliminary excavations in eastern Kalimantan, southeast of Niah, show that the superficial layers of earth surrounding these paintings yield cord- and paddle-impressed pottery as found in the early Neolithic period of the Southern Chinese coast and Taiwan and in central India. A sample, again taken from more recent superficial layers of the Kalimantan site, is around 5500 years old. Similar ceramics have been found in Sabah and Sulawesi.[23] The date for these Neolithic sailors and artists might fit an early dispersal from the south coast of China but would be too early for one coming from the Philippines, which would only have arrived in Borneo between 3000 and 4000 years ago according to Peter Bellwood.[24]

North and east Borneo may hold a clue to the meaning of the spirit boats motif in the island's oral history. The Berawan, a tribal group living in the vicinity of Niah, have a myth of a sacred river that flows through the land of the dead. This land and river are both located well out to sea on the drowned Sunda shelf. A similar myth is shared by the Kayan, who spread into Kaltim (see Chapter 5). The 'boats of the dead' motif appears in designs found as far south as Sumba Island in the Lesser Sundas, west on the famous woven cloths of Lampung in Sumatra (see illustration 22), and as far north as Vietnam, where it is depicted on the sides of Dong Son bronze drums from the first millennium BC.[25] Westerners may recall the River Styx, which, in Greek myth, had to be crossed by ferry in order to reach the land of the dead. Similar boats with the same mysterious nets have a wide distribution as rock carvings in Sweden, where they are associated with the Bronze Age dated between 1800 and 500 BC.[26]

The Swedish Bronze Age also has characteristic crescentic ceremonial bronze axes very similar to the Dong Son style axes found in Indonesia and New Guinea (see illustration 5).[27]

Another feature shared between the rock carvings in Scandinavia and Southeast Asia are cup-mark etchings. One particular arrangement of these is in two parallel rows of seven (see illustration 6). In Sumatra and Flores Island this arrangement found on prehistoric megaliths is identified with the ancient Austronesian board game *Chanka* (also known as *Mancala*) which has spread round the Indian Ocean. Such rows of cuplets are also found on rocks on the east coast of Africa and Turkey. If there is any cultural connection between these art motifs in Southeast Asia and Scandinavia, it is more likely to have travelled over such vast distances via a network of sea traders. As I have mentioned, archaeologist Wilhelm Solheim has suggested just such a network for the entire coastline of East Asia starting from about 7000 years ago – the Nusantao.

D'ou les Chams

While we are in the Bronze Age and before we leave the flooded continental shelf of Sunda I would like to mention a linguistic anachronism posed, under Peter Bellwood's China-Taiwan-Philippines hypothesis, by one of the most brilliant civilisations of Indo-China. Soon after the French established their colonial presence in Vietnam in the late nineteenth century they found ancient Sanskrit inscriptions in an Austronesian tongue still spoken in many dialects along the South Vietnamese coast and into the hinterland. Since then ample evidence has appeared of an advanced civilisation that flourished (as the state of Champa) for a thousand years from the fifth century AD and worshipped Siva and Buddha. The Cham vied with the Khmers and Vietnamese for control of Indo-China until they lost out in the fifteenth century AD. The Chamic languages appear to be most closely related to Malayic tongues, and are regarded, with that group, as the only clear examples of Austronesian migration to the Asian mainland from island Southeast Asia (see Chapter 5).

A few years ago as I drove up the coast road from Ho Chi Minh city to Hue, I could see their huge carved towers standing like bishop's mitres among the hills and limestone outcrops. A mixed Hindu/Buddhist worship was still practised among the ruins. As I peered into the smoke-filled gloom under one tower, garlands and offerings were being placed reverently around a large, smooth, grey granite phallus.

Since the French discovery of an even earlier civilisation, the Sa Huynh, occupying the same area as Champa, there has been speculation as to a prehistoric connection between the two. The early French archaeologists tended to discount any link on the basis of the preconception that the Cham were recent 'civilising' migrants from Indonesia. But recently, Vietnamese archaeologists have proposed a continuous development from the Sa Huynh as far back as a pre-Iron Period in the second millennium BC through to the start of the Cham culture around AD 200. British archaeologist Ian Glover has recently reviewed evidence of the connections between these two periods, and comments: 'One implication of the new Vietnamese reconstruction which is not much discussed is that, if accurate, the Sa Huynh peoples would have spoken an Austronesian language which, though clearly intrusive into Vietnam, must have been established there much longer than the linguists have generally allowed.'[28] According to the linguistic arm of the China-Taiwan-Philippines model, the Cham would not have arrived in Vietnam until around 300 BC.[29]

Sa Huynh was a sophisticated Bronze and Iron Age culture, which, until recently has been overshadowed in popular imagination by its brilliant contemporary neighbour, the famous Dong Son Bronze culture of the Austro-Asiatic speakers of North Vietnam. In spite of their proximity, both cultures appear to have developed most of their skills and style independently of each other and of India and China.[30] Apart from some bronze ornaments that resemble finds in Tabon Cave in Palawan in the Philippines (see below), the Sa Huynh culture is best known for its unusual custom of jar cremation burials. The burials were usually made in coastal dunes. Destruction of the pots and funerary items were part of the ritual. The habit of urn burial passed on into the Cham culture. The remains were usually cast into the sea.[31]

Urn cremation is uncommon in Indo-China and Southeast Asia and is associated primarily with ancient, presumed Austronesian, populations living round the South China Sea during the second and early first millennium BC. These examples include Niah caves in Sarawak, Borneo (from the second millennium) and Luzon in the Philippines (1000 to 500 BC).[32] Other sites in Indo-China, all presumed Austro-Asiatic, are the Plain of Jars in the uplands of Laos and the famous site of Ban Chiang in Thailand. Although there are slightly later parallels of urn burials in India and in Japan (late Jomon cultures), and several examples are also known from Early Neolithic sites in North and South China, the Austronesian jar burials are probably indigenous.

The association of jar burials with the Cham and their predecessors, the Sa Huynh, 3000 years ago hardly supports the linguists' idea of their being late newcomers from the deep south of Borneo to the strand known later by GIs as China Beach. It makes them sound much more like long-standing members of a trading network around the South China Sea. As indefatigable archaeologist Wilhelm Solheim has traced, this took the seafarers further north than Taiwan – to Japan and Korea – as well as west.[33]

To summarise: the Cham and their putative ancestors the Sa Huynh, rather than being relative newcomers to the coast of Indo-China, may have been in Vietnam from the second millennium BC. They may also have been part of a widespread complex Bronze Age maritime trading network. This picture conflicts with the Bellwood/Blust linguistic chronology for the first Austronesian dispersal out of island Southeast Asia, which has the Austronesian speakers arriving at China Beach only in 300 BC.

Long-distance trade between Southeast Asia and Melanesia after the flood

Moving back again to Borneo a thousand or so years after the third post-glacial flood we find another date and activity which does not square with the China-Taiwan-Philippine Austronesian dispersal scheme. This evidence has been obtained from Sabah in Borneo where, it seems, obsidian or volcanic glass was being traded from the Admiralty Islands in Melanesia 6000 years ago and 3500 kilometres away to the east. This dark-grey-to-black, uncommon glass-like mineral is the ideal stone for flaking into knives or spear points. Chipping obsidian produces very sharp and predictable edges, and the mineral was consequently highly sought after and traded over vast distances across the Pacific. It carries chemical and other fingerprints of its origin, so that flakes from one site can be uniquely identified thousands of miles away. This make obsidian a very powerful trade marker.

Archaeologists have known for a few years that obsidian was traded for small distances around islands of the Bismarck Archipelago, north-east of New Guinea, before the Austronesian speakers are supposed to have arrived in the area, implying that the indigenous New Guineans could make short sea trips before the Austronesians arrived with their ocean-sailing canoes. We know that the highlanders of New Guinea were practising horticulture 9000 years ago and that the North Solomons were colonised by people who may have ground their own cereal food at least 28,000 years ago.[34] But these early Melanesian populations seem to have stayed put, perhaps because this was about as far as they could sail at that time. The conventional view is that after the Solomons were colonised, for the next 22,000 years or so, short trading trips across open sea in a limited easy 'voyaging corridor' of the Southwest Pacific region of Melanesia did not much exceed 25 kilometres or a maximum of 200 kilometres and that the sailors hugged the coast.[35]

The Lapita controversy

According to the Bellwood model, the 'limited sailing trips' were all supposed to have changed with the relatively sudden appearance of Lapita pottery in the region 3500 years ago. This so-called 'express train to Polynesia' hypothesis (see Chapter 5) proposes that a complex of Neolithic technologies, coming from Taiwan via the Philippines, rapidly spread throughout Melanesia to central Polynesia from about 3500–3100 years ago. 'Lapita' pottery is defined by a distinctive, dentate (literally tooth-like) decoration and dates from 1600 BC to about 500 BC. Lapita is found in Melanesia and Polynesia and nowhere else (see illustrations 8 and 9). In many peoples' view the pottery also defines the big push of sailing canoes out into the Pacific and Central Polynesia from the previous eastern limits of the Solomon Islands. The Lapita period coincides in Bellwood's view with the first entry of Austronesian languages into the Southwest Pacific. So neatly did the two fit, that the Oceanic Austronesian language group is identified by many with Lapita and the Lapita culture is identified as the forerunner of the Polynesians.

Nothing can be so simple. Academic debates have raged for the past ten years or more as to who the Lapita people were, if they were a homogeneous people and culture, whether they were pure Austronesian or a mixture with indigenous non-Austronesian-speaking people, whether their culture was home-grown, whether the Austronesians came from

Figure 15. **Were the makers of Lapita pottery the first serious sailors in the southwest Pacific?** This map shows the earliest dates (underlined) of human habitation in different regions of Australasia and Oceania up to 3000 years ago. While the Lapita period saw people sailing deep into the Pacific from 3500 years ago, local sailors had made trips over 170 km, 25,000 years before that. Further, long-distance trading of obsidian between Southeast Asia and Melanesia had started at least 6000 years ago.

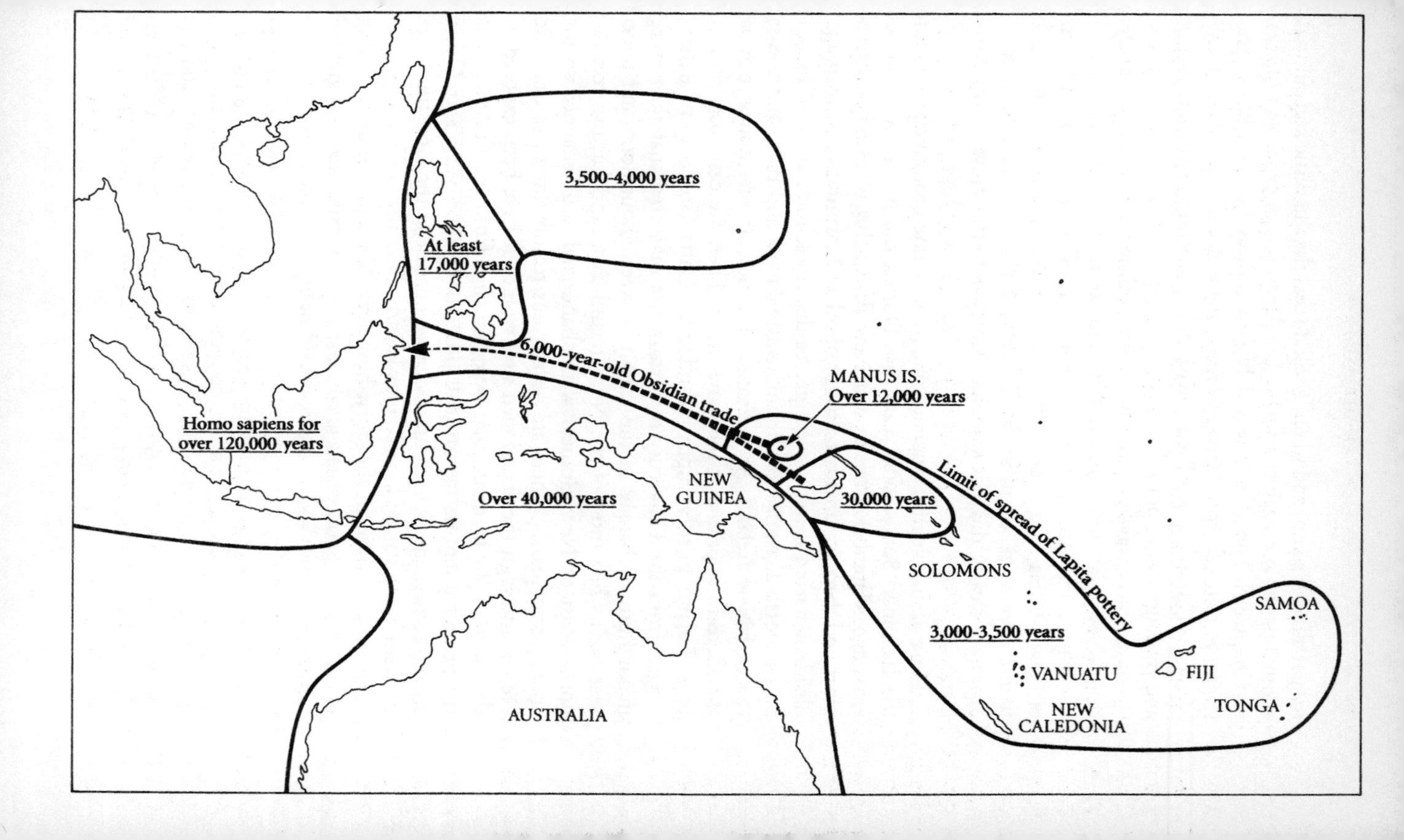
3,500-4,000 years
At least
17,000 years
6,000-year-old Obsidian trade
MANUS IS.
Over 12,000 years
Homo sapiens for
over 120,000 years
NEW
GUINEA
Over 40,000 years
30,000 years
Limit of spread of Lapita pottery
SOLOMONS
SAMOA
3,000-3,500 years
VANUATU
FIJI
TONGA
NEW
CALEDONIA
AUSTRALIA

Asia at all, and so on, and so on. I will discuss the linguistic and cultural arguments for and against a single, late Austronesian expansion further in Chapter 5. The issue I would like to address here is whether the Lapita period of 3500 years ago really defined the start of maritime Neolithic cultures in the Pacific, with deliberate long-distance voyaging and trading: it does not seem to.

For a start, travelling to the North Solomons 28,000 years ago from New Caledonia across 170 kilometres of open sea was no mean feat. The Admiralty group which includes Manus Island north of New Guinea require an open sea voyage of 200 kilometres to reach them; they were occupied at least 12,000 years ago. Those early explorers clearly did not wait for Lapita pottery before sailing long distances.

More archaeological evidence of activity came around the time of the last flood 8000–6000 years ago. During the period 9000–6000 years ago Matenbek Cave in east New Britain began to be occupied more and there was increased use of obsidian.[36] Around 8000 years ago obsidian started being moved greater distances, such as from Talasea on the north coast of New Britain to Panakiwuk and Balof on the east coast of New Ireland. At the same time new animal bones such as shark's teeth appeared at the same sites.[37] Then the east coast sites in New Ireland were abruptly abandoned. Chris Gosden, an archaeologist from the University of Oxford has suggested that there were major human changes in the region between about 8000 and 6000 years ago when most of the New Ireland caves and Lachitu (on the north coast of New Guinea) were abandoned and remained so for about 6000 years.[38] There are no obvious reasons for these dramatic events, although the abandoned sites would all have been exposed to the great Pacific tsunamis that were launched from North America as the great Laurentide ice cap collapsed about 8000 years ago. Other coastal settlements started up or changed nature at the same time, one of them being Pamwak on Manus Island.

Up to this point in the story, however, the change in local trading patterns 8000–6000 years ago could still just be explained by a gradual improvement in short island-to-island hops in simple boats. Geoffrey Irwin, a New Zealand archaeologist with a penchant for sailing, has argued that there is nothing to suggest that these mini-voyagers were foreshadowing the great ocean-crossing exploits of the Lapita culture 4500 years later.[39] And Chris Gosden has pointed out that there is nothing in the archaeological record to connect the cave-dwellers of the Bismarcks 12,000–8000 years ago with the later Lapita culture.

Were the pre-Lapita long-distance traders Austronesian?

Manus island (which is part of the Bismarck Archipelago), however, does seem to have overlapped with Lapita. It is from here that the surprising discovery of 6000-year-old, long-distance, obsidian trading comes. As recently as 1992, Irwin, a world expert in the field of Pacific voyaging, backed up his assertion of only limited voyages before Lapita with the statement, 'Lou obsidian, which requires an open-sea passage, does not appear in circulation before Lapita times.'[40] That assertion has now received a serious blow with the Sabah findings.

Tiny Lou Island near Manus, the still-smouldering remains of a volcano, is and was the Admiralty Islands' obsidian mine. I have reason to remember it well, because on a visit in 1982 I caught a bad dose of drug resistant malaria there. I stayed in a village house with friends. In the morning, they took me to a volcanic hot spring on the shore where there was a permanent hot running bath. On the other side of the island another village had hot muds that were used to cook food, especially the large eggs of the megapode fowl. Walking back to my friend's house the track was strewn with dark-black, glass-like chippings. Picking up a few of these, I realised that they were flakes from an obsidian tool factory. They walked me up a hill to a raw source of obsidian, a large boulder of the glass, among the banana trees, surrounded by flakes and half-finished tools. One man in the village sold me a hafted obsidian knife made by his father twenty years before (see illustration 7).

Lou Island was one source of some 200 obsidian flakes recently found by Malaysian archaeologist Stephen Chia in Bukit Tengkorak on the east coast of Sabah 3500 miles to the west. Talasea in New Britain was the other. The stunning second blow in this discovery was the radiocarbon date for the Southeast Asian archaeological layer in which the Lou obsidian was found.[41] Archaeologists had previously found similar obsidian at the same site but dated 3500 years later at the end of the Lapita period. Clearly this finding needs independent confirmation. At 6000 years ago the new date threatens to overturn the conventional view that the Lapita culture 2500 years later was the start of serious long-distance trading in the southwest Pacific.

The other implication of this finding is that the Sabahan recipients of Melanesian obsidian were trading 3000 years before Peter Bellwood's chronology would allow them even to be in Borneo. Since there are no non-Austronesian tongues anywhere near Sabah today, the first assumption has to be that these traders were Austronesian-speaking. As we shall see in Chapters 6 and 7, the genetic evidence supports this conclusion. Set alongside the evidence of a major change in human activities in the Bismarcks mentioned above, the whole chronology of Pacific voyaging and cultural interchange needs review. Prehistorian John Terrell, who is well known among archaeologists for his objection to the conventional Lapita story, sums up the implications of the Lou obsidian find as follows: 'The new work ... supports the idea that instead of setting out on a one-way eastward migration, the ancestral Pacific islanders opened up a "voyaging corridor" between Southeast Asia, Melanesia, and Polynesia, "with people and ideas flowing back and forth".'[42]

More than people and ideas flowed to and fro between Melanesia and Southeast Asia in those thousands of years before Lapita. Pigs were once thought to be a Lapita import, but their remains have now been found in the New Guinea highlands with a 5000-year-old date,[43] and at Matenbek on the east coast of New Ireland with dates of 8000 and 6000 years ago.[44] Another curious anachronism that had previously been put on one side as too bizarre to be acceptable is the finding of Japanese pottery sherds in the Mele plain in Vanuatu in the 1960s. These cord-marked pottery pieces were originally identified by Japanese experts as from the Early Jomon Period. Exhaustive modern analysis of the sherds has left little doubt that these are indeed Early Jomon and were manufactured in Japan more than 5000 years ago. The pottery tradition in Japan is the oldest in the world, going back to the ninth millennium BC. There is no satisfactory explanation for the finding of Jomon ware in Vanuatu except perhaps that the pots had somehow been transported from Japan a very long time ago. Even older pottery sherds have been found in Matenkupkum Cave in New Ireland, taking the Neolithic there back to the time of the third flood (around 8000 years ago).

Jim Allen, an archaeologist from La Trobe University, recently reviewed all the evidence for an early pre-Lapita Neolithic in Melanesia, arguing that the period 8000–6000 years ago in island Melanesia was one of considerable change, 'albeit with different changes taking place in different areas'.[45] Finding pre-Lapita Melanesian-type artefacts in the Bismarcks and the North Solomons, he concludes: 'On this evidence, ground-stone technology, shell-tool technology, ceramic technology, horticultural technology and efficient sailing technology all occurred in Melanesia well before the advent of Lapita, rather than arriving with Lapita as was widely believed a decade or so ago.'[46]

It is also tempting to wonder if the idea of blow-pipes (see Chapter 2) made its way from Sabah in Borneo to that small pre-Lapita community of ocean traders in the Bismarcks and the North Solomons.

Old Austronesian settlements in New Guinea hidden by the flood

Perhaps the best archaeological evidence of a maritime colonisation of northern Melanesia by pre-Lapita people from Southeast Asia comes from the mainland of New Guinea. Although the clues are found in parts of the Sepik, Madang and Enga provinces that now speak non-Austronesian languages, the style of the shell artefacts and the animal and vegetable remains strongly suggest that the early colonists came from a similar tradition to the later Austronesian invasions. But as in Mesopotamia, China and Southeast Asia, much of the evidence of the pre-Lapita settlements has been buried under metres of marine and estuarine silt resulting from changes in the coastline in the past 10,000 years. Pamela Swadling, an archaeologist based at the Papua New Guinea National Museum, has studied what evidence has survived.[47]

The Sepik River of north New Guinea has the fifth highest annual flow in the world. Some 6000 years ago, when the post-glacial sea-level had reached its peak, the alluvial swamp plain of the Sepik was flooded by a vast brackish inland sea. The narrow mouth of this sea was partially obscured by an island, now a region of low hills known as Bosmun. Archaeologists found a beach settlement at Dongan on the southern shore of Bosmun island, where, along with layers of harvested sea shells, there was evidence of characteristic domestic plants and trees, such as betel-nut, candle-nut, canarium almonds, coconut and pandanus. These plant remains date to 5800 years ago. Betel-nuts were the key import from Southeast Asia and, although now widely used as a stimulant, characterise Austronesian communities. This trade pre-dates the Lapita phenomenon by 2300 years and is currently the oldest-known Asian import to the New Guinea region. There were other islands in the Sepik sea. One of these is now inland on the alluvial plain and holds the famous story-board-carving culture of Kambot which preserves ancient story motifs found throughout Eurasia (see Chapter 16). The other unexpected pre-Lapita Neolithic finds in the same region were pots. Their decorations are typically described as 'Incised and Appliqué'. While this kind of pottery is also found later in Lapita sites, it is not characteristic of Lapita. Pamela Swadling suggests an early eastern Indonesian origin for this style.[48]

As in sites in Asia and Mesopotamia now covered by the rising sea, the finds under the silt layer left by the retreating Sepik sea when levels stabilised provide only a brief window on early coastal cultures as earlier settlements may now lie under the sea. Although the earliest date so far found for this marine culture of the New Guinea north

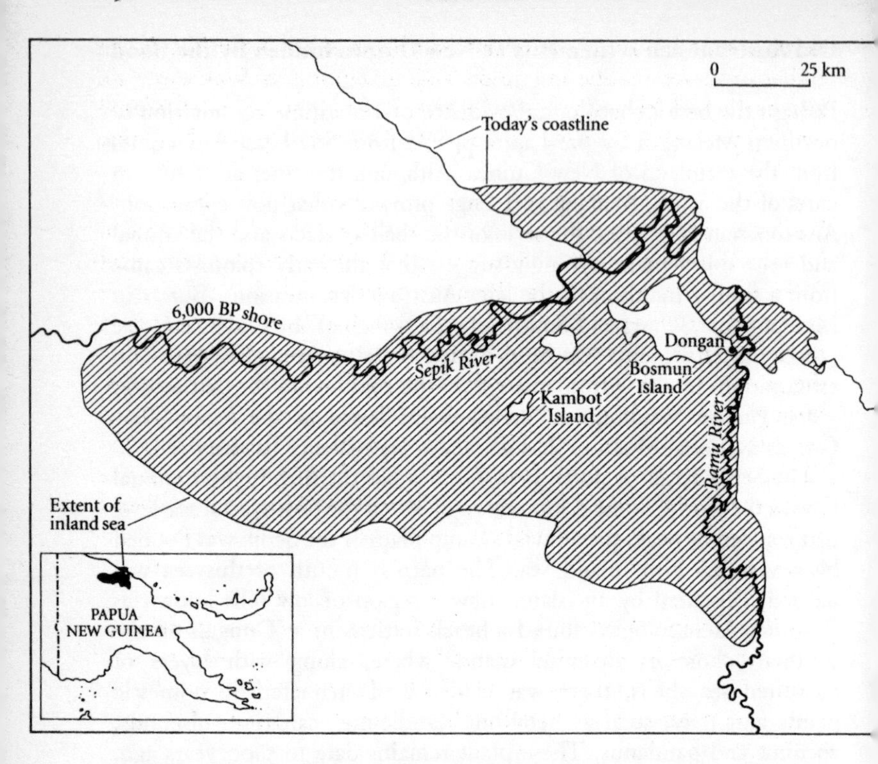

Figure 16. **The flooding and drying of the Sepik plain.** A huge brackish inland sea reached its maximum extent covering the Sepik plain 6000 years ago. The key storyboard-carving inland village of Kambot was then an island. Beach settlements of that time, such as Dongan on Bosmun island, show Southeast Asian imports and Austronesian habits. The subsequent infilling of the sea left a 3-metre layer of silt over the evidence. (Adapted, with permission, from Swadling (1997).[47])

coast is 3800 BC, Swadling points out that earlier sites 'will be found only beyond the area of the inland sea and its 3m-blanket of Holocene deposits'.[49] She speculates from archaeological and linguistic evidence[50] that there was considerable early contact between the colonising marine cultures of the inland Sepik sea and neighbouring indigenous highland populations. This would have been enhanced by the proximity of the highlands to the old shoreline. The highlands had their own start to horticulture 9000 years ago, which has always been regarded by the Lapita Austronesianists as a completely independent development from the Asian and Southeast Asian Neolithic. If the earlier dates for marine migration and agriculture in Southeast Asia and northern Melanesia are substantiated, the highlands horticultural development may turn out to be part of a larger regional Neolithic revolution.

Between 5000 and 3500 years ago the shoreline of the inland sea at Sepik retreated steadily until the lake was dry and a delta protruded into the Bismarck Sea. By the time of the Lapita pottery and the great Polynesian expansion to the Pacific, therefore, all the old sites of presumed Austronesian coastal settlement had been covered by 3 metres of silt and a huge muddy alluvial plain. Swadling argues that the people of the Sepik and neighbouring Ramu riverine swamps, through their contact with the hinterland, adopted indigenous languages, thus losing the linguistic markers of their origins. In Chapter 6 and 7, I suggest that they did not lose their culture or the genes that identify their Southeast Asian origins. Swadling's evidence and conclusions have important implications for Southeast Asian prehistory:

> It is becoming increasingly apparent that the eyes of many Pacific prehistorians have been blinkered by their concern to resolve the origins of Lapita pottery. More attention needs to be directed to the Sepik-Ramu which is culturally the most complex part of the Pacific.[51]

In spite of the loss of most traces of the earlier Neolithic in Southeast Asia, there are now enough clues – and a sufficiently unequivocal trail out to Melanesia by Austronesians – for the primacy of the migration that coincided with the Lapita culture to be doubted. There is evidence in modern peoples and their languages to support the view of two injections of new skills, genes and languages. I will discuss more evidence for this in the next four chapters.

The age of the mangroves

One injection of new blood further south in Australia is less talked about by archaeologists than Lapita. This intrusion was characterised by introduced animals (especially dingoes) and possibly by small new tools called microliths. The trajectory of the third flood in Australia mirrored the one further north but the people involved and the effects on their food-gathering habits were slightly different. Some archaeologists have called it the age of the mangroves.

In Chapter 1, I showed sea-level curves from the Great Barrier Reef along the east coast of Australia that mirror the picture seen elsewhere on continental shelves, with a dramatic oscillation of the sea between 8000 and 7500 years ago. After the big sharp rise of the flood, sea-levels paused for a time at minus 5 metres and then only crossed the present-day mark just under 6000 years ago. There may then have been an overshoot to a metre above today's levels over the next 4000 years.[52] The period from 8000 to 6000 years ago has been labelled the 'big swamp' or 'the time of the mangroves' in the huge Sahul continental shelf of northern Australia and has left characteristic sedimentary sequences.[53] In places such as Arnhem Land and the South Alligator River, mangroves spread over a much wider band of the coastline, penetrating more deeply into the hinterland than now. Harry Allen, an Australian archaeologist, believes that similar changes occurred throughout tropical Southeast Asia:

> Similar sedimentary sequences are known from the Bengal Basin, the Gulf of Thailand, along the coasts of Vietnam and South China, and in the Straits of Malacca. Areas of Kalimantan are likely to have been similarly affected ... In addition, the location, dating and shellfish content (mangrove/mudflat/estuary species) of Hoabinhian shell-middens in Sumatra, now many kilometres inland, suggests that further environmental surveying of the eastern Sumatran Floodplain would provide a sequence of changes already documented for North Australia and the coasts of Central Thailand and South China.[54]

In passing, it is worth reflecting that the time of the mangroves in these flat coasts of Australasia was also 'the time of the crocodiles', a point emphasised by the name of the Alligator River. As I point out later in the book, the dramatic increase in the habitat of one of humanity's most feared natural adversaries, when Southeast Asians were struggling to establish their Neolithic cultures in times of flood, may still be remembered in the water-dragon motif of Indo-China.[55]

What is particularly interesting in the northern Australian studies is the discovery that the diet and technology of coastal peoples changed after the sea-level rose. As on other flooded coastlines 7000–5000 years ago, where the level first peaked then fell back, people did not re-occupy land in the flood belt for 500 years or so. Again, as on the coasts of the South China Sea, the best evidence of marine cultures of the flood period in tropical Australia comes from piles of estuarine shell refuse in caves and open-air sites set far enough inland to avoid inundation. The local Aboriginal explanation for the 'shell caves' found 25–30 kilometres inland from the present mangrove swamps in western Arnhem Land was simple: 'Noah's flood'.[56] How much of this tradition is due to missionary influence and how much reflects a pre-existing story is unclear. Changes in stone-tool technology at this site appeared around 5000 years ago, well after the major environmental change.

The dingo and other arrivals

The post-flood foreign arrivals reached Australia around 5000 years ago.[57] One of the most lively and unmistakable foreigners was the dingo.[58] This animal's spread through Australia may have been complete 4000 years ago; it never reached Tasmania, because the island became separated from the Australian mainland by the rising of the sea. Given the gaps and distances between Asia and Australia, the dingo's ancestors could not have hitched a lift on driftwood and must have come as invited guests in someone's boat or boats. Opinions vary as to which Asian population the dingo is derived from; it could have been derived from dogs anywhere in South or Southeast Asia.[59]

At the same time, or perhaps a little before the dingo arrived, finely made spear points and other small tools – the so-called microlithic industry – appeared in Australia, adding great variety to the Aboriginals' technology. These new high-tech tools spread rapidly over Australia, with a marked regional diversity that did not follow the distribution of the major present-day Aboriginal cultural areas. The wide dispersion and the diversity of these new tools has led to a controversial belief that migrations of newcomers to Australia 4000 to 5000 years ago brought new tools – and the dingo – with them.[60]

The date of 5000 years ago for the arrival of new tools is still much earlier than the earliest dates for the entry of the Lapita culture into Melanesia to the north, and thus underlines the likelihood of an earlier marine dispersal from Southeast Asia. Similar microliths to those that appeared in Australia around 5000 years ago are also known from Sulawesi and Java, and so the concept of two-way as well as one-way interaction between Australia and Indonesia between 6000 and 4000 years ago is favoured by some archaeologists.[61] Microliths are, however, widespread in the Old World and almost certainly were introduced to Australia from Asia. So far, there is still little evidence to say who might have brought the tools to Australia and earlier dates are possible. In many such situations, one can turn to linguists for an answer, or at least an hypothesis; but in this case, all that linguists can say is that there was a rapid spread of different languages throughout Australia sometime between 10,000 and 4000 years ago, which can best be explained by an influx of new people. There are no clear candidates for the new Australian languages from the Old World. The concept of a recent Australian linguistic expansion is supported by a mathematical analysis of linguistic diversity in space and time by linguist Johanna Nichols.[62] According to Nichols, Australian languages are just one of numerous groups around the world that diversified in the post-glacial period. There is also clear genetic evidence for multiple human intrusions into northwest Australia directly from Southeast Asia. This will be discussed in more detail in Chapters 6 and 7.

Josephine Flood offers a suggestion as to the cause of the sudden arrival in Australia of foreign hunter-gatherers with new tools and dogs in her book *Archaeology of the Dreamtime:*

> It is ... probably no coincidence that these new weapons appear at the time the sea had risen to drown huge tracts of land ... the effects on the Sunda shelf were particularly dramatic. Here, a peninsula the size of India, was suddenly turned into the world's largest archipelago. The tremendous loss of territory, particularly if it happened fairly rapidly, may well have been what triggered migration and conflict, bringing new technology, new tools and ideas to Australia, and at least two dingoes.[63]

Not all Australian archaeologists agree with Josephine Flood's model. The microliths may not be as specific a date marker in Australia as she claims, although there was clearly a surge in their popularity. One problem is the dates. If the first of these microlith-carrying visitors did not arrive until sometime between 6000 and 4000 years ago, the last post-glacial flood was all but over at least 1500 years before. On that scale, the flood refugees might have been waiting on Timor or Sumba a long time before taking the final trip across to Australia. An earlier date of between 8000 and 7500 years ago would fit the flood event rather better. It is possible, as Josephine Flood points out, that the continued rising of the sea after the catastrophe as on other continental shelves obliterated the earliest evidence of coastal settlements in northern Australia, thus giving another false horizon. The present eastern beaches of the Great Barrier Reef were not breached until after 6000 years ago, drawing a curtain over new coastal settlements before that date. Josephine Flood's picture of the devastation of that last post-glacial inundation leads on to my final archaeological speculation – just how bad a time was the catastrophe for the coastal dwellers of Sundaland and coastal South China?

Flooded out and nowhere to go

In a recent book *The Austronesians* Peter Bellwood lists seven stimuli for his dispersal of Austronesians, none of which refers to Josephine Flood's unusual suggestion that post-glacial sea-level rise may have literally forced coastal foragers off the Sundaland shelf and into their boats. This is perfectly reasonable given the timescale and chronology he has set for the Austronesian diaspora. All the migratory legs in his model, except perhaps the move from China, came well after the end of the last flood.

Bellwood's seven reasons or motives for leaving the safety and comfort of the Asian continent and sailing out into the blue do, however, deserve close consideration here:[64]

1. *Continuous population growth based on an agricultural food supply, allowing a continuous generation-by-generation 'budding-off' of new families into new terrain;*

If we strip this statement down to motives, it ends up as land shortage when younger siblings move out to establish their own territory. (Bellwood admits, however, that he has moved away from over-reliance on this particular argument.)

2. *The inherent transportability and reproducibility of the agricultural economy to support colonising propagules, especially on resource-poor small islands;*

Translated, this means that the Austronesian colonisers were well able to cope with farming on scrubby islands. This is self-evident but it could not constitute a stimulus to move to those islands.

3. *The presence of a deep and absorbent 'frontier zone' available for the colonisation next to the area of early Austronesian agricultural development, occupied by foraging populations (i.e. Taiwan and the Philippines in the early days of expansion), most of who would presumably have shown little interest in adopting a systematic agricultural economy for themselves;*

Leaving aside the presumption that hunter-gathers are not interested in new ideas, this statement seems to mean that big islands near an Asian homeland, without much local competition, could act as a springboard for further colonisation. This is a reasonable point, but it is a means not a stimulus, and it spoils the 'land hunger' argument in (1).

4. *A developing tradition of sailing-canoe construction and navigation;*

Again this is a means not a motive for exploration. Certainly, when better sailing craft and skills became available, the Austronesian speakers could sail further. This may have been a factor in the dramatic Lapita expansion into the greater Pacific and Polynesia only 3500 years ago. By this time, however, the Austronesian-speaking inhabitants of the small islands and coast round New Guinea would have been, by the choice of their ancestors, living in more cramped difficult environments. They probably also suffered intense local competition from the majority local non-Austronesian inhabitants, as implied in the Kulabob and Manup stories (see Chapter 16). Incidentally, this Southwest Pacific zone is the region where land hunger would have been operating, not the Chinese Coast.

5. *A predilection for rapid coastal movement and exploration, probably to find the most favourable environments for cultivation and sheltered inshore fishing, and thus promoting a colonisation pattern of wide-ranging settlement followed, often only centuries later, by territorial infilling;*

When we peel off the presumed land hunger and the descriptive aspects of Austronesian culture, the only stimulus implied here comes from the *Star Trek* series immortalised by the most-repeated split infinitive of the twentieth century: 'to boldly go where no man has gone before'. The desire to explore is certainly powerful, but most successful explorers into the unknown make sure they are well equipped to come back. In this respect the Lapita expansion of confident deep-ocean sailors 3500 years ago can be seen as a later phase in a process that started 4000 years before that. The earlier dispersals, which included the foragers reaching Australia, sound more desperate in intent. This is backed by their folk-stories of escape from a great flood that swallowed their homeland, as I shall explore in Chapter 10.

6. *A culturally sanctioned desire to found new settlements in order to become a revered or even deified founder ancestor in the genealogies of future generations (presumably this evolved hand in hand with the colonisation process itself);*

Higher motives are required here. I think Bellwood refers to the old issue of primogeniture combined with land hunger. By this is meant that, if only the oldest son (or daughter) gets the chieftainship, the other sons (or daughters) may want to go and found their own colonies elsewhere. (This is basically the same point as (1) above.)

7. *A desire to find new sources of raw materials for 'prestige goods' exchange networks.*

This last point presumes an existing inter-island trade network and therefore cannot be regarded as a stimulus to initial island exploration.

Bellwood acknowledges that some of the 'stimuli' listed above, in particular (4), (6) and (7), could have developed only after the expansion began and as part of the process. At this point in his argument, however, he goes back to his original main premise and theme: 'it is my suspicion that the tap-root of the expansion process, a *sine qua non*, was the possession of a systematic agricultural economy capable of supporting continuous population growth.'[65]

It is now clear why it is so important for Bellwood to establish the provenance of a new successful rice venture for the Austronesian ancestors in Taiwan (see previous chapter). Otherwise there would be nothing to distinguish these Proto-Austronesians from any other stay-at-home Neolithic culture on the Asian coasts. To me it does not seem to matter for the population argument whether the original Austronesian staple was rice or the root crops taro and yams. Both types of agriculture can support large populations although the latter are more suited to Pacific islands (the New Guinea highlands of today and 9000 years ago are good evidence for the success of root crops in the Pacific region). Certainly the means to support rapid population growth is crucial to expansion but it cannot drive people out to sea unless there is a real squeeze at home. The real tests of the agricultural hypothesis are (1) is there any precedent or logic for agriculture driving people out to sea, and (2) was there evidence of extreme land shortage at the time of the hypothetical original dispersal from China?

Colin Renfrew, a prehistorian at the University of Cambridge, has inspired others with his book *Archaeology and Language*. In this popular book he makes a strong case for the gradual spread of Indo-European languages through South Asia and Europe on the back of the new or Neolithic agriculture. Although he draws parallels between Indo-European and Austronesian languages, he is the first to say that the Austronesian dispersal – especially that to Polynesia – was different: 'This was a process, of initial colonisation, in areas previously without human population. In this respect it certainly differed markedly from the demographic processes at work in Europe at the time of the development there of early farming.'[66]

There were other differences. The physical rate of Indo-European expansion was several orders slower than that for the argonauts of the Pacific, and even then the Indo-European speakers did not have to sail. Europe and Asia were and are made of a huge expanse of dry land, some of it very fertile. The Pacific is an ocean and the islands on it get smaller and less fertile the further east they are. China now supports over a billion people on the main staples of rice and wheat. Rice is the staple proposed for the first pre-Austronesian dispersal from Hemudu, and has been a southern Chinese staple since the time of the flood. It is only recently that China has become a net importer of rice. We can thus assume that there was at least some mainland capacity to absorb the burgeoning Neolithic populations 6000 or 7500 years ago. Put more simply, China cannot have been that crowded in Neolithic times; Kwang Chih-Chang from Harvard University and Ward Goodenough from the University of Pennsylvania also disagree with Bellwood's hypothesis: 'Certainly there was great population growth in China during the period in question. But there was still no dearth of agricultural land.'[67] What could have possessed those early coastal farmers to leave their huge and fertile mainland home to seek their future in the unknown? Let us suppose, for the sake of argument, that they were determined for one reason or other to leave the safety and fertility of the mainland. Would they, then, as Peter Bellwood and Robert Blust imply, have first gone through the already inhabited Maluku to the hostile and, in Neolithic terms, densely populated island of New Guinea?[68] Java and Sumatra were nearer, more attractive agriculturally, and also apparently undeveloped. 'Agriculturally attractive' is perhaps an understatement for Java which holds some of the most densely populated fertile agricultural land in the world. Of the 270 million speakers of Austronesian languages today, a hundred million, or more than a third, are supported by the volcanic island of Java.

The motives for the initial stages of Austronesian dispersion – population expansion and land hunger – suggested by Peter Bellwood are thus not convincing, although they may apply to Renfrew's Indo-European model. The means for a successful Pacific expansion, on the other hand, are not in dispute: those were possessed by good farmers, good fishers and good sailors. Since there are clearly objections to the validity of the 'agricultural' model of Austronesian dispersal, whether it was 3500 or 7500 years ago, we can now move on to the alternative which I propose. This is that early explorers were literally driven off their land by the flood.

Getting your feet wet

Archaeologists and other specialists have moved away from the old question of post-glacial sea rise as a cause of Neolithic dispersal simply because it was too long ago and too slow. Over the last two chapters I have argued that the first East Asian Neolithic sea dispersal did after all follow the last great flood. I now have the task of reconstructing the catastrophe. This can be divided into two aspects, as with the myths of the event (see Chapters 9 and 10): the first of these is the big wave; the second is rapid loss of land.

I discussed the strong likelihood of superwaves arising from the crustal strains when the Laurentide ice sheet of Canada collapsed and melted around 8000 years ago in Chapter 1. The release of energy from the Earth's crust would have produced waves rolling across the Pacific and inundating all shores and flat hinterlands in direct line. The east coasts of China, Japan, Taiwan, the Philippines and the northeast coasts of New Guinea and New Ireland would have suffered the brunt of these walls from 50 metres to maybe as much as 300 metres high. Devastation would have been terrible and coastal loss of life near complete, but those who took refuge on the tops of mountains, as in Taiwan and the eastern Philippines, may have survived to tell the tale. On steep coasts, the local destruction would have been great but limited in extent; on flat coasts, the waves would have rolled far inland. Richard Huggett, geographer from Birmingham University, has described the sort of damage caused by much smaller waves:

> And if it be doubted that superwaves of 50 m or less would leave their mark on the landscape, then consider the known effects of a modern floodwave that was produced by a vast rock-avalanche, triggered by an earthquake, in an inlet of the Gulf of Alaska in 1938. The displaced water in the inlet generated a wave with a steep front that rose to a height of 30 m or more and reached a velocity of 210 Km/hr. The wave destroyed forest along kilometres of shore and in places the momentum of the surging water carried it up to 525 m, as indicated by the height to which trees had been stripped of their bark and bedrock had been stripped of its soil cover.[69]

In comparison to the earthquakes of 8000 years ago, this event was very small. As I pointed out in Chapter 1, earthquakes caused by post-glacial faulting are easily the largest known externally induced quakes; one example of these was the earthquake that produced the Swedish pärvie (wave in the ground) 8000 years ago. That quake was produced by an ice cap that was all but played out. Consider then the quakes that accompanied the collapse of the great Laurentide ice sheet of

Canada around the same time. As the pärvie report states: 'Great ice sheets can induce great earthquakes.'[70] These great earthquakes and great waves were the result of energy from the Earth's crust after rapid de-glaciation, so would have followed episodes of particularly fast sea-level rises. In other words, coastal farmers who may have just suffered a bad loss of land were then faced with great waves rolling in. There would thus be some reason for the survivors to associate the two, as happens in many flood stories (see Chapters 9 and 10). We can now answer the question whether the sea was coming in fast enough to be noticed and remembered in legend.

Some worst-case calculations can be estimated on the back of an envelope – anything more precise might assume more accurate information than is available. The Sunda shelf in Southeast Asia is flatter in some places than others, but the maximum horizontal distance between 20-metre depth contours on a bathymetric map is about 2000 kilometres. This represents a sea incursion of a kilometre for every 10-centimetre rise in sea-level. The single most rapid rise in sea-level after the Ice Age happened 8000 years ago with the collapse of a complex of two glacial lakes, Agassiz and Ojibway in Canada. This raised global sea-levels by 20–40 centimetres instantaneously (see Chapter 1).[71]

On the beaches of the Sunda shelf 8000 years ago sea water would have flooded inland up to a maximum 4 kilometres within two days. We can imagine that the sea would not have come in quietly. Further fluctuations in sea-level would have resulted from rebound of the Earth's crust relieved of a heavy load. It is fairly certain, then, that this event would have been 'noticed' by coastal people throughout the world.

The event, of course, did not stop there. As I explained in the first chapter, the Canadian lakes were the high-altitude cistern that flushed out great volumes of water held in the Laurentide ice sheet over several years. The figures estimated from different studies for the subsequent sustained rise in sea-level vary enormously and are worth repeating. The maximum estimate of sustained rise was 8–15 centimetres a year over a range of 25 metres; lesser calculations give 3–4 centimetres a year. These values would translate to a coastal sea incursion of up to a kilometre a year. The exact figure is unimportant; any annual land loss of such an order, sustained for hundreds of years, would be disastrous for a coastal community. I believe that this cause of land loss transformed into land hunger did force people out to sea. I can now start to paint the picture on different coastlines of the Far East 8000–7500 years ago. First though, what did the vegetation of the coastland of South China and Sundaland look like at the time of the last flood?

Three recurrent cycles of dry and cold followed by warm and humid characterised the three post-glacial floods of the last 15,000 years (see Chapter 1). The last of the freeze-ups was extremely short, lasting only 400 years. Then the world warmed up to its most sunny and humid time of the past 100,000 years – the so-called inter-glacial optimum – and the final flood of 8000–7500 years ago was released. Forests and other vegetation are generally very sensitive to changes in temperature. This effect is blunted in tropical regions where temperature changes are less, except at high altitude. Sub-tropical regions, however, develop more seasonal vegetation during cold spells. At the height of the last Ice Age, the dry exposed flat areas of the Sunda shelf were extensively covered in pine forest and grassy plains, except for a core region defined by the northern half of Borneo, and its exposed shelf to the north. These regions stayed 'everwet' and humid throughout the Ice Age.[72] As the post-glacial world warmed up, the pine and savannah was replaced by humid tropical lowland forest with giant dipterocarp trees, beloved of loggers, and coastal mangrove swamps. The tropical region extended further up the China coast than it does today. Hong Kong, for instance, still has small areas of mangroves, but the climate is considerably cooler in the 1990s than it was during the days of the inter-glacial optimum. This time was the beginning of the age of the mangroves I mentioned earlier. We can thus visualise the coasts of South China, and island Southeast Asia at the time of the third flood as extensively clothed by mangroves and backed by dense tropical forests.

Austronesian-speaking peoples living in the traditional coastal way in islands from West Sumatra to Polynesia depend for their food today on a combination of marine produce, foraging and horticulture. Unlike some Inuit tribes, they do not rely solely on marine produce for long periods. The multifarious diet of Austronesians goes right back to the earliest reconstructed Austronesian proto-language. Horticulture requires land. If the hinterland is forested, the forest needs to be cleared periodically by burning and felling. Mangrove swamp cannot be easily cleared and used in this way, and tropical forest requires considerable investment of energy to fell. If the coast keeps moving backwards, this activity becomes fruitless and repetitive. When tropical forest is flooded, as in dam projects, the large dead hardwood trees remain standing as solid ghosts in the water for years. Once the Neolithic coastal people lost the battle to clear the land, the great unfelled forest giants would have remained standing, wet and dead in the new sea, thus preventing easy access from the remaining hinterland to the ocean.

We can imagine the scene: the sea was moving in inexorably at up to a kilometre a year over the flat forested plains; the capacity of coastal Austronesian or Austro-Asiatic speakers to relocate their villages repeatedly inland became exhausted; their only recourse was then to move, in one of the following ways:

1. *Hundreds of kilometres inland to a more mountainous area to continue horticulture.* The Bontoc and Ifugao tribes are a modern-day example of this solution. Their ancestors built the ancient rice terraces of the Luzon highlands in the Philippines. In this context it is significant that the main evidence of Neolithic dispersal into Sumatra 8000 years ago comes from the Batak uplands around Lake Toba, where extensive forest clearance occurred at that time.[73]

2. *Further into the lowland jungle to continue foraging.* Believers in the 'fully agricultural' hypothesis of Austronesian expansion – Peter Bellwood, for example – see the present-day Austronesian-speaking foragers and hunter-gatherers in islands such as Borneo and the Philippines as a problem for their model. They therefore suggest that such foragers may be 'devolved agriculturalists'.[74] But as is clear from the archaeological records of northern Australia, foraging lifestyles do not preclude the use of boats capable of crossing seas.

3. *To sail away to lands with more coastal elevation and less jungle.* These were the first argonauts of the Pacific. The sailing solution appears to have been taken by many different island cultures in Indonesia, who still build their houses to look like boats and say their ancestors were flooded out from a lost homeland and had to migrate across the sea. Those migrants who could not get a foothold in the remaining islands of Southeast Asia had to disperse to the four points of the compass.

4. *Upwards. Some people decided to stay on the strand and build houses and fishing platforms on stilts, thus ignoring the rising water.* The best argument for the original invention and construction of stilt houses in general remains the recurrent flooding hypothesis (see illustration 2).[75]

5. *Some may have chosen to live partly or wholly in their boats.* Modern representatives include the Badgao sea gypsies of the Sulu Archipelago, the Orang Laut of the Straits of Malacca and the Moklen and Moken off the coast of Burma. Wilhelm Solheim in his south-to-north hypothesis of Austronesian linguistic origin proposes that Proto-Austronesian developed as a barter language among the ancestors of these fully marine 'Nusantao' traders.[76]

All of these varied solutions to wet feet have been taken and are still being used as lifestyles by Austronesian and Austro-Asiatic speakers of island Southeast Asia.

In the light of this model of dispersion and diversification, the reason for the lack of coastal Neolithic settlements in Java and Sumatra in spite of other evidence of a rich Neolithic culture in these islands is now clearer. The first argonauts did not miss the north and east coasts of Java and Sumatra. Instead, they found the same problems of progressive land loss there. Where they did settle, their footholds were eventually washed away. We are left with enough evidence of land clearance in the uplands and beautiful polished axes elsewhere to know they lived there after the flood. The surviving ancient Austronesian cultures of Western Indonesia and Burma – The Enggano, the Mentawai, the Nias, the Bataks and the Aceh – are found either on islands whose coasts were too steep to suffer from sea encroachment or, simply, well away from the coast.

Did the flood stimulate a Neolithic Revolution?

Part of the archaeological evidence for a flood-driven dispersal, which I have reviewed, suggests devastation in the suddenly abandoned settlements in the eighth millennium before the present. But another side shows a new horizon, a Neolithic Revolution, suggesting that the floods may not only have stimulated a diversification of food-gathering and culture, as discussed earlier, but also moved these new skills and others around Eurasia.

If the people really had been forced off their land by the flood, each small desperate migration could have spread locally developed skills to other points of the Eurasian and Oceanic coastlines. The enforced process of taking to boats, in turn could have been the start of the so-called voyaging corridors and trade networks of the Southwest Pacific. Thereafter, throughout the Indo-Pacific region, ideas, pottery styles, religious views, stories and technology moved easily from one place to the next.

One example of the new technology transfer may be the disputed site of the first discovery of bronze. Archaeologists believe that happened in the Ancient Near East during the fourth millennium BC and that the same event occurred independently in eastern Asia, but the earliest date recorded from Ban Chiang in Thailand for bronze-making also comes from the beginning of the fourth millennium BC (see above).[77] Surely this is an unlikely coincidence for such an epoch-making discovery? The eastern location had the advantage of greater availability of tin, so may have been the original source of the discovery of alloying copper to make bronze. Afterwards, it would have been easy for the sailors on the trading networks to have compared notes.

The archaeological evidence for an early Neolithic in Southeast Asia and its early dispersal at the time of the last post-glacial flood long before Lapita, finds curious echoes in the story of the spread of languages in the Asia-Pacific region. We will look at the spoken word next before finally asking the same questions of the genetic oracle.

4
BABEL

'And the whole earth was of one language and of one speech'. These words from Genesis sound quaint when measured against the thousands of languages known today, spanning diverse races and cultures. According to the Genesis story, it was the building of the Tower of Babel after the Flood by peoples from the east that led to the 'babble' of tongues known throughout the world today. Their diversity is so great that we might consider the date of that first language too remote to bother about.

We know, however, that much of the geographic distribution of modern languages – at least until the major colonisations of recent times – dates from the end of the Ice Age. The fact that languages of people living in certain regions are clearly related to each other has strongly influenced prehistorians of Southeast Asia and the Pacific in their study of how dispersals of Neolithic cultures came about. Some prehistorians even present 'palaeolinguistics'[1] as their single most powerful microscope upon the past.

From the start, comparative linguists have consciously acknowledged a cultural debt to the Genesis authors. Like the scribes of the Sumerian King Lists, those indefatigable Hebrew genealogists clearly intended to provide a firm provenance for their patriarch Abraham, on the tree of man in the ancient Near East. Like the jumbled foundation wall from a past era of an ancient city, the names of Noah's family, some of whom contributed to Babel both figuratively and architecturally, persist as eponyms in modern linguistic family trees.

Noah had three sons. Shem, who is generally regarded as the father of Semitic tongues, in fact shared this role with Ham. Shem had five sons. These included Asshur (Assyria), Arpachshad who gave rise eventually to Abraham, and Elam (Elamite?) who may not have been Semitic at all. Noah's second son Ham, the eponym for some African (Hamitic) languages, fathered Canaan, Put, Cush (hence Cushitic) and Egypt. While eventually this family gave rise to the North African branches of the Afro-Asiatic (or Hamito-Semitic) language phylum, Cush also fathered Nimrud who was credited, in Genesis, with founding the cities of Babel, Erech (Uruk) and Accad (hence Akkadian) in the land of Shinar (Sumer). The third son, Japheth, is more mysterious. He is popularly regarded as the father of Europeans. However the terms 'Japhetic' languages or Japhetite peoples usually refer to peoples speaking certain isolated Caucasian languages and living in the Caucasus and parts of Asia. From Javan, one of Japheth's sons, descended Elishah, Tarshish, (a Phoenician colony in southern Spain) and the spreading 'coastal peoples'. 'Javan' was a generic Hebrew term for Greek peoples, or literally Ionians. Other descendants of Japheth include Magog who does have a legendary connection in the Caucasus and beyond into central Asia.

We need to know if Genesis was right: in other words that the third great flood after the Ice Age led to a dispersion and diversification of languages throughout the known world. In this chapter, therefore, I will concentrate on exploring the evidence of possible links between the languages of Southeast Asia and India, as well as with the dead language of Sumerian. But I also hope to find out whether an incestuous marriage of linguistics and archaeology has ignored the effect of post-glacial sea-level rise on the evidence on which they mutually rely for their model. Finally, I shall see whether the cultural links that are so obvious in the origin myths (to be explored in Chapters 11 and 12) fit with the theories linking East Asian languages.

The comparative method in linguistics

First, I shall look briefly at the methods of the comparative linguist. There are certain misconceptions among onlookers – for instance, that languages are compared simply by looking at the numbers of shared words, and how similar they are to each other. Curiously, the historical linguist is more interested in the regular ways in which similar words have *changed* between related languages. We can all see history of change in our own languages.

Modern English, for instance, has had many borrowings from different but related branches of the Indo-European language family. While much of English vocabulary is similar to Germanic languages, we can still hear the influence of the Norman invasion in AD 1066. French feudal overlords in early medieval England might well have asked their Saxon stewards and serfs to bring viandes de boeuf, porc, poulet and veau rather than meat of the Saxon cow, swine, chicken or calf. So our modern terms for the dead meats or viands of beef, pork, poultry, veal, etc. were originally from the French, while the terms for the live animals are still Saxon.

This phenomenon is called 'borrowing' or 'intrusion'. It can happen just as easily between related languages, as in the above example, and totally unrelated languages as, for instance, Basque and Spanish. Borrowing will always occur when peoples speaking two languages live in proximity on the same landmass. It can also happen through trade and other forms of contact.

The most extreme form of borrowing would be when a group of people take on a complete language not spoken by their ancestors. This can affect migrants and people who are invaded. Colonial languages such as English and French have spread with minimal modification in this way. Sometimes, however, the indigenous people only borrow the vocabulary rather than the syntax of the invaders, and the result is a Pidgin. In Papua New Guinea, I had to communicate in Tok Pisin bilong Niugini (New Guinea Pidgin). I was able to learn the vocabulary fairly quickly, but the word order and syntax took longer. The most difficult thing was learning to pun.

Languages will also change gradually without any outside influence. In this case the changes – for instance in pronunciation – are usually uniform throughout the lexicon. Thus certain sounds will change *en masse* in a regular fashion. One of the first linguists to record this effect systematically was a German, Jacob Grimm, also famous for collecting European folk-tales. Grimm's Law describes several regular switches in use of consonants particularly between Germanic languages. The 'd' in German 'der, die, das' would thus be expected to be pronounced as a 'th' in English 'the'. Similarly German 'dunne' becomes English 'thin'. It is the very regularity of the sound changes of these so-called cognates[2] that help comparative linguists to establish a true genetic connection between languages with common words, rather than misleading sound/meaning associations based on borrowing or chance resemblance.

Proving that languages are genetically related, using these well-tried methods, is uncontroversial. A recognisable synthetic Latin, for instance, can be reconstructed from modern romance languages. The 'comparative method' can be used and validated in situations of uncomplicated language change and dispersion, even where there are no written records to confirm the language history. For instance, most prehistorians would agree that the pattern of development of Polynesian culture in the small Pacific islands is an example of migratory dispersion. The islands were previously empty and widely spaced, there were no competing outside languages, and the archaeological, linguistic, genetic and anthropological records show good (though not perfect) concordance. In other words all the different cultures, the people and their languages in these small islands are clearly related.

Table 1. Grimm's Laws. Examples of regular changes of labial and dental consonants between different Indo-European languages.

Greek	Latin	Gothic	Sanskrit	Slavic
p	p	f	p	p
b	b	p	b	b
ph	f/b	b	bh	b
t	t	e	t	t
d	d	t	d	d
th	f/d	d	dh	d

The next step in exploring genetic relationships between languages is the process of forming sub-groups of more closely related languages. This is done again, not so much by statistically measuring the degrees of similarity and shared features, but rather by looking for systematic language innovations which are shared by other members of the sub-group. The consonant changes of Grimm's Law are examples of innovation or change. If one change or set of changes are shared by a sub-group of languages but not by all the other related tongues, then it implies that this sub-group shares a common more recent ancestor. The sub-groups defined in this way can then be attached on to larger branches, and eventually a genetic 'family tree' of languages is reconstructed. In this process it is necessary, still using the same techniques, to reconstruct the hypothetical ancestor languages on the nodes further down the tree, since all that is available today are the modern descendants at the twigs.

Finally, although comparative linguists may regard 'shared innovations' as better evidence of close relationship than mere quantitative 'shared features' and shared cognate words, they cannot ignore loss of these latter shared features. If two languages are closely grouped on the basis of shared innovations, but share less than 10 per cent of their vocabulary, there has to be a good reason why. As I shall show in the next chapter, this is particularly relevant in western Melanesia where the languages in the presumed original area of dispersion of the Oceanic group of Austronesian languages are so different from the others in the group that they have been labelled 'aberrant'. The key alternative explanation is that they may simply have split off earlier.

Know your ancestors

The process of sub-grouping and building of the language tree uses the same comparative principles as in the first stage of establishing a genetic relationship (see Chapters 6 and 7). The results of sub-grouping are, however, much more uncertain, variable and controversial. The linguist's decision as to what is a 'language innovation' and what is a 'retained feature' can make radical differences to the prehistorian's interpretation of a tree. I can illustrate this by an example that may seem rather academic, but could change the timescale of Pacific prehistory.

I refer again to the previously near-perfect model of migratory dispersal of Polynesian languages. Since the 1960s the standard family tree of Polynesian languages has shown up to five generations of branching nodes with the 'Central Pacific Homeland' language groups of Samoan and Tongan as 'stay at homes' arising early in the tree. Bill Wilson and Jeff Marck of the Australian National University have reconstructed a radically different family tree, but still using the traditional methodology. The members of the family have not changed but their sub-groupings have, with profound implications for prehistoric dispersals and migrations. The relative prehistoric relationship of Samoan and the so-called Polynesian Outliers is crucial:

> Where previously there had been the implication that the effective settlement of Eastern Polynesia occurred before the Outliers were settled, we are now free to allow the possibility ... [of the] ... Outliers [having been] settled prior to or at the same time as the effective linguistic settlement of Eastern Polynesia.[3]

If we review this dry statement, the new coppiced tree suggests a redrawing of the map of Polynesia. Numerically most Polynesian Outliers do not lie anywhere near Polynesia; they lie scattered much further west among the Melanesian islands of the Solomons, New Caledonia and Vanuatu (see Figure 17). These 'out-of-place' Polynesian settlements have always been thought to represent descendants of Samoans who had all wandered back west again from 'the Central Pacific Polynesian Homeland', after the settlement of central Polynesia. Not only does the new tree release them from this prehistoric renegade label, but it also allows a simpler, more balanced interpretation of the outliers' location in Melanesia, nearer to Southeast Asia. They could just represent the remnants of the trail of earlier Polynesian settlements during their original dispersal through Melanesia from west to east. In other words, the Polynesian language family could have first burst into bloom in the Southwest Pacific rather than in the Central Pacific. As I shall show shortly, there are other westward shifts of 'effective dispersals' resulting from such linguistic reorganisations. They suggest, like the

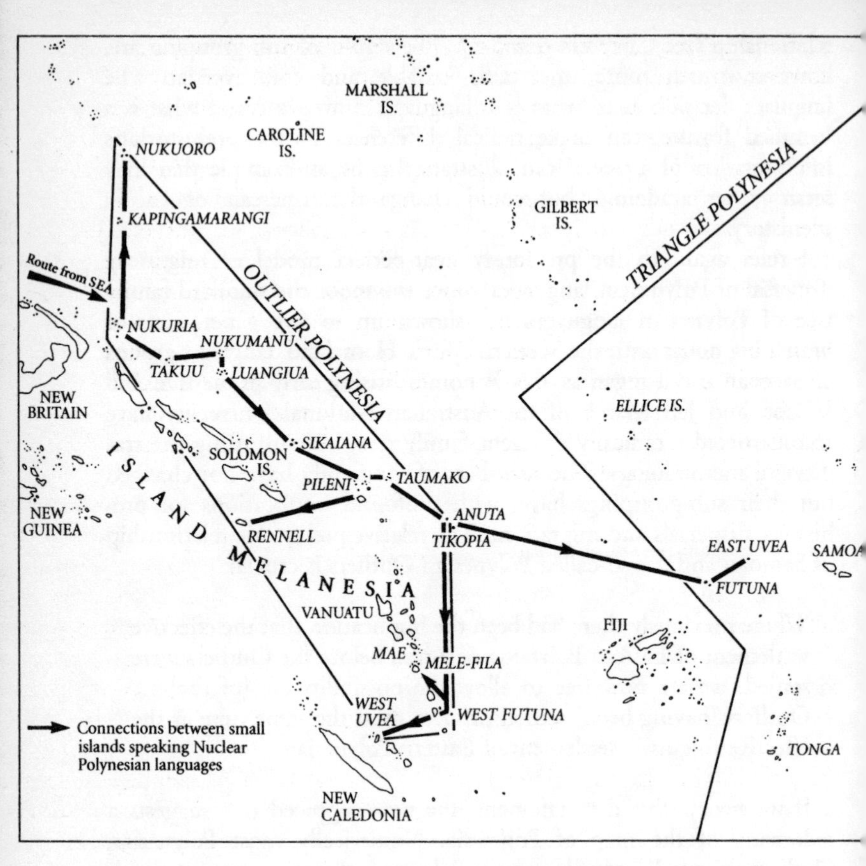

Figure 17. **Polynesian fast track revealed.** Linguists usually assume that the so-called 'Outlier Polynesian' speakers wandered west from Samoa. A recent reorganisation of the language tree classifies them as 'Nuclear Polynesian' (place names in italics) and of a higher order on the tree than Samoan.[3] This promotion allows their tiny islands to be the ancestral stepping-stones that early Polynesians may have taken in their eastward penetration of the Pacific, thus bypassing the larger islands of the Solomons, Vanuatu and New Caledonia, occupied by Melanesians.

archaeological reconstructions I describe in Chapters 2 and 3, that the timeline of spread of the argonauts of the Pacific clearly needs re-writing.

I will return to the reorganisation of the Austronesian linguistic tree a little later; first, I need to put the Austronesian language family in the context of other world and Eurasian groupings. The first stage of language classification, using conventional comparative linguistics, links large groups of languages that are related to each other. The highest-order groupings that result are sometimes called *phyla* by analogy with biological taxonomy. A phylum should have no identifiable other relatives. Austronesian languages, for instance, together form one phylum. In the huge Eurasian mainland there are only eight such phyla, and relatively small numbers of languages in them (see Figure 18). Contrast Eurasia with the island of New Guinea, which has six apparently unrelated phyla of its own, sharing between them only a little fewer than a thousand discrete tongues. This overall lack of diversity throughout much of Eurasia is almost entirely due to the relatively recent post-glacial expansion of particularly successful Neolithic and Metal Age monocultures.

Indo-European and other Eurasian languages

The main phylum spoken in Europe, Indo-European, includes nearly all the languages spoken in Europe. The larger sub-groupings are Italic (the romance languages); Germanic (most of the northern languages down to the Netherlands and England); Celtic (Breton and some extinct mainland languages); and Slavic (languages spoken in many eastern European countries, such as Russia, Poland and the former Yugoslavia). Hellenic, Armenian and Albanian are all single-language sub-groups.

What started the linguistic ball rolling 200 years ago was the exciting discovery that many languages spoken in South Asia combined with European languages to form a larger family, Indo-European. These Asian cousins form a sub-group called Indo-Iranian, which includes Persian, Sanskrit and its many modern descendants such as Hindi, Urdu and Bengali. Romany, spoken by travelling folk thoughout Europe, is included with these last three in the Indic group. Some other older, non Indo-European language groups are also spoken in the Indian subcontinent and include the Dravidian, and the Mundaic languages. Dravidian is placed in its own phylum and the Mundaic languages, as I have discussed, belong to the large, unrelated Austro-Asiatic phylum, with a distribution from Vietnam in the east to India in the west.

Indo-European languages may be relatively recent arrivals to Europe from further east. As an alternative to the stereotypical view of the invading Aryans, Colin Renfrew, a Cambridge University prehistorian,

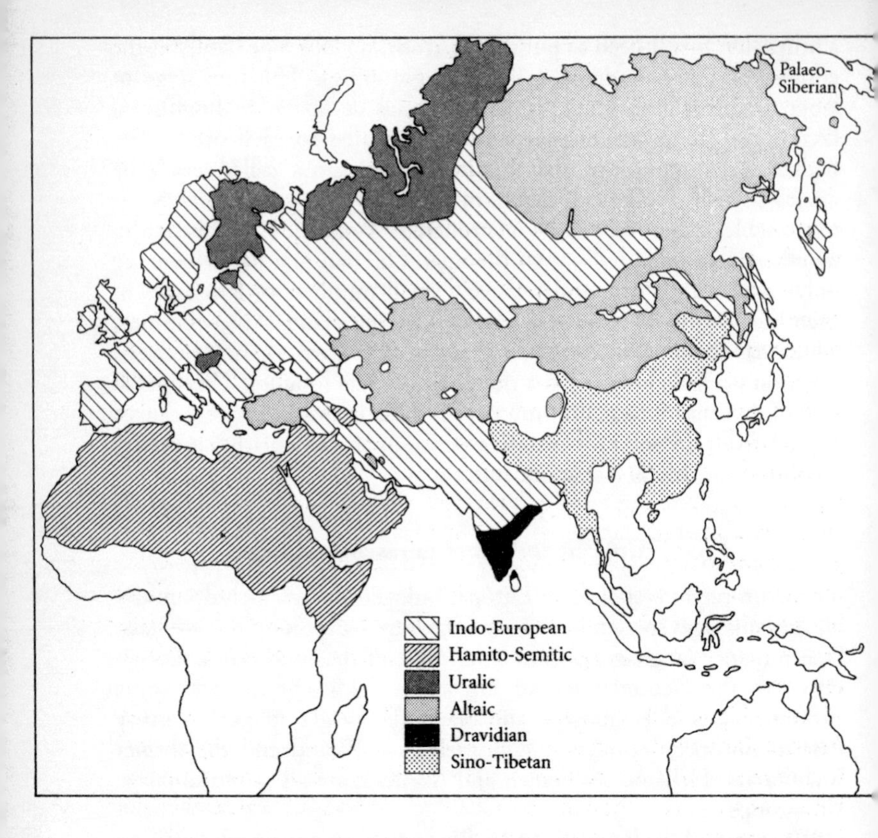

Figure 18. **Major language families in Eurasia.** A simplified map of the distribution of six major language families (phyla) found in Eurasia today. The three families of Indo-China and Southeast Asia are shown in Figures 19 and 26. For clarity, smaller families and isolates such as the Caucasian groups, Basque, Korean, Japanese and the Palaeo-Siberian families are not shown.

has painted a picture of a more gradual spread of Indo-European languages on the back of agriculture, without necessarily a large movement of people. From around 7000 BC, farmers from Anatolia (Asiatic Turkey) may have started a concentric wave of Neolithic technological innovation that gradually carried Indo-European language phylum with it to the rest of Europe and South Asia.[4] It is this model that some Austronesian scholars would like to emulate for the Pacific argonauts.

Indo-European languages are thought by Renfrew and many others to originate around the Black Sea and Caucasus area, possibly in what is now the Ukraine. American palaeolinguist Johanna Nichols, however, places the epicentre much further east in Central Asia and the expansion date more recently, around 3700–3300 BC. She argues that the spread of Indo-European was only the latest of a series of expansions from the east that started by 5000 BC and included the non-Indo-European Uralic and Altaic phyla.[5]

The other languages now spoken in Europe are generally thought to be unrelated to Indo-European and consist mainly of the Finno-Ugric branch of the Uralic phylum, which includes Finnish, Estonian, Saami (Lapp) and Hungarian. These languages have a completely different word structure to Indo-European languages and are sometimes called 'agglutinating' because of the habit of sticking extra particles onto and into words to modify their meaning and use.[6] In this respect Uralic languages resemble Austronesian languages and the extinct orphan language Sumerian. Some linguists even suggest the possibility of a genetic link between Uralic languages and Sumerian.[7] Finally, there is one language that may be the only one with any claim to have belonged to the inhabitants of Europe before the arrival of farming: this is Basque, a language found in northern Spain with no known relatives.

Finno-Ugric languages also spread into Russia, and so did another Asian branch of the Uralic phylum called Samoyedic. Samoyeds live within the Arctic Circle and may have originated in southwest Siberia. Uralic languages are thought to have dispersed from in or near the Ural Mountains as much as 7000 years ago.

In the centre of Asia, to the north and northeast of Eurasia, live speakers of the main Central Asian language family – the Altaic phylum. This Asian phylum, which not all linguists accept as a group, has three main branches: Turkic, Mongolian and Manchu/Tungus. Also agglutinating, the languages of this phylum have been associated, controversially, with Uralic languages and, even more controversially, with Korean and Japanese.

Semitic languages such as Hebrew, Aramaic and Arabic of the Middle East belong to the Afro-Asiatic phylum. This large family includes most of the languages of North and Northeast Africa such as Chadic, Cushitic, Ancient Egyptian and Berber.

Language and prehistory

Study of the relationships between the languages people speak is a powerful tool in the study of prehistory and human migration. Historical linguistics, however, contains pitfalls if too much is expected of the models it produces. Much of the methodology developed by palaeolinguists is, like any archaeological reconstruction, intrinsically untestable. Linguists can describe and quantify similarities between related languages in many different ways. But when it comes to putting related modern languages on a family tree there are a surprising number of ways in which the branches can be attached. This difficulty is compounded by a lack of direct knowledge of the ancestral languages. Except where the older languages have been committed to writing, linguists can make only educated guesses about a mother or grandmother tongues.

Superphyla

The comparative method has arguably a limited time depth of perhaps 7000 years. Before that time, most traditional linguists would argue that relationships become increasingly difficult to substantiate. Larger continental groupings of phyla, to be sure, are suggested, but many linguists cannot agree on the grouping methods used, which do not follow the traditional 'comparative method'. Several of these superphyla have caused controversy and even some bad feeling. One is the 'Nostratic' phylum,[8] which combines all the five Eurasian phyla that I have listed – Indo-European, Uralic, Altaic, Dravidian and Afro-Asiatic – into one big family. The four Far Eastern phyla, Austro-Asiatic, Austro-Tai, Austronesian and Sino-Tibetan (see below) are notably excluded from this grouping.

Populations and distributions, not languages and trees

Linguist Johanna Nichols has focused the comparative linguistic method much further back than 7000 years in her recent book, appropriately entitled *Linguistic Diversity in Space and Time*.[9] This reveals Southeast Asia as the epicentre of language dispersal since the last Ice Age. She manages this extension of the comparative method by a novel use of traditional language markers.

First Nichols avoids direct analysis around existing linguistic family trees. The only tree in the book spans the whole of humanity's time on Earth and has only four branches. Nichols calls this a tree of 'typological' rather than 'genetic', divergence.[10] Second, she avoids language comparisons around specific words. Third, the structural grammatical tools that she uses to classify language can be applied to all tongues and are all well established from traditional linguistics and the comparative method; the descriptive tools are thus uncontroversial. Fourth, although the material is complex, she uses only the simplest and most rugged statistical approach.

It is the very simplicity and lack of sophisticated assumptions that make Nichols's method potentially so novel and powerful. Nichols uses conventional types of grammatical structures seen in a large sample of the world's languages to classify each tongue into generally yes/no categories. A simple example of such a category is:

> Does the language have 'subject-object-verb' word order in its sentences?
> Category answers: English – No; French – No; German – Yes, etc.

Armed with a wide range of simple descriptive ways of dividing the world's languages into 'yes' or 'no' categories, Nichols then shows that some of these grammatical (stuctural) categories show more 'yes' answers in some parts of the world and more 'no' answers elsewhere. She then uses these results in a comprehensive analysis of change across and between continents which stretches over a great timescale.

Although Nichols's models extend way back into the Palaeolithic era, we are concerned here with the post-glacial period. She sees the end of glaciation as a watershed followed by the dispersion of languages from spread zones, an increase in complexity of societies and a consequent reduction in linguistic diversity, particularly in Eurasia.[11] These processes would be the expected effect of the widespread loss of homeland and disruption of coastal communities that followed each of the three floods I talk about in this book. Nichols's analysis is particularly illuminating on how these processes affected East Asia.

Southeast Asia: the centre of the world in prehistory

An important message in Johanna Nichols's book *Linguistic Diversity* is the key role of Southeast Asia in peopling the world as the Ice Age came to a close. After 'emerging early from Africa, spreading slowly to Southeast Asia and undergoing much linguistic diversification there' she writes, people then began 'expanding from there to colonise the Pacific and the New World'.

> It is circum-Pacific colonisation rather than spread from the Old World that has populated most of the world, given rise to most of the genetic lineages of human languages, and colonised

> the New World. The entry point to the New World was of course Beringia [the landbridge across the present Bering Strait]; but linguistic typology shows that the colonisers entering through Beringia were predominantly coastal people involved in circum-Pacific colonisation ... rather than inland Siberian people.[12]

A fascinating aspect of the picture Nichols paints of the colonisation of Asia, the circum-Pacific region and the Americas, is the great antiquity of the Southeast Asian coastline as a centre of language development. In her prehistoric linguistic model Southeast Asia and the east coast of Asia are placed as the main region of human expansion from Late Stone Age times onwards, with Europe and the Near East as late entries and on the periphery of action. We are not looking here at Ice Age hunter-gatherers wandering gradually across the steppes of Asia. Instead, we are dealing with a circum-Pacific coastal spread starting from Southeast Asia – much as I suggested earlier for the later spread of Austronesians into the Pacific 8000 to 6000 years ago. As I explained in the earlier chapters, any evidence of the technological stage of development of those first coastal explorers from Sundaland would certainly be hundreds of miles out to sea now and hidden by over 100 metres of water.

Mechanisms spreading language structural types are not necessarily the same as those of mass migratory movements of people or simple language switches.[13] They seem to flow across the unbridgeable genetic boundaries of language families. This implies continental-scale communication networks, perhaps trade or exchange, rather than mass movements of people. In spite of this qualification, independent evidence to support Nichols's argument that the first Americans were derived from the South Pacific and South Asia rather than Northeastern Asians has recently come from sophisticated analysis of prehistoric skull shapes.[14]

Austro-confusion in East and Southeast Asia

The languages of China and Southeast Asia are different in many respects from those of the rest of Eurasia. Because they are intimately mixed geographically, and have extensively borrowed and shared, it is difficult to disentangle their genetic inter-relationships.[15] Yet this needs to be attempted if the prehistory of the past 10,000 years, suggested by the new archaeological finds I described in the last chapter, is to be unravelled. The 9000-year-old pots and charred rice from Sakai cave in southern Thailand cannot tell us who made them, but a linguistic reconstruction might help suggest who were the cave-dwellers and who, if anyone, took the farming and metallurgical ideas to India and the West.

Before looking at these questions, I should clarify some of the terms and names. The first thing to strike the non-linguist when reading about Southeast Asian languages is the confusion of similar-sounding terms for the language families and people: Austronesian, Austro-Asiatic, Austric, Austro-Tai, Tai-Kadai and Sino-Tibetan are just some of the proposed linguistic phyla and superphyla that need to be considered. Here, therefore, is a brief explanation of each term before I assess the possible inter-relationships of the various languages – or indeed their relatedness to any other families. The first confusing linguistic aspects are the prefixes and suffixes of the phyla names.

The prefix 'Austr-' or 'Austro-' simply means 'south' as in Australia (terra australis incognita = unknown southern land). The suffix '-nesia' means islands.

'Poly-' means many (from the Greek), hence *Polynesia* means many islands in a large region of the Pacific. Confusingly, however, *Polynesian* refers to a language family as well as to the people living in Polynesia. Polynesian languages belong in the sub-group *Oceanic*, which is a higher-order grouping of Austronesian languages.

Austronesian, literally meaning 'southern islands', is a whole language phylum, individual languages of which are spoken by many genetically and culturally different ethnic groups living over the huge Indo-Pacific region. The term is purely linguistic and should not be generically used to identify the people or the region, but it often is used in these ways.

'Melanos' means black and *Melanesian* is a vague, imprecise term that was originally intended to mean dark-skinned, frizzy-haired people living on islands in the Southwest Pacific stretching from New Guinea to Fiji. Where I use the term, it is with this meaning. Sometimes, however, Melanesian is used to mean different things, such as Austronesian speaking people who are also dark-skinned and frizzy-haired, and who also live in a certain island group. Melanesian should definitely not be used as a linguistic term, because the region of Melanesia encompasses at least six different language phyla. In Southeast Asia, Aboriginal people looking similar in many ways to Melanesians and often living as hunter-gatherers are referred to as Negritos.

'Tai' in *Tai-Kadai* is derived from Thai. *Austro-Tai* is a proposed superphylum of Tai-Kadai and Austronesian. 'Sino-' or 'Sinitic' is intended to mean Chinese and closely related tongues. *Sino-Tibetan* is a proposed grouping to include Sinitic and *Tibeto-Burman* languages.

'Asiatic' should mean precisely that, though why Austro-Asiatic speakers, literally 'South Asian', should be any more Asian than their other Southeast Asian neighbours is unclear.

On the language families themselves, linguists agree that there are three large language phyla indigenous to the Far East and Southeast Asia – Sino-Tibetan, Austro-Asiatic and Austronesian – and a fourth, Tai-Kadai, whose affiliations are still indistinct. I will start with the two less controversial groups.

Sino-Tibetan

The Sino-Tibetan family, with over 300 languages spoken by over a billion people, is second only to Indo-European in numbers of speakers. Most Sino-Tibetan speakers belong to one of the fourteen Han Chinese dialects of the Sinitic sub-phylum, such as Mandarin. Although the dialects are not mutually intelligible, they use an identical script in which each syllable has meaning and a unique character. The languages are thus monosyllabic. They are also tonal, which means that each syllable has to be sung in a certain cadence. In these respects they differ from many other world families, such as Indo-European and Austronesian, which are monotonal or atonal and polysyllabic. The most southerly group includes Cantonese or Yue. These tongues spread from far to the north of Korea to include the Pacific coast down as far as Vietnam. Located in the east, they occupy more than half the landmass of China.

To the west we find the far more diverse languages of the Tibeto-Burmese sub-phylum. The area they cover is huge, stretching from Tibet and northeast India in the west, most of Burma (now called Myanmar) in the south, to southwest China in the east. Tibeto-Burmese languages include (1) a western Himalayish group spoken in Tibet, northeast Nepal and Bhutan; (2) a northeastern group spoken in the area around the northeast Indian border, Tibet, Burma and China; (3) the northeast Indian group, which includes the Jinghpaw or Kachin languages; and (4) a southeastern group which includes Burmish-Lolo, Kuki-Chin, Naga and Karen spoken in southwest China, Burma and Thailand.

Although most linguists agree in lumping Sinitic and Tibeto-Burmese families together as relatives, this does not mean that the peoples speaking these tongues have a common origin. Genetically and physically the people come from widely diverse stocks. There is also no agreement on a linguistic homeland. Some linguists, for instance, put Karenic languages, which spread right down into the

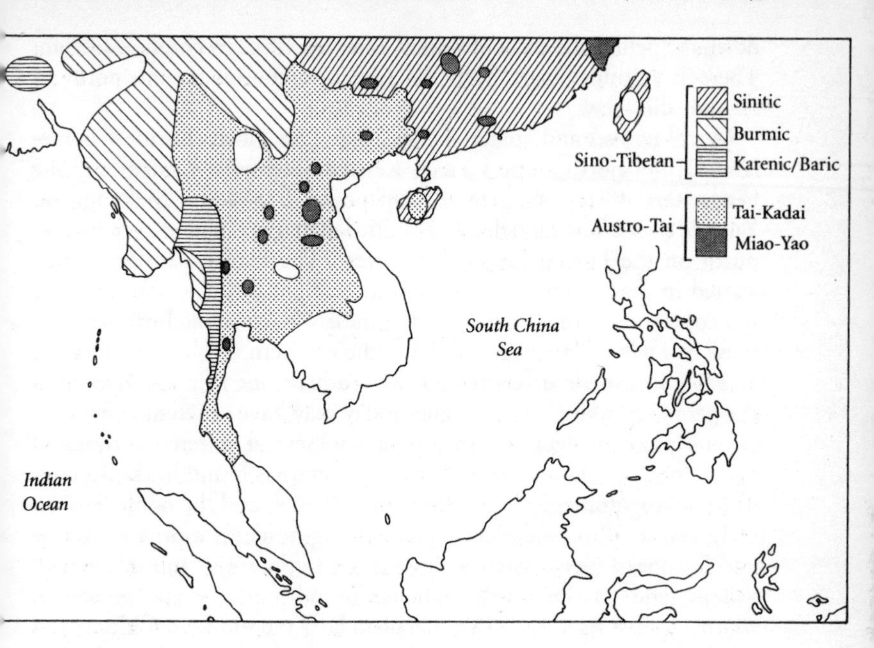

Figure 19. **Two main language families of mainland Southeast Asia and northern Indo-China.** A simplified map of the distribution of Sino-Tibetan and Austro-Tai language families (phyla) found in Burma, Thailand and South China today. The scattering of individual languages is far more complex than shown. For clarity, Austro-Asiatic languages and their spread into Burma are shown elsewhere (Figure 21). (Adapted from various sources, including Higham (1994).[17])

Malay Peninsula, and have the least tonality, in a higher and presumably older subgroup called Tibeto-Karen.[16] Karens, although speaking a nominally Sino-Tibetan tongue, share much territory and vocabulary with the Austro-Asiatic-speaking Mons, who are now reduced to parts of southern Thailand and the region around the mouth of the Salween river on the southeast Burmese coast.

In spite of the wide scattering of the Tibeto-Burmese speakers, however, their flood myths of the 'mountain-landing box' type show remarkable uniformity (see Chapter 10). There is a strong tradition of sea-flood myths among Tibeto-Burmese-speakers but linguists believe that Tibeto-Burmese languages originated in central Asia and migrated southwards to Burma and Thailand. So, for example, Karen, spoken down the peninsular coast of Burma, is regarded as a recent introduction. There is nothing apart from the linguistic cousins to the north to support this view.

Most linguists and archaeologists[17] place the Tibeto-Burmese homeland further north around Tibet, western Szechwan, Yunnan and the headwaters of the Yangtze, Brahmaputra, Irrawaddy, Mekong and Yangtze rivers. The homeland of Sinitic languages is placed even further north on the Huang He (Yellow River). The Han expansion, which started in that region and then spread on right down to south China, has continued throughout historic times. Whatever the birthplaces of these two related language families – the northern one large in speakers and low in genetic diversity and the southern one of great diversity – the people speaking these tongues today may have different origins.

One piece of evidence that points to several different origins of people now speaking Tibeto-Burmese tongues is found in skull shape. Those living nomadically in the north of Tibet, and the noble families of Lhasa, tend to be dolichocephalic (long-headed), more like Turkic and European types, whereas those living in the south and in the river valleys tend to the brachycephalic (round-headed) type typical of south and east Asians. As I shall explain later the southern Chinese and southern Tibetans are genetically closer to peoples speaking Austro-Asiatic and Tai-Kadai languages than to those speaking Mandarin in the north.

The tight area of confluence of the great Southeast Asian rivers between India, China and Burma certainly contains great linguistic diversity, but this encompasses two other large, apparently unrelated, families each with their own characteristics and sharing no intermediate relatives. These other two language families, the Tai-Kadai and Austro-Asiatic, have had their homelands located in this region by some authorities.[18] Linguist Robert Blust also believes the homeland of Austro-Asiatic languages to be the same region (see below). In respect of diversity, however, the eastern Himalayan region seems linguistically more like a vast gathering of unrelated refugees from the progressive post-glacial flooding of the southern continent, as argued by Thai polymath, Sumet Jumsai (see below),[19] than the fount of all East Asian languages. If, as suggested by Johanna Nichols and others, the western Pacific Rim was the linguistic centre of a vast coastal Palaeolithic culture, it is difficult to see all of this as emerging more recently from a rugged, jungly inland area near the Himalayas. A homeland for at least the Tibeto-Karen sub-group at the mouths of the Irrawaddy and Salween rivers, where they are at present, would be a simpler solution, and makes more sense in this context.

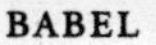

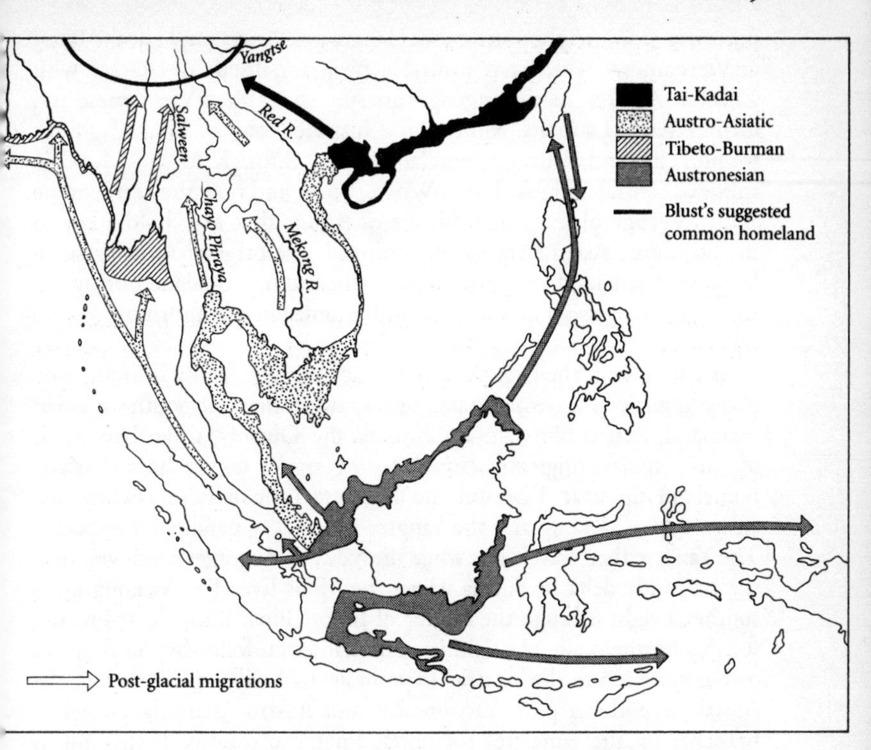

Figure 20. **Coastal homelands of the four Southeast Asian language families.** On the premise that Southeast Asian language families developed among coastal cultures, their logical sites of origin can be derived from present language distributions and Ice Age river systems. For clarity, each homeland is shaded between the 50m-depth contour and the present-day coastline. During the Ice Age this line would have extended beyond the 100m-depth contour.

One of the two other language families on the Southeast Asian mainland, with probably the best claim to a southern Indo-Chinese homeland, is the Austro-Asiatic phylum.

Austro-Asiatic

Austro-Asiatic languages are spoken in two major regions of Asia, India and Southeast Asia. They are generally non-tonal except under influence from neighbouring tonal languages. An example of the latter is Vietnamese, which has probably been tonalised by contact with Chinese. Austro-Asiatic languages are spoken by most Vietnamese and Cambodians, Laotians, Mons and a scattered trail of isolated groups round Thailand, Burma, Bangladesh and through to the Mundaic tribes of central and east India. Where, when and how they came to be split up geographically like this are questions that may hold a key to the Southeast Asian farming revolution. If the original Austro-Asiatic language homeland was centred in northeastern Sundaland during the Ice Age, several archaeological and linguistic conundrums resolve themselves.

As I have said, the large Austro-Asiatic language family is thought by many linguists to have originated further north than the Southeast Asian mainland. Robert Blust, the authority on the 'Out-of-Taiwan' hypothesis of Austronesian origins discussed earlier, argues for an Austro-Asiatic homeland up near Tibet on the Burmese-Yunnan border where the Salween, the Mekong and the Yangtze run closely parallel for a space.[20] The Yangtze then travels east while the Salween disgorges southwest near the Irawaddy delta in Burma where the Mons live. The Mekong flows southeast right through the middle of Indo-China. Blust's stated reason for this northern site of origin is a rationalisation following on from his own conversion to the 'Austric' hypothesis. As I will explain shortly, the Austric hypothesis puts Austronesian and Austro-Asiatic languages as branches on the same tree for purely linguistic reasons. If this link is accepted, then both Austronesian and Austro-Asiatic have to be traced back to one common regional homeland.

There is a major geographic problem here for Robert Blust's 'Out-of-Taiwan' hypothesis for Austronesian origins. According to this, Austronesian languages were first spoken by people living near the mouth of the Yangtze River more than 6000 years ago and thousands of miles away on the east coast of China, whereas Austro-Asiatic speakers live thousands of miles to the west, and spread right over to India. This huge gap spans some of the most hostile mountain ranges in Asia. Blust has taken the only logical way to reconcile his linguistic hypothesis with the difficult land dispersion; that is, to put the grandmother tongue on the site of parallel confluence of three great Asian rivers near Tibet. He then has Austro-Asiatic speakers dispersing in three different directions down the great rivers – west, east and south. A neat patch-up job it might be, but there is no linguistic evidence anywhere along the entire length of the Yangtze to support the model, a fact acknowledged by Blust.[21]

The evidence from prehistoric physical anthropology also does not

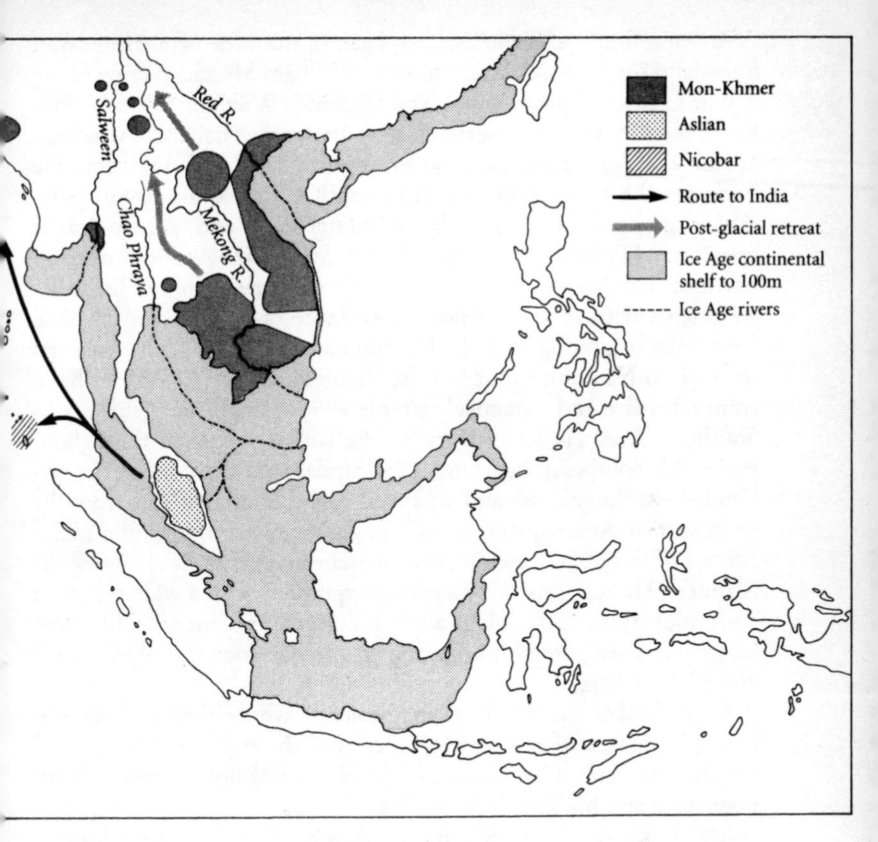

Figure 21. **Austro-Asiatic, the main language family of Indo-China.** A simplified map of its distribution. For clarity, the spread of Austro-Asiatic languages into India is shown elsewhere (Figure 14). (Adapted from various sources, including Higham (1994);[17] Ice Age rivers adapted from Morley and Flenley (1987), note 72, Chapter 3.)

support such a northern origin of the present Austro-Asiatic speakers. The simplest explanation is that the Austro-Asiatic area – and the original Austric homeland – was along the coast of Vietnam, where Austro-Asiatic tongues are still dominant today. It may be even further south on the old Sunda continent. In that case, the Austro-Asiatic-speaking Aboriginals of the Malay Peninsula far to the south might well be the stay-at-homes on the rump tail of the old continent.

At least four archaeologists are against the idea of a Himalayan homeland for Austro-Asiatic tongues – William Meacham from Hong Kong, Charles Higham from New Zealand, Wilhelm Solheim from the United States and Surin Pookajorn from Thailand. Meacham moves the Austro-Asiatic area to south China and Vietnam. He envisages the earlier populations of south China as a polygot, poly-ethnic grouping of Tai-Kadai, Hmong/Mien and Austro-Asiatic speakers.[22] Higham argues strongly for the Austro-Asiatic homeland having always been in Southeast Asia. He supports a range of linguistic arguments with the archaeological evidence of cultural and physical continuity beginning with the Hoabinhian people of 13,000 years ago through to Neolithic groups of the Vietnamese coast.[23] Solheim has a comprehensive and attractively simple view of linguistic prehistory in Southeast Asia. He sees Austric as the language spoken throughout mainland Southeast Asia and the Sunda continent before it was flooded. As the sea rose and separated island Southeast Asia from the mainland of Asia, Austro-Asiatic tongues evolved among the main-landers of Indo-China, while Austronesian tongues evolved among the islanders. He supports this linguistic hypothesis with a wide review of anthropological, archaeological and cultural evidence.[24] This view solves more geographical, linguistic and archaeological problems than any of the others.

Surin Pookajorn, the Thai archaeologist who claims to have discovered evidence of rice-growing as early as the eighth millennium BC in southern peninsular Thailand (see Chapter 2) holds a similar view. Pookajorn and his team have made an intensive linguistic and anthropological study of the Mlabri, an Austro-Asiatic-speaking hunter-gatherer tribe now living in Mae Hon Son province in northern Thailand.[25]

The Mlabri language belongs to the Northern Khmer subfamily, and oral history states that the people migrated to Thailand from Laos in the nineteenth century. Lacking the typical facial features of Thai and Laotian people, their skull shapes have some similarities with those of the Neolithic people of the Malay Peninsula. Pookajorn believes that the Mlabri represent a relict population descended from the Hoabinhian cultures of mainland Southeast Asia. These peoples who occupied Indo-China mainly between 13,000 to 5000 years ago, had a foraging lifestyle with agriculture developing in the later phases. My own memories of a visit to Mae Hon Son in the 1980s are of a river trip through gorges, mountains and jungles, and exploring limestone caves. The richest memory was the early morning market in Mae Hong Son where, in the smoky mist, hill-folk came in their traditional clothes to sell jungle produce. Several women were selling cleaned, cooked rats, tied to sticks and laid neatly in rows.

The fact that two Austro-Asiatic-speaking groups live today in the same region, one still with a hunter-gatherer lifestyle, the other farmers for perhaps the past 8000–9000 years, argues for great local antiquity of Austro-Asiatic tongues in mainland Southeast Asia. The mixed-culture picture is further evidence against a migration of Austro-Asiatic speakers from the Himalayas. This is because hunter-gatherers are supposed always to have had a pre-Neolithic lifestyle and hence may not have migrated along the same routes with the agriculturalists. The situation of parallel societies of agriculturalists and hunter-gatherers is also widespread in the Western Austronesian language areas of the islands of Indonesia, Malaysia and the Philippines and again argues for local cultural evolution of Austronesian speakers in island Southeast Asia, rather than invasion and replacement from the north.

Historical linguists and prehistorians use several strategies to overcome this paradox of migrant hunter-gatherers living alongside migrant farmers. The simplest is to say that the hunter-gatherers previously spoke some other tongue and took on the new languages. Another strategy is to say that they were previously agriculturalists, but for some reason changed back to hunting and gathering. This is possible, but there are no historical examples in Southeast Asia.[26]

The location of the Austro-Asiatic homeland in Southeast Asia thus makes better sense of the anthropology and archaeology than the Himalayan site; but it does force a different view of the timescale and direction of spread of the Neolithic revolution in Southeast Asia. As previously mentioned, the only remaining clue to the identity and language of the first rice-growers in this part of the world (represented by the Sakai cave-dwellers of southern Thailand) comes from the present-day Austro-Asiatic-speaking Aboriginals of the Malay Peninsula (see Figure 33). The Austro-Asiatic-speaking Aboriginal Aslian tribes of Malaya have a variety of physical appearances. The northern Negrito groups resemble Melanesians, the central groups resemble more the island peoples of the Moluccas and the southern group resemble Indo-Chinese. Lifestyle changes in the same sequence from jungle hunter-gatherers in the northern group through hill padi-growers in the central group to farmer-fishermen in the southern group. Wilhelm Solheim sees these Orang Asli groups as the results of a fusion between Hoabinhian cultures and the Neolithic cultures of the Malay Peninsula as represented in the cave remains.[27] Thus in Malaya, as in Thailand, we find a deep diversity in development among people in the same language group, indicating local antiquity.

I will discuss the genetic markers and origins of the Orang Asli further in Chapters 6 and 7.

The three Austro-Asiatic languages spoken by Aboriginal Malaysians are included by some linguists as a sub-group of Mon-Khmer and by others as a higher-order sub-group of Austro-Asiatic.[28] To find apparent representatives of all the three deep ethnic divisions of Australasia speaking related Austro-Asiatic tongues[29] points strongly to the antiquity of this language family in Sundaland, but it also begs the question as to which of the three ethnic Aslian groups were the original Austro-Asiatic speakers. My guess would be the central group, the Senoi, as suggested by local expert in Malaysia Iskander Carey,[30] but this does not directly identify the first rice-growers. The Sakai cave rice-growers clearly did not rely entirely on hunting and gathering, so if they still have any descendants among the present-day Austro-Asiatic-speaking Aboriginals of the Malay Peninsula, it would be more likely to be the central or southern groups.

The concept of Austro-Asiatic Aboriginals wandering south down the Malay Peninsula from the Himalayas, inventing rice culture, and then returning north to teach agriculture to their cousins in Indo-China seems rather illogical. The direction of this piece of cultural diffusion again depends on the location of the first Austro-Asiatic homeland. The picture is simplified if we remember that the putative ancestors of Austro-Asiatic speakers, the Hoabinhians, occupied Southeast Asia roughly from 13,000 to 5000 years ago. Over that period that Pacific coastline of their land changed from an unbroken line south to Bali with a huge flat hinterland, to the thin straggling wisp of a peninsula we see today. In other words, the centre of gravity of the Austro-Asiatic homeland may have been considerably further south than is possible today. The Austro-Asiatic Aslian speakers of Malaya, and the different tribes speaking Austro-Asiatic tongues through Indo-China and north and west to Burma and India, may all be refugees from the flooding of the great southern continent, Sundaland.

A prehistoric retrograde migration of boat refugees up, rather than down, the former great rivers of Indo-China as Sunda drowned has been suggested in a beautifully illustrated book entitled *Naga*, written by the Thai architect-historian Sumet Jumsai.[31] This turns Robert Blust's three-river hypothesis back to front, and still explains the extraordinary polyglot diversity among the rivers around the borders of northern Burma. Jumsai reviews literature on related hypotheses from polymaths as diverse as Buckminster Fuller, Thor Heyerdahl and Paul

Benedict. The great rivers Jumsai refers to are the Chao Phraya of Thailand, the Mekong and the Red River of Northern Vietnam. In addition a prehistoric river flowed between Bali and South Borneo. To these four rivers could easily be added the Salween, the Irawaddy, the Brahmaputra and the Ganges because they all start in the Himalayas; the Yangtze, however, is no longer relevant or needed for the hypothesis.

Clearly, the timescale of this hypothetical retreat of Austro-Asiatic speakers from greater Sundaland goes back more than 10,000 years into the early post-glacial period (see the chronology of sea rise) and can be investigated definitively only by conventional archaeological methods. Jumsai's case rests on the ethnographic, architectural and stylistic motifs that have spread in the region. In his view the most important of these is the 'water dragon', a concept that we will discuss in greater depth in Chapter 11.

If Austro-Asiatic-speakers retreated to the Himalayas after the flooding of Sundaland, does the language chronology fit? Language dating (glottochronology) is not an accurate business, and many linguists have reservations about it. Different languages may change at different rates.[32] The most important structural category in this respect is whether languages are classed as so-called 'head-marking' or 'dependant-marking'. This is rather a technical detail, but the relevance is that head-marking tongues are more likely to lose evidence of relatedness over a given time, whereas dependant-marking languages preserve their evidence of relatedness better. The language phyla of South and Southeast Asia are dependant-marking, so Southeast Asian languages may be more resistant to change than most. In broad terms, this means that the genetic splits in all the four Southeast Asian language phyla could be considerably older than linguists think.

Glottochronology is constrained by the self-doubting conviction that very old language splits cannot be detected by the comparative method. Thus, although the splitting off of the Indian Mundaic branch is consigned well back into the prehistoric past, the subsequent break-up of the large Mon-Khmer branch of Austro-Asiatic languages is dated by glottochronology to only 3000–4000 years ago.[33] On this short timescale, diverse people now living as far apart as Vietnam, Bhutan and the Nicobar Islands as well as the hunter-gatherers in the jungles of Malaya and the builders of Angkor Wat all shared a common ancestor as recently as the time of Homer. Judging from the wide range of lifestyles, the huge linguistic diversity in Indo-China, the geographic spread and available knowledge of the dates of the earliest

Mon-Khmer civilisations in Southeast Asia, this seems rather unlikely. If Indo-China was invaded by a successful Neolithic Austro-Asiatic culture from the foothills of the Himalayas only 3000–4000 years ago, the result would have been a lack of cultural and linguistic diversity such as is found in the monoculture of the Han Chinese dispersal further north. Again, an older, local evolutionary model seems more plausible.

Quite apart from the issue of cultural and linguistic diversity among Austro-Asiatic speakers in Indo-China there is a further question. If Austro-Asiatic languages did not arrive until comparatively recently, what language did the ancient Hoabinhians speak? On the basis of the suggested Himalayan homeland, the Proto-Mon-Khmers would have been living in the eastern foothills of the Himalayas side-by-side with the ancestors of the Chinese and the Thais until 4000 years ago. Even if the date of their dispersal was moved back somewhat from 2000 BC, this would still leave the earlier Hoabinhian and related cultures, and the Early Neolithic of Indo-China without a language. In other words, there is archaeological evidence for continuous cultural development of people in Indo-China during the past 13,000 years, but there is also a linguistic vacuum for the first two-thirds of that occupation.

Tai-Kadai and Miao-Yao

Before we move on to the Austronesian language phylum – the other major player in the coastal spread of Asian culture – we need to look at the orphan Tai-Kadai group, which, like Austronesian, at one time or another has been linked with all the main language families of the region.

Most tourists visiting Indo-China today will come in contact with Thais, who, with their language relatives the Laos, spread over much of the region. Linguists regard these resourceful people as comparative newcomers from further northeast towards China. They may even have constituted the original language substrate of south China. The Tai, Kadai, Miao and Yao[34] languages of south China and Southeast Asia have, like orphans, been passed around nearly all the language phyla of the Far East in the hope of finding their true cousins. Linguists now generally agree with the late Paul Benedict in grouping them together. But their relationships with the other three phyla of the region remain controversial.

Kam-Tai, the largest sub-group of Tai-Kadai languages, includes languages spoken by 76 million people in Southeast Asia. Just one of three well-known and widespread tongues, Thai, Lao, and Shan. The first two are national languages while Shan is spoken in northeast

Burma and in Yunnan province of China. The Kam-Thai sub-group now covers most of central and southern mainland Southeast Asia apart from Austro-Asiatic-speaking Cambodia and Vietnam (see Figure 19). It also extends north and west into Burma, India and Yunnan, Guizhou and Guangxi provinces of China. Kadai languages are less numerous and are spoken on the eastern fringes of the Kam-Tai distribution, notably on Hainan Island, North Vietnam and the Chinese provinces of Guangzi, Guizhou and Yunnan.

The Miao and Yao languages are spoken by only 8 million people in tiny scattered cultural pockets, but have a vast and evenly spread seed-like distribution throughout South China and Southeast Asia – from southwest Thailand, through most of the Kam-Tai distribution and on to cover most of the mountainous parts of South China. They are even spoken in parts of the eastern seaboard of China such as Hainan and, especially, Fuzhou.

Much of the work of dissection and association of the Tai-Kadai group was pioneered by Paul Benedict, a brilliant, linguistically inclined psychiatrist. In 1942 he proposed the 'Austro-Thai' superfamily for not only the tonal language groups Tai-Kadai and Miao-Yao but also Austronesian, a polysyllabic non-tonal family. In creating this linkage he

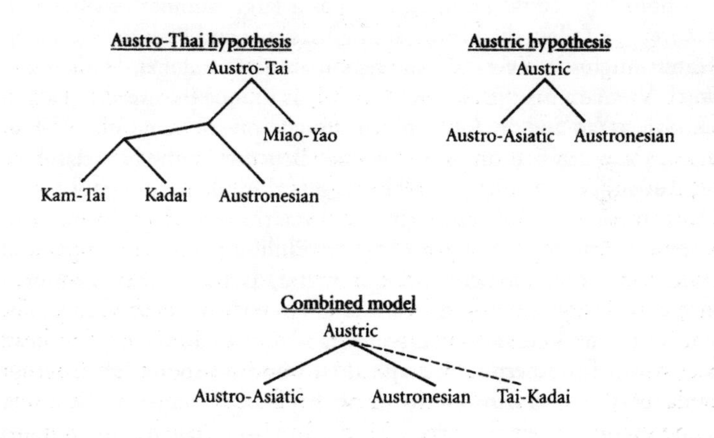

Figure 22. **Three current views of the older relationships of Southeast Asian language families.** (1) Wilhelm Schmidt's 1906 'Austric' hypothesis; (2) Paul Benedict's 1942 Austro-tai hypothesis; (3) a combination of (1) and (2). No consensus exists. The combined view is geographically compatible with the Ice Age east coast homelands shown in Figure 20.

rejected the earlier 'Austric' hypothesis first suggested in 1906 by the Austrian ethnologist Wilhelm Schmidt that connected Austronesian and Austro-Asiatic families genetically. The Austric hypothesis faded from popularity, and Benedict's Austro-Thai link gradually gained a degree of acceptance. The Tai-Kadai group was even recently incorporated by Peter Bellwood, with qualification, in a discussion of the Austronesian dispersal.[35] As I shall explain shortly, the argument has come full circle again and several Austronesian experts, including Robert Blust, have now reverted to the old Austric hypothesis.[36] Although he disagrees with some of Benedict's methods, however, Blust does not reject the Austro-Thai link, allowing for a super-Austric link connecting Austro-Asiatic, Austronesian and Tai-Kadai.

In Chapter 10, I describe the rich Shan version of the flood myth, pointing out similarities with both Taiwanese and Austro-Asiatic versions of the event. Blust's super-Austric group certainly fits this thematic linkage. As with each of the other Southeast Asian language families, the tradition of the flood myth suggests an original coastal homeland. Blust himself makes particular comment about the continued use of stilted houses by Tai-Kadai-speaking peoples even in places where they are no longer at risk of flooding.[37] The common area where pockets of Tai-Kadai and Miao-Yao languages are found is huge, so a homeland could be in any one of a large number of places. If, however, we follow the historical linguist's rule and look for the site of greatest linguistic diversity,[38] the region around Guangxi, Hainan and North Vietnam fits the bill best. Hainan is unique in displaying a Tai, a Kadai, a Yao and an Austronesian tongue on the same island. This region was suggested originally by Paul Benedict as the homeland for his Austro-Thai family, and he suggested multiple migrations of, '[Austronesian-] speaking peoples ... via the island of Hainan, to Formosa [Taiwan] on the north, the Philippines on the east, and Annam [Vietnam], Borneo, Java, Sumatra, and the Malay Peninsula on the south'.[39] From their homeland somewhere around the south coast of China, the Tai-Kadai and Miao-Yao language families spread over most of southern China and then west and south. The western route took them northwest up through Guangxi province. But their major expansion south, which took them to Thailand and eastern Burma, did not occur until the last 2000 years.

Three coastal homelands

Locating the homelands of the four East Asian language phyla is central to understanding the post-glacial prehistory of the region. As far as the comparative inter-relationships of the East Asian language phyla are concerned, most of the possible prehistoric linguistic links and combinations were already pointed out more than fifty years ago. The problem in a region short on prehistoric archaeological evidence, has been to find a geographical chess solution to the prehistoric migrations suggested by different linguistic models.

Charles Higham has described the confluence of the Asian rivers in the rucked-up fold of land in the eastern Himalayas as the centre of a great cartwheel with the rivers radiating out as the spokes. And, as I have mentioned, Robert Blust imagines all the Asian languages radiating out from this remote mountainous confluence, springing up, as it were, out of the steep gorges. His view is based partly on the great number and diversity of languages that occupy the region, and follow the river beds upwards. It is also one logical geographic strategy to solve the linguistic problem of trying to link the Austric hypothesis to the separation of Austronesian tongues spoken in Taiwan and the Austro-Asiatic tongues spoken far to the west in Indo-China and India.

The picture I have drawn of the coastal homelands of the three mainland East Asian language phyla arising in the areas where they are most diverse, is closest to Wilhelm Solheim's post-glacial model. It still uses the big rivers as language conduits, but the direction of dispersal is the exact reverse of the Himalayan centrifugal radiation hypothesis. Instead of starting in the hills, the languages spread there from the flat coasts of Southeast Asia as Johanna Nichols suggests. When their land was drowned by the rising sea, many of the sedentary coastal peoples rushed back past each other. As I discussed in the previous chapter, these coastal cultures had to adapt and seek more permanent pastures to grow their rice and root crops. One of the strategies that some members of all three families could have adopted was to move inland up the rivers into the mountains.

This 'coastal homeland and highland refugee' hypothesis is the simplest and most conservative solution. Geographically it allows several additional options such as Paul Benedict's Tai-Kadai homeland. My model clarifies the geographic links between Tai-Kadai, Austro-Asiatic and, as I shall show, Austronesian in the super-Austric model that Robert Blust favours, and explains the location and dispersal of the modern language families. Moreover, it makes sense of the recent archaeological discovery of the earliest rice-growing in Asia's southern tip, and allows an explanation of the prehistoric Mundaic migrations west to India with their rice-growing skills. The 'stay-at-home' hypothesis for the three family homelands should be testable. For instance, the Austro-Asiatic-speaking Orang Asli of the Malay

Peninsula should have genetic markers which are ancestral to those of the rest of Austro-Asiatic dispersal. Later, I present just such evidence.

The refugee model also explains how the hunter-gatherer peoples of the Indian Ocean coast came to be isolated from the technological discoveries of the presumed Austro-Asiatic Neolithic. From the end of the Ice Age to the breaching of the Malacca Strait 8500 years ago, the evolution of Neolithic skills took place on the east coast of the great Sunda continent. How the skills and ideas reached the coast of the Indian Ocean, and who sailed the boats, I will speculate about next.

5
HOMELAND OF THE ARGONAUTS

Austronesian is geographically the most widely spoken of the Asian language families. Virtually all of island Southeast Asia and the Pacific islands, as well as Madagascar in the Indian Ocean, are populated by speakers of its various languages; exactly how many people this represents is difficult to establish accurately, but 270 million is a conservative estimate. The only significant gap among the Pacific islands is New Guinea, which apart from a thin rim of coastal Austronesian speakers, is almost entirely non-Austronesian speaking.

Western Austronesian languages and their links with mainland Asia

Austronesian or Malayo-Polynesian tongues are broadly divided into two geographic/linguistic groups: a western or Indonesian group with some 200 languages, and an eastern or Oceanic group with about 300 languages. Controversy surrounds their origins, timescale of evolution and their classification, much of the latter related to the relative position of the Taiwanese, Moluccan and certain New Guinean languages.[1]

I have described Austronesian as an Asian language family because it is the main family of island Southeast Asia, and many prehistorians, linguists, anthropologists and palaeogeneticists believe it or its ancestor tongue originally came from the mainland. There is, however, no direct evidence for the view that the Austronesian homeland was situated on the Asian mainland. Apart from the Chamic languages of Vietnam and Hainan, and the Malay languages found at the foot of the peninsula, there are no Austronesian languages on the mainland of Asia. In any case, most linguists regard the Malayic and Chamic languages as relatively recent seaborne introductions.[2] Although it is perfectly possible for languages to be extinguished or replaced, even non-linguists might think it surprising that there is not a single mainland tongue to give firm Asian provenance for the Austronesian family. Asia is after all the nearest continent.

In spite of this poor representation in Eurasia, until the last few hundred years, Austronesian languages had the greatest spread of any known language family ever, covering nearly half the globe. Any theory of their origins thus has to explain their mobility and their associations with Asian tongues, and at the same time why there is no direct evidence of their roots on the mainland. Theories fall into those that propose a mainland origin, single or multiple, and those that have origins elsewhere, either in island Southeast Asia or in Melanesia.

At a conference specifically on the inter-relationships of Asian languages held in 1996, the Hawai'ian linguist Lawrence Reid reported on discussions of the present status of the various theories of origin of Austronesian languages. I will base my discussion around his review.

Starting from the northeast, there is the long-vaunted Austronesian link with Japanese. Reid concluded that the evidence was highly plausible for a contact relationship with Japanese but not a true genetic affiliation: 'Is it conceivable that the great voyagers only headed their canoes south and east from Formosa, and never ventured north to the islands which were only a few days sailing away from their own shores?'[3]

Reid's personal view is that Japanese languages will prove to be Altaic, as predicted by the American linguist Joseph Greenberg, and that any links between the Japanese and the Austronesians will be of a contact nature – through trade – only. The Japanese link could have occurred very early. Several small pieces of evidence combine to support this connection: there are Japanese pottery fragments from the Early Jomon period found in Vanuatu, apparently dating to 5000 years ago; there is Jett's record of blowpipes in southern Japan supposedly introduced by Austronesian traders (see Chapter 2); and there are the jar burials. Archaeologist Wilhelm Solheim, the originator of the Nusantao hypothesis, has written eloquently on the similarities of prehistoric artefacts found in Japan and Southeast Asia. He believes they were carried by the Nusantao sailors operating a maritime trading network throughout the coasts of Asia.[4]

Only a few days sail away south from Japan is Taiwan, linguists' most popular site at present for the Austronesian homeland. This island has more than just language links with Southeast Asia. It holds at least three deep branches of Austronesian tongues, unique to Taiwan and so different from each other and all other Austronesian languages that many linguists, including Robert Blust, place each of them in separate categories. These three thus, in Blust's scheme, rank the same as the fourth huge sub-group holding all other living Austronesian languages, namely Malayo-Polynesian. In these terms, Taiwan with only fifteen living Austronesian tongues, holds three-quarters of the oldest branches in the whole Austronesian phylum which has hundreds of other tongues.[5] This observation, along with Taiwan's proximity to China and Peter Bellwood's archaeological arguments, are the main props of the 'Out-of-Taiwan' hypothesis that I discussed in Chapters 2 and 4.

There are several catches in Blust's argument. One is the assumption that there need be a direct Chinese mainland origin for Austronesian. As I have mentioned, there is no prima facie evidence for this assumption. The second problem is simply that, as many linguists have pointed out and Blust himself acknowledges, there are no languages from the fourth and largest sub-phylum, Malayo-Polynesian, in Taiwan. This might be expected if the languages of the Philippines, and which belong to the main Malayo-Polynesian branch, came from Taiwan. In a recent archaeological review, American archaeologists Kwang-Chih Chang and Ward H. Goodenough point out that although Taiwan may be somewhere near the original homeland, this evidence does not necessarily make it the homeland.[6] If there is no direct provenance for Malayo-Polynesian in Taiwan, there is then no reason why the deep diversity of Taiwanese languages cannot be a result of their remote island location and longstanding isolation. The Taiwanese branches would then become peripheral relicts. If that were the case, the whole Austronesian phylum and its dispersal then become much older; this would fit the archaeological evidence given in Chapters 2 and 3 for the early timescale of Southeast Asian and Pacific voyaging.

Lawrence Reid discusses Paul Benedict's 1942 linkage of Tai-Kadai, and Austronesian as an Austro-Thai superphylum. Once again the verdict is that the links are real but they are more likely to be due to language borrowing than to a true genetic relationship.[7] As has already been mentioned Bellwood still favours this link although Blust has moved towards the Austric connection.

Another link between Austronesian and the south Chinese coast is the so-called Sino-Austronesian hypothesis. First suggested in 1942 at the same time as the Austro-Thai hypothesis, the theory, in Reid's words, 'seems to be difficult for some linguists to even consider'.[8] Just how difficult, I recently discovered at a conference on the so-called Yue languages and cultures to which I was invited in Hong Kong. The 'heretical' Sino-Austronesian view nearly led to a disturbance. Laurent Sagart, a distinguished French linguist, had just presented his well-researched evidence for a genetic link between Austronesian and Sinitic tongues. The heated attack that came from traditional Chinese linguists against this connection of Sinitic tongues with the 'southern barbarians' threatened to get out of hand. The chairman stopped the discussion and hurriedly moved on to my paper. Putting the details of the structural evidence to one side, one of several hurdles is the same as with the Austro-Thai link – namely that Sinitic languages are tonal and monosyllabic whereas Austronesian tongues are polysyllabic and monotonal or atonal.

All these mainland hypotheses still beg the question, however, whether Proto-Austronesian, or even a 'pre-Austronesian' developed on the mainland at all. If the provenance of Malayo-Polynesian from Taiwan is doubtful, then the origin of Austronesian on the nearby mainland is even more shaky. I shall return to this issue shortly. First, though, what other areas along the south China coast have Austronesian links?

At present Austro-Asiatic is the most likely Asian mainland relative for Austronesian languages. As Hawai'ian linguist, Robert Blust noted, however, there are some major problems if the supposed joint homeland is to be placed on the mainland. As I have argued above, the Himalayan foothill site requires a large stretch of the imagination to link with Taiwan, or any other verified ancient Austronesian location. The nearest juxtaposition of Austro-Asiatic and Austronesian languages is in Malaya, where Malay sits side by side with Austro-Asiatic languages, and in Vietnam, where Chamic languages are surrounded by Austro-Asiatic tongues. Both Malay and Chamic tongues are thought to be fairly recent introductions to these countries, as I have said (see Chapters 3 and 4), so they do not count as credible locations for a family split.

Offshore or mainland?

There is, however, an exciting offshore link that Australia-based Austronesianist Alexander Adelaar has unearthed between Land Dyak languages (Austronesian), spoken inland in the western area of Borneo, and the central group of Austro-Asiatic Aslian[9] languages in the jungles of the Malay Peninsula. When he compared the languages, he found evidence of a combination of structural and innovative sharing of vocabulary. This is very unexpected. Austro-Asiatic languages, in complete contrast to Austronesian, are not spoken at all off the Asian mainland, except in the Nicobar Islands of the Indian Ocean. The only previous example of a direct influence of Austro-Asiatic on an island Austronesian tongue was the extensive Austro-Asiatic borrowing of vocabulary found in Achinese on the northern tip of Sumatra. Adelaar suggests that, 'If there was contact, this must have been a very long time ago, as there is, as far as I know, no evidence for it in historical times.'[10] The important structural link with mainland languages that he describes is also found in other languages spoken on the island of Borneo. In addition, the Punans of Borneo share some vocabulary items with Land Dyak and Aslian tongues. As Adelaar points out, however, the links indicate contact and borrowing, not a genetic relationship. His findings do not prove the 'Austric' genetic link – they cannot – but they provide supporting evidence for the geographic site of the split between Austro-Asiatic and Austronesian languages suggested by Solheim. The links appear to place Aboriginal Austro-Asiatic tongues prehistorically *off* the mainland and in the Bornean part of the Sunda continent side by side with Austronesian tongues.

Adelaar's findings not only extend the putative Austro-Asiatic coastal homeland further south, but also support a location near West Borneo for the ancient 'Austric split' between Austro-Asiatic and Austronesian families. We even have a ready-made physical reason for the split, in the rising sea, which separated Borneo from the east coast of mainland Southeast Asia around 10,000 years ago (see Figure 13 in Chapter 3 and Figure 20 in Chapter 4). Adelaar sees the Austro-Asiatic/Land Dyak link as the result of language shift. This could have come about either with Aslian speakers in Borneo shifting to Land Dyak or, as he says, 'It is also possible that once there was a third (unknown and now extinct) language spoken in Borneo and on the Malay Peninsula, and that its speakers in Borneo shifted to Land Dyak while its speakers on the Malay Peninsula shifted to Aslian.'[11] Adelaar's other work on the complex kaleidoscope of Bornean languages may help to resolve much disagreement on the spread of Austronesian languages both within and outside island Southeast Asia. I will discuss this later.

Genetic links between Austronesian and other East Asian language families are the only ones that most Austronesianists generally consider, but genetic links have been suggested between Austronesian tongues on the one hand and Indian and Mesopotamian tongues on the other by a few linguists.[12] First suggested early in the twentieth century, the links have never quite been forgotten, and in a recent palaeolinguistic reconstruction, Irén Hegedus includes Austronesian as an early member of a tree of evolution of the Eurasian Nostratic phylum (see Chapter 4).[13]

Recently, linguist Paul Manansala has claimed links between Austro-Asiatic and Austronesian languages and between both Sanskrit and Sumerian.[14] He argues from structural similarities, such as the shared agglutinative nature of the tongues, and has published long lists of homonyms on the internet. The shared vocabulary that he claims between Sanskrit and Austronesian languages extends out into the Pacific and East Polynesia, way beyond the recognised area of recent Indic influence in island Southeast Asia. As far as I know, these links have not been reviewed or confirmed by any other linguists. The logical arguments against either Sumerian or Sanskrit mothering Austronesian are even stronger than for the other more easterly links.

The best known of the Austronesian words which have travelled west in the past are the most familiar like lemon and cinnamon. Austronesianist Waruno Mahdi has studied the provenance in India of other terms such as those for cloves and camphor.[15] If these and the shared words listed by Manansala are confirmed as simply borrowings, however, then they would complete a chain of Austronesian language contact and borrowing stretching from Japan around the coast of Asia to the birthplace of Western civilisation.

Most linguists, however, still believe the parentage of Austronesian to lie with Austro-Asiatic languages in some hypothetical Austric homeland crib, whatever the fine details of the proposed links. So for instance, a convert to the Austric theory (such as Robert Blust) might disagree with Paul Benedict's 'Austro-Thai' hypothesis but would still agree with the evidence for contact links between Austronesian and Tai-Kadai tongues. Therein may lie part of the answer to the conundrum. There are links between Austronesian tongues and Eurasian phyla so diverse and separated that they cannot all be related; yet no one can agree on a clear genetic relationship with any of them. If all the links are valid, then we are looking at other kinds of language link. Those may well be the contact links of trade, which result in exchanges of ideas and borrowings of language.

Everybody agrees that Austronesian-speaking sailors were the most supremely mobile of any in the pre-Columbian world. In Chapter 2, I described Wilhelm Solheim's proposed Nusantao maritime trading network, and evidence of trans-oceanic trade between Thailand and India from the Neolithic period onwards. Such contact is clearly supported by and supports the linguistic evidence of the Austronesians as Neolithic super-Phoenicians. As I discussed, there may have been a partnership between the Austronesian speakers who ran the shipping routes and spread the religion, magic and concepts of hierarchy and kingship, and the Austro-Asiatic speakers from the mainland who had many of the more down-to-earth ideas of technology and cereal agriculture.

If most of the links between Austronesian and mainland Asian languages were the result of trade, the logical need for a mainland Austronesian homeland recedes. If the split between Austro-Asiatic and Austronesian took place somewhere on the Ice Age Sunda coastline between Malaya and Borneo, the branching of the Austronesian tree changes because the potential time-depth for evolution of Malayo-Polynesian or non-Taiwanic languages becomes much deeper.

How far west was the homeland?

Before I discuss exactly where I believe the Austronesian homeland was, let me summarise the key theories to date. As I have said, they divide into mainland and offshore (see also Figure 12). Current mainland hypotheses include the Austro-Thai hypothesis of Paul Benedict which postulates a homeland somewhere near Hainan; and the China-Taiwan-Philippines theory of Robert Blust; The offshore homelands proposed for Austronesian range from 'near Oceania'[16] (Melanesia) to island Southeast Asia. Two anonymous recent reviews state that the evidence for an Austronesian homeland 'increasingly points to Indonesia and New Guinea'.[17] Archaeological and linguistic arguments for a more westerly homeland are put forward by Patrick Kirch and Peter Bellwood.[18]

An important linguistic method for resolving how far west to place the Austronesian homeland is a study of the use of words to describe placental mammals and marsupials. In using this tool, linguists seem to echo Alfred Russel Wallace, the great nineteenth-century naturalist and co-luminary, with Charles Darwin, of the principle of natural selection. Wallace proposed a line separating the Oriental flora and fauna of the Old World, particularly placental mammals, from the Australasian flora and fauna, which features, for instance, marsupials rather than placental mammals. This line (see Figure 23) passes from south to northeast between Bali and Lombok, between Borneo and Sulawesi, finally veering off to the northeast below the Philippines. It demarcates a watery gap between the Sunda continent and the islands to the east, which was never dry even at the height of the Ice Age. These islands of Maluku and the lesser Sundas which lie between Wallace's Line and New Guinea are still sometimes called 'Wallacia' to differentiate them from the sunken continents of Sundaland to the west and Sahulland (Australia/New Guinea) to the east. Most Old World mammals never made it across this gap. Wallace's Line does not cut the animal cake perfectly, partly because of overlap, and has been modified several times since. For example, Thomas Huxley's Line, which moves the northern part to the west of the Philippines (excluding Palawan), is seen by zoogeographers as a better compromise.

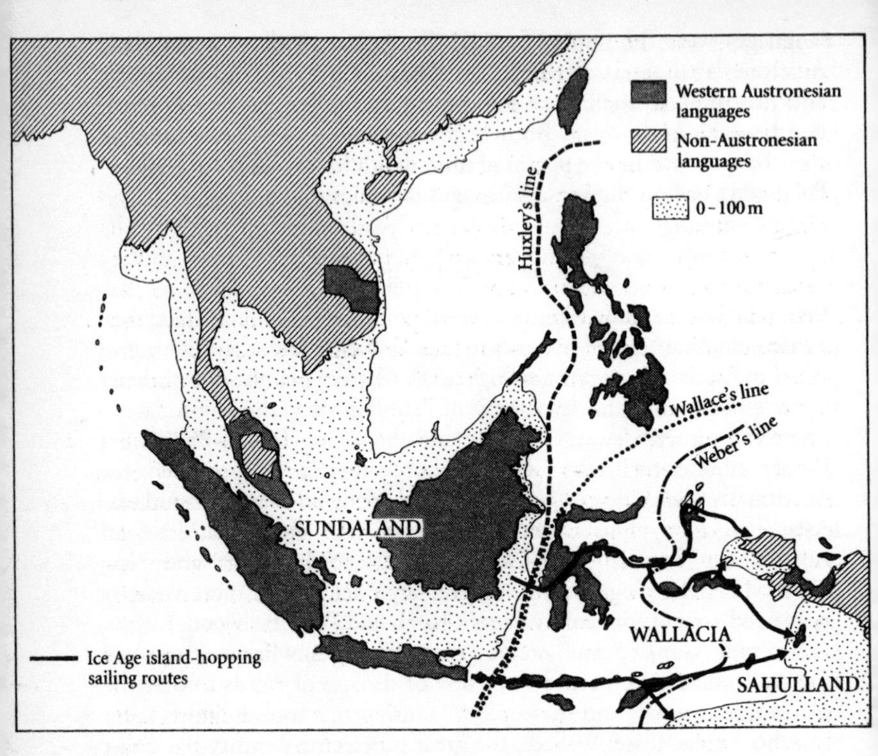

Figure 23. **Wallace's, Huxley's and Weber's bio-geographic lines. Originally designed to show the relative oceanic barriers to movement of plants and animals between Southeast Asia (Sundaland) and Australia/New Guinea (Sahulland), these lines were clearly no obstacle to the first colonisation of Australia during the Ice Age (see the solid black lines). They have, however, been used to speculate on post-glacial human migrations. Weber's Line may delineate the Western Austronesian homeland during the Ice Age.**

Blust has reconstructed Proto-Austronesian terms for several Old World mammals, such as pangolins, monkeys and bovids. Bellwood argues that the Austronesian homeland must lie to the west (that is, in Taiwan or in Sundaland) because, as he implies, these mammals are not found east of Huxley's Line. Wallace's original line would have been more appropriate for this argument, because in this instance all these animals are also found in the Philippines.[19] Following Bellwood's 'faunal logic' the Philippines should also be regarded as a potential homeland. The German linguist Bernd Nothofer uses the same line of argument as Blust, but in a reverse direction, to place the homeland of his 'Palaeo-Hesperonesian' group (discussed later) in Sulawesi, on the other side of the line. He points out that the cuscuses (marsupial phalangers) live no further west than Sulawesi, yet cognates for these animals, although present in all eastern Austronesian tongues, also appear far to the west in other ancient members of his group – in the Mentawai barrier islands off Sumatra – but are there reapplied to the Asian pangolin or scaly anteater, a small placental mammal. Thus, the practice of using animal names to place language splits can be interpreted to locate the Austronesian homeland anywhere from Sulawesi to the Asian mainland.

Apart from Huxley, others have tried to improve on Wallace. Weber's Line, which also attempts to delineate the region where Australasian and Oriental faunal species are equally balanced, also includes Sulawesi and most of the Lesser Sundas as Old World, but excludes the Moluccas (see Figure 23). The floral distribution in Weber's Line is slightly different; it follows Wallace's Line to the north but includes the Lesser Sundas and the Nusa Tenggara together with Java to the south of the archipelago.[20] Both these lines in eastern Indonesia still fail to represent an absolute boundary of sea water to placental mammals on the west side and marsupials on the east. If there is a barrier, it is more permeable for certain fauna and flora. This ease of movement of the latter is determined by the distance between islands rather than the depth of the intervening sea.

Weber's faunal line does, however, describe the easterly limit of western Austronesian tongues (and incidentally the distribution of the blowpipe in Southeast Asia). The whole western Malayo-Polynesian language group is thus bracketed, significantly, with the Lesser Sundas. Hence there may be an analogy between the spread of Oriental flora and fauna across the small distances between islands, defined by Weber's Line, and the limits of the (hypothetical) earliest maritime Austronesian-speaking communities in Sundaland. Put more simply, there must have been a time during the Ice Age when these peoples' sailing skills were sufficiently reliable to cross the small distances of sea from Java and Borneo (then part of Sundaland) through the Celebes Sea to the Lesser Sundas, Sulawesi and the Philippines on a regular basis. They would then have been able to establish long-distance trade routes with Melanesia. The archaeologist and sailor Geoffrey Irwin has made an extensive study of migration routes and island intervisibility in the region. He has shown, first, that such distances were well within the capabilities of Ice Age sailors even back to 50,000 or so years ago, and second, that, for these voyagers, the Lesser Sundas and Sulawesi were the necessary first steps of the only two island-hopping routes to the southwest Pacific. The Lesser Sunda route, which had more but shorter gaps, led to Australia and the south coast of New Guinea, and the Sulawesi route led to Oceania and the southwest Pacific.[21] If this model is correct, the homeland area of the western Austronesian languages in island Southeast Asia could have considerable antiquity back into the Ice Age.

Several archaeologists and at least one linguist argue along these lines for such an island Austronesian homeland. For example, archaeologists Wilhelm Solheim and William Meacham,[22] unlike Peter Bellwood, wish to extend the old Sundaland cultural/linguistic region east to the limits of Weber's Line to include the Lesser Sundas, Sulawesi and the Philippines. In Meacham's hypothesis the homeland is placed somewhere within 'the broad triangular area formed by Taiwan, Sumatra and Timor, where the reputedly oldest Malayo-Polynesian languages are found' (this triangle, incidentally, also coincides with the central distribution of the blowpipe – see Chapter 2). Meacham believes that Proto-Austronesian may have evolved *in situ* out of a 'New Guinea-like diversity ... the early diversity, perhaps preserved in Taiwan, was honed into the more uniform Proto-Malayo-Polynesian'.[23]

Solheim identifies his own archaeological construct, the peoples of the Nusantao maritime trading network, primarily as a mobile culture, dating from before 5000 BC, in other words just after the third flood. In this respect, he is careful to distinguish the culture from the languages they may have spoken or their racial types. But he acknowledges that 'a majority of the people with this culture, at any one time, probably spoke Malayo-Polynesian languages ... The Nusantao were no doubt directly associated with the spread of Malayo-Polynesian languages.'[24] He locates their cultural genesis in the same region around the east of Borneo, where the 6000-year-old obsidian from the Admiralty Islands was recently found (see Chapter 3).

Some modern linguists who support the more recent 'Out of Taiwan' model of Austronesian origins now argue from Bellwood's archaeological construct, for much younger dates in the early branches of the Austronesian tree. To do so, they have had to reject and ignore the dates derived from 'glottochronology' that they accepted and promoted in the 1970s.[25] These placed the dispersal of western Austronesian tongues well back into the time envisaged by Solheim for the early Nusantao in Indonesia. The genetic evidence which supports this older timescale will be given in Chapters 6 and 7.

Drowning Sundaland

On the assumption that the original homeland of Austronesian languages was somewhere on the east coast of Ice Age Sundaland, I will reconstruct the sequence of events as the sea rose to split up the continent. Rather than insisting on a precise location of an offshore/Sundaland Austronesian homeland, I will first follow Johanna Nichols's more general view of the spread-out ribbon of Ice Age Pacific Rim cultures as the coastal source of Asian Neolithic language families. During the Ice Age the continent of Sundaland included three eastern coastal regions centred around the island of Borneo, which were joined, but are now separate from the mainland (see Figure 13 in Chapter 3 and Figure 20 in Chapter 4). The diverse and complex language map of Borneo is central to an understanding of early western Malayo-Polynesian development. Linguist Alexander Adelaar calls it a crossroads.[26] The first of these Sundaland coasts is now represented by the north and northwest coast of Borneo. This region, which was swallowed up by the South China Sea after the Ice Age, lost more land than any other part of the Sunda continent. The second region is the steep northeast coast of Borneo which hardly lost any land in the post-glacial period. The third Sundaland coastline is the south and southwest coasts of Borneo facing Sulawesi and the north coast of Java, which again lost a considerable amount of land as the sea rose.

Taking the northwest coast of Borneo first, during the Ice Age, when the South China Sea was dry land, a river ran northeast below the Natuna Islands and parallel to the present coast of Sarawak, draining the 'North Sunda valley'.[27] As the sea rose and split Borneo from Malaya, the western mouth of this river progressively shifted back towards the southwest and round the western tip of Borneo, eventually ending up as the Kapuas river, which now disgorges below Pontianak in west Kalimantan, in modern-day Indonesian Borneo. The rest of the northwest coast of Borneo was drained by the Lupar river, the mouth of which eventually shifted back to near Kuching in Sarawak on the north coast of Borneo. Adelaar recently argued for the homeland of the large Malayic subgroup of the western Malayo-Polynesian family in the western region of Borneo, drained by these two rivers. The surviving representatives of these ancient stay-at-home peoples, who are linguistically Malayic, include the famous head-hunting Ibans or Sea-Dyaks, the Kendayan and the Salako. So, far from being recent newcomers at the end of a long trail from Taiwan through the Philippines, and then somehow west through Borneo, as suggested by

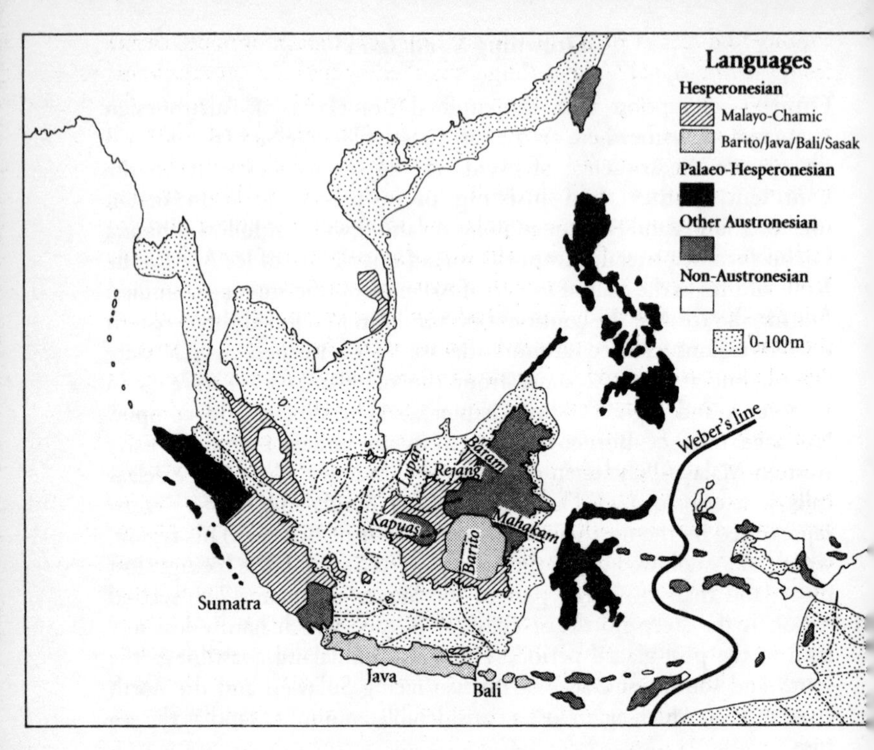

Figure 24. **Post-glacial coastline retreat and the distribution of Western Austronesian languages: a speculation.** The distribution of Bernd Nothofer's 'Hesperonesian' languages corresponds with the north and south catchment areas of two great glacial river systems of Sundaland. Today they are found in two related clusters, Malayo-Chamic to the north and Java-Bali-Sasak-Barito to the south. These two clusters are large in population and small in numbers of languages. The Palaeo-Hesperonesian languages, found on steep shores around the periphery, are by contrast poor in numbers of people and rich in diversity. (Ice Age rivers adapted from Morley and Flenley (1987), (note 72 in Chapter 3.))

Robert Blust, the Malayic tongues may have evolved 'at home' somewhere in their present-day distribution in Malaya, Sumatra, west Java and west Borneo (see Figure 20 in Chapter 4). Adelaar argues on linguistic grounds for the homeland of the Malayic tongues in west Borneo.

Some indirect evidence of the antiquity of Malayic tongues comes from the Aboriginal Malayic tongues spoken by maritime groups living in islands from Singapore, through the Strait of Malacca and up the west coast of the Malay Peninsula to the Mokens and the Moklens off the Burmese (Myanmar) coast. These island sailors represent the western remnants of Wilhelm Solheim's prehistoric maritime trading network. Not only do these populations show considerable anthropological and linguistic diversity, but they also carry evidence of the same kind of prehistoric contact with Aslian Austro-Asiatic tongues that Adelaar demonstrated for Land Dyaks living in western Borneo, also at the headwaters of the Kapuas river. Some of the 'Aslian' features that he described are thus found in Sumatra and in Aboriginal Malayic tongues spoken in the Malay Peninsula and in small islands of the Malacca Strait, from the Riau Islands off Singapore up to Phuket in Thailand.

Linguistic dating of the early splits and movements of the Malayic tongues in west Indonesia and up to Thailand is unlikely to be accurate, given the problems I have already described with glottochronology. Two pieces of evidence, however, may at least constrain the earliest date of movement of Malayic and other north Bornean tongues over to Sumatra and up the western side of the Malay Peninsula. These were, as I mentioned in Chapters 3 and 4, the opening of the Malacca Strait in the seventh millennium BC, and then the forest clearance around Lake Toba in northern Sumatra, which occurred just after it, around 8000 years ago. An older origin of Malayic tongues on the west coast of Borneo also makes more sense of the archaeology of the Chams and their presumed ancestors, the Sa Huynh in the middle of Vietnam. Chamic tongues are generally regarded as a daughter branch of Malayic tongues, and the mother-group for Achinese on the northern tip of Sumatra. These groups have been in Vietnam much longer than allowed for by the 'Out of Taiwan' Austronesian model.[28]

Malayic languages may also have had influence further east. Lawrence Reid sees shared innovations between Malayo-Javanic and Central Philippines languages.[29] If Malayic tongues originated in west Borneo, these links would suggest a language migration northeast along the Malay coast or, more simply, an earlier shared origin on the east coast of Sundaland.

Further east, along the coast of north Borneo from the Lupar River, are two more rivers with their associated indigenous Austronesian language groups – the Rejang and the Baram, which drain two-thirds of Sarawak. The Rejang-Baram group of ten tongues here includes peoples such as the Tutongs, the Punans, and the well-researched Berawans. The languages have absorbed some features from neighbouring Malayic speakers. The Berawans offer one of the most tantalising accounts of the widespread Malayo-Polynesian myth of the journey of souls to the land of the dead across the sea.[30] In their story the soul has to travel down the Baram River to a larger, downstream, but now invisible 'Apek' River located somewhere in the sea. This invisible river flows through their 'land of the dead'. The myth here seems historiographic rather than aetiological in that it echoes a prehistoric land loss for which there is no present-day visible evidence. It also supports the concept that the voyages of the 'boats of the dead', described in so many Austronesian myths and painted at high-water level on the walls of the nearby Niah caves (see Chapter 3), were literally returning to the land of their ancestors on the drowned Sunda shelf. Similar stories are also told by their neighbours the Kayan.[31]

Moving south of Borneo to the region where the invading Java Sea split Java and Bali from Borneo after the Ice Age, there are four large linguistic groups that would have been cut off from each other as the coastline of Sundaland receded. Starting from the southeast Sundas, these are Sasak, spoken in Lombok, and west Sumbawa, Balinese and Javanese. On the north coast of the Java Sea, in southern Borneo, is the Barito group (literally languages on the Barito River). During the Ice Age, the Barito was one of the tributaries of a great river that had its mouth halfway between Bali and Borneo.These four languages are often grouped together, although only the Bali-Sasak link is definite. The so-called Tamanic tongues, a small group of languages spoken right at the headwaters of the Kapuas River in western Borneo, may have taken a long journey along the south coast and up a river as the coastline receded. Although they share much vocabulary with Malay, Adelaar has offered good evidence that they share a common ancestor deep in prehistory with the famous Bugis sea people of Makassar in south Sulawesi in eastern Indonesia. The Buginese-Tamanic split, Adelaar says, 'must have happened so long ago that it allowed the Tamanic speakers to adapt and assimilate to a considerable degree to their Bornean environment, and to forget their exo-Borneo origin'.[32]

The languages bordering the new Java Sea, Malayo-Chamic in the north and Java-Bali-Sasak and Barito in the south, are together also known as the western Indonesian sub-group and include Malagasy languages.[33] With at most thirty tongues, including various regional Malay dialects, this group holds only 3–6 per cent of Austronesian languages, but the bulk of their 270 million speakers. The majority of these people, however, speak just four tongues: Javanese, Sundanese, Malay and Madurese. Numerically, this group is the dominant cultural block in modern island Southeast Asia.

Palaeo-Hesperonesian – the oldest tongues in island Southeast Asia?

In a fascinating reconstruction of prehistoric languages, Bernd Nothofer has reapplied the old term Hesperonesian (literally 'Western Islanders') to these thirty dominant languages of Malaysia and Indonesia,[34] to distinguish them from the older Palaeo-Hesperonesian tongues that he believes were once spoken in most of the area now occupied by Hesperonesian languages. These older tongues are now spoken only round the periphery of Indonesia. Nothofer's argument is based on standard linguistic comparisons, and fits well with an island Southeast Asian origin of Austronesian languages. The Palaeo-Hesperonesian tongues include the orphan languages of northwest Sumatra such as Gayo and Batak, and the barrier islands Nias, Simalur, Mentawai and Enggano. Incidentally the languages of these ancient cultures in west Sundaland have no defined place in Robert Blust's genetic tree, although he acknowledges that they are not Malayic. On the east of Sundaland, Nothofer includes northern Sulawesi and the southern Philippines as Palaeo-Hesperonesian. He also includes some languages of northern Borneo (see Figure 24).[35]

On the east coast of Borneo, three rivers, the largest being the Mahakam and the Kayan, are home to a numerically diverse group of indigenous tongues that spread west across to the north coast. These are loosely termed the Kayan-Kenyah group. The Kayan speakers have a rich mural and carving tradition with elaborate paintings of the tree of life, the cock and the serpent. In the mountains tongues of the Apo-Duat group are spoken, including Kelabit, which may be a more ancient group. The ancestors of the mountain people made large stone burial monuments and erected standing stones with mysterious inscriptions or petroglyphs on them deep and now forgotten in the jungle (see illustration 15). If these megaliths were not surrounded by tropical vegetation they would look eerily similar to their equivalents, the Dolmens and Menhirs of western Europe. Perhaps because there was less land loss after the Ice Age, the north and east coastal Palaeo-Hesperonesian linguistic and cultural diversities are better preserved here than elsewhere in Borneo. Traditional lifestyles in the region vary from jungle hunter-gatherers to swidden farmers. The rivers are the roads and a major source of food. In Sabah, in the northeast of Borneo, live people who are fairer-skinned than the inhabitants of Borneo speak Murutic, Paitanic and Dusunic tongues that share many features with Philippine languages.[36] Finally there are the fully maritime sea gypsies, the Sama-Bajau, who inhabit islands off the north-east and southeast coasts of Borneo as well as islands of the Sulu Sea. The latter are their main home bases.

The Sama Bajau of Wallacia: amphibious foragers and traders

Some years ago I took a five-day trip in a passenger-cargo ferry round the Sulu sea, which spreads between Mindanao in the southern Philippines and Sabah in northeast Borneo. The tiny islands scattered like pearls across the shallow gap are called the Sulu archipelago. In each island village, the large wooden vessel would stop to unload, and pick up sacks of beche-de-mer (sea cucumber) for Hong Kong's restaurants and also take on people. A group of rather menacing armed soldiers on board were there to guard against the pirates that infest the Sulu sea. At one point, well lubricated with San Miguel beer, they seemed more interested in my Chinese fiancée. Luckily the ship's crew kindly rescued us from imminent danger and accommodated us in the bridge area for the rest of the journey. We had, in the first place, been advised to take this 'fun trip' by two Westerners we had met in a hotel bar in the town of Zamboanga, in Mindanao, Philippines. This couple, an American and Englishman, were themselves planning a trip across to Madagascar in a double outrigger traditional sailing vessel. The sponsored expedition was to be a successful attempt to prove that Austronesian speakers could have sailed straight across the Indian Ocean rather than round it.

In spite of our friends' obvious familiarity with the Sulu Sea, I saw no other European tourists throughout the five days. I soon found out why, in a rather forcible way from the military police, who interrogated me on the boat. There was a war on and they were concerned that I was from Amnesty International. I did not notice any other signs of the war during the trip. The villages with their markets and the floating Bajau settlements gave me some experience of how possible it is to live completely over water. One of the largest villages, Sitankai, which was more the size of a small town, was entirely built on stilts on a submerged reef (see illustration 2). Although we were only maybe 20 kilometres from Borneo by this time, I could see no land as we sailed in a complete circle round the houses. From a distance it seemed like a town suspended in the middle of the ocean. Dramatic as the Sitankai view was, there are many other settlements of a similar size and appearance scattered round Southeast Asia that have received the same epithet 'Venice of the East'.

The Sama-Bajau speak a western Austronesian tongue that forms its own sub-group unconnected with the other maritime, trader, forager fishermen of whom I spoke, living to the west. Although their highest concentration is in the Sulu Sea, the Bajau are no respecters of linguistic or political boundaries. They are the most widespread of all the sea-nomads in Southeast Asia. Way down in the Lesser Sundas of Indonesia, the western Flores port where most tourists hire boats to visit the Komodo dragons is called Labuhan Baju or the 'port of the Bajau'. The Flores Bajau speak the same 'Sama' tongue as in the Philippines. Sama-Bajau also live far to the east in the Sula islands of Maluku (the Moluccas).

Wilhelm Solheim sees these enterprising foraging, trading and amphibious people as the descendants of his Nusantao maritime trading network.[37] The existence of such cultures is potentially damaging to the theory of a recent emergence of fully agricultural Austronesian speakers from Taiwan. The same can be said of the Austronesian-speaking, jungle and coastal hunter-gatherers found throughout Malaysia, the Philippines and Indonesia. Not surprisingly, there has been an attempt by the 'Out of Taiwan' camp to redescribe the adaptive lifestyle of these out-of-place, but widespread, non-agriculturalists as a recent phenomenon.[38] At Bukit Tengkorak on the coast of Sabah there is archaeological evidence of coastal foraging populations from the first millennium BC, who not only exploited the marine and inland resources but also engaged in long-distance sea trade. Their portable hearths for use on boats are still a feature of the Sama-Bajau.[39]

As I mentioned in earlier chapters, the time-depth of such communities and their trade with Melanesia has recently been rolled back to 6000 years ago. Such extreme marine adaptation as shown by the Bajau was recorded in Mesopotamia over 4000 years ago, when the Babylonian poets referred to Adapa the fisherman or Oannes and the seven educators from the east as amphibious half-fish, half-men (see Chapter 12).

The first western Austronesians?

Bernd Nothofer draws parallels between his construct of the 'old and the new' with the, now defunct, classification of 'Proto-Malays' and 'Deutero-Malays' as seen by linguists, archaeologists and anthropologists earlier in the twentieth century. Such a net also draws in the Bontok and Ifugao of northern Luzon, the Penans of Borneo and megalithic cultures from east Sumbawa, Sumba and Flores to the south in the Lesser Sundas as the 'Old Ones'. This larger geographic language grouping scattered round the periphery of Indonesia is defined by Weber's Line in the east and nearly coincident with the blowpipe distribution (see Figures 11 and 23).

Nothofer's contrast between Hesperonesian and Palaeo-Hesperonesian can be seen as a paradigm of Johanna Nichols's concept of linguistic expansion and extinction in the post-glacial period. The new and few competitive expanding languages in the centre replaced the old and many on the periphery. The modern language map (see Figure 24) certainly reveals island Southeast Asia in this light.[40] Geographically the region has Borneo at the centre with two overlapping rings of islands. On the periphery, in the outer ring of the barrier-island archipelago west of Sumatra, the northwest of the Sumatran mainland, the Philippines, Sulawesi and the Lesser Sundas with their steep coasts, are small groups of ancient and diverse languages, megalithic cultures, and even pre-rice cultures such as in Mentawai. In the centre of Borneo and on its steep northern and eastern side there is again enormous cultural and linguistic diversity and small linguistic groups. If, however, we look at the Hesperonesian tongues of the inner and greater Sunda islands of Sumatra and Java, and the western side of Borneo (which suffered enormous land loss on their coasts and now border the Java Sea) we see small numbers of languages, with vast numbers of speakers and uniform cultures.

The motive force behind the centrally expanding Hesperonesians to develop their coastal Neolithic in this model, was not a random invention. It was, as Surin Pookajorn noted for the inhabitants of the Malay Peninsula, the sheer necessity of having to adapt to continuing loss of coastline and change of environment. In this model of Austronesian language evolution after the Ice Age, the megalithic Palaeo-Hesperonesians seem to be the ones that took to their boats and sailed to steep rocky islands, while the majority stay-at-home Hesperonesians decided to stick it out and adapt on the shrinking remains of the greater Sundas. That picture is certainly supported by the flood myths of the two groups, as I discuss later in Chapter 10. The Hesperonesian-speaking peoples on the Greater Sundas around the Java Sea have flood myths but no boats, whereas the people of western Sumatra, the barrier islands, northern Borneo, Sulawesi, the Philippines and the lesser Sundas, all of whom speak languages of the Palaeo-Hesperonesian type, had a variety of arks, some very seaworthy.

The lack of boats in the flood myths is not to say that the western

Figure 25. **Spread of the family of Austronesian languages from China to the Pacific proposed in the Bellwood/Blust model.** The relationship of Austronesian to Tai and Austro-Asiatic languages remains uncertain (see Figure 22). Each major sub-group (diagonal) includes all lower-order sub-groups to the right. Movement down, and to the right, indicates expansion in time, and distance east, respectively. (Updated map kindly supplied by Peter Bellwood (1998) and redrawn with permission.)

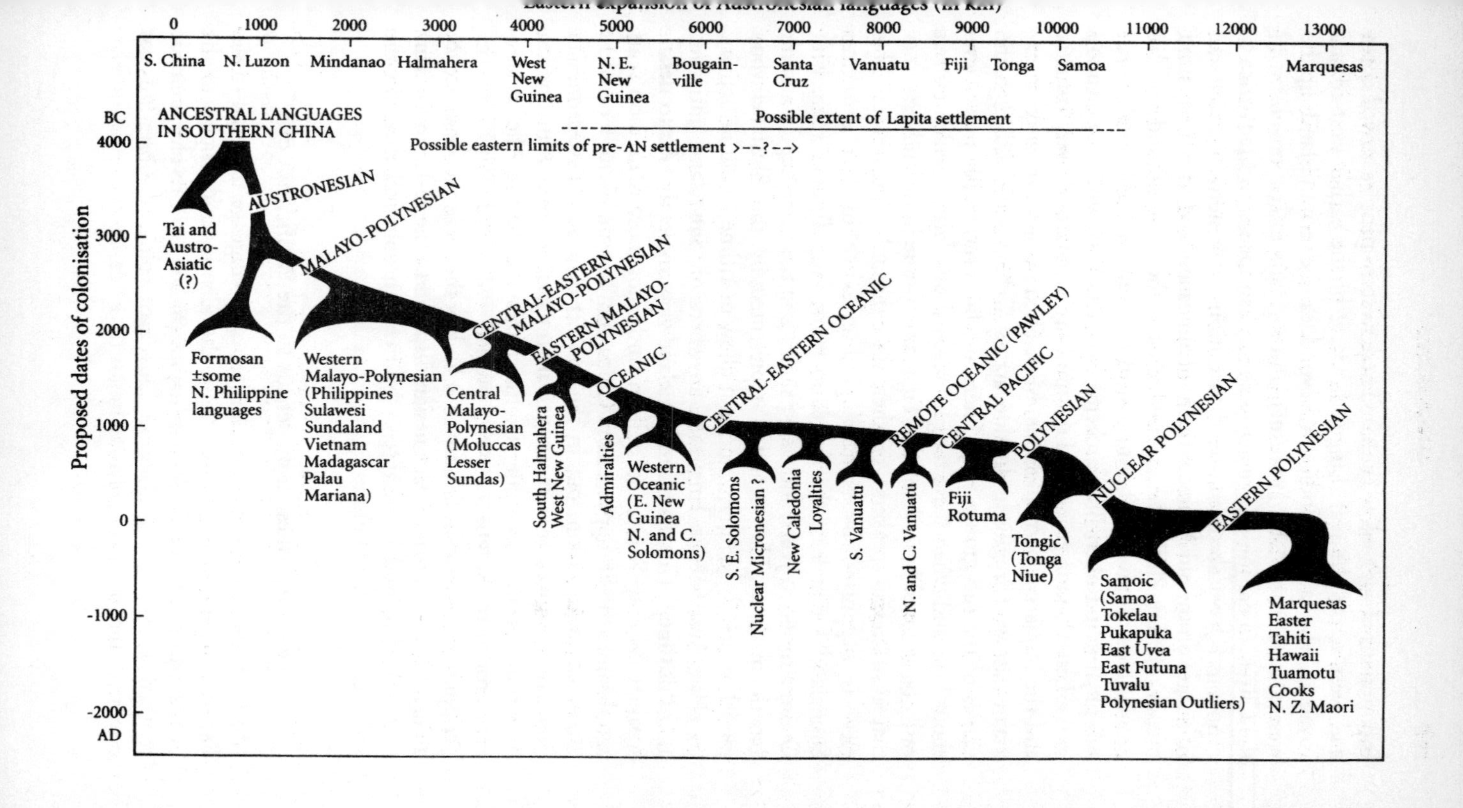
0
1000
2000
3000
4000
5000
6000
7000
8000
9000
10000
11000
12000
13000
S. China
N. Luzon
Mindanao
Halmahera
West New Guinea
N. E. New Guinea
Bougain-ville
Santa Cruz
Vanuatu
Fiji
Tonga
Samoa
Marquesas
Possible extent of Lapita settlement
Possible eastern limits of pre-AN settlement >--?-->
BC
4000
3000
2000
1000
0
-1000
-2000
AD
Proposed dates of colonisation
ANCESTRAL LANGUAGES IN SOUTHERN CHINA
AUSTRONESIAN
MALAYO-POLYNESIAN
CENTRAL-EASTERN MALAYO-POLYNESIAN
EASTERN MALAYO-POLYNESIAN
OCEANIC
CENTRAL-EASTERN OCEANIC
REMOTE OCEANIC (PAWLEY)
CENTRAL PACIFIC
POLYNESIAN
NUCLEAR POLYNESIAN
EASTERN POLYNESIAN
Tai and Austro-Asiatic (?)
Formosan ±some N. Philippine languages
Western Malayo-Polynesian (Philippines Sulawesi Sundaland Vietnam Madagascar Palau Mariana)
Central Malayo-Polynesian (Moluccas Lesser Sundas)
South Halmahera
West New Guinea
Admiralties
Western Oceanic (E. New Guinea N. and C. Solomons)
S. E. Solomons
Nuclear Micronesian ?
New Caledonia
Loyalties
S. Vanuatu
N. and C. Vanuatu
Fiji
Rotuma
Tongic (Tonga Niue)
Samoic (Samoa Tokelau Pukapuka East Uvea East Futuna Tuvalu Polynesian Outliers)
Marquesas
Easter
Tahiti
Hawaii
Tuamotu
Cooks
N. Z. Maori

Indonesians never took to the sea. These western peoples moved north and west across the seas. Linguistic traces of the earlier west-coastal voyagers, who sailed to India and beyond, can be seen in islands up the west coast of the Malay Peninsula, and a great western movement in the Christian era took them across the Indian Ocean to Madagascar.

So far I have sketched the distribution of western Austronesian languages on the old Asian continent of Sundaland and its nearest island masses of the Philippines, Sulawesi and the Lesser Sundas. This geographic grouping is close to that of the western Malayo-Polynesian sub-phylum in Robert Blust's scheme (see Figure 25), with the exception of the Lesser Sunda group, and the minority languages of west Sumatra and the Sumatran barrier islands. Most linguists agree broadly on the major east-west linguistic division across Weber's Line, although the names of the sub-groups vary. There are, however, clearly polar views about how and when these tongues reached Sundaland, which cannot easily be resolved by archaeology. First, an offshore homeland presumes that Austronesian speakers were there since the end of the Ice Age. This view is supported by archaeological evidence of agriculture on Sundaland for at least the last 8000 years; long-distance trade with Oceania for 6000 years; and, as we shall see in the next chapter, ancient genetic markers. The second is represented by the Blust/Bellwood model, which, by contrast, does not allow maritime Neolithic activity, let alone Austronesian languages, anywhere on Sundaland until well after this time.[41] This mainland homeland view argues that Austronesian speakers came to Sundaland quite recently, not more than 4000 years ago through the Philippines from China and Taiwan. Bernd Nothofer's linguistic contribution, put in the context of a Sunda Austronesian homeland, implies that there was an internal western Austronesian dispersal. As the sea split up the Sunda continent, the Palaeo-Hesperonesian languages were pushed west and south, to the periphery of Indonesia. We can now look at the linguistic evidence for an early 6000-year-old Austronesian dispersal to the east into Oceania that was suggested in Chapter 3 by the archaeological finds on the north coast of New Guinea.

Two Austronesian dispersals to the Pacific, not one

Much of the discussion of the Austronesian language dispersal in the Pacific centres round theories about the identity and origins of the people who made the distinctive 'Lapita' pottery with its characteristic toothed (dentate) impressions. This archaeological obsession has obscured and overlaid previous linguistic evidence that Austronesian tongues had been in the Pacific for over 5000 years. Lapita pottery is supposed to define the beginning of the big push of sailing canoes out into the Pacific and central Polynesia from the previous eastern limits of the Solomon Islands. The key features of this pottery style that excite prehistorians are: (1) it was not found before 3500 years ago; (2) when it did appear, it spread through island Melanesia in an incredibly short time; (3) as the pottery reached western island Melanesia it also simultaneously spread out to Vanuatu, New Caledonia and the Central Pacific to previously uninhabited islands such as Samoa and Fiji; and (4) artefacts and other objects found with Lapita pottery suggested a sophisticated marine and agricultural Neolithic technology.

Because the distribution of Lapita pottery also coincides with the present-day distribution of Pacific Austronesian languages, it seemed an obvious conclusion that Lapita pottery was made by an advanced Neolithic maritime culture, speaking Austronesian tongues, which had suddenly swept out from somewhere in Southeast Asia 3500 years ago. Sadly, pots cannot talk, so there is still argument about who made them and what languages the makers spoke. When I introduced the Lapita controversy in Chapter 3, it was in the context of the much earlier post-flood dispersals from East Asia and Southeast Asia. I listed archaeological evidence that people in Melanesia had been doing many of the same things as the Lapita culture at least 6000 years ago and possibly earlier. These included long-distance maritime trading of obsidian, making pots, using advanced shell technology, and growing and eating vegetable and animal foodstuffs imported from Asia such as betel-nuts and pigs. Here I will look at the evidence for a pre-Lapita Austronesian expansion from more of a cultural and linguistic point of view.

Three views of Lapita

The conflicting evidence of old and new skills in prehistoric Melanesia has given rise to two polar views of Lapita pottery. At one extreme is the archaeological theory that Lapita pottery, and its associated technological complex, started somewhere in Melanesia. Archaeologist Patrick Kirch has called this the 'Indigenous Melanesian Origins' (IMO) theory.[42] As Kirch points out, however, this theory does not explain the distribution of Oceanic languages, unless of course they also originated in Melanesia.

At the other extreme is the combined linguistic and archaeological, Blust/Bellwood model (shown in Chapter 3) that argues for one rapid continuous process of colonisation by Austronesian speakers from Southeast Asia, culminating in the Lapita phenomenon 3500 years ago.

This 'express train to Polynesia' (ETP) is the prevalent view held by many linguists.

The third solution to the paradox of pre-Lapita sailors in northern Melanesia is the one I introduced in Chapter 3 – namely, that there was a pre-Lapita Austronesian colonisation from Southeast Asia at least 6000 years ago. That situation could be allowed by the Meacham/Solheim view of the Austronesian language homeland in island Southeast Asia, but not by the Blust/Bellwood 'Out of Taiwan' hypothesis. The arguments for and against these two views were aired earlier this chapter. If there had been an early Austronesian migration, the Lapita expansion would then have been a second migration, adding an improved sailing technology to a pre-existing Austronesian trade network. The physical, genetic and cultural differences between the Austronesian speakers of Polynesia and island Melanesia would therefore result from Polynesians being the latest newcomers from Southeast Asia, and the island Melanesians being descended from the older, mixed Papuan-Austronesian colony from the north coast of New Guinea who took advantage of the new technology to spread out east themselves. This, the 'Two Train' (TT) hypothesis, is my favourite option. It allows the possibility that trading between Southeast Asia and Melanesia continued throughout the period from at least 6000 years ago.

The first of these three models is archaeological and does not really address the linguistic evidence. I will therefore concentrate now on the other two models – the later single express train and the earlier Two Train hypothesis. First, though, I need to explore views on the language tree of the more eastern Austronesian languages in a bit more depth.

The eastern branch of Austronesian languages

The early Austronesian tongues spoken in the island region around eastern Borneo and Sulawesi, along with some Philippine languages, may have been the budding point that gave rise to the more eastern branches. Those spoken in the same region today would be described in Bernd Nothofer's model as Palaeo-Hesperonesian,[43] but all still belong to the larger western Malayo-Polynesian group in Robert Blust's classification.

The main eastern sub-division of Austronesian tongues is the Oceanic eastern group. The Oceanic family includes all Pacific Austronesian tongues roughly to the east of the 138th parallel (except Chamorro and Palau of western Micronesia, which belong to the western Malayo-Polynesian group). This means all of Polynesia, most of Micronesia and the Austronesian-speaking parts of Melanesia, but excludes most of

Indonesian western New Guinea (Irian Jaya). The main Eastern branch of the Austronesian phylum is thus separated from the nearest western Austronesian tongue by over 1500 kilometres.

In the space sandwiched between the western and eastern Austronesian families are the eastern Indonesian languages, also Austronesian. These occupy Wallacia and west New Guinea, an area bounded by Weber's Line on the west and the 138th parallel to the east. These tongues comprise a large number of island language sub-groups not well related to each other, nor to either of their huge neighbours, the western and eastern Austronesian families. Their great variations in vocabulary prompted older linguists to separate them into many sub-groups. Blust, however, has grouped the languages of Maluku (the Moluccas) and the Lesser Sundas into one family, 'central Malayo-Polynesian', a stay-at-home side branch of central eastern Malayo-Polynesian (CEM-P), which he believes split off from Malayo-Polynesian 5500 years ago. But he acknowledges there are problems with their grouping. The long physical gap before the Oceanic languages is partially plugged by a small group of little-known tongues between the island of South Halmahera and west New Guinea (SHWNG). These tongues share half the language innovations that characterise the Oceanic languages far to the east. Blust argues that eastern Malayo-Polynesian, the eastern part of CEM-P, split into Oceanic and SHWNG branches around 4500 years ago.[44]

It will be obvious that although Blust's language-dispersal model forms the central pillar of Peter Bellwood's hypothesis of the Austronesian sweep into the Pacific 3500 years ago, even Blust's dates each antedate Bellwood's by about 1500 years (see Figure 25). This discrepancy between Bellwood's archaeological dates for the Austronesian expansion and calculated dates of language splits is even greater when estimates of earlier linguists are used, and, as I shall show in the next two chapters, does not fit the genetic picture either. A particular area of uncertainty concerns the timing and relative geographic and linguistic position of the split of Oceanic tongues from the rest of the Austronesian family tree. Clearly, the shape of the linguistic tree has to fit the geography and the timing of the split in any proposed model. Furthermore, such a model also needs to explain the origins of the diverse eastern Indonesian languages of Wallacia and west New Guinea.

The express train to Polynesia

I will now look at how Peter Bellwood fits Robert Blust's language tree to his view of Austronesian colonisation of the Pacific. The late express

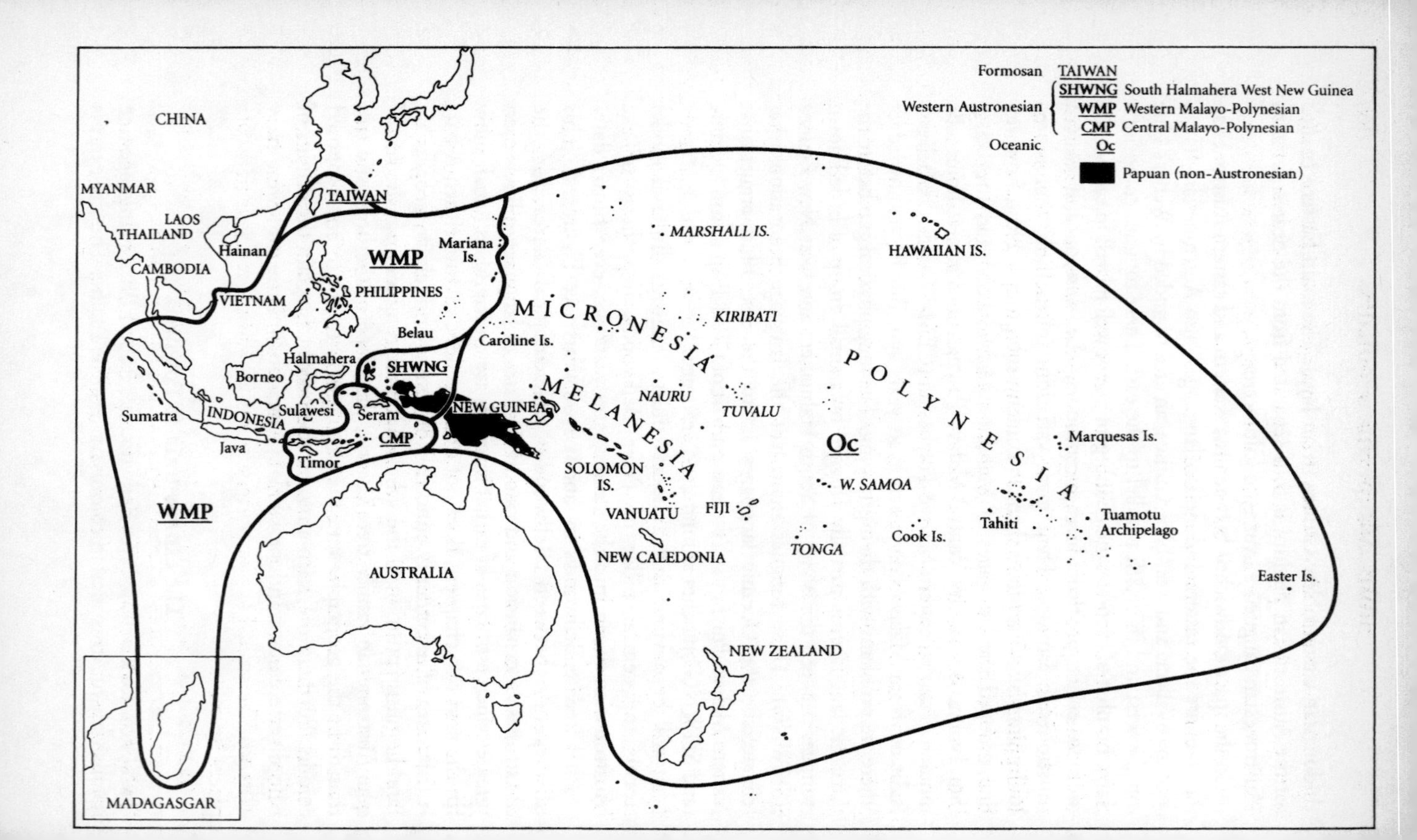

Formosan TAIWAN
Western Austronesian
SHWNG South Halmahera West New Guinea
WMP Western Malayo-Polynesian
CMP Central Malayo-Polynesian
Oceanic Oc
Papuan (non-Austronesian)
CHINA
MYANMAR
LAOS
THAILAND
CAMBODIA
VIETNAM
Hainan
TAIWAN
WMP
PHILIPPINES
Mariana Is.
Belau
Caroline Is.
MICRONESIA
MARSHALL IS.
KIRIBATI
NAURU
TUVALU
HAWAIIAN IS.
POLYNESIA
Halmahera
SHWNG
Borneo
Sulawesi
Seram
Sumatra
INDONESIA
Java
Timor
CMP
NEW GUINEA
MELANESIA
SOLOMON IS.
VANUATU
FIJI
NEW CALEDONIA
Oc
W. SAMOA
TONGA
Cook Is.
Tahiti
Marquesas Is.
Tuamotu Archipelago
Easter Is.
WMP
AUSTRALIA
NEW ZEALAND
MADAGASCAR

Figure 26. **Distribution of the Austronesian language family.** This huge family, as the name implies, is almost entirely located on islands of the southern Indo-Pacific region. Only the main higher-order groupings are shown here. For practical purposes, the most important division is between Oceanic and the rest, the so-called Western Austronesian families.

train to Polynesia follows the trail of the first Austronesian speakers out of Taiwan, bringing the fourth high-order group, Malayo-Polynesian, to the Philippines around 3000–2500 BC. Reaching the south Philippines by 2000 BC, Malayo-Polynesian then split in two, the right branch (which was to give rise to western Malayo-Polynesian) moving into North Borneo by around 2000–1500 BC, and the left branch moving into Sulawesi to give rise to the central-eastern-Malayo-Polynesian group by about the same time.[45]

According to Bellwood's model, after the rather leisurely movement through the Philippines up to 2000 BC, the most extraordinary explosion of migration and cultural/linguistic diversification started from 3500 years ago, and was complete within the space of the next few generations. Nearly the entire Malayo-Polynesian dispersal from Nias in the west to Fiji in the east and New Caledonia in the south[46] (excluding only eastern Polynesian parts of Micronesia and Madagascar) was complete by 1000 BC. In fact, most of the Oceanic settlement (as evidenced by the spread of Lapita pottery) was complete by 1600 BC, apparently instantaneously.[47]

Patrick Kirch has pointed out that the last phase – the Lapita expansion from the Bismarck Archipelago to central Polynesia, a distance of 4500 kilometres – would have been completed in 300–500 years, within 15–25 generations. Thus each successive generation would have moved on average 180–300 kilometres. This whistle-stop progress is the reason the model is often called the express train to Polynesia. But the train is supposed to have stopped to let off colonisers at frequent intervals. I have added the word 'late' to distinguish this single train from the earlier two-train model (see Figure 27). On arrival in central Polynesia the train then stopped again for about 1500 years before the colonisation of eastern Polynesia, which began again after AD 500. The typical Lapita pottery, however, had petered out in most places by 500 BC.[48]

In its Asia-to-Samoa concept, the ETP is clearly a more comprehensive and explanatory archaeolinguistic model for Lapita than the 'Indigenous Melanesian Origins' theory. ETP has, however, some inconsistencies that are difficult to resolve. These problems are imposed by the inalterable rates and dates imposed by the model. They can be resolved if the ETP can be seen as just that, and only the latest of more than one expansion. The sheer rate of the Lapita expansion is exemplified by the uniformity of pottery styles in its wide distribution. Even the few hundred years allowed for its movement from Melanesia through to Polynesia have been called into question by statistical analysis of the radiocarbon dates that suggest an even faster spread.[49] Such a rapid spread and the cultural uniformity of the Lapita complex fit with the general uniformity found in the later Polynesian dispersal after AD 500. But it takes much more explaining when we look at the enormous diversity in terms of linguistics, culture and physical and genetic anthropology found among the peoples along the way to Polynesia, from Southeast Asia.

Enough time for change?

The express train to Polynesia clearly specifies that the entire dispersal of the Austronesian phylum with all its major branches of western Malayo-Polynesian, eastern, central and, finally, the Oceanic sub-branches should have occurred between around 2000 BC, when the Malayo-Polynesian stem reached the south Philippines, and 1000 BC, when the Lapita dispersal reached as far as Polynesia. That is the time gap between the Norman invasion of England and today, or only twice the time that has elapsed since Shakespeare learnt to speak English. The language groupings, large and small, of Robert Blust's genetic tree with its many hundreds of daughter languages are based on shared linguistic innovations, rather than shared vocabulary. All the linguistic innovations that still define the sub-groups, the most radical being Oceanic, must have taken place in the same 1000-year timescale. The Oceanic group, as a whole, represents a major departure from other Austronesian tongues such as western Malayo-Polynesian, not only in terms of innovations but also in terms of massive loss of vocabulary. For instance, Malay, a western Malayo-Polynesian tongue, still retains 74 per cent of the total reconstructed Proto-Austronesian vocabulary compared with Tongan from Oceania, which only has 15 per cent. Further, Oceanic now has nine high-order sub-groups[50] one of which is the Manus group. This means that all must have split at the same time in the Oceanic homeland. Peter Bellwood places this homeland in Wallacia around 1400 BC[51] (that is, at the same time as the Lapita dispersal). Splitting means language change. According to the Bellwood model, these groups of tongues immediately dispersed widely, so the changes must have happened at the time of initial break-up, which was complete in a mere instant 3500 years ago.

Putting aside any general disbelief that all this change and diversity within each group and sub-group could have happened in such a short time, there is another problem with the express train. The model predicts that all the splits in the major and minor branches after Malayo-Polynesian should have nearly the same time-depth; from any point of view, that does not seem to be the case.

In the old days, time-depths of language splits were estimated by glottochronology. So, for instance, authoritative statements still appear in print as follows:

> Glottochronology, a technique for dating the division between languages (known as linguistic splits) based on the assumption that there is a stable rate of basic vocabulary replacement in languages, places the separation of Fijian and Polynesian sub-groups at between 3000 and 4000 years ago. The separation of Proto-Polynesian into separate branches is dated at between 1800 and 2500 years ago.[52]

These two sets of dates are in fact roughly appropriate, first, for the arrival of Lapita to central Polynesia, and then for the subsequent eastern Polynesian dispersal. The problem is that dating by this method makes the previous branches of the Oceanic tree, and the tree itself, much older than the ETP allows. The same source of reference then has this entry:

> These are relatively recent branchings, far down on the Oceanic limb of the Austronesian family tree, and it follows that the separation of the common ancestor of Fijian and Polynesian from more distant branches of Oceanic must have occurred somewhat earlier. Glottochronological estimates indicate that diversification of Austronesian languages began around 4000 to 5000 years ago in the New Hebrides, in New Caledonia, and in the Solomons, and earlier still in the region of New Guinea.

Later we find:

> Comparisons of basic vocabulary show that several New Guinea-West Melanesian groups share less than 15 per cent of a common basic vocabulary with all the other members of Austronesian, indicating a divergence from the parent language at least 5000 years ago.[53]

These statements clearly do not fit the ETP model, because they suggest that Oceanic languages near and in New Guinea, often called 'aberrant', may have been there at least 1500 years longer than Lapita pottery. A linguistic argument for a pre-Lapita Austronesian exploration of the Bismarcks was first made by linguist Isidore Dyen in 1965.[54] His proposal was endorsed in the early 1970s by other linguists such as Andrew Pawley and Roger Green.[55] It was given biological support by physical anthropologist William Howells around the same time.[56] The idea fell out of favour, however, as more was learnt about the deficiencies of glottochronology.

As a result of this change in fashion, the modern genetic linguistic trees for Austronesian languages usually ignore major differences in vocabulary between Oceanic tongues as long as shared innovations can be identified. But there is a flaw in this. If linguists disbelieve their own evidence for a previous dispersal and rely on archaeologists to date their trees, the independence of the disciplines is lost. There are several linguists and archaeologists who acknowledge the possibility of an earlier Austronesian dispersal.[57]

Various strategies have been adopted to explain away the so-called 'aberrant' languages on the eastern tip and the north coast of New Guinea, and in the Bismarcks (see distribution in Figure 29). The main approach has been to blame the intrusive influence of nearby Papuan languages, or to suggest that these tongues are really pidgins. This has been refuted. In a recent book entitled *The Prehistoric Settlement of the Pacific*, Ward Goodenough makes a detailed comparative example of the Austronesian languages of the large island of New Britain in the Bismarck Sea, and those on the neighbouring coast of mainland New Guinea. The gist of his argument is as follows. Two Austronesian languages spoken on the north coast of New Britain, Lakalai and Bulu, share more basic vocabulary with far-away Fijian than with their close neighbours in the centre and south of the island, Bebeli and Mangseng. Conversely, these last two languages share more vocabulary with the languages across the Vitiaz Strait on the north coast of New Guinea than with their neighbours Lakalai and Bulu. Bebeli and Mangseng also share very little with Fijian. Goodenough argues that this difference suggests that the latter two Austronesian languages in south New Britain, and all the Austronesian tongues of the north New Guinea coast, are much older in their separation from the other Austronesian languages in Oceania, as their geographic location also implies.[58]

This research has three important messages. First, it refines the argument of vocabulary loss in the 'aberrant' languages, which in this example are the Bebeli and Manseng of the Whiteman mountain range in central and south New Britain, clustering with the neighbouring New Guinea coast. Second, it counters the Papuan mixing argument by showing a closer vocabulary relationship between the north New Britain languages and Fijian than with their 'older' close neighbours on the same island. Significantly the linguistic division that Goodenough highlights across the Vitiaz Strait between New Britain and New Guinea[59] is also part of the western boundary of Lapita. There are numerous Lapita sites northeast of the line among the Fijian-related tongues of the northern part of the Meso-Melanesian cluster of languages. But south of the line throughout Austronesian-speaking coastal mainland New Guinea there are no sites, except one isolated find far to the west in Aitape, West Sepik province.

Goodenough goes on to show that the source of the ancient trade of Talasea obsidian, which was traded as far as Borneo 6000 years ago, is located in the territory of 'older aberrant' languages, and finally also draws the conclusion that directly contradicts the single express train hypothesis:

> It may be no coincidence that Bebeli is located in the immediate vicinity of the source of Talasea obsidian, which was traded in Melanesia long before and well after the Lapita period. It may be no coincidence that the languages of the North New Guinea cluster are distributed over the area from which sugar cane appears to have originated and where the pig first makes its appearance into Melanesia. And it may be no coincidence that the North New Guinea cluster of languages is distributed along ... a pre-Lapita trade corridor.[60]

In other words, there was a pre-Lapita Austronesian-to-Austronesian long-distance trading route along Geoffrey Irwin's voyaging corridor between Southeast Asia and the Bismarck Archipelago (see above).[61]

The linguistic and ceramic transition region stretching from the Madang province on the north coast of the New Guinea mainland to southwest New Britain that Ward Goodenough discusses here also exactly defines the area of the conflict legend of Kulabob and Manup which I will discuss in Chapter 16.

Two routes out to the Pacific

The concept of Lapita moving through a pre-existing Oceanic

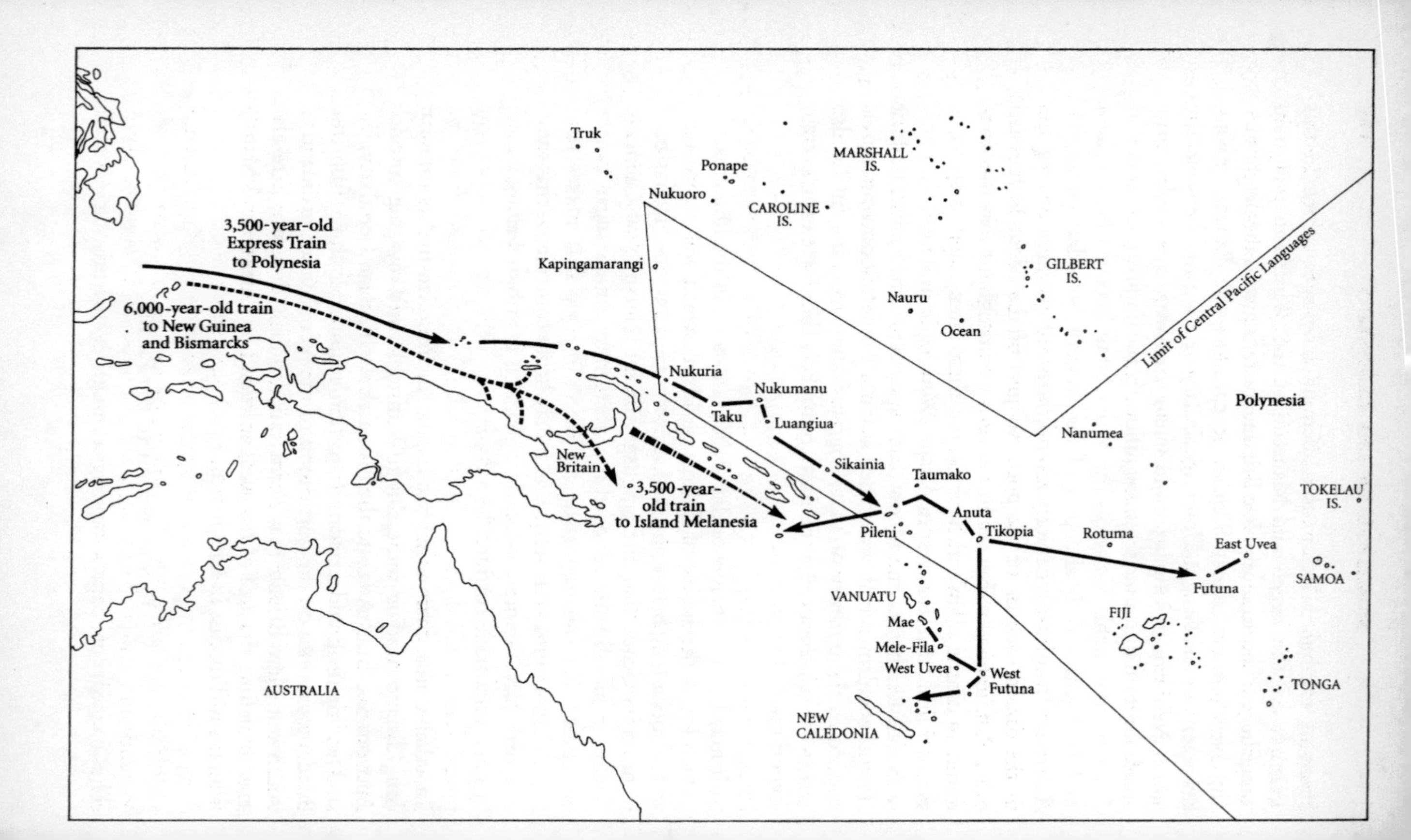
3,500-year-old Express Train to Polynesia
6,000-year-old train to New Guinea and Bismarcks
3,500-year-old train to Island Melanesia
Limit of Central Pacific Languages
Polynesia
Truk
Ponape
Nukuoro
CAROLINE IS.
MARSHALL IS.
Kapingamarangi
GILBERT IS.
Nauru
Ocean
Nukuria
Nukumanu
Taku
Luangiua
Sikainia
Taumako
Anuta
Tikopia
Pileni
Nanumea
Rotuma
TOKELAU IS.
East Uvea
Futuna
SAMOA
FIJI
TONGA
VANUATU
Mae
Mele-Fila
West Uvea
West Futuna
NEW CALEDONIA
New Britain
AUSTRALIA

Figure 27. **The 'two train' hypothesis.** This differs from the current 'Express Train to Polynesia' concept in that the ETP bypassed Melanesia, stopping only long enough to introduce improved sailing and ceramic technology. A previous Austronesian train had already colonised northern Melanesia at least 2500 years before (see distribution of 'aberrant languages', Figure 29). These older colonies, now of mixed race, took on this new technology and sailed on as a parallel train to colonise the rest of island Melanesia 3500 years ago.

Austronesian culture 3500 years ago is borne out by other notable gaps in the distribution of Lapita pots. Manus and Lou islands and the other Admiralties, which were the source of 6000-year-old obsidian found in Borneo, have yielded only a handful of Lapita-style potsherds.[62] Thus the oldest Melanesian centre of long-distance trading with Southeast Asia may have been peripheral to the first Lapita ceramic culture except as a source of obsidian. Many archaeologists regard this region with its 12,000-year occupation as central to Oceanic prehistory. Linguistically, the Admiralties have their own high-order sub-group in Oceanic. But even this grouping may be misleading, because the languages of the tiny islands Wuvulu and Awa are probably isolates.

As I have said, the Lapita pottery culture does not really start until we get to the western end of the Bismarck chain, to the arc of islands including Mussau, Watom, the Duke of Yorks and New Britain.[63] This Austronesian-speaking region also has, as Ward Goodenough points out, some Fijian-related vocabulary. Here the warring-brothers myth has changed somewhat from the Kulabob/Manup deadly end-game into the more friendly Tolai version of the smart brother/stupid brother, and the New Ireland loving-brothers version with its strange forced fratricide. Like an isolated beacon, the Bismarck cluster of Lapita sites also defines the main region of blowpipe use in Oceania (see Chapter 2), thus indicating a diffusional seeding from western Austronesian cultural regions far to the west. Stephen Jett's detailed study of the technological motifs of blowpipes tends to support this hypothesis (see Figure 11). The Bismarck variety of telescopic blowpipe is also found in the Bisayan area of the Philippines. The Lapita dispersal may also have been when that weapon found its way to the Marshall Islands in Micronesia where it is known from oral history.[64]

Moving out to the Pacific, the Lapita ceramics of the Bismarcks are stylistically and geographically isolated by the Solomon Islands from Vanuatu and central Polynesia to the east. The large Solomon island chain from the one Lapita site on the tip of Buka Island in the west to the Reef-Santa Cruz Islands, a distance of 1400 kilometres to the east, is a Lapita void. Patrick Kirch comments in a recent review that, 'It is possible that Lapita colonists simply skirted these islands which were already populated.'[65] Archaeologist Peter Sheppard and colleagues from New Zealand and the Solomons, having found no Lapita remains in the west Solomons, comment that the 'hypothesis of no Lapita occupation in the Central ... [and] Western Solomons ... forces us to consider the effect of interaction of Lapita with established populations in ... Pacific colonisation. It seems possible that the colonisation of the Reefs/Santa Cruz ... may mark a very big first step, leap-frogging previously established populations and cultural networks.'[66]

After the long gap of the Solomons, fourteen Lapita sites are found in the Reef-Santa Cruz Islands to the southeast of the main Solomon group. It is difficult to imagine even the most experienced of canoe sailors regularly skirting the huge Solomon island chain, which the obsidian traders of the Lapita network had to do, without alternative stop-overs *en route*. As it happens, there is an alternative route, which ends up directly at the Reef-Santa Cruz Islands to the east of the Solomons. The trail follows the submarine Ontong Java Rise, which is scattered with tiny atolls in a line to the east but parallel with the Solomons. This chain of atolls includes the Tau'u Islands, Nukumanu Islands, Ontong Java and the Stewart Islands. All these islanders speak Polynesian tongues related to Samoic, and constitute the northern part of a linguistic chain known as Polynesian or Samoic outliers (see Figure 17). Stretching the full 3000 kilometres parallel to the majority non-Polynesian islands of the Bismarcks, the Solomons, Vanuatu and New Caledonia, the southernmost representatives are West Uvea and West Futuna.

As I discussed earlier, these out-of-place Polynesians may not be the renegade Samoans that linguists have always labelled them, but the relict trail of a founder Polynesian region in Melanesia. If this were the case, and the glottochronological evidence were correct, logically we should expect to see old Lapita sites in at least some of the atolls that presently have Polynesian-speaking populations. Indeed, such is the case. The Reef-Santa Cruz Islands hold Pileni, a Polynesian outlier tongue, and a little further east are the Lapita sites of Anuta and Tikopia, again both Polynesian outliers. The picture emerging from this linguistic and archaeological leapfrog race appears to be one of two parallel colonisations of island Melanesia; one by people who may already have spoken Polynesian tongues, carried the Lapita skills and colonised atolls; the other, which I will come back to shortly, was derived possibly from an older, numerically larger, pre-existing hybrid Austronesian/Papuan culture spread along the north coast of New Guinea, who benefited from the new Lapita technology brought from Indonesia 3500 years ago.

The next big geographic leap for the Lapita culture was from the western and southern cultural regions in island Melanesia to Fiji, then to Polynesia 2000 kilometres to the east. Here, Lapita sites abound. All the languages, including Fijian, belong to the Central Pacific Group of Oceanic languages.[67] Using a recent tree suggested by Andrew Pawley and Malcolm Ross, this grouping is one of the nine high-order Oceanic sub-groups. As I mentioned in the last chapter, this rank means there is no linguistic node above linking it with any of the other Oceanic groups. Because there is as yet no single mother candidate among the sibling groups, theoretically the founder tongue could have come all the way from the supposed homeland in eastern Indonesia 3500 years ago with innovations and vocabulary replacement on the way. Eastern Lapita pottery is well represented among the locations of all the central Pacific linguistic sub-groups such as Fiji, Tonga, Samoa and the sister-tongues of the outliers. Both East Uvea and East Futuna between Fiji and Samoa have Lapita sites. Clearly the strong representation of Lapita in Polynesian-speaking islands both in Melanesia and Polynesia, combined with the archaeological and glottochronological evidence of rapid and recent dispersion and arrival, is consistent with a link. The Central Pacific languages thus seem to be the best candidates for a group booking on the Lapita express train to Polynesia. There may, however, have been Austronesian influence in Western Oceania long before then. I will now look briefly at the earlier trains from the north coast of New Guinea to Vanuatu and from the Bismarcks to the Solomons and east Melanesia.

Branch train to south Melanesia from north Melanesia

An old 1975 map of the complex prehistoric linguistic movements in the Southwest Pacific, based presumably on the now out-of-favour glottochronology, shows an earlier train arriving from Southeast Asia 5000 years ago.[68] Several important features of this older view were logically impossible in the later ETP hypothesis. The first is that the author, Stephen Wurm, showed the non-stop express train offshore and moving east somewhere in the islands west of Manus, and then bypassing both the Bismarcks and the Solomons to the east and speeding on to the Santa Cruz Islands. Although Wurm's dates of the ETP are probably too early, this is a similar route to my fast-track spread for the Lapita dispersal.

The second point of Wurm's map is that colonial side-branches came out of the older train along the north coast of New Guinea, and the rest of the train finally ended up in the Bismarcks. The region between the Bismarcks and the north coast of New Guinea and the Papuan tip, Wurm described as the Austronesian/Papuan contact areas. Today, as I have said, they are home to the so-called 'aberrant' Austronesian languages and technologically the oldest and least-seaworthy styles of outrigger canoes. Wurm indicates secondary eastward migrations of mixed 'Melanid' and Papuan speakers out of these areas around 1000 BC to populate the non-Polynesian parts of the Solomons, Vanuatu and New Caledonia.

Wurm's view that multiple migrations of Papuan and older mixed Papuan/Austronesian cultures populated island Melanesia from New Guinea and the western Bismarcks during the Lapita period overcomes a major defect of the express train. That defect is simply that the peoples of southern island Melanesia are culturally and physically very different from the Polynesians. Not only are they different, but they are also much more diverse, showing more links with north coast New Guinea than with their neighbours in Polynesia. The express train, which specifies a single-track, rapid linguistic and human migration from Southeast Asia, has to explain the Melanesian-Polynesian divide. Its adherents try to do this by postulating a gradual post-Lapita diffusion of both genetic and cultural elements from New Guinea. I discuss the population genetic faults in this rationalisation in Chapter 6 and 7, but will address the cultural and archaeological issue briefly here.

Pre-Lapita Austronesian colonisation of north Melanesia

Perhaps the best way to give an idea of some of the cultural links and dissociations between Melanesia and Polynesia is to start with a couple of personal anecdotes. Two of these have a *déjà vu* element. When I was working in the Sepik province of New Guinea as government paediatrician, one of my quarterly tasks was to visit Aid Posts in the two tiny islands of Wuvulu and Awa 200 kilometres north of the New Guinea coast. This involved an overnight trip in the government trawler. After weathering a storm in the night, we woke up to a blue sky and a view on the horizon of a short fringe of coconut trees. I had been warned, but it was still a surprise to arrive in an island that seemed more appropriate to Polynesia. The people looked like Polynesians and culturally they appeared so – in terms of carving designs and many other aspects. In the interior of the islands were the pits their ancestors had dug for the wet cultivation of the giant Polynesian taro. They hardly needed their expert fishing skills since trevally, kingfish, barracuda, rainbow runners and dolphin fish competed for the lures let out behind their boats. Yet these isolated islands were 1300 miles west of the nearest Polynesian outlier in the Bismarcks, and a quarter way round the globe from the nearest island of Polynesia. For me the other out-of-place experience was two dishes I was served, which I can recall eating only in Southeast Asia, certainly nowhere else in New Guinea. One of these the Malays would have called *otak-otak*, literally 'brains'. White fish is steamed or baked, marinaded in thick coconut milk in a watertight rectangular box made of a banana leaf. The other dish was a sweet of glutinous sago balls in a bed of shredded coconut.

If I was ever looking for the lost tribe of a late Polynesian fast track in the Western Oceanic homeland, these two tiny islands would be an early destination. Others have appreciated their unique charm. The islanders told me that a consortium including the film star John Wayne had been negotiating to build an exclusive resort there. Linguistically they speak isolate Oceanic tongues with only tenuous links to the Admiralty Islands to the east. No evidence of Lapita pottery has ever been found on either island, although this may not be surprising because as low-lying reefs they were both vulnerable to sea-level oscillations after the end of the Ice Age.

The other anecdote comes from a later period when I was working in the Madang province on the north coast of New Guinea. Driving back once from an up-country visit, I came across a village in a clearing where a ceremony and get together were taking place. The villagers, dressed in red bark-cloth sarongs, explained that their boys had just returned from a month's post-circumcision seclusion in the bush where they had been educated into various mysteries of manhood. A big party had been prepared with gifts and food. I was invited to join the feast. My hosts explained that although they lived in the bush, their ancestors were originally from Bil Bil village on the coast. The Bil Bils are famous from the Russian anthropologist Mikloucho-Maclay's nineteenth-century diaries, and because they have a unique pottery tradition (I describe their myth of the origin of pottery in Chapter 12). Some years later, I had the same experience with the same-looking people, the same clothes and the same ceremony, but thousands of kilometres to the east, in Tanna Island of Vanuatu. The elaborate exchange of gifts was to the families of the boys' mothers. Throughout the non-Polynesian-speaking parts of eastern island Melanesia are found such diverse counterparts of north coast New Guinea cultures.

In short, the people of these islands are unmistakably recognisable as Melanesian, and those people who speak Polynesian are clearly Polynesians even when not talking. To be sure, there are linguistic and cultural analogies between the Polynesians and Melanesians, such as the story of the creator, Tangaloa. But then Tagaroar is also found in the Sepik province of New Guinea to the west.[69]

My crude anecdotes of north and south Melanesian links are backed up by a recent analysis of cultural and technological links between the people of Madang and Sepik on the north coast of New Guinea. The Swiss archaeologist/ethnologist Christian Kaufmann from the Basel Museum for Folk-Arts found several Sepik and Madang cultural traditions reproduced as separate but related strands away to the east in Vanuatu, the Solomons and New Caledonia. The Sepik river region, which only relatively recently recovered from the great flood of 8000 years ago,[70] has one of the richest cultural traditions anywhere in Oceania. This tradition extends to carving, painting, pottery and oral history. Although most of the region's people speak non-Austronesian languages, there are good reasons for believing that they have been strongly influenced by Austronesian cultures. Apart from the specific Lapita design motifs, which are found on the coast and in the Middle Sepik river region, there are shared motifs in oral myths, such as the hawk and the two brothers linked to an outgoing canoe voyage. I will describe these and other Austronesian Sepik/New Caledonia myths in Part II.

Kaufman notes that pottery from north New Guinea and other traditions, perhaps influenced by earlier migrations from Indonesia up to 5500 years ago, were developing and diversifying in the Sepik long before the Lapita dispersal into the Pacific. The effect of the cross-fertilisation was a rich tapestry of cultural strands. These extremely diverse cultural strands were then transported and reproduced again in island Melanesia to the east, particularly in northern Vanuatu, possibly from 800 BC. Thus from a different perspective, we have again the conclusion of two competing colonisations of Vanuatu, the Solomons and New Caledonia from 3000 years ago – one the new Lapita, the other a diverse hybrid culture of older origin from western Melanesia.

The linguistic and cultural picture thus amply supports Pamela Swadling's archaeological theory of an earlier Austronesian spread to the Pacific at least 6000 years ago (see Chapters 2 and 3). As I shall show in the next chapter this same story is told in the genes, except that there are other surprises concerning the prehistoric movements of the first inhabitants of Sundaland.

6
EVE'S GENES

In the last four chapters I re-examined various archaeological and linguistic models to see if they support the concept of early flood-driven dispersals of Austro-Asiatic and Austronesian-speaking peoples out of island Southeast Asia in all directions of the compass, including to the Pacific islands, around 7500 years ago (see Figure 14 in Chapter 3 and Figure 27 in Chapter 5). Fine, the sceptic should say, but is there any genetic evidence of such migrations and do the dates fit? Now that geneticists can reconstruct the mitochondrial DNA sequence of Eve, our mother of mothers, and forensic molecular biologists can uniquely identify a criminal with DNA fingerprinting, surely such tools can trace population migrations over the last 10,000 years? They should be more powerful and accurate than any amalgam of geology, archaeology, linguistics and fairy tales. But are they? The answer to this is a qualified yes.

The geneticists do have very powerful weapons, but, as in the Vietnam war, dependence on modern technology and fire power can have disappointing results, when faced with a moving and invisible target. An alternative metaphor for the patchy knowledge that can be obtained from population genetics comes from the oracle of Delphi. This fountain of all wisdom had the habit of giving ambiguous or opaque answers. A king was told by the oracle that if he went to war a great nation would be destroyed. He went to battle. The oracle had omitted to tell him which nation would be destroyed – his own. The value of the information given depends on the question and on the interpretation of the answer. When questions as basic as single or multiple evolutions of human beings remain polarised, in the face of such detailed knowledge, there is much more to be learnt about the tools.

Some simple questions have arisen out of my model of post-flood dispersal. We should expect more than half of them to be answered in the affirmative. Any questions with a negative rather than no result should count against the positives. There is geological evidence of three great and destructive floods over the last 15,000 years, the last being 8000–7600 years ago. Were all these associated with worldwide (and Southeast Asian) population dispersals in all directions? This question can clearly be broken up according to the direction of migration:

(1) Was there an early post-glacial eastern maritime dispersal out of island Southeast Asia to the New Guinea coast and the Bismarck Archipelago, 8000–7000 years ago, and can it be distinguished genetically from the arrival in New Guinea – and Melanesia generally – of the first Polynesians 3500 years ago?[1]

(2) Were there similar migrations south to Australia via the Lesser Sundas?

(3) Were there similar migrations north from Indo-China and Burma (Myanmar) into China and Tibet, and up along the Pacific Rim islands of Taiwan, Japan and Korea?

(4) Were there similar migrations west round the northern rim of the Indian Ocean, and northwest, on towards Mesopotamia, the Middle East and Europe?

Before answering these questions in detail I will sketch out briefly the genetic tools for tracing migrations, what they can do, and their limitations.[2]

Down to the colour of our eyes and skin, we are products of our genes and influenced by our environments. Every protein and structure in our body is created on templates held in our genes. To all intents and purposes a complete library record of our genetic make-up is contained in every nucleated cell in the body. The information is contained in a digital code on long molecular strings of deoxyribonucleic acid or DNA looking rather like a zipper. As with any code there is a language. This is encrypted in units called base pairs arranged side by side like the teeth of the zipper. The basic coding group is a triplet, and each triplet codes uniquely for an amino acid, the building blocks of our proteins. Since the base pairs are the basic unit in the DNA string, lengths of DNA, are often described in terms of numbers of base pairs. For instance the deletion of a stretch of DNA containing a thousand base pairs would be called a kilobase deletion. This DNA, the substance of our genes, is parcelled into twenty-three pairs of chromosomes. We inherit half of the information held in our genes from each of our parents. If molecular geneticists had the time to analyse the full library of genetic code in each of us, they would find that everyone was different from everyone else. The strings of DNA are so long that a total genetic fingerprint is impossible on an individual basis. Instead geneticists focus on inherited differences between certain genes, many of which are well understood and easier to study.

Individual genes often vary in people from different countries and are more likely to be shared by those in the same country. In any one population, however, there may be a variety of versions (alleles) of a particular gene. This is because genes, like languages, slowly change or mutate in small ways over the generations. Mutations can be duplications, deletions, insertions or substitutions and may involve one base pair or many. Once a gene in our germ cells has acquired a mutation, that change will be passed down the generations. Once a mutation has occurred, geneticists can use it as an unique human marker through the ages. If several different mutations happen over the generations in the same stretch of DNA, geneticists may be able to reconstruct a family tree by comparing DNA in different members of today's population.

As with linguistics, these marker techniques are rather better at establishing relationships between similar groups than in dating the branches in the tree. Some genetic mutations are more likely than others and may thus happen more than once, or even revert to the original format. To show that this has not happened, when geneticists compare two identical mutations they may look at the DNA on either side of the mutation in each individual. (This is rather like checking a painting's provenance by the style of the picture frame; I will refer to it in this sense later.) There are two main ways of looking at these individual gene differences. The older method is to look at a product of the genes, such as the protein haemoglobin, the red pigment in our blood cells, which can be analysed. The other approach, technically more difficult but often more informative, is to map the DNA of the gene itself.

Each of our cells has two kinds of DNA: that contained in the nucleus, and that in the mitochondria. Mitochondria are small bodies that swim around in the cellular soup outside the nucleus, and act rather like batteries for the rest of the cell. Nuclear DNA is a vastly longer sequence than that in the mitochondrial DNA. Paradoxically, however, mitochondrial DNA seems to give us better information about our past. The reason for this is that mitochondrial (mt) DNA does not take part in the gene swapping, shuffling and duplication that goes on in the nuclear DNA during sexual reproduction. This casual nuclear genetic promiscuity happens because the duplicate chromosomes from each parent line up with each other after fertilisation and do a *pas de deux* of sorts. This genetic dance, teleologically speaking, could be a 'deliberate' function of the sexual reproductive process – to generate variety and experiment with new genes under controlled conditions. But it makes for blurred gene studies.

Because mitochondria inhabit, and vegetatively reproduce in the cytoplasm, their DNA just divides when they do, like bacteria, and therefore it is not 'shuffled'. When the sperm and the egg fuse, the only member of the bridal couple with mitochondria that can reproduce themselves is the egg. So mtDNA of the resulting offspring is derived only from the mother. Mitochondrial DNA can and does mutate – at a relatively rapid rate as it happens – and provides a purer, more reliable measure of genetic change than the 'mutate, shuffle and splice' of the nuclear DNA. Hence mtDNA is a nearly perfect population marker. Being maternally transmitted, each mutation will be carried through from mother to daughter without change until the next minor mutation. Because the length of mtDNA is quite short, only 5523 'coding triplets' long, it can be fully sequenced if necessary. Geneticists end up with a surprisingly small number of unique 'matrilineal clans', which could soon encompass and classify the entire human population. By building trees based on these clans geneticists will be able to reconstruct with some confidence the mtDNA of our first mother 'Eve'.

There is a part of the nuclear DNA that can never do the genetic *pas de deux* because it does not have a willing dancing partner. This surprisingly, is the male Y chromosome, a nuclear chromosome that geneticists have only just started looking at in depth. Although paired with the female X chromosome during the meiotic division of the sex cells, the smaller un-macho Y keeps genetically to itself. Like mitochondrial DNA, the DNA of the male Y chromosome keeps itself pure during sexual reproduction and transmits only its own genetic image, and, of course, any mutations it has developed over the generations. Y chromosomal DNA or 'Adam' genes thus have analogous marker properties to the 'Eve' mtDNA. Maternal and paternal markers do not necessarily give the same migratory patterns, of course, because women and men have different behaviours. Where colonisation occurs by raiding parties of men in canoes, the maternal genetic make-up of a population may reflect the women of the invaded culture. Further, if women are captured by raiding parties in one location, their mitochondrial markers may involuntarily move elsewhere, independently of the Y chromosomes of their former brothers, uncles and husbands.

With such powerful tools can the whole history of human

migrations be written? There are problems. One major problem that has dogged all genetic studies of early populations, is that there seems to be more variation within populations than between them. In other words, individuals of a population in, say, Borneo are more different from each other than Borneo, as a whole, is from its neighbours. This is more of a problem for nuclear DNA than the Adam and Eve genes. The other hurdles, or confounders, for population geneticists are the forces of evolution. Two of these are, of course, mutation and migration. The others are mathematical irritations and include so-called founder effects, genetic drift, and natural selection.

Founder effects typically happened in the history of colonisation of uninhabited Pacific islands. Small groups of related migrants in a few canoes took with them only a few Adam and Eve genes and other nuclear genes. If, therefore, only five women and five men started up a new island colony, there would have been only twenty copies of any nuclear gene in subsequent generations. The colonists were thus not representative of the population they came from – only a small sample of the home population passes on its genes. Other causes of dramatically reduced breeding populations, or 'bottlenecks', are caused by natural catastrophes such as floods, droughts, cyclones and epidemics. A sudden swell of the sea could have reduced the members of a sailing foray by half. Interbreeding of small island populations then had two effects, which together cause genetic drift. Some of the small pool of genes disappeared, for instance, if all the offspring of one family were the same sex, and others became over-represented, magnifying the difference from the original population. The end result would be a population with a different genetic balance and the loss of some key markers. It can also result in harmful variants that were at a low frequency in the parent population becoming more common.

Natural selection also changes the genetic balance of populations. Some of the mutations used as markers by population geneticists are protective against disease. Those, for example, that affect haemoglobin in red blood cells sometimes also protect against malaria. Individuals with these inherited blood disorders may be less likely to die of malaria, and because they survive and breed, the mutation, and neighbouring genes, increase in frequency in the population. These inherited blood disorders are particularly relevant in studies of migrations in the Indo-Pacific. Because of their high frequency, mutations can be used to follow population movements. Very high frequencies of malaria-protective genes in any given population, however, may simply reflect recent selective amplification of an introduced marker.

The genetic mark of Cain

Before putting my questions to the 'genetic oracle' in detail, I would like to tell an anecdote that illustrates some of these population genetic effects, and is also instructive of migrations in the southwest Pacific. It started off when, during my study time in Papua New Guinea in the early 1980s, I found that many babies born in Madang on the north coast of New Guinea were anaemic. This did not seem to be due to iron deficiency. I found a possible cause of it when we analysed the newborns' haemoglobin. Most of the babies in this Madang study were abnormal. More than 80 per cent of the samples that were examined by electrophoresis had an extra band of abnormal haemoglobin.[3]

It is difficult to convey the excitement that this result produced in me; it was somewhat like finding a new range of mountains. I should first point out that the abnormal haemoglobin was already well known in the literature. It is called haemoglobin (Hb) Barts after St Bartholomew's Hospital in London, which is where it was first demonstrated. What was new was the frequency of this finding. Hb Barts occurs in the umbilical cord blood of babies with alpha thalassaemia. This inherited disorder results from deletion of one or more of the four genes (alleles) that code for alpha globin, an important component of the human haemoglobin molecule. When there is just one deletion of the alpha gene, a condition found in New Guinea, the individual has a haemoglobin level 1–2 grams below the rest of the population and suffers a mild anaemia (See Figure 28). Otherwise the condition is compatible with a fairly normal life. In most individuals with single-deletion alpha thalassaemia, electrophoresis screening will detect it only at birth, not later on in life.[4] Therefore until cord-blood surveys such as mine and then gene mapping were carried out in the tropics, the true incidence of alpha thalassaemia was completely unknown. My study showed not only the highest frequency of the alpha thalassaemia ever recorded, it was the highest frequency for any genetic disorder ever found.[5]

When I returned to Madang from a short home visit to my base in the Liverpool School of Tropical Medicine in early 1981, I had cord-blood electrophoresis results on about half of the group of babies that I was following. Because only a few of the babies did not have thalassaemia, it seemed sensible to find out where those normal ones were. Fairly rapidly it became obvious that babies whose parents were migrants from the central Highland plateau of New Guinea were all normal. These Highland babies did not represent a large proportion of the population of Madang Port. About half of the children originating from the nearby mountains known as the Finisterre Range were also

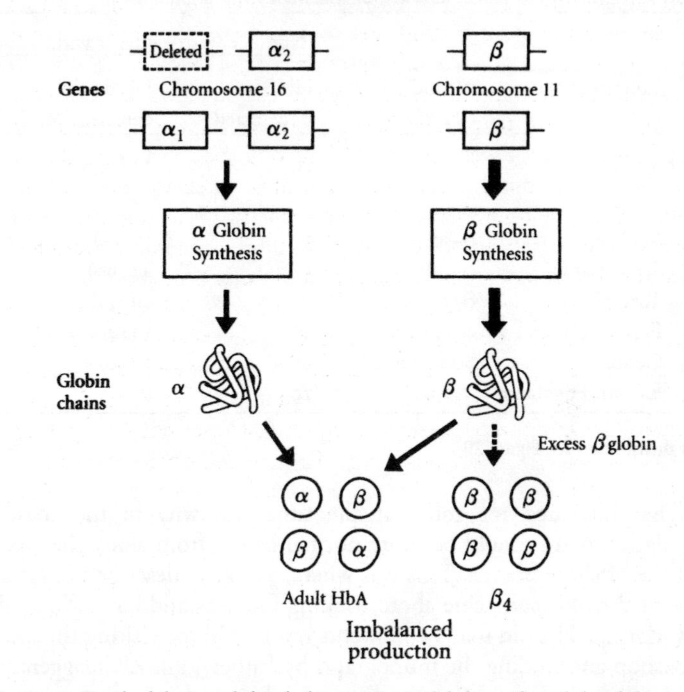

Figure 28. **Single deletion alpha thalassaemia.** A deletion of an alpha globin gene reduces the amount of alpha globin production. The imbalance results in an excess of beta globin over alpha globin production and a mild anaemia (low haemoglobin level in the blood). Either α_1 or α_2 may be deleted and each of the chromosome 16 pair may carry a deletion, thus leaving only two functioning genes.

normal. The remaining normal children came from a strange distribution of villages scattered along the north coast at the very edge of the sea and on some of the offshore islands. Children from inland in Madang province but living in the lowland areas almost all had Hb Barts in cord blood (see Table 2 and Figure 29). The division between the Highlands and the coast seemed to be fairly clear and even at that stage it occurred to me that this might represent a selective effect of malaria; but more of that later.

Table 2. Frequencies of alpha thalassaemia in Papua New Guinea found by testing newborn's blood for the abnormal 'haemoglobin Barts'. Low frequencies found at high altitude reflect absence of malaria in the highlands.

	Language*	Altitude (m)	Number (%) of infants with: Hb Bart's undetected	Hb Bart's detected (%)
Austronesian		0	13	24 (65)
Papuan				
1	Madang	0–500	3	57 (95)
2	Sepik-Ramu	0–500	5	44 (90)
3	Torricelli	0–500	0	2 (100)
4	Finisterre-Huon	0–1500	4	5 (44)
5	Gende	600–1500	3	2 (40)
6	Eastern Highlands	>1500	20	0 (0)

*For distribution see Figure 29.

What intrigued me more at the time was why in the coastal population there should be more normal babies from along the coast and the offshore islands. This was where, as I shall describe in Part II, I heard the old man's clue about looking for the children of Kulabob and Manup. The old man's comments resulted in me visiting the local bookshop and finding the monograph by Father John Z'Graaggen on the languages of the Madang district.[6] This academic work gives a detailed analysis of the 173 distinct and unique languages spoken in Madang province, and also has a very good map of their distribution (see Figure 30). I was immediately able to identify the villages where the babies came from. Those lacking Hb Barts in their cord blood came from villages occupied by Austronesian speakers. These included the offshore islands of Manam, the southern part of Karkar, Bagabag, Long Island and, along the northern coast, Megiar, Matukar, Rempi,

Figure 29. **Distribution of the language groups of the families in the Hb Barts cord blood survey.** Map shows the main linguistic regions of Papua New Guinea from which the families derived. The trans-New Guinea Phylum (groups 1, 4, 5 and 6) represents the main Papuan language family. Austronesian groups inhabit coastal and island areas. Most of the Austronesian families in the study belonged to the so-called 'aberrant' New Guinea language sub-groups discussed in Chapter 5 (lighter shading).

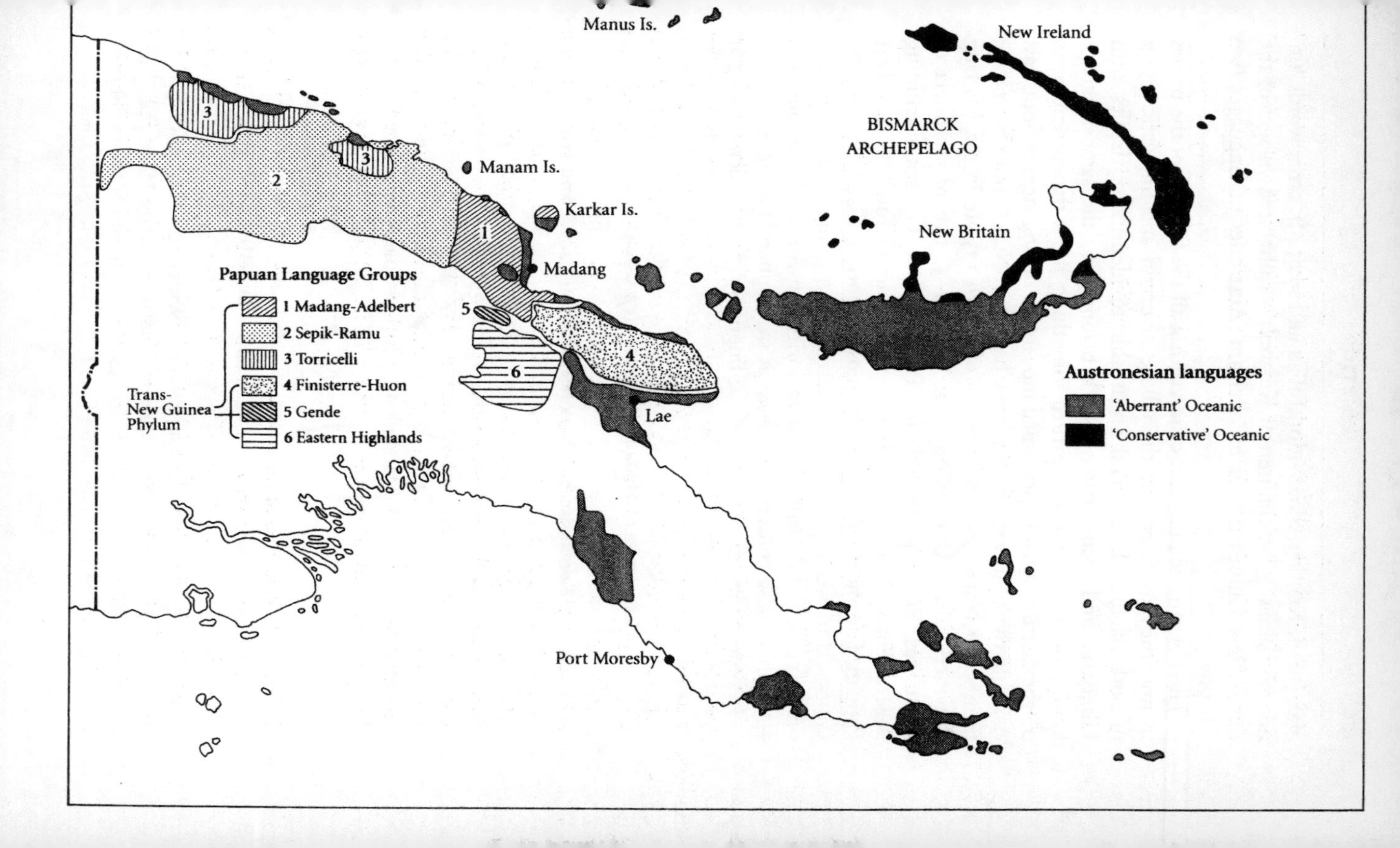

Manus Is.
New Ireland
BISMARCK
ARCHEPELAGO
Manam Is.
Karkar Is.
New Britain
Madang
Papuan Language Groups
1 Madang-Adelbert
2 Sepik-Ramu
3 Torricelli
4 Finisterre-Huon
5 Gende
6 Eastern Highlands
Trans-
New Guinea
Phylum
Lae
Austronesian languages
'Aberrant' Oceanic
'Conservative' Oceanic
Port Moresby

Siar, Bilbil, Kranket, Sio, Saidor, Biliau and so on. In other words, the normal babies – the children of Kulabob – inhabited villages of the north New Guinea cluster of 'aberrant' Austronesian languages (see Chapter 5).

Then began the long task of re-visiting all the families of the babies in my study to determine the village of origin and linguistic group of both parents. In the end I was able to identify 183 babies with Hb Barts, and whose parents both belonged to the same language family. By this time I had learned something about the current views on the distribution and presumed movement of languages in Southeast Asia and the Southwest Pacific (see Chapter 5). New Guinea has a large number of languages – over 750 – of which 173 are in the Madang Province alone. As mentioned in Chapter 5, five major phyla of languages are represented in Papua New Guinea including Austronesian, Trans-New Guinea, Sepik-Ramu, Torricelli and East Papuan. For my purpose here, the most important distinction in New Guinea is between the minority Austronesian group who live mainly on the coast and the others – the majority non-Austronesian languages – which are also collectively known as the Papuan languages.

In order to increase the size of the linguistic groups when looking at

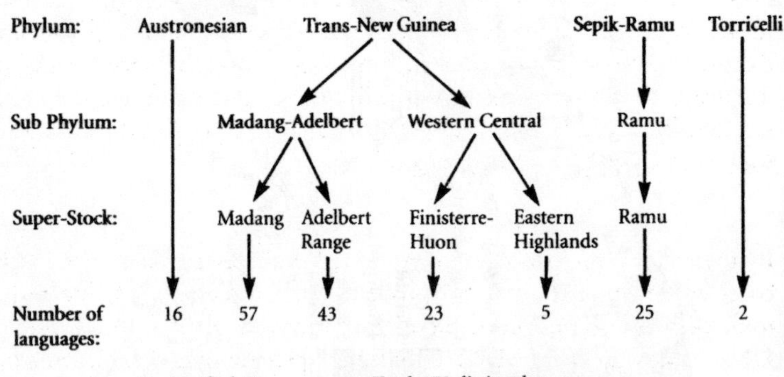

Figure 30. **Languages of the Madang Province, New Guinea.** The majority of the infants in the Haemoglobin Barts study were indigenous to the Madang province. These 173 distinct languages spoken by 250,000 people form a fraction of those in the whole country, yet they derive from four unrelated language families.

the cord-blood results, I divided them into one Austronesian and six non-Austronesian (Papuan) language groupings. The Austronesians, as I have said, occupied scattered villages along the north coast and all around the coast of New Guinea and all the offshore islands. The non-Austronesians consisted of three lowland (1–3) and three Highland groups (4–6). The Madang coastals, numerically the largest of the lowland groups, and the three Highland groups came from populations speaking languages of the largest non-Austronesian family called the Trans-New Guinea phylum. The two other lowland groups belonged to two different language phyla – Sepik/Ramu and Torricelli. Having divided the babies in my study into seven broad linguistic groups, certain patterns emerged. First, all the babies in the three lowland coastal groups (Madang, Sepik/Ramu and Torricelli) had very high rates of Hb Barts in cord blood: 95 per cent for the Madang group, 90 per cent for Sepik/Ramu and 100 per cent for the Torricelli group. Combining these three groups the overall frequency was 93 per cent, much higher than my initial figure. It should be remembered that people from these three lowland populations speak languages as different from each other as English and Chinese. By contrast, all the babies from the Eastern Highlands – linguistically most closely related to the Madang group – were normal. The Austronesian group had rates of Hb Barts intermediate between the non-Austronesian Highlanders and coastals.

There were thus two paradoxical findings: one was that within the non-Austronesian language group the frequency of Hb Barts was inversely correlated with the altitude and not related to linguistic affinities. The other was that within coastal lowland groups a major linguistic division *was* associated with an apparent difference in the rate of Hb Barts. The answer to the second of these paradoxes had to wait until I got back to England in 1983.

By then a lot more people were interested in thalassaemia on the north coast of New Guinea than just myself. When I returned to England I took with me some frozen blood specimens to see if I could obtain DNA maps in the MRC Molecular Haematology Unit in the University of Oxford. There had been a dramatic improvement in the detailed mapping of the sites occupied by the alpha thalassaemia genes on chromosome 16, by the Oxford laboratories. When I visited Oxford from Liverpool with the various bags of frozen blood, one of the senior researchers asked me which bag I wanted results from first. I said that it did not matter, but that he would find alpha-thalassaemia alleles in the bag with the coastal bloods and not in the bag with the Highland bloods. He looked at me strangely, and asked why were the Highlands different? I said because the Highlands have no malaria and would not have selected for the thalassaemia gene. At this wild statement, his expression, which had been mildly patronising, turned to disbelief. He said that they had always found some alpha thalassaemia in any groups of blood from Melanesia: the Highlands were unlikely to be any different. I should point out here that the idea that there was a link between certain abnormalities in the haemoglobin of red blood cells (such as sickling) and malaria protection was not new – the famous Oxford physiologist, J. B. S. Haldane,[7] had suggested as much in 1949. But no one had to that date suggested the same effect for alpha thalassaemia; hence the disbelief.

My boss in Liverpool was rung up urgently two weeks later by Sir David Weatherall, Professor of Medicine in Oxford. It seemed that my prediction of 'no thalassaemia' in the Highland bloods was correct. All the bloods from the coast, in contrast, had some degree of alpha thalassaemia, either heterozygous or homozygous.[8] This exciting finding showed that Highlanders living in an area with no historic records of malaria transmission had zero or very low rates of alpha thalassaemia whereas people living only a day's walk away and mostly speaking languages from the same family had very high rates. On the face of it, this finding supported the malaria hypothesis. We published immediately in *The Lancet*.[9]

Our preliminary report had a major drawback, that my study was small and possibly unrepresentative. The eighteen bloods from the Highlands I had brought to Oxford all came from one province and the thirty-nine coastal bloods came mostly from Madang. Now they had the scent, the Oxford team wanted more specimens, especially from other Highland provinces. Because of my ongoing collaboration with the Papua New Guinea Institute of Medical Research, I went out to New Guinea again in 1984 to collect nearly 600 representative samples from five provinces in the Highlands. This time the result was clear. There was a low frequency of alpha-thalassaemia alleles in each Highland province, this was never greater than 3 per cent. All the coastal malarious provinces had high rates of alpha thalassaemia (see Table 3).

We also got samples for three representative regions of coastal mainland Papua New Guinea: northern, southern and eastern. The specimens from the north coast again confirmed the very high rate (87 per cent). There were lower rates in the eastern coastal region (60 per cent) and in the southern region around the capital, Port Moresby (35 per cent). These graded rates followed the degree of malaria transmission in each region closely.[10] Results from samples taken elsewhere in Melanesia by other collaborators showed the same pattern, but instead of an altitude effect there was a latitude effect. The further south in island Melanesia you go, the colder the climate and the lower the malaria transmission. Concomitantly with the decline in malaria transmission, the rates of alpha thalassaemia in the study fell from 70 per cent in the North Solomons to 12 per cent in New Caledonia in the south.[11] In spite of the clear geographic evidence for protection of alpha thalassaemia against malaria, it has been difficult to work out at the cellular level just how this protection is effected. Just recently, however, a team I set up in Hong Kong to study this problem has come up with a convincing answer; but that is another story.[12]

Table 3. Prevalence of alpha thalassaemia and regional endemicity of malaria in Papua New Guinea. (Areas with high rates of malaria endemicity also have high rates of alpha thalassaemia. This may be due to natural selection.)

Province or region	Percentage with α thalassaemia[§]	Malaria endemicity
North coastal	87	***
Eastern coastal	60	**
South coastal	35	**
Bundi/Gende (highlands)	9	*
Chimbu (highlands)	5	o
Eastern highlands	9	o
Southern highlands	6	*
Western highlands	5	o

§Frequency based on combined heterozygotes and homozygotes; data from Flint *et al.* (1986).[10]

*** intense transmission; ** moderately to highly endemic; * low transmission; o = absent

To return to Madang, we found that there were two kinds of alpha-thalassaemia deletions on the north coast of New Guinea (see Table 4). One of them, the $\alpha^{3.7III}$ type, deletes one of the two genes that encode for the alpha-globin part of the haemoglobin molecule.[13] The $\alpha^{3.7III}$ type constitutes 60 per cent of alpha deletions found in Austronesian speakers of the New Guinea north coast and Bismarck Archipelago. In some instances it does not produce haemoglobin Barts in cold blood, hence the higher rates of 'normals' in coastal villages. It is also the dominant type found throughout the rest of island Melanesia. I call it 'Kulabob's gene' for reasons that will become apparent in Part II. 'Kulabob's gene' is also found in Polynesia, although at lower rates than in Melanesia. It is only found in Oceania. The other type, $\alpha^{4.2}$, deletes the other of the two alpha-globin genes. In Melanesia, this is the dominant type in non-Austronesian speakers, especially of the north coast of New Guinea where it is found either as a heterozygote or homozygote in 76 per cent of the population. It also occurs throughout Austronesian speakers of island Melanesia but is a less common type than the $\alpha^{3.7III}$-deletion. The $\alpha^{4.2}$-deletion is notably not found in Polynesia.

Table 4. Differences between two types of single alpha gene deletion found in northern Melanesia.

$\alpha^{3.7111}$-deletion	$\alpha^{4.2}$-deletion
Distribution:	
Predominant type in Austronesian speakers of the islands and north coast of New Guinea and throughout Oceania	Predominant type in non-Austronesian speakers of the north coast and throughout lowland New Guinea
The only variant in Polynesians	Absent in Polynesians
Occurs nowhere else in the world	Uncommon type elsewhere in the world
Probably a local mutation	Probably a local mutation
Also found in non-Austronesian speakers of island and coastal Melanesia	Also found in Austronesian speakers of island and coastal Melanesia

Our study suggested, then, that there are two alpha-thalassaemia alleles in the Pacific both independently selected for by malaria: one identifies the majority non-Austronesian-speaking population of north coast New Guinea whereas the other, with some overlap, identifies the Austronesian speakers of the north-coast islands, island Melanesia and Polynesia. They thus seemed tailor-made as the Kulabob and Manup genes to correspond with two different ethno-linguistic groups.[14] What powerful migration markers those would be. Unfortunately it proved not to be so simple. In the case of both of these alpha-thalassaemia deletions, the DNA frames they are found on place them very firmly as mutations on local New Guinean rather than Southeast Asian DNA.[15] In other words, the $\alpha^{3.7III}$-deletion may have travelled with Austronesian speakers right out to eastern Polynesia, but it was picked up as a passenger locally somewhere around or off the north coast of New

Guinea. Not only are they local, but these deletions may also be quite ancient. The unique $\alpha^{3.7III}$-deletion has been around northern island Melanesia long enough to acquire a further mutation that produces a variant haemoglobin molecule called Hb J Tongariki, which is found in some people on Karkar Island, off the north coast of New Guinea.[16] These observations confirm that Polynesian ancestors must have stopped at least long enough to intermarry with northern Melanesian populations, and they tell us something more about that supposed genetic interaction. If the Polynesians' ancestors stopped on the north coast of New Guinea long enough to pick up the $\alpha^{3.7III}$-deletion (and some more markers as we shall see) it seems strange that they failed to pick up the $\alpha^{4.2}$-deletion as well because it is present in over 80 per cent of the people living there. The $\alpha^{4.2}$-deletion was carried to the Solomons and Vanuatu and not further into Polynesia. The only possibility – apart from small canoes and extreme founder effects – that could explain this selective genetic divergence in northern Melanesia is that the contact area where the pre-Polynesians took on the $\alpha^{3.7III}$-deletion was offshore from the New Guinea mainland. By offshore we might include the Bismarck Archipelago (Manus Island, New Ireland and New Britain), all places where the $\alpha^{3.7III}$-deletion is the dominant mutation today. But this interpretation would suppose that these sailors bypassed the mainland north coast of New Guinea entirely in their race out to the Pacific 3500 years ago as I suggested in the last chapter. Other genetic markers suggest that maybe that is what happened.

Such an interpretation certainly fits the common archaeological model that identifies the pre-Polynesians with Lapita pottery because with one exception there are no Lapita pottery sites anywhere on the New Guinea mainland. Put another way, although the $\alpha^{3.2III}$-deletion may have originated on indigenous Melanesian DNA somewhere in the Bismarck Archipelago, its subsequent spread out to central Polynesia coincides neatly with the distribution of Lapita pottery sites 3500 years ago. But this interpretation still leaves us wondering who were the ancestors of the people speaking the clusters of Austronesian languages on the north coast and eastern tip of New Guinea coast and who carry both the $\alpha^{3.7III}$ and $\alpha^{4.2}$ markers.

In Chapters 2–5, I argued from archaeolinguistic evidence that the people of northern Melanesia and their 'aberrant' Austronesian languages came out of Southeast Asia over 7000 years ago as a separate migration, long before the Lapita phenomenon. If so, there should be specific evidence of gene flow out of Southeast Asia into the north coast of New Guinea. Clearly such evidence does need to be framed in space and time, because all genetic roads should eventually lead back to the Old World. The evidence does exist, but it points to non-Austronesian as well as Austronesian-speaking tribes of northern New Guinea being the recipients and curators of antique Southeast Asian markers.

One of the striking aspects of any comparisons between the mainly Austronesian-speaking populations of island Southeast Asia today and the Austronesian speakers of Oceania is how little they share genetically and physically. The paradox is even more stark when we look at Austronesian speakers of island Melanesia, who in physical, cultural and genetic terms are closer to (or even indistinguishable from) non-Austronesian lowland speakers of Melanesia than they are to Indonesians, Filipinos and Malaysians. Even Polynesians, who appear so different from island Melanesians, share many physical features and a surprising number of genetic traits with Melanesians (see illustrations 7, 8 and 10).[17]

Susan Serjeantson, a geneticist from the John Curtin School of Medical Research in Canberra, has long argued that several unusual Asian haematological markers found along the north coast of New Guinea are shared between Austronesian and the majority non-Austronesian-speaking lowlanders.[18] These markers, which include some that protect against malaria, are not present in the neighbouring Highlanders nor in most of the island populations of Oceania to the east, but they occur in certain ancient aboriginal populations of island Southeast Asia. The best known of these genetic markers is hereditary ovalocytosis, a blood disorder manifested by oval red cells. In Southeast Asia, ovalocytosis is found in the Palaeo-Hesperonesian-speaking regions of northern Sumatra, the Philippines, eastern Borneo and Sulawesi.[19] It is also found among the Austronesian-speaking Temuans and Austro-Asiatic-speaking Aboriginal groups of the Malay Peninsula[20] and among the Ibans and Land Dyaks of Sarawak in north Borneo.[21] As I discussed in Chapter 5, the last group show an ancient linguistic link over the sea with the Austro-Asiatic Aslian groups of the Malay Peninsula.

This eclectic distribution of the ovalocytosis abnormality includes reputedly some of the oldest Aboriginal groups of Sundaland, but, with the exception of some of the Aslian groups, they are all Austronesian-speaking. In Melanesia the abnormality is mainly confined to the north coast of New Guinea although there is one report from the Solomons. It is notably absent from the Highlands thus indicating it as a post-glacial introduction. The Melanesian distribution of this ancient Southeast Asian abnormality thus excludes the Lapita dispersal areas of 3500 years ago. A measure of the antiquity of ovalocytosis in New Guinea is the evidence that at one point it has moved among non-Austronesian speakers through the mainland from the north to the south coast.[22] On the basis of the ovalocytosis distribution, and some other nuclear genetic markers, Susan Serjeantson argues that the Austronesian and non-Austronesian-speaking peoples of the Madang and Sepik provinces of northern New Guinea together represent a migration discrete from and before the Austronesian migrations to the New Guinea islands. Although she sees the unusual Madang and Sepik gene markers as deriving from the Aboriginal tribes of Southeast Asia (who are, in fact, mainly Austronesian speakers), she argues that this presumably pre-Lapita migration was of people speaking non-Austronesian tongues.[23] Her argument seems to be based on the present numerical majority of non-Austronesian tongues in the north coastal region of New Guinea, although the markers she uses are equally distributed between Austronesian and non-Austronesian peoples of the mainland.

Adela Baer from the University of Oregon has long been looking at similar nuclear genetic links from the Southeast Asian perspective. Five markers, including ovalocytosis, are present in both various Austronesian-speaking peoples of Southeast Asia[24] and non-Austronesian-speaking peoples of New Guinea.[25] Although three of these markers also occur in the Austro-Asiatic Aslian-speaking tribes of the Malay Peninsula, none of them has been found in the Austronesian-speaking Aboriginals of Taiwan. If these mainland New Guinea links indicate a west-to-east flow of genes in Austronesian-speaking Southeast Asians, and Baer stresses the 'if', then the exclusion of Taiwan appears to eliminate the express train to Polynesia migration wave as their source.

We are thus left with the question of why Austronesian genetic markers from Southeast Asia should appear in non-Austronesian speakers of north coast New Guinea. There is no provenance in Southeast Asia either for the Sepik-Ramu language phylum or for the Madang branch of the main Trans-New Guinea phylum. In any case the Highland branches of the latter phylum do not feature the Southeast Asian markers among their speakers. We therefore have to think of Pamela Swadling's suggestion of a 6000-year-old Austronesian immigration to the north coast which subsequently intermarried with non-Austronesian speakers. Some of the descendants lost their original tongues while others still speak the 'aberrant' north coast Austronesian languages. This is the same conclusion reached from archaeological and cultural evidence in Chapters 3 and 5.

Eve's genes

From the evidence I have just discussed, it is possible that some of the older nuclear genetic traits found in Austronesian-speaking Southeast Asians found their way evenly and firmly into non-Austronesian-speaking New Guinean populations as a separate migration long before the Lapita dispersal to Oceania 3500 years ago. In particular, both the Austronesian and non-Austronesian speakers of the north coast provinces of Madang and Sepik form a separate group different from the neighbouring non-Austronesian Highlanders, and may have links with Southeast Asia from before Lapita.

Moving from the promiscuous nuclear DNA markers to the maternal mitochondrial markers ought to bring us a closer view of this ancient migration and even confirm its direction from west to east. Geneticist Mark Stoneking from the University of California at Berkeley, and colleagues from Papua New Guinea have studied mitochondrial (mt) DNA from many mainland New Guineans. They identify at least eighteen 'maternal clans' that correspond with a minimum number of different lineages of founding mothers. This figure is an artificial construct and is not an estimate of the number of unrelated women arriving in New Guinea from Asia over the past 50,000 or more years.[26] Study of diversity within and between these clans helps to determine their relative antiquity. On the basis of Stoneking's genetic tree, these eighteen clans can be re-grouped into six deeply divided groups, the two largest of which are in the New Guinea Highlands and have great antiquity (see Table 5).

The first one of these two indigenous families is made up of Stoneking's maternal clans 1–7. With at least thirty-six different mtDNA types, it characterises the Southern Highlands province and is also common in western New Guinea,[27] but is represented at much lower rates in every other coastal and island region of Papua New Guinea studied.[28] This old New Guinean family, however, does seem to have been picked up and taken out to the Pacific by the Polynesians.[29] Along with its antiquity in New Guinea, the Southern Highlands group has no close relatives to the west in Asia. There are several vague links with mainland Southeast Asia, and a computerised family tree indicates that a common Aboriginal mtDNA type from the Malay Peninsula may be closer to an ancestral form.[30]

The second of the indigenous groups contains only one maternal clan, but at least twenty-six mtDNA types. This group characterises the Eastern Highlands,[31] but is also very common in the neighbouring Southern Highlands Province. Like the latter group, the Eastern Highlands group is found scattered at very low rates throughout the lowlands of Papua New Guinea, although not in any of the north coast Sepik populations studied. This second indigenous Highland group

Table 5. **Deep maternal DNA groupings in New Guinea.** Three groups are indigenous and ancient, the first two being common to all New Guinea populations studied here. Eurasian relatives are genetically distant. The other three, including the 9 bp-deletion, all derive from Asia (since the Ice Age) and are almost exclusively found in lowland and island regions around New Guinea. Although the Asian clans are commoner among Austronesian speakers, they are not exclusive, also being found among lowland Papuans. Numbers are individuals surveyed.

	Indigenous Melanesian clans from Ice Age			Clans introduced from Asia since Ice Age		
New Guinea region	Maternal Clans 1–7	Maternal Clan 10	Maternal Clan 18	Maternal Clan 17	Maternal Clans 8 and 9	Maternal Clans 11–16 (9 bp deletion)
Southern Highlands	23	16	1	0	0	0
Eastern Highlands	7	14	0	0	1	0
North coast (Papuan)	4	1	0	0	0	1
South coast (Papuan)	3	1	0	0	1	3
North coast and islands (Austronesian)	3	4	0	0	0	6
South coast (Austronesian)	1	2	0	1	3	11
Relatives in Southeast Asia (degree of relationship)	Orang Asli in Malay Peninsula (distant)	Orang Asli in Malay Peninsula (distant)	Europe (distant)	Throughout Asia (closer)	Borneo and Malay Peninsula (closer)	Throughout Asia (closer)

Data from Stoneking *et al.* (1990).[26]

again has no close Asian relatives except for two mtDNA types, one found in a Malay individual and the other in a Jeni Aboriginal of the Malay Peninsula.[32] One additional isolated mtDNA type found only in the Eastern Highlands has near relatives mainly in Europe.[33] To summarise, apart from the unexpected European links, the two main Highland groups confirm the great antiquity and relative isolation of the Highlands region of New Guinea from Southeast Asia. Their isolation probably stretches back into the Ice Age, although ultimately they had an Asian origin.

When we turn to the islands and coastal regions in these studies, however, the mtDNA picture shows some intrusions that overlay and partly replace the above two indigenous families. They occur among both Austronesian and non-Austronesian (Papuan) speakers, although more predominantly among the former. That the other four groups of coastal and island maternal clans are more recent multiple intrusions can be seen from their absence from the Highlands, their regionality, and the presence of their many cousins in Southeast Asia. The smallest group, found on the south coast of New Guinea, has one maternal clan (number 17, see Table 5). This may have originated among the Austro-Asiatic-speaking Aboriginals of the Malay Peninsula and then radiated out to Sabah, India, Tibet, Vietnam, Korea and Siberia.[34] Maternal clan 9 is also present on the south coast of New Guinea among both Austronesian and non-Austronesian speakers. Again, the nearest Old World cousin is a Malay mtDNA type from the Malay Peninsula.[35] A further five cousins are found among peninsular Malays and among Sabahans from Borneo.[36] All these latter links, which I discuss in more detail in the next chapter, suggest old immigrations that have become intimately mixed throughout the New Guinea coast and low-lying hinterland.

The Asian deletion

Maternal mtDNA clans 11 to 16 from New Guinea all share a key Asian deletion – the so-called nine-base pair (9-bp) deletion. This Asian deletion is absent in the New Guinea Highlands indicating, again, their relative isolation from the Asian dispersals of the post-glacial period. The 9-bp deletion may have originated in China and is generally not found in Eurasians of non-Asian ancestry. An additional marker identifies a family of Asian migrants that may have spread from Vietnam round the Pacific Rim to Taiwan and America in the north, and Sabah to Oceania in the south.[37] Quite when this particular circum-Pacific radiation occurred is unclear. A date of no less than 6000-7250 BC, possibly much greater, has been suggested for the American wing of spread of this deletion.[38] A recent study in Alaska suggests that the 9-bp deletion reached the Americas well before the arrival of the present circum-Arctic populations of Eskimos, Aleuts and Athapascans, none of whom possess the 9-bp deletion.[39] There is currently a debate about whether the trans-Pacific similarities of the 9-bp variants between Amerindian and Pacific island populations represent evidence for Thor Heyerdahl's South American-Pacific connection.[40] What is under-emphasised in these discussions, however, is the time-depth of the Pacific dispersal implied by the diversity of the 9-bp deletion on both sides of the Ocean. Although all the geneticists quote Peter Bellwood's archaeolinguistic date of the Pacific dispersal of 3500 years ago,[41] their own evidence for dispersal of even the most recent Pacific variants of the 9-bp deletion produces dates well before this and much closer to the American figures.

As I have said, the 9-bp families in both Southeast Asia and Oceania are related to the ancestral American type.[42] This group also includes the commonest types in coastal New Guinea, especially in the south.[43] On the north coast and offshore islands, five other related types predominate.[44] The original Southeast Asian mtDNA type 54,[45] or something very like it, thus appears to have diversified regionally at the same time both on the north coast of New Guinea and in America. The additional evidence of its relative antiquity in America suggests that the New Guinea 9-bp deletion family may also have been in the Pacific well over 5000 years. There is other evidence for this, as I shall show next.

The Polynesian motif

In the last three to four years, additional evidence for such antiquity of the 9-bp deletion in coastal New Guinea has been got from study of another section of mitochondrial DNA called, as it happens, the control region. Geneticists have made much of a variant of the 9-bp deletion found in Polynesians that has three distinct substitutions in the control region. This triple mutation is called the Polynesian motif[46] since it was found at high rates in most, but not all, the Polynesian populations studied, particularly in eastern Polynesia. The Polynesian motif[47] is not, however, confined to Polynesians and also represents 74 per cent of the 9-bp deletion variants found in the coastal New Guineans just mentioned.[48] The highest number of triple substitutions occurs in south coastal New Guinea, among both Austronesian and non-Austronesian speakers. Geneticists have found Polynesian motif substitutions in most lowland places they have looked, not only in

Polynesia but also in Melanesia and Micronesia; in fact throughout the distribution of Oceanic Austronesian languages.[49] So far, the only places outside Oceania where the Polynesian motif has been found as more than a single isolate are the eastern Indonesian islands immediately off the western tip of New Guinea. Here in eastern Indonesia, it features at rates of 20 per cent among both the Austronesian and non-Austronesian speakers in the Lesser Sunda and Moluccan islands of Alor, Flores, Hiri, Ternate and Timor. The Polynesian motif is absent further west in Indonesia, the Philippines, Malaysia and Indo-China. The diversity of the Polynesian motif variant is also at its greatest in the Moluccas (Maluku) and Nusa Tenggara, suggesting the ancestors of that isolated population as the site of its origin. I put this interpretation to Martin Richards of the Oxford University laboratory that has worked on the Polynesian motif. He re-estimated the time of origin of the motif in eastern Indonesians and obtained a figure of some 17,000 years ago.[50]

This distribution of the Polynesian motif thus seems to build some sort of genetic bridge between the linguistic region of Oceania to the east and central Malayo-Polynesian-speaking eastern Indonesia to the west, but it also suggests a different starting point and time of origin of the first Austronesian train to Oceania. The special ticket (Polynesian motif) that was supposed to be held by female Austronesians coming from mainland Asia, and leaving Southeast Asia 3500 years ago,[51] instead has a local Moluccan stamp on it dated 17,000 years ago, and no immediate provenance anywhere to the west of Wallace's Line,[52] let alone in the Philippines, Taiwan or China. Not only is the Polynesian motif confined to the regions of Wallacia that are close to the western Papuan tip, but, as in mainland New Guinea, this presumed Austronesian marker is again evenly mixed into non-Austronesian-speaking islands as well, thus supporting the genetic evidence of much greater antiquity.

The absence of the Polynesian motif in Taiwan, the Philippines and most of western Indonesia and its local antiquity of around 17,000 years in eastern Indonesia are the strongest evidence against the 3500-year-old express train to Polynesia. The hypothesis of an earlier Austronesian maritime expansion out to the Pacific, however, still holds. We have estimated that date of arrival of the Polynesian motif on the north coast of New Guinea from the diversity of its versions found there. The figure comes out at approximately 5000 years ago,[53] which is near the archaeological estimation obtained for the first putative Austronesian settlements in the Sepik province of New Guinea (see Chapter 3). The equivalent genetic date for the arrival of the Polynesian motif further east from Samoa in central Polynesia, is

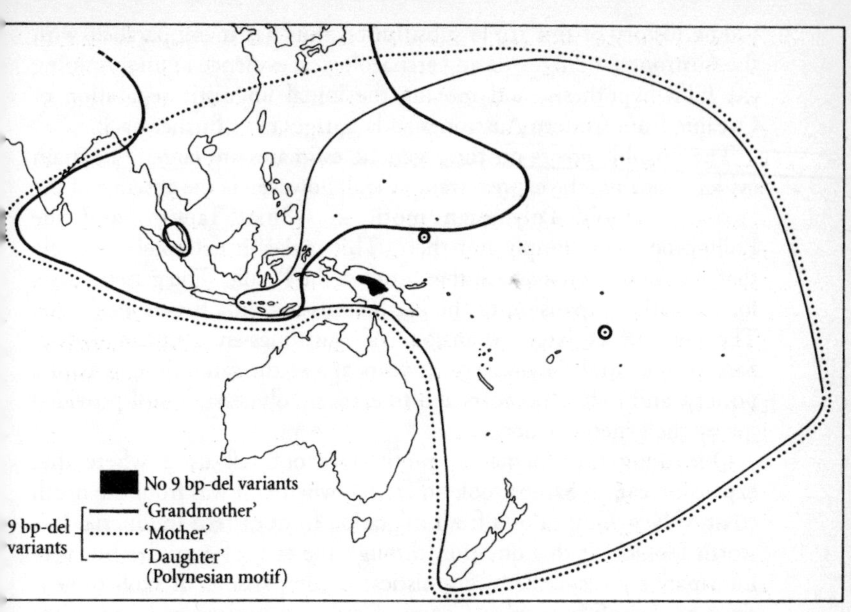

Figure 31. **Genetic history of the 'Polynesian Motif'.** The Polynesian Motif ('Daughter') is the last in a series of three sequential point substitutions in Asian maternal DNA, that already had the 9 bp-deletion. The two previous ancestors in this sequence had, respectively, one substitution ('Grandmother') and two substitutions ('Mother'). Their geographic distributions, while confirming the older Indo-Pacific spread of the mother, show the Polynesian motif to be mainly confined to Oceania and eastern Indonesia and absent from the Philippines, Taiwan and China. Absence of 9 bp-deletions from highlands New Guinea confirms the family as Southeast Asian immigrants. (Geographic distribution data derived from: [46–49])

approximately 3000 years ago.[54] This last figure agrees with the archaeological estimation for the first arrival of Lapita pottery in Samoa 3500 years ago. We calculated the genetic date for the subsequent human dispersal from Samoa to eastern Polynesia at 1000 years, which is again in line with the archaeological estimation of the same expansion of 1500 years ago (see Chapter 3). The genetic dates also correspond well with the linguistic dates estimated by glottochronology for the same dispersals. Those dates were ignored by supporters of the express train to Polynesia theory (see Chapter 5).

The history of this triple substitution thus has many parallels with the Austronesian linguistic and archaeological evidence in undermining the ETP hypothesis, and moving the initial linguistic separation of Oceanic from western Austronesian languages even further back.

The possible errors on these genetic estimates are large. The main evidence against the express train model, however, is the absence of the 17,000 year old Polynesian motif in China, Taiwan, and the Philippines. It is simply not there. This makes it extremely unlikely that the Austronesians took that route to the Pacific. The genetic dates for the earlier expansion to the Pacific thus rest on a firmer local base. The concept of later expansions of Austronesian speakers first to Samoa in central Polynesia 3500 years ago at the same time as Lapita pottery, and then 1500 years ago to eastern Polynesia, is still provided for by the genetic evidence.

One thing the Polynesian motif does not tell us is where that expansion east to Samoa took off from – whether it was from the north coast of New Guinea or a fresh migration from eastern Indonesia. It is worth looking at this question through the eyes of a cruder but very informative measurement. Sophisticated comparisons of skull dimensions have confirmed what Captain Cook first noticed and any visitor can see – namely that Polynesians look alike, somewhat like Southeast Asians, rather different from Melanesians and nothing like the Chinese nor Australian Aboriginals. Anthropologist Michael Pietrusewsky at the University of Hawai'i has refined these studies in Asian and Pacific populations. His findings, plotted graphically, show Polynesians from many locations forming a tight cluster of their own with Micronesians and Admiralty Islanders (see Figure 32). This cluster lies somewhat intermediate between Melanesians and Southeast Asians. The respective extremes are taken up by Australian Aboriginals at one pole and China, Taiwan and North Asia at the other. Significantly, the Asian neighbours who are most like the Polynesians are from the Sulu Sea east of Borneo, and the least alike of all the Southeast Asian groups are the Filipinos. On the other pole, the nearest Melanesians are the Fijians.[55]

The first deduction from this picture would thus be that Polynesians are not recently derived from Melanesia, China, Taiwan or the Philippines, but they could well have originated in Sulawesi in eastern Indonesia. Polynesians share some genetic markers exclusively with Southeast Asians and not with Melanesians.[56] These markers further support the notion of a dispersal of Polynesians out of a local eastern Indonesian population.

Putting all the mtDNA and skeletal evidence together, the simplest model for the late Polynesian expansion 3500 years ago is that it arose

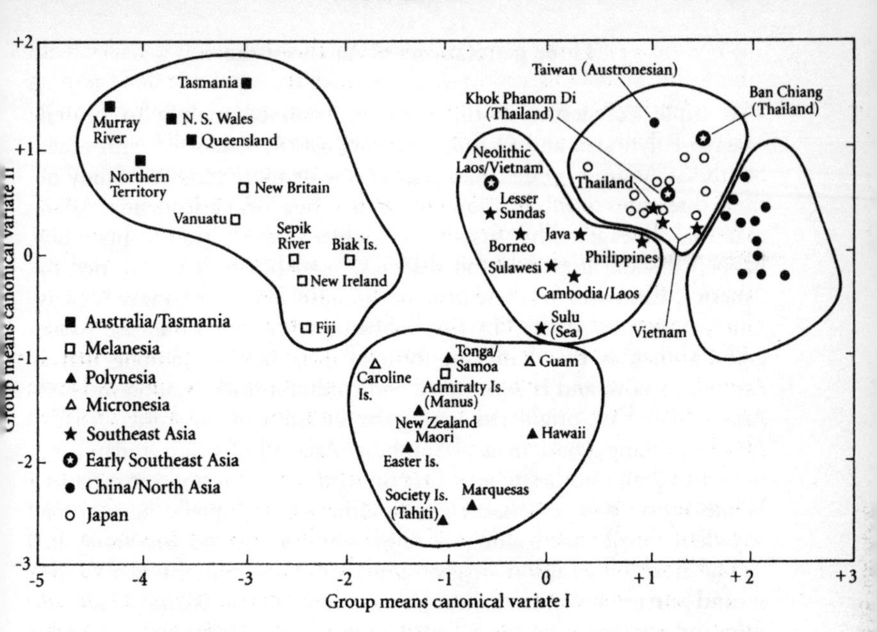

Figure 32. **Physical and genetic relationships can be described by head shape.** Here 28 different head measurements are used, after analysis, to group different populations from Asia and the Pacific in a two-dimensional spread. The clustering of group mean 'points' (solid rings) indicates their degree of genetic closeness. The Polynesian and Micronesian peoples (bottom cluster) are intermediate between Melanesians and Southeast Asians. Their nearest Southeast Asian relatives are in the Sulu Sea and the furthest in Luzon (Philippines). Australia and China (top left and right) are distant. (Adapted, with permission, from Pietrusewsky (1996).[55])

from a pre-existing eastern Indonesian population, moved rapidly east, via the Admiralties, bypassing the north New Guinea mainland but picking up some Melanesian genes before arriving in Samoa. This is the same model that I arrived at from a combination of archaeology and linguistics in Chapters 2–5, and from the alpha-thalassaemia results earlier in this chapter.

The perspective of a 17,000-year-old local eastern Indonesian origin of the Polynesian motif carried by Austronesian speakers to the Pacific now begins to help us unravel the mystery of the Austronesian homeland.

Three generations of Asian mothers

The triple Polynesian motif, although confined mainly to central Malayo-Polynesian and Oceanic speakers, is still connected with other Southeast Asian 9-bp deletions, but at one or more removes. Study of these three sites of substitution reveals that they form a sequential Asian maternal lineage. The first of the three substitutions[57] probably happened soon after the 9-bp deletion,[58] and before it was carried to America. Estimates for these first two mutational events go way back as much as 60,000 years. The first substitution, which I dub the Asian grandmother, is the dominant form of 9-bp deletion among native Americans now, and is widespread and common throughout Southeast Asia. It may have originated among the ancestors of the Austro-Asiatic Aslian-speaking Aboriginals of Southeast Asia, all of whom today have the Asian grandmother type of first substitution, with no later variants. While saying this, the Asian grandmother could equally have arisen anywhere further north along the south Chinese coast 60,000 years ago.

The next substitution in the family produced variant two.[59] The second variant has spread throughout South China, island Southeast Asia and Oceania and even South India. It is thus the most widely dispersed of the three variants in Southeast Asia/Oceania with an epicentre in island Southeast Asia. I call this ubiquitous second model the Southeast Asian mother. Its highest frequency is among Taiwanese Aboriginals, and on this basis, coupled with the high diversity, American geneticist Terry Melton suggests a Taiwanese origin of the Southeast Asian mother from its maternal ancestor the Asian grandmother.[60] The problem with this hypothesis is that some of the Taiwanese Aboriginal populations, such as the Ami, do not have the preceding Asian grandmother frame that is otherwise common in Southeast Asia and throughout the Americas. Such a patchy picture suggests more that Taiwan was the recipient rather than the origin of the Southeast Asian mother. The birth of the Southeast Asian mother from her Asian grandmother is put at 30,000 years ago.[61] This figure, while highly speculative, fits with Johanna Nichols's earliest linguistic estimates for the start of language dispersals round the Pacific Rim. Whatever the real date of birth of the Southeast Asian mother it happened long before the postulated date of arrival of Austronesians into Taiwan from China 7000 years ago, so cannot be used as an argument for that route.

When we look at the distribution of the three maternal generations – the Asian grandmother, the Southeast Asian mother and the Polynesian motif – the key location that holds all three turns out to be eastern

Indonesia (see Figure 31). The older Asian grandmother version, with the single substitution only, has not so far been found in neighbouring Melanesia but is common in eastern Indonesia up to the boundary with Melanesia. The region of the Lesser Sundas and the Moluccas is thus different from the rest of Southeast Asia in that it has all three generations: the Asian matriarch overlaps here with her Southeast Asian daughter and her granddaughter the Polynesian motif with the triple substitutions. This is further evidence of the antiquity of that population.

To summarise, the model of Southeast Asian expansion suggested by the dates of these three sequential mutations is as follows. The oldest of the three Asian 9-bp deletion variants or Asian grandmother may have originated somewhere in Asia up to 60,000 years ago and characterises a circum-Pacific Rim population movement north into the Americas and southeast as far as the Moluccas. The second substitution to produce the Southeast Asian mother happened somewhere in Southeast Asia, perhaps 30,000 years ago, and subsequently also spread throughout southern China, Southeast Asia, and to the Moluccas by at least 17,000 years ago. Finally, the third substitution that produced the Polynesian motif happened around 17,000 years ago in eastern Indonesia and was subsequently carried out to the Pacific by two successive maritime migrations of people who may have spoken Austronesian languages of the Oceanic family. The first of these arrived in northern Melanesia perhaps 6000 years ago, occupied the Bismarck island group and the north coast of New Guinea, and may have spread as far as the northern Solomon Islands.

This first pre-Polynesian Southeast Asian invasion into Melanesia hybridised with local non-Austronesian speakers and over several thousand years gave rise to northern Melanesian coastal and island populations. The subsequent arrival of another wave of Austronesian speakers from eastern Indonesia 3500 years ago carried the Polynesian motif into Polynesia. The introduction of improved sailing technology then allowed the pre-existing hybrid Melanesian populations to colonise the rest of island Melanesia as far as New Caledonia to the south.

Southeast Asians went to Australia

In Chapter 3 I drew attention to archaeological evidence for human and canine introductions into northern and northwest Australia between 8000 and 5000 years ago. Although there is still argument about the Asian region of origin of the dingo, the genetic evidence for origins of the human visitors points mostly to Austronesian populations in Southeast Asia. The best evidence for this comes from the same kinds of nuclear genetic markers that have been used to trace intrusions into New Guinea and Oceania.

Recent genetic surveys of Australian Aboriginals show the northwestern tribes as very different from the more conservative and ancient central peoples. Susan Serjeantson's observation in 1989 that north and west Australia had certain gene markers that were rare or patchy in the New Guinea Highlands raised the question of a Southeast Asian intrusion, bypassing New Guinea, as a possible reason.[62] More recent studies of alpha-globin gene markers have confirmed this surmise. The markers found in northwestern Australia include not only the familiar $\alpha^{3.7III}$ alpha thalassaemia mutation from island Melanesia, but also a Southeast Asian type not present in either Melanesia or Polynesia.[63] These markers point to direct, independent, non-Polynesian intrusions from both island Melanesia and Southeast Asia.[64] Other markers, however, are present in these Australians, and in Polynesians and Southeast Asians but not in Melanesians. These are the same markers that previously identified Polynesians as distinct from coastal Melanesians, and like Southeast Asians.[65]

This welter of inclusive and exclusive genetic links points to possibly three substantial and separate intrusions into northwest Australia. One of these brought genes directly from Southeast Asia, which are not found in Oceania, and the other two brought Melanesian and Polynesian markers. The frequency, nature and penetrating distribution of these markers cannot be explained by sporadic recent Indonesian fishing visitors from Timor. Again the evidence points to more than one Austronesian expansion into the Southwest Pacific.

7
ORANG ASLI: ORIGINALS

The genetic evidence for the spread of people from Southeast Asia round the Pacific Rim points back to two Aboriginal areas, Sabah in northeast Borneo and the jungles of the Malay Peninsula. Part of the reason these areas keep cropping up is the selectivity of the genetic studies that have been done in the past. Sabah, for instance, an Austronesian-speaking region on the eastern tip of Borneo, has received attention because of its location in the supposed region of Austronesian expansion further east from island Southeast Asia. The Malay Peninsula region by contrast has some of the oldest and most diverse representatives of both Austronesian and Austro-Asiatic-speaking populations of mainland Southeast Asia.

Orang Asli – the original Asians

In the Malay Peninsula a group of non-Malay tribal groups live traditional lifestyles in designated areas. Collectively called Orang Asli,[1] they are deeply diverse linguistically, physically and culturally, a fact not always acknowledged or specified in the tabulations created by the big gene labs in the west. An excellent ethnological description of these dwindling peoples is given by Iskander Carey in his 1970s classic *Orang Asli*.[2] Carey, with qualification, divides the eighteen Orang Asli tribes of the peninsula into three very different ethnic groups. These are the Negritos in the north, the Senoi in the middle and the Proto-Malays in the south (see Figure 33). With some misclassification and overlap, the languages spoken by these people can be accommodated in Carey's tri-partite ethnic grouping. The Proto-Malays in the south speak Aboriginal Austronesian tongues; the Negritos in the north speak northern Aslian tongues of the Austro-Asiatic phylum; and the Senoi in the middle speak either central Aslian or southern Aslian tongues of the Austro-Asiatic family. The Austronesian Proto-Malay group in the south of the Peninsula includes the Temuan I mentioned in the last chapter as suffering from high rates of a mild inherited blood disorder ovalocytosis.

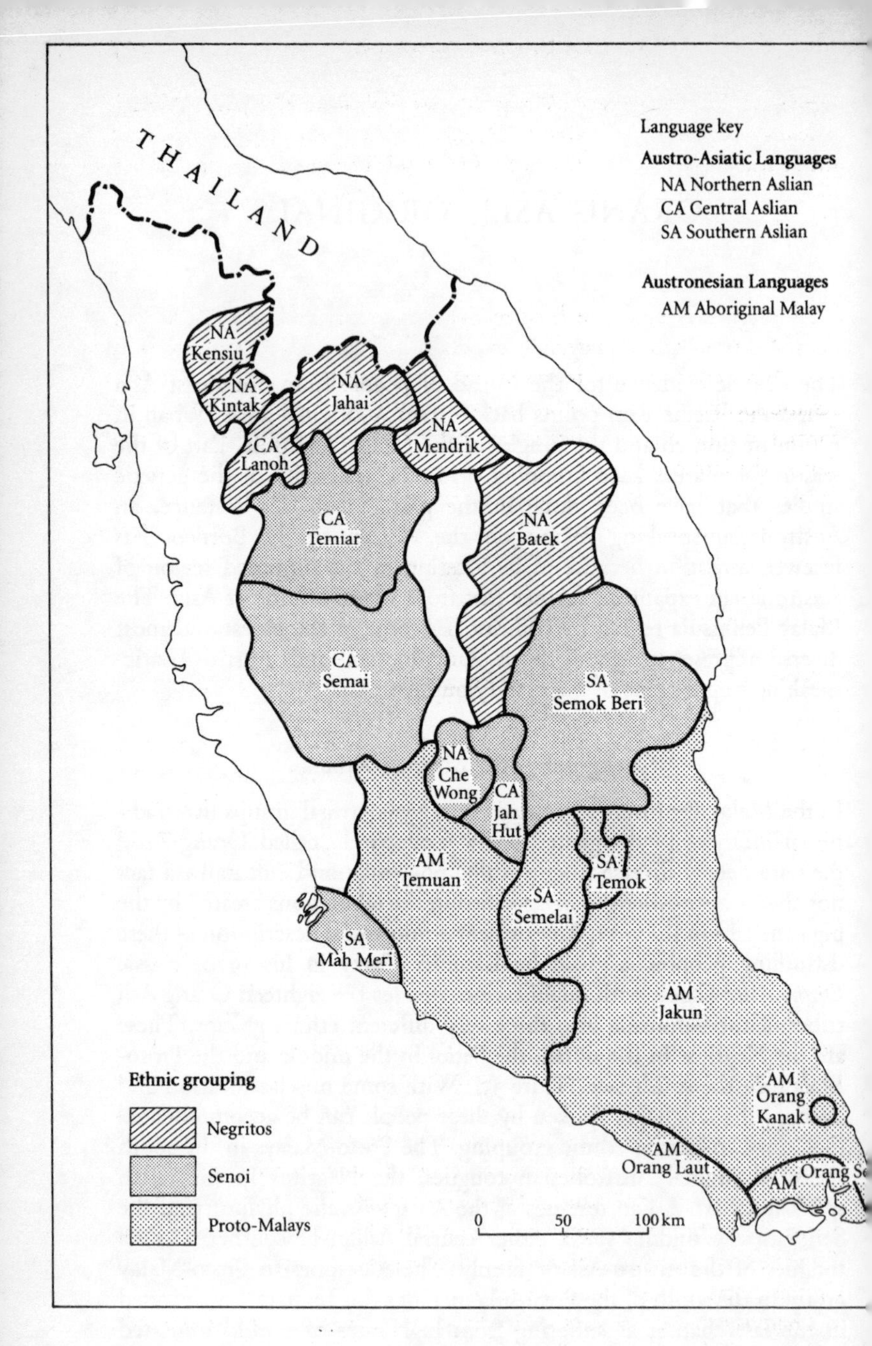
THAILAND
Language key
Austro-Asiatic Languages
NA Northern Aslian
CA Central Aslian
SA Southern Aslian
Austronesian Languages
AM Aboriginal Malay
NA Kensiu
NA Kintak
NA Jahai
CA Lanoh
NA Mendrik
CA Temiar
NA Batek
CA Semai
SA Semok Beri
NA Che Wong
CA Jah Hut
AM Temuan
SA Temok
SA Semelai
SA Mah Meri
AM Jakun
AM Orang Kanak
AM Orang Laut
AM Orang Se
Ethnic grouping
Negritos
Senoi
Proto-Malays
0
50
100 km

Figure 33. **The Orang Asli (Aboriginals) of Peninsular Malaysia.** Although covering a large region, the Orang Asli actually form a very small proportion of the present Malaysian population. Simplified tribal groupings are identified in each area by language and name; physical groupings are shaded. (Adapted from Carey (1976).[2])

Most genetic evidence linking Southeast Asia and the Pacific has come from studies of maternal mitochondrial (mt) DNA mutations in two Aboriginal groups representing, respectively, mainland Austro-Asiatic speakers and island Southeast Asian Austronesian speakers. The former are the middle Aboriginal group on the Malay Peninsula, the Senoi; the latter live in Sabah in northeast Borneo. In these cases three Aslian and two Sabahan representatives nestle at early nodes in the five main Southeast Asian branching networks,[3] with the coastal New Guinea clans that I discussed in Chapter 6 and other Southeast Asian ethnic groups, such as Vietnamese, Malays and Taiwanese, on nearby but later twigs.

This founder location of certain Orang Asli and Sabahan tribes on Asian maternal DNA trees is repeated when we look at the spread north and to the west of Malaysia. A more recent re-analysis of the same Southeast Asian mtDNA types along with many Tibetan and Siberian samples still has Aslian, and Sabahan Aboriginal maternal clans at early nodes of major Asian branches.[4] The Aslian mtDNA type 62, also present in Malays and Taiwanese Aboriginals,[5] was identical with a Tibetan type and apparently ancestral to various Vietnamese, Taiwanese and Sabahan variants.[6] Of particular note among the seven East Asian mtDNA families revealed by this analysis of Antonio Torroni and colleagues, based at the Università La Sapienza in Italy, were their clusters B and F, which had clear roots in Southeast Asia.[7]

Cluster B is defined as those with the Asian 9-bp deletion and, as previously mentioned, spreads from Melanesia round the Pacific Rim to the Americas. As in the local Southeast Asian analysis, Torroni's tree, which includes Tibetans and Siberians, still has the same Sabahan mtDNA type[8] at the root of the branching cluster. This ancestral type is shared with the equivalent nodal type in Amerindian[9] and coastal New Guinea[10] populations. An Aslian type[11] is found nearby on Torroni's B branch, somewhat closer to the ancestral node than Taiwanese Aboriginal, Korean, Sabahan, Malay, Tibetan and southern Chinese types on the same cluster.

There is other evidence that could place the Senoi at the geographic epicentre of the spread of the ancestral Asian 9-bp deletion type round

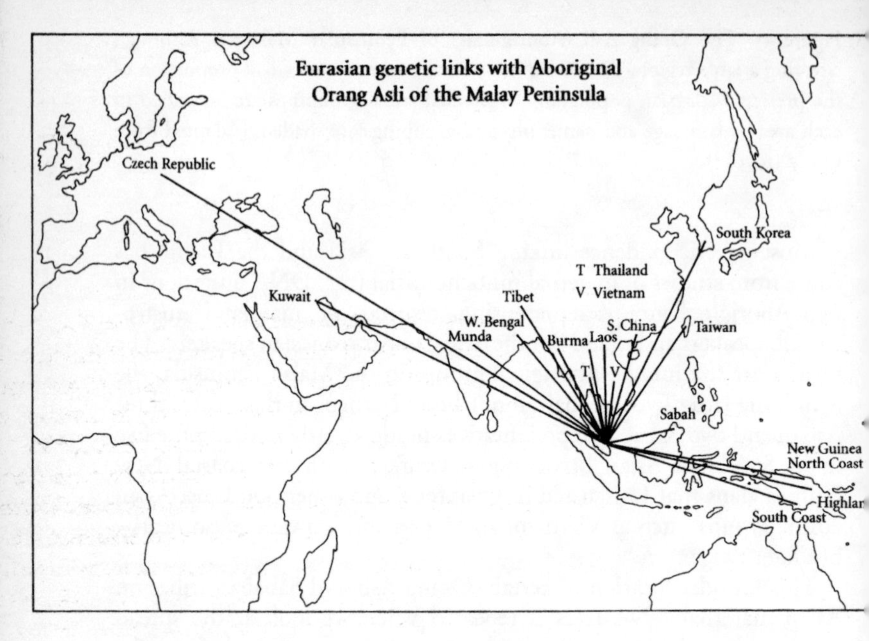

Figure 34. **Eurasian genetic links with Orang Asli (Aboriginals) of Peninsular Malaysia.** Solid lines indicate specific genetic marker links, both nuclear and mitochondrial, identified in Chapters 6 and 7. For reasons of space, markers mentioned in the text (and Asian countries) are not identified on the map.

the Pacific Rim and up the great rivers into Tibet. This comes from the analysis of the three substitutions in the control region of mtDNA which I noted earlier. In Terry Melton's 1995 study the oldest version of the 9-bp deletion or Asian grandmother is the only type present in the Austro-Asiatic-speaking Senoi population, while later variants are admixed in varying proportions in other Asian groups: 90 per cent of these Aboriginal grandmother types are also the commonest 9-bp deletion variant throughout Southeast Asia.[12] This combined evidence suggests the Austro-Asiatic-speaking Senoi of the Malay Peninsula as a possible ancestral focus for all Asian populations with the 9-bp deletion.

Melton's study also shows the Asian grandmother type penetrating along with her daughter (the Southeast Asian mother) into southern Indian populations. Further probes show, however, that the southern Indian grandmother types are not identical with the Orang Asli types.

1 Post-glacial land-raising in Canada. When the Canadian ice-plates flushed off the continent at the end of the Ice Age, the release in pressure allowed the land to rise rapidly. This aerial photograph of the eastern end of Bear Lake in the North West Territories, taken from 3,000 metres, shows multiple raised shorelines. The present shore is seen top right.

2 Stilted huts, with and without water, are a feature of all Southeast Asian communities. These may originally have been an adaptation to flooding. Like an eastern Venice, the town of Sitankai, shown here, is built in the middle of the Sulu Sea on a submerged reef. Everything, including water, is traded. The ship's steward (profile on right) rescued the author and his fiancée from the attentions of the military.

3 Visitors from the east? Terracotta figurine of the type found in graves just above the flood silt layer at Ur in Mesopotamia (4th millennium BC). Features, which might suggest an east Asian origin, include the mongoloid slant, tattoos and raised welts around shoulders. The majority are female. The male versions have been likened to Egyptian representations of Osiris.

4 Cave wall-paintings of the 'Boats of the Dead' motif. Found in Niah cave, Sarawak, Borneo, above the post-glacial high-water level of 5,500 years ago.

)

5 Ceremonial bronze axes: (a) from Jonokom island, Lake Sentani, Irian Jaya, unknown date; (b) from Roti island, eastern Indonesia, unknown date. Although a connection with the Dong-Son bronze culture of Vietnam (c. 500 BC) is suggested for (a) and (b), the designs are closer to those of Lapita pottery (1500 BC); (c) Galstad Axe, Goteborg, Sweden (c. 800 BC).

(b)

)

6 Mancala or Chanka, an ancient board game found all round the Indian Ocean from Africa to East Asia. Usually carved in wood, the game is also found on ancient megaliths in Turkey, East Africa, eastern Indonesia and here near Bukittinggi in Sumatra.[78 (chap.3)]

7 A Melanesian man, from Lou island in the Admiralty islands of New Guinea, holds an obsidian (volcanic glass) knife fashioned and hafted by his father. His ancestors were trading this valuable commodity with Borneo, 3,500 kilometres to the west, up to 6,000 years ago.

8&9 A peninsular Malaysian woman at work in a traditional potting village in the interior of Kelantan State. Techniques include slow-turning wheel, low-temperature firing, black burnish and dentate decorative markings on finished product (above right). Similar patterns are carved on masks and ceremonial spears from the Sepik river in New Guinea.

10 An ancient Austronesian craft. A Polynesian woman in Tonga beating softened bark to make bark-cloth.

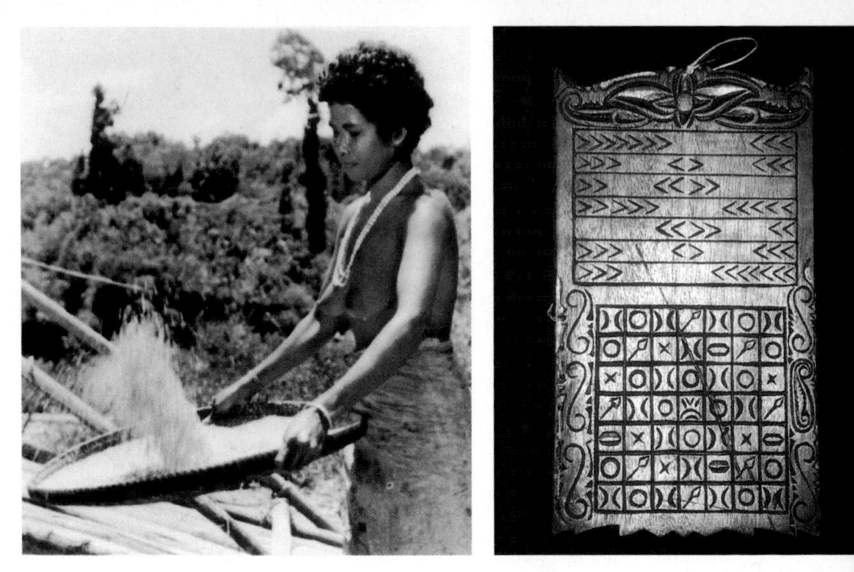

11 ABOVE LEFT Temiar girl winnowing hill rice (aboriginal of the Senoi ethnic grouping in Perak State, West Malaysia). Did her ancestors grow the first domesticated rice?

12 ABOVE RIGHT A hunting almanac of the Benuaq Dyaks of east Kalimantan, Borneo. This divides both the day and the week into seven parts, and indicates propitious times for certain activities. More elaborate 360-day lunar almanacs can be found all over Borneo and Sumatra.

13 Author with Batek guides 1990, in Taman Negara (aboriginals of the negrito ethnic grouping in Pahang and Kelantan State, West Malaysia). Although earning money as guides, these people still have a mainly hunter-gatherer lifestyle.

Shadow puppet-master (*tok dalang*) Hamzah Awang Amat performing the *Ramayana* at the
thor's home in 1990 (Kota Bharu, Kelantan State, West Malaysia). Such Hindu epics, first written
wn over two thousand years ago, are still accurately passed on by word of mouth by the shadow-
ppeteers of Southeast Asia.

Prehistoric megaliths of Europe have their counterparts throughout Southeast Asia and the
cific rim. Here a dolmen (a flat stone supported by two or more upright boulders) is found deep
and in Borneo. The dolmen covered a grave – excavated bottom right.

16 Wain and followers. In the two-brother myth version of Angoram on the Sepik river of New Guinea, the role of cuckold is taken by their paramount ancestor, Wain. After Wain's brother Mopul escapes from the men's house through the hollow central pole, he sabotages Wain's canoe so that it sinks. (Incised bamboo, Kambot village, Papua New Guinea.)

Instead, the South Indian population shows great diversity in that they share six different 9-bp deletion types with those found in nearly every other region of Southeast Asia and South China *except* the Malay Peninsula.[13] These links are predominantly with peoples of island Southeast Asia speaking Austronesian tongues. As there seems to be no other evidence for the 9-bp deletion so far west in Asia, the shared mtDNA types must reflect migration from these regions westwards to Sri Lanka and India rather than the other way round. Notice, however, that the migrations appear to come more directly from Austronesian-speaking stock than from Austro-Asiatic-speaking Aboriginals of Southeast Asia, and perhaps a very long time ago in view of the local South Indian diversity.

The picture for Antonio Torroni's other Southeast Asian maternal mtDNA cluster F tells us more about Austro-Asiatic expansions. The broad picture for group F[14] mtDNA links with the rest of Asia is generally similar to that for group B, except that for F the evidence points directly to the Aslian Austro-Asiatic speakers rather than Austronesian speakers as an early and separate source of migrants west, east and north. Group F has two Orang Asli maternal marker types right at its root.[15] The rest of the twigs of this branching cluster are mainly composed of Vietnamese and Tibetan types, although there are a couple from Malays, a Korean and a Siberian. The genealogical primacy of the Aslian types over the Vietnamese in this group supports the archaeolinguistic theory that there was a southerly homeland of Austro-Asiatic speakers with spread north to the Mon-Khmer speakers of Indo-China.[16] Another prediction of this southern homeland hypothesis was that the Mon-Khmer speakers in the eastern foothills of Tibet are refugees rather than stay-at-homes (see Chapter 4). This is also supported by the genetic tree.

The final prediction of the southern Austro-Asiatic homeland hypothesis is that the migration of Austro-Asiatic speakers to India went through the Strait of Malacca shortly after the rising sea opened it over 8000 years ago. We would, on this argument, expect to see genetic evidence in north India linking back to the Orang Asli groups in the jungles of Malaya. Such is the case: the mtDNA marker 72[17] characteristic of the Austro-Asiatic Aslian speakers is present in northern but not southern India. A recent analysis of Indian mtDNA types reveals not only multiple East Asian intrusions into the Indian subcontinent, but a clear north–south division as well. Another conclusion from this latter study is that the antiquity of East Asian mtDNA markers in India suggests a very ancient migration west.[18]

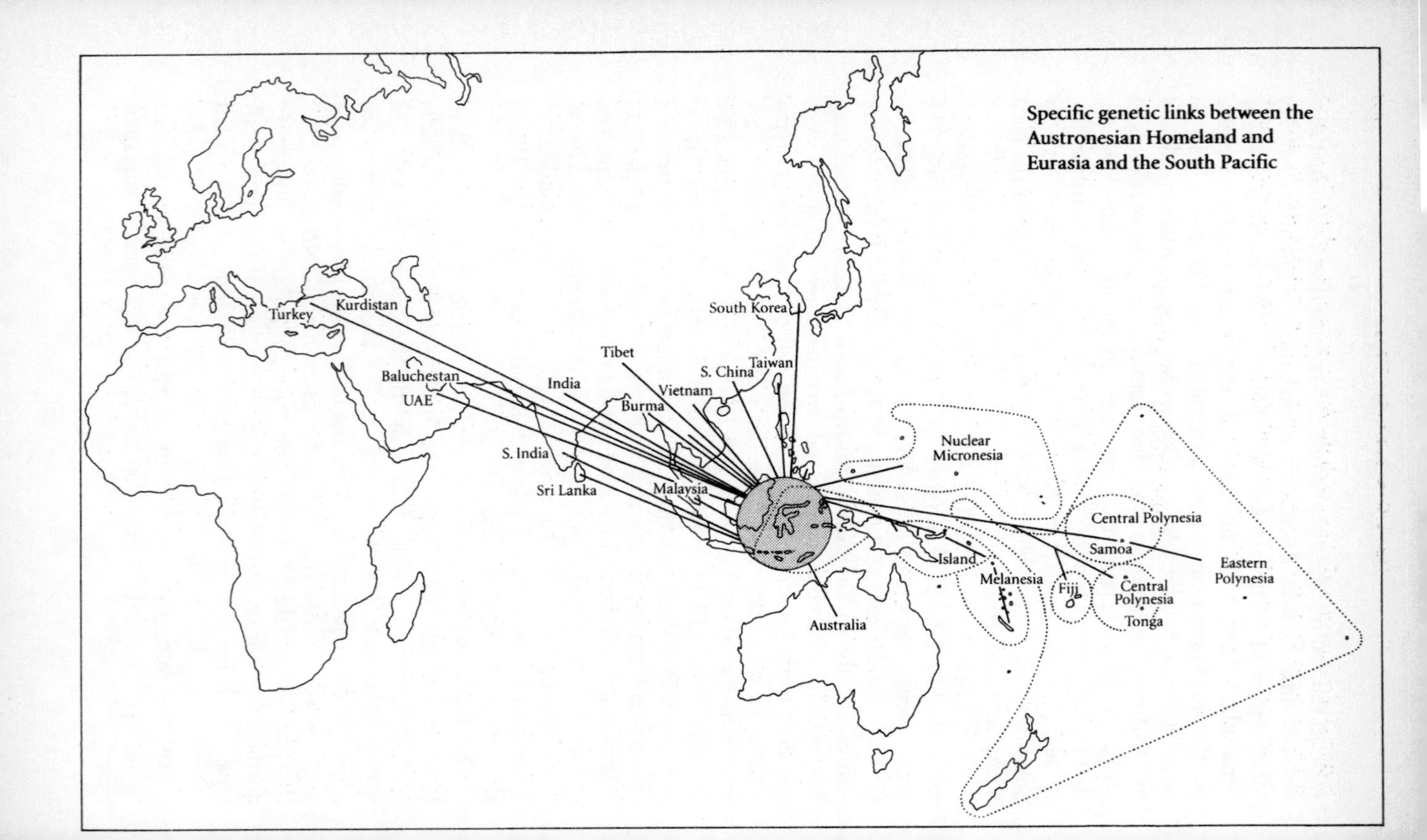
Specific genetic links between the Austronesian Homeland and Eurasia and the South Pacific
Turkey
Kurdistan
Baluchestan
UAE
India
Tibet
S. India
Sri Lanka
Burma
Vietnam
S. China
Taiwan
South Korea
Malaysia
Australia
Nuclear Micronesia
Island
Melanesia
Fiji
Central Polynesia
Samoa
Central Polynesia
Tonga
Eastern Polynesia

Figure 35. **Eurasian genetic links with the Austronesian homeland.** Homeland, shaded area, as discussed in Chapters 3 and 5. Lines indicate specific genetic marker links, both nuclear and mitochondrial, as identified in Chapters 6 and 7. For simplicity, markers are not identified on the map.

Mothers and fathers move west?

The F maternal mtDNA cluster as defined by Torroni and colleagues,[19] also has two isolated cousins among Caucasian types (those in Europe, the Middle East and most populations in the Indian subcontinent). One of these comes from a group of Swedes and Finns.[20] There is another Asian echo in Scandinavia.[21] Generally Caucasian populations have completely different mtDNA from East Asians, but independent evidence of Asian intrusions into Arctic Europe comes from the paternal or Adam's Y chromosome. Tatiana Zergal at the University of Oxford along with her colleagues have linked a unique Asian Y chromosome mutation present in Uralic-speaking populations in central Asia to the linguistically related Finns, Estonians and Saami (Lapps) in northern Europe and Mari in northwest Russia.[22] Several examples of the mutation also crop up in Norway, suggesting local spread into Norse-speaking populations. From the distribution of the mutation Zergal and her colleagues speculate an origin in the Mongolia/China region. One individual has even been found in Japan on the Pacific Rim. Their model suggests that an originally Asian migrant group of males from central Asia retained their Asian language and male chromosomes but replaced much of their nuclear genetic characteristics with European genes in Finland, Estonia and northwest Russia. The Saami, who can be traced back by rock engravings to 4200 BC, may be genetically the closest survivors to the first migrants from the East. A shamanistic culture, their legends record such migrations.[23] Finnish mythology, as seen in their epic *Kalevala*, has clear Asian and Pacific echoes.[24] Clearly those Asian genes linger on in a much wider distribution of northeast Europe.

Curiously the Y chromosome evidence explains the remarkable difference in appearance between the Europe-based Finno-Ugric speakers and their linguistic cousins the Uralics from central and north Asia – presumably because of the dilution of Asian nuclear genetic characteristics in the former. There are other mtDNA links between the Asia-Pacific region and Europe, but these are tenuous and need further study.[25] The whole issue of Asian intrusions to Europe during the Neolithic and Bronze Ages, as evidenced by pottery styles and 'round-headed' skulls, has a long history and remains controversial. It is outside the scope of this book.

I can now summarise the evidence from the Adam and Eve genetic markers for an east-west spread as follows: the Asian 9-bp deletion was carried to south India by the Southeast Asian mother, a woman who may have spoken an Austronesian tongue. The group F maternal clans in Antonio Torroni's classification, which are more clearly linked to Austro-Asiatic speakers of the Asian mainland, spread radially north into Indo-China and Tibet, and west into north India, as suggested by the model in the previous chapter. The maternal and paternal trails suggest possible further spreads of these people into Europe, either via India or through central Asia. The hottest trails in this respect are those to Finland and Sweden.

This suggestive evidence from the celibate Adam and Eve genes is amply supported by study of the more promiscuous and prolific nuclear genetic markers. Again, some of the best population-based evidence comes from the genes coding for the haemoglobin molecule that carries the oxygen in our blood.

The thalassaemia belt from Asia-Pacific to Europe

Haemoglobin contains four protein subunits like coiled chains known as globins. In adult haemoglobin these are made up in sets of two alpha globins with two beta globins (see Figure 28). Mutations in the genes responsible for these two globins and several other types can be used as population genetic markers. In some ways there is an excess of information on the geographic distribution of mutations in the globin genes. Studies are mostly on mutations of the alpha- (α) and beta- (β) globin genes that cause thalassaemias, a group of inherited blood conditions, which, as we saw in Chapter 6, cause varying degrees of anaemia. Maps of the spread of the alpha and beta thalassaemias resemble the maps of distribution of the Genesis myths which I will describe in Part II. Although some of the thalassaemia distributions include Africa separately, Amerindians are unrepresented and the affected regions are spread in a band from the South Pacific in the southeast, through Southeast Asia, south China, India, Arabia, the Middle East and finally into the Mediterranean in the northwest.

Most of these mutations were naturally selected for in the past because they increase the ability of the carrier to resist malaria. Therefore much of the east–west thalassaemia band is defined by the historic distribution of the disease in Eurasia. Malaria is, in turn, dependent on tropical and sub-tropical temperatures, combined with adequate

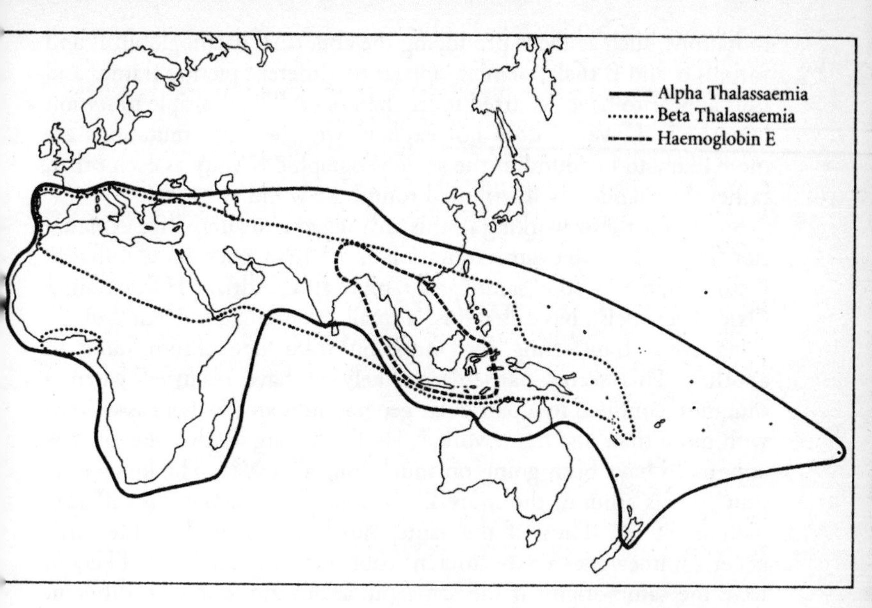

Figure 36. **Alpha and Beta thalassaemias and Haemoglobin E.** Distribution of the commonest defects of haemoglobin genes in Asia. Note that each of the three overlapping areas contains a number of variants. Specific trans-continental links are identified in the text and in Figures 34 and 35.

rainfall; these regions were also natural recipients of Neolithic coastal migrations. From this point of view it would be difficult to determine whether the similar southeast–northwest distribution bands of the Genesis stories, the structural language links and the mutations are coincidental or reflect a common migration pattern.

The unique nuclear globin mutation markers ought to help here. They do, but there are many different markers causing thalassaemia. Well over a hundred β-thalassaemia markers have been described, and more α-thalassaemia defects are being discovered all the time. With such a powerful selective force exerted by malaria, there is a chance that some of the more common population genetic markers may have occurred by mutation more than once. This could render the use of geographic links between markers to prove migration routes fallacious in some circumstances.

The strength of this multiple-mutation argument varies with the type of mutation, and is to some extent an imponderable. Certain mutations, such as those producing the abnormal haemoglobin E and various α and β thalassaemias, appear on different picture frames and thus appear to have occurred more than once. The multiple mutation hypothesis, however, does not explain why the same mutations are more likely to be found in the same geographic vicinity as each other, rather than randomly distributed round the world.

Some geneticists working in this area suggest an alternative explanation for finding the same mutation more than once on a different picture frame in the same geographic area. Adrian Hill, another Oxford geneticist, has called this: 'a small recombination (gene conversion) event transferring the mutation from one chromosome to another. This seems particularly likely to have occurred when a mutation confined to a particular geographical area is there associated with more than one framework.'[26] He further argues that this process appears to have been going on much longer in Asia. The longer any mutation is around, the more likely copies of it appear in different picture frames. Thus, if the same mutation is found in the same genetic framework in two different countries, they are highly likely to have the same origin; if the same mutations are found on different picture frames, it is still possible they had a common origin but a long time ago. In spite of this sleight of chromosome, there are sufficient instances of the same mutation on the same framework, linked across the Indian Ocean, to make a case for substantial ancient Southeast Asian intrusions into Assam, west Bengal, Andhra Pradesh and on to the Arabian Gulf and the Mediterranean.

Beta thalassaemia connections from Southeast Asia to Europe

One of the oldest β-globin gene mutations to have been used to follow Southeast Asian migrations radially outwards is that causing the abnormal Haemoglobin E trait (HbE), which may protect against malaria. Found in over 30 per cent of Austro-Asiatic speakers in Indo-China and among the Austro-Asiatic-speaking Senoi Aboriginals of the Malay Peninsula, HbE is usually regarded as a marker for the Austro-Asiatic language group. This view is reinforced by finding much lower rates among Austronesian-speaking Aboriginals, such as the Temuan, of the same malarious Malay Peninsula jungles. The latter Austronesian group are more noted, by contrast, for their high rates of hereditary ovalocytosis, as I mentioned in the last chapter; I suggested that this disease was imported east into north coastal New Guinea.

On the broader regional basis in Southeast Asia, Lie-Injo Luan Eng, working in Kuala Lumpur, Malaysia, showed back in 1969[27] that although HbE is found at relatively low rates throughout southern China and island Southeast Asia, nowhere does it reach the same uniformly high rates as in the Austro-Asiatic speakers of the Malay Peninsula and Indo-China. An exception to the rather low rates found among the Austronesian-speaking Malays occurs among the Kelantanese on the east coast of the peninsula close to the Thai border and to the Austro-Asiatic Aslian speakers. I once worked in Kelantan for two and a half years in a medical school, and came to know the unique local culture. The Malay-speaking population of Kelantan has an HbE rate of 40 per cent and more genetic and cultural links with southern Thailand than with the Malays further south.[28] Kelantan is also not far south from the ancient Sakai Cave which had an early date for rice cultivation.[29] It also possesses some of the oldest cave remains found in Southeast Asia.

The HbE mutation is found on at least two genetic frameworks (2 and 3). The location on framework 2 has several varieties among Austro-Asiatic speakers, and is thought to be older. The location on framework 3 is found in Kampuchea where that frame is particularly common, and is again thought to be an example of the gene conversion mentioned above.[30] Thus the types found among the Orang Asli Aboriginals may well be the ancestral form.

One anomalous feature of the spread of HbE west out of Southeast Asia are the high rates noted among some Tibeto-Burman-speaking tribes of Assam and Arunachal Pradesh. These contrast with lower rates in some neighbouring Austro-Asiatic-speaking tribes of eastern India, such as the Khasis. This interlanguage spread does not cast too much doubt on the Austro-Asiatic provenance of the HbE mutation here because it is found on the older frame 2 and the same frames, as in the Austro-Asiatic speakers further east.[31] The high rates in a different language group and low rates in Khasis suggest, first, that there was migrant intermarriage in the past and, second, that enough time had elapsed for differential malaria selection in the new hosts to reverse the HbE gene frequencies between the two language groups.[32]

There are several implications of these results. First, migration of Austro-Asiatic speakers out of Southeast Asia and west through Bengal also penetrated north up to Arunachal Pradesh and Assam. Second, the malaria-selective reversal of gene frequencies suggests that this was a long time ago. Third, because the Tibeto-Burmese tribes, such as the Bodos, were the recipients of HbE, they must *also* have been in India a long time ago. This supports the hypothesis I outlined in Chapter 4 that their homeland was southerly, and somewhere around the mouths of the Salween or Irrawadi rivers. If the Tibeto-Burman languages did migrate north into Tibet up those rivers or even up the Brahmaputra from Assam, we might expect to see HbE in Tibet. Haemoglobin surveys in Tibet have indeed shown low rates of HbE in the main Tibetan population, but higher rates in the MenBa and LuoBa minorities on the border with Arunachal Pradesh and Bhutan. The genetic trail here also explains why flood myths are found in Tibet, particularly among the Kuki minorities.[33] HbE is also present in varying frequencies further west in India through west Bengal[34] and into Bihar.[35]

Not confining itself to the Austro-Asiatic language dispersal into northern India, haemoglobin E has spread further west into the Arabian Gulf region, being found in Kuwait,[36] and even in former Czechoslovakia. In this last case the mutation is definitely on a local framework.[37] This and other European occurrences of HbE have been regarded as new mutations because of the frame change, although Adrian Hill's gene-conversion explanation is an alternative.[38]

In contrast to the finding of isolated instances of HbE on local frameworks in Europe, the β-thalassaemias in Southeast Asia show mutations that turn up on the same frameworks across the Bay of Bengal and spread out westwards, even as far as Turkey. If we only look at mutations that share the same beta picture frame, and are thus firmly related, there are five Indian variants derived from Southeast Asia; one Southeast Asian variant has even been found as far west as Kurdistan. There are ten variants linking Burma with its eastern neighbours.[39] One variant, which was the dominant mutation in a survey of Vanuatu (Melanesia), also occurs in China, Indonesia and Turkey on the same picture frame.[40] This widespread Southeast Asian mutation is also particularly common among Arabs of the United Arab Emirates and among Baluchis of Baluchistan, western Pakistan.[41] Mutations of the β-globin gene thus support the view that the thalassaemia belt from the Pacific to the Mediterranean is not just a coincidence of malaria and people, but may also mark an ancient trail of migration or trade.

Alpha thalassaemia connections from the Pacific to Europe

As mentioned earlier, the commonest group of genetic defects in the world are the α-thalassaemias caused by single-gene deletions. Although they show a broad resemblance from East to West, however, they give less clearly defined information than the β-thalassaemia variants. Four α-thalassaemia mutations cause most of these defects over a wide area, including Africa and the band of countries from the Southwest Pacific through Southeast Asia, India, the Middle East to the Mediterranean. These are deletions of 4·2 ($-\alpha^{4.2}$) and 3·7 ($-\alpha^{3.7}$)

kilobases long, respectively. The 3·7-kilobase deletion has three subtypes $\alpha^{3.71}$, $\alpha^{3.711}$ and $\alpha^{3.7111}$. I discussed two of these four ($\alpha^{3.7111}$ and $\alpha^{4.2}$) in relation to migrations in Oceania in Chapter 6. The -$\alpha^{4.2}$ deletion has a wide distribution from the Pacific through to Saudi Arabia,[42] although the highest rates have been found in the north coast of New Guinea and in India. The deletions $\alpha^{3.711}$ and $\alpha^{3.7111}$ both have very localised distributions respectively in the Indian subcontinent and in the Pacific, and the $\alpha^{3.71}$ deletion is very widespread throughout Africa and from the Pacific to the Mediterranean.

I explained earlier that β-globin gene mutations might skip from one chromosome to another. Because these large alpha deletions occur on different picture frames, and such deletions cannot easily be related in the same way as the β-globin point mutations, some geneticists think that each of these occurrences imply separate mutational events. It seems, however, that something analogous to the β skips can happen with alpha deletions. Ricardo Fodde, a geneticist working in Leiden in the Netherlands, has, with his colleagues, given strong evidence for this among isolated tribal groups in southeast India. Intratribal marriages (or endogamy) over a very long time may have contributed to the large number of different picture frames for the same three α-thalassaemia mutations ($\alpha^{3.711}$, $\alpha^{4.2}$ and $\alpha^{3.71}$).[43]

Although the distribution of high rates of thalassaemias across the belt stretching from the Pacific to the Mediterranean may reflect intense selection against malaria in the past, the fact that the same α and β mutations occur repeatedly over such a long and narrow band of Eurasia seems to hint at an old human trail.

The genetic evidence

Three general conclusions can be drawn from this exploration of our oldest library. The first is that the genetic markers that have spread radially out of Southeast Asia, carried by people speaking Austronesian and Austro-Asiatic tongues, had both been in this island region back in the Ice Age if not much more. This contradicts the conventional view of the recent Austronesian dispersal out of Asia through the Philippines, and supports the theories derived from archaeology and linguistics I discussed in Chapters 2–5. Second, where genetic trees have been constructed for East Asian genetic markers, including those in Tibet, Aboriginal populations still found in Southeast Asia and speaking either Austro-Asiatic or Austronesian tongues are placed at the earliest branches. Third, these markers were carried out east to the Pacific, west to India and the Middle East, north to Taiwan, China,

Burma and Tibet and south to Australia since the last Ice Age. All these findings are predicted by the prehistoric models outlined earlier in this book.

Our genes, our mother languages, the archaeological remains of our ancestors are all features of our history and prehistory that we can study with interest, but are largely inert and beyond our control. In Part II, I will explore other more lively traces of a migratory past, those which traders and explorers carried in their heads, and could pass freely from one people to another – namely legends and myths. Although these living stories form only one facet of our many cultures, they pervade the very essence of our views about who we are, where we come from and where we are going. As markers of cultural diffusion, they also have an antiquity, specificity and purpose, which is often not found in genes, bones, tones and stones. They may offer alternative models to those of the comparative linguist in explaining how Austronesian terms such as 'lemon' and 'cinnamon' entered Western vocabularies in prehistory. To give a last genetic example from my personal experience, the high rates of α-thalassaemia in coastal New Guinea suggested to me that thalassaemia had been naturally selected in that region because it protected against malaria. But it was the old man's story of the two warring brothers that set me wondering how the two different thalassaemia variants got there in the first place.

PART II

CHINESE WHISPERS

INTRODUCTION TO PART II

From the history of our own times, it is not hard to argue that one technological breakthrough leads to another. We have only to think of developments in radio communications and computer technology to see how progress has accelerated on a global scale in the past fifty years. In the case of the simpler technologies of our ancestors, though, can we extrapolate back to the big leaps forward that occurred after the great post-glacial floods? Why did the same inventions of pottery, fine tools, agriculture and metallurgy happen throughout Eurasia, if not simultaneously then at least within a relatively short period (in prehistoric terms) of a couple of millennia of each other. This all makes it likely that there was long distance communication of ideas from the end of the Old Stone Age onwards.

As I argue in this book, the answer to this puzzling question lies in Southeast Asia. I believe that it was the centre of innovations after the Ice Age and long-distance seeding of ideas from the region led to technological breakthroughs elsewhere. The Austronesians may have contributed sailing technology, magic, religion, astronomy, hierarchy and concepts of kingship. The Austro-Asiatic speaking people may have contributed the more down-to-earth skills of cereal farming, and even bronze. A combination of all these traits was necessary for the first city-builders of Mesopotamia, who wished to organise and control people.

At the beginning of the twentieth century, such cultural transfer would have been called 'diffusion of ideas'. From the 1930s onwards, however, it became politically incorrect in anthropological circles to talk too much about diffusion. Yet some kind of diffusion must have occurred between populations of modern humans during the past 100,000 years. It may have been motivated by migration or by exchange of tool-making materials and precious goods such as sea shells. People travelled about by foot or by boat. It now seems clear, for instance, that deliberate long-distance open-sea journeys were made over 25,000 years ago, before the peak of the last Ice Age, between the Bismarck Archipelago and the northern Solomon Islands in Melanesia.

And it is likely that people would have needed boats to reach Australia possibly 50,000 or even 60,000 years ago.

This book concerns prehistoric transfer of technology and culture between East and West, leading to the first civilisations of Mesopotamia. As we have seen in the first half of this book, prehistory – history before written records – is studied as a branch of archaeology. This also has to include related subjects such as linguistics, anthropology and, more recently, genetics. Whereas archaeology of the historical period is able to use the abundant information of written text, prehistory is much more dependent on the archaeological record. One of the natural obsessions of prehistorians both in the East and West has been the ancient migrations of people carrying their technology with them. Since such people usually carry their language along as well, historical linguistics has also been used to trace such movements. Clearly people can change their language, so there are pitfalls in that approach. We cannot change our genes, so, as we saw in Chapters 6 and 7, genetics can be used to support models of ancient human movements. All these three disciplines support the hypothesis of early post-glacial migrations out of Southeast Asia to the North, West, South and East. The new results of the genetics in particular confirm that Austronesians had their home in island Southeast Asia back in the Ice Age and then spread early to the Pacific and to south India. These migrations came out of two ethnolinguistic centres of old Sundaland – the Austronesian homeland in eastern Indonesia around Sabah, Sulawesi and Maluku (the Moluccas), and the Austro-Asiatic homeland which may have spread down the old east coast from Vietnam and into the South China Sea.

There is, however, an inherent flaw in following people to trace the spread of their ideas. Although obviously good ideas need to be transmitted by word or example they may otherwise have a life and movement of their own, as many academics have learnt to their cost. The same also applies, to a lesser extent, for artefacts such as pots and obsidian blades, which can travel great distances. Seen in another way, it would be a mistake to assume that, if using some super-genetic marker system we knew exactly where people migrated, we could then explain how farming or metallurgy spread in prehistory. The people as a whole may not have moved much at all yet may still have learned new skills.

A Papua New Guinean man who is first generation out of a Stone Age village may fly aeroplanes in Papua New Guinea today. Since there has been little permanent expatriate settlement in the country, genetic or physical surveys performed in fifty years might give very little evidence of who taught him and where. The flowering of the Indianised Sri Vijaya and Majapahit empires in Southeast Asia during the past 1500 years had an enormous influence on the present day cultures of the region. The cultural transfer from India to Southeast Asia over the past 2000 years, however, was not achieved by military invasion or even by much peaceful migration, but rather through trade links and adoption of culture.

The worldwide effects of the colonial era make it self-evident that religion and language are also not necessarily tied to the ethnic groups in which they arose. There are Catholic Amerindians who speak Spanish, English or Portuguese as first tongues, while Pidgin, the most widely spoken language in Papua New Guinea, derives the bulk of its vocabulary from Europe.

I once had the opportunity to see a deliberate attempt at a specific cultural transfer in process at first contact which may illustrate some of these points. On medical patrol in the upper reaches of the Sepik River of Papua New Guinea, I visited a tribe that had only been 'discovered' the previous year, and who spoke a language unintelligible to their nearest neighbours. They had not yet picked up Pidgin. We were accommodated in a brand-new bungalow, built and occupied by a young couple from the American Mid-West. The couple belonged to a church whose stated mission in Papua New Guinea was to find new tribes and learn their languages so that the Bible could be translated and published in them. Oddly, it was the two Americans who were more shocked by the extended cultural encounter than their Stone Age hosts. One reason for our visit was to follow up the condition of the wife, who had previously been admitted to the provincial hospital with severe vitamin intoxication. We had apparently failed to wean her off this habit. The breakfast table – stocked with orange juice, milk, corn flakes and a dozen bottles of vitamins – told its own story. Two years later, their language-learning task finished, the couple went back to America to debrief to the Bible translators. Subsequently, a New Guinean pastor and primary teacher were installed in the village with a stock of Bibles.

On probing this true story we can see that a cultural transfer with far-reaching effects had been accomplished, which, at least initially, had different directions of flow for the different elements that define people and culture. The Bible was introduced but American English was not. The local language of a few hundred speakers was copied and immortalised for linguistic archives and sent to America. As Pidgin would be learnt in the primary school, the local tongue would vanish in the next two generations, so that a future ethnographer who did not know the context might conclude that a Pidgin-speaking culture had introduced the Bible. As far as I know, there was no gene flow either way. In thirty years there will be no physical trace of the two Americans except for a rotting bungalow in the jungle. I should point out that these examples of genetic and cultural de-linkage are extreme: in Australia and the Americas, for instance, the genetic and physical anthropological evidence for which ethnic group irreversibly changed the culture of native inhabitants in the last few hundred years is overwhelming.

The point of the missionary anecdote is that although linguistics and physical anthropology with its modern DNA tools may be the most appropriate methods to study population movements, their value in tracing diffusion of culture and civilisation should be taken in context. The number of people who took a major cultural advance across a sea by trade routes or otherwise may appear quite small when measured as a proportion of the indigenous people that received it. The modern traces of those seminal transfers when measured as genetic or linguistic markers may thus be quite faint.

If we are looking for evidence of migration of ideas and culture, the best markers should be those of culture rather than those of people. If you are trying to find a rat, you do not look for animals in the sky with wings. The archaeologist's best durable culture markers such as specific pottery styles are useful for relatively short-distance trading. But over longer distances ideas of new technology – such as firing methods – may travel, yet the styles and designs often remain regional.

Surprisingly, by far the oldest provenanced cultural links from Southeast Asia to the Ancient Near East are the non-physical, but more durable traits held in folklore. As we shall see, a number of clear folklore links are preserved in Mesopotamian written texts and seals of the third millennium BC. These complex stories have a distribution covering the whole South Pacific region through Southeast Asia and India up to the Ancient Near East. How such stories can have survived longer than the languages that told them is obvious, on reflection. Language changes randomly: folk-tales are preserved deliberately. For proof of this, we have the evidence of the folklore held in the sacred texts of Mesopotamia and the Middle East. Through most of their life they were passed on by word-of-mouth, yet the stories we read in Genesis today in a thousand different tongues are clearly related to the same stories written down in Sumerian on tablets and buried in Iraq up to 5000 years ago. Alternatively we can take the example of the sacred Indian stories of the *Ramayana* and *Mahabharata*. These are still passed on by word-of-mouth between shadow puppet-masters in the

Muslim villages of the east Malay Peninsula and many other places (see illustration 14). The original tales were told thousands of years ago, and provenanced ancient written copies are found in India. Yet they are still passed on by word-of-mouth, intact and accurate, throughout the Indian Ocean. We explore the ancient treasury of these links with our cultural past in the East in this half of the book.

Since it is my view that sea flooding was the root cause of post-glacial migrations, I will first describe some of the hundreds of flood myths found in every continent of the world (Chapters 8, 9 and 10). Their distribution suggests that they were, originally, historiographic. If so, they provide a folk record of one or possibly two world-shattering cataclysms that may correspond with the last two great post-glacial floods described in Chapter 1. Apart from their arguable value as 'history', they also provide several family trees of story-types, which cross continental, linguistic and genetic boundaries. What concerns us here are the origins of the flood myths of the Ancient Near East. I shall identify, at most, four Eurasian story-types which turn out to have ultimate ancestry in the flood myths of Southeast Asia. Three other continents receive less attention here. One of these, Africa, is lacking in a strong flood tradition perhaps because it suffered less flooding of its continental shelf. The other two, North and South America, have many fascinating flood myths, some of which are related to Eurasian types; but because they are peripheral to the main East-West argument I give only a summary of them here.

Second, we will look at the other core myths of the Western cultural tradition that are also incidentally contained, along with the flood, in the first ten chapters of Genesis in the Bible. For convenience, they have been divided up that way: so, in Chapters 11 to 16 we explore the myth archetypes of the creation of the Heavens and Earth, the creation of Man and Woman, the Garden of Eden (which is an amalgam), and finally, the most revealing of all, Cain and Abel. What transpires is that, not only do we find cousins for the West in the East, but that for every Western archetype there is an Eastern origin and logical explanation either in Maluku (the Moluccas) or in Indo-China. The fantastic, complex and unlikely nature of Western mythology has been thought by many in this century to have emerged from the deep recesses of our subconscious. My analysis has tended to lead instead back to a few basic and simple themes that may have originated in Southeast Asia and subsequently combined and recombined to produce the involved, yet glorious, myths that were first recorded on seals and tablets in Mesopotamia at the dawn of history. This trail, whose first provenanced record is 4500 years old, may take us back at least to the time

3000 years earlier when the sea was still eating up the Southeast Asian and Mesopotamian coastline.

8
FIVE HUNDRED CATACLYSMS?

'The Flood? I'm glad you asked that question; luckily we left that nonsense behind in the nineteenth century. Only fundamentalists still talk about it. There is no geological evidence of a great world flood, let alone one that destroyed most of the world's population, or stayed for a long time, or with waves that topped mountains, or made a great noise. To be sure there have been bad riverine floods. The land between the rivers, known as Mesopotamia, is a good example of a region with frequent disastrous riverine floods. Those must have been the origin of the myth. Tales from all around the world? Well, floods are common things; maybe stories of floods in Mesopotamia spread elsewhere. Oops, sorry, we are not supposed to talk about diffusion. That went out of fashion early in the twentieth century. Anyway, my dear fellow, surely you have heard of parallel development of myths. These sort of stories are part of our subconscious; the Flood was an obvious expression of our deep fear of drowning in our mother's womb...'

Rubbish. There is ample geological evidence for not one but three worldwide floods that would have destroyed any coastal settlements on flat continental shelves, as I pointed out in Part 1. There is also evidence of massive earthquakes sufficient to cause superwaves especially during the most recent of these floods. Signs of the penetration of these superwaves well inland and upland exist in the extraordinary collections of animal debris filling caves and fissures as deep as 200 metres in most continents. Some of these remains have been dated to the second flood around 11,500 years ago.[1] If there were so many bad riverine floods in Mesopotamia, as the sedimentary record shows, one very bad one would not be remembered so long. Instead the recurrent aspects would be recalled. The myths from around the world do not usually refer to periodic river floods. In any case most flood myths come from island Southeast Asia, which, unlike Mesopotamia, lost most of its alluvial flood-plains after the great melt when the Ice Age ended. The 'deep psychological' argument, which is untestable in any case, does not explain the numerous worldwide versions of the myth that separate the floods as a more recent event than creation. If a great flood really was part of some subconscious black box full of a mush of fears and cosmic thoughts, then why separate it from creation?

Yes, there are flood myths from all over the world; more than 500 of them as it happens. In Europe there is the ethnocentric view that if there was any diffusion of stories, it was out of Mesopotamia – or more recently the Black Sea[2] – to the rest of the world. There is nothing to support this view. If there is any single epicentre of the flood myths, which is unlikely, Southeast Asia would be a more obvious choice.

The solid wall of uniformitarian academic opinion that lasted from Charles Lyell's time in the nineteenth century started showing cracks after the 1970s. Geologists, oceanographers and geographers have begun to break rank, using unacceptable words such as 'catastrophic' and 'dramatic':

> the disintegration of the Hudson Bay and James Bay ice [8000 years ago] also resulted in the most catastrophic and dramatic sequence of events ever to have affected the northern hemisphere during the late Quaternary ... the periods of rapid ice melting between 13,000 and 11,000 BP [before present] and between 10,000 and 7000 BP are characterised by very rapid rates of sea-level rise ... The largest catastrophic floods, however, occurred much later at 8000 BP ... and led to an almost instantaneous rise in sea-level ... the melting of the last ice sheets led to immense changes in the redistribution of mass across the surface of the Earth. At present we know nothing about the way the Earth's crust and interior responded to these changes ... it seems inevitable that significant seismicity and earthquake activity may have occurred.[3]

These lines do not come from Genesis, nor from any of the approximately five hundred known flood myths but from a textbook on the Ice Age published in 1992 by a geologist. Increasing knowledge of the extraordinary events of the great ice melts and the possible effects of meteoritic impact has spawned a new breed of 'neo-catastrophists' and 'neo-diluvialists' who are experts in the relevant fields. The argument of the neo-catastrophists is that the flood myths may be based on literally world-shaking events in recent prehistory. They emphasise that the story of the great flood around 8000 years ago, unlike all the rest of creation mythology, is still widely regarded as a historical event. The myth that has launched a thousand books will not go away. The study of people's ideas on this flood is a discipline itself. Historians, geologists, oceanographers, theologians and anthropologists have written countless tomes on the history of 'diluvialism', 'catastrophism', and their antithesis, 'uniformitarianism'. Belief in the historicity of the flood has oscillated between politically and religiously 'correct' to laughable. Just at the moment it seems to be coming back into fashion.

This persistence of the flood myth cannot be due to the intrinsic credibility of the story, which still sounds as fantastic as when it was first put on ancient Sumerian tablets. Nor can its presence in sacred texts of the main religions be used as an argument. There are several other creation themes such as the creation of humanity that are theologically more central but still less popular. The widespread distribution of the flood story and its key position in many creation myths is obviously important, but then the 'clay man' myths[4] are even more widespread and still fail to attract the same attention. Many authors end up saying something vague about the position of flood myths in 'popular consciousness', and add that for many cultures it has never ceased to be 'history'.

One bonus of the latter view for comparative mythologists is that they do not have to apologise for even discussing the idea that the flood myths may have an historical basis. Nor do they have to tackle the theory of the common 'psychic' origin of a motif, because floods are concrete real events and not a by-product of the world psyche. The questions should rather be phrased: Is the flood myth so widespread because of (1) worldwide diffusion of one story (monogenesis); (2) many different floods and stories (polygenesis); or (3) one world-destroying flood with more than one original account (linked polygenesis)?

The ethnologist Sir James Frazer attacked the subject of the flood myth's distribution with even more than his usual enthusiasm and comprehensive cover in his book *Folklore in the Old Testament*. His effort has not been surpassed since. He stated the main questions immediately as antitheses of a type that are common to all comparative mythology:

> How are we to explain the numerous and striking similarities which obtain between the beliefs and customs of races inhabiting distant parts of the world? Are such resemblances due to the transmission of the customs and the beliefs from one race to another, either by immediate contact or through the medium of intervening peoples [monogenesis]? Or have they arisen independently in

many different races through the similar working of the human mind under similar circumstances [polygenesis]?[5]

Frazer then immediately answered his own rhetorical question by saying that the two ideas were not mutually exclusive, and depending on the individual situation it was probably a bit of both. After 200 pages of concentrated flood myths he concluded that such ancient myths were widespread on every continent except Africa; and that while there had been some diffusion of story-types within continents there was no evidence of significant intercontinental diffusion;[6] that is, until recent historic times, when Christian and Islamic missionaries got to work. He also dismissed the idea of one big world-stopping flood as false: 'for, if the best-accredited testimony of modern geology can be trusted, no such cataclysm has befallen the earth during the period of man's abode on it'.[7] With this problem out of the way, he then suggested by elimination that if the individual stories had any basis in history, it was because of many individual locally catastrophic floods that occur from time to time everywhere (polygenesis).

I cannot fully agree with any of Frazer's last three conclusions. First there are and were flood myths in Africa, although not many.[8] Second, concerning diffusion, there was some intercontinental diffusion of flood-story motifs, even of those that he quoted in his review. Third, his qualified faith in the omniscience of Edwardian geologists was unfounded.

Frazer was, of course, echoing the nineteenth-century uniformitarian view that major geological events are slow rather than sudden and catastrophic. This has remained the establishment position until the past two decades. Now various astronomers and Earth scientists have revived the idea that our planet may not be as stable and free from outside influence as we would hope, and that real world-shaking catastrophes such as bombardment by meteorites and comets may have occurred recently.[9] Evidence for a recent significant meteoritic impact remains controversial.[10] We can say, however, that the acknowledged astronomic possibility that the Earth was recently dealt a shattering blow casts doubt on the 'accredited testimony of modern geology' of Frazer's time. Even if Frazer had confidence that a worldwide flood causing near extinction could not have occurred, it does no justice to his normal perceptiveness that he chose to ignore this concept as a possible unifying factor in the myths he so carefully collated. By arguing for unrelated parochial floods as the original historical events behind the myths of worldwide destruction, he did just that.

In contrast to the situation with most fabulous myths, the problem with historicity in flood myths is not whether any individual story could have been based on a real event: that possibility is now self-evident. Sufficient terrible floods have happened during recorded history to make it undeniable. The real problem is that, even if there had been one worldwide mother of all floods that annihilated all but a few humans, the memory of it might have been overlaid in legend by subsequent locally disastrous floods. I will show examples of this from the Pacific later. Crude analysis of descriptions of mythological floods may, therefore, be misleading unless the genealogy of the story-types is explored at the same time.

All this means that we need to review the numerous flood myths again closely. When we do this we must keep several possibilities in mind. Firstly at one extreme all five hundred or more myths may refer to different floods, while at the other they all refer to one flood. Even in the latter case there is the possibility that people living in different places saw the flood in different ways with the result that there may be several versions of the same event. As we shall see not all kinds of floods are the same and not all have the same potential for destruction. I have already discussed the effects of the three world floods fully in Chapter 1. However, I will recap below the main types of floods that we should be looking for in the descriptions of legend. The most destructive floods come from the sea, but other possibilities are land-based, such as a dam burst or river flooding on a large scale.

(A) Sea-based floods

(1) *Post-Ice-Age drowning of continental shelves.* A large proportion of the Earth's surface was permanently lost to settlement and agriculture somewhere between 18,000 and 5000 years ago as a result of the sea-level rising by 150 metres. The rise in sea-level at the end of the last Ice Age flooded vast areas of continental shelf. That event caused more permanent destruction of land-based life than any other that we know of during our time on Earth. It is the only worldwide flood in the past 18,000 years for which there is universal scientific agreement.[11] In the Far East and some other tropical areas, the annual destruction would have been very noticeable, and would have continued to colour the lives of coastal dwellers for thousands of years. In contrast, people moving into the recently thawed-out northwest Europe and Canada experienced a rapid re-emergence of their new defrosted lands out of the sea as an after-effect of the pressure of ice being removed from the underlying Earth's crust. Continents like Africa, with narrow

continental shelves, would have been relatively spared the flooding.

The rise in sea-level after the last Ice Age was not spread out evenly. There were three periods of rapid sea-level rise. One of these followed a catastrophic cold snap called the Younger Dryas event (see Chapter 1). Geologists and oceanographers are now agreed that this globally catastrophic climate reversal occurred between 13,000 and 11,600 years ago, after the end of the last main part of the Ice Age. This event plunged the world back into a very severe but short deep freeze which took temperatures to 20 degrees centigrade below today's. The big freeze came and went rapidly, lasting just over 1000 years. When it ended, the Earth warmed up again within about 50 years, releasing vast amounts of water again to the great oceans. Every new scientific article on this event published in frontline journals such as *Science* and *Nature* competes to say how much worse the melt was, and how much more rapid, than people had thought before.

The rapid rise in ocean levels after the Younger Dryas event has probably not been matched since. But there was at least one other surge afterwards. The final (third) rapid sea-level rise occurred about 7500–8000 years ago on equatorial continental shelves. This final surge raised equatorial sea-levels by another 25 metres to 5 metres higher than they are now. If this kind of flood was the original basis of surviving legends, then there is a definite possibility that more than one worldwide event might have been recorded in some stories.

(2) *Tsunamis*. Sea-born tidal waves arising from earthquakes and volcanic explosions are dramatic, common and extremely destructive.[12] They may involve the coastlines of an entire ocean basin and can wipe out populations living on flat atolls, but they do not usually destroy civilisations. Even the celebrated vulcanic explosion of Thera in the Mediterranean, 3500 years ago, which has been suggested as the origin of the Atlantis story,[13] did not in the end completely destroy Minoan civilisation with its tidal waves. The worldwide waves that accompanied the great earthquakes of around 8000 years ago, when the last ice plates collapsed, may have been several orders greater than even those of Thera.

(3) *Superwaves and superfloods due to bombardment of the Earth.* Tsunamis have big brothers, sometimes called superwaves, that may follow visits by large bodies from outer space. Although no one living has ever seen one of these, their effects can be calculated. Astronomers envisage two types of events, one much more likely than the other. The first and more likely catastrophe is a direct hit in an ocean by a large comet or asteroid. Waves from these may rise to hundreds of metres and may travel hundreds of kilometres inland. The superfloods thus

caused would inundate vast areas of coastal lowland and would even travel up small mountains. Depending on the size of the asteroid or comet, and where it landed, there could be catastrophic conflagrations and rains of fire as a result of volcanic matter thrown into the atmosphere. Increased seismic activity would also inevitably follow. After the initial destructive effects of the waves and increased volcanic activity, there would probably be a prolonged winter as a delayed result of the volcanic matter thrown up into the atmosphere through the breached crust. A short Ice Age could even occur. Depending on the size of the asteroid, such an event may be expected to occur at average intervals as small as every 12,000 years. Larger bodies, such as the one that is thought by some to have wiped out the dinosaurs would strike much less frequently. It is conceivable that the Younger Dryas cold event followed such a bombardment.

(4) *Superwaves and superfloods due to rapid tilt or tumble of the Earth.* The second and much less likely catastrophe that could cause superwaves and superfloods is a near miss by an object of comparable size to the Earth, causing a sudden alteration in tilt of the geographic axis of rotation. This would be like a top suddenly going off its line of spin, and would be the result of the gravitational pull of the visiting heavenly body. In the extreme case, the Earth's axis would turn 'Tippe Top' or upside down. Because the Earth is neither a perfect sphere nor solid, the effect on its crust, let alone on its oceans, of any of these events would be truly cataclysmic. Oceans would run over continents, which themselves would change shape. There would be widespread vulcanism, conflagrations, hurricanes and mass extinction.[14] The chance of a stray planet wandering near Earth with these effects is, however, extremely low.

Rapid tilt or tumble of the Earth's axis of spin may also theoretically be caused by imbalance in the distribution of the world's mass. This could result from an unequal build-up of ice over the poles with a sudden change as the Earth literally tips over suddenly to correct itself. Such an idea causes hilarity among most Earth scientists at present. Recent research has shown the Earth to be a much more wobbly top than was previously thought, however, and these ideas are still put forward as possible reasons for a worldwide flood.[15]

On a less-dramatic scale, smaller cyclical wobbles in the Earth's axis that are known to occur may rapidly alter polar and equatorial sea-levels by up to 100 metres. These wobbles could be the cause of some rapid changes in ice cover rather than the other way round. The resulting large equatorial swings in sea-level would then be more the result of rapid redistribution of the seas than melting of ice. This kind of cyclical change in the Earth's tilt is a reality rather than a fantasy and was discussed in Chapter 1. The effects on people living in the tropics in this case of flooding would be identical to that caused by the drowning of continental shelves, except on a faster timescale.

The after-effects of any change in tilt of the Earth's axis could be one of two things: either the same as the flooding of the continental shelves, with rapid de-glaciation and sea-level rise as ice was exposed to more sun or a cold dry snap with rapid glaciation. This would depend on the direction of the change in tilt. These effects would be noticeable with even minor changes in tilt. Rapid increase in the Earth's tilt followed by correction is another possible cause of the Younger Dryas event.

(5) *Local superfloods of landlocked seas.* Millions of years ago the Mediterranean Sea dried up and was subsequently reflooded by a dramatic torrent through the Straits of Gibraltar. A similar event happened to the Black Sea 7250 years ago.[16] People living on the shallow sloping northern shores of the sea would have had to flee away from the shore to save their lives as the water rose. The huge torrent through the Bosphorus would have made the noise of 200 Niagaras.[17]

(B) Land-based floods

Limited superfloods

1. Lake-bursts: Water which is suddenly released following the unblocking of a dammed lake can cause local superflooding and earthquakes.[18]
2. Periods of exceptionally high rainfall in conjunction with hemispherical anomalies in the atmosphere.[19]

Seasonal riverine flooding

3. Many commentators on Mesopotamian flood myths have concluded that the regular seasonal occurrence of rain-driven flooding of the Tigris and Euphrates rivers must have been the origin of those stories. In some years the floods must have been worse than others. As the same scholars note, although severe and locally destructive, such floods could not have been civilisation-destroying.[20] When we look at the distribution and nature of other flood myths we will see how little this local pluvial/fluvial hypothesis explains. The possibility of local overlay on older legends, however, has to be taken into account in the Mesopotamian myths.

No flood myths in Africa?

We might expect that worldwide floods should have worldwide effects.

In contrast to all the other continents Africa is poor in flood myths. Frazer goes so far as to say that '... it may be doubted whether throughout that vast continent a single genuinely native tradition of a great flood has been recorded'.[21] He did none the less list a small number of stories which in his view were of questionable provenance. Subsequent folklorists have argued that these and others are not just corruptions of missionary teaching.[22] It is worth pausing to consider the importance of this relative gap, since Africa has been subject to as much missionary influence as anywhere in the world, has a large coast and might thus be expected to have more flood myths.

Deluge stories are among the most widespread of any group of creation myths. This is one of the oldest arguments for their historical authenticity. So complete absence of indigenous flood myths in even one continent would obviously have negative implications for any theory of a worldwide flood. In spite of this, the plausible types of grand world flood listed above could just have escaped the ancient mythological record of Africa under certain conditions. Post-Ice-Age sea-level rise would have been less noticeable in Africa than any other continent, since the continental shelf is so steep and narrow, particularly in the crucial equatorial region. For the same reasons and also because of rapid altitude rise in hinterlands round most of Africa, superwaves would also have had less opportunity to invade and devastate the coast land. Finally, if the oldest catastrophic flood myths had really originated in one giant meteoritic impact in the Pacific, as some suggest, Africa would have been least affected since it would be protected on both sides by two oceans and two continental masses.

Apart from the negative arguments I have already given that the floods, although globally destructive, may have affected Africa least, there are still the questions of psychological origin of myths. I have already stated my objections to the theory of an innate psychological tendency to tell various common myths. My objections are further supported in the case of the flood stories by their very paucity in Africa. I assume for the purpose of this argument that there are no innate racial differences in any *hypothetical* tendency to make up such stories.

Flood-myth anthologies

Several anthologies of flood myths are available.[23] Because there are so many stories, these anthologies run to many pages. Attempting the same task here is pointless, as there is simply not enough space here and in any case the reader may wish to read the originals. Many of my references are from Sir James Frazer because, in spite of some objections, I find his approach logical, encyclopaedic, and he has few pre-conceptions. I have, of course, used other sources for my review. The chief impressions I gleaned when wandering through these flood legends was how few basic story-types there were. Before I describe them, however, I will digress to a group of myths that have escaped the attention of the diluvialists – the watery creation-myths that are really flood stories in disguise.

Watery creation myths and land-raisers

The first observation to make about flood anthologies is that few of them recognise the commonest root story of all flood myths – the creation of the cosmos from a watery waste or chaos (this motif will be discussed in detail in Chapter 11). In nearly half of the hundreds of creation myths I reviewed, there was a dark watery start to the world and land had to be created. If the original flood was so voracious and destroyed all but a few handfuls of people it is likely that at least some legends would describe the start of the world in terms of the state the survivors found it immediately after the cataclysm – that is, very wet. It seems illogical to exclude from flood anthologies, myths with a watery start. The watery-start creations were often followed by a later flood. This is the case, for instance, in Genesis. If both of these story-types referred to a worldwide flood then we must at least consider the possibility that the legends were describing more than one great flood. The post-glacial record shows there were three, so it is possible that the watery start referred to the flood that followed the Younger Dryas event around 11,500 years ago. This was the second of the three post-glacial floods described in Chapter 1.

Additional support for treating watery-chaos creation myths as flood stories can be seen in the association of the so-called 'Earth-Diver' creation motif with the flood myths of North America. As I shall detail in Chapter 11, a widespread family of myths describe the creation of land in a watery wilderness by raising it up from the floor of the ocean bed. One mechanism used in these myths is the 'earth diver'. Various animals, including diving birds, are sent down to the ocean floor to pick up the earth there. After a few failures one gets back with some earth or clay under its claws. This scrap of earth then grows rapidly in size, with or without some magic help from a creator. Land is eventually formed from this growing earth. As we shall see, these diver creation myths are found on both sides of the Bering strait. The diver myths are most numerous in sub-arctic regions of North America where they are integral to a universal flood myth found there. Whereas in most places the 'earth raiser' family of stories are structured as creation myths and refer to the sea, among the Algonquian Indians of North America and Canada, the earth diver myths specifically describe the recovery of land from a great and sudden lake flood, which itself followed a prolonged period of cold and famine.

The land-raising creation stories include other methods of retrieving earth from the sea-bed. Fishers of land are common to the Pacific and its west coast, and shovers or plowers of the sea-bed appear in India, Thailand and eastern Polynesia. The concept of land appearing as a mound of earth or slime dries out appears mainly in North Africa.

Birds as earth-raisers and land-seekers

One class of animals repeatedly found both in the land-raising and flood myths are birds. In the sub-arctic myths of North America, as I have said, they are usually recruited as divers, while elsewhere they benefit from the land-raising activities of other animals. An example of the latter appears in the 'clay/devil' stories about the creation of man in Chapter 13. This long creation story, which contains nearly every archaic Eurasian creation theme, comes from the Santals, a Mundaic Aboriginal tribe of Bengal. After a watery start to the world two birds were created in mistake for men and could not find any land to nest on. They flew around the world fruitlessly looking for land for twelve years. The creator recruited various animals to dive for earth. After a few failures the turtle brought up land in the form of an island, which was then planted up by the creator. The birds then nested. The same motif appears in a Digueno creation myth from southwest California.[24] Here the divers are two brothers who were under the sea at the beginning of time. The elder brother created land from packed red ants. The birds that he made next, however, could not find the land he had created because it was still dark. So he then made the Sun and the Moon.

Two widely separated myths record an island that was created for wandering teal (a small duck) to nest, as I shall describe in Chapter 12. One of these is the Finnish *Kalevala*, and the other comes from Samoa. Other non-Christian creation myths have birds in a less passive role being sent out, usually to find land in the watery waste, at the beginning of time. One of these stories was collected from the Bila-an, a non-Christian tribe of the southern Philippines: 'In the beginning, four beings, two male and two female, lived on a small island no bigger than a hat. Neither trees nor grass grew on the island but one bird lived on it.[25] So the four beings sent the bird to fetch some earth, the fruit of the rattan, and the fruit of trees.' The creator beings then fashioned the earth into land and the rest of the story is a variant on the clay-man myth.

The birds are not always sent to find land. A Hopi myth from Arizona records the creation of land in the middle of the ocean by two goddesses, one from on the east side, the other from the west. The Sun during his daily passage noticed that there were no living things. The goddess of the east made a wren out of clay, animated it and sent it all over the Earth to look for life. The wren found none, so the two goddesses set about to create animals. Last of all they made a woman and then a man out of clay.

The extension of the diving-bird motif to include birds that are sent out across the ocean to find seed-earth for land creation, introduces another link between 'wet creation' and flood myths. That is the well-known biblical motif of sending out birds, usually ravens or crows, to locate land after the flood. We find this theme in the Mesopotamian flood stories, throughout Eurasia and also in many Amerindian flood myths. While the rest of the Americas lack the earth-diver story, they are rich in other flood myths including those with bird land-seekers. Some, especially those in Central America, have an uncanny similarity to the main Eurasian types I will describe over the next two chapters. Others, especially in South America, are individually unique; they will be dealt with elsewhere. I do not have space to discuss them in any depth here as it is outside the remit of this book.

To summarise so far, we can include the North American flood/diving myths in a land-raising family of 'earth diver', 'earth fisher', 'earth shover', 'earth drier' and 'earth scratcher' creation stories as all variants on a basic post-flood recovery theme. The diver variant dominates in North America, Northeast Asia and Siberia, and among the Aboriginal Austro-Asiatic tribes in India. We can include 'bird land-divers' in this group. Birds flying out to locate or fetch earth have a more worldwide mythological distribution. The 'earth-fisher' and 'earth-shover' variants are found more in southern Asia and the Pacific, while the 'earth-drier' and 'earth-scratcher' variants come from Africa. (The scratching, incidentally, is performed by birds.)

The 'earth-raiser' myths of the Northern Hemisphere lend themselves well to the phenomenon oceanographers call 'coastline emergence'. This happened on a grand scale in parts of North America. Put in simple terms, after the Ice Age, the land in the sub-arctic rose faster than the sea level as the ice melted. During the Ice Age the huge weight of ice over the northern continents had dented the Earth's crust inwards, like a beach ball, by as much as 500 metres or more. When the ice caps over North America and northern Europe melted, the weight came off and the continental crust rebounded towards its former shape. The springy rise in the land was so much more than the relative rise in sea-level resulting from the ice melting that the land would have emerged out of the sea after the melt. This crustal rise happened quickly, but not as quickly as the melting of the ice, so there was a 'window' when the ice had melted but the land remained dented down. Much of North America, Canada and Scandinavia had been pushed below sea-level during the Ice Age. As a result, if the Amerindian spectators of the ice cap melting had looked north they would at first have seen huge expanses of lakes and sea. Then in turn, these were rapidly replaced by rising land (see illustration 1). Hudson Bay, the Great Lakes and the Baltic Sea and the numerous small fresh-water lakes of Canada and Finland are what is still left over from the Ice Age dents in the crust (see Chapter 1). Maybe old people in Canada compared stories passed down from their great grandparents – of the land that rose out of the sea. Consequently, they felt inspired to credit their animal totems with this impressive feat of land creation.

In contrast to the arctic totemic land-raiser myths, in the southern hemisphere we find the 'Rainbow serpent' stories have been linked in Australia to rapid post-glacial sea-level rise.[26] There is, however, an even larger family of watery creations called the separation myths (see Chapter 12), two thirds of which start from a watery chaos, often with a dragon or serpent representing the sea. The theme of separation of the firmament from the world below is common throughout Eurasia, Oceania and the Pacific. The stories generally feature a dark watery start with the creation of light *before* the creation of the Sun or the Moon – that is, light before the luminaries.

As we shall see in Chapters 11 and 12, these myth types hint at an additional global calamity of another kind. The initial state of watery darkness, and the subsequent separation of the sky from its close cloudy cover over the sea and land, point to the sort of prolonged winter which might follow a more sudden global catastrophe. On the other hand, it may simply be that the separation myths were, as a group, recalling a mini Ice Age. We know that two such events did occur and immediately preceded each of the last two rapid sea-level rises.[27] The former, as we know, was the Younger Dryas event, a millennium of extreme climatic disruption, vulcanism and cold followed by rapid warming and ice-melt 11,500 years ago. The other event was a short 400-year freeze-up around 8500 years ago, just before the last flood.

We will come back to the watery creation myths in more detail in Chapter 11. I should stress here that in recruiting them as flood myths

I am not glossing over the implicit duplication. Many watery creation cycles, such as Genesis, include a flood after creation. There are several possible explanations for this apparent flood duplication, apart from the fact that myths often duplicate important motifs anyway. First, there is the possibility, already mentioned, of the myths recording two catastrophes. Second, there is the phenomenon of overlaying where, as I have described above, a former grand catastrophe is re-told in the context of a more recent relatively minor event.

Earth-moulding and topographical changes

Some legends about a deluge or another world catastrophe specify that the shape and topography of the Earth was permanently altered after the event. One obvious example of this is in the stories telling of an extension or contraction of a coastline and of the formation of many islands where there was continent before. Many of these can easily be related to relative changes in sea-level, either as a result of land emergence and subsidence locally or, more universally, as a result of the global post-glacial events I have just discussed. Others tell of the formation of hills, mountains and river beds where there were none before. In many cases these perceived effects could either follow from the same post-glacial events or belong to the so-called 'aetiological' group of myths. (These are stories supposed to have been invented to explain a natural phenomenon or feature.)

Some modern catastrophists see the mythic descriptions of land change as supporting the concept of massive crustal derangement. One common group of such fabulous descriptions are vanishing continents in the Pacific, Indian and Atlantic Oceans. Certainly, the islands of these three great oceans were much larger during the Pleistocene when sea-levels were lower. Another idea is that many modern mountain ranges were uplifted in the last 10,000 years or so.[28] The crustal derangement necessary for these geological and oceanographic grand changes could only have followed one of the two less likely catastrophes I mentioned above. One of these would be a very large asteroid bombardment that caused more than just a big ripple on the surface crust of the globe. The other would be a major tilt or even Tippe-top (reversal) of the Earth's axis for whatever reason. A number of legends do record the Earth turning upside down, while others record bombardment from the sky or celestial wars. (Mythological and geological evidence for these kinds of events has been recently reviewed.)[29] The disadvantage of such theories is that they depend on an unlikely, and as yet unproven, event to explain things that could have resulted from known events. When reviewing flood myths we thus need to try and distinguish between mythological land changes that can be explained by known sea-level changes and those that require a hypothetical earth breaking event.

World conflagration as the primary or associated disaster

American folklorist Stith Thompson, the father of motif analysis in folklore, defined a major subclass of 'World Calamities and Renewals' to describe 'World Fire'.[30] While this included local fires, he showed that a number of myths and legends from every continent recorded a world-destroying conflagration. These are most numerous in the Indian subcontinent and are sometimes told in conjunction with flood myths. Rains of fire, of boiling water and of flammable matter and also of rocks and gravel may accompany any major vulcanic activity. Fire-storms may also follow earth bombardment by small meteorites or rapid tilt of the Earth. The mythological and geological evidence for these events has been reviewed recently.[31] The fact that legendary conflagrations followed or joined floods means only that we should suspect major seismic disturbance in such stories, not how it was caused.

Having sketched some of the mythic phenomena that may have been associated with floods, or may have held a surrogate description of them, I now move on to the bulk of the world myths which explicitly described a cataclysmic flood.

9

FLOODS IN THE WEST

There is now general agreement that the stories of Noah's Flood and the floods of the Sumerians, Babylonians and Assyrians are related, although there is no agreement on the original source. The story of how the ancient versions were rediscovered is one of the romances of nineteenth-century archaeology. Before telling that, we need to review what the scribes handed down to us in the book of Genesis because, as with other parts of that ancient work, two different versions are knitted together. The superficial similarities between these stories gloss over a worldwide split. In other words, the two traditions describe two different floods.

Noah's Flood

There are at least two different versions of every story in the first five chapters of Genesis. Scholars can identify and separate the two accounts relatively easily on the basis of stylistic clues such as the name used for God by the different authors. They label one the 'Priestly' account and the other – the earlier one – the 'Jehovistic' account. The tale of Noah's Flood is no exception to the rule of parallel versions, except that there are more similarities between the two accounts. The superficial similarity of the two flood myths was, unfortunately, too much of a temptation for the Genesis editors. Whereas early chapters separate the relevant traditions into more or less discrete and contrasting stories, when we come to Noah the two versions have been spliced clumsily together. The result is repetitive and, therefore, rather confusing.

Much of the scholarly output on flood myths has been devoted to minute comparison of the two Genesis versions with some eight other Mesopotamian versions. With 500 or so flood myths to review, I do not have the space in this book for such indulgence. The general case for genetic relationships between the Mesopotamian myths, including Genesis, will be made in later chapters. Each version on its own gives a complete and coherent story.

The first thing to remember is how superficially similar the two flood stories are. Whereas the two creation stories in Genesis Chapters 1 and 2 were clearly different stories with different origins, the two Noah myths just as clearly share many motifs from the same source. The stylistic differences reflect as much the theological agenda of the Priestly writer as anything else. For example, throughout the Priestly version there are detailed references to an improbable calendar of events and ages. In particular, the length of the flood is rounded up from the lunar year by ten days to exactly one solar year. The first dry land appears on New Year's Day. American biblical scholar Norman Habel points out that this timing allows for the familiar annual ritual cycle of creation, battle and destruction, culminating in rebirth.[1] In contrast the Jehovistic version has the flood lasting forty days and nights followed by a three-week wait for the waters to subside.

Several other differences between the two accounts are determined by the theological sensitivity of the Priestly writer. The use of two of each of the clean animals by the Priestly writer rather than the seven of the Jehovistic writer is a logical prudence. The knowledge of clean and unclean was supposed to have been revealed to Moses only long after the flood. Further, the Priestly writer omits the sacrifice of thanks given by Noah after landing. By the time the Priestly version was written, sacrifices were allowed to be made only by the proper priest in the temple at Jerusalem, not by some patriarchal commoner on a hillside.[2]

The most significant differences between the accounts – the details of the flood itself – arouse the least comment from the scholars. The Jehovistic account has a pluvial or rain-driven flood and records a grace period with Noah entering the Ark a week before the flood came up, at which point the Lord sealed him in. The Priestly version, in contrast, described a one-day cataclysm apparently coming from the sea and sky, with Noah and his team embarking on the same day.

In its description of the flood, the Priestly text records that: 'in the second month, the seventeenth day of the month, the same day were all the fountains of the great deep broken up, and the windows of heaven were opened.' These two ringing phrases are somewhat opaque in meaning. The phrase 'were all the fountains of the great deep broken up' has divided biblical scholars into 'sea flooders' and 'subterranean aquifer flooders'. Alexander Heidel and Max Mallowan regarded the breaking of great fountains of the deep as a release of subterranean water after an earthquake.[3] Others have postulated earthquake-driven sea floods with huge superwaves.[4] I find it difficult to get much from the literary wrangles over translations of this poetic phrase, but 'the great deep' sounds to me like the sea. Conversely, 'the windows of heaven were opened' sounds very like a rainstorm, but some catastrophists see in this evidence of a sky-ripping disaster such as meteoric bombardment.[5]

Both of the Genesis accounts agree that the flood was worldwide and destroyed every living thing except the occupants of the Ark, but they give conflicting descriptions of the depth it reached. The Jehovistic writer gives no depth, whereas the Priestly writer gives us a choice: 'And the waters prevailed exceedingly upon the earth; and all the high hills, that [were] under the whole heaven, were covered. Fifteen cubits upward did the waters prevail; and the mountains were covered.' (Genesis 7:19–20)

Fifteen cubits using my own forearm is only 5 metres, a depth that would have been devastating on the Mesopotamian plain but would hardly have covered hills. The King James Authorised Version above does not clarify whether this phrase means a rise of 5 metres above the plain or 5 metres over the tops of all mountains: later translations assume the latter. The depth of 5 metres is, incidentally, a realistic estimate of the peak post-glacial overshoot of sea-levels over the Arabian Gulf coast of Mesopotamia 3500 years BC. This last surge took the sea-level from minus 50 metres to plus 5 metres above the Mesopotamian plain. It took the sea a further 140–170 kilometres inland over the Mesopotamian plain than it is today, and created Sir Leonard Woolley's famous flood layer at Ur.[6] That flood, however, would not have covered even small hills.

If the 15 cubits really represents a separate tradition from the covering of mountains, we are left with an internally inconsistent Priestly story – that is, unless there were two flood traditions, one with a superwave briefly sloshing over high land and the other covering the Mesopotamian flood-plain for a longer period. That is certainly possible from the literary point of view. I have already noted that the Genesis editors usually included contradictory accounts side by side rather than cut out bits of conflicting sacred text. In this respect they followed the practice of folklorists today (except that they still try to make one story out of two). Maybe the 15 cubits is an unrecognised intrusion from the Jehovistic account. Alternatively, the Priestly account was really recording two phases of the same flood – the initial giant tsunamis that accompanied the final collapse of the Canadian ice sheet around 7500 years ago, and the later slower and prolonged sea-level rise caused by the ice-melt.

The end of Noah's flood has a distinctive flavour in the two biblical accounts. The Priestly version tells us that Elohim sent a wind, and reversed the windows of the heavens and the fountains of the deep. As the waters settled the mountains reappeared and the Ark landed on the mountains of Ararat. Eventually, after the waters had left, the land also dried out. The Jehovistic version, as before, makes no mention of mountains, but the rain was stopped, water flowed off the land, and Noah waited for three weeks in the Ark on a featureless sea.

This section of the Jehovistic account also introduces the worldwide 'bird-seeker' motif, which I will explore further in Chapter 11 in my discussion of 'land raisers'; this is not found in the Priestly account. Two birds were sent out, first a raven which did not return, and then a dove which did. An apochryphal Hebrew version has the raven stopping off to eat carrion and thus not coming back.[7] This non-biblical variant reappears in several Amerindian stories from Mexico. In one of these, from Michoacan province of Mexico, Noah's part is taken by a man named Tezpi. Tezpi brought his family along with animals and seeds and took refuge in a large boat when the flood came. When the waters abated, Tezpi sent out a vulture to look for land but the vulture stopped off to feed on corpses and did not return. Eventually the humming-bird was sent out and returned with a green bough in its beak.[8] The Cora indians of Mexico also have this story but, in addition, the vulture was cursed for his act and turned black. The ring-dove eventually reported that the earth was dry but the rivers were still in spate.[9] Although these two stories may appear to be copied from missionary teaching, the Jewish folk motif of the carrion is not in the Bible and is unlikely, therefore, to have been transmitted by missionaries.

The two floods reported in the two versions are thus different in origin, nature and depth. While the Priestly account implies a grand and sudden cataclysm involving both land and sea and covering mountains, the Jehovistic account specifies no more than a pluvial flood that may have affected only alluvial and flat land. Neither mentions rivers, which are the most likely source of floods in Mesopotamia. After the landing, the Jehovistic version, consistent with its previously stated concept of the Ark as a sealed chest, has Noah removing the covering.

God's attitude to the flood after the event is quite different in the two versions. On the one hand, Jehovah talks mournfully to himself, regretting his act because he now realises that man is congenitally hopeless and evil. In this downbeat post-mortem, the Jehovistic version is closer, as we shall see, to other Mesopotamian stories. In the Priestly version, on the other hand, Elohim takes a positive, high moral stance and gives Noah detailed instructions for man's new life. Elohim follows up these instructions with a grand and legalistic covenant. The most interesting part of the covenant is the rainbow, which Elohim provides as a token of the bargain not to flood the Earth again. The rainbow appears in many myths from other parts of the world, and from a climatic point of view is clear evidence of a return of the Sun after any global catastrophe.

I will now extract some general story themes or motifs from both the Jehovistic (J) and Priestly (P) versions in Genesis, which I will compare with the rest of the Mesopotamian family and the other flood story-types from around the world (key words are in italics). In chronological order, these are:

1. *Evil*, corrupt, wicked man was the *reason* for the flood, which was sent as a *punishment* in Genesis. This story-type has to have a *previous creation*.

2. *Worldwide destruction of life by the catastrophe;* in the case of Genesis this was a flood. In some other stories there was a conflagration with or without a flood; in a few stories, the annihilation was complete and life had to be re-created.

3. One just *person* or hero and others were *warned/instructed/saved* by the author of the flood (or another deity). The covenant demanded for this good turn is unique to the Priestly version and need not be considered further. The *Flood hero* was either very *long-lived* or in other versions was made *immortal.*

4. A *period of grace* was allowed in preparation for the catastrophe.

5. The *author* of the flood was also previously the *Creator* and a just deity.

6. The *refuge* from the catastrophe in Genesis was a *sealed boat* or *chest.* Other stories describe canoes, logs, rafts, trees and caves.

7. The *occupants* of the Ark included other members of the family, food and breeding stock. Other stories included seeds and plants, and even priests.

8. The *nature* of the flood in Genesis was either *pluvial* (J) or pluvial with an ill-defined *sea cataclysm* (P). For other stories, I will try to determine whether a sea or land-based flood was specified and which of the types I have discussed could have happened.

9. In many stories there were, in addition to the flood, other *unusual*

climatic, geological or cosmic *phenomena*, such as preceding cold, drought and famine, loud noises, darkness, earthquakes, fire, steam, unnatural falls from the sky, stellar derangements etc. In Genesis there is only the mention of the fountains of the deep 'breaking up', and the wind that passed over the Earth at the end of the flood.

10. The *extent* of the Genesis flood was stated to be *worldwide* rather than local.

11. The *height* of the Genesis flood was stated as over the *mountain tops* (P) with the caveat that in one version it may have only been 5 metres above present sea level (J).

12. The *duration* of the Genesis flood was stated as either a year or sixty-one days.

13. Noah sent out *birds as land seekers* (J). Although they sometimes dived rather than flew, the bird motif is one of the most widespread in the world.

14. The *landing site* in Genesis was unspecified in the Jehovistic version but the mountains of Ararat in Asia minor are mentioned in the Priestly account.

15. At landing Noah made a *sacrifice* and received a *blessing*.

Two other parochial themes anchor the flood myth in the context of Genesis genealogies and are also found in other Ancient Near Eastern flood myths:

16. Noah's family tree includes *ten ante-diluvian patriarchs* including himself.

17. The extraordinary longevity, amounting to near *immortality* of those patriarchs, including Noah, who together reigned for 1656 years or *86,400* weeks.[10] A line in Genesis before the flood implies that God did not wish this state of affairs to last for ever: 'My spirit shall not abide in man for ever, for he is flesh, but his days shall be a hundred and twenty years.' (7:3)

Flood stories of Mesopotamia and Syria

Until 120 years ago, the mosaic account of the flood in Genesis was the only surviving version from Mesopotamia. The only other indication that Noah's story was not unique in the region came from second and third-hand references. A native Babylonian priest historian Berossus, who wrote in Greek in the third century BC, published a version of the flood, which was known in fragmentary copies passed through other Greek writers.[11]

The nineteenth century saw fabulous discoveries in the Ancient Near East. One of the more fantastic was described in a talk by a certain George Smith at the Society of Biblical Archaeology in London in 1872. Apprenticed as a banknote engraver at the age of fourteen, Smith spent his holidays hanging round the British Museum. He showed such interest that the Keeper of Oriental Antiquities gave him a job sorting out thousands of cuneiform inscriptions – the tiny fragments of tablets from Assyrian digs engraved with wedge-shaped writing. With intuitive genius he read the fragments and pieced together the different jigsaws they made up. At one point, realising he was on to something, he asked to have a certain tablet cleaned. This was the eleventh in a series of tablets later to be called the Epic of Gilgamesh. The expert tablet-cleaner, a Mr Ready, was on holiday and Smith, being rather highly strung, was very agitated at having to wait. When the tablet was finally clean, Ready handed it to him. With growing excitement Smith read the tablet. In his own words 'my eye caught the statement that the ship rested on the mountains of Nizir, followed by the account of the sending forth of the dove, and its finding no resting place and returning. I saw at once that I had here discovered a portion at least of the Chaldean account of the Deluge.'[12]

At this point it all became too much for the excited scholar. He cried, 'I am the first man to read that after two thousand years of oblivion.'[13] So saying, he placed the tablet on the table and, in front of some surprised museum staff, ripped off his clothes and danced round the room. When he presented his work on the Assyrian flood legends in 1872 the excitement became a national frenzy. *The Daily Telegraph* even sponsored him on an expedition to Nineveh to find the remaining tablets of the Gilgamesh series with their story of the flood survivor Utanapishtim. He failed in this, but found yet another Assyrian version of the flood, the story of Atrahasis.

The rest is history, sort of. There are now at least eleven related Ancient Near Eastern versions, including the two in Genesis and Berossus's account of Xisuthros. The three Assyrian versions were committed to tablet in the seventh century BC. This was perhaps a hundred years before the writing of the Priestly account in Genesis, but probably well after the Jehovistic account, for which a date is still under discussion. The two surviving Babylonian accounts were written thousands of years earlier somewhere between 1850 and 1500 BC. In one of these the hero was called Atramhasis. Finally, around 2100 BC, over 4000 years ago, we have the oldest two records of all, written by Sumerian scribes. One of these relates the story of Ziusudra, who was clearly the same as Berossus's hero Xisuthros. The other text is the Sumerian King List. This refers to the flood as a historic watershed in Sumerian history with eight ante-diluvian kings and five ante-diluvian cities. Even in these, the oldest written versions, the Flood was seen as something that happened a long time before.

Because we have approximate dates and locations for this related group of the oldest recorded myths it makes sense to start with the earliest, in an attempt to make a family tree. The first Sumerian flood myth was found on a fragmentary tablet at Nippur in Mesopotamia. Many lines are missing and others are incomplete, but enough motifs are present to establish the story-type we have detailed for Genesis. I have highlighted keywords for these motifs in italics rather than comment on each one.

The Sumerian flood

The story of Ziusudra starts with the *creation* of man, vegetation and animals, establishes the divine nature of kingship and names the five ante-diluvian cities and their *five gods*. God-fearing King *Ziusudra ('Long of Life')* carved a god of wood to worship, and stationed himself by a wall where he heard a *deity*, probably Enki, *warning* him of the *decision of the gods' assembly* to send *a deluge* to *destroy the seed of mankind*. No *reason* was found in the tablet for this *punishment*. Translators presume that in the next missing part of the tablet the friendly *deity instructed Ziusudra to build a giant boat to save himself and some animals*. When the text resumes, the *violent storm flood that had raged for seven days was over*. Ziusudra then removed the cover with which the boat was *sealed* and the *sun god* Utu appeared, lighting and warming up the Earth. Ziusudra then made a *sacrifice*, bowing before the gods An and Enlil. In return, he was *blessed with immortality* and was transported to Dilmun, the Sumerian *Eden in the East*, the 'place where the sun rises'.[14] No mountain is named in the Sumerian text. Oxford archaeologist Stephanie Dalley points out that 'in spite of the gaps in the text, it looks as if the sun comes out and dries up the water and the ark does not come to rest on anything but the emerging flat land'.[15]

The other Sumerian reference to the flood is, as mentioned, the Sumerian King List. Written at the end of the third millennium BC this historiographic record numerates again the five pre-flood cities Eridu, Badtibira, Larak, Sippar and Shuruppak, but also *eight* ante-diluvian

Kings of extraordinary *longevity*: 'five cities, eight Kings reigned 241,200 years. *The flood then swept over (the land)*. After the flood had swept over (the land) and kingship had descended from heaven (a second time), Kish became (the seat) of kingship.'[16] The post-diluvian kings in the list had more normal life spans.

The next story, that of Berossus, is chronologically out of place because it was the latest of all versions to be written and came out nearly 2000 years later than Ziusudra's. It is, however, so like the Sumerian flood story that most commentators[17] have concluded that Berossus, having a choice of versions available from Babylon to reproduce, chose the Sumerian one as the most ancient (the italics are mine in the following extract). Berossus:

> begins with the *creation* of the world, [and] points out ten ante-diluvian Kings of *long life*, indicating *Xisuthros* as the tenth, who appears as the *hero* of the *Flood*. According to Berossus, Xisuthros was *warned* by *one of the Gods* of the imminence of the Flood, being *ordered to prepare a ship to save his family and his friends, and also the animals*. Saved in this manner, he disembarked on a *mountain* in Armenia. After having *worshipped the Gods* he and his wife and daughter and the pilot *disappeared from among mortals to be with the Gods*.[18]

Although Berossus, who was writing on the Greek island of Kos, harked back to the 2000-year-older Sumerian flood story, several details are shared only with the Priestly account in Genesis, which appeared just 250 years after he wrote. These are that the flood hero was the *tenth ante-diluvian king*, the month of the start of the flood was named and that the ten kings ruled for a total of 432,000 'years' (that is 86,400 × 5, five years being sixty months).[19] Another detail in Berossus's version shared with the Priestly account rather than with the Sumerian or Old Babylonian versions is the mountain landing of the Ark in Asia Minor. Berossus also inserts a motif shared with the Jehovistic version – the use of birds to find land.

The Old Babylonian flood

The rule of the mysterious and brilliant Sumerians was replaced by a Semitic people, the Babylonians. During the first dynasty of Babylon, some 300 years later than the Sumerian flood story was written, the new scribes tried their hand at writing stories about this flood. Three similar versions exist from this period, two of them fragmentary. The third one, previously known only in fragments, is now available as a near-complete translation.[20] This 'Old Babylonian' flood story was written 3700 years ago, and a thousand years before the Priestly version of Genesis. With Atrahasis (meaning extra-wise) as the flood-hero, it is very close to the 1000-year younger Assyrian version that so excited George Smith in the British Museum. Although only a quarter the length of the great Epic of Gilgamesh, the Old Babylonian story ambitiously attempts a grand history of the world from before man's creation until just after the flood.

The scene starts before mankind's creation, and 5000 years before the flood, when the gods had to do their own work of canal-digging and dyke-building, irrigation and water control in Mesopotamia. After 3600 years of back-breaking work, they went on strike and noisily surrounded the gate of Ellil, god of wind and air, their divine foreman. Ellil dithered and tried to get the support of his senior colleagues. Eventually the gods persuaded Mami the womb goddess and creatrix to *create* a slave race *man* out of clay and the blood of a sacrificed god Geshtu-e.[21] This anachronistic sequence makes me pause to wonder whether the stevedore gods were really so divine, or whether the idea of controlling and using another man's or another race's labour had been imported to Mesopotamia. The fact that the whole story is told from the point of view of the hapless 'humans' implies that the 'gods' may have been former human overlords.

All went well at first, and the new 'men' built bigger irrigation canals to feed themselves and the 'gods'. After 600 years there were too many people and they spread over the country and made a loud noise. Ellil complained to his colleagues again and announced he would send a plague to control the population. At this point *Atrahasis* appeared. From the start he was in confidential and sympathetic communication with the god Enki. Enki advised Atrahasis and his people to make a noisy uprising and 'shame' the god of the underworld with offerings of bread. This stopped the plague and all was well for 600 years but 'men' became too numerous and noisy again, so Ellil sent a *drought and famine*. Again this was stopped by an uprising and 'shaming' Adad, the storm and water god, with a sacrifice of bread. This was followed, however, by a series of ever more dreadful droughts and their attending famines. The degree of drought and famine is told in prosaic tones: 'The dark pastureland was bleached, the broad countryside filled up with alkali ... Their faces covered with scabs ... Let the womb be too tight to let a baby out! ... They served up a daughter for a meal, served up a son for food.'[22] All of these effects would be expected in severe famines. The secondary infertility is particularly characteristic. We can only speculate whether the white sterile fields were purely a result of poor irrigation and alkali/salinisation, or whether there had been sea flooding as well.

At this point the gods, in particular Ellil and Enki, fell out among themselves with mutual recriminations for the famine getting out of hand. In the end Ellil pre-emptively resolved that a *flood* would be sent. In this instance the flood author was neither just, nor the most senior god nor the creator. The *reason* for the flood was still *overpopulation.* Enki refused to have any hand in it. Because *Enki* as a god was sworn to secrecy he could only *warn Atrahasis* indirectly. He therefore did so through the medium of a reed wall. Atrahasis was instructed by the wall to dismantle his house and build a multi-storey boat. The roof had to be *sealed* so that no sun could get in. Since he was to be sealed for seven days, and as we find out later there was *no sun* anyway, Enki gave Atrahasis a seven-day sand clock. He was to reject possessions and save only living things.

Atrahasis gave his people the excuse that he had to go and stay with Enki after a row between the latter and Ellil. They helped him make the boat out of wood, reeds and bitumen. While the artisans were feasting after their work, he stocked the boat with healthy specimens of *domestic and wild animals, birds and his own family.*

The flood was *catastrophic*. The storm came suddenly with a *loud noise* and darkening sky and a raging *wind* from Adad, so Atrahasis embarked, cut the mooring rope and sealed the lid of the Ark with bitumen. Unfortunately at this crucial point there is a damaged tablet and some missing text. One of the gods, Anzu, is described as tearing at the sky with his talons. Something is broken and the flood appears, and then:

> The kasusu weapon went against the people like an army.
> No one could see anyone else,
> They could not be recognised in the catastrophe.
> The Flood roared like a bull,
> Like a wild ass screaming the winds howled
> The *darkness was total,* and there was no sun.[23]

The storm was so terrible that the very gods, who had agreed to it by default, cowered whining and powerless. Mami the womb goddess in particular blamed Ellil for his pre-emptive role. She complained:

> Would a true father have given rise to the rolling sea, so that they [presumably dead bodies] could clog the river like dragon flies.[24]

Another reference to the *sea flood* was that the gods remained thirsty at the height of the flood and there is no direct mention of rain:

> Thirsty as they were, their lips
> Discharged only the rime of famine.
> For seven days and seven nights
> The torrent, storm and flood came on.[25]

At this point in the story there is a large gap and we resume with Atrahasis burning thanksgiving *sacrifices* for his survival. The gods clustered round like flies for their ritual sustenance; for, like Peter Pan, they could not survive without recognition. Ellil turned up for the party and Mami the womb-goddess asked who invited him after all the trouble he had caused. Ellil responded by saying he thought they had all agreed on total destruction; so what was this boat doing here? Anu, the most senior, suggested they all asked Enki who had spoken to the reed wall. Enki defiantly defended his action in preserving life. In the end they all backed down and agreed to have some birth-control laws to solve the population problem. One law was the establishment of a caste of virgin priestesses. It has been suggested that one of the control measures referred to in the text was a withdrawal of the previously enjoyed *immortality* from mankind.[26]

In this Old Babylonian epic story of the flood we have a very different moral tone to the controlled righteous fury of Elohim in the Priestly account in Genesis. There is more of a parallel with Jehovah's self-regret in the Jehovistic version. The Babylonian gods appear to show fear, lack of self-control, disunity, poor leadership, indecisiveness and general incompetence. Although the shared motifs I have highlighted in the text leave no doubt that the stories are related, the context for sending the flood was completely different from Genesis. The problem, as all the gods agreed, was overpopulation. What they could not agree on was how to deal with it. There is a parallel for the overpopulation motif in the Greek poem the *Cypria* attributed to Homer. In this, Zeus planned a war to trim down the population.[27]

The other notable differences from Genesis are in the circumstances and nature of the flood. Dealing first with the ante-diluvian story-line, the recurrent droughts and famines preceding the flood in the epic appear to last over 1000 years, depending on how the chronology and gaps in text are interpreted. The recurrent ante-diluvian cycles of plagues, droughts, famine and sterility of people and fields reappears

1000 years later in an incomplete Assyrian flood myth. In this story the overpopulation excuse for the flood is replaced by the 'evil mankind' motif.[28] Many flood myths from other parts of the world record similar famine/drought phenomena. The flood myths of the Algonquian Indians of northeastern America and Canada have a prolonged period of cold and famine before the flood (see Chapters 10 and 11). If these have any basis in prehistoric reality the story could be taken back to a mini Ice Age like the Younger Dryas episode, as described earlier, when global temperatures were 20 degrees centigrade lower and rainfall was very low. The end of the Younger Dryas event was characterised by a massive ice-melt that produced lots of rain and a rapid rise in sea level.[29] A similar cycle accompanied the third flood only 7500–8000 years ago. Although this sequence fits with the description of a sea flood in the Old Babylonian Atrahasis epic, it does not explain the sudden and cataclysmic nature of the flood that is shared with the Priestly account, unless we suppose superwaves set off by the collapsing ice plate. The duration of one week is shorter than either biblical version. The graphic if incomplete description of the disaster in the Atrahasis epic gives us more the picture of the sea rolling in deep over the land in a superstorm and then draining back down the river beds. The accompanying phenomena of noise, high winds, total darkness and Anzu tearing at the sky serve to emphasise the catastrophic nature of the event but cannot tell us what was the cause.

In the Old Babylonian account of Atrahasis, we are meant to take the flood as a universal event but there is no mention of it reaching the mountain tops nor of sending out birds, nor the boat landing on any mountain. This last motif appears only in the Priestly version and the contemporary versions of the flood found in Asia Minor, such as Berossus's Babylonia, the Greek myths and the Assyrian rendering of the Gilgamesh Epic (see below).

The Assyrian flood

It was the landing of the Ark on Mount Nisir near Nineveh (now Nimush – southern Kurdistan) that first caught George Smith's eye on the famous eleventh tablet of the Gilgamesh Epic. Scholars now agree that the flood episode was added later and did not feature in the original Sumerian Gilgamesh story cycle. Stephanie Dalley argues that it was not present even in the Old Babylonian versions, and was added only when the story got to Assyria.[30] The Assyrian redactors incorporated a description of the flood story as an episode into the Gilgamesh Epic for one reason only, and that was *immortality*. As we shall see in Chapter 14, a main story-line of the Epic was Gilgamesh's search for immortality. In the Assyrian version this quest took him to visit the *Sumerian flood hero Utnapishtim*, a former King of the Sumerian city of Shuruppak, who was the only 'surviving' man to have received this gift of the gods.

Gilgamesh had to tackle many obstacles in his epic journey to find Utnapishtim, 'the far distant' in his retirement home 'at the mouth of the rivers'. The location of this paradise is much debated. One popular view is that the rivers were the Tigris and the Euphrates and that the paradise was Bahrain. Bahrain is also regarded by some as the legendary Dilmun, the paradise Atrahasis was transported to after the flood.[31] But the 480-kilometre journey from Ur to Bahrain could hardly be described as difficult for the seafaring Sumerians, let alone epic. Recently geologists have tried to read a journey to the Black Sea into the text, to tie up with the known flooding of the Black Sea 7200 years ago. The problem is that much of the action in Gilgamesh's journey is symbolic and abstract to the point of obscurity so that one can read virtually any itinerary into it. Stephanie Dalley has noted some common episodes between Gilgamesh's journey and the Odyssey and later Arab trading myths.[32] My own personal choices for Utnapishtim's paradise are further east, either the Indus delta or even as far east as Southeast Asia. The text gives as much or as little support as it does for the other locations. In the final leg of the journey, Gilgamesh crossed a sea with the help of a ferryman. As he neared the land where Utnapishtim lived, he had to drive in three hundred 30-metre pre-measured pine poles with knobs on to navigate the 'lethal' water. Opinions on the meaning of this dangerous water vary from the salinisation of the Black Sea to water that is poisonous to touch (that is, sea of death).[33] The simplest explanation seems to me that he was using depth markers in treacherous tidal muddy shallows.

When the exhausted and bedraggled Gilgamesh finally met Utnapishtim he found himself the target of a patronising philosophical speech from the immortal about life and death. Gilgamesh, a man of action, cut this speech short by offering to have a man-to-man fight and demanding to know how Utnapishtim was lucky enough to get his immortality. Utnapishtim responded with a nearly word-for-word recital of the seven-day catastrophic Atrahasis flood story with himself as flood hero. Utnapishtim's tale of the flood ended with the god Elill giving him *immortality* just before sending him to his retirement home at the mouth of the rivers. The only notable differences from the Old Babylonian Atrahasis story come in some extra details of boat-building, the gold and silver that was brought aboard, a boatman and some of the details of the end of the flood. These last details show two contradictory versions in the same text. The two accounts are analogous in many respects to the Priestly and Jehovistic versions and had been spliced together as in the Bible. I have reproduced them below with my own italics to indicate the conflicting and partially repetitive text:

When the seventh day had arrived the tempest, flood and onslaught
Which had struggled like a woman in labour, blew themselves out.
The sea became calm, the imhullu-wind grew quiet, the flood held back.

I looked at the weather; silence reigned,

For all mankind had turned to clay.
The flood-plain was flat as a roof.

I opened a porthole and light fell on my cheeks.
I bent down, then sat. I wept.
My tears ran down my cheeks.

I looked for banks, for limits to the sea.
Areas of land were emerging everywhere.
The boat had come to rest on Mount Nimush.
The mountain Nimush held the boat fast and did not let it budge.
The first and second day the mountain Nimush held the boat fast and did not let it budge.
The third and fourth day the mountain Nimush held the boat fast and did not let it budge.
The fifth and sixth day the mountain Nimush held the boat fast and did not let it budge.

When the seventh day arrived,

I put out and released a dove.
The dove went; it came back,
For no perching place was visible to it, and it turned round.
I put out and released a swallow.
The swallow went; it came back,
For no perching place was visible to it, and it turned round.
I put out and released a raven.
The raven went, and saw the waters receding.
And it ate, preened, lifted its tail and did not turn round.
Then I put everything out to the four winds, and I made a sacrifice,

Set out a surqinnu-offering upon the mountain peak.[34]

The lines in italics, like the Jehovistic version, tell us of a flat flood-plain of endless horizon and of the birds sent out to find land. In contrast the other verses in plain typescript echo the Priestly account with a landing on a mountain in Kurdistan followed by sacrifice. The inherent contradictions in the text are obvious. A flat featureless flood-plain could not hide the mountain the Ark had just come to rest on; and, as in Genesis, there would be no point sending out the birds to look for land if the Ark had already landed on the mountain.

Three flood stories of the Ancient Near East

The same kind of clumsy splicing of the same two stories makes it likely that the Genesis redactors were using the same double-barrelled edition as the Assyrians rather than tapping from a Mesopotamian source during their exile in Babylon in the first millennium BC, as was formerly suggested. These considerations and the foregoing discussion support the idea that at least two if not three traditions have become merged in the Ancient Near East since the fourth millennium BC. In summary:

1. The first tradition in the Arabian Gulf in Sumerian and Old Babylonian texts was written over 4000 years ago. This *Babylonian* type is characterised by a long period of drought and famine followed by a seven-day catastrophic sea flood over flat land. The flood hero is warned by a god who is neither the creator nor the author of the flood. The message is passed via a talking reed wall. The hero builds a wood/reed ark and seals himself, his family and animals in. After the cataclysm, the flood drains back to the sea, the land dries and the flood hero gets out to make a sacrifice. He and his wife are then made immortal and transported to a far off earthly paradise at the mouth of the rivers in the East.

The two other types are found to the northwest in Asia Minor and Genesis. They were written in the first millennium BC and although they borrowed much from the Mesopotamian versions, two new and separate traditions were added.

2. The first of these, the *Bird*-type, is represented in the Jehovistic account, in part of Berossus and in the italicised part of the Assyrian Gilgamesh. It retains the sealed chest and flat-land flooding of Mesopotamia, but introduces the land-seeking birds.
3. The second of the West Asian types introduces the motifs of mountain drowning and mountain landing. This *Mountain*-type is found in the Priestly version and the un-italicised part of the Assyrian Gilgamesh flood story. Berossus also borrowed the mountain motif

and the ten ante-diluvian Kings from the Priestly version. The mountain-type is also characteristic of the nearby Greek and Anatolian flood traditions, which may be the origin of the motif in this region.

Greek flood myths

Frazer lists fifteen Greek flood stories in his *Folklore in the Old Testament*, twelve of which record a mountain landing.[35] I base the following descriptions of the Greek stories on his accounts. Ancient mythographers have grouped these chronologically into three separate floods: the Boeotian flood of Ogyges of about 2100 BC, the Thessalian flood of Deucalion and Pyrrha of about 1500 BC and the last, that of Dardanus of unspecified date, in which he took refuge on the island of Samothrace.

The earliest of the Greek flood heroes, Ogyges, was said to be a King of Thebes in Boeotia. One account states that the whole Earth was submerged by the flood, even Mount Parnassus and the peaks of Thessaly. Apart from the name of the hero, the lack of specific details and the earlier legendary date, there is not much to distinguish this legend from that of Deucalion, since it occurred in the same region.

The largest group of Greek flood myths relates the story of Deucalion and Pyrrha, son and daughter respectively of Prometheus and Epimetheus. Pyrrha's mother was Pandora, the first being fashioned by the gods. According to Apollodorus, Zeus wished to destroy the men of the Bronze Age. Prometheus therefore advised his son Deucalion to construct a chest or ark and, after stocking it with provisions, to seal himself and his wife in it. Zeus then sent rain and washed most of Greece down. All men perished except those that climbed the highest mountains. Then the mountains in Thessaly were parted and all the world beyond the Isthmus and Peleponnese was overwhelmed. Deucalion and Pyrrha floated in their chest for nine days and finally grounded on Mount Parnassus. When the rains stopped, Deucalion made a sacrifice to Zeus who sent Hermes to ask what wish he had. Deucalion chose men, and at Zeus' command he picked up stones and threw them over his head. The stones became men. Pyrrha did the same and her stones became women.

Other versions of the same myth record post-flood landings at various sites around the plain of Thessaly such as Mount Gerania and Mount Othrys. Gatherings of refugees with other animals such as wolves and cranes on mountains are also mentioned. The stone creation motif is also mentioned in an earlier telling by Hellanicus in the fifth century BC. Much later, the Roman author Ovid livened up the story with details of wind, rain, thunder and a rolling in of the sea. He even used the phrase: 'The fountains of the great deep were now opened' which seems like a steal from the Priestly account. Ovid also recorded that the flood had been sent because of man's wickedness.

The same motifs reappear in Lucian's late description of the Deucalion myth told in relation to the worship of Astarte at Hierapolis on the Syrian section of the Euphrates river. There is a suspicion that the Greek myth had combined somehow with Berossus and Genesis in this region maybe as a result of the Alexandrian conquests in West Asia. This suspicion is increased by the use of the name Sisuthea in the opening lines of Lucian's text, which sounds very close to Berossus's Xisuthrus. Even the dove motif is inserted into a late version of Deucalion written by Plutarch.

The descriptions and clustering of the Deucalion legends around Thessaly and its mountains point to a local flood of the plain of Thessaly. This plain forms an hourglass-shaped basin surrounded by mountains with a narrow low-lying exit to the sea between Mount Olympus and Mount Ossa, the Peneus gorge. Herodotus recalled a legend that the plain of Thessaly was once a huge lake and that the gorge was cleaved by a great earthquake sent by Poseidon. The Mediterranean achieved its present level only around 5500 years ago, so the drop in water level between the lake and sea-level may have been considerable. Whatever the level of the sea, a sudden release of a huge volume of lake water is a recognised cause of a superflood. This theory was disputed by T. H. Huxley, who regarded the Peneus gorge as a typical erosion valley.[36] Frazer suggests that the local details of this myth might only amount to a so-called 'myth of observation'.[37] This term coined by Sir Edward Tylor supposes that people invent myths to explain local features such as natural geographical formations.[38] If that is so, then the other motifs of the Greek myths – for instance the ark – may still belong to a more widespread family. The argument of 'observational myths', however, can hardly be used to explain the fact that half of the world stock of flood myths record a mountain-covering flood.

I have already mentioned above the spread of the Deucalion myth into Syria. One motif shared with the Greek Deucalion versions that recurs in the flood myths in West Asia[39] is the legend of a devastating lake flood with the water finally disappearing down a chasm that opened up in the ground. Ovid recorded the Anatolian folk myth of Philemon and Baucis in his *Metamorphoses* which 'explains' the origin of a particular temple of Jupiter in the Phrygian hills. It tells of two old peasants who welcomed two strange travellers who had been turned away from a thousand doors. Philemon and Baucis were about to kill their last gander for the pot for their visitors, when the bird fled to the strangers, who then changed into the gods Jupiter and Mercury (Zeus and Hermes). The divine pair determined to wipe out the wicked inhabitants of the locality while saving their hosts. They led the old couple up a long slope to the mountains and then they turned round. They were amazed to see the whole valley filled with water except their own house which had changed to a temple. The old couple spent the rest of their days as priest and priestess of the temple and were finally changed to sacred trees.[40] W. M. Calder at the University of Manchester has examined the mythic and geographic background of this story and concludes that it does refer to a lake flood.[41] The identities of the gods in this story are, however, shared with the Deucalion myth, which suggests some diffusional connection across the Aegean Sea.

Whether all these stories of lake floods from both sides of the Aegean Sea can be tied into the recent discovery of the catastrophic spilling of the Sea of Marmara into the Black Sea 7150 years ago[42] is, of course, a tempting speculation. But the only legends of the region that point specifically towards the Black Sea unfortunately (for the theory) describe the flood going in the other direction – that is, through the Dardanelles and into the Aegean Sea.[43] If the myth had the opposite direction it would fit the recent discovery of the Black Sea flood perfectly.

The first and better known of these Aegean flood myths is the legend of King Dardanus who lived in the highlands of Arcadia. When the flood came he escaped on a raft and landed the other side of the Aegean on the mountainous island of Samothrace which guards the opening of the Dardanelles. In another version he was flooded in Samothrace itself and made his way on an inflated skin to Mount Ida on the Turkish mainland where he founded Dardania or Troy. The third and most remarkable version was held by Samothracians themselves, who claimed the original true story. Their tradition stated that in antiquity the Black Sea was separated from the Aegean. Then the waters of the Black Sea rose and suddenly broke the barriers, which till then had kept it apart from the Mediterranean. The enormous volume of water thus released carved a passage through the Bosphorus and through the Dardanelles to make the passage that we see today. As a final result, the torrent that was released washed over a large part of the eastern Aegean coast and the lowlands of the island of Samothrace, forcing the inhabitants to seek refuge on the mountain.

This last Greek tale, fantastic as it sounds, has more credibility than any of the foregoing stories. First it does not belong to the group of 'aetiological myths' since it does not try to explain anything such as a geographic feature or a city foundation. Second, surprising as it seems, the sea-level record does show a time 9500 years ago when the Black Sea was briefly a fresh-water lake 20 metres *higher* than the Aegean.[44] This hypothetical situation occurred 2000 years before the recently proven flood in the opposite direction. There is, however, no evidence for such a reverse flood from the sea-floor record.

To summarise, the flood myths of Semitic-speaking West Asia and Indo-European-speaking Greek cultures show considerable overlap in detail with the Mesopotamian stories. In addition they contain the two motifs of mountain flooding and lake bursting. The lake-burst motif could fit several locations both in Greece and Turkey, but the mother of the legend could have been superfloods surging either way between the Black Sea, the Sea of Marmara and the Aegean.

Flood traditions exist in other Indo-European cultures, but apart from some borrowing of Sumerian and Semitic motifs, they are rather different and idiosyncratic; they are also intriguing.

Iranian flood traditions

There is no strong diluvial tradition in Iranian mythology. In the *Bundahis* cosmogony the angel 'Tistar', the embodiment of the dog-star Sirius, waged war with the Evil Spirit and in the three forms of man, horse and bull he created a thirty-day downpour that left the Earth covered to the depth of a man's height.[45] This cleansed the Earth of all the offspring of the Evil Spirit, who drowned in caves. It was their venom that made the sea salty.

The Persian *Zend Avesta* also has a world catastrophe, which, although not a flood, shares sufficient motifs with other flood myths to justify inclusion. In this story, the reason for the flood was over-population, as in the Mesopotamian flood stories. After a golden age of 900 years, the world was crowded with animals and people. The hero Yima managed to enlarge the Earth thrice at 300-year intervals with the help of the Creator Ahura Mazda. Finally, however, the creator, after consultation with other gods, warned Yima that the world would be plunged into a prolonged winter with deep snow and many creatures would die. He was told to create a *vara*, a protective heated enclosure, and introduce healthy seeds of plants, humans and creatures and keep them going for many years.[46] In this story there are links not only with the the Norse mythology of the big freeze (see below) but also possibly with the Mesopotamian pre-flood drought, if the latter event was truly a result of a short Ice Age. The *vara* or place of safety does sound somewhat like a 'dry ark' and Yima may be cognate with the Indian Yama and Norse Ymir.

Western European floods

Flood myths crop up further west in Europe. Many of these refer to a race of giants who lived there before the flood. The Celtic Welsh have a myth about a lake burst which may have travelled from the eastern Mediterranean and been modified to local tradition. They say that 'once upon a time the lake of Llion burst and flooded all lands, so that the whole human race was drowned, all except Dwyfan and Dwyfach who escaped in a naked or mastless ship and re-peopled the island of Prydain (Britain). The ship also contained a male and a female of every sort of living creature, so that after the deluge the animals were able to propagate their various kinds and restock the world.'[47] This legend sounds closer to those of Asia Minor than any Christian diffusional copy. The Celts have not been in Wales long enough to have experienced any cataclysmic prehistoric flood. The fact that Celts have occupied the British Isles only during relatively recent times has not stopped the local flourishing of flood myths in Ireland, which has one of the richest oral traditions in Europe; and when we examine the motifs and story-types in the Irish tradition, there are clearly two separate non-Celtic sources, one from the Norse and the other from the European Christian oral tradition.

I have already alluded to the watery creation of the Finnish *Kalevala*. The Norse peoples have a much more direct and climatic flood story, which is intimately bound up with their own creation myth. Furthermore, the story is symbolically close to our concept of the dramatic end of the Ice Age. The *Edda* tells that in the beginning there were two regions – Muspell in the south, full of brightness and fire, and a world of snow and ice in the north. Between them stretched the great emptiness of Ginnungagap. As the heat and cold met in the middle, a living giant called Ymir appeared in the melting ice. From under his left arm grew the first man and woman, while a family of frost giants arose from his two feet. Ymir fed on the milk of a cow called Auohumla, who licked the salty ice blocks and released another new being, a man called Buri. He had a son called Bor. The god Bor had three sons, Odin, Willi and We who killed Ymir the giant. All the frost giants except one named Bergelmir were drowned in the giant's flowing blood. His blood became the lakes and sea.[48] The imagery of the melting ice cap with the resulting regeneration of life could not be contrived better as an explanatory myth of the flood in northern regions of Europe. An interesting motif is the pre-flood race of giants who perished. Many flood myths, including the Priestly account, refer to a race of giants who previously lived on Earth just before the flood (Genesis 6:4).

We can only speculate whether the frost giants who grew out of Ymir's feet and disappeared or drowned as the ice cap melted were an earlier European race such as the Cro-Magnon people who may have seemed different or larger to the new arrivals from the Middle East at the end of the Ice Age. Another version of the myth mentioned by Snorri Sturluson, a medieval compiler of Norse myths, tells that the surviving giant Bergelmir escaped the flood with his wife in a boat and founded a later race of giants.[49]

A Lithuanian story relates that the supreme god Pramzimas was so fed up with man's wickedness that he sent two giants, Wandu and Wejas (wind and water), to destroy the Earth. The two laid about themselves with such gusto that after twenty days there was not much left but a few humans and animals huddling together in refuge from the flood on the mountain tops. The creator was eating nuts and let a few shells fall. One of these landed on the mountain top, thus providing an ark for the survivors. Pramzimas then stopped the wind and water and the flood abated. The survivors spread out and repopulated the land. An aged couple was left on the spot, and being too shocked and exhausted to do much about repopulation, Pramzimas came to their help. He sent them the rainbow we heard about in Genesis, and told them to jump over the bones of the Earth nine times. As a result, nine more couples were created who became the ancestors of the nine Lithuanian tribes.[50] There is reference to stones being the bones of the ancestors in one of the Deucalion and Pyrrha versions of the Greek flood stories.

The Voguls, a people speaking a Finno-Ugric language located either side of the Ural Mountains, have a flood version that harks right back to the Sumerian or Babylonian original. The story, which is told of a race of giants, begins with a seven-year drought. The giant elders became aware, from a rumbling noise lasting two days, that a cataclysm with giant waves was about to engulf them. Their elder giant made the following suggestions to prepare for the holy flood:

> Let us cut a poplar in two, hollow it out and make two boats. Then we shall weave a rope of willow roots five hundred fathoms long. We shall bury one end of it in the earth and fasten the other to the bow of our boats. Let every man with children embark in the boat with his family, and let them be covered with tarpaulin of cowhide, let victuals be made ready for seven days and seven nights and put under the tarpaulin. And let us place pots of melted butter in each boat.[51]

Those that did not follow his instructions right down to the length of the ropes and the amount of butter to grease them with, or who tried to take other refuge, perished in the hot flood that swept all before it. The flood started to go down after seven days, but everything had been swept away so had to be re-created.

There are several motifs in this story that are shared with the Old Babylonian version. The flood was preceded by drought, the flood was catastrophic and lasted seven days, the boat was covered over the top so that the sun (and water) could not get in. The grease is also mentioned in the part of the Gilgamesh Epic that copies Atrahasis:

> Three sar of oil they fetched, the workmen who carried the baskets.
> Not counting the sar of oil which the dust soaked up,
> The boatman stored away two more sar of oil.[52]

The similarities may be coincidental, but this story from west-central Asia on the border with Europe concerns a sea flood. Since the migratory route of the Uralic peoples radiated towards the north some 4000 years ago, it seems likely that the myth originated somewhere south round the Indian Ocean. Uralic languages may be the nearest living relative to Sumerian.[53] Furthermore, the content of the legend appears to describe superwaves and a superflood.

The five flood traditions in the West

So far I have tried to reconstruct five separate deluge traditions of Europe and the Ancient Near East: the Sumerian, which was adopted by the Semitic Babylonians, two from Asia Minor and two Indo-European, from northern Europe. All but the Norse myths involve the survivors taking refuge in some form of ark. Apart from the flood and the ark there are insufficient motifs to relate these stories back to one type or even a family. That was certainly Sir James Frazer's view.[54] But I think we should at least explore the possibility of a common ancestor or archetype. One obvious potential diffusional source, apart from Semitic or Sumerian, is an Indo-European tradition from South Asia. We might expect that India, which is a recipient of Indo-European speakers relatively unaffected by Semitic traditions, might at least help us to determine an original Indo-European sub-stratum. In the event the Indian flood stories give us much more of a window on East Asian traditions, as I shall discuss in the next chapter.

10

FLOODS IN THE EAST

India may well have had its own flood myths before the time of Sumerian King Gilgamesh in the third millennium BC. Without the earliest written records we can look at this possibility only by comparing the flood stories. As with the other Eurasian origin myths, this approach shows that although local experience colours the tales, there is clear evidence for diffusion of motifs from the East.

Genetically, geographically and linguistically India bridges the deep divide between East and West. This key position could help determine the direction of East–West cultural flow. Given that the earliest written reference to the flood in Mesopotamia was more than 4000 years ago, it would be very helpful to know the relative roles played by local experience and regional diffusion in India. Because Europeans share language families and physiognomy with a large part of the Indian subcontinent, they often think of India as more West than East. In Chapters 6 and 7, I showed that there is a surprisingly high frequency of Far Eastern genetic markers both in north and south India.

The West has clearly had enormous cultural influence on India resulting from the Aryan invasions through Iran into the subcontinent. These started around 4000 years ago, which was after the first Sumerian and Babylonian written versions of the flood. If the latter were the original source of all flood stories, as some scholars suggest, flood myths in India might be expected to derive their content and structure from the Old Babylonian type or one of the western Indo-European types.

As I noted in the last chapter, the Sumerian or Old Babylonian flood tradition has a long period of drought and famine followed by a seven-day catastrophic sea flood over flat land. The flood hero was warned by a god who was neither the creator nor the author of the flood. Upon instruction, the hero built a wooden ark or chest and sealed himself, his family and animals in. After a cataclysm, the flood drained back to the sea and the land dried. In the Middle East, one variant of this basic story had land-seeking birds. The other Middle Eastern variant, which was shared by both Semitic and Greek (that is, Indo-European) versions, introduced a different flood motif – the 'mountain-topping flood and mountain-landing ark'. Finally there were several highly idiosyncratic western European versions. The Iranians, who we might expect to hold a similar or even ancestral story to India, had little in the way of a diluvial tradition, telling instead of a series of droughts, as in the early part of the Sumerian flood story.

Manu's flood

The best-known of the Indian deluge stories is that of Manu and the fish. The flood hero, Manu, was actually the seventh of a series of fourteen Manus that represented mythic cycles of creation and destruction by flood stretching back hundreds of thousands of years. According to Hindu chronology, we are still in the seventh Manu cycle with seven more to go. The story of Manu appears in at least five sacred Hindu texts, the *Satapatha Brahmana*, the *Mahabharata*, the *Matsyu Purana*, the *Bhagavata Purana* and the *Agni Purana*. In spite of the text link, however, it seems that the story is not an Indo-European Ur-myth. Although the story appears in texts written in the first half of the first millennium BC and 300 years before Alexander's conquests in India, it does not appear in the earlier Vedic hymns. These were the oldest Aryan texts written between 1500 BC and 1000 BC before the Aryan spread south and east out of the Punjab. By the time of the earliest written record of the myth around 600 BC, the Aryans had reached the Indus Valley.[1] These dates preclude a Greek diffusional connection either way. This makes it more likely that we are dealing with a pre-existing indigenous Indian flood myth picked up by the expanding Aryans. Thus Manu's flood was derived from either the indigenous Dravidians or the Austro-Asiatic cultures of the Munda (see below), or even from the Indus Valley civilisation itself. If there was any diffusional connection for the myth with the Ancient Near East, it would thus be more likely to have been through trade with the latter civilisation or through a more ancient third source. In this latter case we should expect to see a relationship with the Babylonian myth.

The earliest provenanced record of the myth comes from the *Satapatha Brahmana*, written between 800 and 500 BC and before the Priestly account in Genesis. Although it has the motifs of a sea flood, the warning god (in this case in the form of a fish) and the advance instructions to build an ark, there the similarities with the Old Babylonian or Sumerian version cease. The hero waits until the flood has risen before embarking. This implies that there were no great waves or sudden catastrophe. There is clearly a mountain landing, which follows the Middle Eastern mountain type, rather than the Sumerian drying plain. Finally, a rope is tied to the mountain as in the Uralic myth of the Voguls which I described earlier.

When they brought water for Manu to wash his hands with, a small fish came into his hands. The fish promised to save Manu from a great flood, which would carry away all animals, if only he would save him. Manu asked how? The fish asked to be reared in safe containers of increasing size. It soon became the largest of all fish. Before Manu released the fish into the sea, the fish told him when the flood would come. The fish further ordered Manu to build a ship and said that he, the fish, would save him. The text is ambiguous here and in some translations the fish instructed Manu to worship him as well. Manu made the ship in the same year, and when the flood had risen he entered the ship. The fish then swam up to the ship and Manu attached the bow rope to the fish's horn. The fish towed Manu over to 'the northern mountain' where it announced that he was saved. It instructed him to tie up to a tree and not to let the water 'cut him off' from the mountain as he descended. The water gradually settled and the boat on the mountain with it. The mountain slope is now called 'Manu's descent'. Manu alone remained, for everything else had been swept away.

The next part of the story described a re-creation. Manu, the sole survivor and lacking a wife or partner, practised austerities, and offered up in the waters clarified butter, sour milk, whey and curds. Within a year a fully formed woman with rather buttery footprints rose from the sacrifice as a blessing for Manu. She greeted him as his daughter and encouraged him to use her as an intermediary in sacrifices to regenerate men and beasts. All this was successful and the race of Manu or man was generated.[2] In spite of the niceties of ritual, there is an implied incest in this last part of the tale that hints at Austro-Asiatic origins, which I will discuss shortly.

Several hundred years later around 500 BC we find nearly the same story encapsulated in the world's longest epic poem, the *Mahabharata*. This version varies in small details such as the additional seven sages and various seeds Manu was obliged to take with him on the boat from the Ganges delta. This ark tossed about on the waves for many years, until the fish brought it to the highest peak of the Himavat. We also find that the fish identified itself as Prajapati Brahma and because Manu had great skills he did not need the help of a divine daughter to regenerate the world.[3] Tales from the *Mahabharata* were later included without much change in *puranas* or written legends. In all versions the flood is clearly described as coming from the sea and world-destroying. The fish always towed the boat by a rope tied to its horn, although it became increasingly like a serpent in some versions. This last motif implies an influence from the sea snake of the Nagas of Assam, which in turn derives from East Asia (see Chapter 15).

The other common motifs of the later *puranas* featuring Manu's flood are the seven sages, the addition of seeds on the boat, the identity of the fish/serpent with Vishnu, seven days warning before the flood, and universal darkness after the cataclysm. The sea flood and rope, however, remain constant. In the last five added features there are now hints of shared motifs with the earliest Sumerian and Old Babylonian stories (see last chapter). The proximity of the Arabian Gulf with India could support a late diffusion of these motifs from Babylon via trade, but this would still leave the earliest Indian versions with provenance discrete from the Mesopotamian ones. Certainly the only European myth with both a fish-associated flood and also a warning from its author, comes from Transylvanian gypsies,[4] who are an Indic-speaking group in any case. The consensus view is that the Manu/fish/flood story does not have an Indo-European origin.

A fiery catastrophe

In one of the *puranas,* the *Matsyu Purana*, completely different motifs appeared, pointing further to the East. The main story was well preserved but more features had crept in. For instance, Manu was now the son of the sun-god and lived in Malaya or Malabar[5] before the deluge. This version also has a prolonged drought and tormenting famine preceding the flood, and various conflagrations suggestive of intense seismic activity. These include rains of burning charcoal and:

> the submarine fire shall burst forth ... Thus kindled, the world shall be confounded. When, consumed in this manner, the earth shall become like ashes, the aether too shall be scorched with heat ... The seven clouds of the period of dissolution ... produced from the steam of the fire, shall inundate the earth. The seas agitated, and joined together, shall reduce these entire three worlds to one ocean.[6]

We are left to wonder where this description of global fire and tectonic convulsion, beloved by catastrophists, came from. The pyrotechnics do not feature in any other Manu version. The details suggest a grand disaster, such as may follow a meteorite strike or rapid tilt of the Earth. Southeast Asia and Australia have common rocks, dating from the Old Stone Age, containing tectites – small silica-rich particles probably thrown up by meteor impacts, which could have given rise to stories of rains of fire.

Other support for a Far Eastern source of the fire motif – as I shall elaborate shortly – comes from the Aboriginal Mundaic tribes of central India. Speaking Austro-Asiatic tongues related to Mon-Khmer, the Hos Kols, a Mundaic tribe from West Bengal, say that after the first creation, people became incestuous and disrespectful of their god. So Sing Bonga, the creator, resolved to destroy them all, some say by fire and others by water.[7] Another group of Kols, the Mundaris from Chota Nagpur, have a fuller version. After the first creation when people were made from dust, mankind grew wicked and hedonistic. Sing Bonga repented making humans and resolved to send a flood to destroy them. To this purpose he sent a stream of fire water down from heaven and killed everybody. Only two were saved, a brother and a sister who hid under a tree. God thought better of his act and stopped the fiery rain by creating a rainbow snake called Lurbing who puffed himself up to hold up the showers.[8] This motif also appears in Australian flood myths, as we shall see.

Another Austro-Asiatic Aboriginal tribe, the Santals of Bengal, have three distinct versions of a deluge of '*Fire rain*' sent by their creator Thakur.[9]

An Austro-Asiatic fish motif from the East?

Finally, there is one more piece of independent, non-fiery evidence from India that points to an Eastern origin of the fish motif and may yet hold the key link to the origin of the Manu fish/flood story-type in India. This is the fish/flood story of the Bhils, a jungle Aboriginal group in central India. First recorded at the turn of the century,[10] this legend was re-checked just before the Second World War by Wilhelm Koppers. The story type is of particular interest not only because of the modified fish motif but also because of the explicit incest motif. The bird-finder with the sealed chest may also link with the Middle Eastern flood type found in the Priestly account of Genesis and in Gilgamesh. The Bhil tribe speak a dialect of the Indo-Aryan tongue called Gujarati, but they are regarded as pre-Aryan in origin and culture. Kopper could not tell from non-Indo-Aryan elements of their language whether they had been Dravidian or Austro-Asiatic speakers originally:

Bhagwan created two washer-people, a brother and sister, who were to become the progenitors of mankind. When drawing water at the stream the sister made friends with a fish, Ro, by feeding it rice. One day the fish asked her what reward she desired. The girl had no particular request, and so the fish said:

> 'Through water the earth will be turned upside down. Take pumpkin seeds with you and make a cage. Then do you and your brother step into the cage, taking seed and water with you. And do not forget to bring a cock also.' The rains then began to fall, slowly at first, then in ever greater torrents. It was as if earth and heaven had merged into one. Then God spoke: 'Thus have I turned the world upside down. But has not someone survived? The crowing of the cock informs me of it.' Bhagwan ... came to where the cage was and asked, 'Is anyone inside?' Then the girl answered ... Then God spoke: 'I have destroyed the whole world. Who warned you and gave you the advice to build such a cage?'[11]

Bhagwan then encouraged the brother and sister to commit incest, and they became the progenitors of the human race with all its different languages. In the first generation there were seven brothers and seven sisters.[12]

The key motifs in this story are the fish warning, the sealed cage, the bird-finder, the encouraged incest of the siblings and the seed. In spite of the missing linguistic link, there is good thematic evidence that the Bhils derived their story from a very ancient Austro-Asiatic stock thousands of miles to the east among the Bahnar Aboriginals of Vietnam. The Bahnars, who live in the highlands of Vietnam, speak Austro-Asiatic tongues which, although in the Mon Khmer family, form a distinct group separate from Vietnamese. Their story, which includes the brother and sister, the sea flood, the sealed chest and the crowing cock, has the fish replaced by an avenging crab. They

> tell how once on a time the kite quarrelled with the crab, and pecked the crab's skull so hard that he made a hole in it, which may be seen down to this very day. To avenge this injury to his skull, the crab caused the sea and the rivers to swell till the waters reached the sky, and all living beings perished except two, a brother and a sister, who were saved in a huge chest. They took with them into the chest a pair of every sort of animal, shut the lid tight and floated on the waters for seven days and seven nights. [Then] the brother heard a cock crowing outside, for the bird had been sent by the spirits to let our ancestors know that the flood had abated, and that they could come forth from the chest. So the

brother let all the birds fly away, then he let loose the animals, and last of all he and his sister walked out on the dry land. They did not know how they were to live, for they had eaten up all the rice that was stored in the chest. However, a black ant brought them two grains of rice: the brother planted them, and the next morning the plain was covered with a rich crop. So the brother and sister were saved.[13]

The Bahnars have other related versions of this story, including one with an ante-diluvian Golden Age. The parallels with the Bhil flood story seem too close to be a coincidence and cannot be explained away by any missionary diffusion, whatever religion. This Austro-Asiatic bird/trunk/incest story type reappears over a broad swathe of Austro-Asiatic minorities in northern Thailand, Laos and southwest China. Swedish folklorists have studied the flood myths of the Kammus in northern Thailand in detail.[14] There are many variant traditions, but the core myth is preserved. In some the trunk is replaced by a gourd or the sister is delivered of a gourd which gives rise to the races. Elements of these stories are also found in neighbouring tribes speaking completely different languages. The Kams, a group of tribes speaking Tai languages in southwest China, tell of a big flood which was sent by the thunder god and a dragon after a prolonged drought. This killed everyone except a brother and sister who hid inside a gourd. They had to commit incest to recreate the race.[15] There is also a small Dravidian tribe, the Kamars in Central India, which holds a version of the brother/sister/bird/sealed box story type.[16]

Three archetypes in the Far East

If the foregoing links are accepted, we can now identify two Austro-Asiatic sea-flood traditions that may have influenced later Hindu legends. One of these is an earth-shaking grand disaster with a conflagration, the second is the fish, the sealed box, the brother and sister, the bird-finder and landing on a flat drying plain. These two have some analogies with the two flood traditions from the Ancient Near East and the eastern Mediterranean that I mentioned in the last chapter. These were the Old Babylonian 'famine/warning/catastrophe/ark' type and the eastern Mediterranean 'bird-land-seeker/sealed chest/flat plain' version. The Babylonian version has a rather clearer counterpart, however, among the Shans in Assam.

These peoples speak a language belonging to the Tai-Kadai family. They are nowadays better known in relation to opium and guerilla warfare, and live mainly in the northeastern part of Burma (Myanmar). The story I quote here comes from the Ahoms, a Shan tribe living way to the west in Assam who migrated from Indo-China 800 years ago. In its entirety it is one of the longest flood legends. The early parts contain motifs that link it closer to the Old Babylonian Atrahasis epic than any Austro-Asiatic account. These include the plagues, the preceding drought and famine, the collusion of the wind, storm and river gods, the violence of the rolling flood and the descriptions of dead bodies in the water. The legend is, however, rich in other motifs that anchor it firmly in the Far East with its Austronesian and Austro-Asiatic fellows:

At the beginning there were many worlds. In the middle world of men at first there were no Shans. Bamboos cracked open to produce animals. Then the first Shan King and Queen came down from heaven to create the first men, but soon they fell behind in their sacrifices. So Ling-lawn the storm god – the Shan equivalent of Ellil – sent waves of beasts including cranes, lions and serpents to devour them. This was unsuccessful so a drought was sent that went on to a terrible famine. The dry watering places stank with the bodies of the dead. The storm god took counsel with other gods and they agreed to destroy the human race. They recruited the help of Hkang-Hkak, the god of streams, ponds, crocodiles and all water animals. The water god was first sent to warn one sage among men, 'Lip-long'. Lip-long was not surprised at his visitor's message, because he had been consulting the augury of his chicken bones. Hkang-Hkak told the sage that Ling-lawn would send a flood to overwhelm the Earth. Everything would be destroyed. Against the flood Lip-long was instructed to make a strong raft and bind it firmly with ropes. The saddest thing of all was that he could not warn his wife and family. He could only take a cow with him on the raft.

A few days more and the flood came, sweeping on and increasing like the onward rush of a forest fire. Then follows a gruesome description of mass death by drowning, 'All animals were swept away and the race of man perished' and then finally 'Lip-long and the cow, alone floated safe on the water. Drifting on he saw the dead bodies of his wife and children ... Thus perished the kingly race (the Shans). Paying their ferry hire, their spirits passed over to the mansions of heaven ... But now the stench of dead bodies, glistering in the sun, filled the earth.' Ling-lawn sent serpents and tigers to eat the dead bodies, but there were too many, so he sent the gods of fire to burn everything up. 'They sent forth a great conflagration, scattering their fire everywhere. The fire swept over earth, and the smoke ascended in clouds to heaven.

'When he saw the fire coming, the sage Lip-long snatched up a stick and knocked down the cow at one blow.' He hid in the cow to escape the fire, and while there found a seed of the gourd plant. 'The fire swept over the dead cow roaring as it went.' His divine mentor Hkang-Hkak advised him to plant the gourd seed. This grew in three directions, up, down and out, into a vast vine of life. The middle growth was the most luxuriant. Ling-lawn was by this time, like Ellil, reconciled to man's re-creation, so he dried out the earth and sent gardeners to tend the vine and prepare the earth. When the gourds were ripe, Ling-lawn sent bolts of lightning to break them open. All life including the Shans came out of these gourds.[17]

Although the beginning of this flood myth recalls Atrahasis in the Old Babylonian Epic, the fire and the gourds at the end of the story are features more characteristic of the Mundaic and Mon-Khmer traditions, respectively, that I mentioned earlier. The story of the Kams referred to above also shares most of the Babylonian features with their linguistic relatives the Shans.

The third flood story-type I discussed from the Middle East had the mountain motif. This is not represented in any Austro-Asiatic tradition, although it fits the landing scene in the Manu myth. There is, however, an extensive mountain tradition in east India among minorities speaking Tibeto-Burman languages. Hence various routes to a mountain refuge from the flood, such as boats, logs, rafts, caves and trees, appear in stories told by Tibeto-Burman-speaking tribes in India, Burma and China. These people include the Lepchas of Sikkim, the Singphos, the Lushais and Anals of Assam, the Chingpaws (Singphos) and Karens of Burma and the Lolos of Yunnan province in China.[18]

The myth of the Lolos has several other surprising elements shared with the Greek mountain and Mesopotamian traditions. These are: (1) *Pandora's Box* – Pandora was the first human and also the flood hero Deucalion's mother-in-law, who opened a box that released woe on mankind; (2) *immortality* of ante-diluvians lost by post-diluvians; and (3) the flood hero as the only man who gave *flesh* to the gods when requested (although in the Anatolian story of Philemon and Baucis the flesh given to Jupiter and Hermes was goose and pig rather than the human flesh in the Lolo story).

The flooding of Adam's Bridge

One independent flood tradition in India that is unlikely to have influenced the earliest Manu stories directly comes from the Tamil region in southeastern India. The Manu story was written before the Aryans got anywhere near southern India. The converse, that the Tamil traditions were entirely derived from Manu, is, of course, possible, but unlikely. The Tamil tradition, first seen in the so-called three Cankam legends, is historiographic and relates the local effects of a worldwide sea flood. These ancient legends claim to describe a progressive loss of southern Indian coastal land over some 10,000 years. In particular, two legendary cities disappeared, Maturai and Kapatapuram:

> Atiyarkkunallar informs us that the sea swallowed up forty-nine provinces of the old Pantiya land from the Pahruli River to the north bank of the Kumari River. In other words ... the ancient antediluvian Tamil land stretch[ed] far to the south of the present southern border at Cape Cormorin [the southern tip of India].[19]

As flood-myth expert David Shulman has discovered, other ancient Tamil sources tell a similar story. The epic *Manimekalai*, for instance, describes the destruction of the ancient Cola port city Pukar by a flood. The Tamil Nadu state of southern India has two large tongues of flat and shallow submerged continental shelf, one pointing due south from Cape Cormorin, and the other stretching all the way to Sri Lanka. The former corresponds directly with one of the Tamil traditions mentioned above. The latter, which is now represented by a narrow reef called appropriately Adam's Bridge, stretches across the Palk Strait between India and Sri Lanka. Adam's Bridge was the legendary land link created by monkey king Hanuman in the *Ramayana*. In another version of the story, Rama asked the sea of the Palk Strait to recede so that he could get across to Sri Lanka and, when this did not work, started shooting arrows at the sea. The sea asked for a compromise with the monkey Nala, building a causeway.[20]

The numerous legends of sea flooding and sea retreat along the southern, western and eastern coasts of India have been woven repeatedly into Hindu religious literature. Several different traditions are often conflated into one text. An example of this is found in the *Mahabharata*, which, as mentioned, contains one of the earliest versions of the Manu story. In the last verses of the *Mahabharata*, *Dwaravati*, a legendary port of the west coast south of the Indus outlet, was swallowed up by the sea. Marine archaeologists now claim to have found the original port, under water and showing signs of great antiquity.

There are three story threads which reappear in the different south Indian legends:

(1) *Seaflooding as a result of conflict, rivalry or competition.* The conflict is often waged between a land based hero or god and a sea god, serpent, demon or fish. A feature of the conflict is the throwing of a spear or axe or shooting of arrows at the sea and coastline. The results of these symbolic acts are either to force the sea to retreat or to destroy land and create new coastal features. In the Tamil myth of Murukan, the hero casts his spear once against a mountain and once against the sea demon Cūr thus conquering the sea creating more land and clearing up Chaos and darkness. The name Cūr and other motifs of this last tale are rather close to the flooding sea monster Kur who was killed by Ninurta (Nimrud) in the Sumerian myth of the defeat of Sea and Chaos, which I shall describe in Chapter 11.[21] As in other sea-dragon-slaying stories, there are themes of drought preceding the flood and the poisoning motif which comes from the salt on the land.

(2) *Fratricide, incest and conflict over women.* The Mahabharata contains most of these elements. In some cases the woman is a Nagini or daughter of the serpent deities, the Nagas. In several legends she bears an illegitimate child who she sends across the waves to claim his inheritance of land from a land based father. In the myth of the flooding of *Pukar* the woman was a daughter of the Naga King. Linguist Waruno Mahdi has suggested that this story-type refers to alliances between the Nagas' Austronesian forebears to the east and the indigenous aboriginal Indian tribes. Versions are found as far northeast as the Shans of Burma. However, the fratricidal triangle, which we will see again in Chapter 16, is more likely to have originated in the Moluccas.

(3) *The flood as a cyclical cause of destruction and re-creation or rebirth.* In many of the southern flood stories certain sites, shrines and cities are preserved from the flood or recover and become foci for regeneration. The regeneration motif is also seen in the Adonis Gardens[22] or 'creative pots' which come into the myths.

In summary, the Manu myth of a world deluge is derived from up to three pre-Aryan flood-myth traditions found throughout the north-central and eastern parts of India and reaching out to Burma and Vietnam. A separate and possibly unrelated Dravidian legendary complex in the south may well recall the post-glacial inundation of the coastline. They also recall the widespread Oceanic and Eurasian motif of the defeat of a watery and serpentine Chaos by a cult hero.[23] Finally, nearly all myths and legends of the Indian subcontinent specify a sea flood.

Fish floods and island-cutting in Maluku

The fish/flood motif, the land-carving spear and the coast-drowning serpent are not confined to India and Austro-Asiatic-speaking minorities of the Far East. They both reappear far to the southeast in a distinctive complex of stories which explain the formation of the lesser Sunda Islands and Maluku in eastern Indonesia. As we shall see, that is where they may have come from. I am indebted to Dr Aone van Engelenhoven for the following information:

Briefly the stories tell of floods caused by sea-creatures when they destroyed or chipped off bits of islands in the process of creating the geography of the region. This motif is widely spread in eastern Indonesia, throughout the eastern Nusa Tenggara and southwestern Maluku, centering around the Timor region. The stories not only 'explain' the post-glacial drowning of this part of Indonesia, but also the reasons for migration between islands. The westernmost variant is found in Amarasi, a domain in southwest Timor, where the form of the present coastline is explained as being caused by a huge fish that smashed off parts of the mainland with its tail.[24] The fish turns into a whale in another tale of southeast Maluku, and created a lake on the island of Kai Minor.

In a nearby island, the Alorese tell of the destruction of another island near their coast by a fish. The interesting element is that some Alorese trace their origin back to that event and consider the sunken island as their previous homeland. These non-Austronesians are closely related linguistically with the Timorese. Further east lies the island of Atauro that belongs to East Timor. The many holes and caves in the mountains there are explained as caused by a huge eel, who was hunted by the forefathers of one of the three peoples living on the island. They have the idea that Atauro used to be part of a larger landmass of which Timor and the nearby island of Kisar, further east, were also a part.[25]

Off the eastern tip of Timor the islanders all state that the present geography of the region was caused by a fierce sailfish who destroyed a much larger island, called Luondona-Wietrili. Now only the tiny islet of Luang has remained from the former island. It takes about three hours to tell the condensed version of this myth and maybe a week for the full story. All immigrant clans to the island, the so-called boat-owners start with this story before they can start their own migratory myths. On the other hand all inhabitants of the island, both boat-owners and indigenous landowners accept the legend as true. A very condensed account of the story runs as follows: Once upon a time two brothers were adopted by different foster parents. The older stayed with the king and the youngest, who was the good fellow in the story, stayed with an old woman. The younger brother once saved a sailfish from being killed, and therefore had gained its eternal friendship. Later, the two brothers became enemies, after a contest on Timor. The youngest ended up at the bottom of the sea and was then brought back to Luondona by the sailfish who happened to be the king of the depths. On the way back to Luondona the sailfish destroyed some places, hewing off Leti from East Timor, for example, and blasting the original Roma island into a group of tiny islets. Since the older brother had run off with the fiancée of the youngest, the sailfish retrieved his protégé's family from the north (Damar) and punished the elder's treason by destroying/ drowning the entire continent. Because nothing was left but a tiny islet, the population had to go. After a game of dice, the losers, representing further clans also left Luang.[26]

The last motif of the dice game pre-empts the famous Indian epic the *Mahabharata* which, as I mentioned earlier, holds a version of Manu's fish flood. In the opening chapters of this epic, a kingdom and a wife were lost in a dice game while, at the end, the Indian legendary port of Dwaravati on the Indian west coast, disappeared under the salt waves.

There is no record of any Hindu influence in the area round Timor that could explain any resemblances with the Indian flood myths. If there is any genetic connection it is likely to be much more ancient than any Hindu influence of the last 2000 years.

While there may be some shared motifs between the *Mahabharata* and southern-Indian flood stories and the geographic myths of the islands of the southwest Maluku and Nusa Tenggara, there are stronger links between the latter and Melanesia and Australia. First there is evidence that immigrants took along variants of this story to southeast Maluku (the Kei Islands) and to Australia (Arnhem Land), because it is found there with the same migration motif: 'our original home was destroyed, and therefore we migrated'. There are Aboriginals in Arnhem Land with Leti as a first name, who stress that their forefathers had come across the Alafuru Sea before the Macassans did.[27] Second, as regards Melanesia, in Chapter 16 I describe the story of the warring brothers Kulabob and Manup along the coasts and islands of northern Melanesia. The story contains the fratricidal motif along with a triumphant return of the defeated sibling as in the sail/fish story. The fight is about a wife, and Kulabob, during his final migration, sliced off the Barrier Reef islands of Sek and Kranket from the north New Guinea mainland with his spear. The connection between the Kulabob and Manup story and the Timorese legend has been pointed out by several anthropologists.

The land and sea modelling spear of Kulabob was also wielded in southeast Maluku by the Tanimbar Austronesian cult hero Atuf,[28] who is credited with slicing off the Lesser Sundas from Borneo with his spear during his eastward migration. Geologically this is just what happened to Bali in the post-glacial flooding (see Chapter 1). The Tanimbar people have their whole culture centred round the escape of their ancestors from a catastrophe that obliterated their great homeland somewhere to the west. That terrible event happened at a time when the earth was 'unstable'. Thereafter they had to migrate ever eastwards from island refuge to island refuge. As if to emphasise this, visitors will find huge symbolic stone boats as ritual centres of the villages.[29]

Further north in Maluku, in Austronesian-speaking Ceram and Banda islands, we find the same motif of the 'geographical weapon' in a flood story about a princess Boi Ratan. This also has some similarities with the Tamil stories of the Naga princess.[30]

Pausing briefly from tracing the fish/serpent flood motif ever eastwards, we can surmise what mechanism, in general, gave rise to these stories of sea rise and land loss in India and the East Indies. It is easy for folklorists to dismiss such stories as 'aetiological' or 'explanatory'. In this context that would mean that local people observed many islands and then, without any other reason, created myths to explain how they were all part of a continent before. I cannot see any automatic logic in this. The mythological island groupings in the East Indies and the inundated lands off the Indian coast *do* correspond with shallow waters that were previously land more than 6000 years ago. The legends record events that we know happened, from oceanographic information unavailable to the local story holders. Australian Aboriginals are credited with preserving this ancient reality of post-glacial flooding in their stories of the 'rainbow snake',[31] so why not the Timorese and Dravidians? But how have the specific motifs of sea-flooding serpents and fishes, fighting brothers, incestuous pregnancies and regenerative tree spirits come to be distributed so widely outside the known area of Hindu influence? The Melanesian and Australian links suggest that, in eastern Indonesia, we are looking at a far more ancient and deeper layer of connections than the Indian influence of the last 2000 years. This supports the genetic evidence of genetic links from that region towards south India given in Chapters 6 and 7.

In these last few tales I have strayed from the ancient Austro-Asiatic cultures of South and Southeast mainland Asia to the inhabitants of the island region, the Austronesians, who also have a rich flood tradition. I will discuss them next.

Austronesian flood stories

The Austronesian speakers of Southeast Asia and the Indo-Pacific region have more flood stories than peoples of any other single language phylum.[32] The majority of the tales are held by the minority who live on the smallest islands. This might be no coincidence. Island folk, particularly those living on flat atolls, are continuously threatened by the restless sea, so they could have been flooded many times and told many stories. On the other hand one story may have been taken out from Southeast Asia. We can explore that dichotomy. The Austronesian dispersal has proved one of the few near-perfect models of cultural diffusion. This is so whether one looks at language, social anthropology, or archaeology; so a myth starting on the Asian mainland or Southeast Asia could have spread out with the people. Here we ought to be able to put to the test questions of polygenesis versus monogenesis.

Unfortunately the answer is not as clearcut as the language tree suggests. On the one hand, there is some evidence that stories of the oldest branches of the Austronesian language phylum in Taiwan are shared with eastern Polynesia at the outermost point of the radiation. On the other hand in the intervening regions of island Southeast Asia and Melanesia there is profusion of at least three different traditions, as in India and the Ancient Near East, but with greater diversity. In attempting to trace the migration of flood stories, we have to be careful, as before, not to confuse story-type with flood-type. The story-type is made up of combinations of characteristic signature motifs such as incest of the survivors and the land-finding bird. If the flood-type stays constant with movement of the story, well and good; it supports a diffusion model. If, however, the holders of the story are themselves subject to recurrent serious floods, we may expect the flood-type to change.

Hawai'ian linguist Robert Blust has argued that Taiwan is the homeland of the Austronesian language phylum. Whether this is actually true or not was discussed in Chapter 5, but it is clear that the Aboriginal Austronesian languages of Taiwan are the most archaic and deeply diverse of the surviving members of the phylum. Taiwan is a mountainous island off the east coast of mainland China, which was part of the mainland up until the end of the last Ice Age. The Taiwanese Aboriginals living off the China coast, may have been physically and culturally separated from the rest of the Austronesian diaspora for more than 6000 years. We should therefore logically start with their versions of the deluge. In common with their neighbours who, by contrast, speak Sino-Tibetan languages, all Taiwanese deluge myths record that the flood topped the mountains.

The Ami of Taiwan have a group of flood myths that share some features with both the Tibeto-Burmese 'mountain' and Austro-Asiatic 'sealed chest' myths from eastern India. The legends all describe a brief cataclysmic flood, a mountain-landing in a wooden mortar and post-flood incest. In one version there is a sea flood with superwaves reaching to mountain tops:

In ancient times the god Kakumodan and goddess Budaihabu descended with two children, a boy Sura and a girl Nakao, a pig and a chicken. There was a disagreement over the domestic animals with two bandit deities Kabitt and Aka who, in revenge, called on the four sea gods to send a flood. The sea gods readily agreed and warned the plotters: 'In five days from now, when the round Moon appears, the sea will make a booming sound; then escape to a mountain where there are stars.' On the fifth day Kabitt and Aka did not wait for the sound but rushed up a mountain with stars. 'When they reached the summit, the sea suddenly began to make the sound and rose higher and higher, till soon Kakumodan's house was flooded. But Kakumodan and his wife escaped from the swelling tide, for they climbed up a ladder to the sky.' Unfortunately they left their two children behind in their hurry. The children found a wooden mortar and floated in this to the Ragasan mountain. They found they were alone in the world. Aware of the crime of incest, they nevertheless procreated but placed a symbolic mat between themselves on the marriage bed. In due course the wife also produced a grain of millet from her ear, and they learnt the rituals for cultivating that crop.[33] This rainless flood legend appears to describe destruction by a Pacific superwave.

Another Ami version has a boiling flood after an earth-opening earthquake: 'They say at that time the mountains crumbled down, the earth gaped, and from the fissure a hot spring gushed forth, which flooded the whole face of the Earth ... few living things survived ... the inundation.' The rest of the story is similar to that above with the wooden mortar, a mountain-landing and incest. In this case the brother and two sisters at first separated on the mountain, were re-united, and then lost one sister on the mountain. The remaining sibling pair then asked permission from the Sun to commit incest. Having received the Sun's blessing, they obtained instructions from the Moon for a comprehensive world re-creation. The couple were rather upset with the Moon that their first two offspring were abortions which gave rise to fish and crabs, and the third was a stone. To their relief, the stone then gave rise to the different races.[34]

The strange gestation the incestuous first mother endured in this story is analogous to that of the Austro-Asiatic Kammus in northern Thailand who obliged her to deliver a gourd. The other theme we are reminded of is in the Greek 'mountain' myths where Deucalion and Pyrrha re-created man from stones after the flood (see Chapter 9). The wooden bowl and flood motif may appear under a different guise in another part of the Austronesian diaspora. In Chapter 16, I describe Kulabob's creatrix mother sailing away from Arop island in a wooden bowl on a flood that came from the crater lake.

Two other Taiwanese Aboriginal tribes, the Tsuwos and the Bununs, have stories of sudden cataclysmic mountain-topping floods with mountain refuge. The details are somewhat different with the introduction of some other motifs that could have been picked at random from cultures throughout South and East Asia. Where a mechanism of the flood is specified, two versions are given. In one, a great snake dammed the river and a giant crab sliced the snake in two to release the flood. In another the crab and snake fought until the snake escaped to sea, and then the flood came. The refugees were groups of villagers who scrambled to the mountain tops, so neither a boat nor incest were necessary. In one story, the motif of the stars on the mountains became a source of the first fire on a neighbouring half-submerged peak, which had to be retrieved by brave animal swimmers, rather like the land-divers. In another, the swimmer was a pig that released a dam, thus letting water drain away. The animals – in particular the birds – helped to remould the land by dropping stones from a height. The only bird that refused to help was the eagle. The defluvescence of the flood also carved and contoured the land, which had been flat before. At the end the stalk of millet remaining was used to bring back agriculture.[35] Both the crab and the 'last millet' motifs are shared with the Austro-Asiatic story from Vietnam held by the Bahnars.

The motif of the animals seeking fire has an extraordinary connection with a flood-myth from the Andaman Islands in the Bay of Bengal, a continent and two seas away. This isolated Aboriginal group tells a story that: some time after creation, the creator angered at man's disobedience sent a flood which covered all except their 'Saddle Peak'. Only a man and a woman who happened to be in a canoe were saved. The creator re-created all animals and birds for them, but they had no fire. The ghost of one of their departed friends, taking the form of a kingfisher, flew to the creator's fire and tried to steal a brand. He failed, but the creator threw the brand at him which fell to the couple on the ground.[36]

Table 6. **Distribution of the six basic Flood myth types around the world.**

	Watery Chaos; Land-splitting Hero; Battle with Serpent	Overpopulation; Drought-Famine; Warning: Catastrophe; Ark and rope; +/– Fire	Bird Land Seeker; Sealed Chest Incest of First Children	Superwave; Mountain High Flood; Mountain Landing; Stone Recreation	Lake Flood	Land-Raise
Sumerian/Babylon	+	+ +				
Assyrian (2)	+	+ +	+ (1)	+ (2)		
Genesis (3)	+ (Chap 1)	+ + (J&P)	+ (J)	+ (P)		
Greece/Anatolia				+	+ +	
Western Europe	+ (Norse/Finn)	+ (Voguls)		+ (Lithuanian)	+ Celtic	Rumania
N. Africa (Egypt)			+/– Cameroun			
Sub-Saharan Africa						
India (Aryan)	+/–	+ +				
India (Dravidian)	+ +		+/–			
India (Austroasiatic)		+	+ +			
SEA (Austroasiatic)			+ +			
SEA (Tibeto-Burmese)				+ +		+
SEA (Tai)		+ +	+	+		
Taiwan (Austronesian)		+	+	+ +		
Island Southeast Asia W. Malayo-Polynesian	+	+	+	+ +		+
Eastern Indonesia C. Malayo-Polynesian	+ +	+	+	+		
Melanesia (AN)	+					
Polynesia (AN)	+			+ +		+
North America	+/–	+	+	+	+	+ +
Cent. America+Aztec	+	+	+	+ +		
South America		+ +	+/–			
Australian Aboriginal	+ +					

Key:

+/– = Occasional version

\+ = Secondary version

\+ + = Dominant version

(J) = Jehovistic version; (P) = Priestly version; (1)&(2) = equivalent Assyrian version

Deluge myths of Taiwanese Austronesian-speaking Aboriginals thus appear to share themes common to the 'mountain-topping' and the 'Old Babylonian Catastrophic' types with Tibeto-Burman and Tai-Kadai speakers respectively. Yet in complete isolation from the cultural traditions surrounding the Indian Ocean they also share some of the oldest themes or motifs of the Austro-Asiatic 'sealed-chest and bird-finder' and 'fire/catastrophe' and even the Moluccan types. It is possible that Taiwanese Aboriginals, as relict groups of the most ancient Austronesian stock, still hold archetypal myths which were originally common throughout Southeast Asia and Indo-China (see Table 6). The three traditions may originally have been one. This possibility might be supported partly by the hypothetical Austric and Austro-Tai linguistic super-families (see Chapter 5).

Mountain-topping myths in east Polynesia as well

Before further compounding the confusion of mixed motifs I have uncovered, by plunging into the varied Austronesian flood myths of Indonesia and the Philippines, I would like to jump next to the eastern limit of the diaspora in east Polynesia. Here the flood myths have a curious uniform likeness to the first Ami Taiwanese tradition a quarter of the globe and 6000 years away in space and time. First of all, the east Polynesian legends without exception describe a rainless sea flood. Second, in more than half of the tales the flood has every aspect of a superwave like that of the Ami; in others, the sea just rose very rapidly. Third, where the islands have mountains, the flood is always mountain-topping.

There are several problems to an easy genetic link between these similar flood myths at the two poles of the Austronesian diaspora. For example, many of the mythological descriptions of the giant waves in these islands that were told to the first ethnographers included local topographical features. Thus individual descriptions varied, depending on whether the islands were flat atolls, uplifted atolls, mountainous islands or large landmasses as in New Zealand. As far as we know, eastern Polynesia was colonised by people only during historic times, when the only big waves would have been the numerous Pacific tsunamis, not the mountain-topping superwaves of a grand global cataclysm. So it could be argued that the local story-tellers were simply recording relatively recent tsunamis, and exaggerating a lot. But the story-tellers were clearly not talking about tsunamis. Tsunamis do not keep the sea-level raised for hours, days or weeks, nor do they top mountains, and the story-tellers were well aware of this. What makes it more likely that the local topographic touches in the stories were simply overlaying a deeper more ancient story are the other unique shared motifs.

A fairly typical east Polynesian flood myth comes from Tahiti, which was luckily collected on the eve of proselytisation. Apart from the lack of rain in these pre-Christianisation legends, a particular feature is the lack of the use of a boat or ark as refuge. In the majority of such legends the survivors scrambled to a place of safety such as a mountain. This lack of faith in boats is really surprising for a culture that could sail rings round Captain Cook; yet it agrees with the Taiwanese mountain-topping flood/mountain refugee stories, which did not use any boats either. Tahiti, a mountainous island in the mid-Pacific, was destroyed by the sea. No animal nor man nor tree survived, and the deep was over the land. A husband and wife only were saved. They took all their domestic animals, dog, pig, and chicken to the top of Mount O Pitohito, which was higher than the neighbouring Mount Orofena, that the husband had chosen. This was lucky, for when the sea came, it out-topped Orofena. They stayed on O Pitohito for ten days until the sea subsided and they saw the little heads of the mountains. When the land reappeared, everything was sterile and unproductive. 'The fish were putrid in the caves and holes of the rocks. They said, "Dig a hole for the fish in the sea." The wind also died away, and when all was calm, the stones and the trees began to fall from the heavens, to which they had been carried up by the wind.' They therefore dug a shelter with a stone roof and waited till the hail of stones finished. There was a small mountain of stones when they finally emerged, but everything living was totally destroyed. The woman brought forth two children, a boy and girl, and all men and women came from them presumably as a result of incest. The food plants of breadfruit, coconut and others suddenly reappeared in three days.[37]

For comparison, the Tsuwo legend from Taiwan described a boatless mountain refuge from a sea flood and also had birds dropping numerous stones from the sky onto the emerged land. The Bunun myths from Taiwan also had the theme of the total devastation of the vegetation and the miraculous rapid recovery of crops. Other characteristics I have not yet mentioned that are shared with Taiwanese deluge myths include incest of the survivors, the noise made by the flood, the flood resulting from a divine argument and the way that the flood carved river valleys during its defluvescence. These latter features, although found in both traditions, are not universal. For instance, the survivors were not always a brother and sister. In both traditions there are stories of groups of villagers surviving on mountains. In summary, concerning eastern Polynesian myths we may say that although local topography colours the individual legends, the deep structure, which includes various distinctive motifs, shows a number of similarities with Taiwanese Aboriginal mountain flood myths.

Austronesian flood myths in island Southeast Asia

Robert Blust's model for the spread of Austronesian languages and people has Taiwan as the original homeland. Geographically the nearest Austronesian populations are in the Philippines, and they are also the closest linguistically. Blust has put them as the first port of call for the start of the diaspora over 5000 years ago. As I have said, there are other explanations for similarities between neighbouring Austronesian cultures. However, this simple diffusional radiation model of the flood myths through the Philippines is supported only partially by similarities between the flood myths. Far greater diversity of story type is found in island Southeast Asia than Taiwan, as I shall show below.

Not surprisingly, the myths in the northern Philippines are the closest to the Taiwan stories. The Ifugao, who live in the high cordillera of Luzon, have a story that contains the incestuous brother and sister, the mountain refuge, the two mountains with the fire on one of them, the reuniting of the pair and their shame of incest allayed by the god:

> The Ifugao ... tell of a great drought which dried up all the rivers. The old men suggested that they dig up the river ... For three days they dug when suddenly a great spring gushed forth. It came so fast that many died before they could get out of the pit. In their joy over the waters, the Ifugao celebrated a feast. But while they were rejoicing it grew dark; the rains fell, the rivers rose up so that the old men finally advised the people to run to the mountains for the river gods were angry. The people were all overtaken by the waters except two, a brother and a sister, Wigan and Bugan. Wigan was safely settled on top of Mt Amuyao, and Bugan on the summit of Mt Kalawitan. The waters continued to rise until the entire earth was covered except the tops of the mountains. For six months the flood covered the earth ... only Bugan had fire.. Wigan was cold because he had no fire ... after the waters had receded, Wigan ... was reunited with his sister ... Bugan realised

> one day that she was with child. In her shame she left her home ... the god Maknongan who came to her in the guise of a benign old man ... assured her that her shame had no foundation. What she and Wigan had done was right because it was through them that the world would be repeopled.[38]

The motif of the preceding drought, which appears first in the Babylonian stories, may come to this myth through its Austro-Tai ancestry because it also features in the Shan myth.

Birds, incest and mountains

In Mindanao, the large southern island of the Philippines, two related stories were collected in the early part of the twentieth century. The Atás in mountainous central Mindanao are said to be descendants of an invading people who had intermarried with Negritos and other Aboriginal tribes.[39] In their flood myth, the incest motif persists but, in addition, the bird motif resurfaces. In this case the eagle is helpful, in contrast to the Tsuwo story of Taiwan. The trio that lost the redundant member echoes an Ami story from Taiwan. Manama, their great spirit, had made the first men by weaving blades of grass. He made four couples from which all the Atás and neighbouring tribes came.

> Long afterwards the water covered the whole earth, and all the Atás were drowned except two men and a woman. The waters carried them far away, and they would have perished if a great eagle had not come to their aid. The bird offered to carry them on its back to their homes. One of the men refused, but the other man and woman accepted the offer and returned to Mapula.[40]

In the second related myth, this time from the Mandayas, another mountain tribe, the trio is replaced by a single pregnant woman. She prayed that her child might be a son. Her prayer was answered and she gave birth to a boy she called Uacatan. When he grew up he took his mother to wife and all Mandayas are descended from that incestuous pair.[41]

The motif of the birds is a central feature of tales from the Bisayas, the central island region of the Philippines. In one story the flood took place as a result of a quarrel between the supreme god Bathala and the sea god Dumagat. Bathala's subjects, the crow and the dove, were stealing fish which were the subjects of Dumagat. The upshot was that Dumagat opened the big world waterpipe and flooded Earth, the dominion of Bathala, until nearly all people were drowned.[42] In another variant of this story we find, surprisingly, a nearly word-for-word repeat of an equally strange Mexican story I discussed in Chapter 9 under apochryphal Hebrew versions of the flood:

> ... Pavon tells a story of how the crow got its black colour ... In very remote times ... God ... sen(t) a great punishment to man ... a great internal war took away the lives of many ... a river overflowed its banks and took the lives of many more. The judge of the dead Aropayang ... sent out the crow and the dove to examine and count the dead. The dove came back and gave a faithful account of the disaster. The crow, who came back much later, could not do so because it forgot to count the dead in its eagerness to peck at the eyes of the dead. Furious, Aropayang hurled a bottle of ink at the bird and thus stained the feather of the crow for ever, and he cursed it to be lame on one foot where it was hit by the inkwell.[43]

My first reaction to both this story and those of the Cora Indians in Mexico, where the black carrion bird is a vulture, is that they were both derived originally from Catholic missionary teaching. The inkwell betrays a modern corruption in any case. The trouble is that Genesis, although it uses a dove and a raven, says nothing about carrion birds eating the corpses nor about how they became black. The corpse-eating motif appears in an apocryphal Jewish legend but not the blacking of the bird. The other point is that the 'bird-seeker' motif is also established in different non-mosaic contexts in both of these widely separated cultures.[44]

The bird-finder and bird-seeker motifs crop up a few times further south among the flood myths of Maluku and Nusa Tenggara. The people in this region mostly speak languages belonging to the central Malayo-Polynesian branch of Austronesian languages. As we saw in Chapters 6 and 7, the genetic evidence seems to identify their ancestors as the ones that started the great eastward sea migrations of the Austronesians. These stories still mostly fit into the 'mountain-topping flood, mountain refugee' group like the Taiwanese myths. One tale from the Alfoors of Ceram in Maluku is similar to that of the Atás in Mindanao, in that the surviving refugees were three persons who were helped by a sea eagle who located the first dry land. There is an additional anthropomorphic tree-of-life motif, which crops up again in Ceram.[45] The first mountain to reappear was 'Noesakoe' with its sides covered with trees on which the leaves were shaped like the female genitals. In a novel and typically Ceramese twist to the tree-of-life motif, the three survivors then used these generative leaves to re-populate the world.[46]

The mountain-refugees and bird-finder version reaches as far south in eastern Indonesia as Roti in the Nusa Tenggara. An osprey sprinkles some dry earth on the waters and the man and his family descend from the mountain to the new land. The osprey then finds all kinds of domestic crop seeds so that they can farm.[47]

Western Malayo-Polynesian mountain floods

Still following mountain flood myths, we move slightly west from eastern Indonesia into Sulawesi, the beginning of the territory of the main western Malayo-Polynesian branch of Austronesian languages where the Minahassa name a mountain-landing and a land-seeking bird.[48]

Another 'mountain-topping' flood myth comes from the Bare'e speaking Toradjas of the central highlands of Sulawesi. This tale shares the incest and animal rice donor motifs found both in the Taiwanese (Austronesian), and Vietnamese (Austro-Asiatic) versions to the north. The incest is, however, of the Oedipus type, (mother/son), like that of the Mandayas' mountain myth in the southern Philippines. The animal that donates the seed rice after the flood is a mouse, and the Taiwanese Ami ark has changed from a wooden mortar to a pig trough.

Further west again, to the former centre of the submerged Sunda continent, around Borneo, we find a 'mountain-topping' myth of the Ot-Danoms in the Barito district of southern Borneo. Near by, the Sundanese have a missionary-corrupted myth, where the flood covered all except their two highest mountains. On the east coast of the Malay Peninsula we find another simple 'mountain-topping and mountain-refugees' story among the Kelantanese. Here, it was the menials who had been sent up into the mountains to collect firewood who escaped with their lives when the flood came. 'After the event, the Sun, Moon and stars were extinguished and there was a great darkness. When the light returned, there was no land but a great sea and all the abodes of man had been overwhelmed.'

Finally, moving to the west coast of the ancient Sunda continental shelf, we find 'Mountain-topping floods and refugees' among the megalithic Austronesian tribes of Sumatra. In a Batak flood myth there is the 'mountain top' motif alongside a typical 'land recovery'.

The people of Nias island off the west coast of Sumatra may have an even older megalithic tradition than the Bataks. In their mountain-topping flood story, the use of the immortal crab as author of the flood echoes both the Taiwanese and Vietnamese stories which we have explored. A neighbouring island, Enggano, has another island-covering flood myth, but in addition has the post-flood 'stone re-creation' motif common to mountain-topping myths from the rest of Asia and Europe.

The bird, the snake and the tree

Although the bird land-seeker motif is clearly apparent in the central Malayo-Polynesian stories of Sulawesi, Maluku and Nusa Tengara, the bird has changed from a willing servant of the human survivor to assume more of its creator role present elsewhere in Southeast Asia in the form of the bird/snake/tree-of-life triad.[49] This creative theme may be seen further to the west in a flood story of the Bataks in Sumatra. I shall describe in Chapter 15 how the Batak place the 'tree of life' central to their creation mythology in a way that closely mimics the great ash tree (Yggdrasill) of the Norse sagas. The Batak, one of the world's last-surviving megalithic cultures, speak an Austronesian tongue that is not closely related to the majority Malayic tongues of Indonesia. Further, their proximity to Aboriginal Austro-Asiatic cultures of the Malay Peninsula may have opened them to other mythic traditions in the past. A flood myth is incorporated into one of their tree-of-life cycles in the form of a watery serpent creation; but most other Eurasian flood motifs, such as an earthshaking catastrophe, the mountain, the bird-seeker and bird-diver and even a sealed container are also woven in. To finish off there is an 'end of the world' scene that is strangely close to the Ragnarok of the Norse myths as the serpent at the base of the tree shakes himself free of his fetters and tears the world apart in fire and flood:

The Naga Padoha is the buffalo serpent at the base of the tree of life who holds up the middle world on his horns (see Chapter 15). Early in time the Naga Padoha became weary of this task and shook his head, submerging the Earth. The god of the upper world, 'Batara Guru set about recovering it from the watery abyss. For that purpose he sent down his daughter Puti-orla-bulan [princess of the moon] … so down she came, riding a white owl and accompanied by a dog.' Since the Earth was flooded she could not walk, so her father sent a mountain for her to walk on, 'and from it gradually sprang all the rest of the habitable Earth'. In another version her husband, whom she had abandoned for this mission, was sent down from heaven packaged in a bamboo container. Ever since then, Naga Padoha has grudgingly continued to carry the Earth on his horns, shaking his burden from time to time in an attempt to free himself, thus causing earthquakes. Since these are so frequent in Sumatra, Batara Guru sent his own son 'diving swallow' to bind the monster with fetters. The earthquakes none the less have continued in spite of the fetters. 'And he will go on shaking himself till he snaps his fetters. Then the Earth will again sink into the sea, and the Sun will approach to within an ell of this our world ... At the destruction of the world, the fire of the cauldron will join with the fire of the Sun to consume the material universe.'[50]

The motifs of the mountain, the potent tree, and the irritable Earth snake reappear without the bird in a complex Iban flood myth from Sarawak in northern Borneo: Some Dyak women were cutting up young bamboo shoots on a tree trunk in the jungle. They noticed that with every cut of their knives, the trunk exuded blood. Some young men came up and pointed out that it was not in fact a tree trunk, but a giant torpid snake. The men soon killed and cut up the snake, taking the flesh home to cook. While they were frying the meat, strange noises came from the pan and all of a sudden it began to rain torrentially. This wet punishment for their crime continued until all but the highest hills were covered by a flood. All mankind perished except one woman, who fled to a mountain peak. She found a dog warming itself under a creeper where it scraped against a tree trunk. The woman imitated the action of the creeper and discovered the fire drill, the first production of fire after the great flood.

For lack of a mate she resorted to wood, and married the fire drill. By this potent staff she had a son, or rather half a son because he only had one of every pair of body parts. Every central feature was also half.[51] This half-man, Simpang-Impang, or Wanleg as he is called in a similar myth of New Guinea,[52] had several trickster adventures. There was a rat that, like the mouse in the Bare'e story from Sulawesi, had the foresight to retain some rice at the time of the flood. Simpang-Impang did not wait to be offered the seed rice, but took it. The rest of the story relates how he outwitted the Spirit of the Wind in competitions to get his full complement of limbs and also to regenerate domestic crops.

Arks – sealed chests, tubs and ships

In this catalogue of mountain-topping flood myths of island Southeast Asia, several motifs found both in Austronesian myths from Taiwan and Austro-Asiatic ones from Vietnam keep reappearing. These include the snake, the crab, incest, the finding of fire, the last grains of crops and, of course, the mountain-topping flood. There is, however, a leaning towards the Tsuwo/Bunun model from Taiwan, in that most of the flood survivors manage without boats by scrambling to the mountain tops and there are frequent recurrences of the snake, bird and crab motifs. The Ami flood myths of Taiwan, with their constant use of the wooden mortar as an ark, the incest and their stone re-creation that all link them more to the Austro-Asiatic models, are less well represented in island Southeast Asia. They do, however, have some representatives. I have already mentioned one from the Bare'e Toradjas in Sulawesi, where the 'mortar ark' was replaced by a pig trough.

Another comes from the Ibans of Sarawak. The Iban, or sea Dyaks, have a flood myth recorded in early colonial days. It is not a mountain-topping flood, and has instead retained the floating wooden grain mortar and the stone re-creation of the Ami in Taiwan. The Iban Noah was called Trow and floated about in his makeshift ark with his wife and some domestic animals. When the storm abated he and his motley crew disembarked. Trow must have made some calculation of the task he faced, since he decided that one wife could not bear enough of his children to repopulate the world. He therefore resorted to polygamy using wives he had created out of stones and bits of wood. The ethnographer who collected this story was well aware of the analogy with the Greek mountain-topping, sealed-chest flood-myth of Deucalion and Pyrrha, where re-creation of humans relied on stones.[53]

The Benua-Jakun, an Aboriginal group of the jungles of the southern tip of the Malay Peninsula, have a flood myth of the Austro-Asiatic or Jehovistic sealed-chest type. Unlike most other jungle Aboriginals of this region, who speak Austro-Asiatic languages of the Aslian group, the Benua-Jakun speak an Austronesian tongue. Their story appears at first to show a preternatural knowledge of plate tectonics. Looked at in another way, it might echo the Sumerian concept of the 'Apsu' as some kind of underground fresh-water cistern that welled up on the land to cause the flood. The myth also manages to combine the flat drying plain of the sealed-chest myth type, with a dark 'light before luminaries' watery creation.

> [They] say that the ground on which we stand is not solid, but is merely a skin covering an abyss of water. In ancient times Pirman, that is the deity, broke up this skin, so that the world was drowned and destroyed by a great flood. However, Pirman had created a man and woman and put them in a ship of Pulai wood, which was completely covered over and had no opening. In this ship the pair floated and tossed about for a time, till at last the vessel came to rest, and the man and woman, nibbling their way

> through its side, emerged on dry ground and beheld this our world stretching on all sides to the horizon. At first all was very dark, for there was neither morning nor evening, because the sun had not yet been created. When it grew light, they saw seven small shrubs of rhododendron and seven clumps of grass called Sambau.[54]

Foreseeing that their children would have to commit incest to procreate, the woman overcame the problem in an ectopic fashion that also appears in New Guinean mythology. She conceived a son in her right calf and a daughter in her left, thus avoiding the chance of two children of the same womb marrying. All mankind descended from that first pair.

It can be seen that there is a general lack of arks of any description in most of the flood myths of the central region of island Southeast Asia – that is, the Greater Sundas and Borneo. In contrast, the Lesser Sundas or Nusa Tenggara, the most southeastern part of the Malay archipelago and the least developed, have some very seaworthy ships in their flood myths. I have mentioned the stone-cult ships of the megalithic Tanimbar culture and their attached stories of flight from an inundation to the west.

Another megalithic culture in the Nusa Tenggara, this time in Flores, had a Noah as their great forefather. The Nages, in the highlands of Flores, 'say that Dooy, the forefather of their tribe, was saved in a ship from the great flood. His grave is under a stone platform, which occupies the centre of the public square at Boa Wai, the tribal capital.' At the time of the harvest festival there are great celebrations around the ancestor's grave. People come from far and near and many buffaloes are slaughtered. The chief of the tribe is gorgeously decorated 'and on his head he wears the golden model of a ship with seven masts in memory of the escape of their great ancestor from the flood'.[55] Flores is not unique for these kinds of ceremonial head-dresses. They are found in dance groups all along the north coast of New Guinea, along the route Kulabob took.

Several conclusions may be drawn from the flood myths of India and the Far East. First the three basic types of flood story of the Ancient Near East – the catastrophic, the mountain-landing and the land-seeker types – are found again, but this time defined by culture, geography and language. Second the diversity is much greater. Southeast Asia and the east coast of China make more logical sources for these flood traditions. A fourth flood tradition, which we can call the equatorial type, appears both in South India and the Moluccas. This tells more directly of land loss and the splitting up of continents into islands.

Five hundred cataclysms?

Clearly it would be perverse and ethnocentric to insist that the diversity catalogued in these two chapters could be attributed to Christian missionaries. Yet, what general and local conclusions can we draw from this selection of the hundreds of different deluge stories from every continent in the world? Could they all have originated from one story? Were there instead multiple limited diffusions of stories of a number of unrelated local floods? Or was there just one mother of all cataclysms, either a huge meteoritic impact or some dramatic axis wobble that spawned all subsequent stories that have combined and recombined since? Or, finally, were there two types of grand floods in the legends, one catastrophic as just stated due to sudden cracks in the Earth's crust, and the other due to the more gradual but also possibly oscillatory rise in equatorial sea-levels as the great ice caps melted and the globe gently wobbled? My own view is the last one, but to get there we have to take an overview of the phenomenon.

If we take a story-type as one containing three or more shared motifs or themes and look at the distribution of those story-types across and between continents, we can start to suggest answers to questions about the number of floods and the number of original stories (see Table 6). On this basis, there are a maximum of six flood-story types which are distributed on a global scale. One of these, the 'lake-flood type', which is found both in North America and in the eastern Mediterranean countries of Greece and Turkey, is likely to have had separate local origins. A second type, the 'land-raiser family', shows a distribution over North Africa, Eurasia, the Pacific and North America. The wide distribution of this group both in the Old and New World suggests a very ancient origin. The 'land-diver' variant, which is found in northern Eurasia and North America, supports this concept of antiquity. They may even reach back as far as the second of the three postglacial ice-melts over 11,000 years ago. The land-raiser myths thus seem to hint at a much older cataclysm than the rest of the stories.

The other four flood story-types, because of uniquely shared motifs, have a claim to be related. They all reappear in some form throughout Eurasia. They have also all been found in the most ancient of written literature in the archaeological sites of Syria and Mesopotamia. In the three main regions I have reviewed, they take the following parallel forms:

Europe and West Asia

1. Watery creation, sometimes with a dragon/sea serpent, and/or followed by the separation of sky and land/sea. (Babylonian creation/ Genesis Chapter 1)
2. Sumerian and old Babylonian catastrophe, with drought/ famine/warning/sealed boat and anchor rope/catastrophe/restitution. (Noah's flood – both Priestly and Jehovistic)
3. Bird-seeker type with sealed chest/landing on a flat plain/two-bird land-seeker; (Noah's flood – Jehovistic/Assyrian Gilgamesh version 1)
4. Mountain-topping flood/mountain-landing survivors/stone re-creation. (Noah's flood – Priestly/Assyrian Gilgamesh version 2)

South Asia

1. Permanent coastal land loss with a hero versus sea-serpent battle and land-carving spear. (Dravidian/Aboriginal)
2. Manu fish-saviour with drought/famine/warning/catastrophe-fire and mountain-topping flood/boat and rope/sea serpent or fish/ mountain-landing. (Hindu Sanskrit – derived from Tai/Austro-Asiatic/Tibeto-Burmese/Dravidian)
3. The creation/fire storm/sealed chest/incestuous children/bird-finder. (Austro-Asiatic: Indian Mundaic). The sealed chest/bird-finder/ incestuous children. (Dravidian)
4. Mountain-topping flood/mountain-landing survivors/wood or stone re-creation. (Tibeto-Burmese)

Indo-China and Southeast Asia

1. Rising sea/island- and continent-shattering spear/conflict with sea gods and sea-serpents. (Austronesian: Maluku, Nusa Tenggara, Iban, Batak, north New Guinea coast, east Polynesia)
2. Creation/drought/famine/fire storm/sea flood/raft/serpent (Tai: Shan); creation/fire/mountain/catastrophe/sea superwave/mortar/incest/ millet grains. (Austronesian: Taiwan, Iban, Batak, Malay peninsular Aboriginals)
3. Sealed chest/incestuous children/sea flood/bird-finder/rice grains/ gourd re-creation. (Austro-Asiatic: Vietnam and Thailand)

Creation/fire/mountain/catastrophe/sea superwave/mortar/incest/millet grains/stone re-creation. (Austronesian: Ami Taiwan, Batak, Nias, Maluku, Iban, Sulawesi, south Philippines)

4. Mountain-topping flood, mountain-landing survivors/incest/

grains of millet. (Tibeto-Burmese/Austronesian: Taiwanese-Tsuwo and Bunun/north Philippines, south Borneo, Sulawesi, Batak, Enggano, Malay, Nias, Maluku, east Polynesia)

I will discuss the first of the above four story-types in more detail in the next chapter. This watery chaos and serpent tradition, although widespread elsewhere, features as the dominant flood variant in Australia, western Melanesia, eastern Indonesia and south India, thus lending support to its antiquity. These latter stories appear to be historiographic and refer to the permanent rise of the sea, flooding the coastal plains and continental shelves. Because they usually give local details of the land lost it could be that, of all the flood myths, they have the best claim to be historiographic. If they really do refer to the loss of coastline and breaking up of islands on the Sunda shelf of Southeast Asia, we may be looking at not one, but the last two rapid post-glacial sea-level hikes.

The remaining three story-types (numbers 2–4) are typically catastrophic and fantastic. Although they are worldwide and overlapping in distribution, they are commonest and achieve their greatest diversity in Southeast Asia. The largest number of variants of the mountain-topping flood (number 4), in particular, are found among Austronesian speakers of island Southeast Asia. Although all four types are represented in the literature of Mesopotamia and Assyria, the variety is much less apparent in the west. This general observation of diversity in Southeast Asia supports that region as the homeland of the stories, by analogy with historical linguistics.

Because of the overlap of distribution of the story-types in Asia, there is some difficulty in proposing any individual homeland for each variant, but we can note certain links. The familiar first part of the Old Babylonian flood with its warning and building of the ark, followed by a sudden catastrophe (number 2), is the dominant type among tribal people speaking Tai languages, such as the Shan. The third variant on the other hand, with its bird land-seekers, sealed chest and incestuous children is typical of Austro-Asiatic peoples in India and Indo-China. Finally, the mountain-topping flood, usually following a giant wave with refugees on the mountain top (number 4), is the dominant type among people speaking Tibeto-Burman languages.

In conclusion, the multiplicity and distribution of flood stories far outreaches any other common origin myth in the world, and crosses more geographic and ethnic boundaries than any other. The distribution and nature of the stories suggest at least one worldwide sea flood, if not two. There is not one but many story-types, of which six have an inter-continental spread. It is more likely than not that they refer to a real cataclysm or cataclysms. Of particular relevance are those stories from South and Southeast Asia which link sea floods with permanent migrations of coastal people.

II

WATERY CHAOS WITH DRAGONS

Respect for authority is not one of my strong points. I first read Genesis to myself as a teenager, rather than listening with half an ear from the pew. I remember feeling cheated that the first two chapters, so familiar to many readers, described two distinct and contradictory creations. There was no apology for the inconsistency, and no religious instructor ever mentioned the error. They are so dissimilar that scholars have consigned them to different ages. In this and the next few chapters I will retrace my own voyage of discovery through the archives of our folklore. Although I started off walking well-trodden paths of comparative biblical and folklore analysis, I soon found that all but a few of the many paths had been hedged off. In fact further exploring was discouraged by signs saying 'beware: diffusionism'. I persevered and found, first, that both stories are much older than civilisation in the ancient Near East; and secondly that they form part of a family of stories that have travelled east into Oceania and west through Eurasia. The opening lines seem to describe the recovery from some great watery catastrophe.

Two creations

The first story, with a seven-day creation from watery chaos, is thought by some to have been put together during or after the exile in Babylon. It is sometimes called the Priestly account:[1]

> In the beginning God created the heaven and the earth.
>
> And the earth was without form, and void; and darkness was upon the face of the deep. And the Spirit of God moved upon the face of the waters.
>
> And God said, Let there be light: and there was light.
>
> And God saw the light, that it was good: and God divided the light from the darkness.
>
> And God called the light Day, and the darkness he called Night. And the evening and the morning were the first day.

> And God said, Let there be a firmament in the midst of the waters, and let it divide the waters from the waters.
>
> And God made the firmament, and divided the waters which were under the firmament from the waters which were above the firmament: and it was so.
>
> And God called the firmament Heaven. And the evening and the morning were the second day.
>
> And God said, Let the waters under the heaven be gathered together unto one place, and let the dry land appear: and it was so.
>
> And God called the dry land Earth; and the gathering together of the waters called he Seas: and God saw that it was good. [Genesis 1:1–10]

The second story then leads on to Adam and Eve and the Garden of Eden. In this latter case, creation of the cosmos, which starts from dry barren land, is complete in one day, apparently ending with a flood. Some scholars believe this second version to be much older. It is known as the Jehovistic account:

> These are the generations of the heavens and the earth when they were created, in the day that the Lord God made the earth and the heavens,
>
> And every plant of the field before it was in the earth and every herb of the field before it grew: for the Lord God had not caused it to rain upon the earth, and there was no man to till the ground.
>
> But there went up a mist or flood from the earth, and watered the whole face of the ground. [Genesis 2:4–6]

The stark contradictions between the two Genesis Creations, while they may cause Fundamentalist Christians some confusion, are at the same time a key to a past that reaches way back before the age of the biblical patriarchs.

The oldest layer in creation myths

Cosmogony, the birth or creation of the Universe and its parts, is one of our most enduring obsessions. Physicists steal the television screen from nature documentaries in their eagerness to tell the world in which second after the Big Bang each primordial particle was made. Pictures of the birth of a new star thrill all ages, and increasing knowledge of origin of the Universe does not dim the magic of thinking about it.

In most creation myths the creation of the Universe is intimately connected with the appearance of the first God or gods (theogony), and the creation of humanity. In spite of this, cosmogony needs to be dealt with separately, because most commentators believe this aspect of creation may have a different provenance. Cosmogonic myths are often more conservative and show less variation between related cultures than their respective theogonies. For example, the cosmogonic myths of Babylon, Greece and Israel are clearly related, while their gods appear on the surface to be very different. A simple interpretation of this divergence is that the first parts of individual creation stories contain earlier and older material. Thus if the cultures are really related but diverging, then the older parts of their mythology would be expected to show less change than the later parts. This would be particularly likely to occur if the new gods were introduced either as god-kings or as new blood from merging cultures.

In this chapter I am not primarily concerned with the *reasons* for most cultures having elaborate cosmogonies. The questions are more *whether* and *how* the cosmogonies are genetically related and if this can shed any light on the origins of civilisation. In general such questions have ceased to tax folklorists' minds since the early part of this century. They still sometimes argue, however, that any similarities between mythologies are the structural result of the common subject matter and humans' innate psychological response to their environment and natural phenomena. I therefore need to digress briefly to review possible reasons for cosmological and cosmogonic myths. Then I will compare different ancient views on the origins of such phenomena as light, day, night, sky, Sun, Moon, stars, sea and land.

Myths of cosmogony – explanatory or irrational

A persisting nineteenth-century view of folklore held that creation myths were products of naive, irrational or 'pre-logical' minds. Our tendency to invent explanations for impressive cosmic objects and phenomena, however, need not necessarily be seen as irrational nor mystic nor even as uniquely human.

Every higher organism requires an internal operational framework of the environment that it grows up in. Otherwise it would constantly be faced with confusions of decision, which would interfere with life's main functions of survival, feeding and breeding. Put in other words, any animal that can learn has to make some sort of empirical sense of the world it lives in to function adequately. This functional framework is built up by a combination of innate skills, parental teaching and experience. A simplistic example of functional knowledge through 'phenomenal experience' might be a bird in a glass-fronted cage at a zoo. The bird cannot have been prepared genetically for its unnatural environment, but it learns very quickly not to fly into the glass. We cannot picture the bird's empirical concept of glass when it finally adapts its behaviour. We may feel that the bird can never understand glass as we do, but the bird's new concept of glass is functionally appropriate and is not irrational.

Knowledge of the effects of phenomena such as day and night on everyday activities are essential to land animals. These effects are not always realised instinctively. The hunter-gatherer requires to know how the different times of day affect his chances of success in the field. An attempt to formalise this is still seen in the hour calendars inscribed on plaques of wood used by various Dyak tribes in Borneo. These almanacs are usually based on a seven-hour day (see illustration 15). They inform the hunter of auspicious and inauspicious times to hunt; they inform the villager of the right times to plant, marry their daughters off and engage in other activities. Much of the information on these calendars seems as irrelevant and illogical to the modern city dweller as the Christian or Islamic calendar might have seemed to the original creators of the Bornean calendars. However, the various tribes-people who use them somehow manage to be more successful hunters and farmers than a city clerk would be if put in the same environment today. The point is that knowledge and skill, obtained empirically over a long period, will inevitably contain much redundant and wrong information along with good ideas. It is illogical to regard such an approach to knowledge as irrational.

The idea of cosmogonic myths being early man's empirical attempt to explain the unexplainable in his perplexing environment is not new. Oxford academic Sir Maurice Bowra, for instance, had a similar view, although he stressed the emotional and irrational components in the process.[2] As will become apparent, even the most fantastic creation myths have a discernible basis in attempts to describe or explain natural phenomena.

Cosmogony – the explicable and inexplicable

If cosmogonic myths were rationalisations of natural phenomena, the more inaccessible to testing and understanding particular phenomena were, the more fantastical explanations could result. Thus at one extreme the *origins* and *means* of motion of powerful heavenly bodies like the Sun were beyond explanation and could be anyone's guess. In many cultures – for instance that of the Ancient Egyptians – we find extraordinarily naive and bestial imagery of the events of cosmogony. The descriptive mathematics of the annual and monthly calendars and the regular movements of heavenly bodies were, however, amenable to prehistoric testing and analysis, although with great effort. Thus the astronomy of the Egyptians and some pre-Columbian cultures seems sophisticated and sensible beside their mythological ideas of cosmogony. I discuss this further later.

At an early stage of human evolution, we may imagine individuals in pre-urban societies each with their own ideas about the seasons, years, the length of day and night and so on. Inevitably some people's ideas and models were better and more predictive than others. Evidently, the better models survived. One most amazing achievement of prehistoric people was the creation of functional annual calendars and observatories such as Stonehenge. The very size of such monuments suggests that sufficient solution of the mathematical relationships of the heavenly bodies had been achieved for confident planning and co-operative massive construction in prehistoric times. As pointed out by Colin Renfrew in *Before Civilisation*, the layout of Stonehenge as an observatory before 3000 BC *predated* the conventional date of construction of the Great Pyramids of Giza by at least 500 years, making it unlikely that they were influenced by Near Eastern civilisations.[3] The accepted function of the Giza monuments themselves as mausolea has recently come under doubt. Further evidence has been produced of their use as ancient ritual observatories.[4] Other sites proposed as ancient observatories include Tiahuanaco in Bolivia and Teotihuacan in Mexico. The Mayans left written evidence of advanced calendrical and astronomical knowledge that they apparently inherited from their predecessors the Olmecs.

With such tantalising evidence of ancient and anachronistic sophistication, several writers and the occasional archaeologist have extrapolated to lost technologically advanced societies during prehistoric times. Investigative journalist Graham Hancock, in his recent best-seller *Fingerprints of the Gods*, suggested flying machines may have been available to the well-to-do in predynastic Egypt.[5] The calendrical and astronomic evidence, however, needs to be seen in the perspective of what was possible with the resources that might have been available in, say 3000 BC. Remember it is the lack of prehistoric evidence of advanced technology that forms the backbone of the establishment's scorn of the proponents of the wise men of prehistory.

If sites such as Stonehenge, Giza and Teotihuacan were built as observatories, their builders did not apparently have the benefit of lenses and telescopes and fine, metal astrolabes. Otherwise why were they so dependent on huge, line of sight monuments to make their observations? That these monuments were used as working observatories is suggested at least in Stonehenge: there are rows of experimental post holes in a narrow avenue just anti-clockwise of the line of midsummer sunrise.[6] On the other hand, several writers argue that the ancients did have the use of telescopes. One lynchpin of this view is the apparently detailed ancient knowledge that the Dogon tribe of Timbuctoo (in Mali) have of the dual star system of Sirius and also Saturn's halo. Neither feature is detectable by the naked eye. Such views, although provocative, remain to be proved. Given that there is no overwhelming evidence yet of the use of telescopes before 3000 BC, the best working hypothesis is that celestial alignments were assessed using the naked eye.

Another piece of evidence used to claim that prehistoric people had access to advanced technology is the size of the stones used in their megalithic monuments. Some of these stones would still defy the largest modern crane. Perhaps this paradox holds the answer. Twentieth-century civilisation has the wrong technology for such feats. There are other ways of building large monuments nowadays. Large stones are, however, still manhandled by the surviving megalithic cultures of Southeast Asia and the Pacific. Only a few hundred years ago, huge blocks were carved and moved in Easter Island, with only men, rope, wood and stones as tools.

If we accept that the means of construction and the methods of celestial observation of these ancient sundials were within the reach of a determined and intelligent Stone Age culture, the question still remains: how could they have achieved the knowledge they are credited with, using the equipment they had? This knowledge includes determining the cardinal points of the compass, the length of the year, the solstices and equinoxes, prediction of the Moon's movements, the annual rotation of the twelve stations of the Zodiac and, as a final pinnacle, calculation and prediction of the precession of the equinoxes. The last mouthful refers to the slow cyclical wobble of the Earth's axis of spin that occurs over a cycle of about 26,000 years (see Chapter 1). Surprisingly all these calculations could theoretically be made, given time, using naked-eye alignments in the observatories.[7]

An important additional fact is that prehistoric people had time on their hands. For at least 35,000 years, and possibly for 100,000 years, they had the same brain as ours. There was plenty of time for protracted observations, since we cannot assume that the monuments seen today were the first observatories.

Ancient uses of astronomy

The question of why any Stone Age society should want to measure the movements of the celestial bodies so accurately has often been asked. A common and sensible answer is that the early astronomers were also sailors who needed to navigate. The ancient use of the seven stars of the Pleiades by sailors is one of many examples that connect navigation with Eurasian and Oceanic mythology.[8] Another practical and self-evident reason was to predict the seasons and best times for planting and harvesting. As we shall see, the interactions between the Sun's and the Moon's movements were the key to this in Eurasia and Oceania. But another more sinister development may have been the desire of an elite to impress and control their fellows.

The acquisition of advanced astronomical and calendrical knowledge may have been the point where smart shamans and priests hijacked the whole process of discovery of knowledge for their own agenda. From a brilliant prediction of seasons and equinoxes and days in the year it was a small step to secret societies that controlled such knowledge. From there the priests could impress outsiders with their magical ability and supposed power. Then in turn they could have introduced the concept of god-kings and deities of the various components of the cosmos.

The history of the Old World misuse of astronomy for controlling people is preserved in the two words, 'Astronomy' and 'Astrology'. The first of these Greek derivations implies naming the stars while the second implies talking about them. The Greeks learnt about the stars from Mesopotamia. Their star-gazers had, at an early stage, described how the Sun rose serially among the twelve different constellations of the Zodiac during the course of the year. It was clear that these celestial changes were associated with the regular changing of the seasons and nature in general. Priests could claim that the stars also influenced the destiny of people. This was where the hijackers came in. Armed with the magical ability to predict both the seasons and celestial phenomena, they were in a strong position to dominate their ignorant colleagues. The picture of a caste of experts who use privileged knowledge and gobbledegook to control and take advantage of their fellows is still with us today. This confidence-trick hypothesis of early religion implies a 'hijack' of the original purpose of knowledge.

One of the most entertaining and erudite of discussions on prehistoric people and their gods is H. R. Hay's *In the Beginnings*.[9] In this book he elaborates on the well-known theme of the 'trickster creator' who was usually a coyote or fox in American Indian mythology. This character is also often significantly identified as a shaman. In Norse mythology the god Loki has the contradictory roles of creator, trickster and shaman. Jan DeVries has interpreted the first three syllables of the Norse pre-creation chaos 'Ginnungagap' as meaning 'deceit through magic'.[10]

In summary, myths of cosmogony form the oldest layer of creation stories, but could still have originated in practical and intelligent attempts to explain and predict the behaviour of the Universe. Such recorded behaviour of the cosmos may have included sudden and catastrophic events as well as the more regular seasonal ones. Later embellishments may represent on the one hand ill-informed speculative elaboration, or, on the other, deliberate lies. Once the ancient priest-kings had tasted the power of 'people control', the useful triad of magic, religion and politics could have developed in parallel with the continuing practical use of astronomy.

One of the most powerful forces for elaboration and change of myths would have been diffusion. A myth changes most rapidly when it moves. This elaboration results from new agenda and new contexts. Thus an explanation for some natural phenomenon may become progressively more fantastic with repeated telling; there need be no arcane and irrational motives behind these unbelievable stories. How much the simpler, explanatory model is supported by the following analysis of the stories, I leave the reader to judge. I should stress again, however, that the primary goal in this part is to demonstrate the diffusion of story motifs from Southeast Asia. The prehistoric motives for telling the stories, although interesting, are of secondary interest and do not affect the diffusional hypothesis.

Chinese whispers

Anyone who has read even a fraction of the hundreds of cosmogonic myths from around the world will admit the extraordinary resemblances of such stories from vastly different cultures. Such similarities may be due to chance, common subject matter, common cultural and physical environment, or finally common origin. The question can be simplified to diffusionism versus neo-evolutionism. In other words, myths are similar either because they are related to a common source, or because people tend to tell stories like that. The materials we have are the myths, as recorded by ethnographers, wanderers, administrators and others, and, lastly, the ancient texts. The most objective approach to the question is to take a statistical view of the content of the myths and see which of the above reasons for similarity best fit the observations.

For example, the Sun and the Moon can be seen throughout the world. Therefore, cosmogonic stories of their origins and powers would, on a non-diffusionist model, be expected to be widespread and random in actual content. The sea would be an important subject only for people who live by it or whose ancestors did. But stories of the sea in Tibet, for example, could have arrived there only by some mode of diffusion. Animals would be likely to appear in all stories of people whose ancestors hunted or domesticated them; this could apply, of course, to any culture. Plant foodstuffs would feature in origin myths of ancient horticulturalists or cereal-growers. But if a certain agricultural theme had a particular regional dispersion rather than a random distribution, a diffusional origin could be inferred.

If a particular theme of cosmogony – for instance the 'Sun as a creator' – occurred in a uniform distribution throughout the world it would be difficult to prove or disprove either a diffusionist or evolutionist origin. But if this particular theme occurred only in a restricted regional distribution and nowhere else, then a diffusionist explanation becomes more likely. And if two or more particular themes shared the same regional distribution, and even appeared in the same stories, then the coincidence would be too great, and the argument for diffusionism becomes much stronger. In this kind of analysis, regional absence of themes is as important statistically as their presence.

Clearly, stories change over thousands of years, although surprisingly little. In order to tell if a particular theme or motif has persisted, and appears in several versions, we have to abstract the essence of that theme. Themes are also known as 'motifs' in folklore jargon, and groups of motifs as 'story-types' – many creation stories start with the separation of the sky and earth. This is the essence of the *separation motif.* In different stories, the sky and earth have different names, and the means of separating them change, their sexes even change or may be irrelevant; the metaphor may have become a breaking eggshell. Sufficient other features of these stories persist, however, for folklorists to define 'separation' as a clear motif. The more varieties of separation motifs we find, the more we know that they form a family. If members of the family appear only in certain countries, we can suggest they arrived in those countries by diffusion.

One way of viewing this process is to see it as playing multiple games of 'Chinese Whispers'. A story is passed by whispers along a line of people. The story is progressively distorted. If a series of lines of people start with the same story, the lines of narrators will all end up with different versions. Although these final versions may bear little superficial resemblance to each other, we should still have a better chance of discerning the original version by comparing them for common themes than if we looked at only one.

I have studied collections of cosmogonic myths with the aim of identifying common themes. I analysed 190 cosmogonic myths from a number of sources that include all the major language families and all inhabited continents. This represents a valid statistical sample of known myths. While this is not an original method, I took the less-common analytic approach of looking at the material before studying Stith Thompson's Index of Motifs.[11] Initially, I did this to identify common motifs subjectively and avoid selective bias of existing literature. After reading the source material, I was subsequently relieved to find that the twenty cosmogonic themes I identified in the first trawl were close to those already identified by authorities in the field.

I also soon realised that North and South America and Sub-Saharan Africa differed profoundly from Eurasia and Oceania in their subject matter and also in having rich pantheons of animal creators. To do justice to such a treasure of diversity would occupy more space than I have here and would deflect from the main argument that concerns the prehistory of Eurasia and the Indo-Pacific region. So although I have included a representative sample of creation myths from Africa and the Americas for statistical comparison, I admit to having condensed some of their many and unique themes into more general categories. The other regions I found with a combination of rich internal variety and lack of Old World themes were Australia and the non-Austronesian speaking parts of the island of New Guinea.

As can be seen in Table 7, Eurasia and Oceania share a number of themes of creation. The themes not only unify half the globe but also combine and recombine in the same complex story-types. These themes or motifs can be broadly divided firstly into those that deal with an initial cosmic chaos, usually wet and dark. Secondly we have those that deal with the recovery from this mire by a process of separation of the heavens from the earth which lets in the light and the heavenly bodies. These two story-types are often combined in the same myths, but we can deal with chaos first.

Watery chaos and dragon-slayers

Worldwide themes of cosmogony include the origins of the heavenly bodies (the Sun, Moon and stars), land, sea and sky. Most creation myths specify a primeval cosmic state. In about half of the cosmogonies I reviewed the world starts off as vast watery chaos. Thus, in the Priestly

Table 7. **Story motifs in the creation of Heavens and Earth.** Motifs grouped into those that characterise Eurasia and Oceania, and those that are found in other continents or have a more general worldwide distribution.

Eurasia and Oceania	Other continents & worldwide
Watery chaos with dragon at start	Watery chaos at start
Apsu (a body of fresh water)	Dry rocky start
First light before luminaries	
The word as a creative force	
Separation of sky and earth	Sun
Moon/lake complex	Moon
Mother earth (+/– father Sky,	
Land raisers (fishers and ploughers)	(divers, driers and scratchers)
Parricide	
Use of body parts to make elements of cosmos	
The wind as a creative force	
Incest at creation	
Use of seven in describing aspects of cosmogony	
Cosmic egg	

version of creation the Old Testament starts: 'In the beginning … the earth was without form, and void; and darkness was upon the face of the deep … And the Spirit of God moved upon the face of the waters …' This theme of original watery chaos, usually without light, appears in every continent and in over half of creation myths in each of the main language phyla. It is perhaps not a surprise to see watery chaos motifs in Oceania and in various coastal cultures. Yet, the theme's presence in central Asia and in Tibet takes some explaining without diffusion (see Table 8 in Chapter 12). In some cultures the primeval sea is calm and featureless, but in others it is chaotic, with malignant, violent and even poisonous aspects. These features have a distinct regional distribution.

The idea of a malign and powerful primeval ocean appears several times in the Bible although the two Genesis creations specifically exclude any reference to troublesome forces:

On that day the Lord will punish
With his sword, which is hard great and strong,
Leviathan, the fleeing serpent,
And Leviathan, the tortuous serpent,
And he will slay the crocodile (*tânnin*) that is in the sea.
[Isaiah 27:1][12]

Thou didst divide the sea by thy power;
Thou didst crush the heads of the crocodiles (*tannînîn*) by the waters.
Thou didst shatter the heads of Leviathan, ... [Psalms 74:13–14][12]

Four other Old Testament sources refer to this ancient conflict between God and the deep (Tehom in Hebrew). These battles involved reptilian sea monsters named variously Rahab and Leviathan, although, in several places in the extracts above, they are also identified as sea crocodiles. The first biblical scholar to collate and discuss this material was Hermann Gunkel in 1895. The parallels were further enlarged in a series of essays from Chicago University, by Alexander Heidel, a Mesopotamian specialist. These were intended to show that the myths of the Old Testament had cousinship with, rather than descent from, those of Mesopotamia. Heidel also raised the possibility that Leviathan and Rahab were both synonymous with the mythical creatures Labbu and Lotan in Babylonian and Assyrian literature.[12]

In Babylonian mythology the primeval mother Tiamat was the apotheosis of the bitter salty chaos of water. She was espoused to Apsu who was identified with sweet fresh water.[13] Etymologically her Ionian Greek equivalent was Tethys, who appears as progenitor with her husband Okeanos in a creation myth told by Homer nearly 3000 years ago. In this story the original sea encircled the Earth like a stream. Okeanos was also seen as the father of all river gods.[14]

In several verses of the Babylonian creation, Tiamat assumed a dragon-like form or generated cohorts of dragons. One of her descendants, the young hero-god Marduk (Assur in the Assyrian version) was volunteered by his relatives to defeat her in all these forms.[15] The Babylonians' forerunners, the Sumerians, had a birth-goddess Nammu associated with primeval water, but they also had a separate myth of a god-hero conquering a water dragon. Versions of this story appear in several epics, including Gilgamesh.[16] The story of 'Ninurta and Kur', which is at least 5500 years old, relates how the god-hero Ninurta (also known as Nimrod) battled with the serpentine demon Kur from the netherworld. During the battle, the sea rose and inundated the land, poisoning it with salt. Ninurta raised a stone mound over Kur's corpse, thus creating a dyke against the sea and allowing the Tigris to flush away the salt.[17] Some writers have seen in this ancient story the archetype for a group of legends of dragon-slayers including such familiar but diverse Indo-European figures as Heracles, Perseus, St George, Beowulf and Krishna.

The Lernean Hydra, or water-snake, that Heracles slew was an offspring of Typhon and lived in a hole in marshy grounds, poisoning the surrounding countryside. To add to Heracles' problems was a giant crab that grabbed him by the foot.[18] Hydra's nine heads have been equated with Lotan's seven heads as described in a tablet from Ras Shamra in Syria.[19] Perseus, another Greek hero, rescued Andromeda from a rock on the sea shore, where she had been exposed as a sacrifice by her father to appease a sea monster. The monster that Perseus killed had been sent by Poseidon the sea-god to terrorise the countryside.[20] St George carried out a similar feat except that his dragon lived in a lake. St George's dragon also demanded regular sacrifice. This Western European myth may have been brought over from Asia Minor during the Crusades.[21]

The song of Beowulf is well known as the earliest complete surviving poem in English. The scene of action however is Denmark. An obliging hero, Beowulf, offered his services to Hrothgar whose court had been terrorised by Grendel, a man-eating monster from the flood marshes. Grendel, who symbolised a dark formless world inhabited by monsters, was tormented by the singing of the joyous song of creation in Hrothgar's hall. As a result he had a bad temper. After mortally wounding Grendel by ripping off his arm, Beowulf found that he still had to deal with Grendel's mother, who was even more terrifying. When Beowulf finally got to Grendel's lair in a marsh lake, he had to dive under water to do battle with the mother, while everyone stood round on the bank wringing their hands, fearing he was dead. In the end, however, he chopped off her head with a sword he found in the lair.[22]

A similar tale of entry into the monster's lair is found in Hindu mythology with Krishna, a child-like incarnation of Vishnu as the hero. In this case, the monster serpent Kaliya lived in a deep pool on the side of the river Kalindi. He destroyed crops and animals with his poison. The boy Krishna eventually subdued Kaliya with his music after being dragged into the churning depths for a long time by the monster.[23]

Moving east, China has various stories where dragons, which are normally useful creatures in Chinese folklore, were associated with the malign effects of water and flooding. In one of the two main Chinese cycles of creation myths, Nu Wa the creator goddess slew a black dragon of the Yellow River Valley that had been stirring up floods.[24] Another myth tells of the ancient State of Shu in Sichuan that was prone to floods. The cause of these was a lustful river-god in the shape of a dragon who demanded the regular sacrifice of two beautiful young girls every year to be his brides. A local hero, prefect Li Bing, offered his own daughters as decoy and battled the monster under water. Amid much churning of water he was eventually successful in bringing the monster under control without killing it. During the fight he turned briefly into a bull.[25] This myth, which has ancient provenance, is surprisingly close to other dragon-slayer myths and clearly labels the water-dragon as the personification of river floods.

Creation myths from most of the Indo-Iranian branches of the Indo-European language areas have some reference to watery chaos and serpents but not to dragon-slayers. So in the Zend Avesta of Zoroastrianism, Ahura Mazda created all lands and good things, after which his antithesis Angra Mainyu, who lived in the abyss, counter-created many bad things including, first, a serpent in the river.[26] In a Brahmanistic version of creation in India, the original state is a vast watery chaos on which floats a giant water snake with the creator-god Vishnu asleep in its coils.[27]

A cosmic serpent is ubiquitous in early Egyptian mythology. It takes on both sexes and various roles such as creator, a primeval sea monster to be overcome during the chaos of creation and as guardian of the underworld.

In Norse mythology we are most familiar with gold-hoarding dragons, but there was also an ancient and poisonous serpent in the depths of the ocean called 'girdle of the Earth'. Among the other fearsome deities of the sea, it was the chief enemy of Thor who protected humanity and the gods from chaos and anarchy. When it lashed itself into a rage at the end of the world, the sea covered the land and men and gods perished.[28]

Chaos and water monsters also rear up in Southeast Asia, Oceania and among Sino-Tibetan cultures. A widespread myth among various Dyak tribes of Borneo tells that the supreme god Mahatara has a helpful son called Jata who lives in the deepest parts of the river (or in the underworld) and is a crocodile, or can generate them. This blends in some cultures of that region with another story about the tree of life, which has a crocodile at the base and a hawk in its branches.[29] The Dyak's crocodile god is not entirely benign because he waits fiercely for souls entering the netherworld. Curiously the Fijians also have a story of a creator serpent Degei, who previously lived alone in the sea (and now lives in the world of the dead). His first companion was a creator hawk.[30] In the Gilbert and Ellis Islands of Micronesia, the creator deity Narreau the younger enlisted the help of a giant conger eel Rikki from the depths of the ocean to separate the sky from the land. After this Narreau the younger killed his father.[31] Serpents do not feature in eastern Polynesian myths, presumably for reasons of their absence from the fauna of those islands. The pre-creation watery chaos, however, appears in 90 per cent of cosmogonies from this area.

A widespread creation myth from northern Australia, which is thought to derive from sea flooding 9000–7000 years ago, describes a creator goddess who turns into a gigantic rainbow serpent in a fight with her son Chinimin. During the fight, rivers, lakes and mountains were formed. Another story of this region tells of a creator shark who separated the Milingimbi and Crocodile islands from the mainland as the sea-level rose.[32] In the high Himalayas, the Kuki tribes of Tibet believe that the world was originally covered by a single sheet of water inhabited by a huge worm.[33]

In spite of the universal distribution of water dragons in Eurasia, Australasia and Oceania, they are notable for their absence from myths of the African continent and their relative scarcity in the Americas. Among the thirty-five American creation myths that I reviewed, I found only four references to water monsters and in only one of these does the myth start with a primeval sea. In the Navaho creation, trickster creator Coyote steals the water monster's children. The bereaved monster responds by causing floods from which everyone had to escape by repeatedly climbing ladders into successively higher worlds.[34] Eskimos of the Bering Strait mention an amorphous black sea creature, which they cut up with the raven creator's help to make islands.[35] Iroquois Indians have a celestial water dragon, which is a personification of the Milky Way.[36]

The Aztecs of Mesoamerica were alone in the Americas in having a water dragon that would have been recognisable to the Babylonians: Cipactli, the great Earth Mother, was a terrifying monster from the other world in the shape of a huge alligator whose scales were mountains. As she emerged from the primeval water she engaged the sun-god Tezcatlipoca in battle. He tore off her lower jaw while she ripped off his right foot.[37] Interestingly, as in Southeast Asia, the Aztecs also had a myth of a world tree with a hawk in the branches and a reptile at the base (see Chapter 15).

These stories of ancient conflict between creator gods and heroes on the one side, and water dragons on the other show several common features. First, the threat of the dragons is always directed against the land and people living on the coast or near rivers and marshes. There are virtually no references to conflicts with fishermen or sailors whom, one would have thought, should have most to fear from monsters in the water. Secondly there is a strong association with flooding. The monsters were often poisonous to people, animals and crops. In the north Australian myths the floods are circumstantially linked with the rise of sea-level. In the oldest written Mesopotamian dragon story, 'Ninurta and Kur', however, sea floods were actually specified. This myth, composed just after the high point of sea-levels after the Ice Age (see Chapter 1), identifies the monster's poison as salt left by sea floods. Elsewhere such as in China and India river floods are mentioned.

Human sacrifice, particularly of girls, to the dragons and the sea appears in several of these stories as an ineffectual means of controlling the threat. It is curious in this context that many ancient petroglyphs (drawings and marks on rocks) occur throughout East Asia on seaside rocks at 5 metres above the present sea-level. This level coincides with the high point of sea-levels 5500 years ago.[38] It is difficult to imagine that peoples who lived on flat continental shelves did not make some ritual attempts to stem the apparently relentless loss of coastland. Our own international meetings to discuss global warming may be analogous in their Canutian inefficacy.

The question remains as to why dragons are so often the personification of flooding. The sinuous shape of rivers has an obvious analogy with serpents. There is, however, a much simpler explanation provided in the stories themselves, namely crocodiles. Alexander Heidel, in his analysis of biblical and Babylonian parallels, noticed a contradiction in the biblical references to Leviathan and sea-crocodiles, because there were and are no such creatures in the Mediterranean nor in the Red Sea.[39] The Nile crocodile was clearly a potential candidate reptile in its behaviour towards people, but since it remains in fresh water it could qualify only as a river dragon. The biblical reference would cease to be contradictory if it was put in the context of the Indo-Pacific region, where the cosmic water dragon also has a wide distribution (see Table 8 in Chapter 12). This is because there are estuarine and salt-water crocodiles (*C. palustris* and *C. porosus*) in India. *Crocodylus porosus* occurs throughout Southeast Asia and the southwest Pacific. It has even been seen as far out in the Pacific as Fiji. Salt-water crocodiles still occasionally terrorise villagers living near estuarine swampland, but in the recent past when their numbers were greater, they had a significant impact on village populations. One could imagine then a picture soon after the end of the Ice Age when a rapid incursion of the sea over flat tropical plains converted huge areas to mangrove swamps. The crocodile's habitat would have then tended to encroach over the villagers', thus posing an even greater threat.

To summarise: rapid sea flooding of broad tropical and sub-tropical continental shelves after the Ice Age caused an increase in the crocodile threat to coastal and island Indo-Pacific populations. Besides the progressive loss of arable land, due to the rising sea, there were also annual floods. During these, brackish water contaminated the land, causing salt marshes (which can still be seen in southern Thailand). These effects of a malignant sea and its cohorts of crocodiles would have been a regular feature of life for coastal populations for thousands of years. Then, about 5500 years ago, the sea stopped rising, it could be brought under control by dykes, and it then even started to fall. We can be sure that some hero then claimed credit for this reverse.

If this hypothesis of the origin of the sea-dragon and sea-crocodile myths is correct, it provides an explanation as to why similar myths are found in places where there are no large crocodiles, such as Sichuan, Mesopotamia and Europe. We have to suppose diffusion of the myth motif.[40] Apart from the meaning and origins of the sea-dragon myths, we can note the pattern of their distribution for, apart from the Aztec myth, they are confined to Europe and the Mediterranean, Mesopotamia, India, Southeast Asia and Fiji (Table 8).

A dry start to creation

In contrast to the more common watery creation, a dry start is specified in less than one in ten cosmogonies. We have already seen that in the second chapter of Genesis the Jehovistic one-day dry cosmogony is a short prelude to the Garden of Eden story. Curiously this is the only clear reference to a dry creation in any of the early Near Eastern civilisations – or any other part of the Old World for that matter. Island Southeast Asia has several dry creations, one in an inland Dyak tribe in Borneo.[41]

Not surprisingly there are dry creations in central Australia and dry parts of Africa and the Americas. But the peoples with the highest frequency of myths with waterless origins are the non-Austronesian speakers of Papua New Guinea, who frequently refer to a stony barren start to the world, often with people emerging from a hole in the ground. This is surprising since New Guinea is one of the wettest places in the world, and estimates of the antiquity of these cultures vary from 15,000 to 50,000 years. Another feature of their myths is reference to a time when the Sun was so hot that people and animals died. This theme is also found in northern Borneo in a story of two suns. The Earth was so hot in those days that an Iban hunter came home to find his wife roasted, bleeding and dead. Enraged he shot one sun, which has been weakened ever since and is now called the Moon.[42]

From these last stories, a dry start to the world can be seen to be the exception to the rule of a watery primeval chaos.

The land-raiser myths

Along with the worldwide distribution of stories of a primeval watery chaos, there are also various explanations as to how land was created from the midst of water. I have already briefly introduced these in the flood myths because of their shared motifs with the latter (see Chapter 8). Where the land creation mechanism is actually specified, there are five main versions: (1) a creator fisherman hooks and pulls the land up from the bottom of the sea; (2) a creator god, usually as an animal avatar, shoves or plows the Earth up from the sea floor; (3) a diver, either animal or human, is sent by the creator to get some earth from the ocean floor; the harvested earth is then made to grow by the creator; (4) the ocean partially drys up leaving a mound of earth or slime. A third of watery creation stories have such sequels.

The first two versions are both found in the same distribution of Eurasia and Oceania and represent nearly half of the stock. In central Polynesia the Tongans have Tangaloa as the creator fisherman *hauling up* their islands from the sea-bed, while in eastern Polynesia, the cult hero Maui is generally credited with this feat. In some versions Maui uses his sister's hair as a line while in others the 'land' is actually a large bottom-dwelling fish.[43] In the Micronesian creation from the Gilbert and Ellis Islands, which has already been mentioned in this chapter (see also the next chapter), there was a two-stage process. The initial

Figure 37. **Land raisers of creation.** The four main varieties of cosmogonic land-raiser myths have different continental distributions. The stories with fishers and ploughers of the ocean bed tend to be associated with an initial watery Chaos or Flood and follow the distribution of that theme from South Asia to the south-west Pacific. The diver stories are found in central and northeast Asia and North America, while the scratcher and dryer variants are African.

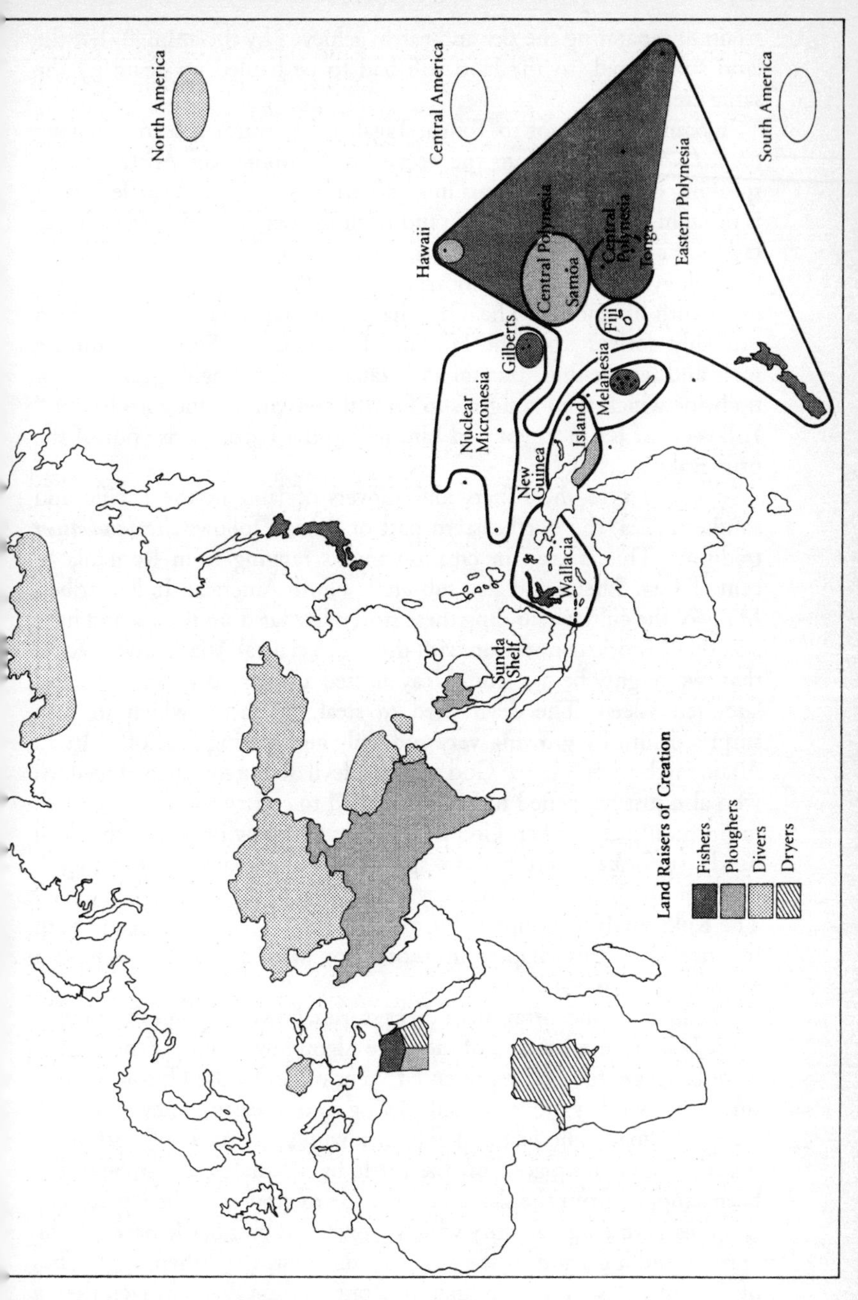
North America
Central America
South America
Hawaii
Central Polynesia
Samoa
Central Polynesia
Tonga
Eastern Polynesia
Fiji
Gilberts
Nuclear Micronesia
Melanesia
Island
New Guinea
Wallacia
Sunda Shelf
Land Raisers of Creation
Fishers
Ploughers
Divers
Dryers

strain of separating the sky and earth, achieved by the animals, left the land submerged, so the land still had to be hauled up again by the same creatures.

In Samoa next door to Tonga, Tagaloa the creator is seen as having *pushed up* the earth from the ocean bed.[44] Among the Austronesian-speaking Orokolo of Kerema in southern New Guinea, a turtle creator is thought to have pushed up sand from the sea-bed.[45] In Hawai'i this task was accomplished by a boar, a story that recurs in Hindu Vedic mythology where Vishnu, incarnated as a boar avatar, shoved up the earth with his snout.[46] The Thais have a similar story of a boar which probably derives from the Hindu.[47] In a Japanese Shinto creation a male and female duo, Izanagi and Izanami, use a magic spear to draw up brine which then congeals to form the mythical Onogoro Island.[48] Followers of Ra in Egypt had him telling the Earth to rise out of the primeval waters of Nu.[49]

In contrast to the fishers and shovers of land in the Pacific and southern Asia, the northeastern part of Eurasia follows the *land-diver* tradition. This is seen in creation myths ranging from Romania to central Asia, Siberia and also sub-arctic North American Indian tribes. Many of the cultures holding these stories live far from the sea and have no other historic connection with the sea. A central Asiatic myth recalls that two mighty beings from Heaven used a frog to dive for earth and later fell asleep. The devil tried to steal the earth, which in turn surprised him by growing very suddenly and scaring him off.[50] In an Altaic myth from Siberia, God sent the devil diving for earth. The devil who also just happened to be a man tried to secrete some of the earth in his mouth, but when God made the earth grow into land the devil nearly suffocated and had to spit it out thus forming the bogs.[51] Another of the same kind of story is found far to the west in Romania.[52] The Kuki myth from upper Burma and Tibet which has already been mentioned in this chapter in connection with serpents also has an earth-growing motif.

The largest concentration of diver stories, however, comes from sub-arctic North America, and of these the Algonquian tribes of the eastern woodlands are the best represented.[53] For example, the Huron tell of a turtle that sends various animals diving to find earth. They all drown except the toad, who just makes it back with some traces of earth in its mouth. These are placed on the turtle by a female creatrix, who has been dropped from the sky, and are made to grow into the land.[54] The Iroquois have a similar story which is preceded by a battle between the creatrix and a dragon in the sky.[55] To the west, the Athapascan tribes of the upper Yukon have a man on a raft sending first a beaver, then a muskrat diving for earth which is then blown away to make the land.[56] As mentioned in Chapter 8, in some of the Algonquian stories the event follows a great lake flood that has occurred after the original creation. In these versions the animal sent to find soil is usually a bird rather than a diver and the author of the flood is referred to as a water serpent.

There are thus clear parallels between such stories from northern and northeast Asia across the Bering Strait to their counterparts in North America. The land-diver motif has the most clearcut linguistic distribution of any of the flood themes in the Americas. With a few exceptions,[57] it is only found in two linguistic groups right up in the sub-arctic north of America. In one of these, the Algonquian Indians of the Northeast, who are Amerind speakers, it is at the core of their definitive flood myth, being found in over 90 per cent of versions. In the other group, the Athapascan Indians who are Na-Dene speakers, it is found in 30 per cent of versions. The motif is not found in Eskimo flood myths nor in any of those of South nor Central American Indians.

This highly focused distribution of an Old World creation theme among the flood myths of sub-arctic North America may help to illuminate one aspect of a hot linguistic and genetic debate as to the origins and dates of migration of the different American Indian tribes. The distribution of these land-diver stories partly coincides with the absence of the Asian 9-base-pair deletion genetic marker (see Chapter 6) in sub-arctic North America. Various views are held concerning these northern groups, one of which is that they represent an expansion of circum-polar Asian and American populations around the time of the Younger Dryas event over 11,000 years ago.[58] Such a date might explain the period of extreme cold and famine preceding the flood, that is described in the Algonquian myths. Fascinating and controversial as this topic is, it is outside the remit of this book.

To recap, in the land-diver myths we have reviewed, the subject matter is the same as in the land-shover and land-fisher stories, although the presentation of the theme is distinct. The fourth type of land-raiser stories, the partial *drying* of the sea to reveal land seems to be a particularly African variant, and is found both north and south of the Sahara.[59] Since the land-raiser stories are essentially sequels to a watery creation, four-fifths are found in that connection. The others seem to be found in association with versions of creation that specify the moulding of the first man and woman from clay. That will be dealt with in Chapter 13.

Summary

The dominant 'watery starts' of Eurasia do thus appear to be surrogates for a prehistoric marine flood or floods. Counterparts for the flood serpents and dragons of the Ancient Near East can be seen in Southeast Asia, the Pacific and even in Australia. Furthermore, if the creation myths were referring to more than one legendary world flood then the first may have been the rapid sea-level rise that followed the thousand year freeze up of the Younger Dryas event over 11,000 years ago. Circumstantial evidence for this may be seen in the widespread land-raiser stories of Asia, which reappear as land-diver myths in the circum-Arctic region.

As we shall see next, the motifs of watery chaos and dragons are linked in the same stories with the other main Eurasian creation theme of separation, in a broad band from Europe to Polynesia. The separation myths appear to be the mythological metaphors for the recovery from that dark, misty, watery chaos.

12
HEAVEN AND EARTH

The female sex of the land is an idea ingrained in European and Middle Eastern cultures. So it may come as a surprise to find that an Earth deity, although widespread, is mentioned in only a quarter of all creation myths. Even in these, not all are Earth Mothers, some are Fathers. Many readers will be familiar with Gaia, the Earth Mother of Greek mythology. By contrast, the best example of an Earth Father comes from Egypt in the form of Geb, who was forcibly separated by Shu, the wind, from his union with Nut, the female sky. Curiously, in one version of the Egyptian separation of Earth and sky, Geb assumed the form of a serpent and swallowed seven cobras. This formed the ring of the world, and the rule of Geb.[1] Several Indo-Iranian and North American myths also contain a male Earth deity. Generally, however, North American and Meso-American myths speak of Earth Mothers. China assigned no particular deity to Earth. Instead Chinese myths have a creator goddess Nu Wa, who appears in a separate myth cycle from the creative giant Pangu.[2]

Earth Mothers take on clear regional significance in the context of cosmogony only when they are found in association with a Sky Father, as in some cosmogonies of Classical Greece, Micronesia, eastern Polynesia and parts of the rest of the Austronesian diaspora. The Austronesian locations include a limited part of eastern Indonesia, where among the non-Islamic tribes of the Nusa Tenggara, Mother Earth is invariably associated with Father Sky (see below). During original chaos, there was literally a physical association between these Earth Mothers and Sky Fathers. The love affair was generally short-lived and usually had a gory end when the bridal couple were ripped apart or separated. The separation theme that I turn to next can be grouped with a core cluster of other themes characterising Eurasia and Oceania, which are discussed in the rest of this chapter.

Separation of the Sky Father and Earth Mother

After watery chaos, separation – usually of the Sky from the Earth – is the

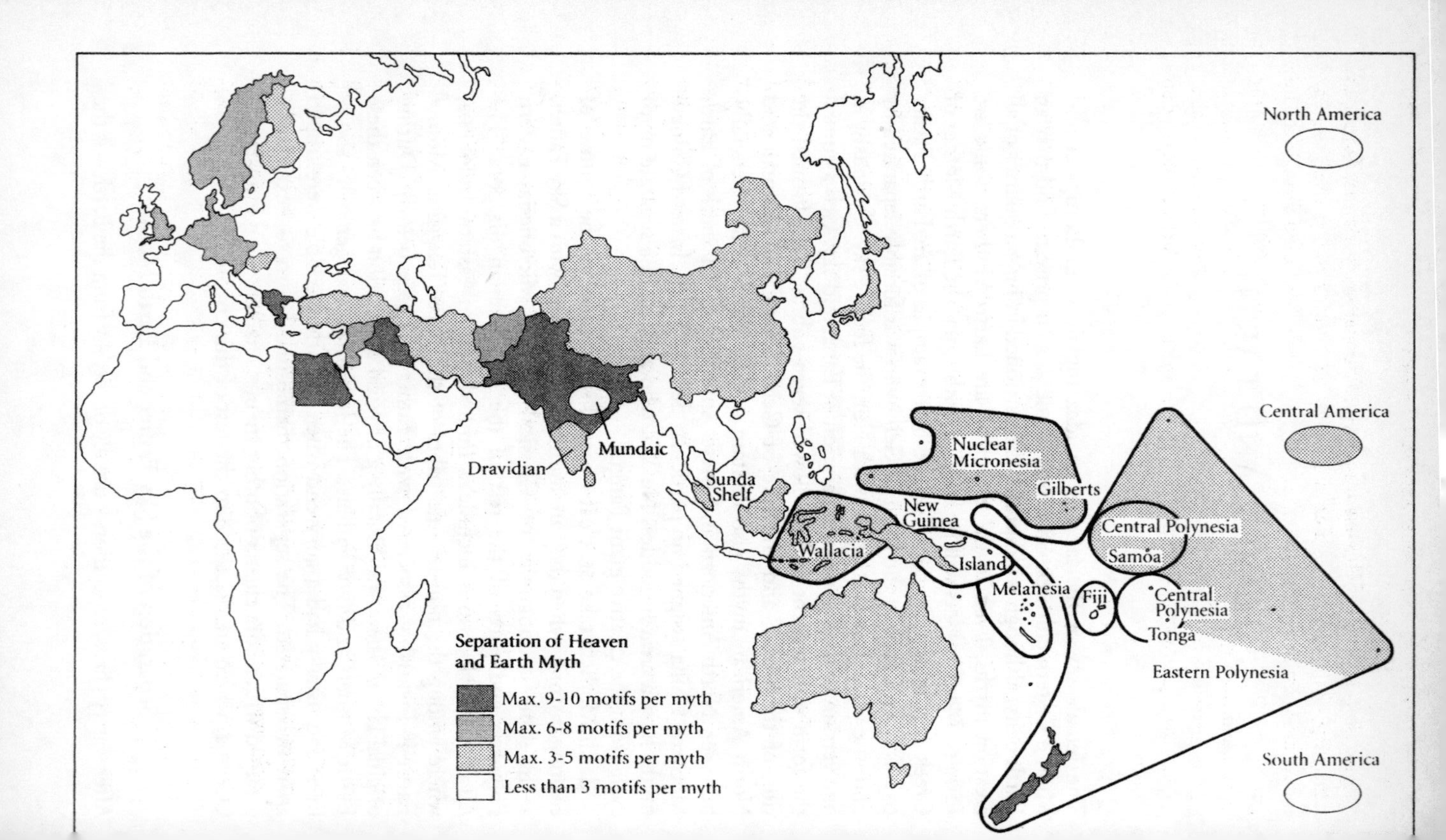
North America
Central America
South America
Nuclear Micronesia
Gilberts
New Guinea
Central Polynesia
Samoa
Wallacia
Island
Melanesia
Fiji
Central Polynesia
Tonga
Eastern Polynesia
Sunda Shelf
Mundaic
Dravidian
Separation of Heaven and Earth Myth
Max. 9-10 motifs per myth
Max. 6-8 motifs per myth
Max. 3-5 motifs per myth
Less than 3 motifs per myth

Figure 38. **Separation of Heavens and Earth.** This map shows the distribution of the story of the 'separation' after the watery serpentine darkness of chaos. The story has a distinctive distribution stretching from the South and West Pacific up to the northwest through China, South Asia and then the Middle East, finally ending in northern Europe. The ten story motifs (listed in Table 8) are not generally found in Africa, the Americas nor Central and Northeast Asia. Indo-China, with its Austro-Tai and Austro-Asiatic speakers, also lacks the separation story.

next commonest theme in cosmogonic myths, appearing in over a quarter of those I reviewed. As with the watery serpentine chaos, the motif occurs predominantly in the regions of Eurasia and Oceania. A particular version of the separation theme, which may even be an archetype, starts creation with Sky Father locked in close and dark sexual union with Mother Earth.[3] This story is found in a band stretching from New Zealand to Greece. The locked-couple picture is seen at its fullest in a little-understood string of islands, the Lesser Sundas of eastern Indonesia.

Beyond the imprint of Hindu influence, in eastern Indonesia and not too far from Australia, we find the surviving megalithic societies of Sulawesi, Maluku and the Nusa Tenggara. Here, a concept of Father Sky and Mother Earth, who were previously locked in a tight embrace, remains central to cultural beliefs. According to the Mappurondo faith of the Torajas of Sulawesi, Heaven, as in other megalithic groups of the archipelago, is called Langi; Mother Earth is Padang or Pongkapadang. These names are cognate with Rangi and Papa of the Maoris.[4] Langi appears as a sky god further west among the Donggo of Sumbawa, but this time as the primary god of a trinity that includes a water god Oi and a wind god Wango.[5] In the mountainous island of Flores there are myths telling of Mother Earth and Father Sky who were previously bound together by a sacred vine. The vine was chewed up by a dog. As a result, the lovers flew apart and were permanently separated. According to people in western Flores, the proof of this is seen in the behaviour of the bamboo, which bends towards the earth as if it is still pushed down by the weight of the sky on his lover. The period immediately before the separation was regarded as a plastic time when 'rocks were young and earth was soft'.[6] Throughout this region the ideas of the duality of godheads and the duality of their sex are explicit in the architecture and arrangement of houses. In the highlands of Flores each village has two sets of shrines, one phallic and the other box-like, to represent the two sexes. Menhirs and dolmens also take on the respective gender symbolism in this area.

Table 8. Motifs of the Creation Story of Separation divided by Geo-Cultural Area.

	Water Dragon	Light	Creative Word	Separation of Heaven & Earth	Parricide	Use of Body	Creative Wind	Sevens	Creator Incest	Cosmic Egg
C. America+Aztec	–	–	–	+	–	+	–	–	–	–
North America	–	–	–	–	–	–	–	–	–	–
South America	–	+	–	–	–	–	–	–	–	–
Sub–Saharan Africa	–	–	–	–	–	–	–	+	–	–
North Africa	+	+	++	+	+	++	+	+	+++	+
Europe	+++	++	+	+++	+++	++	+++	+++	++	+
Jew/Arab/Phoenicia	+++	+	+++	+++	+	+	+	+++	–	+
Mesopotamia	++	++	++	++	+++	++	++	+++	+++	++
Indo–Iranian	++	+	–	++	+	+++	–	+++	+++	+
Central Asia/Siberia	–	–	–	–	–	–	–	–	–	–
Japan	–	–	–	+++	–	+++	+	+	+++	++
China–Tibet	++	++	–	+++	–	+++	–	–	+	++
SEA (Austro–Asiatic)	–	–	–	–	–	–	–	–	–	–
SEA (Austro–Tai)	–	–	–	–	+++	–	–	–	+++	–
Island SEA (AN) W. Malayopolynesian	–	–	–	+	–	–	–	+	++	–
East Indonesia (AN) C. Malayopolynesian	–	–	–	+++	–	–	–	–	–	–
Melanesia (AN)	–	+	–	+	–	++	–	–	++	+
Micronesia (AN)	–	++	+	++	+++	++	–	–	+	+
C. Polynesia (AN)	+	+	+	+++	–	–	–	+	+	+
E. Polynesia (AN)	–	+++	–	+++	+	++	–	–	–	–
Melanesia (Non–AN)	–	++	–	–	++	–	–	–	–	–
Australian Aboriginal	+	–	–	–	+	+	+	–	–	–

Key:

–	Motifs found in 0–10% of stories.	AN=Austronesian
+	Motifs found in 10–30% of stories.	SEA=Southeast Asia
++	Motifs found in 30–50% of stories.	
+++	Motifs found in over 50% of stories.	

This architectural symbolism is equally evident in Timor. Among the Mambai of Timor, physical representations of the sky god's phallus and Mother Earth's vagina mark the centre of an altar complex, which includes separate houses for each god.[7] This practice of genital worship curiously seems to echo the more ancient aspects of the Sivaistic worship of the Linga and Yoni in Hinduism. In the Mambai cosmology in Timor, Mother Earth fell ill and died after her incestuous union with her brother Father Sky. He for his part recoiled and separated from the black, decaying but still-fertile corpse. During the annual pre-monsoon festival the reunion of the pair is ritually caused by ceremony and drums. The resulting rains represent the Father's semen that mixes with the Mother's milk in the soil.[8]

Although it is a feature of Austronesian cultures, the concept of the separation of Sky Father and Earth Mother is virtually absent from non-Islamic Austronesian cultures of Borneo, the Philippines, western Indonesia and the Malay Peninsula. In these regions it is instead replaced by stories of a sky god creating the Earth. This sky god has various names such as Mahatara, Bintara, Batara, Petara, Bathala and Siwa Mahayogi. Authorities generally regard these deities again as versions of Siwa, which derive from the Indian influence of the past 2000 years.[9] How much this is true and how much of the material in the stories pre-dated the period of Hindu influence, is unclear. The worship of Siwa probably existed in the Harappan civilisation of the Indus Valley before the Aryan invasions of India. The conventional view is that the recent 'Hindu' influence affected all of island Southeast Asia to a greater or lesser extent and therefore the sky god or Mahatara is explained as an import. The Hindu influence of the past 2000 years did not, however, extend to the southeastern part of the archipelago to islands east of Bali or the Nusa Tenggara, which hold the Sky Father/Mother Earth version. Given that these two ancient traditions have some features in common, such as a Sky Father and bi-genital worship, an alternative explanation is that some elements of Siwa worship originated in Southeast Asia.

I return to the separation of the cosmic couple later in this chapter under the gory sub-heading of 'Parricide and the use of the body'. Meanwhile I will look at less sanguinary and more ethereal archetypes of separation that have a similar band of distribution. In the first case it was the Word.

The Word, separation and light before luminaries

'And God said, Let there be light: and there was light'. (Genesis 1:3)

The use of speech by a creator to call light into being is associated in every cosmogony I could find, with a version of the separation theme. Similarly, nearly every time the word is used as a tool of creation even without producing light, there is a separation story or the body of the creator was used to build the cosmos. Thus, Ptah the creator god of Memphis, created the entire cosmos from his mind and speech and then made the gods from his heart and speech.[10] In the Sama Veda of India, self-creation by the Universal Soul was achieved by speech. The first two lines of the Babylonian creation epic *Enuma Elish* read: 'When the skies above were not yet named, Nor earth below pronounced by name'.[11]

Did the magical power of the first words of the creator cause the separation of Heaven and Earth, resulting in the appearance of light before the Sun or Moon? The three motifs of the word, separation and light before luminaries are commonly bound together in different contexts and combinations throughout Eurasia and the Indo-Pacific region. They can be dealt with individually and in context. Their order varies and we can look at the various combinations.

First light before the luminaries

To us, the Sun is self-evidently the source of all useful natural light. It comes as a surprise, then, to find that a fifth of all cosmogonic myths do not record the Sun as the source of the first light of creation. The Priestly creation of the Bible, for instance has light 'talked in' on the first day, but does not get round to creating or separating the Heavens until the following day:

> And God said, Let there be light: and there was light.
> And God saw the light, that it was good: and God divided the light from the darkness.
> And God called the light Day, and the darkness he called Night. And the evening and the morning were the first day.
> And God said, Let there be a firmament in the midst of the waters, and let it divide the waters from the waters.
> And God made the firmament, and divided the waters which were under the firmament from the waters which were above the firmament: and it was so.
> And God called the firmament Heaven. And the evening and the morning were the second day. (Genesis 1:3–8)

This was no slip of the stylus or imprecise wording. In his comparison of the biblical and Babylonian myths, Alexander Heidel called the arrangement 'light before the luminaries'[12] and further noted the same order of events in the Babylonian creation *Enuma Elish*.[13] Although primeval darkness is not specified in *Enuma Elish*, it is inferred from Berossus, a Babylonian priest of the cult of Marduk, who wrote, in Greek, a history entitled 'Babyloniaca' in the fourth century BC. Berossus described the watery chaos of Tiamat as shrouded in darkness.[14]

In many myths the creation of light was a particularly important and early aspect of the change from the unpleasant darkness of the initial chaos. In Greek mythology, light also came earlier than the Sun.[15] Phoenician (Canaanite) myths contain a selection of Babylonian, Judaic and Greek elements but keep the distinction of light (Phos) from the Sun.[16] Malay mythology, which is an amalgam of Islamic and pre-Islamic tradition, puts *light* right at the beginning: 'From the supreme being first emanated light towards Chaos'.[17]

First light before both separation of Heaven and Earth and luminaries

As mentioned, the 'first-light' theme is closely associated with the separation of Heaven and Earth. The separation motif appears in three-quarters of the myths that also include the 'first-light' theme. If we look only at Oceania and Eurasia then the association rises to 90 per cent. In some of these coincidences, particularly in the Pacific and China, the act of separation itself created or let the light in, but separation was not always the agent of light.

The Judaic creation is a Near Eastern example where the separation of the skies and earth come *after* the first light. Also in one Phoenician creation the first light appears from air as lightning.[18] Heaven and Earth then separated and the Sun appeared. Similarly in Hesiod's Greek *Theogony*, the gory separation of Heaven (Ouranos) and Earth (Gaia) came a divine generation later than the creation of light.[19]

Light called forth before separation of the Heavens

In about half of these situations of light before separation of the Heavens, the word of the creator is the agent that calls forth light, as in Genesis. This mechanism is repeated in the Pacific. Thus, in eastern Polynesia, a common myth of this type, holds that:

> Io, the Creator who has always existed, lived at first in a time

when there was only dawnless darkness above the shoreless waters. It was Io who spoke first, calling light into existence so that day came. When he had contemplated the light for a while, he spoke again, calling the darkness back, so night reappeared. The first day had ended. Then Io again dispelled the darkness and established the rule of light. He raised the sky, separating it from the earth. Then he separated the waters so the land became visible. Then he made Ra the Sun and Marama the Moon, and the bright Pacific stars.[20]

The stunning identity between this story and the first ten verses of the Priestly creation in Genesis might make the sceptic suspect a missionary influence. Even the name of the sun god has a Mediterranean touch. The same story has, however, multiple sites of provenance in eastern Polynesia. This could not be the result of a recent local missionary influence. In another tradition in Tahiti, Ta'aroa takes on a role like Io the Creator, calling everything, including light, into existence by himself.[21]

Light engendered by the gods before separation of the Heavens

The austere monotheistic cosmogony of Io the creator competes in Polynesia with the more exotic, sexual and polytheistic Tangaroa myths, which, according to location, echo variously the Greek, the Phoenician and the Babylonian cosmogonies. These will be discussed in more detail below. As far as the creation of first light is concerned, however, there are two main versions, corresponding roughly with the Greek and Phoenician.

The first of these is the Greek cosmogony where light is engendered during the first incestuous generations of the gods: Immediately after Gaia emerged from Chaos, Erebos (infernal shades) and Nyx (night) appeared and the two of them incestuously produced Æther (light) and Hemera (day). Phoebus, Apollo and Helios (divine aspects of the Sun) did not appear until later.[22]

A Pacific example of this light-engendering story-type comes from Tahuta in the Marquesas of eastern Polynesia. Tanaoa was the god of The Primeval Darkness or Chaos. On a given morning 'Atea, 'Space' emerged, freeing himself so that there was room for Atanua, 'Dawn' to arise. She married Atea, since light can only exist in, or together with space'.[23]

Another Pacific example of the engendering of light by the gods, comes from Samoa, one of the oldest parts of Polynesia. The 'Word' is used only for the creation of the sky in this myth. Tagaloa, in this story the ocean god, called everything forth from the primeval rock that he had pushed up from the ocean bed. He also called up:

> Mamao, 'Space', [who] is female; and Ilu, 'The Firmament', [who] is male; together they formed the sky ... The sky-couple had two children: Po, 'Night', and Ao, 'Day', who together had two children: Rangima, 'Bright-sky', and Rangiuri, 'Night-sky'.[24]

Ilu is identified with the firmament elsewhere further west. 'Ilai' in the Torajas applies to the sun god who married Indara the Earth Mother, while in Phoenician mythology, 'Ilus', from which the heavenly bodies shone, was generated from chaos by the wind.[25]

Separation of the Heavens and Earth lets in light

In the second and more logical of the two Pacific accounts of first-light production, the separation of Heaven and Earth created or let in the light. In the Pacific, this idea is confined mainly to eastern Polynesia and Micronesia. In the Maori version the male sky Rangi was locked in a tight embrace with his female consort Papa or 'Earth', thus excluding light from their divine offspring who were trapped between (see below, p.331). The children ganged up on their father with varying degrees of resolve, and eventually Tane Mahuta, fierce god of forests, took the lead to lift up his father with the others' help. Subsequently, as his father split painfully away from Papa his mother, and the light flooded in on the Earth, Tane Mahuta also became the god of light.

The Hawai'ian version renames Tane as Kane, the head of a trinity of gods that splits asunder Po, the primeval chaos of night.[26] In a Samoan version it was a snake that carried out the separation.[27]

The Micronesian story of how Narreau the Younger separated the Sky from the Earth with the help of a conger eel was mentioned in the last chapter. The separation of the Sky from the Earth in this myth from the Gilbert and Ellis islands was performed in order to bring light to the creatures and people who were trapped in a hole in earth.[28]

Cracking the cosmic egg lets in the light

A parallel string of traditions in the East has non-Sun light let in by the cracking and separation of the cosmic egg. The symbol of the world egg that floats in dark chaos and splits to create light, the skies and Earth appears in the main Chinese cosmogony of Pangu. The giant creator Pangu woke up to find himself trapped in a dark egg. Infuriated by the dark, Pangu somehow found an axe and split the egg with a great crash. The light and clear part rose to become Heaven while the cloudy, heavy substance sank to become Earth. This separation did not happen immediately and the young world needed Pangu's help as he cleaved and chipped away. Eventually he stood up and physically held the sky apart, like Atlas, for thousands of years. When he died, all the parts of his body changed into natural features. In particular, his eyes became the Sun and Moon.[29] In the same language family but from Tibet, a pre-Buddhist Bon creation myth also has the world cosmic egg bursting with the release of non-Sun light and a magical, all powerful man/creature.[30]

Japan is physically close to China and has had much Chinese influence over the ages including a few shared elements in the creation myths. The ancient origins of its language and culture, however, although a mystery, are certainly not Chinese. Some scholars have detected links with Polynesian cultures: in a Shinto Myth from the Nihongi there is a preface of Chaos and an egg separating into Heaven and Earth, which sounds very like the Chinese version without Pangu. However the scene soon changes and two related creator deities of opposite sex appear. They perform ritual acts of creation (like Brahma and Vishnu) with and around a spear, which has phallic properties, including the production of semen. During these acts Heaven and Earth separate and the Heavenly bodies are formed.[31]

The Chinese and Japanese stories of the splitting of the cosmic egg to bring first light are cognate with the Pacific traditions of separation of the firmament from Earth, as evidenced by a hybrid version of the separation of Heaven and Earth that comes from the Tuamotu Islands. This account of separation makes the world a cosmic egg-shell, which is split from the inside by Ta'aroa (Tangaroa) acting as a Polynesian version of Pangu.[32] In this egg version, however, which is clearly related to both the Pacific and Chinese stories of separation, there is another twist: the first light does come from the Sun.

These egg-cracking myths from the East have echoes in a Phoenician creation recorded by Eusebius, which implies both Sun and non-Sun light.The firmament in this cosmogony is referred to as Ilus, as in Samoa:

> Zophasemim – that is, the overseers of the Heavens ... were formed in the shape of an egg; and from Mot (Ilus) shone forth the Sun and the Moon, the less and the greater stars.[33]

The myth of the cracking of the cosmic egg is also found even further to the northwest in the Finnish creation *Kalevala.* In this cosmogony, separation results in the appearance of the celestial luminaries:

> From the cracked egg's lower fragment,
> Now the solid earth was fashioned,
> From the cracked egg's upper fragment,
> Rose the lofty arch of heaven,
> From the yolk, the upper portion,
> Now became the sun's bright lustre;
> From the white, the upper portion,
> Rose the moon that shines so brightly.[34]

Separation reveals the Sun as the source of first light

Clearly, then, the first-light theme and its different temporal associations with separation occur throughout the ancient Near East, China and the Pacific. The first light in separation stories may, however, still come from the Sun, as it did in the egg myths from Finland and the Tuamotu Islands. This concept is also found, without the egg, in Tanimbar Island of the Nusa Tenggara in eastern Indonesia, from a time

> long ago when the world was undifferentiated. The sun encompassed the moon and the stars and was caught on the eastern rim of the horizon, pressed down by the sky which hovered low over the earth. A perpetual darkness hung upon the land. The mainland likewise encompassed the offshore islands, and the life-giving springs of fresh water had not yet begun to flow ... the culture hero Atuf ... sails into the eastern horizon and spears the sun into pieces [with his magic lance], thereby releasing both the moon and the stars. The sky is separated from the earth ... thus allowing the passage of the heavenly bodies in their cycles. The lance is also stuck to the front of the boat like a plow thus effecting the separation of the islands from the mainland.[35]

The variant of the Sun's release by separation is repeated when we look at the land between the Far and Near East – in the Indian subcontinent. Although the themes of the cosmic couple and cosmic egg, the wind and word, and separation are well represented, the appearance of first light is generally attributed in the later Vedic myths to the Sun. It is possible that this is the result of the Aryan influence on the pre-existing indigenous myths of India. In some Hindu myths involving the cosmic egg, light originates either from the egg or a lotus or from Brahma.[36]

A creation myth of the Muria, an Aboriginal Dravidian tribe in central south India, seems to bridge the 'first light before luminaries' and 'first Sun' versions by a complex transformation involving sacrifice:

> When this world was first made there was neither sun nor moon and the clouds and the earth were like husband and wife, they lay so close together ... Then Lingo and his brothers raised the clouds into the sky and there was room for men on earth, but there was no sun or moon and everything was dark. There was a tree called Huppe Piyer. When this tree blossomed it was day, when it dried up it was night.[37]

There follows a complicated sequence by which the light-giving qualities of the tree are taken by Lingo and his brothers and transferred to the Sun and Moon through the blood of a sacrificed child.

Even more so than with our previous themes, the complex of first light and cosmic separation finds no adequate parallels in the myths of Africa or the Americas. There are American stories of primeval darkness, but in these people generally emerge from the darkness by climbing up into another world.[38] Once again, the distribution of the first-light theme and its variants in Eurasia and Oceania seem to suggest a common cultural origin.

Separation, parricide and the use of the body to build the cosmos

Besides first light and separation, several other elements are also associated with separation, such as wind, incest, parricide and use of the deity's body and fluids as building material for the cosmos. Where there is an egg in the story, the shell and contents are used in the same way as the deity's body. One of the fullest versions of the separation story, referred to already under 'first light', comes from New Zealand:

> In the darkness of chaos before the creation of the cosmos exist two primordial and self-created beings, Te Po, the personification of night, and Te Kore, the empty void. In the cosmic night they engender the prime parents of the Polynesian pantheon, Ranginui (father of the sky) and Papatuanuku (mother of the earth).[39]

> 'In these days the Heaven lay upon the Earth, and all was darkness. They had never been separated.' Heaven and Earth had children, who grew up and lived in this thick night, and they were unhappy because they could not see. Between the bodies of their parents they were imprisoned, and there was no light. The names of the children were Tumatuenga, Tane Mahuta, Tutenganahau, and some others. So they all consulted as to what should be done with their parents, Rangi (the heavens) and Papa (the earth). 'Shall we slay them, or shall we separate them?' 'Go to,' said Tumatuenga (the god of war), 'let us slay them.'
>
> 'No,' cried Tane Mahuta (the forest god), 'let us rather separate them. Let one go upward, and become a stranger to us; let the other remain below, and be a parent to us.'
>
> Only Tawhiri Matea (the wind) had pity on his own father and mother. Then the fruit gods, and the war god, and the sea god (for all the children of Papa and Rangi were gods) tried to rend their parents asunder. Last rose the forest god, cruel Tutenganahau. He severed the sinews which united Heaven and Earth, Rangi and Papa.[40]
>
> It … [was] … left to Tane Mahuta, the god of forests, and subsequently of light … [to use] … the great trees to lift Ranginui off Papatuanuku and to support the sky for ever more.
>
> Then wailed Heaven and exclaimed Earth, 'Wherefore this murder? Why this great sin? Why destroy us? Why separate us?'
>
> Light spreads over the Earth and all the creatures, once concealed between the bodies of the prime parents, begin to grow and multiply.
>
> Only the storm god differed from his brethren and followed his father into the sky.[41]

This tragedy tells of the divine couple, torn apart and mutilated by their trapped offspring, who end up donating their body parts to the New World. It forms a key link with Western myths. Apart from the parricidal intent of the son and use of body parts, the Maori cosmogony shares other common story motifs with Hesiod's Greek *Theogony* 3000 years earlier.

In our Greek story the equivalent copulating couple were Ouranos (Sky) and Gaia (Earth). The myth starts with the familiar dark, watery chaos. In this bloody story, Kronos, one of their sons, was trapped with his siblings in the cave Tartarus within Gaia. This incarceration was effected by his father Ouranos who in his sexual passion also forcibly overlaid Gaia. The wily Kronos, helped by his mother, sliced and separated Ouranos away with an obsidian knife, incidentally castrating him. He hurled his father's genitals into the sea, where the foamy semen created the goddess Aphrodite. Curiously in the Greek myth this ripping act of parricide is not the source of first light.[42]

Again in this ruthless Greek creation, we can see the familiar themes of chaos, darkness, first light, a Sky Father and Earth Mother whose embrace smothers their divine offspring, who in turn rebel murderously against their father thus achieving release by separation of their parents. The use of one fluid aspect of the father's body – semen here – may echo the Timorese rite of monsoon.[43]

The Phoenicians had a similar but theologically more complex creation. The names and roles of Gaia (Ge) and Ouranos, and their son Kronos (Cronus or Ilus) were the same as in the Greek version, although the action was given particular locations in the Middle East: 'Ilus, who is Cronus, laid an ambuscade for his father Ouranos … and dismembered him over against the fountains and rivers … and the blood flowed into the fountains and the waters of the rivers.'[44]

Significantly in the Phoenician story, one of Cronus' brothers was Atlas who in Greek mythology was a Titan. He had the punishment role, in the Greek version, of keeping Heaven separate from Earth on his shoulders in the west.[45] In spite of these cognate parallels, Phoenician mythology has the event of separation of Heaven and Earth represented by the alternative method of splitting the cosmic egg.

Norse myths have retained many of the elements of creation such as parricide, use of body and separation, but with a frosty flavour. As in the Chinese and Greek cosmogonies, a long-suffering giant was used. The Norse Chaos or 'Ginnungagap' stretched from the frozen north to the fiery south. As the ice melted, the giant 'Ymir' was defrosted. Apart from man, he gave rise to a family of frost giants. A man named Buri was also defrosted and also his grandsons, the three gods: Odin, Vili and Ve, who slew Ymir the giant. Nearly all the frost giants were drowned in his surging blood. Ymir's vast corpse was then used piecemeal by this delinquent trio to create the world of men. His skull in particular was used to make the dome of the sky. They placed four dwarves, one at each corner, to support it high above the earth.[46] It is tempting to place Norse cosmogony in the immediate post-glacial period since the melting of the ice and the resulting floods are so conveniently implied.

The Finns, although in many other ways close to the Scandinavians, have a completely separate linguistic tradition. Their epic creation myth *Kalevala* also has different provenance (see also Chapter 13). The

Eurasian themes of watery chaos, separation, cosmic egg, trapped offspring and use of body are preserved, however, in an involved cosmogony. Creatrix Ilmatar, the virgin daughter of Air, descended to the primeval ocean. Here as 'Mother of the Waters', buffeted by the wind and sea, she conceived. In this role she was analogous to Vari-ma-te-takere of eastern Polynesian mythology. Unfortunately her gestation threatened to become eternal and she complained to heaven of her boredom and unfruitfulness. A teal was sent roving over the waters to find a spot to lay her eggs. Eventually she found Ilmatar's knee, which was raised above the waves as the goddess reclined. Here she laid seven eggs, six golden and one iron.[47] In this early part of the *Kalevala* we find echoes of a Samoan version of the creation, which has already been mentioned in another context: 'Tagaloa, the ocean god, had a son who was born in the shape of a bird named Tuli. Tuli hovered over the waters but found no place to nest, so Tagaloa pushed up a rock from the sea-bed called Papa Taoto, "The Earth Reclining".'[48]

After the teal had laid its eggs on the reclining creatrix, the epic then goes on to two different versions of separation, one of which is the broken-egg type, while the other follows the New Zealand tradition. Ilmatar's unborn son Vainamonen, after a long while, began to feel constrained and claustrophobic with his extended period in his mother creator's womb. He therefore burrowed his way out. He then created all the features of the land, in particular the trees. In this role we can compare him with Tane Mahuta from New Zealand.[49]

Separation of the waters above from the waters below

I have left discussion of the biblical and Babylonian versions of separation until last because, although both traditions have accounts of separation of the sky, as biblical scholar Alexander Heidel noted in *The Babylonian Genesis,* they both have more than one separation.[50] In each case the first separation is concerned only with water. These parallel versions may give us a clue to the allegorical meaning of the primal darkness that appears in so many of the separation myths.

The great Babylonian epic of creation was probably written well over 3500 years ago, and long before Genesis. It contains two episodes during which divine offspring rebelled first against the primal father Apsu and then against their primal mother Tiamat. Apsu of sweet water and Tiamat of salt water were the Babylonian progenitor parents. The first couple of generations of their divine children were very troublesome, although trapped in their mother's womb:

> The gods of that generation would meet together
> And disturb Tiamat, and their clamour reverberated.
> They stirred up Tiamat's belly ...
> They were annoying her by playing inside[51]

Apsu, Tiamat's husband, was more upset by this behaviour than she was and plotted with his vizier Mummu to get rid of his turbulent offspring. Unfortunately news of his plans leaked out to the gods, their sons, in particular to Ea (Sumerian: Enki), who was later the god of water:

> Ea who knows everything found out their plot ...
> Put Apsu to sleep, drenched with sleep ...
> He held Apsu down and slew him;
> Tied up Mummu and laid him across him.
> He set up his dwelling on top of Apsu,
> And grasped Mummu, held him by a nose rope.
> When he had overcome and slain his enemies.[52]

The above excerpts from the Babylonian creation seem to contain the familiar story of parricide of the creator god by one of his sons, who along with his brothers was incarcerated inside his mother. Alexander Heidel saw in this story an analogy with the biblical account of division of waters in Genesis 1:6 and 1:7 – Mummu represented the fog-mist and clouds that rose from Apsu and Tiamat and hovered above them. This scene is familiar from the Pacific myths of a dark and cloudy beginning, and can also be seen in Genesis:

> In Genesis, God created a Firmament 'in the middle of the waters' to cause a division between the waters under the Firmament and those above it (cf. also Psalms 148:4). The biblical account appears to imply that the waters of the earth and those of the clouds originally commingled, like the waters of Apsu, Mummu and Tiamat, without a clear intervening air space, thus producing a condition like that obtained during a dense fog on the water.[53]

Heidel also drew a brief analogy to the Egyptian story of the separation, by the wind god Shu, of the sky goddess Nut from the earth god Geb.[54] The analogy is much closer than this because in Egyptian cosmology, as for the Hebrews, the primeval waters were also seen as dark and all pervasive, with no boundaries or surfaces. The firmament was necessary to 'divide the waters from the waters'. The sun god's dominion was only a temporary rolling back of the eternal night. This scene is also familiar from the Pacific myths of a dark and cloudy beginning, as we have seen. The Phoenician creation is more explicit. After their cosmic egg was formed there was a series of catastrophic climatic effects sounding rather like the deluge account that culminated in separation:

> And when the air began to send forth light, by its fiery influence on the sea and earth, winds were produced, and clouds, and very great defluxions and torrents of the Heavenly waters. And when they were thus separated and carried out of their proper places by the heat of the sun, and all met again in the air, and were dashed against each other, thunder and lightnings were the result.[55]

We may speculate on an allegorical meaning of such a strange, stormy and claustrophobic start to the world. The myths imply a chaotic period of misty, cloudy, windy darkness with light eventually appearing before the Sun. The catastrophists would have a ready answer for this scenario in the climatic disruption and global winter that would follow a meteoritic impact or massive seismic activity.[56] The widespread global extinction that might have followed this sort of disaster would further add to the idea of the beginning of all things.

Alexander Heidel's search for a description of the original undivided chaos as 'fog on water' reminds me of a curious experience I had in Malaysia in 1991. I had been invited to a conference in Kuala Lumpur. As the flight from Hong Kong descended, the whole Malay Peninsula was covered in a low, uniform fog. Once beneath this cloud the Sun disappeared from sight and I did not see it again until I flew out ten days later. We were told that this haze had been going for some time and was due to forest fires raging out of control in Kalimantan. Whether this was true or we were experiencing smoke from the oil wells burning to the west, I do not know. One of the tourist events organised during the conference was a boat trip to a village on the mangrove islands off Port Klang. It was warm but the Sun could not be seen and the light was somewhat dimmer than usual. The sky was a uniform luminous muddy brown, and the sea was the same colour. The most notable effect was a loss of the horizon. We could not see where the sky stopped and the sea started. There were few reflections and the mangrove islands, villages and boats all appeared to float suspended in mid-air.

Whether my experience describes in any way the horizon our forefathers might have seen during the extended winter recovery from one of the three post-glacial flood catastrophes, I do not know. It would, however, make sense of the worldwide mythical obsession with a dark chaotic watery beginning of time – if this was a recovery from some global catastrophe. The Chinese, Phoenician, Babylonian, Austronesian and other descriptions of the chaos have aftermaths of low sky, light before luminaries, separation and, finally, the Sun. These all have a climatic and catastrophic ring. Some ancient cultures even appear to have recorded catastrophic events in their cosmogony. For instance, in the Australian story of the rainbow snake referred to above, the snake fell to earth from the sky causing a huge crater and a period of storm.[57]

Although Heidel's scholarly analysis finds links between both the biblical and Babylonian accounts of the separation of the waters and the firmament, and also incidentally with other separation stories, he seemed to be puzzled by the fact that the next section of the Babylonian creation has another murdered parent and yet another separation. This is the famous battle between Ea's son Marduk and his grandmother Tiamat. Tiamat is no longer the indecisive wife who had watched her husband slaughtered by his son, but a serpentine, terrifying and stormy monster, the apotheosis of the bitter sea who enlisted half the gods inside her to be 'on her side', and created a bestiary of serpents and demons. It did not do her any good. Marduk choked her with winds and threw a net. Then like watery dragon slayers and cult heroes from Denmark to Melanesia he split her open with an arrow. He then calmly butchered and filleted the corpse:

> He sliced her in half like a fish for drying:
> Half of her he put up to roof the sky,
> Drew a bolt across and made a guard to hold it.
> Her waters he arranged so that they could not escape[58]

After these culinary acts of separation, Marduk went on to some sophisticated astral arrangements. His cosmogony was literally 'inaugural' because he used her liver and ribs. He arranged the relative movements of the Sun, Moon and the twelve star clusters of the Zodiac, which had by now appeared. He did not waste any of the body, using her eyes for the two rivers of Mesopotamia and her udder for mountains.

ABOVE The tree that grew people?
›earded god pulls the (fruit?) tree
:r until it forms an arch.
mediately to the right a figure with
ıany-horned head-dress and
.ndishing a mace emerges either
m the bole of the tree or the
›und. Around the tree are bulbous
ects; a star is seen above. To the
ıt of this, a female figure carries a
:ket. Other versions have one or
› people under the arch. (Cylinder
from Mesopotamia, 2390–2249 BC.)

RIGHT Statue of the goddess
emis at Ephesus: the bulbous
ects round her midriff are thought
epresent bull's testicles rather than
it. Her image had stood in the
ıple for at least 800 years before
Roman statue of the second
tury AD. A fertility goddess
›ciated with the moon, childbirth,
etation, hunting and dogs,
emis/Diana has many parallels in
tern mythology.

19 LEFT *Tumbuan* mask, embodiment of a female spirit used in rituals of the Duk Duk secret society i New Britain, Papua New Guinea.

20 BELOW LEFT Ritual neck rings in Nias island, west of Sumatra, are here depicted both round the neck of the male ancestor image and suspended below the spirit boat. The masts of the boat represent the tree of life. An identical carved wood panel is built into the chief's house in Bawomataluwo village, south Nias. Young men in Nias island still wear these neck rings or *kalabubu* (made of tightly woven coconut fibre and brass). The ritual importance of these ornaments in Nias is seen in the universal use of the rings in wood and stone carving.

21 BELOW Torc of Death. Danish archaeologist Professor Glob has pointed out ritual connections between woven halters (seen on top), used to strangle victims such as those found in the peat bog at Borre Fen (Denmark), and neck torcs (below) associated with the fertility goddess, as depicted on the famous Gundestrup cauldron found nearby.

22 Soulship or 'boat of the dead' motif on a ceremonial *tampan* woven cloth from Lampung in south Sumatra. The motif is also found in cave paintings, on bronze drums of the Dong-Son period and in diverse ritual designs throughout Southeast Asia. Key motifs seen here include the ship's masts doubling as the tree of life, the birds, the house and people on the boat.

23 Kenyah Dyak mural with the tree-of-life motif in Sarawak. Note the snake in the lower branches; the hornbill can just be seen at the top.

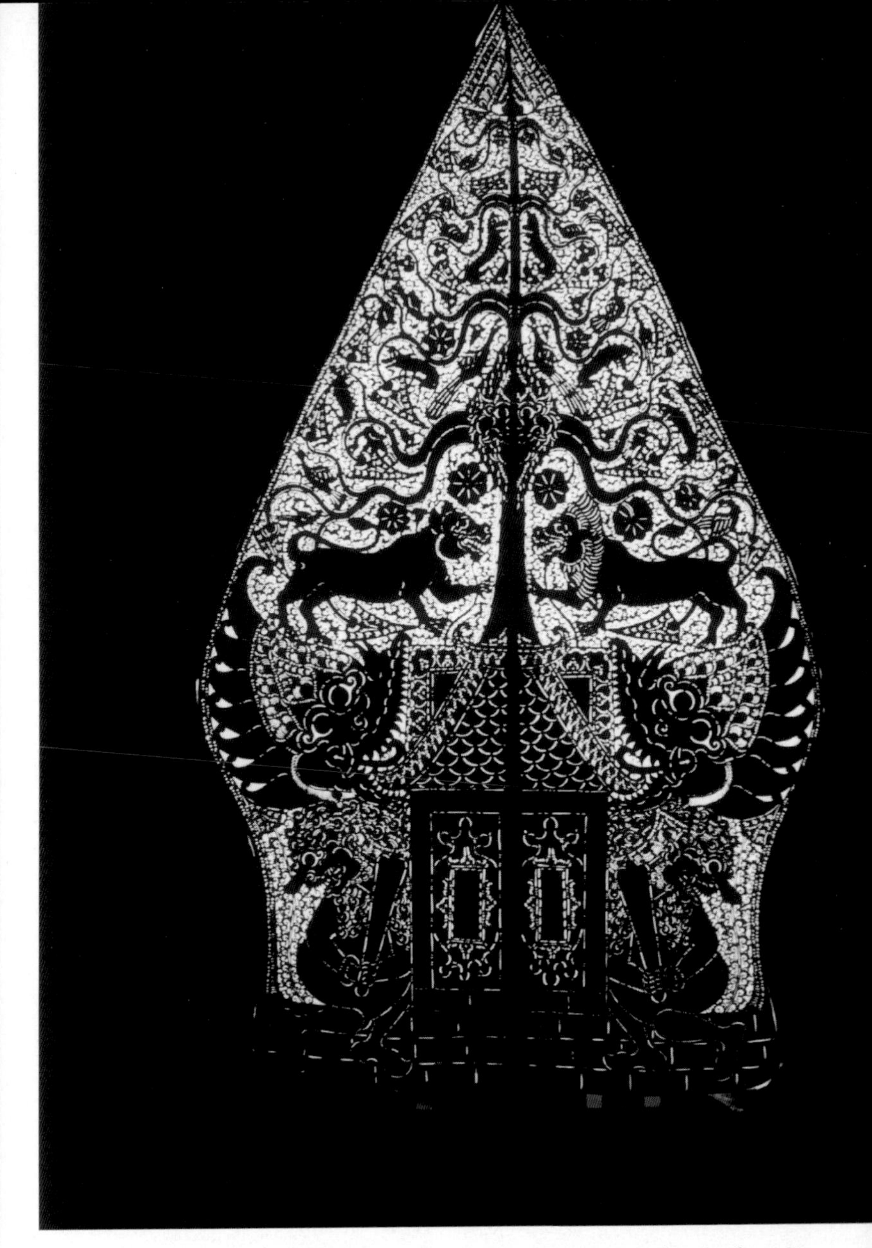

24 *Pohon beringin* ('Wishing Tree', also known as Benjamin tree, banyan, fig or *Ficus benjamina*). The 'tree of life' is the most important piece of scenery in the ancient shadow-puppet plays of Southeast Asia. The concept, however, antedates the introduction of Hinduism. This elaborate version is Balinese. Note the two serpents near the base.

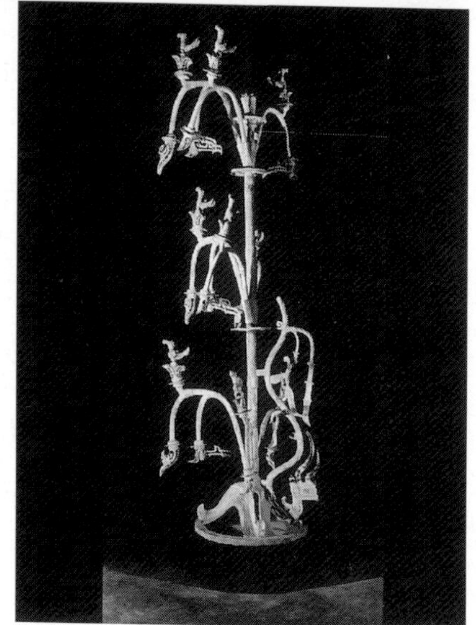

25 ABOVE LEFT Bronze mask from the sacrificial pits at Sanxingdui, Sichuan, southwest China (*c.* 1200 BC). One of a number of masks, some with grotesque protruding eyes, the culture styles are unlike anything of the same period in China and share more with Southeast Asia and Oceania.

26 ABOVE Tree-of-life triad in China: four-metre bronze tree found in the sacrificial pits at Sanxingdui, Sichuan, southwest China (*c.* 1200 BC). Several similar trees were found. A snake curls up from the base. An elaborate anthropomorphic bird slotted into the apex (not shown here). The tree cult is not found elsewhere in China from the same period.

27 LEFT Tree-of-life triad in the late Han dynasty (*c.* 25–220 AD). A one-metre bronze money tree found in Sichuan, southwest China, so-called because of the coins and people in the branches. The ceramic mountain at the base is guarded by a horned, clawed beast with wings. The apex holds a bird, coins and the sun. The central deity of the tree is the 'Queen mother of the West' receiving herbs of immortality on a dragon and tiger throne.

28 Tree-of-life triad of the Ngaju Dyaks of Borneo: in this case the tree is a banana and the birds at the top are hornbills; the serpent at the base, although present in the Ngaju creation myth, is not shown here (engraving on bamboo container).

29 Etana of Kish: cylinder seal from Mesopotamia (2390–2249 BC) depicting the ascent of King Etana of Kish to heaven on the back of an eagle. Two lions prowl round the base of the tree, which also has another bird in it. The snake of the Etana myth is not seen here.

30 Party in 1982 to celebrate the building of a house for the author by the 'bigman' of Kamba village, Madang Province, Papua New Guinea. (The author is sitting on the right in the picture.)

31 The eternal triangle. In the two-brother myth on the Sepik river, Kulabob and Manup's roles are taken by Wain and Mopul. The man on the right, possibly Mopul, holds a spear and has boar tusks in his nose. Motifs of bird and snake are seen lower right. (Incised bamboo from Kambot village, Papua New Guinea.)

32 The story of the two spirit brothers, Lawena and Dawena; key motifs are the snake, the half-man/half-crocodile, bird-men and two cockatoos, one of which holds a severed head. The coconut tree, on which all the action takes place, is not usually depicted. (Incised bamboo from Kambot village, Papua New Guinea.)

33 Massive underwater stone structures in the Pacific, east of Taiwan. Six such structures have been found in the Okinawa area. The largest, at Yonaguni island east of Taiwan, is 200 metres long by 150 metres wide by 30 metres high, and 25 metres below the sea-level. Stepped, tiered and chanelled, these structures could be natural erosion phenomena, or partly man-made; geological opinion is divided. If they are artefacts, then they may be 8,000 to 12,000 years old.

This second separation involves land and is analogous to the second separation in Genesis 1:9 and 10. Heidel argues that the versions of separation in the Babylonian epic and the priestly account of Genesis are both related to some common ancestor.[59] The fact that they each contain sky/water and sky/land separations makes a common ancestor or ancestors even more likely.

Which is the original separation story?

Having traced the parallel strings of the various separation myth-types from Hawai'i, Tahiti and New Zealand to the arctic frost of Finland, we should be able to draw some conclusions about relationship. Linguistic links and thematic similarity would argue that the Austronesian separation myths are all related to a common source. Historic and geographic links would argue the same for those from Greece, Phoenicia, Egypt and Mesopotamia. Thematic links show that all these stories are related from Australia and Polynesia through China and India and all the way to Scandinavia (see Table 8 and analysis at the end of this chapter). The question I would like to pose here is, can the stories themselves tell us how the original went? A similar question that historical linguists ask about related languages is, 'What did the common ancestor or proto-language sound like?' We can do the same for the separation myth.

There is little to tell which tale might have been the nearest to the original except from the content and context of the story. Several themes cluster in the same geographic distribution and often in the same stories. These themes can change, lose their original context or disappear. If the same themes are found at opposite poles of a radiation – for instance, Europe and the Cook Islands – it is reasonable to suppose that they were there in the original source. The Maori cosmogony of Rangi and Papa has the advantage of sharing most of the themes of chaos, Sky Father and Earth Mother, incest, separation, first light, parricide, use of body and wind that are present in the Greek and Mesopotamian myths. The Maori version while sharing the Sky Father and earth Mother with the more sexually explicit Timorese story has many more motifs (see above). There is a paradox here. Timor is closer to the supposed homeland of the Austronesian diaspora than New Zealand and might thus be expected to hold a greater variety of motifs.

There need not be a paradox. As Southeast Asia is the geographic centre of the Austronesian diaspora, so one might look for the 'original' there. Since the start of the diaspora 5000–6000 years ago, however, the Pacific peoples have spread into virgin territory with little external non-Austronesian influence. Southeast Asia, by contrast, has been a melting pot for different cultural influences, so the Polynesian versions may be 'purer'.

The other evidence of originality comes from the context and juxtaposition of the motifs. The older versions should hold these in a way that makes sense as one story. The best example of this internal evidence is 'light before luminaries', which makes better sense when it is incorporated into the event of separation of the skies and Earth. Again the Maori version satisfies this principle. The nearest Western version to the Maori cosmogony in terms of structure is Hesiod's *Theogony*.[60] The Maori tale's similarity to events at the start of Hesiod's *Theogony* validates the version and the preservation in both stories, but the separation of Ouranos and Gaia in Hesiod is not the event that brought light; so the Greek account could have been corrupted in this respect.

In the Eurasian and Oceanic cosmogonies the Sun and Moon seem to arrive when most of the action is over. Yet popular concepts of Polynesian culture place the Sun high in their theology. We can now move on to the Sun and the Moon, the brightest of the objects we see in the cosmos.

The Sun

Much has been made of the distribution of myths of a paramount sun god by early twentieth-century diffusionists. Notable (notorious in some people's view) among these are Sir Grafton Elliot Smith and Thor Heyerdahl. In the 1920s Eliot Smith, with others, derived a unifying hypothesis of the 'heliolithic' cultures radiating from Egypt to all continents. The term heliolithic was meant to imply both the making of megalithic monuments and the worship of the Sun as a god. This idea achieved such prominence at the time that it was included in H. G. Wells's *Outline of History* in 1925.[61] The heliolithic torch was taken up after the Second World War by Thor Heyerdahl, and still arouses strong feelings among the archaeological establishment.[62]

I disagree with the use of the term heliolithic because the Sun itself is not a statistically specific or useful marker in cosmogonic myths. Fifty per cent of creation stories I reviewed mentioned the Sun; 28 per cent had the Sun as a deity, while in only 12 per cent was the Sun a primary creator deity. These different categories had a similar random and universal distribution in all continents and language families. The use of the Sun as a primary deity was not significantly associated (more likely than chance to be found) with any of the other themes I have mentioned except for Mother Earth, and then the association was not strong. The statistical argument does not mean that the Sun was not an important god in Eliot Smith's selected cultures; it was and is, but that it was important elsewhere as well.

One other aspect that needs re-mentioning in this context before we move to the Moon, is the extraordinary, and well-known, coincidence that the name of the sun god 'Ra' is identical in eastern Polynesia and Ancient Egypt. The chance of this being a random coincidence rather than an example of diffusion would seem remote. The extraordinary aspect of this coincidence is the implied time separation of more than 5000 years. Even then the point of departure for the Austronesians was the Far East, not Egypt. Another name likeness is found in the two cult heroes Maui and Mandi. The former is found in eastern Polynesia while the latter appears in the mythology of the Prasun Kafir, an Aboriginal tribe in Northern Pakistan. Both of these characters have adventures rescuing and catching the Sun. In many ways they are both identified as apotheoses of the Sun.[63]

The Moon

The moon goddess in contrast to the sun god really does seem to have a distinctive character niche in Eurasian and Oceanic mythology:

> Hina-Keha (Bright Lady) is the Polynesian Goddess of the Moon in her full phase. As sister of the sun god Maui she is comparable to Artemis-Diana the 'Radiant Goddess', sister of Apollo [= the moon].
>
> In one of the versions of the Maori moon mythology, it is related that in her 'dead' phase, 'Hina Uri' the Moon Goddess drifted into the sea and was covered by weeds. She was washed ashore [as was Diana as Diktynna] and a man discovered her in human form under a tangle of kelp and seaweed ... The prince's name was *Tini Rau* or Rupe ... She fell in love with him, like Artemis in Endymion falling in love with a mortal man. However, like the prince in Andersen's tale ['The Little Mermaid', and also in 'Swan Lake'], he was already married. Nevertheless they loved each other on the shore of the lagoon, and in due course Hina gave birth to a son, Tuhuruhuru ... Hina Keha is also the Goddess of Childbirth, like Diana. Also like Diana she is often seen in the company of a dog.[64]

Hina-Keha is also known as 'Hine-te-iwa-iwa. Iwa means nine, which

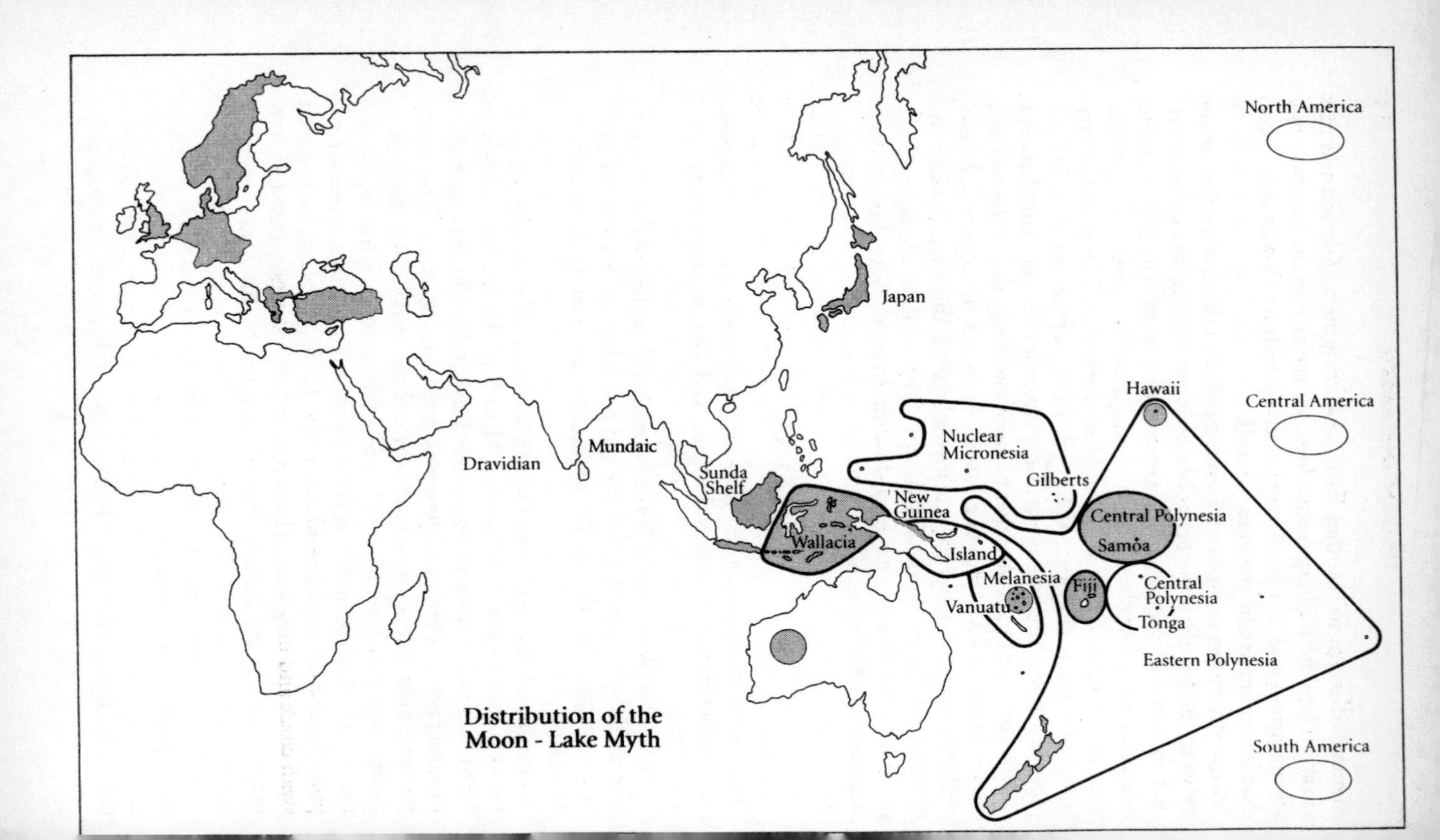

Distribution of the Moon - Lake Myth

Figure 39. **The Moon/lake story.** This characteristic story of the waterside tryst in its various forms, the commonest being the seven girls spied on by a man, is found in its greatest diversity among both western and Oceanic Austronesian speakers. Unmistakable accounts, however, appear in Greek and Norse mythology. The woman or women involved are almost always connected with the Moon or the Pleiades and with fertility. The distribution of the Moon/lake story is broadly the same as the separation story (see Figure 38). These two story types always appear independently.

may be a reference to nine months of carrying. Another Greek analogy for the role of lakeside lunar lover was Zeus' mistress Io, who met with him secretly at lake Lernaea. Wandering Io was also a personification of the Moon and was further obliged for secrecy to be disguised as a white cow.

Other versions of this lagoon or lakeside Moon tryst crop up throughout the Pacific and Southeast Asia. A particular variant is of the goddess being caught without her clothes on. This has a direct parallel in Greek mythology: the goddess Diana was seen bathing naked by the hunter Aktæon. In her outraged modesty she turned the hunter into a stag so that he was killed by his own dogs.[65] In contrast to Diana's frigid and vicious response to this exposure, the Oceanic versions have kinder outcomes for the peeping Toms.

In Java there is the following story: the moon goddess Nawang Wulan (Wulan = month) descends to Earth having donned her swan-feather cloak. She lands on the waters of a lake, where she discards her cloak and begins to bathe, but the cloak is stolen by Kyai Agung. When she cannot find her means of returning to the sky, she is obliged to stay with the man, so she marries him and they have a daughter, Nawang Sih. The goddess generates rice for the household using her magical powers and Kyai Agung is expressly forbidden to look in the pot where the rice is stored. One day curiosity overcomes him and he discovers that the pot only contains a single grain of rice. Now the magic will work no more and the goddess is forced to collect and pound rice each day as would a mortal wife. She does however find her swan cloak and uses it to fly back into the sky. At night she stays there, but during the hours of daylight she returns to earth to be with her husband and child.[66]

In Java and Bali a similar tale records seven heavenly angels bathing, one of who had her garments taken and hidden in a rice granary, with the same ensuing motif of marriage with the peeping Tom and eventual return to Heaven. Many similar stories occur further east in the Moluccas, but here, as with the genetic picture, there is deep diversity. In some of the eastern Indonesian legends, the roles of goddess and mortal are reversed and we find versions of the story of Psyche and Cupid.[67]

Another story was recorded by Henry Ling Roth in a remarkable ethnographic account of Sarawak and northern Borneo. It was told by an old man in Brunei, of a man who lost his way and saw seven nymphs bathing. He noosed one and brought the girl home to be brought up as a wife for his son. All went well but the son had a violent temper. One day he took off his jacket to beat the nymph and another jacket fell from Heaven. His fairy wife disappeared leaving her child who became the ancestor of the tribe.[68] Southern Borneo has a rich variety of these myths which ring the changes on lakeside virgins but seem to have lost the direct role of the moon goddess except in the numerous references to months, menstruation and childbirth. The Barito district has a complex myth of a virgin descending from Heaven into water in the form of a mangrove seed. Another floating tree form changed into a man who married the virgin on a rocky island. Their union produced seven floods of blood from the goddess which generated other virgins who in turn begot creatures of omen. In another story from southeast Borneo, seven angels, 'The Santang Goddesses', were sent down from heaven by the sky god on golden broomsticks to teach and discipline men.[69]

A more explicit reference to the menstrual (monthly) connection comes from the north coast of New Guinea in the Madang and Sepik provinces: 'The women took off their skirts and went into the water to take a bath.' In the Sepik-province version of the story they are cassowaries who change into naked women when they take off their feathers to bathe. 'A man "Nimuk" … happened to come by. In hiding he watched the bathing women. All the women had taken off also their genitals before they had gone down into the water. This man took away one of their skirts … with the genitals. The man put it into a bamboo tube.' Later he found that he could use this tube as a torch to hunt at night with. His brother misused the torch and the Moon escaped from the bamboo and climbed up a breadfruit tree to escape to the sky.[70]

In Vanuatu the same story has winged women sent from Heaven by Tagaro. They take a swim in the ocean and have their wings hidden by a group of men. In this story only one woman makes it back to Heaven.[71]

The styles of these Melanesian myths are typical of the locale and have impeccable provenance. However bizarre the stories sound to Western ears, the message seems to be the same as in the lady of the lake stories of

Greece, Polynesia and Southeast Asia: the moon goddess is somehow connected with bodies of water, the mysteries of female gender, food and fecundity, and seven women who can change into birds. She also possesses power that needs to be concealed to retain its potency. The connection between the Moon and menses is clear enough; the relationship of the Moon's cycle to agriculture is a possibility; the importance of water may be simply that the Moon is reflected in it; or may be there is an allegory for the effect of the Moon on tides. Whatever the allegorical origin of the story, the pattern is found only in the familiar distribution of Eurasia and Oceania that I have described, thus suggesting diffusion of the myth rather than separate origins. Whether the number seven in these stories symbolises the lunar week or is related to the Pleiades is not clear. An Aboriginal story of seven girls who, pursued by a man, ascended to the sky as the stars of the Pleiades constellation, is similar to the Greek story for the same stars.[72]

Another echo of the Moon-lake story is related in Japan:

> A fisherman once found a robe of white feathers on the beach. No sooner had he picked it up than a beautiful shining girl emerged from the sea, begging him to restore her property, for: 'Without my plumage I cannot go back to my home in the sky. If you give it back to me I will sing and dance for you.' The fisherman returned to her the lovely robe of feathers. She put it on, took her lute, and sang a hymn to the Moon, where she had her palace. Gradually as she danced she rose up into the sky, then she unfolded her white wings and flew away to the full Moon.[73]

Curiously, although the lake story is found in the same regional distribution as the 'creation by separation' myths, it forms a part of a different cycle and is not found together in the same stories. Other aspects of the worship of Diana appear in a much wider distribution, as Sir James Frazer found in his twelve-volume classic of comparative mythology, *The Golden Bough*.[74]

As is pointed out elsewhere in this book, the finding of ancient themes of Classical and Near Eastern mythology duplicated and preserved out in the middle of the Pacific suggests a common source. At a conservative estimate the ancestors of the people who tell these stories left Southeast Asia for good at least 5000 years ago. The only known Indo-Aryan influence on Southeast Asia has been in the last 2000 years in the form of the Hindu empires, such as the Sri Vijaya. It is difficult to imagine a diffusion of Aryan myths tailing the Polynesians out into every corner of the Pacific 3000 years after they left Asia. When people from the west did finally get there the myths were Judeo-Christian in any case. One is thus left with the conclusion that stories such as the 'chaos/separation' complex and the 'moon goddess and the lake' derive originally from east of India and perhaps in Southeast Asia. (Figure 39 shows the distribution of the Moon/lake myth.)

A dramatic survival of Moon and fertility worship occurs in the Nusa Tenggara of the Malay archipelago. These rituals reveal why the Moon was so revered. In islands from Lombok to the Moluccas, an annual cycle of festivals begins around the southern autumn equinox with the swarming of the nyale worms in the sea.[75] Also known as the palolo worm in Fiji and Samoa, *Eunice viridis* normally hides in coral crevices and is a relative of the nereid worm (ragworm) we know in the West. It chooses one or two days in the year to shed the female half of its body to be fertilised by swarming sperm. The timing of this event is closely related to the Moon's cycle, occurring at the neap tides closest to the southern equivalent of the harvest Moon and hunter's Moon of the autumnal equinox in Southeast Asia. In central Polynesia, 60 degrees of longitude eastward, the event occurs at the neap tides nearest the southern vernal (spring) equinox. This event in the surviving megalithic cultures of the Nusa Tenggara marks the start of the lunar ritual year. Although the exact month of first swarming varies slightly with locality, the event can be predicted to the day in each village by a knowledge of the relative positions of the Sun and Moon. The annual variation is determined by the regular interplay of the solar year (365 days) and the lunar year (354 days) whereby the lunar cycle gains a month approximately every three years. In each village there are hereditary priests of noble birth, part of whose ritual duties are to observe the Moon and count the years. These priests predict the day of swarming, and on that morning perform augury on the worm numbers in order to predict the success of crops.

The nyale phenomenon serves several practical functions. First, it reconciles (adjusts) the lunar and solar years on an annual basis thus neatly allowing the villagers to use a lunar calendar for ritual and agricultural planning for the rest of each year. The event marks the change of season and determines the time of rice-planting. Second, the worms are good to eat and are distributed as ritual fertility food. This custom occurs in Polynesia as well. Third, the prediction confirms the authority and ritual power of the priests. Seven nights after the 'welcoming of the nyale worms', a ritual but very real battle, the Pasola, is staged near the beach. This fight, conducted with wooden lances on horseback, stops only when blood is drawn or someone is killed. The blood or death is apparently sufficient sacrifice to appease the gods. Other customs practised at this time of year are ritual hunting and a temporary ritualised increase in sexual licence.

With all these references to the Moon, fertility, agriculture and hunting, it is interesting to explore the mythological explanation of these customs. With certain regional variations, nyale worms generally represent the body or hair of a princess who sacrificed herself in the sea either to avoid too many suitors or to bring crops to people. She was either a daughter of the Moon or, like the nereids of Greek mythology, daughter of the sea god. The annual calling of the nyale is intended to bring her body back to bring fertility to the land. Curiously, the Greek equivalent animal embodiment of nereid daughters of the sea god (that is nereid ragworms) have a similar swarming behaviour in the Mediterranean. There are many Western parallels to the customs surrounding the autumnal equinox.

In contrast to these romantic and, in some cases, slightly prurient versions of the Moon's story, there is another more bloody version of the Moon's ravishing prevalent in Southeast Asia, which has every evidence of more recent provenance from the Indian subcontinent. The story is set in the context of a separation myth. As found in Bali, it relates that the giant 'Kala Rau' tried to get a sip of 'The Water of Life' that Vishnu doled out daily to the gods. The giant was spotted hiding in the queue by Dewi Ratih, the moon goddess, who informed on him. Vishnu threw a chakra at the giant, slicing him in half. The upper half became immortal and went up to the sky. There it chased and swallowed the Moon, later passing it out of its neck.[76] Variants of this story are found in Thailand, Java and Madagascar, but significantly not in the Pacific. The story has recognisable Hindu character names, has an equivalent in Hindu mythology and is only found in areas known to have had recent Hindu influence. It is thus reasonable to place the most recent radiation source in the Indian subcontinent.

A number of the Moon stories I have sketched contain the number seven. I have suggested the lunar week as a possible origin for the use of this numeral. This needs some justification. After one, two and three, the number seven appears more frequently in Old World sacred texts than any other number. This applies particularly for the Bible, the Koran, Babylonian texts and the Egyptian Book of the Dead. There are three *a priori* reasons for any particular number to occur more frequently in such texts. The first is linguistic: low numbers such as one, two and three naturally occur more frequently in speech and all texts. The second is numerological: they may have unique mathematical properties such as the prime numbers 1, 2, 3, 5, 7, 11, etc. The third is that they may be naturally occurring such as five, ten and twenty (digits). Although five is a prime, however, the number of fingers on a hand and a half unit in the decimal system, it is not more common in sacred texts than expected from its numeral rank.

The origin of the week

The only regular natural occurrences of seven are found in the relative motions and numbers of the heavenly bodies. Seven is generally recognised as having been an important number in the Old World at least since Chaldean (Babylonian) days for just such reasons. We saw earlier how, after Marduk had butchered Tiamat, he set the relationships of the heavenly bodies. The relevant part of the translated text of *Enuma Elish* which mentions seven, runs as follows:

> He made the crescent moon appear, entrusted night (to it)
> and designated it the jewel of the night to mark out the days.
> 'Go forth every month without fail in a corona,
> At the beginning of the month, to glow over the land.
> You shine with horns to mark out six days;
> On the seventh day the crown is half.
> The fifteenth day (Sabattu) shall always be the midpoint the
> half of each month ...'[77]

This passage concisely describes the approximate length (seven days) of the first quarter of a lunar month – that is from the new Moon to the first quarter (half-Moon), and the fifteen days to full Moon. The Babylonian text then goes on to explain, poetically, that a solar correction needs to be made for the difference between four weeks (twenty-eight days) and the thirty (29·5) days of the true lunar or synodic month.

Genesis may have been committed to writing around the same time and incorporated a seven-day creation. It is generally assumed that the Judaic choice of seven and sabbath derives solely from the seven-day Genesis creation myth and not from any astronomical observation. The term 'sabattu' in the Babylonian verses quoted above, however, is in fact cognate with 'sabbath', although it refers to the fifteenth day of the lunar month not the seventh. Moreover, there is some circumstantial evidence to link the Judaic choice of sabbath (and hence of seven) with the Chaldean. This can be found in five separate verses in the Bible where the new Moon and the sabbath are put in the same verse and context as two similar holy days, for example: 'And he said,

Wherefore wilt thou go to him to day? it is neither new moon, nor sabbath' (2 Kings 4:23), and 'When will the new moon be gone, that we may sell corn? and the sabbath, that we may set forth wheat. (Amos 8:5).[78]

Whether the origin of the Judaic sabbath is the Chaldean lunar week we may never know, but in any case a large proportion of the prolific occurrences of the number seven in the Bible refer to multiple units of time, either days or years. When groups of seven animals are referred to they may also be surrogates for time, as explained by Joseph in his famous analysis of Pharoah's dream of the sevens. For most of the rest of the occurrences (over 99 per cent), seven is used freely as a favourite multiple for a variety of objects including people. This habit reaches an extreme in Revelations.

Outside the ancient Near East, another apparently independent use of seven as a unit of time is in the Kayan wooden hunting almanacs of Borneo, which have a seven-hour day and a seven-day week. The Batak calendar in Sumatra has twelve thirty-day months for their lunar-year calendar. Periodic adjustments, based on natural seasonal events, are made to correct to the solar year. Superficially this calendric scheme has Indic influence in that the first seven-days of each month carry the Sanskrit names of the seven visible planets in the same name order as our own week.[79] The rest of the thirty days are named similarly, but with adjustments of two days for the full Moon at fifteen days and new Moon at thirty. But beneath the superficial resemblance to the Javanese-Indic calendar this is really an oracular almanac instrument which is closer to the Bornean seven-day hunting almanacs. Auspicious days are given for different activities such as sowing, harvesting, building and marrying. The important unit in the cycle of auspicious days is really seven; thus the important weekly cycle runs independently and is staggered by about two days every month. This implies that the lunar monthly calendar is a later addition on top of the basic weekly cycle.[80]

There is little evidence in the Old Testament to suggest that the Jewish week is any other than a lunar week. It would be tedious to review here the 280 pages of the Bible that mention seven. In any case, I can find only three occasions in the Bible where the use of seven may mean anything different from a lunar or sabbath-inspired unit of time or a randomly applied auspicious multiple. One of these is the story of Moses meeting the seven daughters of Midian by water:

> Now the priest of Midian had seven daughters: and they came and drew water, and filled the troughs to water their father's flock.

And the shepherds came and drove them away: but Moses stood up and helped them, and watered their flock ...

And Moses was content to dwell with the man: and he gave Moses Zipporah his daughter.

And she bare him a son ... (Exodus 2:16–17, 21–2)

The reason for picking out this story is the similarity with the Moon/lake and seven sister stories of Southeast Asia. The structure of this episode could be explained, as in the Australian stories, either by the seven maidens symbolising the Pleiades or the lunar week.

The seven sisters

The lunar week is not the only astronomic occurrence of seven. The seven visible planets (including the Sun and Moon) have given their names to the days of the week. Mythologically, however, the most famous astronomic occurrence of seven is the Pleiades constellation, seven stars of which are visible to the naked eye. 'Pleiad' is even used as a term to describe groups of seven (usually illustrious) persons such as the 'seven wise men of Greece'. The constellation was mentioned by Homer in *The Odyssey*. In Greek mythology the Pleiades or seven sisters were daughters of the Titan, Atlas and of Pleione, the daughter of Oceanus. In several versions of the myth they were attendants of Artemis who were pursued by the giant hunter Orion, but were rescued by the gods and changed into doves. After their death, or metamorphosis, they were transformed into stars, but are still pursued across the sky by the constellation Orion. Their sisters the Hyads, also seven, form part of the Taurus constellation, but are less well known. The Lapps in the Arctic Circle also regard the Pleiades as maidens.[81]

The Pleiades are well recognised in the Asia-Pacific region and we can compare these 'seven sisters' directly with the seven feathered bathers in the Moon/lake myth cycles from Southeast Asia and Melanesia described earlier. Indeed, there are several links between Artemis-Diana and the moon goddesses of the Austronesian diaspora. Typologically the Australian Aboriginal story of the seven girls who were chased by the hunter into the Pleiades is the closest of the Eastern stories to the Greek myth of Orion.[82] There is, however, another version of this Pleiades story in Western Australia where the male pursuer was the Moon, Kidilli. The Moon was making the girls bleed. The twin male stars or Gemini, known here as Wati-Kutjara, came to their rescue by persuading the Moon to marry one girl properly.[83] The mythological use of the Moon (and hence seven from the lunar week) thus appears in some way linked in both the Greek and Australian stories to the seven Pleiades.

Although Westerners are most familiar with the Greek stories, the use of the movements of the Pleiades for navigation and for agriculture has a widespread ancient provenance, including Austronesian cultures.[84] It is a good example of an archaic astronomic tool that retained its practical value, while its ritual and mythological significance developed in parallel. The recurrent Eurasian astronomic connections between the seven stars of Pleiades and the technical skills of agriculture and navigation find their focus in other ancient Western myths of the seven educators from the East.

The seven sages from the East

The earliest Mesopotamian reference to seven divine persons is in cuneiform traditions. These record that Ea (Sumerian = Enki), god of fresh water and wisdom, sent seven divine sages in the form of fish-men from Apsu to teach the arts and crafts (Sumerian = Me) to mankind before the flood. They were each paired as 'counsellors' in the texts with an ante-diluvian king. In this capacity they were credited with building walled cities. They were banished back to the Apsu for ever, after angering Ea.[85]

Foremost among these seven sages was Oannes (Uan or Adapa) who was said to have come from a great egg. Historian Robert Temple has explored connections between these amphibious sages and other cults around the Mediterranean in a book called *The Sirius Mystery*.[86] Looking for an Eastern mythological counterpart for the amphibious god/sage Oannes we find the eastern Polynesian god 'Vatea', firstborn of six[87] from the primordial mother Vari-ma-te-takere, who lived inside an egg.[88] Half-man half-fish, his eyes were the Sun and Moon. His youngest sister Tu-metua was the tutelar goddess of Moorea who dwelt with her Great Mother 'Vari' in the very lowest depths of 'Avaiki', the silent land. To her the fourteenth day of every month was sacred.[89]

The astronomical connection of the number seven with the agricultural and sailing skills, of the seven sages from the East, does not explain their amphibious nature unless this term is simply a code for sailors. A possibility is that the term 'amphibious' is connected with the 'Apsu', the mysterious watery land of origin of the seven sages. One speculation is that the visiting educators to Mesopotamia and the Mediterranean, with their technology and astronomy, were accomplished sailors, whose original land was swamped by the rising sea.

The Ancient Egyptians also traced their origin to a marvellous island far to the East in the sea of the rising Sun. In their texts, there are many examples of seven deities, supervisory or otherwise. Thus in the Egyptian Book of the Dead we find: '... The Osiris, the scribe Ani, whose word is truth, saith:- I flew up out of primeval matter ... I am Yesterday of the Four Quarters of the Earth, and the Seven Uraei, who came into being in the Eastern land ...' There are numerous other references to the 'Seven Spirits' and 'Seven Gods' in the same text.

Stories of seven educators are also found in Indo-European mythology. For instance, the Prasun Kafir of the Hindu Kush have Imra the creator engendering the 'seven daughters of Mara' to oversee agriculture in the Hindu Kush.[90] In the Vedic (Hindu) mythology 'Aditi' originally meant 'the illimitable space of sky beyond the Far East, whence the bright light gods sprang'.[91] Then, in later myths, Aditi became the mother (by Daksa, the sun god) of the first gods, the seven Aditya who fashioned the world.

Moving to the Far East, where, in reverse direction to Eliot Smith's diffusion hypothesis, some of the mythical educators are said to have come from,[92] we do find equivalent examples of educators. Several of these have already been mentioned above such as the seven 'Santang goddesses' of southern Borneo, and seven angels with their ability to make rice as a general component of the Moon/lake myth. Elsewhere we read of the seven Malay sages.

Further east in Melanesia we find the famous story of the Yabobs of Madang. In this story, the origin of their pot making skills came from the teaching of Honpain. This Austronesian teacher was a beautiful woman from the seven stars of the Pleiades constellation who came in a canoe to live secretly with a Yabob man. She returned to the stars after a family dispute.[93]

Apart from its connection with mythical educators in the Far East, seven also appears there in ritual and magic contexts. It is frequently used as an auspicious number in non-Islamic traditional Malay magic. In the megalithic cultures of the Nusa Tenggara referred to above, seven is often used as a magic number. A clue to a Lunar origin of this practice may be seen in a Sumban ancestor myth. This story has the Sun and Moon producing fifteen creator offspring, seven daughters and eight sons.[94] Fifteen days is half a lunar month and was the Chaldean sabbath.

Sevens from the South Pacific to the Sami

From this short sketch of the practical, religious and ritual use of seven, several generalisations can be made. There are repeated allusions to fertility, the Moon, skills such as agriculture and sailing and wise men from the East. Whatever the actual use or symbolic meaning of the number, its distribution is confined mainly to Eurasia and Southeast Asia. In this distribution the only definite common factor seems to be the Moon's cycle and the lunar week, understanding of which extends out into the Pacific. There are Melanesian and Australian stories that refer to the seven Pleiades and Polynesian mythology includes some named planets. Astronomical derivations of seven from the Moon, the Pleiades and the seven Planets can thus be found in an arc from the Southwest Pacific to the ancient Middle East and the Mediterranean. Whether the myths found scattered in the megalithic cultures of eastern Indonesia – and echoed in folk cultures of the West – represent related survivals of the earliest attempts to use the movements of heavenly bodies for practical agricultural planning is a matter of speculation.

Creation story-types as prehistoric intercontinental cultural markers

As we have seen in the last two chapters, the well-known creation themes of chaos, water dragons, first light, separation, parricide and use of the dead body and other motifs such as the number seven are found mainly in a band stretching from Oceania and the Pacific to northern Europe. The similarities of story-types are too many and in many cases too detailed and bizarre to have occurred independently. They thus demand explanation. The sceptic, however, may not be convinced by the subjective similarities alone. Few folklorists would argue that the creation myths in different parts of Polynesia arose independently of each other since the archaeological records, the languages, oral history and other aspects of cultural and physical anthropology indicate close relationships across the Pacific. On the other hand there might be strong objections to a concept of a common origin for Polynesian and Greek or Babylonian versions of the separation story, where there are neither contextural nor geographic nor historical links.

In the end where context is lacking to explain trans-global thematic similarities we must analyse the thematic content of the stories themselves systematically. If the same story motifs arose independently in different parts of the world, then they should be randomly distributed and randomly associated with other motifs. This random picture is exemplified by the motif of the Sun as a god. The concept appears in myths of all continents, in a random distribution, at more or less the same rate, and in no particular association with other motifs or gods. The concept of a sun god could thus have arisen independently many times throughout the world.

Other themes by contrast have a distinctive regional distribution and tend to group together with each other. A number have already been described, for instance the water dragon, Moon/lake and separation myths. The most important of these, the 'separation' story-type uses ten, and even up to twelve, distinct story motifs in a string (see Figure 38 and Table 8).

The ten motifs tend to be found grouped together in distinctive story-types in the same geographic/cultural areas. These areas are distributed from the South and West Pacific up to the northwest of Eurasia through China, South Asia and then the Middle East, finally ending in northern Europe. The ten motifs are not generally found in Africa, the Americas nor Central and Northeast Asia.[95] I have performed statistical testing for each motif. This shows that the east–west distribution band is extremely unlikely to have occurred by chance.[96]

Table 9. **Mutual association of 10 individual motifs of the story of 'Separation'.** Each value indicates the chance or 'odds' of finding a pair of motifs in the same story. An odds ratio of 1 (i.e. 1:1) or less means no association. A high value with one or more asterisks shows a significant link.

	Water Dragon	First Light	Creative Word	Separation of Heaven & Earth	Parricide	Use of Body	Creative Wind	Sevens	Creator Incest
Light	2.4								
Creative Word	4.9*	5.9**							
Separation of Heaven & Earth	3.5*	16***	15***						
Parricide	3.0*	3.1*	1.6	4.0***					
Use of Body	2.4	6.2***	3.4*	8.1***	9.3***				
Creative Wind	4.0**	2.8*	5.3**	2.7*	5.9***	4.1**			
Sevens	5.7***	3.1*	3.3*	3.1**	2.5*	3.7**	3.9**		
Creator Incest	3.2*	0.7	1.6	1.3	4.4***	3.8***	2.5*	2.3	
Cosmic Egg	2.5	1.7	2.9	3.0*	2.4	3.2**	3.3*	2.1	1.2

Key: * Chances of random association less than 1 in 20.
** Chances of random association less than 1 in 100.
*** Chances of random association less than 1 in 1000.

Having shown that the individual motifs or themes are found in the same places, the next thing is to see if they are found grouped together in the same stories more often than not. This is quite simple. The chance of finding two or more individual themes together in the same story can be tested. When I did this analysis, the results showed that it was extremely unlikely that the same complex story-types arose more than once (see Table 9).[97] Put in plain English, similarities such as those between the Maori story of Rangi and Papa, and the Greek story of Ouranos and Gaia are so unlikely to have occurred by chance that we can ignore the possibility.

I also applied the same analysis to the less complex stories of the Moon/lake tryst and the land-raiser myths (see Chapter 11). Although the four main varieties of land-raiser myths have different continental distributions (see Figure 37 in Chapter 11), they tend to be associated with an initial watery chaos or flood. This is particularly the case with the diver and sea-bed-plowing versions of land-raising. The Moon/lake story is strongly associated with the number seven, and the woman or women involved are almost always connected with the Moon[98] or the Pleiades, and also with fertility. As mentioned above, the distribution of the Moon/lake story is broadly the same as the separation cosmogony. However, these two story-types always appear independently.

Conclusion

Over the last two chapters I have identified families of myths, which stretch in a distinctive swathe from Polynesia to Finland. These include some of our oldest myths. The most important of these is a narrative complex which starts in a dark serpentine watery chaos and culminates in the separation of the Heavens from the Earth and sea. This is also the one found in the first or Priestly account of creation in Genesis. One allegorical interpretation of the story is that it is historiographic and refers to the recovery from a real catastrophe, possibly separate and even older than Noah's flood, which disrupted the lives of Stone Age people round the world. This is supported by the nearly universal distribution of the motif of initial watery chaos. The land-raiser myths in Chapter 11 also seem to describe the recovery from some past inundation and have a wider spread.

The second group of myths in the Eurasian Oceanic distribution is the 'Moon/lake tryst'. Familiar and faintly prurient as these swan-lake stories are, the component motifs reveal a more serious and sophisticated purpose. The use of the Moon and the seven stars of the Pleiades for agriculture and navigation, which are implicit in the myths, links early Neolithic knowledge of celestial movements from the megalithic cultures of Southeast Asia to the far away stone circles of northern Europe. The second, or Jehovistic account of creation found in Chapter 2 of Genesis, is more concerned with the creation of man than that of the Heavens. We will move on to that in the next chapter.

13
THE CREATION OF MAN

And did God first mould a model from blood and clay and blow into it to give it life? Did he take the bone, Ivi, from man's side among the dark rainforest trees of Southeast Asia? Mesopotamia would be many people's choice, and yet all the evidence suggests that it couldn't possibly be. Southeast Asia and the Pacific both have a greater claim to hold the birthplace of this particular story.

Stories of the creation of humanity are universal. They can be divided into two main varieties, people evolving from a totem, such as a tree or animal, and the creator fashioning man from clay. These two archetypes have distinct distributions which overlap most dramatically in eastern Indonesia. The merging of these two themes in that location eventually resulted in the beautiful and mysterious story of the Garden of Eden as we shall see in Chapters 14 and 15. In this chapter we trace the origin of the Genesis version of the clay-man myth from Southeast Asia.

In Chapters 11 and 12 on cosmogony, I covered the complex of myths, generically related to the so-called 'Priestly account' of creation in Chapter 1 of Genesis. I said little about the 'Jehovistic account of creation', found in Chapter 2 of Genesis, which devotes barely two verses to the topic of cosmogony – and that only to state that the Earth was created dry – and is concerned instead with the creation of man.

For human creation, the tables are turned. The Priestly account has God create man by simple fiat on the sixth day:

> And God said, Let us make man in our image, after our likeness: and let them have dominion over the fish of the sea, and over the fowl of the air, and over the cattle, and over all the earth, and over every creeping thing that creepeth upon the earth.
>
> So God created man in his own image, in the image of God created he him; male and female created he them.
>
> And God blessed them, and God said unto them, Be fruitful, and multiply, and replenish the earth, and subdue it: and have dominion over the fish of the sea, and over the fowl of the air, and over every living thing that moveth upon the earth. (Genesis 1:26–8)

Meanwhile, the Jehovistic account uses the world's most widespread folk version of mankind's creation to start a continuous narrative, which takes us right through to the Tower of Babel. As a prelude to one of the more beautiful texts of the Book, the Lord God forms man from the dust of the ground and breathes into his nostrils to give him life:

> These are the generations of the heavens and of the earth when they were created, in the day that the Lord God made the earth and the heavens,
>
> And every plant of the field before it was in the earth, and every herb of the field before it grew: for the Lord God had not caused it to rain upon the earth, and there was not a man to till the ground.
>
> But there went up a mist from the earth, and watered the whole face of the ground.
>
> And the Lord God formed man of the dust of the ground, and breathed into his nostrils the breath of life; and man became a living soul.
>
> And the Lord God planted a garden eastward in Eden; and there he put the man whom he had formed. (Genesis 2:4–8)

> And the Lord God took the man, and put him into the garden of Eden to dress it and to keep it. (Genesis 2:15)
>
> And the Lord God said, It is not good that the man should be alone; I will make him an help meet for him.
>
> And out of the ground the Lord God formed every beast of the field, and every fowl of the air; and brought them unto Adam to see what he would call them: and whatsoever Adam called every living creature, that was the name thereof.
>
> And Adam gave names to all cattle, and to the fowl of the air, and to every beast of the field; but for Adam there was not found an help meet for him.
>
> And the Lord God caused a deep sleep to fall upon Adam, and he slept: and he took one of his ribs, and closed up the flesh instead thereof;
>
> And the rib, which the Lord God had taken from man, made he a woman, and brought her unto the man.
>
> And Adam said, This is now bone of my bones, and flesh of my flesh: she shall be called Woman, because she was taken out of Man.

Therefore shall a man leave his father and his mother, and shall cleave unto his wife: and they shall be one flesh.

And they were both naked, the man and his wife, and were not ashamed.(Genesis 2:18–25)

In the sweat of thy face shalt thou eat bread, till thou return unto the ground; for out of it wast thou taken: for dust thou art, and unto dust shalt thou return.

And Adam called his wife's name Eve; because she was the mother of all living. (Genesis 3:19–20)

The difference in order of events in these two versions has not been lost on scholars who have compared these stories.[1]

Most secular commentators agree that the two biblical accounts represent ancient and radically different traditions.[2] The purpose of this chapter is to explore the family origins of the 'creation of man' myths. I will argue that although the two main themes of construction and totemism in these myths are generally universal, certain extra motifs allow speculation on their spread and relationships. A key conclusion of this discussion will be that the version of humanity's creation cherished by the three great monotheistic religions of the Middle East, (Christianity, Islam and Judaism) originated east of India.

An early writer on biblical folklore parallels, Sir James Frazer, had a simplistic and symmetrical view of the classification of origin myths. In his view (and we should remember that he was writing in the early 1900s) the stories divided neatly into two categories. One of these implied a theory of creation and the other a theory of evolution. In the former a great artificer or 'divine potter' fashioned us usually from earth or clay. In the latter, we evolved out of animals and plants. In this last category of the story Frazer put the totemic myths, with humans descending from a whole range of different animals and even plants. Frazer was using the terms 'tongue in cheek' and did not claim that totemic tribes had hit on the true nature of the origin of species before Darwin and Wallace; however, he felt that the evolutionary view was no more sophisticated than that of the Jehovistic account.[3] I should make it clear that the ideas of 'creationist' and 'evolutionist' introduced by Frazer here were his esoteric invention, and should not be confused or equated with their modern-day usage in North America. 'Constructive' and 'totemic' are less-loaded terms to label these stories of our creation.

Frazer's classification satisfactorily accounts for most of the myths where the mechanism of our creation is specified. But there are other categories – for instance, the widespread story of humanity's birth after a sexual union of divine beings. This is found at low frequency in all continents, but is a particular feature of Austronesian and Japanese origin myths. There are also the myths where humans were made endogenously by a creator without the use of external materials such as clay. The mechanism of creation in these cases varies from pure thought to words or the production of certain bodily secretions. These endogenous creations are really constructive in type. Binary fission of the creator into male and female is another method appearing in several early Hindu (Vedic) texts. Both Meso-America and India feature multiple or cyclical human creations. In just 7 per cent of myths mentioning man's creation, no mechanism is given. The creator 'just makes' men and women in an unspecified way. The Priestly account of creation in Genesis is one of these types.

Totemic and 'Divine Potter' motifs of man's creation are mutually exclusive in over 90 per cent of origin myths. Also, although they may share some geographical locations, neither the divine potter nor the totemic motifs tend to associate in the same story cycles as the complex cosmogonic myths described in Chapters 11 and 12. The Book of Genesis is no exception to this rule. There was no attempt there to reconcile or merge the two versions of creation. One is concerned primarily with cosmogony, while the other is about man, God and nature, with the devil appearing in snake form.

Analysis of the creation of man myths from a diffusionist standpoint is complicated by the possibility of multiple religious diffusions in recent times through missionaries, traders and colonisers. This sort of effect is a particular problem in Southeast Asia, where, over the past 2000 years, there have been successive waves of cultural influence from Hindus, Buddhists, Muslims and Christians. These partially related religions have left mixed layers of confounding evidence. An obvious example of a cultural relic from previous times is Hindu-style shadow puppetry, which still hangs on among the Islamic Malay cultures of Malaya and Java. Conversely, the Malays have several versions of the creation of Adam that might at first be thought to derive entirely from Islam – that is until we look at the details, which have a distinctly local ring.

An awareness of the possibility of recent diffusion may bias ethnographic observers to ignore and reject valid evidence of older influences. Examples of this selective attitude occur throughout the Pacific where many early recorders of myths were Christian missionaries. Polynesian informants insisted on the antiquity of stories stating that the first woman, who came from a bone in the man's side, was called Eevee/Ivi (the word for a bone in many eastern Polynesian languages). Yet most of the Christian ethnographers assumed a missionary source for these stories rather than the disturbing possibility of a more ancient origin. It is curious that missionaries should show such a sceptical and careful approach to the ultimate origins of the oldest mystery in their sacred book. It is likely that they were unaware of the widespread ancient distribution of the story elsewhere and thus could simply not believe their informants. This selective bias is discussed at length by Sir James Frazer.[4] In the end we have to look at each story on its provenance and context.

I will now summarise the results of my analysis of a world sample of 364 creation stories: 292 (80 per cent) of these mention man's creation.

Totemic origins

The totemic idea of a tribe being descended from one or more animals should be distinguished from stories of animal creator(s) that may co-exist in the same regions. The latter are well known in North America where a raven or very often the trickster coyote feature in rich and often humorous creation stories. There are other stories where creative shamans change at will between man and different creatures.

Although tales of animal origins occur in all continents and feature in 20 per cent of stories that I sampled, their distribution is distinctive. They are the dominant mechanisms of man's creation in nineteen stories from Australia (68 per cent) except for four clay myths.[5] Over a third of stories from the majority Papuan-speaking population of New Guinea are totemic in my sample. Six of sixteen stories from the New Guinea mainland were totemic, with a similar number of clay stories. A particular motif in Papuan or non-Austronesian-speaking New Guinea stories is the emergence of the clan from a hole in the ground, at the beginning of time. In both New Guinea and Australia, totems appear to reflect locally available foodstuffs, both animal and vegetable.

In the American sample, totemic myths are about half as frequent as the clay versions but are particularly common among eastern woodlands and plains Indians. They are uncommon among the Aleuts, the Inuit and Indians of the southwest.

In sub-Saharan Africa, the frequencies of totemic and clay myths were about 20 per cent and 50 per cent respectively. There was an abundance of gods with animal form in Ancient Egypt, a feature that distinguishes Egypt from non-African Mediterranean civilisations.

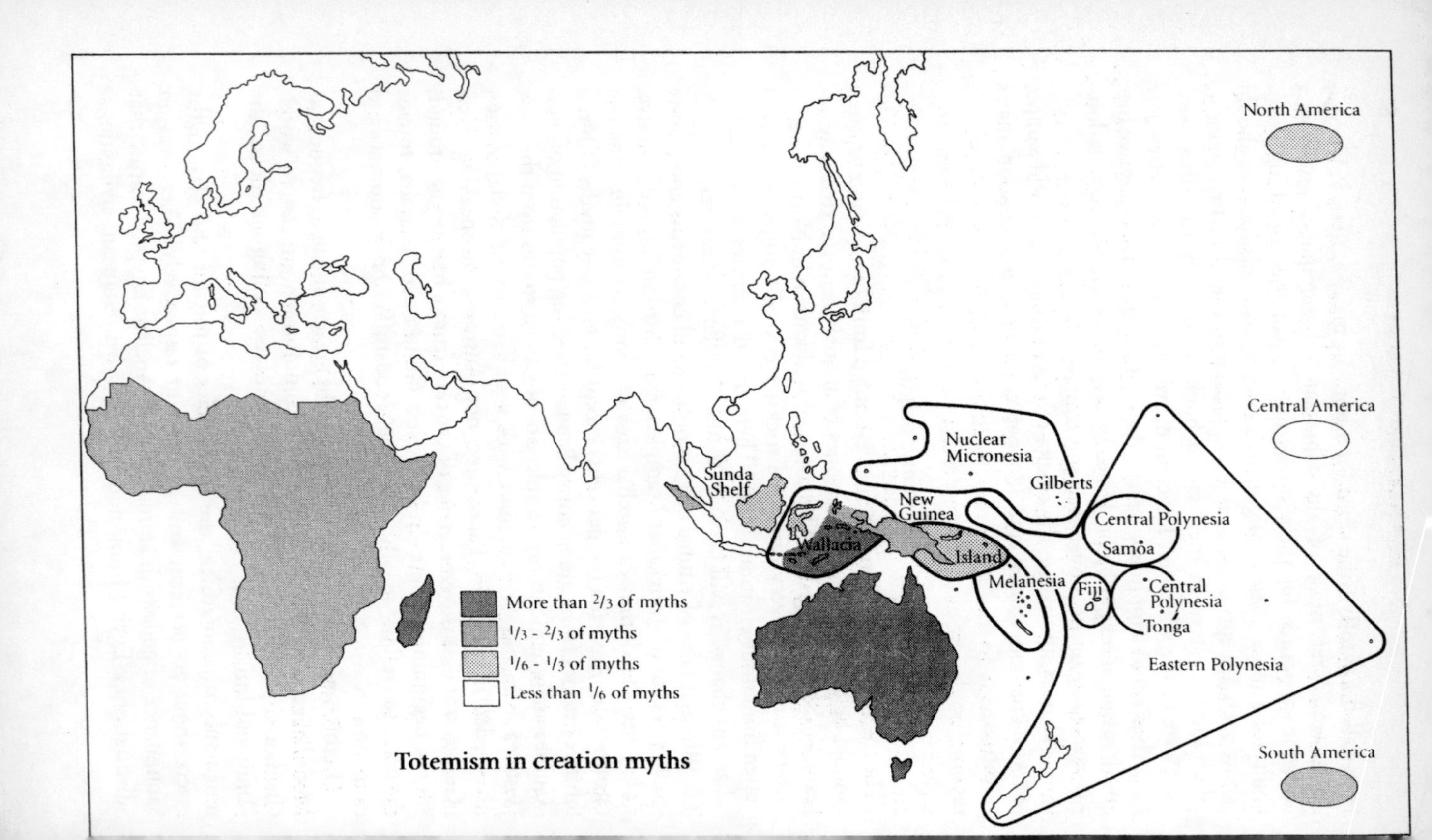
North America
Central America
South America
Nuclear Micronesia
Gilberts
Sunda Shelf
New Guinea
Wallacia
Island
Melanesia
Central Polynesia
Samoa
Fiji
Central Polynesia
Tonga
Eastern Polynesia
More than 2/3 of myths
1/3 - 2/3 of myths
1/6 - 1/3 of myths
Less than 1/6 of myths
Totemism in creation myths

Figure 40. **Totemism, the oldest theory of human creation.** Totemism is the dominant mode of creation in the Southern hemisphere among some of the world's oldest cultures. Although uncommon in most of the societies discussed in this book, it has a distinct role at their interface with Australoid cultures in eastern Indonesia. Tree totemism may have been the precursor to the tree of life.

Generally, however, this trait did not amount to totemism. In a creation myth from Heliopolis, Amun was credited with engendering rulers (who were themselves gods) in Egypt. He was also symbolised variously as a snake, a goose and a ram.[6] Use of clay, tears or the power of thought are other methods recorded in Egyptian mythology.

In contrast to the American, Australian and African continents, totemic myths are notably rare throughout Eurasia both in ancient sacred texts and in recent ethnography (six of ninety-six stories); they are also rare in eastern Polynesia (one of twenty-nine stories). There is a more complex situation in Southeast Asia and the Southwest Pacific, nearer to the origin of the Austronesian diaspora. Some of these areas have unexpectedly high rates of totemic myths.

Totemism in island Southeast Asia

The situation clarifies a little if totemic myths in the Austronesian-speaking areas of Southeast Asia are analysed according to conventional linguistic divisions (see Chapter 5) and location (Figure 26 in Chapter 5). The bulk of Austronesian speakers (more than 95 per cent) belong to the large western Malayo-Polynesian (WMP) group. This includes all the languages spoken in the Philippines, Borneo and from Java to Lombok and covers the geographic centre of the Austronesian diaspora. Within the large WMP language grouping I found only five instances of 'evolutionary' or totemic stories in the forty I analysed. The rest of the stories of humankind's creation in the sample were of the constructive divine artificer type. Two of the WMP totemic stories came from North Borneo and three from Sulawesi.

One Bornean story from the Land Dyaks is a variant of the Moon/lake myth similar to the one from Brunei and described in Chapter 12: An old man went fishing and caught a 'Puttin' fish in the river. The fish changed in his boat to a very pretty little girl whom he took home to be brought up as a wife for his son. She eventually consented to the arrangement but cautioned that the son should treat her well. Of course this did not happen and later the son struck her. She escaped back to the river but not without leaving a daughter who became the tribal progenitor. Such fish are taboo since eating them would be the same as eating one's relatives.[7]

In a second story from north Borneo, the Kayan have a myth that the first man and woman were born from a tree.[8] In another tale found in some tribes of Sulawesi, the crocodile is the totemic creature;[9] and two further myths from northeast Sulawesi both have apes as totemic creatures.[10]

There is a distant western outlier of the WMP language group in Madagascar-Malagasy. Three of four myths sampled from Madagascar are totemic. One of them concerns a crocodile again.[11]

Sumatra and its chain of offshore islands represent the western edge of old Sundaland, and have a mixture of Austronesian languages. To the west are several orphan languages such as Nias, Aceh, and Batak that do not belong to the majority WMP group, and are hard to place anywhere else on the Austronesian family tree.[12] These peoples have preserved distinctive megalithic cultures.[13] Eight of thirteen human creation myths sampled here are totemic, and all belong to the Batak.

The reasons for totemism in Borneo, Sulawesi and western Sumatra may lie further east and south. In the east of Indonesia we find the central Malayo-Polynesian language group (CMP) which includes the Lesser Sundas from Sumbawa eastwards, and most of Maluku. In the first half of this book we saw that eastern Indonesia with its CMP tongues represented the key launching ground for the eastward spreads of the Austronesian diaspora through northern Melanesia out into the Pacific.[14] The other important feature of these islands is the close interface between the Austronesian speakers and non-Austronesian New Guinean (Papuan) speakers. The CMP language area abuts the western end of Melanesia that is the western tip of New Guinea. Non-Austronesian (Papuan) influence in the CMP region is clearly recognisable in terms of physical anthropology and linguistics. From Flores eastwards there are increasing numbers of Papuan physical types. Pockets of the west Papuan language phylum are also found within the CMP region of the eastern Moluccas and Lesser Sundas, in Halmahera, Timor, Alor and Pantar.[15] Some of these islands, such as Timor, are also very close to Australia which has the highest rate of totemic stories.

With this evidence of Papuan influence and proximity to Australia it is perhaps not surprising to find totemic stories in the eastern Moluccas. All eleven totemic stories sampled in the CMP region came from Ceram and Amboin in the east while the other mechanisms of creation varied from divine union to clay and even the power of writing. These latter came from further west towards Bali. As we shall see in the later chapters on the Garden of Eden, tree totemism in Maluku may underly the early stages of the development of the Tree of Life motif. Such non-Austronesian influence may also explain the patchy occurrence of totemic stories that we have just seen in the western Malayo-Polynesian language area.

Moving further east through northern Melanesia along the supposed route of the Austronesian diaspora, 3000 or more years ago, we find the Western Oceanic area of Austronesian languages (WO) which includes parts of the north and east coasts of New Guinea, the Bismarck Islands and north and central Solomons. In areas that have had most contact with Papuan-speaking cultures, we might expect to find more totemic myths. In my sample, however, only five of twenty-two stories sampled, are totemic. These all came from the northeast coast of New Guinea where Papuan and Austronesian-speaking villages live side by side. As already discussed in the first half of this book, this region may have seen over 6000 years of interaction between Austronesian and Papuan speakers.

In the western Pacific, totemic myths persist among Austronesian-speaking peoples as a small minority as far east as the parallel spread of non-Austronesian influence. So in Fiji, for example, we find the story of Degei the serpent who co-created man with the help of a hawk.[16] On moving out into eastern Polynesia, however, totemic stories disappear more or less completely.

From this short sketch, I can make several generalisations about the distribution of totemic myths. First, they are the dominant explanation for the human creation in Australia and Papuan-speaking New Guinea and are common in Africa and the Americas. Second, they are extremely rare in Eurasia and among the majority of Oceanic peoples speaking Austronesian languages. This is consistent with a cultural continuum and corridor from Eurasia to the Pacific. The exceptions to this last observation can be seen in areas such as Maluku where there has been prolonged contact between Austronesian and non-Austronesian cultures with totemic myths.

I mentioned earlier that totemic stories rarely occur in the same context as the complex separation myths. This is usually because they do not share the same territory. Even when they do, however, as in Southeast Asia, they are still discrete from cosmogonic stories in local folklore. The situation is slightly different for the other much larger main group of myths, where man is made from clay or other matter, because here the geographic territory is often shared with separation stories. But more often than not, these two groups of myths still have separate context. I move on to these next.

The divine potter

The commonest version of humanity's origin tells of a creator, often but not always in human shape, who used clay or earth, sometimes moistened, to mould the first human. These tales account for just over a half of the creation stories I sampled, in which man's making is mentioned at all. The extraordinarily wide distribution of this story in every continent could lend support to the idea that this motif at least was a natural and automatic result of human interaction with the environment. In other words the motif could have had many spontaneous evolutions. The opposite and equally likely diffusionist view – namely that the myth had one origin – could make its composition date so remote that the concept, even if true, would cease to have any functional historical value. There is a middle road. The myth has several well-characterised variants with distinct distributions. Analysis of these mean that we can look at possible routes of diffusion without having to make the assumption of one origin.

The skeleton story of the modelling of humanity is fleshed out in different parts of the world by special touches, such as the choice of modelling material, repeated or false starts and the secondary creation of woman (or in some cases man). The details allow us to identify certain story-types or variants. We can look at the materials first. The commonest of these by far is clay, accounting for 38 per cent of such stories. The clay is red in a third of cases. Another 20 per cent have earth as the stuff of man. A smaller proportion of both earth and clay stories have blood, usually sacrificial, as a moistener or temper for the clay.

Bloody temper in the clay

The bloody clay stories with the oldest known provenance come from Mesopotamia. They contain rich imagery of the sacrificial blood of hapless gods. They fall into two groups, both of which involve the bloody sacrifice of a god or gods. The commoner type had a mother womb-goddess variously known as Ninhursag, Nintu, Mami and Ahuru (the potter) as the constructive creator of man. In one Babylonian myth, the unfortunate divine victim was Geshtu-e, who represented intelligence. A long description of the event is found in the *Atrahasis* epic. In this version, the modelling of new people took place after the flood in order to effect a more speedy repopulation of the earth. In the other tradition Ea was the male creator, sometimes with the help of various other gods. In one version it was with Aruru.[17] In *Enuma Elish*, Ea was instructed by Marduk who had just killed his own grandmother Tiamat (see also Chapters 11 and 12).[18] In several of these stories the divine victim who involuntarily donated his blood was Kingu the former chief of Tiamat's forces.[19] Another version mentions two Lamga gods as the source of blood.[20] Berossus the Babylonian priest relates that the god Bel cut off his own head and the other gods caught the flowing blood and mixed it with earth to make men.[21] This was claimed as the reason that men were so wise since their mortal clay was tempered with blood divine.

Mesopotamia was not the only part of the world to indulge in such bloody imagery. There were other cultures of the world where blood featured as an ingredient of man's creation. These included the Aztecs, Hindus and the peoples of the Austronesian diaspora. Quetzalcoatl the feathered serpent of the Aztecs used his own blood to engender man. He is also credited with using bone and ashes of people from previous worlds as substrate for the moulding of a new mankind.[22] In Hindu Vedic literature, sacrifice of gods and the use of blood to make people feature in several places. In one example from the *Rig Veda* a gigantic creator Purusha was sacrificed and various parts of his body used for creation. From his fat came all living things and from his mouth came the four castes of society.[23] Such motifs overlap with the cosmogonic myths that describe the use of the creator's body mentioned in the last chapter.

The use of blood in human creation is a widespread motif in the islands of the Austronesian diaspora. In island Southeast Asia, the geographic heartland of this language group, most bloody myths are found in Borneo. There are many versions, but they group into two main variants in this vast and diverse island. The first has already been introduced under the moon stories in the last chapter.

Among the Ngaju Dyaks and others there is a belief that the supreme god Mahatara produced a progenitor man and woman from wood and dropped them to earth. The woman created six different races of demons from floods of her menstrual blood but was finally persuaded by Mahatara to wed her man. After this seventh attempt she produced two divine children in the conventional way. In other versions, the first humans were made variously with earth and stone for flesh, water for blood and wind for breath.[24]

The other story given by, among others, the Dyaks of Sakarran and Barito, concerns two creator birds, male and female, which were themselves originated by a primordial being Rajah Gantallah. After creating the cosmos they made various attempts at fashioning man, using first wood, then stone. Since these efforts were unsuccessful at producing a fully functional man, they finally used earth and water. To give the man blood they infused in his veins the red gum of the Kumpang tree. He was thus called Tanah Kumpok or 'Moulded Earth'.[25] One version of this story incorporates and precedes a separation myth.

Further east among the Palau islanders we find a story of a brother and sister who moulded men from clay mixed with the blood of various animals. The characters of these people followed from those of the animals that supplied their blood. So rats became thieves, and so on. Although this area is part of western Micronesia, the language spoken still belongs to the large WMP group of island Southeast Asia.

Moving out into the Pacific we find a 'western-oceanic' Austronesian story in New Britain that tells of a creator who drew his own blood and sprinkled it upon the earth. From this earth he moulded the first man To-Kabinana.[26] Finally in eastern Polynesia we find a group of Maori stories of the creator variously named as Tu, Tiki or Tane who took red riverside clay and kneaded it with his own blood into his exact likeness. He then breathed into the mouth and nostrils of the model which sneezed and came to life.[27] I discuss these last two motifs of breathing and sneezing in more detail below.

It is curious that from the rather complex moulding myths of Borneo, if we move right out into the eastern Pacific, the details, and simplicity, of the Jehovistic creation of Adam are preserved along with the addition of the supposedly Mesopotamian motif of divine bloody temper. As with the stories of separation discussed in the last chapter, one explanation of this is that the stories have common provenance, but that the Southeast Asian versions are more adulterated due to multiple cultural influences over the last 2000 years.

Red clay or bloody temper?

The use of red earth and clay to make humanity does not follow with the distribution of laterite and red soils exactly. Some areas such as Africa have the soils but not the story. The main areas with the story of man made from red earth are Southeast Asia, Oceania and some Mundaic tribes in India.[28] All these areas, except eastern Polynesia, have abundant red and laterite soils. But the highest concentration of red-earth stories is in eastern Polynesia, particularly in Tahiti and among New Zealand Maoris. In both these regions the red clay use is usually combined in the same story with the creation of woman from a rib in the man's side.[29]

Another Oceanic myth of red clay comes from Mota of the Banks Islands of Vanuatu in the southwest Pacific. In this Austronesian-speaking Melanesian culture there is a story of the cult-hero Qat, who moulded men from the red clay of the marshy riverside at Vanua Lava.[30]

Since the distribution of the red-clay motif does not follow the distribution of red soils, it is obviously tempting to associate it with the use of divine blood as a temper. Both of these motifs have an identical distribution in Asia. Such an association suggests that the red colour is in fact a surrogate for blood. In favour of a real connection are the following observations: First, the use of blood in creation occurs almost exclusively where clay or earth are the modelling substrates for the making of a human; second, both bloody temper and red clay are strongly associated with the motif of sneezing of the quickening model in the spare-rib motif that I discuss below.

Sir James Frazer, among others, was certainly convinced of the connection between red earth and blood. He even went so far as to assert that the dust from which Adam was made was coloured red in the biblical author's eyes. The justification for this was on the basis of an elaborate pun. 'For the Hebrew word for man in general is *Adam*, the word for ground is *adamah* and the word for red is *adom* ... down to this day the soil of Palestine is a dark reddish brown.'[31]

Ribs, breaths and sneezes

The full Maori story of human creation by Tu/Tiki or Tane has five motifs – red clay, the god's (own) blood, the breath of life and sneezing, and, finally, the making of woman (Eevee) from a rib. Of all these things the most important according to tradition was the clay model sneezing. It was said that when men sneezed those present should say the words of Tu: 'Sneeze, O spirit of life' or as Westerners say, 'God Bless!' although in most cultures, including European, sneezing was traditionally a sign of mortal ill omen. Breath and the soul or spirit are interchangeable concepts in Oceanic Austronesian languages. The root nyawa- in Proto-Oceanic Austronesian tongues means 'soul breath' or breath as a life force. So like himself was the man whom the Maori creator Tiki fashioned that he called him Tiki-ahua.[32]

The Jehovistic account lacks three of the five motifs unless we accept Frazer's argument about red earth and *adom*, in which case there are three out of five. The concept of sneezing, however, to indicate a quickening is found elsewhere in the Old Testament. The prophet Elisha is said to have revived the dead child of the Shunammite by mouth-to-mouth breathing, following which the child sneezed the magic number of seven times. The other missing motif of the god's blood is, as already mentioned, found in the related non-Judaic Mesopotamian creations.

Sumerian expert, Samuel Noah Kramer argues that the rib motif is also to be found hidden in another elaborate pun in the Sumerian myth of Enki and Ninhursag: The god Enki was mortally struck by

Ninhursag the creator goddess, in eight organs for the crime of eating eight forbidden fruits in paradise. The earth goddess was induced to relent and created eight healing deities to salve his eight sick organs. One of these was a rib. The Sumerian term for a rib is 'ti', so the relevant healing goddess is named 'Nin-ti' or lady of the rib. 'Ti' also means 'to make live' in Sumerian, so that Nin-ti could also mean 'lady who makes live'. Kramer argued that this play on words has carried over to Genesis in the name Eve which can mean, in Hebrew, 'she who makes live'.[33]

Personally, I feel that the Polynesian explanation that 'Ivi' means a bone involves fewer assumptions. In the Tahitian version, after he had formed the world:

> [Ta'aroa] created man out of red earth which was also the food of mankind until breadfruit was produced. Further, some say that one day Taaroa called for the man by name and when he came made him fall asleep. As he slept, the creator took out one of his bones (ivi) and made of it a woman, whom he gave to the man to be his wife, and the pair became the progenitors of mankind. This narrative was taken down from the lips of the natives in the early years of the mission to Tahiti ... Some have also stated that the woman's name was Ivi, which would be by them pronounced as if written Eve. Ivi is an Aboriginal word, and ... signifies a bone.[34]

The missionary ethnographer of the above story William Ellis wrote in his book *Polynesian Researches*:

> This always appeared to me a mere recital of the Mosaic account of creation, which they had heard from some European, and I never placed any reliance on it, although they have repeatedly told me it was a tradition among them before any foreigner arrived ... Notwithstanding the assertion of the natives, I am disposed to think that Ivi, or Eve, is the only Aboriginal part of the story as far as it respects the mother of the human race.[35]

Ellis condemns himself by his own words here. The only aspect he was clearly correct in, was that ivi is the regular term for bone in various Polynesian languages. Such patronising statements are reminiscent of the previous attitude of the caring professions to children who repeatedly complained of parental sex abuse, before it became generally recognised that child sex abuse was common to all societies. The usual phrase, 'children tend to lie about these things', was the reverse of the truth. For most children betraying their parents to a stranger is an intensely painful process. For a religious people to share the treasured knowledge of their shattered culture with the priests of the invader and to have it disbelieved and derided could be seen as a similar insult.

The common assertion that any similarities between Genesis stories and indigenous origin myths must be due to missionary influence, ends up by crediting these worthy people with generating two-thirds of the world's stock of folklore archetypes including, incidentally, some extremely inventive sexual behaviour. Not only is such a view uninformed and ethnocentric, but it has the same obligation of proof as any other diffusion model.

Sir James Frazer was clearly of an opposite opinion to Ellis the missionary ethnographer. In his encyclopaedic review *Folk-lore in the Old Testament*, after mentioning Ellis's contribution, he went on to quote other Polynesian 'ivi'/rib stories:

> Thus the natives of Fakaofo or Bowditch Island [near Samoa in central Polynesia] say that the first man was produced out of a stone. After a time he bethought him of making a woman. So he gathered earth and moulded the figure of a woman out of it, and having done so he took a rib out of his left side and thrust it into the earthen figure, which thereupon started up a live woman. He called her Ivi (Eevee) or 'rib' and took her to wife, and the whole human race sprang from this pair.[36] The Maoris are also reported to believe that the first woman was made out of the first man's ribs (Hevee). This wide diffusion of the story in Polynesia raises a doubt whether it is merely, as Ellis thought, a repetition of the biblical narrative learned from Europeans.[37]

To this Polynesian spare-rib catalogue, we may add one from Namoluk in the Caroline Islands of Micronesia where there is a story of a man who in the early age of the world was created out of the rib of a man and married the daughter of the creator.[38] A further three Pacific ivi/rib stories from the coast of Papua New Guinea have all been regarded by their collectors as tainted by twentieth-century Christian diffusion. Two were collected recently by a Catholic priest, Father John Z'Graggen, in the Madang province on New Guinea's north coast; one of them was from the Austronesian village of Malmal:

> ... Dodo [or Anut the creator] lived alone ... Then Dodo wanted to make a man. But that man appeared like a frog. He watched that frog and said: 'Not that thing! That doesn't look right. Man has to be like me.' Then he tried again and formed a man with earth, gave

> him his breath and it appeared like a man. Dodo sat down with this man for some time. Then Dodo made a woman. He made the man sleep. He took a bone or what else from the man and made a woman. Then the two existed a man and a woman and they lived together ... The name of the woman is Suspain.[39]

This story has a dry stony start like the Jehovistic creation and continues with graphic detail through the fashioning of the female's genitals by Dodo's foot, and her womb by an eel and into the most widespread ancient story of the New Guinea north coast – that of their offspring, the two warring brothers Kulabob and Manup. The creation of a garden for them to live in occurred after the woman's creation, and they were given food much later.[40] I have, with permission, listened to the original Pidgin tape-recording of this story and can personally vouch that the translation is faithful to the original. In any case Father Z'Graggen is a trained and experienced comparative linguist. But I can find no basis for his assertion that the details of the creation of man and woman in this story are the result of biblical influence. Certainly there was evidence of mixing of religious themes in Madang during the twentieth century. In his classic monograph on the Madang cargo cults, Peter Lawrence traced such effects in detail. The mixed borrowings and distortions of the cargo cults, however, were concerned with the Kulabob/Manup myth rather than the first man and woman. Although he mentions several related versions of the creation of woman among neighbouring Austronesian language groups, Lawrence does not suggest any biblical borrowing in these stories.[41]

In the same anthology I found an even more complex and explicit creation in a neighbouring non-Austronesian village Murupi. Many elements are common to the Malmal story, such as a primordial stone, the frog, the use of an eel to sculpt internal organs, the delay before the man and woman are capable of reproduction and before the creation of a garden for them to live in. As in the Malmal creation, the first couple bore two sons, Kulabob and Manup. Nestling in a welter of sexual and culinary detail I read:

> The one who had this man created, pondered about that and said to himself: 'What else shall I do for this human?' ... The human man slept, and he [the creator] took a bone from the side and also part of his body, and made with it a second human being ... And the eel went in and formed the inside, the liver and everything ... Then this man breathed again in this second being. The second human being stood up, and he named it woman.[42]

In these two complex myths from different language groups there are many more shared concordances than the two biblical details of rib and breath; in particular, the use of the eel is identical. It would seem perverse to insist that the two biblical details are independent intrusions and have been separately introduced by missionary influence twice over.

Other Southeast Asian rib stories come from the Karen hill tribes in Burma. Here even Frazer agreed that there was a strong possibility of European influence. Again the ethnographers were Christian missionaries collecting in the middle of the nineteenth century:

> The Karens of Burma say that God created man, and of what did he form him? He created man at first from the earth, and finished the work of creation. He created woman, and of what did he form her? He took a rib from the man and created the woman ... How did he create spirit? ... He took a particle of his life, and breathed it into their nostrils, and they came to life.[43]

Frazer felt that suspicion of European influence became a certainty with a myth of the Ghaikos', a branch of the Karens, that introduces Adam by name with a thinly disguised Tower of Babel:

> For the Ghaikos trace their genealogy to Adam, and count thirty generations from him to the building of a great tower and the confusion of tongues. According to them, 'In the days of Pan-dan-man, the people determined to build a pagoda that should reach up to heaven. The place they suppose to be somewhere in the country of the Red Karens, with whom they represent themselves as associated until this event. When the pagoda was half way up to Heaven, God came down and confounded the language of the people, so they could not understand each other. Then the people scattered, and Than-mau-rai, the father of the Ghaiko tribe, came west, with eight chiefs, and settled in the valley of the Sitang.[44]

It is difficult to argue against some recent intrusive elements in these tales, but the question is how much? Why did the Karens, who speak a Sino-Tibetan language, concentrate on these two themes of Genesis? As I will show shortly the Austro-Asiatic minorities of Burma and India abound with closely related and distinctive myths of humanity's creation. Further, it should be remembered that the biblical tale of the Tower of Babel describes linguistic chaos as consequent on the migration to Mesopotamia of enterprising monument builders from the East.

I have only been able to find two other locations of the rib story, one in Siberia and the other in southwest California. The Bedel Tartars of Siberia have a tradition that God at first made a man, who lived quite alone on the earth. But once while this man slept, the devil touched his breast; then a bone grew out from his ribs and, falling to the ground, it grew long and became the first woman.[45] Although this story has been regarded as a cynical distortion of the Genesis story, it should be remembered that the devil acts as an important foil to the creator in the land-diver myths of central and northern Asia (see Chapter 12). In southwest California the Kawakipais tribe have a complex creation starting from primeval ocean, with land created from red ants (a feature in some Melanesian stories). The creator Tcaipakomat creates Sun and Moon from multicoloured clay and then proceeds to create man and woman using a lump of light-coloured clay. 'Then he took a rib from the man and made a woman of it. The woman thus created was called Sinyaxau or First Woman.'[46] Although the American Indians have many clay stories, this is the only one I could find with a rib.

The practice of the creator breathing into the clay models to give life, although statistically associated with the four other motifs, is also found

Table 10. **Consistency in the blood/clay/rib creation of people.** This correlation matrix shows the high odds in favour of finding combinations of the five story motifs in one myth. Asterisks show how unlikely these pairs are to be chance associations; the figure in each box (odds ratio) shows how strong the association is.

	Model made of first Being	Bloody Temper &/or Red Clay	Breath of Life From Creator	Model Sneezes as it Quickens
Bloody Temper &/or Red Clay	23***			
Breath of Life from Creator	27***	5**		
Model Sneezes as it Quickens	4*	57***	48***	
Rib/Bone for Second being	10***	11***	6**	22***

Key:
* Chances of random association less than 1 in 20.
** Chances of random association less than 1 in 100.
*** Chances of random association less than 1 in 1000.

occasionally on its own in other areas of the world apart from Eurasia and Oceania, for example in North and Meso-America, Africa and Australia. But sneezing of the model that the Maoris felt was so important is rarer and more specific in its association with blood, red earth and ribs.

To summarise, there is a version of the Adam and Eve story found most frequently and in its fullest form in eastern Polynesia which we can call the Tiki creation. This tale has five motifs: (1) the use of clay to make a model man and (2) the red colour of the clay and/or bloody temper from the god's sacrificial blood, (3) animation by breath and (4) signs of quickening evidenced by sneezing, and finally (5) creation of woman Ivi or Eve from a rib or bone in a man's side. These five motifs are each significantly associated with the others thus supporting the concept of unity of this widespread story-type.[47]

All five motifs are found piecemeal among the Mesopotamian creations (which include the biblical Genesis). There are traces of this story in other parts of the Austronesian dispersal such as central Polynesia, Micronesia, Melanesia and Southeast Asia. Although recent missionary influence may have introduced biblical elements in some Asian stories, there is sufficient evidence and context to indicate that the Adam and Eve story was indigenous to Polynesia before European contact. The fact that Tiki's creation story was more complete and internally coherent than the Mesopotamian versions supports the view that the diffusion pattern may have been from East to West rather than the other way round. In other words, Mesopotamia may have originally received rather than donated the story. Implicit in this conclusion is a time depth of at least 5000 years of divergence since the ancestors of the Polynesians started moving east.

The most complete stories come from eastern Polynesia, while best versions of the Ancient Near East are the Phoenician and Mosaic. Between these poles is another clay-model man myth. This story has a very different flavour, which I will move on to next.

Clay models, devils, horses and dogs

There is a widespread and consistent clay story in eastern India and the Burmese border which differs significantly from the biblical account. I will call this the 'broken models myth'. Apart from the riddle of its symbolism, the most interesting features of this myth complex are the linguistic associations. The ethnic minorities who share the myth all speak Austro-Asiatic languages. We saw in Chapters 4 and 5 that these languages have been indigenous, since antiquity, to an area stretching from India through Burma to Indo-China and down to the Malay

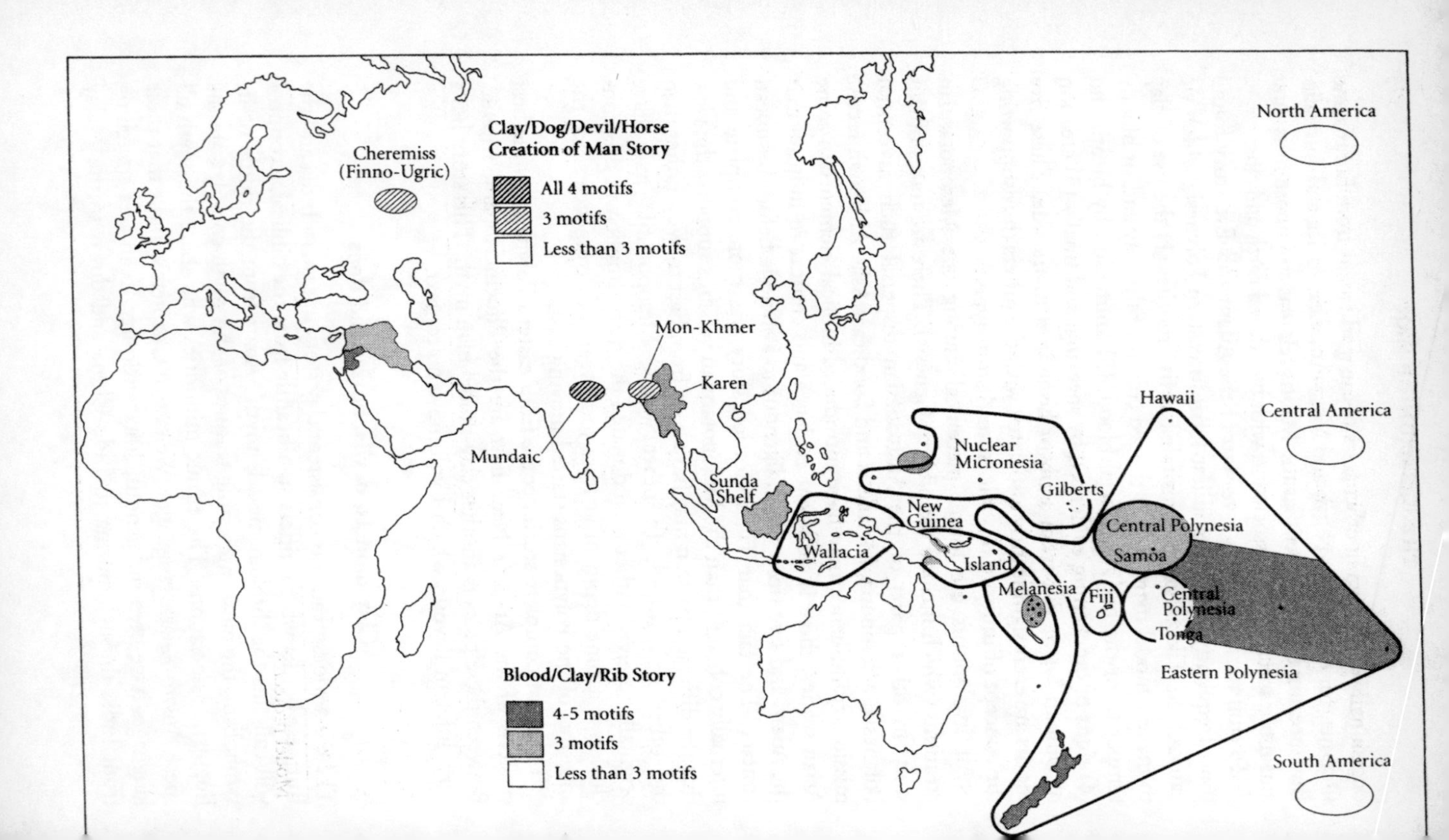

Clay/Dog/Devil/Horse
Creation of Man Story
All 4 motifs
3 motifs
Less than 3 motifs
Cheremiss
(Finno-Ugric)
Mon-Khmer
Karen
Mundaic
Sunda
Shelf
New
Guinea
Wallacia
Island
Melanesia
Nuclear
Micronesia
Gilberts
Central Polynesia
Samoa
Fiji
Central
Polynesia
Tonga
Eastern Polynesia
Hawaii
North America
Central America
South America
Blood/Clay/Rib Story
4-5 motifs
3 motifs
Less than 3 motifs

Figure 41. **The creation of humanity from clay.** This map shows the distribution of the two distinct Eurasian versions of this universal theme. The bloody clay/rib version found in Genesis and among Mesopotamian civilisations reappears among Austronesian peoples of island Southeast Asia and the Pacific. Sandwiched between these poles, the dog/devil/horse version is found spread across Austro-Asiatic-speaking peoples of India and Burma, and in an isolated occurrence among the Uralic-speaking Cheremiss in Russia.

Peninsula where their first epicentre of expansion may lie. They were probably dispersed to their present areas before the Aryan, Thai and Austronesian expansions into these regions over the past 4000 years.[48] In this sense the Austro-Asiatic speakers may be regarded as aboriginal to India, Burma and Indo-China. The largest modern representative groups of Austro-Asiatic speakers come from Cambodia and Vietnam.

The basic tale has the creator make a man or a couple out of clay. He/she leaves them overnight to dry, and a malign creature, usually either a horse or a devil, destroys them. This may happen more than once but then the creator makes another creature, usually a dog, to protect the images overnight and so the models that are made finally

Table 11. **Consistency in the clay model/devil/dog creation of people.** This correlation matrix shows the high odds in favour of finding combinations of the four story motifs in one myth. Asterisks show how unlikely these pairs are to be chance associations; the figure in each box (odds ratio) shows how strong the association is.

	Clay Model made of first Being	Model destroyed by Devil or Snake	Model destroyed by Horse or Indra
Model destroyed by Devil or Snake	6**		
Model destroyed by Horse or Indra	7**	20***	
Model protected by Dog	5**	4*	142***

Key:

- * Chances of random association less than 1 in 20.
- ** Chances of random association less than 1 in 100.
- *** Chances of random association less than 1 in 1000.

survive. The individual motif elements of the stories form a tight and significant association which underlines the unity of the story-type (see Table 11).[49]

One of the fullest and most colourful versions of this type comes from the Santals, a Mundaic tribe of Bengal. This story is remarkable in that it also contains two other well-characterised but uncommon creation motifs that I introduced earlier. One of these is the bird creator wandering the seas without a place to lay its egg; this is found in both Samoa and Finland (see last chapter).The other is the land-diver motif from central Asia, Siberia and North America (see Chapter 11). Another important motif in the Santal version is the island Garden of Eden.

The Santal story starts with an adviser creator, 'Thakur Jiu', in a primeval ocean. His servants requested a blessing or the gift to start creating humans. He recommended they ask for help from a female-creator being, 'Malin Budhi', in a rock cave under water. She used some special froth and stiff clay to make two human bodies, and laid them out to dry. The day-horse, 'Singh Sadom', passed that way and trampled the models under foot. Thakur Jiu recommended the pieces to be kicked into the Ganges and into the sea. With Thakur Jiu's blessing, Malin Budhi tried again. However at this second attempt there was another hitch. Thakur Jiu had left the human spirits on top of a door-frame next to the spirits intended for birds. Malin Budhi, being short, fetched the wrong ones and, when animated, her models turned into birds who flew away over the seas for twelve years looking for somewhere to nest. Thakur Jiu asked a number of sea creatures to raise the land above the sea, but they were all unsuccessful. Finally the earthworm, who had swallowed earth only to pass it out from his rear end, suggested asking Prince tortoise from the sea. The subterranean land was hitched up by four chains to the turtle and raised as an island. Thakur Jiu made a garden by planting grass and trees on the island. The birds landed and laid their eggs, which were then eaten by 'Raghop Buar'. Thakur Jiu then sent 'Jaher-era' to guard the eggs. Finally the eggs hatched to produce two human beings, a male and female, 'Pilchu Haram' and 'Pilchu Budhi', who were the progenitors of the species.[50]

The horse as the destroyer of the first human creation is a particular feature of all the versions held by the scattered Mundaic tribes of India. So among the Korkus Aboriginal tribes in central India we find the following version with some Hindu context:

> Rawan, the demon king of Ceylon, [in an uncharacteristically constructive role], observed that the Vindhyan and Satpura

ranges were uninhabited, and he besought the great god Mahadeo to people them. So Mahadeo, by whom they mean Siva, sent a crow to find for him an ant-hill of red earth, and the bird discovered such an ant-hill among the mountains of Betul. [The god took a handful of the red earth and made images of a man and a woman.] ... But no sooner had he done so than two fiery horses, sent by Indra, rose from the earth, and trampled the images to dust. For two days the creator persisted in his attempts, but as often as the images were made they were dashed in pieces by the horses. At last the god made an image of a dog, and breathed into it the breath of life, and the animal kept off the fiery steeds of Indra. Thus the god was able to make the two images of man and woman undisturbed, and bestowing life upon them, he called them Mula and Mulai. These two became the ancestors of the Korku tribe.[51]

The Bir-hors and the Asurs, Mundaic tribes of Chota Nagpur far to the east, all have similar stories without the references to Rawan, Mahadeo/Siva, crows or red ant-hills. Their creator was a sun god, Singbonga, and he used clay to make his models. The roles of destroyer and protector were a flying horse and a dog, respectively. One more Mundaic tribe in that region, the Mundas, have the same story with a horse, but the dog is replaced by a spider that spins a protective cocoon round the models.

Further east on the other side of the Ganges delta we find Mon-Khmer-speaking tribes with a closely similar tradition. Belonging to the same branch of the Austro-Asiatic language family as the Cambodians, these tribes do not have a horse as destroyer. The Kumis of Arakan have a snake that devours the images while the dog is created to guard them. The Khasis of the Chittagong Hills, on the other hand, have the images destroyed by an evil spirit; again a dog is created to guard them. The Garos, another tribe living further north towards Tibet, have the spider motif, but in their case the web is stretched over the water as an abode for the creatrix of the land Nostu-Nopantu. There is no dog, devil or horse but some of the other motifs are common to the Santal story, such as a watery chaos, a male creator-adviser called Tatara-Rabuga, an elaborate diver story and a prepared garden in which man was placed.[52]

These creations have been remarkably well preserved considering the complete geographic and cultural isolation of the Austro-Asiatic tribes holding them. Both the Mundaic and related Mon-Khmer tribes mentioned here live in small ethnic islands surrounded by a sea of other cultures. The one main difference between the Mon-Khmer and Mundaic versions is the horse. The Santal myth gives the clue as to the possible meaning and origin of this motif. Horses are not aggressive to people unless they are ridden by other people. The Santals state that the horses were sent by Indra. Indra was the great Aryan war god from the north who, in the Vedic poems was symbolised by a horse, and destroyed forts and citadels without number in old Harappan India. Horse-riding invaders were present in Baluchistan even in 3000 BC. We must assume that the effects of the Aryan invasions of India in the second millennium BC were at least as devastating to the Mundaic Aboriginals as to the majority indigenous Dravidians:

> And at his deep neigh, like the thunder of heaven,
> the foemen tremble in fear,
> for he fights against thousands, and none can resist him,
> so terrible is his charge.
> *Rig Veda*, iv, 38, 5–6

Thus in this family of creations it seems that the horse is a later addition, arriving a mere 4000 years ago. The horse motif is specific to India while the Mon-Khmer dog/devil/snake versions may be older. If the horse is for the Mundas, a symbol for the Aryan invasions of India, then the benign role of Ravana, who in the Aryan Vedic literature is a baddy, is explained. Further, Siva and his aliases Mahadeo, Tatara-Rabuga and Singbonga are then synonymous with the creator in an Austro-Asiatic context and in opposition to the Aryan invasions. While Mahadeo could have been borrowed locally from the Dravidians, we may pause to wonder why his homonym, Mahatara, is so common in Borneo and the Philippines outside the known areas of Hindu-Aryan (or Dravidian) influence of the past 2000 years. Maybe Mahatara has a more ancient provenance in east Asia than in India, for instance Austro-Asiatic?

I noted above the motifs of the roving teal and land-diver which were shared respectively with Finnish and some central Asiatic creations. This might suggest support for the long-distance genetic links we saw between Austro-Asiatics and Uralic speakers in Chapter 7. There is a more direct story link found nearer the Urals. The dog/devil clay-man type of the Khasis crops up again far to the north among the Cheremiss in the middle Volga region of Russia, a people speaking an Uralic language related to Finnish. As Sir James Frazer noted, this creation has elements both of a Toradjan legend[53] and of the 'broken-models myth':

> They say that God moulded man's body of clay, and then went up to heaven to fetch the soul, with which to animate it. In his absence he set the dog to guard the body. But while he was away the devil drew near, and blowing a cold wind on the dog he seduced the animal by the bribe of a fur-coat to relax his guard. Thereupon the fiend spat on the clay body and beslavered it so foully, that when God came back he despaired of ever cleaning up the mess and saw himself reduced to the painful necessity of turning the body outside in. That is why a man's inside is now so dirty ...

To summarise, the broken-models myth appears among Austro-Asiatic language groups in India, Burma, Indo-China and Malaysia. The dog and devil motif appears to be the archetype, and could date back to the domestication of the former. The horse motif appears to be a later variant that occurred in India possibly as a result of the Aryan invasions 4000 years ago. Elements of the story as told in both the Mundaic and Mon-Khmer versions appear among other peoples as far apart as Sulawesi, Samoa and two different Finnic tongues of northern Europe, thus supporting the genetic evidence for an ancient diffusion from the south to the north through Central Asia. The Finnic languages are a northwestern branch of the Uralic family which is thought to have radiated from Central Asia 4000 years ago. The association with the other creation motifs – the primeval sea, the creatrix and birds, the diver myth and the prepared garden – are discussed in Chapters 11 and 15.

The only feature that the broken-models myth has in common with the blood-and-rib myth is clay. There is no cross-association between the other motifs of the two stories, yet the former is found geographically in the middle between the two main locations of the latter. There is no trace of the broken-models myth in Mesopotamia except for the clay-and-garden motifs, although there is good evidence of ancient commercial contacts between the Harappan civilisation and Sumer. This geographic gap implies that the cultural connections between Mesopotamia and ancient Austronesia, evidenced by the rib story, were not the result of simple local diffusion of ideas but more likely by the long-distance sea route.

Conclusions

In this brief analysis of the creation-of-man myths, Frazer's concept of two kinds of myths, totemic and constructive, covers the majority of the 364 myths I studied, where a mechanism is specified. Totemic myths tend to be exclusive of cosmogonic myths both in terms of overall distribution and in terms of association in individual creation stories. Totemic myths are found as the rule in Australia and Papuan-speaking mainland Melanesia. They are also found in Africa and the Americas. Totemic myths are neither a feature of Eurasian nor of Austronesian cultures except where there is evidence of non-Austronesian influence, such as is found around New Guinea. The uneven distribution does not support the view of an innate human tendency to tell this kind of story. In the next few chapters we will see how some of the totemic tree myths of eastern Indonesia have been woven into the Garden of Eden story.

Constructive or clay myths are found evenly distributed throughout the world except for Australia and non-Austronesian parts of New Guinea. This could be due to great antiquity or to a natural tendency to make up such myths. In general, these myths are not associated with cosmogonic legends. Analysis of the distribution of two particular variants does support limited diffusion models.

Two clay-man variants are found in Eurasia and Southeast Asia. One of these, the 'rib story', is found throughout the Pacific radiation of Austronesian languages and also in Mesopotamian cultures and the Bible. In its fullest form the creator uses a god's blood and red clay to create a model of man in his image. He breathes into the model to animate it. The man then sneezes. A rib (ivi) is then taken out of the man to make the first woman. There is contextual evidence that this myth started east of India, and may have spread from there to Mesopotamia.

The other Asian variant, the 'devil/dog story', appears to have originated among Austro-Asiatic speakers of India and Southeast Asia. It may be very ancient, and has spread through central Asia to northern Europe and east out to the Southwest Pacific. These two variants are discrete with no overlap except for the use of clay.

In the bloody-clay-man and spare-rib story, once again we find a Mesopotamian origin myth type leading an independent existence in the middle of the Pacific. Again the implication has to be that the eastern Polynesian and Micronesian versions were somehow preserved at the beginning of one-way trips that started more than 5000 years ago. It is significant that although the Austro-Asiatics were nearer to Mesopotamia than the Austronesians, yet it was the Austronesian variant which moved furthest west, thus suggesting a sea route.

The other anomalous pattern for the blood/clay/rib story, which was also seen for the separation story in the last chapter, is the somewhat fragmentary evidence of provenance from Southeast Asia in comparison to that from the Pacific and Mesopotamia. This may not affect the hypothesis of the Asian origin of the Polynesian story since the Polynesians, Micronesians and Melanesian Austronesian speakers were ultimately derived from Southeast Asia (see Chapter 6). Given these links, however, we might expect to see fuller versions of Oceanic-origin myths in the western Malayo-Polynesian language group than the few esoteric bloody clay stories of Borneo and the Palau Islands.

Part of the reason for this paucity of evidence from island Southeast Asia must be the competing cultural influence of the past 2000 years from Hindus, Muslims, Christians and Buddhists. Another possibility may be that the population movements and cultural influences in Southeast Asia over the past 4000 years may not be as simple as suggested by the linguistic trees. The possible influence of the Austro-Asiatic people and traditions of Cambodia, Vietnam and Laos in Indo-China on Austronesian island Southeast Asian myths cannot easily be assessed, but their cousins in Burma and India hold the rival devil/dog/clay-man myth. Indo-China was also the odd region out in the Far East for the distribution of the separation myth. In the next chapters we will see both links, and contrasts, between Austro-Asiatic, Austronesian and Mesopotamian origin myths. I will show both Austro-Asiatics and Austronesians shared in the Garden of Eden.

14
THE QUEST FOR IMMORTALITY

The Garden of Eden story holds a cherished place in Western literature. Its morality, beauty, brevity and profound balance denies any artifice or plagiarism in the telling. Yet the Genesis writers assembled this story less than three thousand years ago from a selection of fertility and immortality myths that were in common circulation at the time. The separate elements of these myths are still to be found today in Southeast Asia and Melanesia.

In the previous chapter we saw how the creation of a man from clay, as related in the Jehovistic account of Genesis, belonged to one branch of the world's universal clay-man myths. The other chief representatives of this 'bloody-clay-and-rib' story were found in eastern Polynesia. Sandwiched between ancient Mesopotamia and the Austronesians of the Pacific were the Austro-Asiatic minorities of India, Burma and Southeast Asia who shared a rather different and older set of clay-man stories. In these stories a malign creature, originally either a devil or snake, interfered with the attempted animation of the clay models by the creator. A third variety of human creation in the Austronesian cultures of Southeast Asia was totemic. A result of competing influence from Australia and New Guinea, totemism found its strongest expression in the ethnic melting pot of Maluku in eastern Indonesia. Here among various animal totemic ancestors, we also heard of the tree which produced people. In this chapter we shall see how a symbolic tree of life was the mythic stage-prop which, when combined with the legend of the lost homeland, set the scene for the drama in the Garden of Eden.

When I looked at Sir James Frazer's well-known analysis of the biblical story of the Fall with its motifs of snake, tree, life, death, knowledge and sex, this turned out to be descended from related and ancient Southeast Asian traditions. One was concerned with immortality and the other connected trees, fertility, death and rebirth. The concept of the Garden of Eden as a lost paradise was a later addition from the Austronesians and derived from their own drowned homeland. This motif links with other Mesopotamian motifs of an underworld and the fountain of youth, which also originate further east. The tree of life and the snake motifs, both originating in the East, underlie all ancient Western myth cycles of fertility, death and renewal. The structure and development of these myths supports a general hypothesis of Southeast Asia as the source, and the Ancient Near East as the recipient of Neolithic religious culture. Archaeologists' ability to date the oldest recorded versions of the Mesopotamian immortality and paradise stories nearly 5000 years ago, places their East Asian forebears even further back in time. We can start with immortality.

The Fall

The association of the Fall with a lost paradise is so ingrained into the Western psyche that it may be difficult to conceive of the two themes having a different origin. Yet, even a cursory examination of creation myths revealed that paradise generally does not precede a fall, and that the loss of paradise may not be because of humanity's transgression. Once again, Frazer was there before me.[1] He paints a convincing picture of the family of myths, in which humanity had lost or missed out on immortality. The biblical Fall was but a recent and deliberate re-synthesis in this tradition. Whilst re-analysing Frazer's work, along with stories that have been translated from Mesopotamian tablets since his time, I discovered more. Not only did this family of immortality stories have a connection with the Austro-Asiatic dog/devil/clay myths of the last chapter, but their family tree demonstrated an extraordinary communication between the cultures that surrounded the Indian Ocean even before Babylon. Three archetypal creative themes, all originating in Australasia, have run in parallel throughout the development of the immortality myths. These are, respectively, the secret creative powers of the *Moon*, potent *Trees* and *animals that shed their skin or feathers*. In the next chapter we shall see how, eventually, the concepts of resurrection and immortality merged into those of fertility and renewal of seasons, throughout Eurasia and Oceania.

The dog/devil/clay creation of man has as its archetype the story of clay models broken, before animation, by a devil or snake and then later protected by a dog. In one variant of this Southeast Asian creation, an agent of the creator mistakenly gave the wrong spirit of animation to the models and they turned into birds who flew away.[2] These two motifs of the snake/devil who interferes with man's quickening and the agent who confuses the essence of life are also present in the family of myths that Frazer felt was the origin of the Fall story. He argued that the Fall was at heart a myth of the origin of death.[3] In the proto-story the creator intended to offer man immortality. Unfortunately, for one mischance or other, often caused by the snake, man missed out.

The Fall as a confidence trick

In the Garden of Eden, Adam was presented with several choices of fruits. He could have eaten from any or all of the unnamed trees, but he could not eat of the tree of knowledge of good and evil. Nothing was said about the tree of life, so by implication its fruit was available to that first couple. The tree of knowledge played centre stage throughout the snake's temptation of Eve. The tree of life, however, remained in the wings unnoticed until it was nearly too late and Jehovah realised that Adam and Eve could eat from that too, and become immortal like Him. He therefore shooed them out of the garden before they could gain immortality as well as knowledge:

> And the Lord God said, Behold, the man is become as one of us, to know good and evil; and now, lest he put forth his hand, and take also of the tree of life, and eat, and live for ever' … therefore the Lord God sent him forth from the garden of Eden … (Genesis 3:22–3)

The tree of life thus played a passive role in the wings of Genesis, and in the end symbolised a lost immortality. Frazer is not alone in considering that the archetypal version of the Fall was different, and probably stressed the tree of life more. He thought that an earlier story had been clumsily modified by the Genesis writers to suit their moral and cultural agenda. Frazer's view was that there were originally two trees, but that the tree of knowledge of good and evil had really been the tree of death contrasting with the tree of life. This hypothesis may explain the verses:

> And the Lord God commanded the man, saying, Of every tree of the garden thou mayest freely eat;
>
> But of the tree of the knowledge of good and evil, thou shalt not eat of it: for in the day that thou eatest thereof thou shalt surely die. (Genesis 2:16–17)

Clearly, humankind did not die on that day of the Fall, but instead became mortal. With complementary trees of life and death, Jehovah's instruction would have had a more open-handed and simple content:

'Eat of the tree of life and you will gain immortality, eat of the tree of death and you will be mortal.' Frazer interpreted the snake's role in tempting Eve to eat the wrong fruit in the earlier version as not just malign interference but rather as a competitive confidence trick; in cheating Adam and Eve out of their entitlement to immortality the snake was laying the ground for his own. He further suggested that in a prior version the snake was actually God's messenger who perverted the message he was carrying to man to his own benefit. Although there is no direct evidence for this hypothesis in Genesis apart from a comment on the snake's subtlety, there is ample analogy in other related myths as we shall see.

Frazer identified other variant motifs in his family of immortality myths, of which the most important are the four alternative secret mechanisms of achieving immortality – the new Moon, the tree or plant of life, the 'cast skin' and a message from God. Imitation of the Moon's monthly renewal after three days' death was seen as a divine recipe for immortality in Africa, Australia, some parts of the western Pacific islands and among Aboriginals of the Malay Peninsula. Second, the mythical concept of eating a magical plant or the fruit of the tree of immortality was prevalent in central Australia, Indo-China and in ancient Mesopotamia and Arabia.[4] Third, the periodic shedding of an old skin or moulting was seen as evidence of immortality in those animals such as reptiles, crustaceans and insects that had this ability. Imitation of casting the skin might have been humanity's lot if things had been otherwise. Stories of the cast-skin abound in Southeast Asia but also occur further out into the Pacific, in Africa and in ancient Mesopotamia.[5] Finally, another important element in the immortality stories was the mode of transmission of the message from the creator to man. In some stories, particularly in Africa, the delivery of the correct message by itself was potentially sufficient for man to achieve immortality. Somehow, however, the message was always perverted in transmission, thus losing its effect. Because stories with this last mechanism were always derived from one of the other three, it was almost certainly a more recent development.

Before tracing and analysing these motifs in different stories, I will look at the symbolic nature of some of the immortal animals. As I have said there was a widespread belief in Eurasia and the southwest Pacific that animals who shed, moulted and renewed their skins or coats were immortal. This view certainly also existed in Mesopotamia and the Mediterranean. So we find the Phoenician writer Sanchuniathon stating that, 'the serpent was the longest lived of all animals because it cast its skin and so renewed its youth'.[6] In the Bible, Psalm 103 states, 'so that thy youth is renewed like the eagle's'. In the Gilgamesh epic, the snake promptly shed its skin after stealing the plant of immortality that Gilgamesh had dived for. This example clearly connects the cast-skin with the plant of immortality thus establishing a thematic link for both in the same story. Another Mesopotamian instance of dual immortality mechanisms in one story is the combination of the serpent and the tree of life in Genesis. We find serpents, usually snakes which probably originated in the cast-skin stories, in immortality myths throughout their Asian distribution.

The Moon's gift of immortality

Probably the oldest of all the immortality motifs in Frazer's grouping is that of the Moon's cycle of renewal. In certain Aboriginal cultures, the Moon was regarded as a deity with the secret of immortality because it 'died' for three days every month, subsequently renewing itself during the first half of the next month. In the traditions of the Wotjobaluk, an Aboriginal tribe in South East Australia, it is said that men used to follow the same cycle of renewal on the Moon's instruction until an elder, for some malign reason said, 'Let them remain dead'; and since then nobody has ever come to life again, except the Moon, which still continues to do so until this very day.

The Mantras, Aboriginal Austro-Asiatic speakers in the jungles of peninsular Malaysia, have this same concept of man originally waxing and waning with the Moon. In their version the lord of the underworld decided that the practice should cease. The Caroline Islands of western Micronesia had a similar tradition. But in their version an evil spirit contrived that when men slept the sleep of death they would wake no more. In a Fijian myth the Moon and the rat discussed the possibility of giving man the Moon's gift of immortality. The rat was against the idea and prevailed in the final decision.

The big surprise is finding the Moon motif repeated among the Aboriginal tribes of southern Africa. In these examples, however, the central action revolves around the theme of the 'Perverted Message': 'the Namaquas or Hottentots [Khoisan] ... say that once upon a time the Moon wished to send to mankind a message of immortality, and the hare undertook to act as messenger. So the Moon charged him to go to men and say, "As I die and rise to life again, so shall you die and rise to life again." '[7] Needless to say the hare got the message the wrong way round saying, 'As I die and do not rise to life again, so you shall also die and not rise to life again.'[8] As a result of receiving the wrong message, man was condemned to mortality. The Moon was cross at

Table 12. **The Fall: a lost quest for immortality.**

Three different routes to immortality and four stages in the development of the story of how humans lost it.

(A) MOON'S WAXING AND WANING	(B) TREE OF LIFE	(C) REJUVENATION BY CAST SKIN
I. **Man already had Moon's immortality by direct imitation of waxing and waning.** It was *lost* as a result of either: (a) An old man's curse or bad temper (Australia) (c) 'Father Death's' decision (Mantras: Orang Asli) (d) Evil Spirit (Caroline Is. Micronesia)	I. **Man already had immortality by 3-day burial under a tree in imitation of Moon.** It was *lost* as a result of either: (a) cranky old man (Australia) (b) lizard's 'advice' to bury under tree of death, thus avoiding overcrowding (Vietnam)	I. **Man already had immortality by casting own skin.** It was *lost* by: (a) personal decision of an old immortal person (many island and coastal Melanesian tribes, from New Guinea to Vanuatu) (b) decision of 'death' because of overcrowding (Santa Maria – Vanuatu, Melanesia)
II. **Man never had the Moon's immortality**; since is was denied him by: Committee decision of Moon and Rat (Fiji)		II. **Man never had immortality through skill of casting skin;** since it was denied him by: (a) Curse of old man or creator, and skill given to snakes and crustaceans. (Bismarcks & British Guiana) (b) God's committee decision; skill given to shellfish (Samoa)
III. **Earth missed opportunity for immortality:** by turning up late for the Creator's free 'waxing and waning' offer; Moon was on time and is now immortal through skill of waxing and waning (Upotos: Congo)	III. **Gilgamesh missed opportunity for immortality;** (a) by allowing snake to eat plant of life; (b) by dropping pukku and mukku wood (Sumer)	III. **Man missed opportunity for immortality through skill of casting skin:** because: (c) Creator ate bananas rather than crabs when creating man (Nias) (d) Snakes ate the crabs and got the skill (Nias)
IV. **The Moon offered Man its immortality via one messenger;** Man missed out because: (a) the messenger perverted the message (Hottentots – S.Africa, Nandi – E. Africa); (b) Man had a tiff with the Moon **The Moon offered Man its immortality via a two-messenger race;** Man missed out because: the first messenger perverted the message (Hottentots – S. Africa) **God offered Man immortality via a two-messenger race;** Man missed out because: the first messenger perverted the message (Bantu tribes)	IV. **Adapa missed opportunity for immortality:** by refusing bread and water of life on false or perverted advice of Ea (Sumer) **Adam and Eve missed opportunity for immortality by:** (a) Snake's false advice to Eve to eat from tree of knowledge (or death) rather than from tree of life. (b) God's curse (Genesis – Hebrew)	IV. **Man missed opportunity for immortality through skill of casting skin**; because: (a) One of two brothers betrayed message of cast skin to snake and perverted the message to men (New Britain) (b) Snakes intercepted message and got the skill (Wabende tribe: East Africa) (c) Snakes intercepted message, passed on perverted message to man, and kept immortality to themselves (Vietnam) (d) Bird on tree sold message to snakes for carrion (Gallas – East Africa)

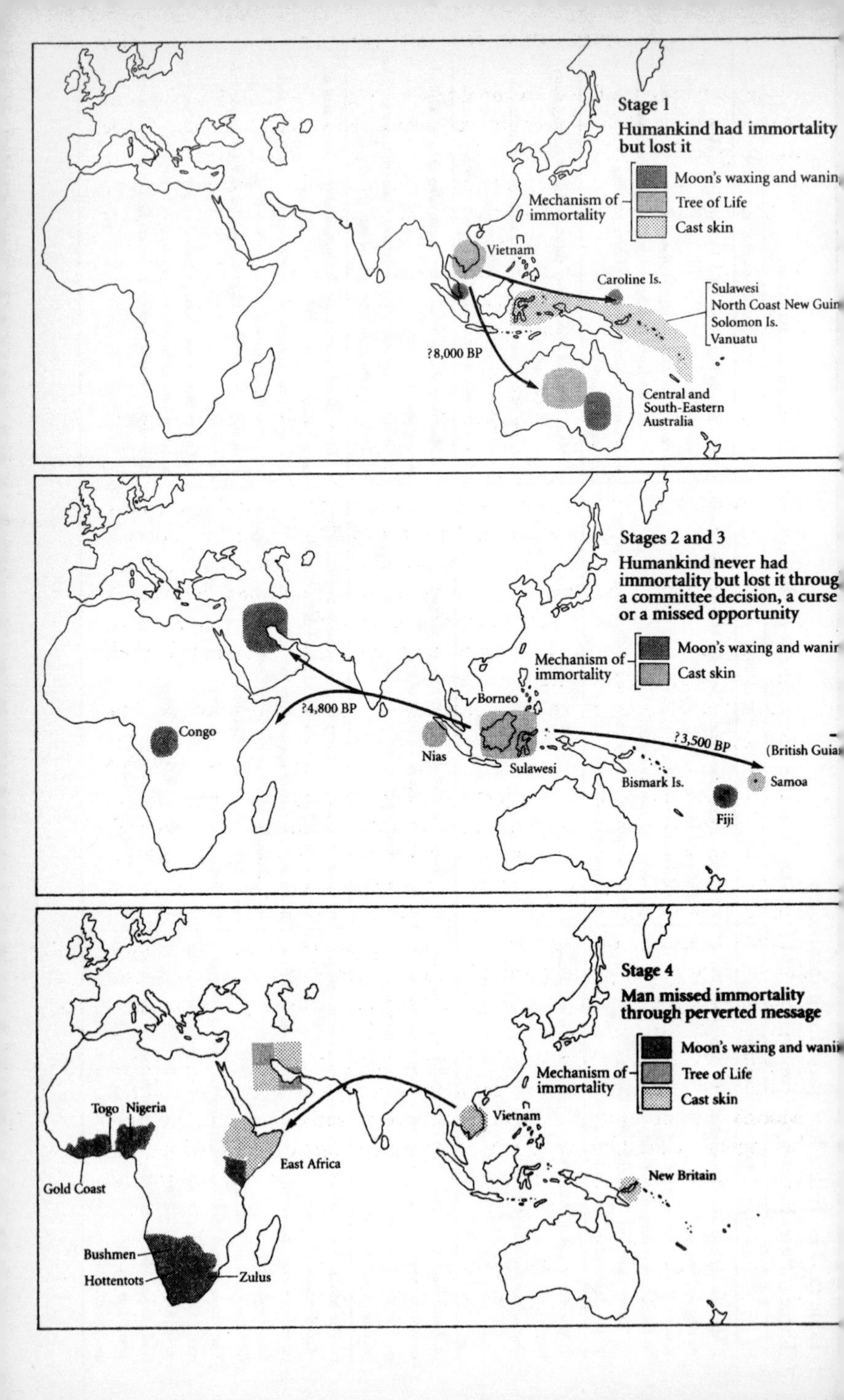

Stage 1
Humankind had immortality but lost it
Mechanism of immortality
Moon's waxing and wanin
Tree of Life
Cast skin
Vietnam
Caroline Is.
Sulawesi
North Coast New Guin
Solomon Is.
Vanuatu
?8,000 BP
Central and South-Eastern Australia
Stages 2 and 3
Humankind never had immortality but lost it throug a committee decision, a curse or a missed opportunity
Mechanism of immortality
Moon's waxing and wanir
Cast skin
Borneo
?4,800 BP
Congo
Nias
Sulawesi
?3,500 BP
(British Guia
Bismark Is.
Samoa
Fiji
Stage 4
Man missed immortality through perverted message
Mechanism of immortality
Moon's waxing and wani
Tree of Life
Cast skin
Vietnam
Togo
Nigeria
Gold Coast
East Africa
New Britain
Bushmen
Hottentots
Zulus

Figure 42. Humankind's lost immortality. Four stages of structural development characterise each of the three story types which spread round the Indo-Pacific region, probably out of Southeast Asia (see Table 12). The earliest stage was confined to the East and may have spread from mainland Southeast Asia to Australia and the southwest Pacific around 8000 years ago. Stages 2 and 3 may have spread out of island Southeast Asia up to 5000 years ago, this time east to the central Pacific and west to Mesopotamia and the Congo. The final stage, the perverted message, still found in Vietnam, spread extensively in Africa and is also the basis of the Fall in Genesis.

this gross incompetence and gave the hare a split lip. The men were also upset and hare flesh is thus taboo in that tribe.

The Bushmen (San) have a variant on this story. The Moon gave the same message directly to them, but a quarrelsome man did not believe her. He was turned into a hare and given a split lip for his impudence. As usual man missed out on immortality. Far away from these aboriginal folk, a Kenyan story of the Nandi tribe links the Moon's immortality with man's lost chance through a surly messenger, the dog, who tried to extort favours from men and, when he failed, took revenge by giving the wrong message.

In several stories from these tribes there are two messengers. The Tati Bushmen or Masarwas of the Kalahari say that the Moon sent the message initially with a tortoise who was so slow that she (the Moon) sent another messenger, the hare. The hare was fast but forgetful and got the message the wrong way round. As a result men became mortal. The tortoise eventually turned up with the correct message, but by this time it was too late and, as before, the hare got a split lip for his error. I find the context of this story hangs together rather better than Aesop's 2500-year-old cut-down version of the hare and the tortoise; the bushmen's story could indeed be the older of the two. In another two messenger version, this time from the Hottentots, an insect takes the place of the tortoise.

The perverted-message version also appears in several Bantu tribes of the Congo and the Upper Zambesi, among whom the story of the Moon's gift of immortality occurs. Several variants occur. In one, belonging to the Upotos, the Moon and the Earth competed for the gift of immortality from the god, but the Earth turned up late for the gift and missed out.[9] The other story has a two-messenger race with the Moon as the donor.

The majority of immortality myths among the Bantu tribes of east, west, central and south Africa have dropped all mention of the Moon's role in immortality; instead there is simply a creator whose message of immortality is perverted from 'you shall live' to 'you shall die', usually in a two-messenger race. A number of animals appear as messengers including reptiles and man's own domestic animals, the sheep, goat and dog.

The tree of life and edible immortality

The motif of the perverted message is an explanation for another immortality story set down in ancient times, but translated only since Frazer's time. This is a bizarre tale whose significance has puzzled students of Mesopotamian literature: the myth of Adapa. Based on a Sumerian original, several fragmentary Akkadian written versions have survived from the second millennium BC. The story, which is set in ante-diluvian times, may, however, be much older than 4000 years. Although the moral of the story is ambiguous, it has been described as the 'Babylonian Fall' with Adapa likened to Adam who, having received knowledge, was denied the gift of eternal life by a jealous god. In both cases the gift of immortality was edible:

Adapa or Oannes was the first of seven amphibious ante-diluvian artisan/priest/sages sent from the Apsu by the god Ea to civilise mankind in Mesopotamia. Ea, god of the Apsu, gave Adapa great skills but specifically not immortality. Both a baker and a fisherman, Adapa, who was based at this time in Eridu at the ancient mouth of the Euphrates, had his boat upset at sea by the South Wind, also sent by Ea, and was forced to take up residence with the fishes. Adapa in self-defence broke the South Wind's wing and calmed the weather. Adapa was then summoned by the sky god, King Anu, to answer for his crime. Prior to going before the god's court, Adapa was coached by Ea on how to dress and behave in Heaven. This treacherous advice resulted in Adapa dressing up as a dead man and pretending to mourn two gods who had disappeared from Earth. Ea warned Adapa that he might be laughed at. To complete the sting, Ea told Adapa to refuse any offer of bread and water from the gods, since these would be the 'bread of death' and the 'water of death'.[10]

When Adapa arrived at Heaven's gate for his hearing, he gave his mourning lines to the very gods, one of whom was Dumuzi,[11] for whom he was supposed to be mourning. They, of course, laughed at him. At his court hearing before Anu, Adapa explained that he had been fishing for the house of Ea when he was sunk in a storm sent by the same Ea. He only broke the South Wind's wing in self-defence. With the intercession of Dumuzi, Anu was appeased concerning

Adapa's 'crime', but was also annoyed with the god Ea for stirring up trouble:

> Why did Ea disclose to wretched mankind
> The ways of Heaven and Earth,
> Give them a heavy heart?
> It was he who did it!

Anu then wanted to do something to recompense Adapa for his trouble:

> What can we do for him?
> Fetch him the bread of (eternal) life and let him eat!

Naive Adapa, of course, refused the offers of both the bread of life and the water of life, explaining to Anu that Ea had told him not to eat or drink! Anu gave up on Adapa as a hopeless case at this point:

> Anu watched him and laughed at him ...
> Take him and send him back to his earth[12]

In these fragments of one of man's oldest-written myths, Ea was the intermediary who, by a series of contradictory actions and perverted advice, made a complete fool of his skilled expatriate servant. Adapa was supposedly also his son, and Ea also deliberately cheated him out of immortality. Maybe the technicians from the East were not needed any more. Ea is thus cast in the story of Adapa as the 'snake' with the perverted message. In other texts we are told that Ea finally got fed up with all the seven sages and sent them packing back to the Apsu.[13]

We are also given a tantalising clue in the Adapa story as to one Sumerian view of the 'tree of knowledge'. Unlike the key role of the tree of knowledge in the Genesis account, in this story Adapa was forgiven for becoming knowledgeable but not for lacking common sense. He lost the 'bread of life' through naivety. None the less, Anu's comments about Ea's trouble-making echo the Genesis horror of 'knowledge'. The disclosure of newfangled technical and religious knowledge of the 'ways of Heaven and Earth', brought in by Ea and the seven sages from the Apsu (wherever that was) to Eridu, was seen by the god Anu, whose temple was based in Uruk, as a source of 'heavy heart' for 'wretched mankind'.[14] Such a gloomy minority view of the civilising benefits of religion, politics and technology has somehow survived to this day in spite of propaganda by theologians, politicians and technocrats.

In Adapa's story, the 'bread and waters of life' were the central prize, as it must also have seemed to Mesopotamian cereal farmers threatened by political control from the new cities. The bread and water of life appear in another Sumerian passion story, 'The descent of Inanna into the underworld'. Fertility goddess Inanna had made the great mistake of confronting her sister in the underworld. Consequently she was killed and impaled on a stake. As a preliminary to her resurrection after three days of death, the god Enki sent two sexless creatures with the food of life and the water of life to resuscitate her.[15] The change from a tree of life to a crop of life could be regarded as a Neolithic agrarian development, separate from the Genesis writer's reference to the 'tree of life' which has older roots in East Asia.

The Adapa myth is both a Fall story and a typical immortality myth. It has recognised connections with other Mesopotamian immortality stories such as the Fall in the Garden of Eden.[16] It thus provides a genetic link between the perverted message from further south in the Indian Ocean to the Mesopotamian tradition, thereby introducing three immortality motifs: the perverted message, tree of life and the cast-skin. The adaptation of the plant of life from a tree to a cereal also shows how ancient motifs are often preserved in their route of diffusion, by incorporation into local context.

Frazer believed that the perverted-message motif of Africa was related to another group of immortality stories on the eastern side of the Indian Ocean.[17] He called these the 'cast-skin' stories.

Immortality through the cast-skin

Since the story of the cast-skin relates most appropriately to reptiles, it is no surprise to find a snake or lizard in most cast-skin stories. But this is not always the case. The cast-skin stories group into two main types. In the older of these, humanity already had the immortal gift of changing his skin but voluntarily relinquished it. Reptiles do not feature as characters in these stories.

The first of these versions, which we can call 'cast-skin before loss', is found among Melanesians speaking tongues of the Oceanic branch of the Austronesian language family. A typical tale of this type comes from the Banks Islands in Vanuatu. Qat, who was mentioned in the last chapter as the creator of red clay-men, had a powerful mother. This woman, when she grew old, went to a stream and cast off her skin into the water where it caught on a twig. Arriving home, her child refused to recognise the young woman as his mother. To pacify her child, the mother went back to the stream and put on her old skin.

From that time humans became mortal. In another Vanuatu village she was known as Ul-ta-marama, 'Change-skin of the world'.

We find very similar stories elsewhere over a wide Oceanic distribution among Austronesian speakers of island Melanesia. These include the Shortlands Islands of the Solomons, the Trobriand Islands, among the Kai, and the Matukar of north-eastern Papua New Guinea. Thousands of miles away to the west of Melanesia in Sulawesi, the To Koolawi have an identical story to the Banks Islands. A variant from the Admiralty Islands, north of New Guinea, has two rival sons arguing immoderately about their newly skinned and rejuvenated mother; with the inevitable loss of immortality for the race. In Aneitum, another island of Vanuatu, the old woman is replaced by an old man whose two grandchildren idly make holes in his night skin which he has folded away before gardening. As a result immortality is lost.

These similar cast-skin stories, scattered in the huge area of dispersal of the Austronesian language family in Melanesia, provide a regional thematic link with the Australian Moon stories, which also have humans losing a previously enjoyed immortality. They are not held by any Polynesians and may thus antedate the Lapita dispersal of 3500 years ago, which we explored in the first half of this book. Their distribution around the north coast and mainland of New Guinea might suggest an ancient recombination of two immortality motifs at the coastal cultural interface of Austronesians and Papuans. This is unlikely however since there are no equivalent mainland Papuan myths. An alternative view is that the 'cast-skin before loss' is simply an older version of the cast-skin story which, like the 'oval red-blood cell marker' (ovalocytosis) and others mentioned in Chapters 6 and 7, survived in the southwest Pacific among the peoples of the first Austronesian dispersal 8000 years ago.

In later cast-skin versions, humans never had immortality. Although a well-meaning deity publicly offered it to humans, the snake usually managed to beat them to it. And while their distribution overlaps the 'cast-skin before loss' type, these 'never-cast-skin' stories, where the vital offer was missed, are centred around island Southeast Asia. We now find the 'never-cast-skin' stories chiefly among speakers of the western Malayo-Polynesian branch of Austronesian languages, although they may well have originated among Austro-Asiatic speakers.

A typical story in Frazer's collection comes from the Dusun people in northern Borneo who say that when the creator had finished making things, he called out, 'If anyone is able to cast off his skin, he shall not die.' Only the snake answered that he could. Meanwhile the

Dusuns did not hear the question and offer, so missed out.[18] So now the snake does not die unless a man kills him. Similar tales are told by the Todjo-Toradjas of Sulawesi where a deaf old woman represented humans at the address and did not hear the message. The serpents and shrimps *did* hear, and closed on the offer.

This Southeast Asian development of the unheeded cast-skin offer spreads to a limited extent east into northern Melanesia, and is found in one instance as far into the Pacific as Vuatom of the Bismarck Archipelago. In this case there was a curse as well. A certain To Konokonomiange told two boys to fetch fire, with the promise of eternal life: they refused and he cursed them to die although their spirits would pass on. Instead the reptiles got the gift of immortality and renewed their lives by changing skin.

The people of Nias Island, off the western coast of Sumatra, have an intriguing variant. It has neither message nor announcement. In it, the Heavens sent down a certain being to finish off creation. He ought to have fasted before his work but, being hungry, ate bananas. This was a bad choice for, if he had eaten river crabs that cast their skins, humans would have cast their skins also and achieved immortality. As it is they are mortal. A further Nias version has the serpents eating the crabs, thereby acquiring the secret of ecdysis and hence of immortality.

The never-cast-skin motif also appears in one instance right out in central Polynesia in Samoa. Rather like in the Fijian Moon story, a divine committee made the decision against humankind. On the proposal of the god 'Palsy', they voted that man, unlike the shellfish, should not cast his skin and become immortal.

Samoa is the only location of the numerous never-cast-skin stories that does not have or mention a serpent. It is also incidentally the most eastern Pacific spread of any of the family of immortality myths.

Mysteriously, though, there are two never-cast-skin versions from Guyana on the opposite side of the globe in the northeast of South America. The Arawaks of Guyana have a disappointed creator punishing humanity for its iniquity by bestowing immortality instead on serpents, lizards and beetles. The Tamanachier Indians of the Orinoco have a visiting creator from the other side of the great salt water, who, on returning home shouted, in a changed voice, from his boat:

> 'You will change your skins,' by which he meant to say, 'You will renew your youth like the serpents and the beetles.' But unfortunately an old woman, hearing these words, cried out, 'Oh!' in a tone of scepticism, if not of sarcasm, which so enraged the creator

that he changed his tune at once and said testily, 'Ye shall die.' That is why we are all mortal.[19]

The setting of this story explicitly claims an influence from outside America (presumably pre-Columbian), although we are not told which country the creator is supposed to have originated in.

In contrast to the island Southeast Asian never-cast-skin stories, in which humanity incompetently missed its opportunity of eternal life, all the Oceanic and South American versions have a clear decision by a deity or committee to deny humankind its right to eternity. The distribution of these includes Polynesia, so maybe this younger branch went out to the Pacific 3500 years ago with the Lapita dispersal.

Links between the cast-skin and the perverted message

The anti-diffusionist would argue against Frazer's unifying hypothesis of immortality stories and for the idea: that the perverted-message myth is uniquely African, while the cast-skin stories are Asian; in other words, that we are dealing with nested groups of similar but unrelated myths. Against this view are certain key features and stories that link these motifs together.

As already mentioned, probably the clearest link across the Indian Ocean is the Moon's immortality motif, which we find among the Aboriginal hunter-gatherers of Africa, Australia and Malaya and also in Fiji and the Caroline Islands of the southwestern Pacific. In Africa, the Moon's immortality consistently links with the perverted message among the Bushmen and Hottentots (Khoisan), suggesting an ancient association. In addition, this link lingers on thousands of miles north among the Nandi of East Africa.

Frazer saw the link between the perverted message and the cast-skin as thematic and self-evident. This is clear in the Southeast Asian cast-skin stories where the creator made a direct announcement, and the serpent got hold of the secret first. There are, however, more direct connections.

In Sudan, East Africa, the Galla tribe speak a Cushitic language, which is a branch of the Hamito-Semitic family.[20] Their immortality story shares both the cast-skin and the perverted-message motifs with a serpent and a bird in a tree: the god sent the message of the cast-skin secret of immortality to man via a blue bird, 'The Sheep of God', who was given a crest for his role. On his way, the bird stopped off to watch a snake devouring carrion on the path. Tempted by the carrion, the bird offered the snake the secret. When the snake accepted the trade, the bird perverted the message to the snake's benefit as follows: 'When men grow old they will die, but when you grow old you will cast your skin and renew your youth.' The snake got the immortality instead of man. For his error the bird was punished with a painful internal illness and now sits on the tops of trees bleating like a sheep.[21]

Another immortality myth that clearly shares both the cast-skin and perverted message comes from a third of the way round the globe on the other side of the Indian Ocean. The Tolais, a Melanesian tribe in New Britain in the southwest Pacific, say:

> that To Kambinana, the Good Spirit, loved men and wished to make them immortal. So he called his brother, To Korvuvu, and said to him, 'Go to men and take them the secret of immortality. Tell them to cast their skin every year. So they will be protected from death, for their life will be constantly renewed. But tell the serpents that they must thenceforth die.' However To Korvuvu acquitted himself badly of his task; for he commanded men to die, and betrayed to the serpents the secret of immortality. Since then all men have been mortal, but the serpents cast their skins every year and never die.[22]

Two more clear skin/message links emerge, in an Austro-Asiatic-speaking area of eastern Indo-China: Vietnam. In one of these the snakes hijacked the message, an event which Frazer suspects happened in the predecessor of Genesis:

> Ngoc hoang sent a messenger from Heaven to say that when they reached old age they should change their skins and live for ever, but that when serpents grew old they must die. The messenger came down to earth and said, rightly enough, 'When man is old he shall cast his skin; but when serpents are old they shall die and be laid in coffins.' So far so good. But unluckily there happened to be a brood of serpents within hearing, and when they heard the doom pronounced on their kind, they fell into a fury and said to the messenger, 'You must say it over again and just the contrary, or we will bite you.'[23]

The rest of the story was inevitable and now all creatures except the snake are mortal.

Clearly here we have a coherent story that links the perverted message, the never-cast-skin, and the serpent's competitive role together. There is, however, another key myth from a minority Austro-Asiatic-speaking tribe in Vietnam. The Bahnars' immortality myth dramatically pulls in the 'Two Trees of Life and Death' as well as the false advice of a wily reptile, thus linking all three immortality motifs as in Genesis. This story retains the older 'Immortality before Loss' variant:

> They say that in the beginning when people died, they used to be buried at the foot of a certain tree called Long Blo, and that after a time they regularly rose from the the dead, not as infants, but as full grown men and women. So the Earth was peopled very fast, and all the inhabitants formed but one great town under the presidency of our first parents. In time men multiplied to such an extent that a certain lizard could not take his walks abroad without someone treading on his tail. This vexed him and the wily creature gave an insidious hint to the gravediggers. 'Why bury the dead at the foot of the Long Blo tree?' said he; 'bury them at the foot of the Long Khung, and they will not come to life again. Let them die outright and be done with it.' The hint was taken, and from that day men have not come to life again.[24]

This Voodoo-style use of the tree of life may be very old. It is echoed in two Central Australian myths that Frazer regarded as related to the Moon myth of the Wotjobaluk mentioned above (p386), because of the three-day interment period. The tribal ancestors' hope, that by burying their dead appropriately with all their daily accoutrements, they should pass uneventfully into their new life, has provenance back into the Palaeolithic period:

> The Unmatjera and Kaitish, two tribes of Central Australia, say that their dead used to be buried either in trees or underground, and that after three days they regularly rose from the dead. The Kaitish tell how this happy state of things came to an end. It was all the fault of a man of the Curlew totem, who found some men of the little Wallaby totem burying a man of that ilk. For some reason the Curlew man flew into a passion and kicked the corpse into the sea.

Of course after that, dead men could not come to life again.[25] This is not the only place that we find the motif of kicking the corpse into the sea. The Austro-Asiatic Santals in Bengal have it in their dog/devil/clay myth. What is more, this myth contains another perverted message in the form of the mix up over the spirits used to animate the clay models.

The two Vietnamese stories not only establish the perverted message and cast-skin motifs as both indigenous to Austro-Asiatic-speaking Indo-China but the tale from the Bahnars also provides an archetypal link between three immortality motifs – namely, the cast-skin and perverted message as represented by the lizard on the one hand, and the trees of life and death on the other. This link in itself is one example of provenance for the association of the serpent with the tree of life in the Mesopotamian stories of the Garden of Eden and Gilgamesh. But before I review the distribution of the tree-of-life motif, I will first discuss possible family trees of the immortality myths collated so discerningly by Sir James Frazer.

Layers of immortality

The myths of immortality that Frazer identified on all sides of the Indian Ocean are clearly related to each other, and we must assume a diffusion to be the reason. It is not immediately clear, however, how and when they arrived at their present locations; that is until we look closer at the evidence. Although not necessarily the original versions, the oldest provenanced stories are those recorded by the Sumerians – namely the Epic of Gilgamesh and the story of Adapa. Gilgamesh, the hero of the epic, was a real king, who lived between 4500 and 4800 years ago. The epic was committed in writing around 4150 years ago; however, seals depicting a lion-killing hero may even antedate Gilgamesh's reign.[26] Gilgamesh visited the Sumerian Noah in his quest, and the story of Adapa is supposed to be ante-diluvian although the earliest tablets recording it are only 3400 years old.[27] Mesopotamian immortality stories may be over 5000 years old. But even these hoary tales may be structurally and thematically the youngest.

As with historical linguistics, it is important to construct diffusional models or family trees for these stories, based on the available information, making the fewest possible assumptions. The simplest and perhaps most rugged approach in looking for a homeland is to look for the region with the deepest and greatest diversity of story-types. Of the three regional borders of the Indian Ocean, Africa clearly has the least diversity, Australasia and in particular Indo-China, has the most diversity; and the Arabian Gulf region is intermediate. Not only does this strongly suggest an east-west Neolithic expansion, but information in the stories themselves allows us to construct a family tree.

Two essential factors in any models are a logical sequence and a feasible timescale of geographic diffusion. In Sir James Frazer's family of immortality myths, the story of the Moon's resurrection may be seen as thematically and chronologically the oldest layer in the group. There are obvious reasons for this. First there is the internal evidence of the stories themselves. The Moon theme develops progressive complexity with addition of other motifs such as messengers, only to disappear completely as the newer themes develop themselves. Second, the peoples that held the simplest myths, the Aslian tribes in Central Malaya (the Mantra – see above) and the Central Australian Aboriginal tribes, led isolated land-locked lives until recent contact in the last couple of hundred years. It is therefore unlikely that they hold the most recent versions of a mobile and evolving story. In particular, the isolation of the Central Australian Aboriginal tribes may have extended back to the time after the partial land-bridges with Asia were swamped by the rising sea-level. The distribution of the original Moon's immortality myth could have spread out from mainland Southeast Asia down to Australia during the post-glacial dispersals over 7000 years ago.

The distribution of the Moon's immortality myth spreads from Australia, Oceania and Indo-China across the Indian Ocean to Africa. We may further speculate on the original site of the Moon motif. Again the argument would have to be thematic. The messenger motif appears to be an elaboration, as does the cast-skin. If so, then the Bushmen and Hottentot 'Moon versions' would represent later layers than the Australian Aboriginal stories which do not possess either motif. Apart from the three-day death before resurrection implicit in the 'Moon' motif, there are two other distinctive features of the Australian and Aslian myths: the fact that man already had immortality before he lost it; and secondly, the concrete necessity in the stories for ritual physical burial to acquire immortality. The practice of ritual burial goes back to Palaeolithic times. The Australian and Aslian feature of 'immortality before loss' is present only in the most simple unadorned stories of Southeast Asia and the Southwest Pacific and may thus also be regarded as characteristic of the oldest layer of the story.

Although the primacy of the Australasian Moon and tree motifs seemed straightforward, I spent a long time studying the groups of related stories around the Indian Ocean before I saw the obvious logical progression. This was imposed by the fact that each theme went through the same stages of structural story development. Whether we start from the Australian Moon myth or the ritual burial under a tree, or the cast-skin, the subsequent order of development of the stories is clear and consistent.

There are four structural stages of development of the myths that affect the variant motifs in a similar way (I have shown these in Table 12). The deepest layer of the myths have humans already possessing the secret of immortality. This immortality was usually lost by the bad temper or curse of an old man. In some cases, as in the Australian stories the old man was a totemic figure; in others, as in the Caroline Islands, the old man was a spirit. In the Austronesian Aboriginal story from Malaya, he was Death: the 'Grim Reaper' himself. From the sharing of motifs in Australian and Vietnamese myths it seems that at some time in this early stage, the variant that involved burial at the foot of a tree developed from a merging of the Moon myth with tree worship. This was probably also the point at which the cast-skin motif entered the stream as a variant since many versions of the cast-skin story are found throughout Melanesia, where a man (or more usually an old woman) previously had the skill of rejuvenation and then voluntarily gave it up to pacify a querulous child. One Melanesian cast-skin myth from Santa Maria has 'Death' making the decision as in the Moon and tree versions.

The first thing to notice about the distribution of these stage one variants is that they are confined to Southeast Asia and Australasia and exclude Africa and the Ancient Near East. Second, although the origins of the Moon and tree motifs could equally be in Australia or Indo-China, the stage one cast-skin version is confined to Melanesia, with the crucial exception of Sulawesi where we find an identical myth. The western margin of this distribution coincides neatly with that of the so-called Polynesian genetic motif described in Chapters 6 and 7 and would thus fit the postulated first Austronesian dispersal of 8000 years ago.

In the second stage of development, death or a committee of animals or gods denied humans their immortality, before he even received it. Such versions are found in island Melanesia, central Polynesia and the Caroline Islands. From this point on snakes and lizards frequently appear, even in stories lacking the cast-skin motif. While the second stage has spread out east to include central Polynesia and also British Guyana, there are still no representatives in Africa or the Near East. If this spread coincided with the Lapita expansion to Central Polynesia then we might be looking at a date of 3500 years ago for stage two.

At the same time as, or possibly before, the eastward spread of the stage two variants, there were other stories, mostly in Southeast Asia, where humankind missed its chance for immortality from the start. The latter belong to the third stage which involved an opportunity for immortality, usually an open announcement, that was taken advantage of by reptiles and arthropods but missed by humanity. Geographically the nearest of these stage three myths to the Oceanic stage two myths are those in Sulawesi and Borneo. Thematically similar stories now turn up both in the Arabian Gulf and in Africa, the most important of these being the Gilgamesh version, for which we have an estimated date of 4500–4800 years ago.

In the fourth stage, the secret of immortality was sent by a messenger who perverted the message so that humans did not receive it correctly. These single-messenger stories are mainly found in Africa, but the Vietnamese complex of stories linking the cast-skin, the trees of life and death *and* the perverted message indicate that the perverted message may well have originated in the East. The final fifth twist in Africa has a two-messenger race, exemplified by the tortoise and the hare, where the wrong message got to humans first. In Frazer's construct for pre-Genesis, the story is stage four – that of the perverted message with a single 'false messenger', the snake. Adam and Eve's Fall was thus also in this stage. A similar argument would hold for Adapa's lost quest for immortality.

These four stages of story development can be traced for all three immortality mechanisms – the Moon, the cast-skin and the tree of life. The 'message' only becomes the 'mechanism' by default in the Bantu stories as a result of the loss of the Moon motif. In my scheme, we can locate the oldest layers of the immortality myths to the Southwest Pacific in the approximate distribution of the Austronesian and Austro-Asiatic language families. The exclusion of the Polynesians, however, suggests that we are looking at a dispersal of stage one myths *before* that of the Lapita culture 3500 years ago. The African myths would thus be later than most of the Australasian myths since humans never achieve immortality in any of the former. Austro-Asiatic areas of Indo-China and Malaya show not only the 'earlier' versions but also a greater variety of mechanisms in the inclusion of early forms of the perverted message and the trees of life and death. This last point of diversity gives further evidence that the area of origin of these myths was on the eastern side of the Indian Ocean. An analogy may be drawn from historical linguistics. One of the essential ingredients linguists look for in a language homeland is deep diversity. This means not only the number of languages spoken but also the number of major divisions among those language groups. This sort of evidence depends as much on the degree of variation found as on the supposed branch structure of the tree.[28]

If the Moon myth, the cast-skin and perverted message all appeared earlier on the eastern side of the Indian Ocean, several questions have to be addressed. *How and when did the stories get to East Africa and Mesopotamia?* We are very fortunate to have dated, and even autographed, copies of the immortality myths of the Ancient Near East. The Mesopotamian myths of Genesis, Adapa, and the relevant sections of Gilgamesh, however, contain complex amalgams of the three independent mechanisms of immortality in the third or fourth stage of development along with much parochial detail. The only explicit mechanism given even in the oldest recorded Mesopotamian myths is the tree of life or food of life. The mechanisms of the Moon and the cast-skin only appear circumstantially and in modified forms. This all weakens the Mesopotamian claim to hold the originals; instead it serves to underline the overall antiquity of the story-types. Even if the Mesopotamian versions are thematically the most recent and complex of Frazer's family of immortality myths, they are among the oldest of all written stories, stretching back well over 4000 years.

Although the rest of the Australasian 'family' of myths were mostly collected by ethnographers over the last 200 years, they have a structural claim to represent earlier and older nodes and branches. The question of antiquity is more difficult for the African immortality myths, for which there are are no written records to obtain dates. Again, for lack of any other evidence, interpretation has to rely on the structure, content, context and complexity of the relevant stories. Although the African stories are nearly all derived originally from the ancient Moon theme, most of them belong to the fourth and latest structural type, namely the perverted message. The only earlier version appears among the Upotos of Congo and is at the same stage as the nested story in the epic of Gilgamesh. This could place the first diffusion into Africa over 4000 years ago.

Coming back to the start of this chapter, Frazer's argument – that the Fall in Genesis also belongs to the family of immortality myths that he collated from around the Indian Ocean – is particularly convincing when we look at the number of shared motifs. These are the *tree and fruits of life*, with the universally sneaky and *immortal snake* at its foot *perversely* advising Eve, ending up with a *curse* from the creator. The same motifs also apply collectively to the Sumerian myths, with the possible addition of the Moon motif represented by goddess Inanna. The patriarchs and scribes who composed these stories may, however, have been borrowing from the East.

Wisely, Frazer did not tackle the origin of the paradise motif since it does not feature much in his examples of the Fall/immortality myth from Southeast Asia, Oceania or Africa. His suggestion of the twin trees of life and death in a pre-Genesis version of the Fall, however, is well supported by the Vietnamese myth of the Bahnars, and this may be a clue to the origin of the paradise motif in the Garden of Eden.

Paradise

Before we explore the origins of paradise in the Garden of Eden myth, it may help to know what we are looking for. The term paradise has a remarkably elusive meaning both in ancient legends and in our own books of literature and reference. The English word is derived from an Indo-European root meaning a walled park.[29] More important aspects than the wall are who inhabited it and when. In Genesis the garden was made for, and occupied by, the first man and woman and then only for a short time. It was then locked and lost. Elsewhere we find paradise occupied by the spirits of the worthy dead, or gods and other privileged persons. In the former case the meaning overlaps with Hades or the netherworld, depending on the degree of comfort, while in the latter, the concept is closer to Heaven.

Many Austronesian (usually Polynesian) cultures refer to a dual role: their paradise is not only the abode of the spirits of their ancestors but also their original, and now unattainable, homeland in the west.[30] In many legends the distinctions are not clear cut. In most cases the paradise is a circumscribed region that is at the same time beautiful, lush, and well stocked. It is difficult, if not impossible, to get there except by a journey of no return across water. Descriptions of the general greening of the Earth, such as are found in the Priestly account in Genesis and many other creation myths, cannot be counted as paradise.

In the story from Vietnam, recounted above, of the burial of man at the foot of the trees of life and death, the reason for inclusion in Frazer's family of immortality myths is the possession of the motifs of serpent (hence implied cast-skin) and perverted message. A Timorese tale from Southeast Asia preserves the duality of the secrets of life and death, but this time the agent of immortality is water: a prince found two wells, one shouted life while the other groaned death. He filled a bottle from each and became a famous doctor.[31] We find the eternal water and tree motifs again out in the Pacific, but this time they are clearly associated with paradise.

Although a concept of paradise is not a feature of Frazer's immortality myths from Southeast Asia, it reappears again out in the Pacific in various guises which include the tree of life and waters of life. Several peoples from eastern Polynesia refer to trees of paradise in their creation myths. In Hawai'i the first couple, Kumu-Honua, were not allowed to eat of a certain fruit.[32] Haumea was the Hawai'ian Mother

Goddess (from whom Honua may be derived). She also attended women at childbirth, although she was at the same time a goddess of death. She had an

> orchard full of magical trees, some of which she gave to her children on earth. Whenever the owner needed something, he could order the tree to produce it for him. Haumea also owned a fish tree. In those times there were no fish in the ocean yet. She gave her fish tree to one of her sons, who was the first fisherman. It had to be placed in the sea, where its fruits became fish. However its owner became greedy, so he shook his fish tree whereupon the fish fruits swam away instead of falling into his hands. So now fish have to be caught by fishing.[33]

A common Polynesian concept of paradise is double-stranded: it is both a lost homeland whilst being a place of departed spirits at the same time. Central Polynesia has a tree of life nested in their story of Polutu/Bolotoo (paradise). This tree is called Pukatala and can supply all one's needs. Its fruits are better than any on Earth and it produces honey or nectar on which the spirits live.[34] Also found in this paradise is Vai-ola, a lake containing the water of life that rejuvenates those who bathe in it or drink it. 'One arrives in Polutu by floating down a narrow river. All the spirits of the dead pass through that gorge into the Nether World, old and young, rich and poor. After bathing, and so regaining their youthful beauty, they live in perfect happiness.'[35] Wai-ora is also the Polynesian goddess of health. Bathing in her pool will heal a sick person.[36] In this role she is exactly equivalent to the Greek goddess Hygieia, who is depicted with healing plants and an immortal serpent wrapped around her.

As we shall see next, the motifs of trees, waters and foods of life are found side by side with snakes and perverted messages in many different Mesopotamian immortality stories; and these stories also feature visits to some paradise or the afterworld.

In the myths of ancient Mesopotamia from over 4000 years ago, we often find the two types of recipes for immortality – the vegetable and aqueous together or singly with other immortality motifs including paradise. On the vegetable side in the Jehovistic account in Genesis, we have the tree of life, while in the Sumerian epic, Gilgamesh dived for the plant of immortality. In 'Enki and Ninhursag: a Sumerian paradise myth', we have Enki eating the eight precious plants, plucked by Isimud, to the fury of Ninhursag. Fresh water was the essential additional ingredient in the agricultural success of Ninhursag's Sumerian paradise.[37] Adapa was also offered the 'bread of eternal life' and the 'water of eternal life' when he visited Heaven.[38] The 'food of life' and the 'water of life' also appear together in the story of the goddess Inanna's resuscitation after her descent to the netherworld in a vain attempt to raise the dead.[39]

Stephanie Dalley in her recent commentaries on translations in *Myths from Mesopotamia*[40] draws parallels between the Gilgamesh quest for immortality and later Greek and Arabian epics. The 'tale of Buluqiya' from the *Arabian Nights* is of pre-Islamic origin and has an episode with a parallel in Gilgamesh's visit to Atrahasis to search for immortality. This is a passage where Buluqiya travels through a subterranean passage and reaches a paradisical kingdom with jewel-encrusted trees. He finds a King, Sakhr, who has obtained immortality by drinking from the 'fountain of life'. As in Atrahasis's conversations with Gilgamesh, Sakhr tells Buluqiya the history of the world. The 'fountain of life' is, unfortunately, guarded by Al-Khidr (thought to be the Arab equivalent of Atrahasis), so Buluqiya is sent home empty handed.[41] The last tablet (XII) of the Gilgamesh epic describes a fatal visit by Enkidu, close friend of Gilgamesh, to the underworld. The passage shows similarities not only with the Adapa story but also with Odysseus' descent to Hades and an episode in the 'tale of Buluqiya', where Buluqiya loses a bosom friend in a search for Solomon's ring.[42]

Three underlying immortality themes can be detected in these stories. One, as already mentioned in the Adapa story, is the functional agricultural and staple symbolism of bread, food and fruit. The second is the fountain of life, while the third theme is 'visits to the otherworld' which, although in one case is identified as Heaven, is usually a dangerous variety of hell.

The location of paradise has always worried Bible scholars, particularly since the lush forest description given in Genesis fits so poorly with anything we know about the environment of ancient Mesopotamia. Rainfall may have been better 6000–7000 years ago, but nothing fits the picture of paradise as well as tropical jungles such as in Southeast Asia. Both ancient Mesopotamians and Egyptians described their respective sites as far across the water towards the rising Sun, that is in the East.[43]

Greek mythology records several different locations for paradise, one of them in the 'Western Gardens of Ocean'. Here grew a sacred apple tree, the Greek tree of life, with golden apples. Seven maidens called the Hesperides, along with a dragon Ladon, who never slept, guarded the tree. Hercules later killed the dragon. Aphrodite was said to have obtained some of the apples too, thus echoing the Genesis myth.[44]

Other European locations of paradise in the 'western ocean' may have been related. These include the Elysian fields where Greek heroes went. In Hesiod's *Theogony* we find the Isles of the Blessed, ruled by Cronus, which then became part of the underworld in Roman mythology.[45] Such islands in the West reappear in English and in Celtic folklore – the lost island of Avalon is one example.[46] This Western tradition may also have been part of the puzzling mythic reason for placing the lost island of Atlantis outside the Mediterranean, in the legend of the same name. The explosion of the Greek volcanic island of Thera in the Mediterranean about 3500 years ago may well have been a focus for reappearance of this myth type, as some suggest. The motif of lost islands of paradise is, however, much older.

The other aspect of paradise myths that may help locate their origin is context. This mainly means analysis of the other motifs found in the same story complexes to explain how such complexes arose by diffusion and mixing. Although I have used this method with all the creation myths, it is particularly relevant to the Garden of Eden because the paradise motif is only rarely associated with 'clay men' and Fall stories outside Genesis. Both Sir James Frazer and Alexander Heidel in their respective mythological comparisons of Genesis with other folklore avoided discussion of the provenance of the 'Garden' motif, concentrating instead on the creation of humans and the Fall. The reason in each case appeared to be the same: they could find no parallels for the Garden of Eden with credible context outside Genesis.[47] This view is echoed in a qualified way by Sumerian expert Samuel Noah Kramer: 'No Sumerian parallels to the story of the Garden of Eden and the Fall of man have yet been found.' But, as the same author acknowledges, 'There are, however, several paradise motifs [in Sumerian literature] that are significant for comparative purposes...'[48] but in a different context. These have the oldest provenance of any of the paradise stories.

Dilmun – abode of the founder gods of Sumer

In the last chapter I briefly mentioned the Sumerian myth of Enki and Ninhursag in connection with the rib story. This ancient story has other firmer connections with the Garden of Eden and Fall motifs. To introduce the characters: Enki (Ea in Akkadian) was the god of sweet water and lived in the Apsu (domain of fresh water). He was also the helper of mankind who sent the seven sages to teach man the arts and skills of civilisation. Ninhursag, also known as Ninmah, Nintu, Mami, Aruru and other names, was the supreme creatrix and womb goddess, and was also mentioned in Chapter 13 as one of the Babylonian deities who modelled man.

The story of Enki and Ninhursag concerns *Dilmun* which: 'is a land that is "pure", "clean" and "bright", a "land of the living". [Dilmun] knows neither sickness nor death,' but lacks fresh water. Enki has this supplied from the earth and:

> Dilmun is thus transformed into a divine garden, green with fruit-laden fields and meadows. In this paradise of the gods, eight plants are made to sprout by Ninhursag, the great mother-goddess of the Sumerians ... But probably because Enki wanted to taste them, his messenger, the two-faced god Isimud, plucks these precious plants one by one and gives them to his master, who proceeds to eat them each in turn. Whereupon the angered Ninhursag pronounces the curse of death upon him.[49]

Thus is immortality lost.

In another Enki/Ninhursag myth, man is made from clay. These stories link a paradise, albeit of the gods, with the mist on the earth (Genesis 2:6), the clay-man myth, the rib, the forbidden fruit, a snake substitute, the Fall and loss of immortality and other motifs. The similarities with the Jehovistic account are too many to avoid the conclusion that the two have the same origin. Yet this is the only paradise myth outside the Judaic tradition that has such a complement of motifs, thus suggesting a close relationship at the time of composition. Samuel Kramer suggests that this Sumerian story was the model for the biblical account.[50] The significant thematic differences are the sex switch and the divine nature of the participants. For the latter, it is possible that, as with other ancestor myths, the earliest founders of the culture adopted or were given divine roles. If Enki and his seven sages really were migrant civilisers from a lush homeland, it becomes even more interesting to know the historical locations of the Apsu and Dilmun. Kramer reiterates that both the Sumerian and Mosaic accounts place paradise *in the East*.

Another source for the location of Dilmun is found in the last extant lines of the Sumerian deluge myth, according to which Ziusudra, the Sumerian flood-hero, is given eternal life and transplanted by the great gods An and Enlil, to Dilmun, which is described as 'the place where the sun rises...'[51] By implication Kramer identifies Dilmun as 'the Cedar Land' east of Elam where Utu the sun god reigns. He speculates, reasonably, that this was the same as the land to which Gilgamesh and Enkidu made their dangerous journey in the Gilgamesh epic – they went to visit Ziusudra (or Utnapishtim). One purpose may have been the quest for immortality.[52] Elsewhere in the Gilgamesh epic, Utnapishtim advises Gilgamesh on his departure for home, that he can obtain immortality by diving for a magic plant. Gilgamesh succeeds in obtaining the plant, only to lose it to a snake that steals it while he sleeps. The snake sheds its skin after that, indicating the acquisition of immortality.[53] One curious seafaring detail found in the Gilgamesh epic is that towards the end of his sea voyage to visit Utnapishtim, Gilgamesh has to navigate treacherous shallow waters by making multiple soundings with poles.[54] Such a description could apply to any estuary or flat continental shelf such as could be found in Bahrain, the mouth of the Indus or, for that matter, the Strait of Malacca.

Much has been written about Dilmun and its supposed geographical origin. One tantalising set of clues relates to how the concept of Dilmun changes with time. In the earliest Mesopotamian documents we read of a fabulous home of the founder Sumerian gods in the east. This place of dreams changes to a powerful and real trading partner in Babylonian times. In Semitic times, no longer was it seen as an unattainable paradise but it appeared regularly on humdrum manifests and bills of lading as a source of exotic trade. Goods coming from Dilmun included gold, copper, bronze, lapis lazuli, wood, ivory inlay, jewellery and onions! Unfortunately these documents still do not locate Dilmun, which is often mentioned with two other great trading partners, Magan and Meluhha, which are also not clearly identified.

The most popular hypothetical location for Dilmun is Bahrain. This view, proposed by Danish archaeologists, is supported by the rich subterranean aquifers that supply fresh water on the island, thus offering a real counterpart to the Apsu.[55] Samuel Kramer, however, rejects this view mainly on the basis that Bahrain is due south of Sumer, not east. One might add that Bahrain was rather too near Sumer to fit the epic sea voyages that the heroes were supposed to have made to Dilmun. Kramer is more in favour of somewhere further east, such as the Harappan civilisation in India.[56] Curiously, some of the archaeological finds in Bahrain of the period do show more cultural affinities with the Harappan civilisation than with the Sumerians.

With so many linkages it is reasonable to suppose that the Mosaic Eden is genetically related to Dilmun. It is often assumed that the biblical Garden of Eden story is descended from the Sumerian myths either through the patriarch Abraham, whose family is originally supposed to have lived in Ur, or from the time of the exile in Babylon. There are other possible routes – for instance, via the Assyrians. Alexander Heidel, although acknowledging the relationship between the accounts, argued for cousinship rather than descent.[57] One thing seems clear from the Jehovistic account – Eden, whatever it represented, was identified like Dilmun as being in the East: 'And the Lord God planted a garden eastward in Eden' (Genesis 2:8). Since the account was supposed to have been written in Mesopotamia, East must have meant east of Iraq, not east of Israel. This conclusion seems at odds with the identifiable locations of the four rivers that flow out of Eden, two of which, the Tigris and the Euphrates, define Mesopotamia. The rivers do not feature in any other paradise myth so we have to assume that they were Judaic embellishments, while the direction 'east' has hung over from a former version. When we look for descriptions of paradise in other Eastern traditions there is not much to find anywhere except in Southeast Asia and the Pacific.

The presence of the Moon/skin/tree cycles of immortality myths in Indo-China and Southeast Asia but not in eastern Polynesia – where a tradition of fountains of youth, paradise, and visits to the underworld prevail – suggests again two separate traditions that have none the less both independently found their way to Mesopotamia. The first of the traditions may be Austro-Asiatic, while the second or paradise motif associates with the Austronesian dispersal. Once again the provenanced dates of the story-types in the Ancient Near East, back in the cuneiform documents of the fifth millennium before our time, can only hint at the true antiquity of the first East–West contact.

Although the dominant mechanism in Southeast Asian immortality stories is the cast-skin, the tree of life comes into its own in another tree-based ritual tradition that is undoubtedly Austronesian. This is the bird, the snake and the tree-of-life triad, which we shall look at in the next chapter.

15
THE DYING AND RISING TREE GOD

In Genesis, the tree of life waited quietly in the background as a stage prop to remind Jehovah that He should banish Adam's family from Eden before they ate of it and became immortal. After the Fall, the tree was forgotten, its fruits apparently uneaten. Maybe He had forgotten that this remarkable tree had more skills of self-generation than dreamt of by our biologists. From parthenogenesis and budding like a yeast to self-insemination, this tree, usually female, could do it all. Species was no barrier; a hawk could have human children in her branches, and could even fertilise snakes in her roots. In the oldest Eden, the tree was both goddess and creatrix of humankind.

The three Southeast Asian themes of the *waxing and waning Moon, the tree of life* and the *cast-skin* all provided parallel mechanisms for the ancient family of immortality myths that spread out radially to the Indo-Pacific regions in Neolithic times. All these motifs had their own independent origins and history in Southeast Asia. Probably starting from the Neolithic, well over 5000 years ago, they have each given rise to their own families of myths, which recombine in a variety of well-known more complex story-types that reappear in Western folklore as well. The connection of the Moon with seasons and fertility in Eurasia was explored in Chapter 12. The Moon reappears along with her three-day resurrection motif, however, in many tree-related stories of the Ancient Near East and the Mediterranean. The tree-of-life theme manifests itself mainly in three related complex story-types both in the East and West. The oldest of these is the 'creative tree', which I introduced first under totemism in Chapter 13 on the creation of man;

Figure 43. **Development and interactions of the three immortality themes with the Two Brothers story.** The three immortality motifs of Southeast Asia may originally have been independent routes to creation, fertility and resurrection. Their combination and recombination with the Two Warring Brothers story and the motif of the copulation of the sky and Earth, could have given rise to the diverse constellation of such myths found later throughout Eurasia.

Interactions of three Creative/Immortal/Fertility motifs with the Two Brother myth in the Indo-Pacific region

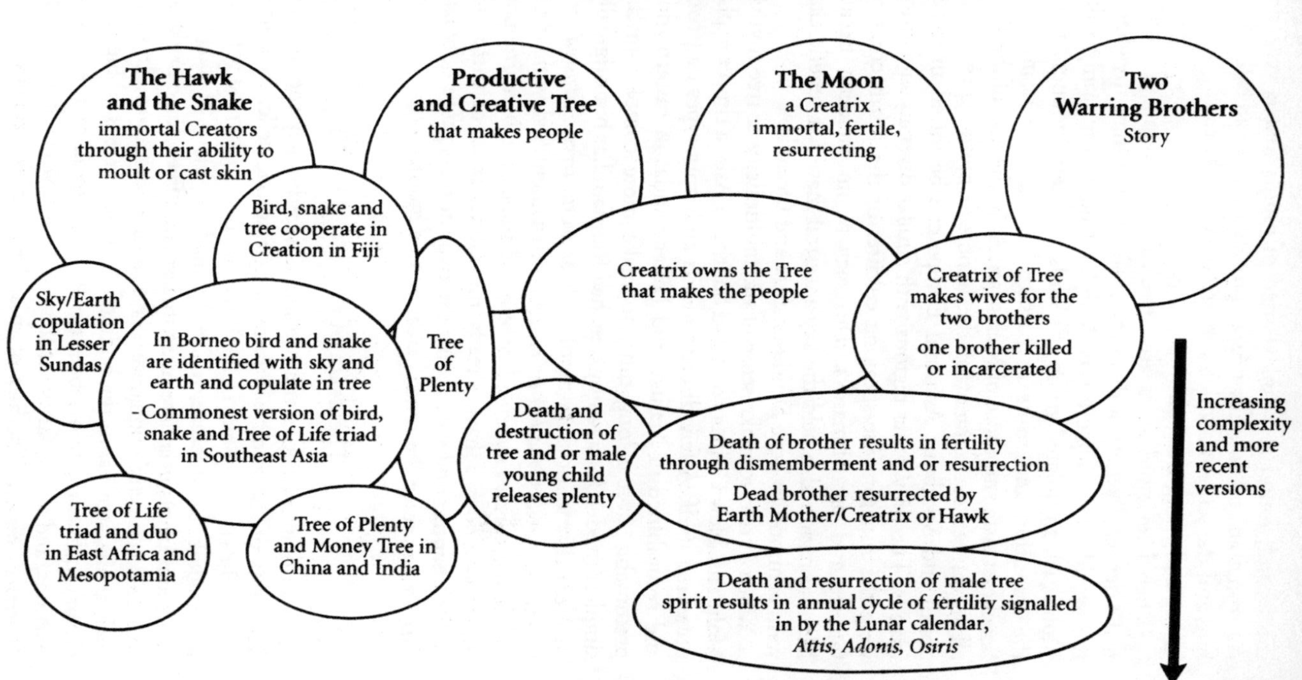

the second, found as a linked triad of motifs that is very clearly of Austronesian and Southeast Asian provenance, we can call 'the tree, the bird and the serpent', which I return to later. The third complex is the 'dying and rising tree spirit'.

When I reviewed all creative-tree stories, I found that one region had a deeper diversity and variety of story-types than anywhere else in the world. This region was Maluku (more commonly called the Moluccas), an isolated group of islands in eastern Indonesia that marks the transition and route of passage between the Asian cultures of Southeast Asia and those of Melanesia. As in the case of the Eve genes, all stages of development of the basic tree-myth types of Western, South and Southeast Asia and Europe can be found in these small islands. The only other regions with similar diversity and story-types were the Austronesian-speaking cultures of the north coast of New Guinea and the Bismarcks. This may be no accident, because the Maluku region also held the key ancestral maternal genetic clans that were common to both Southeast Asia and Oceania.[1]

When I tried to make sense of the multiplicity of tree myths in the Moluccas, New Guinea coast and Southeast Asia, a simple explanation presented itself. A few discrete motifs and story-types had combined and recombined in Maluku and Lesser Sundas of eastern Indonesia, presumably over a long time, to make more complex myths. The simplest model, for a family tree, had four familiar but originally independent themes or story motifs. These were: *trees that produce people*; a *creative fertility goddess* or *creatrix* often identified with the Moon, and a story of *two warring brothers*; and finally the *immortal* powers of *snakes and birds*. I have already introduced most of these motifs in earlier chapters and will discuss the two brothers more fully later. But first we can trace the central creative-tree motif.

The death of the tree of plenty

Trees in Southeast Asia and Melanesia were literally the source of life. The trees of the Southeast Asian jungle sprout delicious fruits whose variety the stay-at-homes in the West cannot comprehend without going to Bangkok, for instance, to see the markets. Many of today's tropical fruits and plants originate in Southeast Asia. Even some of their names such as 'lemon' and 'cinnamon' have Austronesian roots.[2] In some cases, such as the sago palm, the body of the whole tree is edible whereas in others, such as the taro tuber, it is the root. In all such vegetable food, Asia was, and still is, far richer than Melanesia whose flora belong to the Australian region. The idea of these new potent trees is dramatised in stories of the 'Tree of Plenty' along the north coast of New Guinea: the Garus people of the Madang Province in New Guinea have one such story of a mythical Banag tree which had all kinds of fruits and roots hanging from it 'like a supermarket'. At first the villagers viewed the fruits as only good for pigs. Later their children experimented and found the fruits good to eat. The parents decided to cut the tree down to get the fruits. Later, by the agency of the wood chips, the individual types of fruits were spread to the rest of the country.[3] In these tales, the cutting down and destruction of the sacred tree often acts as a trigger, or is necessary to the general distribution of its product.

Sago is an important staple foodstuff of the north coast of New Guinea. The sago palm fits the bill as a tree that needs destroying to be eaten. It has to be cut down and split first before the starch in the pith can be harvested by macerating and sluicing the hollowed trunk in running water. We find the inquisitive and interfering child, as well as a recurrent reference to a generative snake, in stories about sago.

The fecund combination of the snake motif with the tree of life in this Oceanic story from Madang on the north coast of New Guinea contrasts with the snake's negative role in the Southeast Asian immortality stories of the last chapter: women of Giri village used to tap Sago from the living tree, like latex from a rubber tree, until a child spotted her granny at this activity and asked questions. The child then hid and watched the sago flowing. Thinking it was a snake, the child shot at the tree with a bow and arrow, and the flow stopped. Ever since then, villagers have had to cut down the sago tree to get at the starch in the pith.[4]

The concept that the tree has to be destroyed before food results often transfers itself to the death of the interfering child in these stories along the northeast coast of New Guinea. In a related group of myths, a child or sibling has to be killed before new staples and foodstuffs such as coconuts and root crops can be generally distributed. In some of these stories an itinerant woman, who materialised from a floating log, distributed both bananas and root crops, which fell from her skin, fingers and hair. In one version her own child was killed by her husband out of sexual frustration, and, as in many fertility stories, she brought the child to life again by magic and ritual bathing. The fertility goddess later migrated further west.[5] These tales, which are close to the most basic form of tree worship, already hold the earliest introduction of the dying and rising tree-spirit motif, to which I will return. The fact that the woman herself grew out of a log and then produced food, also shows the blurred boundary between potent tree and female creatrix that developed further in other stories.

People from trees

From wonder and reverence for strange new trees that produced food for the tribe, only a small step took them to the belief in the creative tree that made the tribe. The Moluccas region is the centre of diversity for this motif today. The most basic form of this origin myth is totemic; in other words, certain Maluku tribes believe they originally descended from trees.[6] Possibly as a result of the logical connection between the discovery of a new dietary source and population growth, the ancestral trees were often both fruit-bearing and literally 'people-bearing'. The earliest provenanced record of such a concept in the world appears in impressions of cylinder seals excavated in Mesopotamia (see illustration 17).[7] These beautifully sculpted seal stamps reveal much religious imagery from the ancient Sumerian period of the fifth and sixth millennium before our time; along with other themes, we can see the creative tree. One seal actually shows a fruit-bearing tree bent over and a man emerging from the roots.

Three kinds of domestic tree appear repeatedly in creation myths of Southeast Asia and Melanesia – the banana, the coconut and the bamboo. Marco Polo in his travels in India remarked upon the use of the name 'Adam's apple' for the banana. Originating in the Indo-Malayan region, or, as some think, in New Guinea where the greatest variety of wild types exist, the two main domestic varieties of banana were also named *Pomum sapientum* and *Pomum paradisiacum* (knowledge and paradise apples) by the Swedish naturalist Carl von Linné. Incidentally, the banana has as much right to a role in the Garden of Eden as the apple or any other fruit for that matter, because, contrary to popular supposition, the fruit on the tree of knowledge was not specified in the Bible.

In a New Guinean variant, we find another tree that produces people. In this case it is bamboo. Together with competing siblings, and the fertile sago snake, it appears in a melancholy vegetation myth from Kambot village in the Sepik province. Kambot is hundreds of miles to the west of Madang (see Figure 16), near the north coast of New Guinea.

When I first worked in New Guinea as a government paediatrician, I visited this up-river village several times by canoe when on patrol. I met several of the master carvers who had resonant missionary names such as Sigmund and Zacharias. They were famous for making the 'story boards', relief friezes (illustration 16) which held and illustrated their myths. This particular story may refer back to the original visitors from Southeast Asia in the west who intermarried with local Papuan speakers: a visiting man, Wain, lost his wife, as a result of his brother

Mopul, and also his son at sea, and his boat sank under him. He then struck out for shore. While swimming he saw two girls on the bank fishing for eels. Their names were Sisili and Yiripi. He managed to land without being noticed, and hid himself in a length of bamboo which he caused to fall in front of the girls. The girls picked up the bamboo to use as spear-head material. It was rather heavy and they began to realise it was unusual when they left it behind and it rolled towards them. Back at their hut the bamboo behaved strangely, throwing betel-nut at them (a traditional sexual advance). Finally the bamboo changed back to a man. The girls were charmed by his appearance and argued over him, the older claiming priority.

At that time the people used to eat clay, but Wain told them to get their pots and receptacles, made magic and drew prepared sago from the surrounding bush. It came as a long white snake and filled their containers. Everyone had enough to eat. When the sago was finished Wain told the girls to go into the bush and call for the sago snake. Not heeding his instructions they kept silent in the bush, and one of the girls saw what she thought was a snake. She struck at it. Unfortunately it was the sago snake which retreated back to its tree. Wain was cross with them, and from then on sago had to be prepared in the same laborious way it is today by cutting and sluicing.[8]

The motif of people emerging from fruits or trees is not confined to Melanesia and Maluku in Southeast Asia. In Nias off the west coast of Sumatra it is said that the wind god Sihai gave rise to the tree god whose only two fruits bore the first man and woman. These were then animated by the wind. People also emerged from trees in a story from Tanimbar, an island in the Lesser Sundas just south of Maluku.[9]

Mother Tree

The next stage in story development was to give the creative tree a sex and a sense of direction. In the simpler origin stories, the tree itself thus became the female creatrix. A typical creative-tree story of this type comes from Ceram in the Moluccas. Here, the the Alfurians believe that the world was first inhabited by women. The original creatrix was a female banana tree named Patinaya Nei or 'Queen Mother', who produced people from her bananas.[10] The common identity of the fertility goddess or creator with the Moon in some of these stories indicates that this development resulted from the Moon and creative-tree motifs merging early on. It is tempting to draw a parallel between the Alfurian fertility goddess and the statue of Artemis at Ephesus, which is garlanded around the midrif with rows of bulbous fruit-like objects the size of mangoes (see illustration 18). Archaeologists now suggest, however, that these baubles represented bulls' testicles from another related fertility rite.[11]

From a tree that was itself the creative goddess, it was a small side-step to a separate anthropomorphic creatrix who owned the creative tree. Examples of this kind also come from Melanesia. A typical story from the north coast of New Guinea tells of a fertility goddess who rewarded an obliging lad by creating a wife for him from her coconut tree. This tale comes from the flying-fox clan of Amber village in the Ramu River valley. At first, Amber village had no women. One day an Amber man strolled into the plains of the Ramu River and met an old woman who lived by herself. She asked for a favour and then offered him a coconut from her tree, with instructions not to drop it. He took it away and, while he was bathing, the coconut turned into a beautiful, splendidly ornamented young woman who was determined to marry him. He was soon persuaded and took her back home at night. After a certain amount of concealment back at the men's village of Amber, the secret was out and all the other young single men went to visit the old woman for coconuts. These men were pleased to be able to share in their brother's success, one even getting two wives. The traditional narrator of this story explained at the end that the coconuts were really the children of the old woman.[12]

Bananas give more direct 'service' as the fruit of life in a curious tale of a creator goddess from the island of Nehan off Papua New Guinea. Here the Great Mother Creator Timbehes became the mother of all things by impregnating herself with a banana. Several key new motifs now appear in this story. The origin of coconut trees resulted from the *death* of her second *son*; a *bird* motif appears in the name of his *sister*, and *incest* is specified: Mother Timbehes lived in Hohou, the 'Place of Sleep', and had food but no children. 'One day she took a banana and put it in her vagina. After that she became pregnant and gave birth to a son whom she called Bangar. She liked him, so she used a second banana in the same way. In due course she had a second son, Lean. Then she used a third banana. This time she had a daughter Sisianlik ("Songbird"?).' Timbehes then instructed Bangar and Sisianlik to commit incest and have many children. Thus was the world populated. The story then goes on to describe the origin of the coconut. The second son Lean was burnt to death in a cooking fire and his head became the mother of all coconuts.[13]

We might think that the charged use of the banana as a human fertiliser by Mother Timbehes was not a motif that could appear randomly elsewhere. However the theme also appeared in antiquity in the eastern Mediterranean. This was in a common version of the Phrygian myth of Attis and Kybele, where Attis's mother impregnated herself with a fruit.[14] We shall turn to this shortly.

The two-brothers theme

In Chapter 16 I will explore more fully the origins of the widespread myth motif of the two warring brothers, Cain and Abel. Here I will enlarge on the idea that this theme reflects early Neolithic conflicts between Asians and Melanesians in the contact region of Maluku and north New Guinea. One of the positive results of this interaction may have been the new knowledge and types of roots and food trees brought into Melanesia by the migrants. In any case, the two-brothers theme has combined inextricably with the simple-totemic and female-creatrix tree stories from Maluku, the north coast and islands of New Guinea. The result is a saga of incest, fratricide, rebirth and fertility that spread in various forms halfway across the globe.

The female creatrix story-type, from Ceram island in the Moluccas, introduces sibling rivalry and fratricide in a story of two young men, Maapita and Masora, of opposite temperament. An old woman told them that they could pick their brides from the fruits of her langsap tree if they cleaned her skin of huge lice.[15] The obliging youth Maapita got a pretty girl for his kind behaviour, while the lazy impatient Masora received a hag for his rudeness. Like the biblical Cain, the jealous Masora then killed his brother Maapita. Luckily for Maapita, the old woman was in reality the lizard goddess Kuwe and, like Isis in Egypt, she restored life to Maapita by magic rites and ritual washing. This creation story from the Moluccas, which results from a merging of the *two warring brothers* myth with the *creatrix and tree* story, also produced two important story-types that spread West in antiquity. One of these is the kind/unkind sibling motif,[16] the other is that of the dying and rising tree spirit who, murdered by his brother, was then magically resurrected by his mother. Before exploring the widespread distribution of both of these archetypes in the West, I shall discuss the development and distribution of their local variants in Southeast Asia, the Moluccas, Northern New Guinea and the Bismarck Archipelago.

The motifs of creative and regenerative trees and fruits, the Moon, fertility creatrix, sibling rivalry, the dying brother, the sago snake and the bird creator all appear in various combinations and recombinations in the same region. For instance, the two siblings of different temperament are found in Sulawesi as creators climbing up a coconut tree. One of them is identified, through his name, with the Moon. We can still find this story among the Minahassa of Sulawesi, where the dominant brother Wailan (Moon) Wangko climbed a coconut tree and from this vantage instructed his suspicious brother Wangi (Sky) how to make and animate clay models. The models were later called Adam and Ewa.[17]

The motif of the young brother or other male killed in or near a tree for the purpose of distributing fertility also appears in the Phrygian myth of Attis. The event occurred both in myth and grisly ritual reality in the peat bogs of northern Europe and in the Philippines with gibbeting as the favoured method (see below). This theme reappears with chilling detail, the gibbet included, in a variant of the warring-brothers epic of Kulabob and Manup on the north coast of New Guinea.[18] In this version the two warring brothers had a third and younger brother who had received more skills and magic from their father (the first man) than they had. During a lull before their own big fight, the two of them, jealous of the youngest, lured him into the jungle, killed him and hung him up on a tree. To hide this fact they told their father, who was asking after him, that he had been eaten by a dog and showed him a bloodstained leaf. When the boy's body had hung for a while and was already stinking, they dismembered it and divided the bones and body parts between the leaders of the surrounding villages. These actions brought the magic and power of growing crops and producing rain and wind into general distribution in the region.

Lemakot in New Ireland has a tradition of the origin of coconuts embedded in a long cycle about two devoted brothers who were shark-catchers. The motifs include two brothers who are different, the sacrifice of one brother by the other, and the new staple coconut tree growing from the dead boy's head, as in the Mother Timbehes myth from the New Guinea island of Nehan further west. Finally there are the two motifs of a sea monster and birds in the tree: the younger of the two brothers, Ringantinsen, had stolen the rope of a man-eating sea monster who pursued the two of them in their small canoe and ate all their fish. Tougouie, the monster, demanded the sacrifice of one of them for him to eat. Between them the brothers decided that Ringantinsen would submit to be killed by his older brother Natelimon who would then feed him to the monster. All that remained of Ringantinsen was his head which Natelimon buried by the shore. After a few years the buried head grew into the first coconut tree, but what a tree! It grew into the Heavens past the clouds, the Sun and the Moon. Natelimon, previously the reluctant fratricide, now adopted a Jack-and-the-beanstalk role and climbed the coconut tree past the clouds, beyond the sight of Earth, to find the coconuts at the top. He picked them all and threw them down through a hole in the clouds. Where they landed more trees grew. Later, like Jack, Natelimon killed the monster in the land at the top of the coconut.[19]

In another version of this story, we see the introduction of two other characteristic motifs of the tree-of-life myths, dismemberment and immortal birds. In this tale, Ringantinsen and Natelimon were twins who originally came out of eggs. A sorcerer killed Ringantinsen with a spear, cut him up, and tried to feed his liver to Natelimon. Rather like Isis and her murdered brother Osiris (see below), Natelimon found the pieces of his brother Ringantinsen, and put him back together. The two boys then turned into Malip birds and flew up into the coconut tree for safety and have remained there since.

Finally in this group of fertility myths from Melanesia that combine the two brothers, or sisters, with the magic tree, birds and serpents, we come back to a story-type in New Guinea and West Irian that changes fratricide to incarceration and the creatrix to a hawk, but is otherwise similar in structure to the Moluccan story of good Maapita and bad Masora. The motif of young men or young women coming out of segments of bamboo appears in Marindineeze of southwest Papua[20] and again in the coastal region of the Madang province of northeastern New Guinea.[21] Two of these stories are Austronesian, while one is Papuan. In each story there is fierce sibling rivalry over the opposite sex, with the younger brother winning the pretty girl and being incarcerated on a tree. A constant feature is a powerful protector bird. In the north coast versions the bird is a hawk who acts as a saviour or resurrector.

A typical account comes from the island Austronesian village of Arop off the north coast of New Guinea. A group of young bachelors went down to the reef for fishing. They left a length of bamboo on the beach. While they were fishing, girls came out of the bamboo, ate their betel-nuts and prepared food for the men; after that they slipped back into the bamboo. The young men were puzzled, so next time they left a young boy in the bushes to spy on what happened while they were fishing. The young boy saw the girls coming out of the bamboo, and called his friends. They took the bamboo back to the village and sent the young boy out to the bush to get betel-nut. While he was away they broke open the bamboo and got one girl for each man. When the young boy came back, he realised he had been cheated, but asked for the tip of the bamboo which had been thrown into the bush. He went off to find it and obtained a very pretty young girl from the shoot.

Not satisfied with his own girl, his elder brother wanted to play a trick on him to steal his pretty wife, and led him off into the forest. He told his younger brother to climb a breadfruit tree to get the fruit, while he and the two wives remained at the bottom of the tree. When the young boy was up the tree his elder brother hit the tree at the base and caused a swelling to appear on the trunk, thus effectively marooning his brother on the tree. He then went home with two wives. The boy stayed in the tree for a very long time. He was befriended by an old scabby hawk who told the boy to pluck a feather from his wing and lay it under a leaf. This feather became an egg which hatched to become a hawk that grew up and eventually released the young man.[22]

As I mentioned earlier, two distinct complexes of familiar Western myths arise out of these stories. The most obvious is the good boy/bad boy (or girl) type while the second is Frazer's complex of the dying and rising tree spirit, also known as the Adonis, Attis, Osiris cycle. The sibling rivalry and tree-prison motif followed by a hawk saviour is very close, as we shall shortly see, to the Osirian passion cycle of Isis, her lover Osiris and jealous brother Seth.

Mother Holle

One of the best-known Western accounts of the good/bad or kind/unkind story-type is Grimm's version of Mother Holle. Mother Holle is a Germanic earth fertility goddess who is sometimes equated with her Greek counterpart Persephone. In this story she lives in the underworld and is, by implication, the owner of the talking apple tree and talking staff of life: A stepdaughter lost a spindle down a well. Her stepmother threw her out of the house telling her not to come back until she had found it. In despair she cast herself into the well and fell into an underworld. On arrival in this magic country she was first asked by some cakes to take them out of an oven to stop them burning, and then by some ripe apples to shake them from a tree. She did these tasks with good grace; then she was employed as a maid by Mother Holle. A particular task was fluffing up the duvet feathers on Holle's bed, in order to make snow in the upperworld. At the end of her one-year employment the girl was showered with gold which stuck to her skin, and returned to the upperworld. Her stepsister wanted the gold too and attempted to follow the same path. However she was so bad tempered in her tasks that she ended up showered with pitch, which stuck hard to her skin.

A Balinese folktale links the Germanic Mother Holle story firmly into Southeast Asia. Like Mother Holle, this story has lost much of the explicit creation motif, but has retained the talking vegetables and the reference to skin. Both of the named edible bulbs, onion and garlic, originated in Southeast Asia. One of the sisters, in this case the bad one, was killed through skin damage. Mother Holle's role is split in this story between a kind grandmother and a magic bird in the forest. This tale, for which I am indebted to Dr Adrian Clynes, a linguist specialising in Balinese, is called the story of the Yellow Crukcuk Bird:

> There were two sisters, the older named Onion and the younger Garlic. The younger one Garlic was bad and spoiled by her parents. She was also lazy and vindictive to her older sister. The older sister Onion was good, hard working, obedient and did her best although treated harshly and cruelly by her parents and younger sister. One day the mother asked the girls to prepare some rice (dry it in the sun, thresh it, winnow out stones etc., pound it, and cook it) while she was out at the market. Onion did all the work; Garlic repeatedly said she would help 'later', but never did. Back from the market, the mother was tricked by Garlic, who said that she had done all the work, and that Onion had refused to help. The mother beat Onion, and told her to go away and never return. Devastated, Onion wandered off into the forest asking the people she met to kill her. Eventually she met the yellow Crukcuk bird. Onion asked the bird to peck her, which the bird did – and gold jewellery appeared wherever she was pecked. At night she went to her grandmother's. Garlic later visited her grandmother too and saw Onion's jewellery. She asked and Onion told her how she got it; however Onion refused when Garlic asked for a piece. Garlic went home, asked her mother to beat her and then went off weeping to the forest. She asked the bird to peck her – each time it did, scorpions, centipedes, wasps and snakes appeared on her. She then went home apparently not realising what had happened to her, and was driven off by her mother. Garlic was then bitten to death! – Moral of story: 'That is what happens to people who like slandering others.'[23]

With a few local modifications this cautionary tale from the Indian Ocean is closer to the Germanic tale of Mother Holle than to the neighbouring tree-based creation myths from Ceram that I have just mentioned. But Maluku also abounds with such stories, some leaning towards the good stepsister/bad stepsister type while others sound closer to Cinderella. In Halmahera, near the western tip of New Guinea, Cinderella is 'Damura', and the fairy godmother's role is taken by a mother crocodile.[24] The first part of the story follows the Mother

Holle type while the end is typical Cinderella. The point is not so much that the kind/unkind motif is widespread – Stith Thompson, the famous American folklorist, was well aware of that[25] – but that a logical Southeast Asian origin can be seen for the inclusion of the fertility goddess with the two siblings. The strange and symbolic Mother Holle story makes more sense if the original myth had a female tree-based creatrix combined with the motif of the two siblings.[26]

The Germanic analogy of combining fertility goddess Holle, and the kind/unkind motif with skin damage is found in a side story about the Egyptian fertility goddess Isis. Here the lice/scorpion/skin motif of the Southeast Asian stories is found in association with Isis who goes visiting, accompanied by seven scorpions that bite the son of an ungracious host. Isis relents her hard line and comes to the rescue by resuscitating the dying boy.[27]

The Mother Holle story-type is also echoed east of the Moluccas in Papua New Guinea in association with a creative tree-of-life motif. The coconut story I sketched above from Amber village in north New Guinea echoes the Mother Holle story in that the fertility goddess rewarded the obliging lad by creating a wife for him from her tree. In general, the kind/unkind story-type has survived in the West only in the minor form of Märchen or fairy stories; the 'dying and rising tree god' complex had greater impact on the history of Europe and the Middle East than any other story-type, as we shall see next.

Adonis, Attis and Osiris

Some time since the Ice Age, the Maluku and Melanesian amalgam of the Moon creatrix, the man-making tree, the warring brothers, the snake and the hawk produced a complex, symbolic and idiosyncratic story: 'the dying and rising tree god'. It would be difficult to imagine the inventiveness of even the human mind coming up with this same story twice. Yet there was another family of tree-related myths in the West with just the same structure. These had already been recognised as a group by ancient Greek writers, but they were made famous again by ethnologist Sir James Frazer at the start of the twentieth century. Frazer devoted much of his classic *The Golden Bough* and also a three-volume book *Adonis Attis Osiris* to the widespread family of fertility cults, which, he argued, had originally derived from tree worship. If we accept Frazer's additional suggestion that the Christian Passion of Jesus, Mary, the Crucifixion and three-day Resurrection belongs to the same family, then this story complex has claims to be the most important religious theme of all time. Although many myths and cults throughout the Near East and the Orient fitted into the family, Frazer hung much of his discussion around three archetypes from the Mediterranean. These are named after their respective male victims and female fertility creatrices, Adonis and Aphrodite, Attis and Cybele, and Osiris and Isis. Frazer's insight lay, not so much in highlighting their diffusional links with each other, which had been known since Herodotus' time, but in tracing their origins back to tree worship. Vestigial evidence of this tree root remained in the oldest Sumerian and Egyptian records from well over 4000 years ago.

Adonis and Attis, of the Greek and Phrygian cultures of the eastern Mediterranean respectively, were clearly descended from their much older Sumerian ancestor in Mesopotamia. The Passion of Osiris and his mother/sister/lover Isis also had great antiquity. They were recorded in the earliest Egyptian Pyramid texts 4150–4650 years ago. However, although they shared many motifs with their Middle Eastern cousins, their story itself was rather different and closer to the Moluccan archetype. This suggests a direct and separate fertilisation from Southeast Asia. I will therefore start with Osiris and Isis first.

In his thematic encyclopaedia, *Myths of the World*, Michael Jordan recounts that: 'Osiris may have begun his career as a tree spirit or as the spirit of corn. By the time of the eighteenth dynasty at the beginning of the New Kingdom period (*circa* 1567–1085 BC), however, he had become a god almost equalling Re in importance, personifying the Sun as it passes through the darkness of the underworld at night and becoming both god of the dead and perennial victim of nature's curse. Thus he presides paradoxically over fertility and death.'[28] In this latter role he is also connected with Babylonian Tammuz or Sumerian Dumuzi.

Osiris, the first-born son of Nut, married his sister Isis and was continuously threatened by his belligerent and jealous brother Seth, a hunter and a god, among other things, of Chaos. Seth eventually succeeded in incarcerating Osiris in a wooden coffin that was cast into the Nile. The coffin eventually embedded deep in the bole of a tamarisk tree in Lebanon. After Seth slew his brother Osiris, Isis was determined to bear a son who would avenge his father. She searched for the corpse of Osiris and eventually found the coffin embedded in the tamarisk tree. She fled to a sanctuary in the mountains where she performed magic rituals over the dead body of Osiris to bring his seed of life to her womb. Isis took the form of a lesser bird of prey, the kite, to perform the necessary magic to allow her insemination from her dead husband-brother. Isis then hid in the papyrus swamps to give birth to Horus, the hawk god, who killed Seth in the end. In Plutarch's later Hellenised version of the myth, Seth found the coffin and cut the body into fourteen pieces, which he scattered throughout Egypt. Isis then had to collect these dismembered body parts together but lost the penis.[29] According to Plutarch, Osiris's biological father was Thoth, the moon god. This incestuous triangle is repeated in several other related stories not only, as I have shown, in the Pacific, but also in the Ancient Near East.

In this Egyptian passion, Osiris may be discerned alternately as the dying and rising fertility god, who goes to the underworld and is revived seasonally as in the Mesopotamian tradition of Dumuzi, or the Greek versions of Adonis and Aphrodite or Persephone and Hades, or as the triumphant god of a paradisical underworld that all Egyptians aspired to reach. All the key Southeast Asian motifs are there. These include Osiris's origin as a tree spirit, the Moon, the incest with Isis, the two warring brothers and fratricide, dismemberment and incarceration of Osiris by Seth, the resurrection of Osiris by Isis in the form of a hawk and the general fertility resulting from death and resurrection.

As I have said, the Greek Adonis descended from the demi-god Dumuzi who was lover of Inanna, the great Sumerian fertility goddess. We have already seen Inanna in an immortality story, 'Inanna's descent to the underworld'.[30] The original Sumerian version was already a complex story over 4000 years ago, in which both Inanna and her lover were killed and resurrected, as Samuel Kramer recounts: Inanna decided to visit the underworld to confront the forces of evil in the person of her sister Ereshkigal. After a mock coronation, she was stripped naked, killed and hung on a stake on arrival. She was then resurrected after three days through the use of the food and water of life. However, she was still trapped and, in order to leave the underworld, Inanna had to find someone to take her place in the world of the dead. Callously, she volunteered her husband Dumuzi.

Dumuzi, who was thus sacrificed as substitute, pleaded in his last moments for his hands and feet to be changed into the snake equivalents to save him from death.[31] This tragic scene was not always represented as a final death because other stories have Dumuzi spending only half of each year in the underworld.[32] The seasonal resurrection echoes the story of Persephone, daughter of Ceres who, after forcible abduction, married Hades and had to spend half the year underground, again linking with the seasons and fertility. Dumuzi was thus identified with the motif of the dying and rising god.

The god Tammuz and his wife Ishtar were the direct descendants of Dumuzi and Inanna. They were worshipped during the Babylonian period, which followed the Sumerians in Mesopotamia. Their story was written down in the Semitic language Akkadian during the late Bronze Age. Part of the myth included instructions for the annual ritual bathing and annointing of a statue of Dumuzi lying in state in Nineveh.[33] In poetry Tammuz was often symbolised by a tamarisk tree.[34] Every year Tammuz was supposed to die and travel to the underworld. He was followed by his mistress Ishtar, with the resultant loss of Earth's fruitfulness. Both his midsummer death and his annual Easter return to life were celebrated. Tammuz was later known in the eastern Mediterranean by the Semitic term *Adon*, meaning 'Lord'. The Greeks converted 'Adon' to a proper name, 'Adonis' during the first millennium BC.

The Greek version of the Tammuz story is best known: Adonis was a beautiful youth, born of a Myrrh tree according to the Syro-Phoenician version. He was loved by Aphrodite, the goddess of love, who hid him in a chest during infancy. This chest she entrusted to Persephone, Queen of the netherworld. When Persephone peeked in the chest, she was so overcome by his beauty that she refused to give him back to Aphrodite, who had gone to the netherworld to claim him back. Zeus made a ruling that Adonis should have four months with Aphrodite, four with Persephone in the netherworld and four on his own.[35] In another version of the myth, Adonis was gored to death by jealous Ares, Aphrodite's former lover in the form of a wild boar. In this variant, Zeus then interceded to allow Adonis to live, but in compensation he had to spend part of his life below Earth every year.[36]

Persephone, the daughter of Demeter or Ceres, was herself the female subject of a similar myth of annual burial.[37] The female equivalent of the annual rising of the fertility goddess is also found among the Tomori people of central Sulawesi near the Moluccas. Here they annually sing a song to their Moon goddess, Omonga, in the rice barns in order to ensure the next rice harvest. In the hymn, she announces herself as 'queen rising from the *Nether World* to help her people'.[38]

Gardens of Adonis

Several curious features of the ancient ceremonies surrounding the Adonis myth, which Sir James Frazer stressed, were the ritual marriage of Adonis and Aphrodite, the making of the 'gardens of Adonis', religious harlotry in adoration of Aphrodite, and royal incest. The latter appeared to originate in an attempt to perpetuate the male line in a matrilineal society. Such societies are found in the Trobriand Islands of Melanesia and among the Minang Kerbau of Sumatra.

Frazer was only reiterating an ancient view when he linked these

Table 13. The story of the dying and rising tree spirit, his loving earth mother/sister and jealous brother, with their tree and fertility connections. This is an incomplete list; the Western versions of the tradition are given in the first part of the table followed by their, probably older, Eastern counterparts.

Mother Goddess	Dying Person	Other Sibling	Tree/death	Culture
Isis (mother)	Osiris	Set(bro)/Isis(sis)	tamarisk/hawk	Egypt
Inanna	Dumuzi		Impaled on stake	Sumer
Ishtar	Tammuz			Babylon
Astarte/Astar	Adonis		Adonis gardens	Phoenicia
Aphrodite	Adonis		myrrh	Greek
Artemis				Greek
Atagartis				Syria
Ashtoreth	Tammuz			Hebrew
Demeter (Ceres)	Persephone		Cereals	Greek
Kybele	Attis		pine+pomegran.	Phrygia
Freya	Odin/Balder		Oak/Ash	Norse
Mary	Jesus		wooden cross	Hebrew
Semele	Dionysus		Vine	Greece
Mother Timbehes	Lean	Bangar(bro)/Sisi(sis)	Banana/coconut	Papua NG
Crukuk Bird	Onion-sister	Garlic-sister	Tree	Bali
Holle	Good sister	Bad sister	Apple Tree	Germany
Patinaya Nei			Bananas	Moluccas
Kuwe	Maapita	Masora	langsap tree	Moluccas
	Wailan/moon	Wangki/sky	coconut	Sulawesi
Old woman	man	fellow males	coconut	Papua NG
Earth Mother	To Kabinana	To Korvuvu	coconut/banana	New Britain
Dodo/Anut	third brother	Kulabob+Manup	hung on tree	Papua NG

Middle Eastern tree-based Mediterranean dying-god cults together.[39] Others have since agreed with him in adding to Adonis and Aphrodite, Attis and Cybele (Phrygian), Osiris and Isis (Egyptian), Dionysus-Zagreus (Thracian or Cretan), Jesus and Mary (Hebrew) and, moving north, Balder and Frigg (Norse), John Barleycorn (Saxon) and Lemminkainen (Finnish).

Frazer moved further east, however, when he compared the ancient Mediterranean custom of making gardens of Adonis with similar customs in Austro-Asiatic Aboriginal tribes of India. The gardens of Adonis were small earth-filled baskets or pots containing rapidly growing foodstuffs. These pots were tended by women at the sowing season and contained images of Adonis. After eight days they were cast into the sea or some other water.[40]

Frazer inferred that this practice was an imitative magic, invoking Adonis' vegetative powers, and was intended to bring fertility to the fields. He assumed that the casting into water invoked rain. He drew analogies with the ancient European customs of throwing water on a leaf-covered person and of throwing water on the bearer of the last-cut corn or the corn itself.[41] I have seen a leaf-covered magic figure leaping around in secret-society rituals thousands of kilometres to the east in Melanesian New Britain. Called the 'Duk Duk' figure, this representation of a tree spirit always has a conical dunce's hat (see illustration 19). The cone was also the symbol for Artemis, the fertility goddess in the eastern Mediterranean.

Frazer also found a version of Adonis' gardens ritual among Austro-Asiatic-speaking Aboriginals of Bengal which pointed more directly to the origin of the ritual in tree-worship. When the time comes for planting out the bunches of rice seedlings among the Oraons and Mundas of Bengal, a party of young men and women go to the forest and cut down a 'Karma tree' and bring it back to the village with much ritual. In the village, the magic tree is planted in the middle of the dancing ground and danced around with ribbons like a maypole. Pots of rapidly growing barley seedlings are then offered to the tree to ensure good growth of the barley. It is the tree that is subsequently thrown into water and the grove spirits are then held responsible for the crops. Incidentally, the implicit phallicism of both the European and South Asian custom of dancing round the pole becomes more explicit in this version. Frazer argued by analogy that the Mundaic Indian Karma-tree was ancestral to Adonis.[42] If this was indeed the case then he really did find the end of the rainbow of these beliefs coming out of Southeast Asia, since that is where the Mundas originated.

Echoes of the casting of Adonis gardens in water at planting time can be seen in Japan and in the picturesque Thai festival of Loi Krathong; water-throwing comes in the later Thai festival of Songkran. The Mundaic and European custom of bringing in a carefully selected 'wild' tree to be a cult focus in the village, however, reappears thousands of miles further to the east among the megalithic cultures of the Nusa Tenggara in eastern Indonesia. We also find typical examples in Flores and Timor. The Ngadhu pole of the Ngada in the highlands of Flores is a tree trunk that has been carefully selected and gingerly brought back to the village. They regard the trunk as hot and dangerous until it has been cut down to size, covered in carvings and placed in the middle of the village. The phallic symbolism implicit in the maypole and Karma-tree becomes even more explicit in the ngadhu-tree which is placed in juxtaposition to a 'female' womb house called a bhaga.[43] On a visit to the Nusa Tenggara of eastern Indonesia in 1996, I found the ritual, belief and practice still very much alive.

It is sometimes assumed that the fertility cults of Europe were Aryan in origin. But their presence in Egyptian and Sumerian myths as well as from megalithic cultures of the East suggest a much older stratum. To be sure, certain Hindu worshipping areas show examples of the Adonis/Aphrodite cult model, but the gods used in the rituals are pre-Aryan. So, for instance, in Kanagra district, Siva and Parvati are ritually married and buried in a fertility rite, while in Oodeypoor in Rajputana, gardens of Adonis are made in honour of the god and goddess, Isani and Iswara.[44] The names of these both sound rather close to Sumerian Inanna and her Japanese equivalent brother and sister, Izanani and Izanagi.

Attis and Cybele

The beautiful Attis was a male god of vegetation and corn, probably modelled on the Mesopotamian dying-and-rising god Dumuzi, while Cybele was the great Phrygian mother-goddess. In one version of the story, Zeus, in a clumsy attempt at intercourse with Cybele, let his semen drip on the ground. His seed gave rise to the hermaphrodite Agdistis, who was later castrated by a group of drunken revellers including Dionysos. Agdistis' severed penis grew into a tree, either an almond or pomegranate. Nana, the daughter of Sangarios, then took one of the fruits of the tree and placed it in her vagina. As a result, she conceived and gave birth to Attis, who was then fostered out to a nanny goat. In another version Cybele was herself Attis' mother and incestuously fell in love with him. When he was about to marry Midas' daughter, Cybele and Agdistis argued so fiercely about Attis that he castrated himself beneath a pine tree and bled to death. In yet another version, a boar gored Attis to death;[45] the same fate awaited Adonis.

The ancients recognised the parallels between this story and that of Adonis and Aphrodite. Attis died or was killed and resurrected annually; his mother/lover was Cybele the fertility goddess. The association with a tree, this time a pine under which he bled to death, was emphasised in some cults by his effigy being hung up on a pole until the next year. The sacred pine reappears in the epic of Gilgamesh and in eastern Polynesia.[46] Frazer saw the symbolism of the pine as clear evidence of Attis' original role as a tree spirit. He also saw the killing of the tree spirit to ensure vegetative renewal as central to the original ancestral myth.[47]

Humans and animals were sacrificed often by hanging from trees to ensure fertility. That humans, often priests of the fertility cult, were hanged we do not have to rely on Roman hearsay for evidence. There are the grisly but well-preserved remains found in the peat bogs of northern Europe. Ritually hanged victims had carefully plaited collars or neck rings that served not only to send them to the netherworld but also to admit them on arrival there because these rings symbolised the fertility goddess.[48] I have seen elaborately plaited male neck rings in the Megalithic cultures of the Nias islands in Indonesia (see illustrations 20 and 21), although their original function has been forgotten.[49] When I asked the young men what the plaited neck ring was for, they were not sure, suggesting that they were protection against head-hunters. Frazer recounts an ancient Scandinavian custom of dedicating human victims to Odin often by a combination of hanging and stabbing with a spear, and that the Greeks annually hung an effigy of the goddess Artemis.[50] He also quotes an ancient fertility custom in Mindanao Island of the Philippines that exactly parallels the Western practice. Prior to the sowing season, a slave was sacrificed by hanging up in a tree and then dispatched to the netherworld with a spear in the side. The body was then cut in half and the torso left hanging. The repeated analogy with the Crucifixion did not escape Frazer.[51]

Common motifs in fertility myths and cults

Frazer managed to fill thousands of lucid and flowing pages on the ramifications and variations of the family of fertility myths summarised above. I cannot do justice to the erudition required for this task and certainly do not wish to repeat it. What is relevant here is that many of the themes and motifs he identified indicate an origin of the cults from outside of Mesopotamia, the eastern Mediterranean and northern Europe. We have already seen how tree-of-life myths from Southeast Asia and the Southwest Pacific share story themes that could well have been ancestral to the Adonis/Attis/Osiris family.

To Frazer the central elements that united the Old World fertility cults were magical/religious beliefs expressed in ceremony – as passion dramas that were imitative of the seasons, death and rebirth. The key characters and action in these dramas were (1) the fertility goddess; (2) her son or brother, and usually lover, originally a tree spirit; (3) their fruitful union; (4) the sad and violent death of one of the divine partners (usually the male); and (5) his joyful resurrection. The dual aim of the ceremonies was ensuring the generation of children and food.

On reviewing his evidence, we can confidently add certain other distinctive features. The symbolic death of the deity, usually with resurrection, seemed more important in achieving fecundity than the conventional sexual union. Dismemberment and distribution of the corpse was a common event and also a mechanism to spread fertility although there was usually some attempt by the bereaved partner or mother to collect the pieces together. The death or symbolic death, when the lover was sequestered in a chest or tree or the netherworld, usually came about through jealousy. This, at least in the Egyptian case, resulted from sibling rivalry between a good and bad brother (kind/unkind motif). Incest was frequent with the incestuous triangle a special feature of the Osiris story. Another element in the Osiris/Isis passion is Isis' metamorphosis into a bird to perform her resurrection magic and her own child's symbolic identity as a hawk.

Where trees or wood were involved, which was nearly always, there was usually an event of incarceration or hanging. One of the more unpleasant methods of ritual killing that appears in the Attis myths was flaying of the skin while hung on the tree. The introduction of skin damage is not casual. It is also found in association with Isis who, in one story, goes visiting accompanied by seven scorpions that bite the son of an ungracious host. Isis relents and comes to the rescue by resuscitating the dying boy. A curious reaffirmation of the omnipotent generative power of vegetables in the Attis story is seen when Nana inseminated herself with a pomegranate, which in turn grew from Agdistis' severed penis. As we saw in Melanesia, this was not a unique mythological extravagance.[52] The above motifs and themes are all to be found in the tree stories from Southeast Asia and Oceania.

The use of the kind/unkind sibling motif as a mechanism to dispatch or incarcerate the victim in the Moluccan fertility stories tends to put them in a group with the Seth/Isis/Osiris story-type rather than with the Middle Eastern 'Dumuzi' group that diffused from Sumer. The Egyptian passion also shares several other motifs with Melanesia, such as the tree prison and the hawk saviour, that are not found in the Dumuzi/Tammuz/Adonis/Attis complex. As with comparisons of other early cultural elements of Egypt and Mesopotamia, there is an impression of cousinship. The ideas are similar but the details are not the same; that is, they shared a common ancestor. The Melanesian and Maluku fertility stories may be closer to that same ancestor because they actually describe the original tree spirits that Frazer detected only as remnants in the Mediterranean and Mesopotamian stories. If we accept that the Mesopotamian and Egyptian dying-and-rising god traditions, which are well over 4000 years old, descended from a Southeast Asian amalgam of Moon, tree, immortality and two-brother stories, then we are looking a long way back.

Before we leave the Garden of Eden, it would be fitting to introduce an animal which, although not mentioned in the Genesis version, had an important role in a common eastern Eden. This was the bird that sat on the tree-of-life.

Birds, serpents and the tree of life

In reading Sir James Frazer's list of immortality stories in *The Golden Bough* that linked together two or more themes, I was struck by the version held by the Gallas of East Africa.[53] They tell the story of a crested blue bird on the top of a tree that, prompted by greed, sold the cast-skin message to the snake in return for carrion. Not only are most of the Southeast Asian motifs present in this tale, but the immortality mechanism is, uniquely for Africa, the Austronesian cast-skin trick. Apart from these confirmatory links across the Indian Ocean, another exciting aspect of this story was the choice of the bird as the messenger from Heaven. I found that this triad of creative actors – the bird, the snake and the tree – features in another Southeast Asian belief complex. Although related to the immortality myths, it has its own diffusional history, stretching from Fiji to Scandinavia.

I knew that the image of a bird from the top of the tree consorting with the snake is widespread in the context of the Southeast Asian 'tree, bird, serpent triad'. The triad appears in graphic forms throughout the imagery of non-Islamic peoples of Indonesia: in relief carvings on wood and stone, on shadow-puppet stage props (see illustration 24) in Batik design; in Ikat weaving patterns of Sumatra (see illustration 22);[54] and in the huge baroque murals of the Kenyah and Kayan in Borneo (see illustration 23). Other Bornean tribes such as the Bidayu and Iban also hold the motif,[55] and in the south of the Malay archipelago, you can see the triad embedded in the designs of the famous Ikat cloths of Sumba and in the Ngadhu posts of Flores. The tree of life inaugurates all the performances of the theatre of shadow puppets throughout Malaysia and Indonesia (see illustration 24). There are cosmic representations of the tree further north on the island of Palawan, and as far as the Ifugao in northern Luzon of the Philippines.[56] Even further north in the Austronesian distribution, we find an instance of the motif among the Tsou of Taiwan.[57]

The roles of the three actors in the triad vary according to the region of distribution in Eurasia and Oceania and even within Southeast Asia. For a family tree we need to identify a basic archetype. The simplest tradition is that found in Melanesia and is also represented in the Fijian creation, which I will describe shortly. The Melanesian versions have the advantage of less complexity. In addition, the presence of each participant has a logical origin. The tree of life in several versions was the banana, which reproduces itself vegetatively. The two immortal creative animals, the hawk and the snake, had already been given their roles in the cast-skin myths and have a valid ticket as creators.

Earlier, I explored how the four discrete eastern Indonesian themes of the immortal Moon, potent domestic trees, two warring brothers and the immortal hawk and snake could have combined and recombined to produce the 'dying and rising god' story-type. The last of these themes, contributing the sky-hawk saviour with its gift of immortality, and the sago snake with its promise of high yield, came from Melanesia. This region, we recall, was the homeland of the cast-skin myth. The triad of the creator or protector bird, and a productive snake with the tree of life, may be the original motif. A second look at the Fijian creation, already mentioned in Chapters 11 and 13, introduces us to another tree.

In Fiji, the female hawk and Degei, the male serpent, acted as co-operative creators. The female hawk laid the two eggs in a local species of strangler fig (*Ficus species*).[58] These hatched to become the first human couple. The male serpent, for his part, kept the eggs warm and created the banana tree and taro and yams for the children to eat.[59] Austronesianist and linguist Waruno Mahdi, based in Berlin, has studied in depth the Asian distribution of fig-tree cults, in particular the beringin (wishing tree) or Benjamin tree.[60] He argues that its presence in Fiji indicates an origin way back in the Neolithic period before the split of Oceanic and Western Austronesian linguistic families. One piece of evidence for this is that the earliest reconstructed Austronesian name for the Benjamin tree **nunuk*, meaning *spirit* or *shadow*, is common to both east and west language branches. Austronesian-speaking island Melanesians regard the fig variously as an origin tree, sacred, creative and dangerous. It forms the centrepiece of Megalithic circles in Vanuatu, a practice that repeats in Maluku.[61] The distribution of the fig as a sacred tree in Oceania matches the distribution of Lapita pottery. It does not, however, feature in the tree myths of the north New Guinea coast, which, as I discussed earlier in this chapter, concentrate on sago, bananas, coconuts and bamboo. This suggests that the tradition arrived later in Melanesia with the Lapita culture, that is 3500 years ago, but no earlier. The concept of the triad may, however, have come on an earlier boat, because the actors appear in various combinations in the north New Guinea area, albeit without the fig tree. The tree, the creative snake, the boy and girl, and the bird also appear in a slightly different form on Manus in the Admiralty Islands. As with north New Guinea, the tree was not identified as a fig.[62]

Mahdi gives ample and closely argued linguistic, archaeological and literary evidence that worship of the Benjamin tree may have arisen very early among Austronesian speakers. It may even have started before their earliest megalithic cultures. Nowadays, however, the cult of the sacred Benjamin tree is coincident with, and integral to, Southeast Asian megalithic cultures, where it often sits on a pyramid as a centrepiece of megalithic worship. This practice extends to both Austronesian and up to Austro-Asiatic-speaking cultures in Indo-China. What is apparent is that the Indian worship of the sacred Banyan tree was secondary to the Southeast Asian practice, arriving there with the 'Nagas' only shortly before the Christian era.

The real origins of the Nagas, literally the 'snake people', who appear in different contexts in south India and in Assam, are a mystery. The high genetic frequencies of the variant blood pigment haemoglobin E in Assam Nagas indicates a strong Southeast Asian influence.[63] Mahdi identifies early Naga culture closely with Austronesian influence on India. In contrast, the peepul or bo tree, a fig (*Ficus religiosa*) without the aerial roots of the banyan, was worshipped in India from early times, appearing on clay tablets from the ancient Indus Valley civilisation in Mohenjo-daro.[64]

Waruno Mahdi also links recorded instances of the ritual tree of plenty or the wishing tree, a kind of Christmas tree in the same diffusional process out of Southeast Asia north into China and west into India. There are also examples of the triad motif moving up the

Salween River to the Tibeto-Burman-speaking Shans of northern Burma.[65] At present the oldest dated occurrence of both the tree of plenty and the bird, snake and tree triad lies with a striking bronze sculpture from Szechuan in southwest China. Excavated in the last few years, the bronze hoard of Sanxingdui, one of the great finds of the last twenty years, dates from the twelfth century BC. It had treasures like nothing else in China. These and many others were exhibited at the British Museum in 1997.[66]

The most startling items are the huge bronze masks and figures, which look more like Tiki carvings from Polynesia (see illustration 25).[67] Clearly very different from the contemporary Shang dynasty further north, the origin and ethnicity of this ancient shamanistic culture remain a puzzle. One of the most striking features in the hoard was three bronze trees. When reconstructed, a single tree measured 4 metres. Other fragments of similar trees were found and the form was clearly of symbolic importance. At the base there was a dragon. Fruits hung from lower branches, while exquisitely crafted birds perched on the higher branches. At the very top a strange bird-like creature with claws, wings and an anthropomorphic head was slotted into the apex.[68] Nothing else like this tree has been found anywhere else in China for that early period. Links with the well-known bronze 'money trees' of the late Han period, also in Szechuan and dating from over a thousand years later, are speculative (see illustrations 26 and 27). Here again, the Han trees have an elaborate peacock-like bird at the top. This represents the Sun. The Queen Mother of the West presides over the branches on a dragon and tiger throne, attended by a hare and a 'moon toad', who are offering her foods of immortality. Fantastic creatures guard the base. These trees have numerous humans, coins and creatures on the branches.[69] A snake-and-tree fertility motif also appears on exquisite bronzes from the first millennium BC in the southerly Chinese province of Yunnan.[70]

The presence in Melanesia, Southeast Asia, Burma and China of the tree, bird and serpent triad is clearly more than a coincidence. The dates from Southwest China of over 3100 years ago may not be the oldest example of the motif. As we shall see, this triad has provenanced antiquity in Sumerian myths from the fifth millennium before our time and even has links with Frazer's ancient immortality myths.

The creative functions of the bird and serpent are preserved in island Southeast Asia, particularly in Borneo. But the simple Melanesian concept of the two creative animals tends to diversify with the overlaying of other traditions. The traditions found in Borneo and Sumatra represent the two main variants. Earlier, I mentioned a complex of myths found in southern Borneo with both man and woman being created from trees. Variants of this creative-tree myth include both a bird and a crocodile who assist in the creative process. Some of the earliest collections of these Dyak myths appear in H. Ling Roth's classic monograph on Sarawak and British North Borneo of the last century. Roth remarks: 'Besides this account of the creation of the first man, the Dyaks have several traditions regarding the Deluge, one of which, curiously enough, connects it with the universally diffused story of the dragon, the woman, and the fruit of a tree for which she longed.'[71]

A beautiful version of creation is told by the Ngaju Dyaks of southern Borneo. This poem still holds the creative hawk, the serpent and the banana tree (see illustration 28). But the hawk now represents the sky and the hornbill from Dyak mythology is added. The creation of man and woman and all nature results from the destruction of the tree.[72]

A widespread western Indonesian version of the tree-of-life triad takes the identification of the bird with the sky god and the Sun several stages further. In this development, we see a merger with the tradition found in the Lesser Sundas, where the sky god has to copulate with the female Earth Mother annually to bring fertility. I have already discussed the belief in this sexual duality of the godhead in Chapter 12 with the myths of separation in Flores and Timor. In the merger with the triad, which is best described in western Borneo, the hornbill becomes the male representative of the Sun and the sky god. He then runs down the three-level tree to impregnate the serpent in the underworld at the base of the tree. In turn, the serpent adopts a female receptive role. The typical tree in these stories is the sacred 'Benjamin' fig, which 'bridges' the upper and lower worlds. The aerial roots of the Benjamin, which drop vertically from the branches to penetrate the soil, are symbolic of the sexual union between sky and Earth.[73]

While the thick mature banyan with its forest of aerial roots is usually a place of veneration, it also has sinister connotations. A malign female spirit may inhabit the tree, whose habits include the snatching of newborn children. Her Malay name is Puntianak – hence the name of the western Bornean port Pontianak. She is also found as far afield as Vanuatu in the Pacific, with the name Leplepsepsep. As we shall see, the Sumerians and Semitic peoples knew her well. Melanesian peoples often refer to bamboo clumps as the 'place of death' or the 'place of spirits'.

The Batak of the northern Sumatran highlands have one of the most detailed accounts of the East Asian tree of life. Speaking an older

Austronesian tongue than the Malayic peoples, this sophisticated and ancient Megalithic culture managed, through a combination of isolation and belligerence, to avoid external religious influence until recently. In particular, Hindu and Muslim influences are minimal.[74] We are particularly fortunate that a native Batak, Ph. O. L. Tobing, trained as an anthropologist and wrote his doctoral thesis in 1956 on the structure of traditional Batak religious beliefs.[75] A three-level tree of life straddling the underworld, middleworld and upperworld is central to Batak concepts of creation, the cosmos and an omnipotent trinity of gods. The tree itself is identified as the Southeast Asian strangling fig (*Ficus benjamina*). The symbolic use of the fig as the tree of life is the rule in Southeast Asia although in India *Ficus benghalensis* is sometimes called the 'Tree of Knowledge'.

In the Batak creation, the tree originated in the upperworld. The high god of the upperworld, represented by three birds, sent his messenger down to the middle of the sea to plant the banyan tree in the centre of the eight points of the compass. Initially there was no land in the middleworld, so the high god sent some earth[76] to the middleworld with a runaway bride, who had let herself down the tree on a yarn, to make her dwelling place. This earth was initially swamped by a huge buffalo serpent and it took seven days to make the middleworld solid. Her erstwhile husband, meanwhile, was cut into pieces, put in a bamboo container and thrown down from the upperworld to the middleworld. Here it split open, producing a beautiful young man. He then joined up again with his former wife from the upperworld. The middleworld is ruled by a second manifestation of the trinity, who was responsible for originating the Batak from three fruits or eggs of the tree.

The third manifestation of the trinity – a world serpent coiled up among the roots of the tree – rules the underworld. It is responsible for thunder, lightning, waves, the fertility of the fields, the almanac and holding up the middleworld on its head. These three gods form a three-in-one trinity that is not only symbolised by, but *is* identical with the tree of life.[77] Transfer between these three worlds is possible as in other parts of Indonesia via the tree or a bamboo. Other aspects of the tree of life include the conviction that all living things are derived from it, and the concept that its parts, such as the leaves and branches, represent the lives of men of different rank. We still find this latter belief on the western coastline of the Indian Ocean among the Swahilis.[78] Many of the individual story themes of the Bataks are also found in Iban and Dyak mythology.[79]

The above beliefs can be seen enshrined in the carving and rituals of the Bataks. For instance, the fronts of their boat-shaped houses are covered in fine foliate patterns representing the tree of life, with images of the cosmic serpent below and monsters subdued. The whole tree is summarised in the magic wands, or *tunggal panalua*, with a bird on the top and a subdued serpent below. In the past, this wand contained rendered body fat from a ritually murdered child to capture the spirit. They dance with this staff to pray for rain, fertility of the fields and the gift of children. When making preparations for augury using an 'oracle-cock',[80] the Toba-Batak represent the cosmos as a tree; and when preparing for the '*bius*-celebration', they carve a slaughter pole, '*borotan*', decorated with leaves to resemble a living tree.[81]

The sophistication of the Batak tree of life has obviously come a long way from the Melanesian creator-tree stories. Certain motifs remain, however: the bird and serpent and ritual dismemberment.

The bird/tree/snake triad in the West

The Batak construct of the world tree of life has clear analogies with that of the Norse peoples, who named their mighty tree of life *Yggdrasil.* This huge ash tree spread its branches over Heaven and Earth. Three roots passed down from the tree into three realms – one for the frost giants – one for Aesir and the last the realm of the dead. The realm of Aesir contained the magic springwater of knowledge, while that of the giants held the spring of fate, which also preserved the life of the tree. The tree was continually threatened by its inhabitants. On the top of the tree sat an eagle with a hawk perched on top of it. At the bottom lay a great serpent, which gnawed at the roots. The serpent was at constant war with the eagle, and a squirrel ran up and down the tree carrying messages and insults between the two.[82] This angry intercourse between the immortal bird at the crown and the snake at the base of the tree contrasts with most Southeast Asian versions where there is a more sexual element. There is no way of dating the arrival of the tree-of-life triad motif in northern Europe. The direct thematic links with Southeast Asia suggest a diffusion that somehow bypassed Mesopotamia where dating is easier.

The Chinese bronze finds in Sichuan places the triad in East Asia back at least 3000 years. While this might coincide with the flowering of the various cults in Southeast Asia and the Lapita expansion, the sacred-tree mythological complex in north New Guinea hints at a much older substratum. Hard evidence that the triad had been around at least 4000 years comes from the West, especially Mesopotamia. The mortal conflict between the snake and the eagle in the tree, found in northern Europe, is repeated in one of the oldest written myths from Mesopotamia. This is the story of Etana of Kish, which, although told by a King of Ur more than 4000 years ago, is probably much older.[83] Several versions survive.

As the tale starts, the eagle nesting in the crown of a poplar and a snake lying at its base both had offspring. Although lacking true trust they swore an oath of mutual protection of young. The eagle quickly broke this trust, ate the snake's young and escaped to Heaven. Echoing the Galla myth from East Africa, the snake lured the eagle with carrion and, clipping its wings, threw it in a pit to die. Etana, King of Kish, had been searching for the 'plant of birth' to provide him with a son. On the advice of 'Shamash the warrior', Etana found the crippled eagle and promised to feed it until it could fly and find the plant of birth. At first when the eagle looked for the plant of birth he could not find it, so, instead, he carried Etana to the high god Anu three miles (five kilometres) up in Heaven. The rest of the story is lost here, although Etana was succeeded by his son Balih, (according to the Sumerian King Lists), so presumably he was successful in his quest. This fragment of a story holds an immortality motif with the bird/tree/snake triad, as in the East African version of the Gallas. It has one of the oldest provenanced dates of any Sumerian myth. Cylinder seals of the Akkadian period (2390–2249 BC) that followed show the motif of Etana carried to Heaven on the eagle's back (see illustration 29). The simple motif of man's ascent to Heaven lived on in the Greek myth of Ganymede, the eternally young or Juventas. This was then incorporated into the 'Alexandrian Romance', and Persian stories and Islamic legends.[84] The motif of the 'Eagle and Baby' can even be seen on the signs of British public houses today.

Etana of Kish and the Galla myth are not the only examples of the bird, tree, snake triad in the western Indian Ocean. Other stories exist with ancient provenance. While only the snake and tree motifs appear in the Jehovistic account of the temptation of Eve, the full triad is found elsewhere in Mesopotamia. This is the very ancient story of the Halub or Huluppu tree, part of which is found nested in the 'Gilgamesh, Enkidu and the Nether World' myth.[85] The tree motif is not immediately recognisable as an immortality theme, until we find out that the fragments of the chopped tree had immortal power. The first part of the myth deals with a condensed version of the separation of Heaven and Earth.[86] This is followed by a struggle between Enki, the Sumerian Poseidon, and the netherworld represented by a monstrous dragon, and the abduction of the goddess Ereshkigal (like

Persephone) to the netherworld. The main part of the story then follows:

> Once upon a time, a tree, a huluppu, a tree –
> It had been planted on the bank of the Euphrates …
> The Euphrates carried it off in its waters.
>
> The woman …
> Took the tree in her hand, brought it to Erech:
> 'I shall bring it to pure Inanna's fruitful garden.'
>
> Inanna tended the tree with her hand and placed it by her foot,
> 'When will it be a fruitful throne for me to sit on,' she said,
> 'When will it be a fruitful bed for me to lie on,' she said.
> The tree grew big, its trunk bore no foliage,
> In its roots the snake who knows no charm set up its nest,
> In its crown the Imdugud-bird placed its young,
> In its midst the maid Lilith built her house –
> The always laughing, always rejoicing maid,
> The maid Inanna – how she weeps![87]

In this crowded tree, the notorious Lilith, first wife of Adam, mother of demons, temptress, succubus and snatcher of newborn children, made her first (un-explained) appearance in world literature as a tree spirit. In this baby-snatching role she was identical with Puntianak of Southeast Asia and Leplepsepsep of Vanuatu to the east. Fertility goddess Inanna was not happy with the crowded unfruitful tree in her garden and got Gilgamesh to strike the tree down with his great axe. The snake was also struck down, whilst the bird escaped with its young to the mountains, and Lilith was banished to the desert. Inanna used the wood of the tree to make a bed and throne, and she made two magic implements, the *pukku* and the *mikku* from the crown and roots of the tree for Gilgamesh. Thought to be a drum and sticks, these items were related to Gilgamesh's search for immortality. By some accident he dropped them through into the netherworld. It was during a trip to retrieve them that his best friend Enkidu was snatched by death.[88]

Enigmatic as this early Sumerian myth is, the context places a genetic link with Genesis, with the tree-of-life triad and with the Moon goddess. The destruction and use of the tree and its occupants implies the resolution of a conflict of religious beliefs by cannibalising an older cult. Tree-spirit Lilith shares some of her child-snatching manifestations with a dark side of Mother Holle, and could represent in the Sumerian myth a displaced and vilified mother fertility goddess. Holle's other sinister identity is as a furious witch who snatches the souls of newborn children, although she is also credited with bringing babies. Like Artemis, Holle is also sometimes associated with the Moon/lake motif of bathing in a lake in the manifestation of a beautiful white lady.[89]

The frequent appearance of the great Sumerian love goddess Inanna in these Mesopotamian immortality stories may indicate the Moon motif. Elsewhere we read that Inanna was resurrected after three days and three nights of death in the netherworld.[90] This episode is reminiscent of the Aboriginal belief in the Moon's resurrection from a monthly three-day death motif, but Inanna is not usually seen as personifying the Moon. Identified with Babylonian Ishtar, Phoenician Astarte, North African Dido, biblical Ashtoreth and Greek Artemis and Aphrodite (the morning star), she is often viewed as a mother goddess, overseeing the Earth's fertility and childbirth. Astarte is sometimes represented as a wandering white-horned cow, that is, in the same form as Io, who personified the Moon.[91] Other authorities have specifically rejected such connection with the Moon as erroneus.[92]

In the last two chapters I have described how the obsession of Neolithic people with death, life, resurrection and immortality brought together various freelance actors into the Garden of Eden and other related and exotic stages. These actors included the Moon, cult heroes, powerful birds and serpents. Throughout, the tree of life wearing many different costumes, acted as the main stage prop. In every story complex, the immortality myths, the Adonis/Attis/Osiris group and the bird, the serpent and the tree-of-life triad, a logical origin can be traced for their otherwise bizarre symbolism to the prehistoric clash of cultures between Southeast Asia and Melanesia.

Two actors stand out with more reality from the cardboard backdrop of magical animals and trees. These are the contrasting characters of the two brothers or sisters. In the West they were Osiris and Seth and the two stepsisters who visited Mother Holle; in Bali they were the sisters Onion and Garlic; in Maluku they were Maapita and Masora and the mother of the langsap tree; and in Melanesia we heard of Wain and Mopul, Ringantinsen and Natelimon. In all the examples I have given, the two siblings were woven into fertility stories; the conflict motif, however, was often secondary. In the next chapter we move to myths where the conflict motif becomes the primary plot. The familiar story of Cain and Abel belongs to this latter group. The tree and fertility motifs never quite disappear, however, thus giving the pointer to their common eastern origin. The oldest of these stories holds the clue to that first conflict.

16

CAIN AND ABEL

A man from New Guinea once called me the equivalent of 'son of Cain.' He was neither insulting nor flattering me but stating what he believed was a fact. I did and do not carry any visible mark of Cain's line, but he knew what he was looking for. At the time I thought it was a strange misunderstanding, but as I learnt more about his culture I began to see the truth in his statement. I also think that Western civilisations may have borrowed the allegory of the two fighting brothers from the Far East more than 5000 years ago. It needs some explaining why north coastal New Guineans regard Europeans as long-lost brothers.

In our discussion of the 'Garden of Eden' (Chapters 14 and 15), the tiny islands of Maluku were the epicentre of the immortality myths, the creative tree and its main descendant – the dying and rising god. The added motif that gave the 'dying and rising god' story its tragic flavour was the myth of the two brothers. The genetic and linguistic mix in Maluku gives a much older glimpse of the transition between Asia and Melanesia than the conventional dating of the Austronesian dispersal allows, as I explained in Chapters 6 and 7. If ever there was an early Neolithic clash of expanding cultures and races, the Moluccas and the north coast of New Guinea are the places to look. The Moluccas are a key location whether we stick to the rails of the Polynesian express train or accept much earlier Austronesian dispersals.[1] Anthropologists now begin to wonder whether the story of the two brothers, in all its myriad forms, is really a historiographic remnant of that resounding clash of cultures rather than some deep instinct of sibling rivalry. The co-development of the creative tree-of-life myths with the two-brothers motif into the universal story of the dying and rising god supports the antiquity of the latter. The wide distribution of the two-brothers myth into northern Melanesia, as the dominant story-line in a variety of combinations with the tree motif, again hints at the great diversity and time-depth of these themes. At a conservative estimate these myths antedate Genesis by several thousand years.

Shepherds or farmers?

Most commentators on the Cain and Abel archetype, including Sir James Frazer, miss the point that this was a clash of cultures not personalities:

> And Abel was a keeper of sheep, but Cain was a tiller of the ground.
>
> And in process of time it came to pass, that Cain brought of the fruit of the ground an offering unto the Lord.
>
> And Abel, he also brought of the firstlings of his flock and of the fat thereof. And the Lord had respect unto Abel and to his offering.
>
> But unto Cain and to his offering he had not respect. And Cain was very wroth, and his countenance fell. (Genesis 4:2–5)

The story motif of fratricide held in the story of Cain and Abel is as familiar as any in Genesis:

> And Cain talked with Abel his brother: and it came to pass, when they were in the field, that Cain rose up against Abel his brother, and slew him.
>
> And the Lord said unto Cain, Where is Abel thy brother? And he said, I know not: Am I my brother's keeper? (Genesis 4:8–9)

Although we find the motif in many places outside Genesis, folklorists write more on themes such as the Fall, the flood and the two creations. This lack of interest is surprising since 'Cain and Abel' has more anthropological clues than any of the other ante-diluvian myths in Genesis. Frazer, normally so eloquent, contributes a short essay on the ritual meaning of the mark of Cain:

> And the Lord said unto him, Therefore whosoever slayeth Cain, vengeance shall be taken on him sevenfold. And the Lord set a mark upon Cain, lest any finding him should kill him. (Genesis 4:15)

Frazer does not refer to any of the other motifs in the story.[2] Several other authorities also discuss the origins of Cain's mark or tattoo. Some of these agree with Frazer's argument that Cain was the ancestor of a Nomadic tribe of the Sinai Peninsula, the Kenites. This conclusion, incidentally, does not tally with the description of Cain's descendants as city builders and artisans. It also contradicts the biblical comment that Cain went to live in the 'land of Nod' on the east of Eden after his punishment:

> And Cain said unto the Lord, My punishment is greater than I can bear.
>
> Behold, thou hast driven me out this day from the face of the earth; and from thy face shall I be hid; and I shall be a fugitive and a vagabond in the earth; and it shall come to pass, that every one that findeth me shall slay me...
>
> And Cain went out from the presence of the Lord, and dwelt in the land of Nod, on the East of Eden. (Genesis 4:13–14, 16)

The text in Genesis referred to a time before Abraham moved his family on their western migration from Ur; so Cain's dispersal with his family to the land of Nod should at least be east of Mesopotamia if the literary statement has any basis in reality.

Two other related aspects of the story get attention in reference books. The first is the significance of Abel's blood sacrifice being better than Cain's agricultural produce.[3] The second is the contamination of the Earth's body by Abel's own blood.

> And He said, What hast thou done? the voice of thy brother's blood crieth unto me from the ground.
>
> And now art thou cursed from the earth, which hath opened her mouth to receive thy brother's blood from thy hand;
>
> When thou tillest the ground, it shall not henceforth yield unto thee her strength; a fugitive and a vagabond shalt thou be in the earth. (Genesis 4:10–12)

The spilt-blood theme, incidentally, is a major feature of a version of Cain and Abel still told as local folklore in Syria, and parallels the same detail of the Adonis myth in that region.[4] All these details, although important, seem to miss the significance of the conflict. The fight involved two people who, having different cultures, were clearly anything but blood brothers.

Two different motifs are encapsulated in this well-known story of fratricide. One of these is the symbolic ritual theme of sibling rivalry and death discussed in the fertility myths in Chapter 15. The other motif is that of the ethnic and cultural conflict that occurred because of population expansion and migration towards the end of the Neolithic Revolution. In this chapter, I explore these motifs and also question the evidence behind the assumption that Mesopotamia was the source of these two related themes, for the logical origin of both was east of Mesopotamia. Again, the southwest Pacific is the logical site of origin along with the tree-based fertility myths that echo the Osiris and Isis passion.

Who was the hero, Cain or Abel?

The period from Abel's death to the flood appears to cover the whole Neolithic period, because the last generation before this third cataclysm were already making bronze. A common presumption that Cain and his line were the banished baddies receives a knock when we look at the Genesis words a bit closer. Before dissecting the story motifs, a bit of text analysis is needed because the fractures in Genesis reveal more than just bad sub-editing. Chapters 4 and 5 in Genesis contain two different versions of Adam's life story and genealogy with a clear break between the chapters.

Genesis 4 carries on from Adam's and Eve's banishment from the Garden of Eden. It tells of Adam's two first sons involved in mortal combat followed by six generations of Cain's descendants. The first five generations include Enoch, Irad, Mehujael, Methuselah and Lamech. Adam and Eve at this point, and a hundred years after Abel's murder, decided to replace their dead son with a third son, Seth. Seth, unlike his Egyptian namesake, was obviously too late to kill his brother, and had a son, Enos. The story then breaks at Genesis 4:26 and we are left in the dark about whether Noah finally descended from Seth or Cain in this version. The final generation in Genesis 4 consists of Lamech's talented children by his two wives. One of these was a nomadic herder; another played the harp and organ, and a third (Tubal-Cain) was skilled in both bronze- and iron-making – yet more cultural contrasts and social development. The scribes tell us that Cain's line, in spite of being condemned to wander, had in contrast done quite well in their dispersal; they had built an ante-diluvian city and moved out of the Neolithic Age.

Genesis 5 is in effect a third creation. It takes place in one day and God names the first couple collectively 'Adam'. We learn that after 130 years they had a son, Seth. There were others, but the scribes do not name them. Seth then had eight generations of descendants up to and including Noah. Some of the names of Seth's descendants echoed Cain's genealogy in Genesis 4. Sequentially, these generations were: Enos, Cainan, Mahalaleed, Jared, Enoch, Methuselah, Lamech and Noah. In the Genesis 5 version, we are left in no doubt that Seth was

Noah's ancestor and neither Cain nor Abel feature in Adam's line. We also found this kind of inconsistency of text between the first two chapters of Genesis. The scribes, when presented with two different oral traditions, put both in with a crude cut-and-paste technique to suit their agenda: they did not reconcile the conflicting text. This may imply some degree of respect for the integrity of the earlier text. We are left in no doubt later, however, that the Hebrews did not want to regard themselves as descended from Cain. This motive may explain why the story in Genesis 4 cuts off at the birth of Seth. The confusion or reversal of identity between roles occurs frequently in other variants of the family of conflict myths. As we shall see, the name of the villain may depend on which ethnic group is telling the story. In other words, Cain may have been a cult hero to the original story-holders of Genesis 4.

There are other Hebrew apocryphal stories. One, for instance, uses incestuous sexual jealousy as the pretext for the fight. It tells that both Cain and Abel had twin sisters and that Adam planned to cross-marry the boys. Cain's sister was the prettier one and so he personally objected to the deal. He killed Abel by stoning and, taking his example from a raven who had just killed its colleague, buried his brother. God cursed the Earth for accepting Abel's body and banished Cain and his sister to the land of Nod.[5] In another story, blind Lamech shot Cain with an arrow. Lamech did this on the request of his son Tubal-Cain, who thought he saw antlers on Cain's head and mistook him for an animal.[6] This last puckish motif is a curious but not unique variant on the 'Mark of Cain' theme. There are other related Semitic myths of conflict.

Are Cain and Abel motifs related to the Adonis/Attis/Osiris type?

The overlap in Maluku and New Guinea between the motifs of the two brothers and the dying and rising god repeats itself in the Near East. In the Canaanite story of Aqhat, a youth of that name was killed for possessing a magic bow by a henchman of Anat, the goddess of hunting. She and her thug had taken bird forms for the ambush, and vultures ate the victim. The result of the murder was that the Earth was contaminated with blood and became infertile. The goddess regretted her act, since the prize bow was lost anyway, and resolved to revive Aqhat. By this time Aqhat's family was involved, and his father killed all the vultures to retrieve his son's body parts before burial and resurrection. Meanwhile Aqhat's sister got the thug drunk and killed him.[7] This story contains the bloody-infertile Earth motif of Abel's killing, but folklorists also group it with the Adonis/Attis/Osiris fertility family, because of the dismemberment and resurrection.

Some folklorists also regard the Canaanite myths of Baal and Môt as part of the Adonis/Attis/Osiris family although they share motifs with Cain and Abel.[8] The 'Poem of Baal' describes how the god Baal, master of fertility and rain, got dominion over the world.[9] His first act, of defeating Lammu or the Leviathan, parallels Marduk's slaying of Tiamat in the Babylonian creation epic *Enuma Elish*. He then moved into a grand palace and set about the defeat of his rival Môt. He achieved this by consigning him to the barren places (the land of Môt) and the netherworld. Môt then trapped Baal in the underworld. He thus effectively killed Baal and by that caused the loss of the land's fertility. Following that, Môt was killed and chopped up by the same goddess Anat.[10]

The last two Semitic stories have murder and the resultant blighting of the soil, in common with the Cain and Abel story, but otherwise, have closer links with the Adonis/Attis/Osiris resurrection and fertility myths. This argument has two sides, however, since the Egyptian story of Seth and Osiris also shares fratricide with Cain and Abel. The other biblical story linked with Cain and Abel is the episode of Jacob and Esau.[11]

Sumerian parallels

The most obvious and well-accepted Near Eastern parallels to Cain and Abel come from the Sumerians. Curiously the ancient Sumerian tales are also still concerned with agriculture, fertility and immortality. They codify the most important decision for the god/kings of the first organised societies – namely whether to intensify farming or pastoralism. Two of the myths come as 'Dispute poems'. The first is 'The dispute between Summer and Winter'.

Enlil, the Sumerian high god, wanted to increase agricultural production, so created two demi-gods, Emesh ('Summer') and Enten ('Winter'). Enten was responsible for animal husbandry, fishing, the growth of plantations and the growth of crops. Emesh on the other hand was responsible for plowing, planting, harvesting, storage and making cities and temples. When they had completed their mission, they went to Enlil with offerings. Emesh brought some wild and domestic animals, birds and plants as his gift, while Enten chose precious metals, and stones, trees and fish. At the door of the 'House of Life', Enten picked a quarrel with Emesh and eventually they asked Enlil to say who was 'Farmer of the Gods'. Enlil chose Enten, the pastoralist, and the brothers made it up.[12]

In this story, the tasks of the two brothers were not clearly divided between pastoralist and agriculturalist, and although there was a quarrel no one was killed. However, in the next dispute poem, 'the dispute between cattle and grain', the two ways of life were more clearly compared but the competing deities were female.

A Sumerian gods' creation committee, 'The Duku', created Lahar, the cattle goddess, and her sister, Ashnan the grain goddess, to improve food production. They did the task well; but then the two divine ladies got tipsy on wine and had a noisy row in the fields about who was better. Enlil and Enki had to intervene between the warring women, and declared the grain goddess, Ashnan, the winner. This was the reverse of Jehovah's choice of Abel the pastoralist in Genesis.[13]

In a third Sumerian poem, Inanna made the choice of a pastoralist over a farmer when she wooed Dumuzi. We have met these two before as the archetypal fertility lovers in the Adonis/Attis/Osiris family of myths.

Inanna the goddess of love, war and fertility had two suitors, one was the handsome young shepherd, Dumuzi, while the other was the farmer god, Enkimdu. The former was successful after quarrels and threats of violence from his rival. Little did Dumuzi realise that marriage to Inanna would lead to his own Mantis-like death. We learn later that he became a sacrificial replacement victim for his own wife, who had allowed herself to be killed in a quest for immortality.[14]

An eastern origin of the two-brothers conflict

Looked at from the perspective of these and other Mesopotamian myths we can see the story of Cain and Abel as a fertility allegory set in the structural metaphor of fratricide. The historical message of the allegory is conflict of peoples with different agricultural technologies; the structure of the metaphor is the story-type of the Osiris/Seth/Isis passion. With this perspective in mind we can enumerate the motifs in the Cain/Abel/Seth and Osiris/Seth/Isis story-type. They are:

1. contrasting siblings who are rivals; leading to
2. threatened or successful fratricide; (1) + (2) associated with
3. cultural differences in methods of food production; and/or
4. sexual jealousy with or without incest;
5. the potent tree spirit.

The symbolic uses of the death motif in these stories in the Ancient Near East are:

6. as a symbol for land infertility or winter and

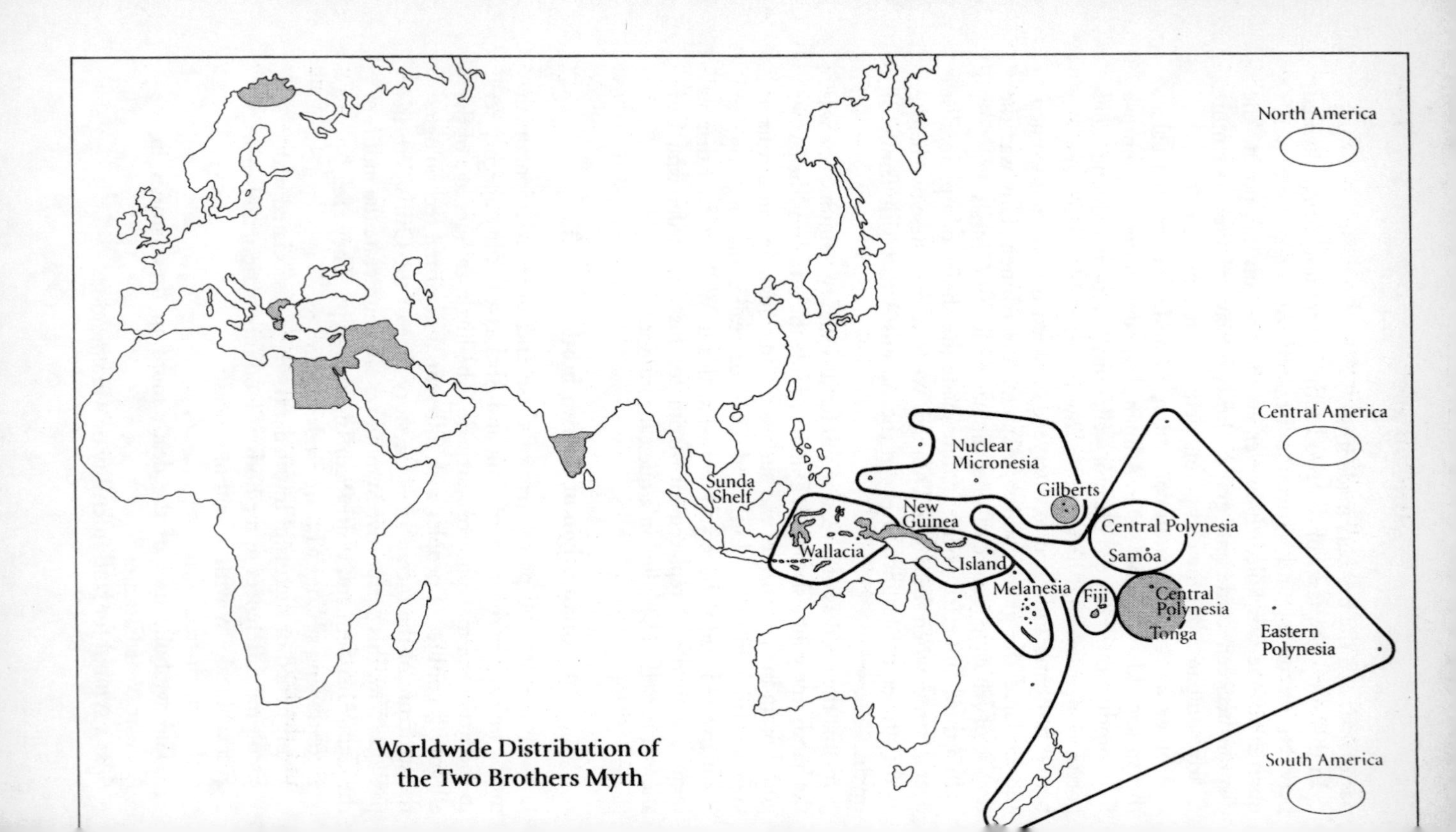

Worldwide Distribution of the Two Brothers Myth

Figure 44. **The story of the Two Warring Brothers.** Famous in the myths of the Ancient Near East, Egypt and Greece, this story is also found in India and among the Saami. The good sister/bad sister versions of northern Europe are not included here. It finds its greatest diversity among both western and Oceanic Austronesian speakers, in particular eastern Indonesia, and along the north coast of New Guinea.

7. as a prelude to resurrection and renewal, or a general (non-seasonal) improvement in production. This latter symbolism is one justification of the practice of sacrifice.

The Western distribution of these two-brother stories spreads from Mesopotamia, through Syria and the Eastern Mediterranean to Egypt (see Figure 44). Where else do we find these stories? The answer is, of course, in a band down through India to the Moluccas and Melanesia.

Some of the Indian tales come from the south and are woven into the flood myths of that region.[15] The recurring tale that was introduced by Naga influence in south India is of rivalry over a Nagini princess. In these tales, which I have already mentioned in Chapter 10, the loss of her son at sea and/or fratricide is followed by a devastating flood.[16] Similar tales appear in the Lesser Sunda Islands of eastern Indonesia such as Timor and Leti but with more specific reference to the two-brother conflict. The princess and her child persist in these tales and the flood is caused by a sea serpent, who breaks up the continent into islands. The famous ancient Indian epic, the *Mahabharata* from further north, shares some of these Naga motifs, such as the intermarriage with the Nagini princess who comes out of a fish, and the devastating flood that destroyed the port of Dvaraka after the fratricidal massacre of the Yadavas. Austronesian linguist Waruno Mahdi has argued convincingly that the true origins of the maritime, coconut-eating 'snake people', the Nagas, who had so much influence on Indian culture, are Austronesian and from Southeast Asia.[17] He shows that the cultural transfer may have pre-dated the later Indian influence on Southeast Asia. If this is the case, then the origins of some of the shared story motifs – the princess, the brothers, the sea serpent and the flood – may be in eastern Indonesia rather than India. The footprints of the two-brother myth in Indian soil thus seem to be pointing East–West.

The two warring brothers in Maluku and Melanesia

This East–West flow of culture, possibly through the ancient trade routes of the Austronesian sea-gypsies, explains the next stage of our search for the origin of the two brothers. The later influence of Aryan overlay on such ancient and complex Indian epics as the *Mahabharata*, makes it difficult to disentangle the different legendary strands. We might thus attribute the links between Indian stories and those of eastern Indonesia to later cultural influence the other way – that is, until we follow the two-brother stories through the Lesser Sundas and Maluku, and into Melanesia. In these regions of contrast and ancient conflict between Melanesia and Asia, the story of the two brothers and the girl in between takes on a life and mobility of its own. Here, well outside any possible later influence from India, we find stories sharing all the complex motifs of both the Cain and Abel and the Osiris and Seth types. In Chapters 14 and 15, we saw Eastern examples that stressed rebirth and fertility, like the Osiris cycle. The Melanesian and Moluccan stories, however, are unique. Not only do they feature both of the two Ancient Near Eastern story-types but they are also explicitly concerned with the conflict of race and culture. What is more, their context gives every sign of being home-grown.

In over ten of the fertility stories from Melanesia and Maluku there are contrasting siblings who are usually, but not always, boys. A good example is the Moluccan story from Ceram of Masora who kills his brother Maapita out of jealousy.[18] This tale mirrors the story of Osiris, and has five out of the seven Cain and Abel motifs enumerated above. There is the unlikely tale from Arop off the north coast of New Guinea. Here the jealous older brother stranded his younger brother on the tree to get his wife. This surely mirrors Osiris and Seth, and also has Cain motifs. The tragic myths from New Ireland introduce a sea monster or devil, as in the Canaanite poem of Baal and Môt. The two devoted brothers Natelimon and Ringantinsen are here forced into fratricide and dismemberment. Resurrection and fertility then follow on from the tragedy. In addition, comic myths from neighbouring New Britain, where a foolish brother To Korvuvu repeatedly acts as the foil to his wise and creative brother To Kabinana, lend a softer touch to the conflict motif.[19]

Kulabob and Manup

These conflict myths from the Moluccas and Melanesia have a curious distribution. They occur in the areas that linguists postulate were the primary contact sites between the migrating Austronesian sailors and the indigenous Papuans over 5000 years ago. One famous myth of the north coast of New Guinea may serve to illustrate this. This is the epic of Kulabob and Manup. I would like to tell this story as it was first presented to me.

On my first visit to New Guinea in 1976, I developed an interest in ancestor myths told in villages. This brought unexpected fruit when I returned in 1979 to carry out research on iron-deficiency anaemia in children. As a sideline of my work on iron deficiency, which I explained in Chapters 6 and 7, I found that 95 per cent of the north coastal people had alpha-thalassaemia, an inherited cause of anaemia.[20] I also found evidence that this blood condition had become so common because of natural selection by malaria.[21] What I found more fascinating when I was in New Guinea was how the genetic results and the linguistic evidence both agreed. They acted together as population markers, corroborating the ancient migration myth, 'Kulabob and Manup'.

My first introduction to the divide between the migrant Austronesians and the indigenous Papuans came from an old Papuan village, 'Bigman' or elder.[22] During my study I had to visit many villages in the hinterland of low jungle-clad hills going up to 500 metres. This involved driving up tortuous mud tracks in a four-wheel drive Jeep, sometimes in heavy rain. In one such visit to a village called Kamba with a magnificent view over the northern coast, I met an old man. We were standing at the edge of the village on a bluff overlooking rolling hills of jungle. The panorama included 48 kilometres of coastline, with the volcanic islands of Kar Kar and Bag Bag standing out in the sea near the long turquoise coral lagoon that stretched some 24 kilometres from Madang to Sek. To make conversation, I remarked that it was a fine sight and a house on this point would have a grandstand view. The old man said that as matter of fact it was his land and he would build a house for me (see illustration 30). Not sure how serious he was, I muttered something about paying for it. Huts of bush material were fairly cheap, and this was a good place for a weekend cottage. He immediately responded with a price. Worried that this was moving too fast, however, I changed the subject.

We discussed variations in custom between different parts of New Guinea. I then mentioned the names of certain villages on the beach and offshore islands laid out beneath us. These were where babies had a different form of alpha-thalassaemia from most of the other Madang villages, including Kamba. He looked at me curiously and said in New Guinean Tok Pisin,[23] 'Ah, those villages are descendants of Kulabob,' as if they were another race. He then looked hard at me again and touched my forehead. To an outsider like myself his statement was a surprise because on casual inspection there were no obvious differences between these villagers and their neighbours. I was to find out later that his surprise was as great as mine, but for different reasons. He wondered how I had come to know about something he regarded as a secret.

The next time I went to Kamba to follow up a child in my study group, the old man came up and greeted me as 'pikinini' (my son). He waited until I finished my work and then took me to a large house. This consisted of a thatched roof reaching down to the ground with no windows either end. He called it 'Yali's House' which, if I had known better at the time, would have identified it as a 'cargo cult' house.[24] I went in with him and with two other men. We all sat down cross-legged in near darkness, and then, in solemn tones, they interviewed me. The questions were leading, but I could not at first see where. They asked where I came from, and I told them. Dissatisfied with my answers, they repeated, 'No, where do you really come from? Kar Kar? Siassi? Sio? Manam?' (all offshore volcanic islands or coastal villages). Not getting anywhere with this line, they then asked if my parents visited me. I answered that they just had, and that they had also come from England. This was a breakthrough because they all nodded at each other. The old man then called me 'son' and 'Kulabob'. I asked him what he meant by that. He said, 'You know, don't you?' I said that I did not, and he prompted me by suggesting that I was a reincarnation of his firstborn who had died in infancy. I said that I did not think so, but that he was entitled to his own opinion.

Seeing my resistance, the old man relaxed. In soothing tones he said that he realised that I could not reveal the whole truth and that he would respect this. Disarmed by this last formula, I knew that anything further I said would be self-incriminating. There was more of this every time I went to that village. I soon realised that my own behaviour in coming to the village to examine children, speaking Tok Pisin and asking leading ethnic questions, and even discussing houses, was to blame. They had somehow concluded that I was a descendant of Kulabob. I assumed, I think correctly, that if I failed to match up to the role in the long term the identity would probably be only temporary.

I went to the Kristen Bookshop run by the Lutherans to see what more I could learn about the different tribes living in the Madang district. As it happened this was the only bookshop in Madang port. Almost immediately I hit gold-dust in the form of two books. One was the seminal work on cargo cults by Peter Lawrence, *Road Belong Cargo*.[25] The other, which I looked at first, was a monograph by a Swiss priest-linguist, Father John Z'Graggen, on the languages of the Madang district.[26] This gave a detailed analysis of the 173 distinct languages spoken in the Madang province. It also gave a good map of their distribution. One thing was clear in the mass of information. The villagers who had the locally rarer type of alpha-thalassaemia, whom my informant had spoken of as Kulabob's line, were Austronesian speakers; the rest of the local hinterland and coastal villagers spoke Papuan languages.

Putting this together there were two independent, mutually supporting observations. First, the 'descendants of Kulabob' were Austronesian speakers. Second, I had found that the mutation causing alpha-thalassaemia in the New Guinean Austronesians was different from that causing the condition in the Papuans who also lived along the north coast.[27] Other Austronesians in the Pacific, including Polynesians, also shared this mutation which is called $\alpha^{3.2III}$.[28] In other words, the $\alpha^{3.2III}$-thalassaemia mutation was a unique migration marker for the Austronesian dispersal into the rest of the Pacific. This is now incidentally among the best evidence against Thor Heyerdahl's vision of the colonisation of the Pacific westwards from South America.[29]

My next task was to find out who this chap Kulabob was. Over the next few months, I found several informants, including Father Z'Graggen himself, and also various texts such as Peter Lawrence's book that opened the door on this famous rogue. The story of Kulabob (or Kilibob) and Manup is the most important myth along the north coast of New Guinea.

The Kulabob and Manup story tells of two very different brothers. One of them, a sailor, seduces or is seduced by, his brother's wife, and after a fight migrates east. Existing as dozens of variants often held secret by different village elders, the myth-type spreads over three provinces and 300 kilometres of coastline. Crossing many language boundaries and five major language phyla, the story seems to hug the coast and offshore islands. Normally it might take hours or days to tell, with all the details and breaks for betel-nut chewing. As I have said, certain of the roles tend to be reversed according to the language of the story-teller. So to avoid confusion I will stick to the commonest orientation. The site of action is variable; in one story all the action, including creation, took place on the coast in an unidentifiable Eden, 'Subambe'.[30] The commonest actual location stated is Kar Kar, a volcanic island off the north coast. A line through the middle divides the inhabitants of this island into Austronesian and Papuan speakers. Here the two populations both agree with the broad outlines of the story. They also agree that Kulabob was the ancestor of the Austronesian speakers (Takia) while Manup was the ancestor of the non-Austronesian speakers

(Waskia).[31] (The Kar Kar islanders, incidentally, leave out the preceding creation story.) No single version would be representative but I will give the core story with an indication of the main variations.

Kulabob and Manup: the core story

Anut, Ludo or Dodo the creator made the first man and woman from earth.[32] In one version Anut took the first woman, Suspain, as a bone out of the man's side. He then had her private parts and womb made by an eel.[33] Kulabob and Manup were their first two sons.[34] In some versions there was another generation before these boys. Alternatively Anut made Kulabob and Manup directly.[35]

Kulabob and Manup were very different men. Kulabob was the younger brother. He was tall and fair in comparison to Manup who was stocky and dark.[36] Kulabob invented canoe-building, in particular the large ocean-going sailing canoes. He was a skilled fisherman. He invented planting magic and pot-making and useful arts. He invented tattooing, magic dances, war gods and magic to settle the reef gods.[37] Further, Kulabob was responsible for work done in the men's house, for spiritual matters. He knew how to make carvings and all the marks (designs), shapes and colours of posts, spears and other artwork. After he had given people their culture, ritual formulas and language, he empowered certain men and women to preside over various food plants and artefacts. Manup was responsible for giving laws and customs, a man of the land and a hunter. In some versions he was also a fisherman.[38] He had a wife and a son.

One day, Kulabob was hunting in the forest near a garden clearing where Manup's wife was harvesting taro. While she was resting, Kulabob shot his arrow at a bird of paradise and missed. The arrow landed near Manup's wife. She picked it up and admired the colour and design of Kulabob's 'mark'. The word used in New Guinea Tok Pisin is *mak* and means, in this context, his own signature design carved in relief on the shaft of the arrow. Kulabob went into the garden looking for his arrow but Manup's wife claimed she had not seen it. Then he saw it. She then asked him to put his mark on her skin, or, to be more specific, as a tattoo on her genitals. Kulabob was ashamed to do this thing, since she was his brother's wife, and refused. Manup's wife pressed him strongly and reluctantly he agreed, saying it was not his responsibility. He tattooed his mark on her pudenda and, when finished, wiped the blood off the tattoo onto a leaf that he threw in a stream. Other versions are more explicit saying that they also had sexual intercourse.[39]

The bloody leaf floated down the stream to the sea where Manup saw it, when returning from an island in his dug-out. While his wife was helping him pull up the canoe, her grass skirt slipped off and he saw the tattoo on her genitals. Furious at his own cuckoldry, he copied the design onto a slit-gong drum pole and went round comparing it with other designs. Eventually he asked Kulabob to decorate a pig-killing stick, and the mark was identical to the one he had. Kulabob realised Manup was going to kill him and prepared defensive magic. They had a big fight. Manup tried to kill Kulabob by crushing him with a house pole. He failed because of Kulabob's magic and ability to change into a rat, and escape.[40]

When we pause in this saga of two warring brothers to count up the shared motifs with the Adonis/Attis/Osiris and Cain/Abel story-types, we find a full house. The rival siblings are, of course, the centrepiece, while fratricide is attempted. The two brothers clearly belong to different cultures particularly in terms of food production. The story-tellers stress Kulabob's special skills; and sexual jealousy and incest are of the essence. In the West, the mark of Cain was commonly thought to have been a tattoo. Tattooing is a feature of cultures speaking Austronesian tongues and Kulabob's skill in this decoration is not surprising. Whether there is any connection between the erotic tattoo in this story and the mark of Cain, I leave the reader to decide. The symbolism emphasises sexual possession. The tree-spirit motif is hidden in the house pole in this story, but in other variants that I will move on to now, it becomes more obvious and dominant.

Besides the tattoo story, Kar Kar islanders also have several alternate tree-based versions of the seduction. In one, Kulabob changed Manup's two wives into beautiful young women and, like some Melanesian Krishna, drew them out of his house holding on to flower petals.[41] In a Waskian (Papuan) variant he lay in a tree dropping leaves on the women's bare breasts when they come to draw water, thus making them pregnant.[42] Another tree-based motif centres round Kulabob's escape from the first skirmish. This has an immortal reptile, and a tree that has to be destroyed, but then keeps regenerating. Kulabob changed into an immortal lizard and ran up the Ngaul tree. Manup's men chopped away at the tree, which kept regenerating itself. Eventually they burnt the chips of the tree and it failed to regenerate. The tree was felled and crashed into the bay, throwing Kulabob into the water.[43]

Finally Kulabob realised he had to leave. He fashioned the felled tree underwater to make a canoe, which surfaced mast tips first. The branches became smaller canoes. He built a huge ocean-going outrigger sail canoe. He then created pale-skinned men, pigs, dogs, fowl, food plants and artefacts, all of which he installed on the ship. The Kar Kar version has Kulabob making people out of bamboo containers of his mother's blood. Kulabob then sailed away east under cover of a volcanic eruption. Manup tried to do the same but his canoes sank, drowning his men.[44] In most versions Manup made a dug-out canoe just when Kulabob made his ship. The dug-out was not very seaworthy and Manup had to turn back home. In others he made his way north and west along the north coast to found the Sepik (Papuan-speaking) culture.[45]

As he was sailing east, Kulabob shot his arrows at the mainland to split it. This created the huge coral lagoon of Madang and Sek with its chain of barrier islands and various channels out to the ocean. He then sailed southeast along the Rai coast again, leaving new islands and reefs in his wake. In these last two actions he imitated, on a small scale, the achievement of Atuf, the Austronesian cult hero of Tanimbar in Indonesia. Atuf also sailed east towards the rising Sun using his spear as a plow, thus separating the island chain of the Nusa Tenggara from the Ice Age continent of Sunda.

At each village east along the Rai coast, Kulabob put a man ashore from his ark. He gave each the power of speech (Austronesian), food plants, a bow and arrows, a stone axe and adze, rain and his ritual formulae.[46] In another version he offered the colonists from his boat a choice of technologies – his own or the more primitive culture of hunter-gatherers. The light-skinned colonists chose the former while the dark-skinned colonists chose the latter.[47] In one story there was a fight at a Rai coast village where Kulabob had his spear broken.[48] There are many tales of artefacts and relics left over from this odyssey. Some of these were metal, others were wood or ceramic. East of Saidor at Sio, Kulabob crossed over to Siassi, another volcanic island in the Vitiaz Strait, and then on to New Britain. In the Kar Kar version he eventually discarded his wife and took his sister with him as lover.[49]

The Yam people of the Madang lagoon say that when Kulabob was sailing, Manup and his people had great trouble. They had no food plants and were starving. The brothers' mother went to find Kulabob. He told her the secret hiding place of the food plants and she returned to give the food to Manup's line. She later went out to sea again in an attempt to reconcile the brothers. This was unsuccessful and she still lives somewhere in the sea. Kulabob never came back, although there are prophesies that he will, following some portent.[50] The loss of fertility after Kulabob disappeared after the fight is curiously reminiscent of the blasted Earth myths from the Ancient Near East. Kulabob's mother going out to find him and the restoration of fertility after her mission again shadows the Adonis/Attis/Osiris resurrection motif.

Pale-skinned brothers from the West?

Speculation about Kulabob's return has caused many misunderstandings, including my own experience. The first of these from a European perspective occurred in the nineteenth century. In 1871, Miklouchо-Maclay, a Russian anthropologist, was the first European to stay in this part of New Guinea. He built a cabin on the coast (which is named Rai after him). People thought he must be a descendant of Kulabob since he came on a large ship, was pale skinned and had some kind of mark on his face, as if he had been in a fight.[51] This last method of identification sounds closer to the mark of Cain, as discussed by Sir James Frazer.

The predictions that Kulabob would return, coupled with his folk image as a paler-skinned man, have meant that local leaders often scrutinised white visitors as potential cousins. Recurrent cargo cults, which have appeared on the Madang coast since the Russian Maclay first stayed in 1871 with his accoutrements, always had this hypothesis. The local view was that, as cousins, the Europeans should share the magic of their technology and goods. The reverse was usually the case. Europeans took local land and never shared their luxury imports with their brothers. Whites even enslaved local people by putting on a 'head tax', which meant that men had to work in the plantations to earn money to pay their tax. In spite of such bad experiences, hope of Kulabob's return has never quite died. Miklouchо-Maclay had tried to warn the Rai coasters that the next Europeans would not be as passive as he had been, and the German planters who came pretended to be his brothers.[52]

Expatriates often assume that cargo cults of the Madang coast emerged simply as a result of the great contrast between the European and Melanesian technology. They all centred, however, round the Kulabob/Manup story, which is much older than the European invasions. Another interpretation is that the story itself is part of the local intellectual mechanism for understanding and explaining any foreigner coming from the sea. The anthropologist Peter Lawrence saw the cargo cults as a rational extension of the local magico-religious framework of knowledge. This framework, which included the local creation mythology, was used to explain all phenomena, natural and human, including their own success as horticulturists.[53] Many European expatriates think that these beliefs are simply stupid, and say so. But they should look closely at their own history of ignorance and religious bigotry in the Middle Ages. Somehow, against all odds and with the intellectual help of our Classical ancestors, we thought most of our way out of that mess after the Renaissance. In any case the

Melanesians were right about one thing in their Kulabob/Manup analogue: Europeans had the same rapacious instinct as Kulabob.

The start of the odyssey

Returning to the trail of Cain, it is easy to dismiss the saga of the two brothers from Madang as a quaint local legend until it crops up again in those islands Kulabob was supposed to have sailed to. For Madang people, the story is still left hanging, waiting for his return. As far as those people to the east on the Rai coast, Arop and Siassi Islands and New Britain are concerned, however, Kulabob arrived a long time ago and had even more adulterous adventures. The peoples who hold these stories are usually well aware of the analogies with neighbouring cultures along the coast and islands. They even collect the episodes together in the form of odysseys. Anthropologists have recently woken up to the historiographic implications of these migration sagas and a whole issue of the anthropological journal *Pacific Studies* has been devoted to 'Kilibob' and his children.[54] The character of Kulabob is preserved but his name changes in each story. Sometimes the reason for the name change is obvious because the torch was carried from mythical father to son. The first name change is at Sio about 160 kilometres east of Madang.

Male, an Austronesian speaker, had skin covered with sores and lived on the north coast with his mother. While he was resting on the beach, two playful mountain women (Papuan) splashed his sores with salt water. Later he wanted to join them at a traditional dance (sing-sing) in their village, against the advice of his mother. He removed his skin, painted his body and donned an aphrodisiac bird costume made by his mother. His mother then invoked the magic *papa* tree to transport him to the dance. Dancing all night he entranced the girls. Then, like Cinderella, he got the *papa* tree to whisk him home where he put back on his old scabby skin. The girls came looking for him, and did not take long to penetrate the disguise when they saw some red body paint through a hole in the skin. He threw off the skin and they all got married.

Unlike the European version they did not live happily ever after. The Papuan mountain-village men came looking for their girls and declared war on Male. His mother helped him with weapons. After a few days shooting arrows at his attackers, Male was worn out and decided to migrate. He left his mother and one pregnant wife behind but took all his secret technology with him in his canoe to his next destination. In another version of this story Male and his brothers had already cuckolded the men from the other village before he met the two women. They were massacred by the cuckolded husbands who had bows and arrows. Male alone survived under his brother's corpses.[55]

Another 160 kilometres east, the Siassi Island group abounds with stories of the creative philanderer. One island, Aromot/Mandok, has the epic separated into six episodes, starting with a close rendering of Kilibob and Manup.[56]

Episode 1: Kilibob leaves Madang

The first episode starts with the story of Kilibob and Mandep in Madang. The standard Madang version of Kulabob/Manup is followed faithfully except that there were three brothers, and the story specifies that Kilibob had sex with his sister-in-law before he tattooed her groin area. After the fight, Kilibob sailed with his mother and all the plants and supplies to Arop Island, which is halfway to Siassi. He also carried sand, soil and wood on the canoe.

When they arrived at Arop, Kilibob created a beach out to the canoe with his sand. He then put down earth and planted the food plants. Although he carved out a fertile niche for the two of them, Kilibob was lonely, so he created people from sand and blew lime dust into their mouths to animate them. He invented a dance called the Sia, which Siassi people admit they got from Arop. He married one of the women he had made but she became jealous and angry with him. Such was his restless character that he immediately decided to leave Arop for Siassi. As he was leaving, he noticed a group of women bathing near the trunk of a fallen tree that sloped into the water. They had left their grass skirts on the trunk to dry. He liked one of the women, Gainor, and, like the Peeping Toms described in the Moon/lake stories, he took her grass skirt. He hung the skirt on a remote branch of the fallen tree and, when she waded out into the deeper water to retrieve it, Kilibob leapt on the tree and drove the log like a jet ski with his prize east to Siassi.

This episode serves, among other things, to confirm that the myth travelled with its creative hero, his mother and his fertile technology. We also see the familiar creative motifs of the clay man, the tree spirit and the Moon/lake story.[57]

Episode 2: leatherskins, trevally and kingfish

In the second episode, Kulabob's mother shows her true colours as a fertility creatrix and fish-mother. Somehow Kulabob had impregnated

Gainor, causing instant twin birth, and had then left their two sons on Arop, all in the few seconds he was pushing off the log: some tree. He also left three species of fish. The grandmother looked after the two boys as they grew up on Arop, and demonstrated clever secret technology in schooling and catching fish for them. Like the interfering children we met in Chapter 15, these two scamps spied on her and then spoilt everything. The fish went away to other Austronesian islands in a gushing flood, with the old woman chasing after and schooling them, like the Russian witch Baba Yaga, in her large wooden bowl.

Episode 3: Mala's travels on Umboi

The third episode takes up the story of Kilibob and Gainor as they arrive on the west coast of Umboi, the main island of the Siassi group. His name changed to Mala. They stayed there for a long time with Mala fishing and Gainor growing taro. Then Gainor made the mistake of serving Mala pig's food and he walked off with a smile, and left her. Coming to another village Mala, like Odysseus, donned the disguise of an old man. He did this at several villages in order to gain admission without trouble. His motives had not changed. He eyed women at the outskirts of the villages and, at one, he climbed up into a tree standing over a spring. Two beautiful women came to draw water into their gourds. They were so beautiful that he had to have them. In the tree he chewed betel-nut until the juice was red and then spat between them.

Anthropologists studying these myths interpret the betel-nut chewing as a symbolic prelude to sex. The girls certainly felt the same and, looking up, called out to the very handsome man in the tree to come down. They both wanted to make love with this Adonis, but after getting him down from the tree went straight back to their village to share the news with their married friends. All the married women then came every day to make love and talk to this young man in the tree. The men of the village, getting suspicious, sent a child as a spy. When they realised what was happening to their wives, the men laid an ambush. Mala changed into an eel in the scramble, but was still caught. In the end the men decided Mala was more use to them alive with his technology, magic and brains, and married him to the first two girls he had met, who were luckily single. As the story-type develops, we can see the Cain and Abel version giving place to the dying and rising tree spirit of Adonis/Attis/Osiris. The tree motif is even garnished with snake and a fig.

Episode 4: Ambogim

With a flashback technique worthy of Homer, the story-teller takes us back to Gainor, who, again heavily pregnant, was looking for Mala. She came upon Tarawe, the first village he had been to. While on a shrimping trip with the Papuan inhabitants up the river she went into labour. She abandoned the baby under a fig tree where it was brought up by the resident snake of the tree 'Ambogim'. The child took the name of the snake and grew up in the bush under the reptile's protection. A long time later the women went shrimping in the same place and, when they were under a huge branch of the fig tree, they heard some rustling in the leaves. One of them spied a handsome young man in the leaves and they were all excited about enticing him down to go with them.

The snake demanded payment for his trouble, which they gave him, and young Ambogim went back to Tarawe with them and married two of the women. Ambogim went to a trade meeting at a neighbouring village, where his father Mala recognised him by his variety of betelnut. Mala morosely said to his son Ambogim that he would know when he was dying by seeing a breadfruit leaf spiralling towards him. In due course the prediction came true and the son buried his father with the correct ceremony, but first removed his dad's skin and folded it up. He used the old skin as a disguise on a couple of occasions, and later tested his wives' fidelity at a dance. They failed the test by flirting with him, thinking he was a stranger. So he got up and left the village.

An ethnographer would here note that both the immortality and continuity of the character are demonstrated in the skin sub-plot. In the next episode, we see the introduction of the tree of plenty,[58] which, in the villagers' attempt to kill Ambogim, is destroyed to spread its produce. The final member of the bird/snake/tree triad also now makes an entrance in the shape of the three birds at the top. Kulabob's descendant finally shows his true colours as a potent and immortal tree spirit by magic use of the cast skin.

Episode 5: the tree of wealth and plenty

Ambogim moved on away from Tarawe and on to another village. The first thing he did here was to make love to a menstruating woman, and then to a woman who had just delivered. This second woman produced another child who grew up instantly and called Ambogim 'Daddy', and ran after him. Ambogim then walked to a place where a group of men were chopping down a magic *maraz* tree and donned his father's skin.

This 'tree of plenty' had every kind of wealth in its branches. At the top were a cassowary, a cockatoo and a bird of paradise. In its branches were black ochre, clay pots, pigs, dogs, wooden bowls and black beads, bows and arrows, boars' tusks and obsidian. It had everything of worth you could want to trade, and they were chopping it down for these goods.

In his father's skin disguise, Ambogim joined the group of old men and made the rain fall. Everyone except him took shelter. When the rain stopped, the woman who had just given birth to his child came looking for him and ignored her real husband. They then all looked for the 'old man Ambogim' under the tree but could not see him. Then the adultress saw him first, high up in the tree dressed in all his feasting finery. He had discarded the old skin and appeared on a branch as a spectacularly handsome young man. The men were furious seeing this Adonis who had fooled them, and hacked away at the tree in order to fell it and kill him. The tree started to sway and Ambogim encouraged this from the branch by shaking it. The movement at the top of the huge tree was so great that the treasures and birds fell far away to the neighbouring mainland and islands before Ambogim came off himself. As a result Umboi and the other Siassi Islands were left barren, and Ambogim himself was thrown another 96 kilometres east over the Dampier Strait to Kilenge in New Britain.

In the next episode which takes the myth east, to west New Britain, many of the original Kulabob motifs are preserved including the attempted murder in a post hole. However, the key theme in this story is the technology that carried Austronesian tongues not only from the north coast of New Guinea to west New Britain, but from the rest of the Bismarcks out to the Pacific. This technology was the means of migration – that of building ocean-going canoes. The villagers consciously refer to this story as analogous to that of Noah's Ark.

Episode 6: Namor's Ark

In New Britain, in the village of Kilenge, Ambogim's name changed to Namor, and he lived on Mount Naventame. For some reason (best known to the Aromots) he felt sorry for causing all the trade goods and skills to flee from Siassi and wanted to return something. He built a double-masted canoe, the 'Erevel Time'. He cut a groove with a pig-bone knife down to the sea, and the river thus formed washed the canoe to the sea. They say that just as Noah's Ark landed on Mount Ararat, so Namor built his two-masted canoe on Mount Naventame. He wanted to sail the canoe as a gift to Aromot, an island in the south of the Siassi group. Although he was using Kilenge villagers as carpenters and crew, they were none too happy about this loss of technology back to Siassi.

When they were about to leave Aromot and return to Kilenge, they sent Namor down into the hull to guide the replacement masts into their holes. They intended to crush his skull with the mast in the hole. Like his previous incarnation, Kulabob, in the men's house in Kar Kar, Namor did not plan to end up with his skull at the bottom of a post hole. He had prepared some red sap from the *isis* tree to look like blood, and some white sap from the *simbam* tree to look like brains. These slops he had put into a bamboo container which he slipped into the mast hole at the last minute to give the effect of splattered brains. After this ruse had worked, again like his predecessor, he changed into a mouse and swam back to Kilenge ahead of his would-be murderers in the canoe. When they saw Namor the man strolling along the beach at Kilenge back in west New Britain, they were scared stiff and took off, leaving the canoe for Namor to return in to Aromot.

The tradition of Kulabob is carried on still further east among the Bariai-Kabana, Lusi-Kaliai and Anêm of northwestern New Britain. These peoples speak the 'aberrant' or ancient Austronesian tongues of the north New Guinea coast cluster, which may have arrived long before the Polynesian migrations of only 3500 years ago.[59] Here the names of Kulabob change variously to Moro, Aragas, Ava and Titikolo.[60] The story-tellers are, however, clear that they all refer to the same deity or spirit who is the same as Kulabob. Manup's name is taken by a village bigman (self-appointed leader), Alu. The old story of the 'decorated spear' tryst in the taro garden and the tattooing of the bigman's wife's vulva is preserved. The episode of the post hole and the escape through the medium of a rat is also preserved.

A couple of familiar ancient twists are added, though. In one episode, Moro is killed and his liver fed to one of his sons, Aikiukiu. The boy is then transformed into a powerful snake-man and provides his mother and brother with shelter, food and domesticated animals. Apart from this resurrection/fertility motif, Moro also earlier turns his wife and son into crab and snake, respectively, thus merging with older creative immortality motifs.[61]

History or myth?

By this stage with all my hints, the reader will realise that this epic is not simply a repetitive tall tale of adultery. Before giving my own views, I would like to summarise what the anthropologist listener and village informant thought it was all about.

For once in the history of folklore collection, both ethnologist and story-teller of this epic agreed about the main purpose of myth: the Namor legend was, and is, history. The guru of Melanesian anthropology, Bronislaw Malinowski, insisted that myths were a coded social charter; that is, they contained rules for everyday living.[62] This was clearly not the case with the antics of the over-sexed Austronesian sailors of Kulabob's line; they broke every rule. Like another invader, Genghis Khan, once said, they were not completely happy unless they lay on the bellies of the wives of their rivals. Unlike Genghis they preferred the bellies to be Papuan, and browner rather than paler than their own. Kulabob's social crime of sleeping with his brother's wife was only topped by Ambogim, who in quick succession broke three taboos of the Gauru people.[63] The first was sleeping with other men's wives, while the other two were sleeping with menstruating and parturient women.

Kulabob and his line had even less regard for social convention than medieval peasant prankster, Till Eulenspeigel, of German folk fame. The ancestors of the indigenous Papuan men of the villages holding these myths certainly had not approved of the behaviour of the Austronesian Adonis. On the contrary, they were always trying to kill him and bury his head under a post as a sacrifice. However embarrassing these episodes might have been to the memory of their ancestors, they were regarded as history by villagers speaking both Papuan and Austronesian languages.

The anthropologist who recorded the legend of Namor from the Mandok of Siassi, Alice Pomponio from St Lawrence University, also saw the content as history but qualified herself by calling it 'coded history'. She coined the phrase 'mythical metaphor' to explain what she meant by this.[64] The sexual odyssey not only followed the ever eastward migration of the Austronesians, but described in metaphor the complex trading relationships established between the colonies of Papuan and Austronesian speakers. The items of trade included rights to Austronesian skills and technology as much as the finished products themselves, such as canoes. The swaying tree of plenty that threw its treasures around the islands actually described in detail the trade routes of the Vitiaz and Dampier straits between New Britain and New Guinea.[65] We should not, however, see the Papuans as lacking in their own special technology. After all, they were draining swamps and planting root crops when most of the World Tribe were hunter-gatherers 9000 years ago.

The village informants were at pains to explain to their receptive

Western anthropological observers that this saga was their history. They used the example of Western mythological tradition, as told in Genesis. They regarded Genesis not only as the same sort of stuff but more literally as the Western version of the same story: 'When discussing significant Mandok concepts communicated in the Legend of Namor, people continually stressed the analogues of their oral historical tradition with Western "historical" tradition as documented in the Bible (and as taught by Roman Catholic missionaries).'[66] They point to the history of the flood and the Garden of Eden, which they locate to the west, as elements present in both mythical traditions.

The conclusion that these myths somehow codify the history of Austronesian expansion along the north coast of New Guinea into the Southwest Pacific, I first heard from Father Z'Graggen in 1982. A group of anthropologists have written up the phenomenon recently as a 216-page issue of the journal *Pacific Studies*, entitled 'Children of Kilibob', and dedicated it to the memory of the late Peter Lawrence.[67] They were at pains to emphasise that they discovered these myths in the course of their other studies and did not call themselves folklorists. Maybe this was an advantage, because they had less prejudice as to the meaning of folklore. One crucial issue echoed by different anthropologists in the book was the fear that their colleagues, the folklorists, had somehow taken a wrong turning early in the twentieth century by rejecting the ideas of Sir Edward Tylor and Sir James Frazer. Frazer's was called the intellectualist approach.[68] Crudely speaking, the intellectualist approach to myths considered their content, however bizarre, as an attempt to explain events and natural phenomena. The later approach considered myth content too bizarre to be taken literally or seriously, and concentrated on the psychological, social, functional and structural symbolism of myths instead.

The idea of the Kulabob myths encoding history seems neat and simple, until we consider the staggering time implications. At a conservative estimate the Austronesian invasions of this part of the Pacific happened 5000 years ago,[69] and almost certainly more. They then moved on out to the rest of the Pacific. This would mean that Kulabob moved east out of Madang at the same time as Sumerian Inanna was wooing Dumuzi or before Gilgamesh went looking for immortality, or just 3000 years before Christ. It is difficult to believe that ethnic distinctions and rivalry could last that long; but they may have.

The conventional anthropological evidence of different languages and different technologies and ethnic consciousness are still there to see all along the route of Kulabob, as if it had happened only yesterday. The Austronesian villages are noted for making pots and ocean-sailing

Table 14. Analogues between the Mesopotamian two-brother story types (Cain/Abel and Osiris/Seth, etc.) and the northern Melanesian complex as epitomised by Kulabob and Manup.

Mesopotamian Motif	Melanesian Analogue
(1) Contrasting siblings who are rivals: leading to	*Kulabob and Manup or their descendants.*
(2) Threatened or successful fratricide:	*Kulabob and Manup's fight and Moro's death.* *Kulabob and Manup kill younger brother*
(1)+(2) associated with	
(3) Cultural differences in methods of food production: and/or	*Austronesian versus Papuan*
(4) sexual jealousy with or without incest	*Kulabob and Manup's wife*
(5) The potent tree spirit (*Adonis/Attis/Osiris*)	*Ambogim/Kulabob/Mala, etc.*
The symbolic uses of the death motif in these stories are:	
(6) As a symbol of land infertility or winter	*Kulabob's disappearance causes famine*
(7) As a prelude to resurrection and renewal, or a general (non-seasonal) improvement in production; this symbolism is one justification of the practice of sacrifice.	*(a) Kulabob and Manup kill their youngest brother and distribute his bones to improve crops* *(b) Kulabob's (or his descendant's) miraculous reappearance after a fight heralds return of technology and/or food* *(c) Moro's liver makes his son powerful and productive*

canoes. They have sophisticated fishing technology, their political structure tends to be hierarchical and hereditary. The Papuan-speaking villages have less sophisticated fishing technology, buy pots from the Austronesians and have self-appointed 'bigmen' who are leaders of opinion rather than hereditary chiefs. On the other hand, they are supreme horticulturists. One Papuan garden holder may grow numerically more genetic varieties of taro root than the entire American wheat machine. Obviously there are exceptions to these generalisations and overlaps in technology. That exchange is partly what these stories are about, but the conscious distinction between Austronesians and Papuans remains as palpable as any religious division.

To me, however, what clinches the antiquity of these tales with their special Melanesian flavour of trade and debauchery are the same old-enshrined motifs that we found in the earliest myths of the Ancient Near East. When we review the motifs that were common to the Cain/Abel and Adonis/Attis/Osiris traditions (see above) in the perspective of the Kulabob/Manup family, we get 100 per cent concordance with bonus interest (see Table 14).

The bonus links we find in the Kulabob/Manup story connect with both the Adonis/Attis/Osiris family and the older immortality mechanisms. The stories constantly refer to magic trees, trees of plenty, regenerative trees, trees that turn into potent torpedoes to carry off brides and, most of all, beautiful and potent men in trees. This is an unmistakable confirmation of Frazer's hunch that Adonis and his kind were originally tree spirits.[70] The main reason he devoted so much space to Adonis/Attis/Osiris stories in his *Golden Bough* was his conviction that their traditions had grown out of tree worship and tree spirits. The immortality motifs of regeneration – skin-changing, snakes and crabs – which are woven into the fabric of the stories also tie the myth-type firmly back into the ancient traditions I described in Chapter 14.

Two brothers in the Sepik Basin

One north-coastal version of the Kulabob–Manup story has Manup migrating with his daughter to Sepik province to the west of Madang. There she gave them her language and the custom of wearing the skin of a flying fox (a bat) as a waistcloth.[71] This variant may hold the clue to the presence of the two-brother myth among the non-Austronesian-speaking Sepik peoples.[72] One well-known two-brother story comes from the famous carving village of Kambot in the Sepik province, which is now around 70 kilometres inland. Two thousand years ago,

Kambot was on the coast of a large brackish sea inlet; 4000 years before that, at the peak of sea rise after the end of the Ice Age, Kambot was an island in a vast inland sea. Evidence has recently come to light of probable Austronesian settlements dating back 5800 years in this locality. Remains of introduced betel-nut have also been traced to this time.[73]

Kambot now nestles on the Keram River in swamps. The story-tellers and carvers have a tradition that includes the motifs of the two brothers (both bad in this instance), birds, a reptile, the self-healing tree, and death and dismemberment represented by an innocent young man who has his head cut off in the crown of the coconut tree. The Kambot language is closely related to the Ramu River family from which the flying-fox clan of Amber village story comes. In that tale, women came out of coconuts. The Kambot story has modified the explicit Austronesian two-brother theme to that of unwanted intrusion and conflict. I include it not only for the combination of the motifs and evidence of Austronesian influence, but because of the fine relief story board and incised designs surrounding the story for which this village is famous.

Lawena and Dawena were two men in Kambot who, in addition to plundering their neighbour's produce, had magic powers. They killed two cockatoos and covered their own heads with the bird's heads. They made lime from shells and chewed betel-nut with it. Whereas betel-nut is chewed in every New Guinean village today, for these ancestral brothers it had the special effect of making them invisible. The two birdmen then climbed a coconut tree to get the fruit and made a loud shrieking noise in the top of the tree. The villagers threw up spears, which the birdmen caught. Finally, a young man was sent up the tree to solve the mystery. He had his head cut off by the birdmen, and the body fell to the ground. The two birds flew off into a nearby *garamut* tree to eat the head. Their invisibility was now wearing off and the villagers tried to cut down the hardwood tree. To their surprise the tree kept on healing itself. On the fourth day the tree came crashing down. Lawena flew off, but Dawena was caught in the branches and thrown into the Keram River. When Lawena tried to find his brother, Dawena, he heard a barking noise indicating that Dawena had changed into a crocodile. He could not change back. The two demons are represented in the Kambot carvings as a half-man/half-bird and half-man/half-crocodile.[74] The other Kambot two-brother myth, Wain and Mopul, part of which we considered in Chapter 15, is much closer to Kulabob and Manup (see illustration 16).

As anthropologist/archaeologist Christian Kaufmann points out with other examples, the intrusion of Austronesian motifs, like the two-brother myth deep into the Sepik region, hints at influence long before the Lapita expansion associated with the Polynesians 3500 years ago. This is supported by recent findings of early pre-Lapita pottery in the Sepik.[75]

Kulabob/Manup analogues occur across New Guinea and have been labelled locally by anthropologists as the 'Myth of the two brothers' or 'Hostile brothers'. They are also recognised by the same pundits as far southwest as Timor and as far northeast as Micronesia in the trickster stories of Oliphat.[76] This obviously leaves the minor question unanswered, whether the first two-brother story was in the Moluccas or on the north coast of New Guinea (see Figure 44).

Two Brothers spread east to the Pacific

We can trace the two-brother story still further east into the junction zone between Melanesia and central Polynesia out in the Pacific. Melanesia, under its loose label of 'island peoples with dark skin and frizzy hair', spreads out as far east as Fiji.[77] In this context we can make a rough approximation that the Fijians, with their combination of Papuan and Austronesian features, represent the mixed-race descendants of both Kulabob's and Manup's lines who sailed southeast from New Guinea. A little further east from Fiji and we are out of Melanesia and into central Polynesia, where Polynesian features and culture predominate. The first island Polynesian groups we meet are Samoa and Tonga. These are thought by many to be the heartland of all later Polynesian migrations. Tonga holds many artefacts and potsherds from the mysterious pre-Polynesian Lapita people dating to 3500 years ago. I was stunned when travelling through Tonga a few years ago to find a text of pre-Christian Tongan mythology that was closer to Cain and Abel than any of the Kulabob/Manup family. Stripped of the local New Guinean spice and colour, this story goes right back to the elements that underlaid the fight of the two brothers: culture, migration and race.

The Tongan conflict story was so like Cain and Abel that its recorder, the English adventurer William Mariner, had difficulty at first believing it was original, so I will give some context to the time of its telling. Until Mariner's enforced detention on the islands in 1806, no Europeans had lived there except for a short and disastrous visit by some ten missionaries nine years before. Far from proselytising, they had always shut themselves up in their cabin to pray and sing their songs, and vigorously refused access to the Tongans. Eventually the Tongans, believing that the missionaries were an evil bunch who practised witchcraft and spread disease, attacked them and killed three. Six fled to Australia and the one remaining survivor renounced Christianity and married locally. It would therefore be safe to say that up to Mariner, there had been no significant Christian influence, and there was certainly not enough time to embed the tale I will tell into their local mythology.

Mariner's own arrival in Tonga was the stuff of nineteenth-century adventure fiction. In early teenage he was employed as a clerk on the privateer *Port au Prince*. After many adventures the ship arrived in Tonga. Shortly afterwards it was over-run by Tongans and most of the crew were clubbed to death. Mariner was spared by a chief who took a liking to him and he spent the next few years in Tonga as an adopted son. Later he set down a history of his time and observations in Tonga with the help of an amanuensis.[78] His accuracy was considerably greater than that of Marco Polo who had a similar but greater task of memory. The Tongans apparently have no argument with the authenticity of his record, since the last two editions of the book have been published there. Although much of the book is devoted to events of his stay in Tonga, Mariner made a study of Tongan customs, beliefs and myths. One of their myths that surprised him most was the peopling of the Tongan islands. His open-minded record was a model from which some of the early missionary ethnographers in Polynesia could have learnt. As if to pinch himself and remind his reader that these were undoctored accounts, at the start of the story he put the footnote: 'The following is as nearly as possible a *literal* translation of the language in which they tell it.'[79] At the end he again metaphorically pinched himself, using the third person:

> Mr Mariner took particular pains to make enquiries respecting the above extraordinary story, with a view to discover whether it was only a corrupted version of the Mosaic account; and he found that it was not universally known to the Tonga people ... This led him at first to suspect that the chiefs had obtained the leading facts from some of our modern missionaries, and had interwoven it with their own notions; but the oldest men affirmed their positive belief that it was founded in truth. It seems strange that they should believe an account which serves so much to degrade them ...[80]

Anyway, on with the story. As related in Chapter 14, the Tongans believe in a very large paradisical island far to their northwest called Bolotoo. This was not only the resting place of the spirits of their departed but also the land their ancestors had inhabited prior to their migration, and which has now disappeared. Their creator god Tangaloa, who lived in the west in Bolotoo, had created the Tonga Islands by fishing them up from the ocean floor.[81] He had put plants and animals on them, but of an inferior type compared with those on Bolotoo. Wishing to populate the new territory with intelligent beings, he had sent his own two sons:

> Go, take with you your wives, and dwell in the world at Tonga: divide the land into two portions and dwell separately from each other. The name of the eldest was Toobo, and the name of the youngest was Vaca-acow-ooli. [He] was an exceeding wise young man; for it was he that first formed axes, and invented beads, and cloth, and looking glasses. The young man called Toobo acted very differently, being very indolent, sauntering about and sleeping, and envying very much the works of his brother. Tired at length with begging his goods, he bethought himself to kill him, but concealed his wicked intention. He accordingly met his brother walking, and struck him till he was dead. At that time their father came from Bolotoo with exceeding great anger, and asked him, why have you killed your brother? could you not work like him? Oh thou wicked one! Begone![82]

Up to this point we are told again the simple story of the contrasting brothers with different skills, but Mariner also tells us that they both came from the large paradise homeland far to the northwest that is now both invisible and inaccessible (a universal belief among Polynesians).[83] Moving in that direction from Tonga, the first large island we come to is New Guinea. The tale of Kulabob and other more conventional sources, however, all tell us that New Guinea was not the Austronesian homeland and that we should look further west, maybe in Southeast Asia. The simplicity and preservation of the Tongan tale is consistent with the original story having travelled more or less intact through Melanesia, bypassing the colourful and sexually explicit embroidery of north coast New Guinea. The next part has important clues, but obviously caused Mariner some puzzlement:

> go with my commands to the family of Vaca-acow-ooli; tell them to come hither. Being accordingly come, Tangaloa straightaway ordered them thus: Put your canoes to sea and sail to the east, to the great land which is there, and take up your abode there. Be your skins white like your minds, for your minds are pure; you

> shall be wise, making axes, and all riches whatsoever, and shall have large canoes. I will go myself and command the wind to blow from your land to Tonga; but they (the Tonga people) shall not be able to go to you with their bad canoes.
>
> Tangaloa then spoke thus to the others: You shall be black, because your minds are bad, and you shall be destitute; you shall not be wise in useful things, neither shall you go to the great land of your brothers. How can you go with your bad canoes? But your brothers shall come to Tonga, and trade with you as they please.[84]

What confused Mariner was the implication that, in their story, the Tongans were painting themselves as 'bad black men'. This seemed self-debasing, and in any case the Tongans that he knew had no sense of personal inferiority towards whites. If anything, they felt the other way about whites, eating them when they had the opportunity.

The context of the Kulabob and Manup story offers one solution to the paradox. Kulabob (the Austronesian) was said to be paler-skinned than Manup. Similarly, the Polynesians tend to be paler-skinned than the Melanesians. Maybe this story was a carry-over of the Austronesian/Papuan ethnic conflict from further west in Melanesia. There are other cognates in the stories – for instance, the 'bad canoes' of Toobo's line remind us that poor old Manup had a little dug-out that sank. We have already heard of the pale-skinned argonauts from the fatherland in the west, in the Micronesian creation mentioned in (Chapters 11–13). The Micronesians go so far as to say that the original inhabitants of the western homeland, the 'Men of Matang', had red hair and blue eyes and may also have gone to Samoa as well.[85]

Before I am accused of suggesting that a white super-race sailed the Pacific 4000 years ago, I should say that I think that all these politically incorrect and recurrent myths of colour and technology differences are all still consistent with an Austronesian/Papuan or Asian/Melanesian dichotomy. Polynesians who are presumed by many to have been in the vanguard of Austronesian expansion are paler-skinned than Papuans. An enormous range of physical appearance exists in the contact area of Melanesia. Blond hair and round blue eyes are seen among the children of the Tolai of East New Britain, who otherwise have dark skins and physiognomies similar to other Austronesian speakers of Melanesia. There is still another possible explanation for the origin of the colour-conflict motif because the conflict stories are also found further west in Maluku and the Nusa Tenggara:[86] there may well have been conflict further west between the 'southern Mongoloid' and the original Australoid and Negrito inhabitants of Southeast Asia, and at an earlier stage before the Austronesian Pacific migrations ever started. In this model, which I prefer, the Austronesians would have carried the story with them when they entered Melanesia.

Another intriguing feature of the Tongan two-brother myth, is the 'great land to the east' that Vaca-acow-ooli's line could and did sail to. There is no great land to the east of Tonga until one gets to South America. Could this strange statement indicate that Thor Heyerdahl's Kon-Tiki raft was sailing the wrong way and that South America was colonised by the Polynesians? There are several such pointers to Austronesian intrusions into Central or South America, such as the cast-skin myth in Chapter 14, the distribution of blowpipe types and numerous themes in Aztec mythology; but they are outside the remit of this book.

In many ways, the motifs and stories in this chapter are an extension of the same topics in the previous chapter on the dying and rising tree god. The difference, however, is that the myths of the latter group have mostly been divorced from their original context, both in the West and East. They thus remain as arcane and powerful but symbolic vestiges. This is the case even in the examples from the Moluccas where the first clash of cultures may have taken place. In the case of the Kulabob/Manup cycle of stories from northern Melanesia, the myths are still very much alive and in logical context. They have a major role in determining attitudes to outsiders. The concepts of conflict, compromise and trade between Austronesian and non-Austronesian speakers are also still very much alive. Trade continues in both the barter and cash form and, in the Trobriand Islands (between New Guinea and New Britain) and similar places, long-distance cycles of symbolic, reciprocal exchange of precious heirlooms, such as shells, still takes place. Certain ethnic groups are acknowledged to possess the rights and skills for unique items of local technology, or magic formulas and ritual dances. Their very vitality is seen in the new cults that have arisen to accommodate the first major influx of a new mythological framework for thousands of years, namely Christianity.

The story of the indigenous and invading cultures would clearly fit either of the multidisciplinary migration models, namely the express train to Polynesia – or the earlier and several trains that I suggest. The fact that different outsiders have listened to these stories, and have independently realised that they immortalise a migration from thousands of years ago, vindicates the views of the local people that this is history. It is also, in the absence of a written record, the best form of provenance. Put in simple terms: if archaeologists propose the ancient Austronesian migration that the story describes, if local people say this story tells their history, if anthropologists agree with them, and if even a casual observer like myself comes to the same conclusion, then we may be looking at the regional origin of the Western myths of Cain and Abel, and the huge tree of the Adonis, Attis and Osiris myth that ramifies throughout India, Europe, the Middle East and North Africa.

The complex traditions of the two-brother myths from the East and West that I have described in this and the previous chapter have too many shared motifs to have developed randomly in parallel. If we accept this, we also have to agree that the stories could not have been synthesised less than 3500 years ago, because no other Southeast Asians dispersed into the Pacific after that time until very recently. The direction of cultural flow must therefore be east to west, on both contextual and chronological grounds. There is no evidence that Westerners migrated to the Pacific that long ago, and nobody suggests this. Even if the contact was as recent as the Lapita dispersal into the Pacific 3500 years ago, it would have been well before the known Indian influence on Southeast Asia. The date of dispersal, however, must surely be even earlier. The 5800-year-old sites recently found in Sepik province of Papua New Guinea suggest much earlier.[87]

Among these 'ifs' there are several well-attested Western dates, which antedate the Lapita dispersal by at least a thousand years. These are the written stories of Isis and Osiris from Egypt and the Sumerian stories of Inanna and Dumuzi from Mesopotamia. As with other myths from the dawn of civilisation in the West, both of their written records go well back into the fifth millennium before our time. These myths were already old when they were written down. How much older, then, if they were derived from somewhere east of Borneo?

EPILOGUE

'Oh, East is East, and West is West, and never the twain shall meet,
Till Earth and Sky stand presently at God's great Judgment Seat ...'
These words of Rudyard Kipling (1865–1936) echo down to us from the colonial period. Archaeology, linguistics and genetics all seem to prove him over 90 per cent right: there is a deep, hard and ancient line between the Far East and the rest of Eurasia. My story has concentrated on that 5 to 10 per cent of contact. Using evidence from these three disciplines in Part I, I have suggested that there was an interlinkage between the prehistoric populations of Southeast Asia and the rest of the world. People from Southeast Asia were forced to flee westwards after the Ice Age to India, Mesopotamia and possibly beyond, and influenced the West far beyond their numbers. I have also shown (Part II) that besides the evidence of the physical movement of people from Southeast Asia, cultural links back to the region are detectable in many Western folktales and other stories. Only in the past 2000 years has the cultural flow been the other way round – from West to East.

I am not asking for the archaeological, genetic and folklore markers I have described in this book to be accepted without question. There are too few of the former, as yet, for their provenance to be sound. And is their dating accurate? More work clearly needs to be done. What I am suggesting is that the prehistory of Southeast Asia deserves a closer review without what archaeologist Pamela Swadling calls the 'blinkered' view of many prehistorians of the region.

Filling in the gaps

For archaeology, with its semblance of accuracy, there is the special problem of gaps in continuity caused by rising sea-levels, especially around 8000 years ago during the early Neolithic period. These give a false picture of the timeline and spurious horizons. The most notable gaps are in the Neolithic period in China and Southeast Asia, the former appearing to be delayed and the latter nearly obliterated. A whole era in Southeast Asian prehistory is missing. There is for example the puzzling concept that a sparse population of hunter-gatherers were occupying parts of island Southeast Asia such as Borneo from 9000 to 3500 years ago when New Guinea, to the east, was practising sea trade and horticulture. Against this primitive view of the region is the evidence of extensive upland forest clearance in Sumatra and Java 8000 years ago.

As we have seen, however, there is an alternative view suggested, among others, by archaeologist Wilhelm Solheim, that the early peoples of island Southeast Asia at this time grew root crops, domesticated animals, harvested trees and became experts in marine technology. They may well have spoken precursors of Austronesian tongues if the Moluccan provenance of the Polynesian gene motif is confirmed. They could have developed a maritime trading network which reached as far north as Japan and Korea 7000 years ago. Traces of that network appear to linger on today among the sea-gypsies of the Malay archipelago. Their cousins, probably speaking Austro-Asiatic tongues, became separated on mainland Southeast Asia and left their remains. Long thought to be rather backward hunter-gatherers, these so-called Hoabinhians and Bacsonians developed land skills such as horticulture, rice-growing and pot-making.

I have devoted much space in Part I to arguing for an earlier Austronesian dispersal to the Pacific over 6000 years ago. There is a purpose in this. While the Pacific dispersal is not directly relevant to East–West diffusion, the issue of timing underpins the whole of the conventional view of Southeast Asian prehistory. Put in simple terms, the present 'express train to Polynesia from China' theory depends on a late entry-date to the Pacific of 1500 BC. If the train not only never went near China but left Southeast Asia just after the last flood, then there is every reason to suppose that the argonauts were capable of sailing west at the same time.

The archaeological record of the East's achievements before history is more gap than fact, except for the scraps suggesting that they lost more than the West realises. Some of the earlier scraps include the sailors of the Pacific who reached the Solomon Islands nearly 30,000 years ago, the Japanese pottery from 12,500 years ago, the New Guinea Highlanders who, as mentioned, were draining swamps to grow taro 9000 years ago, the astonishingly early rice-growing dates from the Malay Peninsula which may have presaged the spread of the craft to India. A little later, we have the third flood of the eighth millennium. This was followed by a relative archaeological silence from inundated island Southeast Asia, as the sea-level rise overshot by five metres for the next 2000 years. The exceptions are some early Neolithic cave dates from Borneo and the Philippines, and the appearance of obsidian on the east coast of Borneo 6000 years ago, traded from Lou Island thousands of sea miles to the east, long before the Austronesian sailors were even supposed to have reached Borneo, let alone Lou Island.

On the Asian mainland, from the end of the flood onwards, we begin to see 'new' Neolithic settlements all along the east and south coast of China and in Vietnam. Perceptive Oriental archaeologists, however, have thought to peer under the layer of silt laid down by the flood in these coastal flats, and found out that earlier Neolithic cultures were already there before the flood. Inland agricultural settlements in Thailand and Vietnam also appear from the fifth millennium BC, in places such as Ban Chiang. Perhaps these colonists had moved in from the coast when the flood came; at any rate, these Far Eastern agricultural settlements dating back to the fifth millennium BC went on to smelt and cast bronze around the same time as – and apparently independently of – the Ancient Near East and China. Metal Age cultures of Vietnam later produced exquisite pieces which were traded around Southeast Asia and as far as Melanesia, long before the advent of Indian influenced cultures of Southeast Asia. The exotic 3200-year-old Bronze Age culture of Sanxingdui in China also had more cultural links with island Southeast Asia than with the north.

As more pieces of the jigsaw puzzle are put together, a contrary picture emerges of the great technical advances since the end of the Ice Age appearing simultaneously throughout Eurasia and spreading towards Oceania. Such a pattern confirms the suspicion that ancient routes of intercontinental communication in the East were considerably more effective than previously realised. The linguistic and genetic picture of Austronesian dispersals into Melanesia and Australia support a much earlier initial spread out of Southeast Asia than argued by supporters of the '1500 BC express train to Polynesia'.

The same process of inundation went on in the swampy Sepik province of north New Guinea over 6000 years ago; again locally based archaeologists have dug under the silt and found that cultures with typically Austronesian shell technology and betel-nuts arrived there up to 6000 years ago, and not 3500 years ago as was thought. They may even have arrived considerably earlier, but any evidence of that would now be under the sea. Maybe this explains the 5400-year-old Jomon pottery from Japan found further east in Melanesia. Whatever the cause, there was a great movement and mixing of people all round the western Pacific Rim during, and immediately after, the flood. Most of the evidence of this was then inundated by a further gradual rise in sea-level until 5500 years ago.

Thousands of kilometres to the west, the flood affected the Arabian Gulf, as Sir Leonard Woolley found both in text and fact; but the 'Ubaidian Mesopotamians, not having dense tropical rainforest to prevent their retreat, were able to move back with the water. Consequently, their literature tells us that they stayed in the Gulf, and played host to straggling traders and skilled refugees from the East. As we saw, at the flood-silted baseline of the 'Ubaid culture 7500 years ago, there were similar collections of Neolithic artefacts and pottery, connected with spinning and fishing, and also mysterious Oriental-looking figurines.

The trail West

It is hard to conceive that the sailors and traders who moved with comparative ease into the Southwest Pacific so long ago did not venture west along the safer north-coastal rim of the Indian Ocean. They did. As far as proof of movement of peoples to the West is concerned, we have the physical presence of Mundaic peoples in central India in the same regions that rice-growing first appeared there, possibly as much as 7000 years ago. Sharing their genes and their language family with the Mon-Khmer peoples of Indo-China, these tribespeople, separated by thousands of kilometres and years, share terms for rice culture and bronze-copper as well. This is good evidence that they took a preformed culture west with them. Linguists agree that the split between these branches of the Austro-Asiatic language family occurred in the depths of prehistory.

We also find genetic and linguistic links between the sea-faring and trading Austronesians and certain southern Indian peoples. Although the language links are less obvious than those further north, the ancient genetic markers clearly lead back to island Southeast Asia. It is possible that those early visitors from the East were the same as the legendary 'Nagas', who brought spices and the worship of serpents to the area. There is evidence of Austronesian linguistic introductions to India; but while a Sumerian connection with Austronesian tongues has been suggested, it remains controversial. The genetic links from Southeast Asia along the trade routes through India to the United Arab Emirates and Mesopotamia and on to the Mediterranean, however, reveal an unequivocal trail of ancient, small and focused migrations.

Problems with dates of migration

While the linguistic and genetic trail from Southeast Asia to the West is certainly there, a major problem for both of these kinds of markers is in dating their movements. Both historical linguists and geneticists can, and do, make estimates of the ages of the branches or nodes in their family trees, but they cannot easily say where and when the branch occurred. In simple terms, any given branch in a family could occur either before, or after, that family migrated: there is no easy way of telling which. For the genetics of population migrations, the difficulty of dating means having to give time boundaries of thousands of years.

A special case exists, however, where the new family members are exclusively found at and beyond a certain point of a migration route but not before. These help to date how long ago the first arrivals landed. This situation holds for the so-called Polynesian motif. It shows that, rather than defining recent Polynesian movements out of China, the motif defines a much earlier Austronesian spread into the Southwest Pacific more than 6000 years ago. The Polynesian motif far from defining recent emigrants from China, places the ancestors of the Polynesians and other Pacific Islanders at the edge of the drowning Sunda shelf at the end of the Ice Age. The same argument also holds for the related maternal genetic markers from Southeast Asia that are found in South India. These show unique local diversity, thus indicating prolonged presence of the migrants in South Asia. A number of other unique genetic markers of the globin genes indicate East-to-West flow through India and on to Mesopotamia.

The same kinds of marker reveal a flow of genes directly south to Australia since the end of the Ice Age. Markers also travelled northwards into the genetic melting pot of the eastern Himalayan foothills. These support the concept that this polyglot population were upriver refugees from the south rather than progenitors of a Tibetan dispersal. The genetic picture is thus of an ancient dispersal radially emerging from Southeast Asia as the sea-levels rose.

Some stories can be dated

That there has been exchange of ideas, genes, tongues, artefacts and cultural practices between East and West is not in question. The problem that still remains with all these markers is accurate dating of the first diffusion. Surprisingly, the marker system that produces the strongest links from East to West is also the one with the earliest provenanced and most accurate dates. This marker system is, of course, our religious and secular folklore and is the subject matter of half of this book.

There are two aspects of my use of folklore that must be distinguished: its use as a culture marker and its role as history. The most important of these to me is the former. If we put aside all questions of why folklore was created, we are left with the issue of irrefutable similarities of traditions across great distances and over ethnic boundaries. In their partial rejection of diffusion as the reason for these links, folklorists of the twentieth century have had to propose the only two other possible causes of similarity: chance and the inner workings of the human mind. While chance may operate for single obvious motifs, such as the worship of the Sun, I have shown that it is statistically extremely unlikely that complex story-types, sharing from three to ten distinct motifs, could have occurred more than once. Yet this is what would have to happen for the distribution of myths in a diagonal band across Eurasia – with Polynesia at one end and Finland at the other – to have all occurred independently. That these were the core myths that were preserved so carefully by the Mesopotamian, Middle Eastern and Egyptian civilisations can also be no coincidence. All the main stories in the first ten chapters of Genesis are found in this cultural band and all occur in the Far East: the watery creation, the separation of skies and earth, the creation of man from red earth, and Eve from his side, the Fall, Cain and Abel, and, of course, the flood. With the exception of the flood, the relative paucity of evidence for these complex story-types elsewhere in the Americas and Africa not only supports diffusion as a reason for the distribution, but also argues against both chance and the 'inner workings of man's brain' for their similarities.

While Frazer's methods in folklore were being rejected, the psychological approach to explaining the similarities of such stories, using the ideas of Freud and Jung, became popular and respectable. Time has not proved the latter's promise. Such theories were intrinsically unprovable, unhelpful or irrelevant and can no longer be taken seriously in this context. To take just one example, the story of the separation of Heaven and Earth discussed near the beginning of Part II has frequent references to the previous sexual union of Father Sky and Mother Earth. This might be a source of inspiration to a Freudian interpretation, but the dramatic sexual event or image is widely different in each story. This indicates that although the separation motif has been deliberately conserved in different versions of the story, they have not each arisen spontaneously as a response to a deep need to castrate one's father, or any other such fantasy. The structuralist approach to folklore, which has been in the ascendant in the latter part of the twentieth century, has been equally unhelpful, and in any case ignores the questions of origin of myths.

If we can accept the statistical evidence of trans-continental relationships in myths, then the dating of the first written versions of the Eurasian myths becomes crucial. We are lucky here, since the Sumerians and Babylonians were so assiduous in recording the motifs on tablets and cylinder seals. The date bracket that comes out of such an enquiry reveals that the myths, with their religious connotations, were among the first of all written records in the third millennium BC. Since in the majority of cases the structure and content of the Mesopotamian myths show them to be derived from earlier Eastern versions, we may suppose that the direction of diffusion was East-to-West, and that the date of diffusion may be even earlier than the beginning of the third millennium. This means that East–West cultural links may be older than 5000 years. Such cultural links could only have occurred if there were people in Southeast Asia to hold the stories, and that they were capable of travelling to India and Mesopotamia to transmit them.

If we take just one example of a myth-type which has good claim to have arisen in eastern Indonesia – namely, the 'two warring brothers' – the time of dispersion may be at least 6000 years ago. This Austronesian story found its way east to Kambot village which, 5800 years ago, was an island in the great inland sea of northern New Guinea. The language of the villagers has changed to non-Austronesian, and they are now a long way inland in swamp, but they, like others in Australasia, have preserved the core story. This myth also moved west at a very early stage to Mesopotamia and Egypt, where it developed separately into the two different but related archetypes of 'Cain and Abel' and 'Seth and Osiris', both of which have provenance from the earliest stages of civilisation in those regions.

If we then turn to the content of the shared Eurasian myths, much of it is less arcane than the folklorists would have us think. Some are obviously historiographic. The flood myth is found on the coasts of every continent, especially those with wide continental shelves. There are a limited number of variants which tell of the different ways the last post-glacial flood affected different coastlines. They have every claim to represent a real marine inundation which happened not too long ago. Certain unique details of the East Asian flood stories have again found their way into the Middle Eastern traditions. The watery creation and separation of Heavens and Earth is certainly a very constant story from the Pacific to the West. While it could be another version of the flood, the picture hints at an even grander cataclysm. The content, however, is too stylised to allow interpretation. The story of the two warring brothers clearly describes a clash of cultures and races throughout its Eurasian distribution. The New Guinean and Moluccan versions have more verifiable local detail in their structure, and therefore have good claim to be nearer the archetype. These stories have become intertwined with fertility, death and rebirth cults, both in the East and West. A key player in the two-brother tradition was a tree with a dying male tree spirit who brought fertility by his death and resurrection.

The tree motif was derived from the 'Tree of Life'. This concept, in its various forms – ranging from totemism to temptation – again originated somewhere between the Moluccas and New Guinea. It probably arose as a result of the fertile impact of bananas, sago, coconuts and fruit trees that were dispersed in this region and led to population growth. An amalgam of two immortal animals, the hawk and the snake, with the tree of life to form a potent triad is recognised as a characteristic Southeast Asian product, but travelled to Mesopotamia over 4000 years ago and to China over 3000 years ago.

The idea of the Garden of Eden being a fertile lost Paradise is a peculiarly Austronesian concept which has found its way into the West more than once. The Polynesians had a geographically understandable view of Paradise. It was a big, lush continent in the west that was originally a homeland. It is not really there now, but is inhabited by the spirits of their ancestors and, maybe certain heroes. To get there you have to make a dangerous water crossing which is commemorated in the 'boats of the dead' motif found in caves, on bronzes, and cloth designs throughout Southeast Asia. It could only be the drowned Sunda continent.

The Fall in the Garden of Eden, which has been closely identified with Western concepts of guilt and original sin, in the end turns out to be only one version of the tree-based immortality myths that Frazer described in various forms round the Indian Ocean from Australia to the Kalahari desert. The family of immortality myths may be the oldest of all, recalling the importance of ritual burial which goes back to well before the end of the Ice Age. When we analyse the story development, the family as a whole shows good evidence of having originated in Southeast Asia or the Southwest Pacific.

Sir James Frazer argued that the 'Tree of Knowledge' was a Mesopotamian corruption of the 'Tree of Death'. The Sumerian view of the potency and danger of knowledge appears again in the older Mesopotamian version of Adam's Fall, 'The Myth of Adapa'. The 'knowledge' that was so carefully guarded could have been either technology or magic or both. In many traditional societies the two are inseparable; claims of the supernatural enhance the power of the clever artisan, priest ruler or astronomer. Secret knowledge held by a ruler priest-caste may have been one of the seeds that changed Mesopotamia and Upper Egypt from successful Neolithic agricultural societies to the rich hierarchical cultures that we know from the archaeological record. Source books remark on the striking similarities between pre-Islamic Malay magical practices, such as augury on chicken livers, and that of the ancient Babylonians.

Just what did the East teach the West?

I have argued in this book that the roots of the great flowering of civilisation in the fertile crescent of the Ancient Near East lay in the sinking shorelines of Southeast Asia. The Sumerians and Egyptians themselves wrote about the skilled wise men from the East, a fact often dismissed as the embellishment of a fertile imagination. We might ask just what seed it was that produced such an explosion of cities, monuments, arts, writing and empires 5000 years ago. Apart from the astounding underwater stone structures found recently off the east coast of Taiwan (see illustration 33) and widespread megalithic cultures, there is little direct proof of cities, writing or monuments of that date from Southeast Asia. Rather there is a collection of origin myths and Neolithic/Bronze Age skills shared between the two regions.

My personal view is that although there was much technology transfer over a prolonged period, the most important new lessons from the East were those Marx wrote about in *Das Kapital* – namely, how to use hierarchy, politics, magic and religion to control other peoples' labour. However, before discussing those, we can look at the more solid traces and requirements of civilisation which were acquired progressively rather than in one package. As I have stressed throughout, the suddenness of any revolution in prehistoric societies based on a flat coastline may be illusory. This certainly applies to the coast of the Arabian Gulf, which may have had a long lead-in period to the era of the first cities. As we saw in Part 1 the rising sea-level there only levelled and started to recede around 5500 years ago, and many earlier settlements and cities built in the Gulf may be lost under the sea.

The first pre-requisite for an urban society is a successful agricultural base to feed the population; and from other evidence in the region, this had been present from much earlier times in the Middle East. The first farming village, Çatal Hüyük in Turkey, has been dated to 7000 BC, around the time when swamps were being drained in the New Guinea Highlands and when rice was dated in a cave in the Malay

Peninsula. By the time of the appearance of the Sumerian civilisation 3500 years later, pastoralists and farmers were well established throughout the ancient world, supporting large populations both in the East and West. The Sumerian 'Cain and Abel' traditions, embodied in the story of 'Emes and Enten', were concerned with the conflicts of pastoralist versus agriculturalist.

Farmers, generally speaking, are independent people, and need the city less than the city needs them. While the city dwellers can specialise in organisation, and skills such as artefact production, they cannot make food without land. The second pre-requisite for urban development is thus the creation of a state where the farmers and other citizens are obliged to owe allegiance to the city state and to supply that city with food.

There are many ways in which this subjugation can be achieved, by coercion, by force, by taxes, by religious persuasion or trickery, and finally by the use of war and spies. All are used. It is no mistake that one of the most famous books of the Renaissance, *The Prince* by Machiavelli, was a frank analysis of such methods in affairs of state. Yet this was a comparative late-comer; *The Art of War*, written nearly 2500 years ago by Sun Tzu, a Chinese ruler, made such an effective manual that it is still said to be required reading for Eastern businessmen.

To maintain this state, the ambitious rulers had to establish their organisation and authority by the same combination of force, feudal protection and religious coercion. In both Egypt and Mesopotamia early rulers were deities or priests, and were supported by a priestly caste. At an early stage, the practical navigational and agricultural science of astronomy, which Easterners were certainly skilled in, was hijacked by priestly 'astrologers' for the purposes of fooling and scaring people. This practice, of course, continues today. The addition of magical procedures, such as divining the future through examining an animal's intestines, was used in Mesopotamia, in the same way it is still used throughout Southeast Asia today, from village to regal level.

Consolidation of central authority in a city state is helped by tradition, hierarchy and concepts of kingship. 'Knowing one's place' is a familiar phrase which only faded out a few decades ago in England. Yet the class structure, which still cripples Britain more than any other European state, is as nothing compared with the stratified hierarchies still surviving in Austronesian traditional societies from Madagascar through Bali to Samoa. Ranks of honorific titles are preserved in Balinese to define how each class should address the other. Every Samoan village still has nobles. This consciousness of rank is thus clearly not something that was only picked up by Austronesian societies from later Indian influence.

My journey told in this book started with a chance comment by an old man in a Stone Age village in Papua New Guinea. It took me from the rather technical considerations of human genes and malaria in that island to a realisation that dispersals of Southeast Asian coastal cultivators and sailors followed a succession of post-glacial floods, and led to the cultural fertilisation of the rest of Eurasia. Echoes of this are still detectable in the West in such ancient texts as the Epic of Gilgamesh and the first ten chapters of Genesis. Themes from these myths still permeate the whole corpus of literature from ancient to modern.

And what remains of Southeast Asia today can only give us a glimpse of the Eden that once was.

NOTES

Chapter 1: An Ice Age and Three Floods

1. For a general introduction to Ice Ages, see Windsor Chorlton, *Ice Ages*, Time Life Books, Amsterdam, 1983, pp. 83–109.
2. Sir James Frazer, *Folklore in the Old Testament*, Macmillan, London, 1918, p. 343.
3. See Immanuel Velikovsky, *Worlds in Collision*, London and New York, 1950; also Immanuel Velikovsky, *Earth in Upheaval*, London and New York, 1955.
4. For the best description, see A. G. Dawson, *Ice Age Earth*, Routledge, London, 1992, Chapter 13.
5. See A. Berger, *Modeling the Astronomical Theory of Paleoclimates*, in 'Holocene Cycles: Climate, Sea Levels and Sedimentation', *Journal of Coastal Research*, Special Issue no. 17, 1995, pp. 355–62.
6. Berger, op. cit., p. 356.
7. Paul Blanchon and John Shaw, 'Reef Drowning During the Last Deglaciation: Evidence for Catastrophic Sea-Level Rise and Ice-Sheet Collapse', in *Geology*, vol. 23, no. 1, 1995, pp. 4–8.
8. Richard A. Kerr, 'How Ice Age Climate Got the Shakes', in *Science*, vol. 260, 1995, pp. 890–92.
9. See Richard A. Kerr, 'Ice Rhythms: Core Reveals a Plethora of Climate Cycles', in *Science*, vol. 274, 25 October 1996, pp. 499–500; also Andrew McIntyre and Barbara Molfino, 'Forcing of Atlantic Equatorial and Subpolar Millennial Cycles by Precession', in *Science*, vol. 274, 13 December 1993, pp. 1867–70; and Richard A. Kerr, 'Ice, Quakes and a Wobble Shake San Francisco', in *Science*, vol. 267, 6 January 1995, pp. 27–8.
10. McIntyre and Molfino, op. cit., pp. 1867–70.
11. Hartmut Heinrich, 'Origin and Consequences of Cyclic Ice Rafting in the North-east Atlantic During the Last 130,000 Years', in *Quaternary Research*, vol. 29, no. 2, March 1988, pp. 142–52.
12. McIntyre and Molfino, op. cit., pp. 1867–70.
13. Paul Blanchon and John Shaw, 'Reef Drowning During the Last Deglaciation: Evidence for Catastrophic Sea-Level Rise and Ice Sheet

Collapse', in *Geology*, vol. 23, no. 1, January 1995, pp. 4–8.

14. P. A. Mayewski *et al.*, 'Climate Change During the Last Deglaciation in Antarctica', in *Science*, vol. 272, 14 June 1996, pp. 1636–8.
15. A. G. Dawson, *Ice Age Earth*, Routledge, London, 1992, p. 229.
16. Calibrated date from Mayewski, op. cit., pp. 1636–7.
17. E. Bard *et al.*, 'U-Th Ages Obtained by Mass Spectrometry in Corals From Barbados: Sea Level During the Past 130,000 Years', in *Nature*, vol. 346, 1990, pp. 456–8.
18. Blanchon, op. cit., pp. 4–8.
19. Mayewski, op. cit., pp. 1636–8.
20. Richard A. Kerr, 'Ice Bubbles Confirm Big Chill', in *Science*, vol. 272, 14 June 1996, pp. 1584–5.
21. R. L. Edwards *et al.*, in *Science*, vol. 260, 1993, pp. 962–8.
22. Kerr, op. cit., pp. 1584–5.
23. Blanchon, op. cit., pp. 4–8.
24. Charles H. Fletcher III and Clark E. Sherman, 'Submerged Shorelines on O'ahu, Hawaii: Archive of Episodic Transgression During the Deglaciation?', in *Journal of Coastal Research*, Special Issue no. 17, 1995, pp. 141–52.
25. Ibid., pp. 141–52.
26. Andrew D. Warne and D. J. Stanley, 'Sea-Level Change as a Critical Factor in Development of Basin Margin Sequences: New Evidence from Late Quaternary Record', in Ibid., pp. 231–8.
27. Fletcher, op. cit., pp. 141–52.
28. Fletcher, and Sherman, op. cit., pp. 144–51.
29. T. Blunier *et al.*, 'Variations in Atmospheric Methane Concentration During the Holocene Epoch', in *Nature*, vol. 374, 2 March 1995, pp. 46–8.
30. H. F. Lamb *et al.*, 'Relation Between Century-Scale Holocene Arid Intervals in Tropical and Temperate Zones', in *Nature*, vol. 373, 12 January 1995, pp. 134–7.
31. P. Larcombe *et al.*, 'New Evidence for Episodic Post-Glacial Sea-Level Rise, Central Great Barrier Reef, Australia', in *Marine Geology*, vol. 127, 1995, pp. 1–44.
32. Fletcher and Sherman, op. cit., p. 148.
33. For full details, see ibid., pp. 141–52.
34. *American Association of Petroleum Geologists*, Bulletin, 1995, 79/10, p. 1568.
35. S. Jelgersma and M. J. Tooley, 'Sea-Level Changes in the Recent Geological Past'. in *Journal of Coastal Research*, op. cit., pp. 132–3.
36. Ibid., p. 132.
37. Larcombe, op. cit., pp. 1–44.

38. AAPG Bulletin, op. cit., p. 1568.
39. Fletcher and Sherman, op. cit., pp. 144–51.
40. Blanchon and Shaw, op. cit., pp. 4–8.
41. M. A. Geyh *et al.*, 'Sea-level Changes During the Last Pleistocene and Holocene in the Strait of Malacca', in *Nature*, vol. 278, 29 March 1979, pp. 441–3.
42. See Juris Zarins, 'The Early Settlement of Southern Mesopotamia: A Review of the Recent Historical, Geological and Archaeological Research', in *Journal of American Oriental Society*, 112.1, 1992, pp. 58–9, 61.
43. All dates are corrected absolute calendar years BP, (before present), see M. Stuiver and B. Becker, 'High Precision Decadal Calibration of the Radiocarbon Time Scale, AD 1950–6000 BC', in *Radiocarbon*, vol. 35, no. 1, 1993, pp. 35–66.
44. W. B. F. Ryan *et al.*, 'An Abrupt Drowning of the Black Sea Shelf', in *Marine Geology*, vol. 138 (1–2), 1997, pp. 119–26.
45. Dawson, op. cit., p. 231.
46. See Arch C. Johnston, 'A Wave in the Earth', in *Science*, vol. 274, 1 November 1996, p. 735; also, Heinz Kliewe, 'Chronologic and Climatic Indicators in Sediments of the Southern Baltic and Estuarine Coasts of Western Pommerania', in *Journal of Coastal Research*, op. cit., pp. 181–6.
47. Dawson, op. cit., pp. 101–3.
48. Mayewski, op. cit., pp. 1636–8; also Christine Mlot, 'A High Glacier Opens a View of the Ice Age Tropics', in *Science*, vol. 269, 7 July 1995, p. 32.
49. A. G. Dawson, *Ice Age Earth*, Routledge, London, 1992, p. 157.
50. Ibid., p. 200.
51. Windsor Chorlton, *Ice Ages*, Time Life Books, Amsterdam, 1983, p. 164.
52. Dawson, op. cit., p. 205.
53. See Kurt Lambeck, 'Shoreline Reconstructions for the Persian Gulf since the Last Glacial Maximum', in *Earth and Planetary Science Letters*, vol. 142, 1996, pp. 43–57.
54. Shoreline data taken from Juris Zarins, 'The Early Settlement of Southern Mesopotamia: A Review of Recent Historical, Geological and Archaeological Research', in *Journal of American Oriental Society*, vol. 112.1, 1992, pp. 58–9, 61.
55. Samuel N. Kramer, *The Sumerians: Their History, Culture and Character*, University of Chicago Press, 1963, p. 40.
56. See Zarins, op. cit., pp. 55–77.
57. For further details, see Charles Higham and Rachanie Thosarat, *Khok Phanom Di: Prehistoric Adaptation to the World's Richest Habitat*, Harcourt Brace College, Fort Worth, 1994; also William Meacham,

'Origins and Development of the Yueh Coastal Neolithic: A Microcosm of Culture Change on the Mainland of Southeast Asia', in D. N. Keightley (ed.), *The Origins of Chinese Civilisation*, Berkeley: University of California Press, 1983, pp. 147–75.

58. For further details, see Patrick D. Nunn, *Oceanic Islands,* Blackwell, Oxford, 1994, sections 2 and 3.
59. Ibid., section 4.
60. See Edward M. Weyer, in *Nature*, vol. 273, 1978, pp. 18–21.
61. Patrick D. Nunn, 'Holocene Sea-Level Changes in the South and West Pacific', in *Journal of Coastal Research*, Special Issue no. 1, 1995, op. cit., p. 317.

Chapter 2: The Silt Curtain

1. See Chapter 1 for further details.
2. Cuneiform, from the Latin, literally means 'wedge-shaped'. Early cuneiform 'writings' were actually created from impressions made by a wedged-shaped stylus onto clay tablets.
3. Leonard Woolley, *Ur Excavations, vol. IV, The Early Period,* British Museum, 1955, p. 17.
4. In fact copper metallurgy was already known in the earlier Halaf and Samarra cultures of Western Asia. See *Past Worlds: The Times Atlas of Archaeology*, Times Books, London, 1995, pp. 98–9, 120.
5. Quoted from *The Times*, London, 16 March 1929.
6. Woolley, op. cit., p. 16; see Chapter 9 for further details on Gilgamesh.
7. M. E. L. Mallowan, 'Noah's Flood Reconsidered', in *Iraq*, vol. 26, 1964, pp. 62–83.
8. Woolley, op. cit., p. 17.
9. Mallowan, op. cit., p. 74.
10. See Chapters 8–10 for further detail.
11. See for example Juris Zarins, 'The Early Settlement of Southern Mesopotamia: A Review of Recent Historical, Geological and Archaeological Research', in *Journal of the American Oriental Society*, vol. 112, no. 2, 1992, pp. 55–77; and Kurt Lambeck, 'Shoreline Reconstructions for the Persian Gulf since the Last Glacial Maximums', in *Earth and Planetary Science Letters*, vol. 142, 1996, pp. 43–57.
12. This elevation depends on the hydro-isostatic correction term at Ur.
13. Zarins, op. cit., pp. 58–9.
14. Mallowan, op. cit, p. 83, Table XX.
15. Ibid., p. 64.
16. See Chapter 11 for more discussion.
17. A. G. Dawson, *Ice Age Earth*, Routledge, London, 1992, p. 158.
18. See Michael Rice, *The Archaeology of the Arabian Gulf: c. 5000–323* BC,

Routledge, London, 1994, pp. 75–6.

19. Zarins, op. cit., p. 61.
20. See Sir Thomas Malory, *Le Morte D'Arthur*, J. M. Dent, London, 1978.
21. S. N. Kramer, *The Sumerians: Their History, Culture and Character*, University of Chicago Press, p. 42.
22. Stephanie Dalley, *Myths From Mesopotamia: Creation, The Flood, Gilgamesh and Others*, Oxford University Press, 1991, p. 320; see also Chapter 12.
23. Benno Landsberger, *The Beginning of Civilisation in Mesopotamia*, in *Three Essays on the Sumerians: Monograph on the Ancient Near East*, vol. 1, Fascicle 2, Oxford, 1945, pp. 8–9.
24. Kramer, op. cit., pp. 41–2.
25. Henri Frankfort, 'Archaeology and the Sumerian Problem: Relations with the East and with the North', in J. H. Breasted and T. G. Allen (eds.), *Oriental Institute of the University of Chicago: Studies in Ancient Oriental Civilisations*, p. 40.
26. Brachycephaly literally means 'broad-headed'. The study of skull shape in this context was somewhat impressionistic in the past, and went out of fashion. The more mathematically based work of Howells and Pietrusewsky, particularly in Far Eastern populations ancient and modern, has recently changed this attitude. See, for instance, W. W. Howells, 'Cranial Variation in Man', *Papers of the Peabody Museum of Archaeology and Ethnology 67*, Harvard University, Cambridge Mass., 1973.
27. For further comment, see Colin Renfrew, *Archaeology and Language*, Penguin, London, 1989, pp. 86–94.
28. See Chapter 9 for further details.
29. Landsberger, op. cit., pp. 9 and 17.
30. Ibid., p. 12.
31. William Meacham, 'Defining the Hundred Yue', in *Indo-Pacific Prehistory Association Bulletin 15 (The Chiang Mai Papers)*, vol. 2, 1996, pp. 93–9.
32. William Meacham, 'On the Improbability of Austronesian Origins in South China', in *Asian Perspectives*, vol. 25, no. 1, 1984–5, p. 100.
33. Li Guo, 'Neolithic Sand Bar Sites Round the Pearl River Estuary Area and Hainan: A Comparative Study', in *Indo-Pacific Prehistory Association Bulletin 15*, vol. 2 (*The Chiang Mai Papers*), pp. 211–18; especially p. 214.
34. Charles Higham and Rachanie Thosarat, *Khok Phanom Di: Prehistoric Adaptation to the World's Richest Habitat*, Harcourt Brace College, Fort Worth, 1994, p. 140.
35. Ibid., pp. 140–41.
36. See H. W. Chau, 'Periodization of Prehistoric Culture of the Pearl River

Delta Area', in *Collected Essays on the Culture of the Ancient Yue People in South China*, The Urban Council, Hong Kong, 1993, quoted in Li Guo, op. cit., p. 211.

37. Li Guo, op. cit., p. 216 (dates corrected for Carbon 14 calibration).
38. Meacham, op. cit., p. 96.
39. See Li Guo, op. cit., and Chen Xingcan, 'Xiantouling Dune Site: Its Significance in Understanding the Coastal Area of South China in Prehistory', in *Indo-Pacific Prehistory Association Bulletin 15*, vol. 2 (*The Chiang Mai Papers*), pp. 207–10.
40. Leonard Woolley, *Ur Excavations, vol, IV, The Early Period*, British Museum, 1955, pp. 7–14.
41. Wilhelm G. Solheim, 'The Nusantao and North-South Dispersals', in *Indo-Pacific Prehistory Association Bulletin 15*, vol. 2, 1996 (*Chiang Mai Papers*), pp. 106–7.
42. Both Solheim and Kwang-chih Chang, an archaeologist in Harvard, concur in viewing the Taiwan move as separate from, and incidental to, the spread of the China south coast 'corded-ware' culture elsewhere to insular Southeast Asia and the Pacific; see ibid., p. 106.
43. Robert Blust, 'The Austronesian Homeland: A Linguistic Perspective', in *Asian Perspectives,* vol. XXVI, no. 1, 1985, p. 49.
44. Meacham, 1984, op. cit., pp. 89–106.
45. Peter Bellwood, 'Austronesian Prehistory in Southeast Asia: Homeland, Expansion and Transformation', in Bellwood (ed.), *The Austronesians*, National University of Australia, Canberra, 1995, p. 102.
46. My discussion of Bellwood's work is not intended as a personal attack. As an outsider, I have the highest respect for his central and seminal work in illuminating Austronesian studies both for his colleagues and for the general public. As far as possible I look at his arguments and presented evidence, rather than his technical work.
47. Peter Bellwood, *Prehistory of the Indo-Malaysian Archipelago*, Academic Press, Australia, pp. 218–9.
48. See Surin Pookajorn, 'Human Activities and Environmental Changes During the Late Pleistocene to the Middle Holocene in Southern Thailand and Southeast Asia', in L. G. Straus *et al.* (ed.), *Humans and the End of the Ice Age: The Archaeology of the Pleistocene-Holocene Transition*, Plenum, New York, 1996, pp. 201–13.
49. Ibid., p. 208.
50. See Wilhelm Solheim, 'Southeast Asia and Korea: from the beginnings of food production to the first states', in *The History of Humanity: Scientific and Cultural Development*, vol 1: *Prehistory and the Beginnings of Civilisation,* Unesco/Routledge, London, 1994, pp. 468–81.
51. Joyce C. White, 'A Brief Note on New Dates For the Ban Chiang

Cultural Tradition', in *Indo-Pacific Prehistory Association Bulletin 15*, vol. 3, 1996 (*The Chiang Mai Papers*), pp. 103–5.

52. Higham and Thosarat, op. cit., pp. 10–12. Incidentally, Hemudu was occupied before the flood more than 7000 years ago, as is confirmed by deposits of oyster shell below the level of Hangzhou City.
53. Ibid., p. 10.
54. Ibid., pp. 9–10.
55. See Bellwood, 1995, op. cit, 100–102. See also Peter Bellwood, 1985, op. cit., p. 223.
56. Kwang-Chih Chang and Ward H. Goodenough, 'Archaeology of Southeastern Coastal China and its Bearing on the Austronesian Homeland', in Goodenough (ed.), *The Prehistoric Settlement of the Pacific*, in *American Philosophical Society*, vol. 86 (5), 1996, p. 39.
57. Solheim, 1996, op. cit., p. 105.
58. Charles Higham, *The Bronze Age of Southeast Asia*, Cambridge, 1996, p. 300; all dates corrected.
59. Bellwood, 1985, op. cit., p 232.
60. Solheim, 1996, op. cit., p. 105.
61. Bellwood, 1985, op. cit., pp. 213 and 223.
62. Bellwood, 1985, op. cit., pp. 213 and 223.
63. Chang and Goodenough, op. cit., pp. 40–41.
64. See Jean-Michel Chazine, 'New Approach in Kalimantan Rock Art and Prehistory', from *IVth Borneo Research Council*, Brunei, 1996, pp. 1–15; see also next chapter.
65. Bellwood, 1985, op. cit., p. 218.
66. Chang and Goodenough, op. cit., p 52.
67. Bellwood, 1985, op. cit., Chapter 5.
68. Stephen C. Jett, 'Further Information on the Geography of the Blowgun and its Implications for Early Transoceanic Contacts', in *Annals of the Association of American Geographers*, vol 81 (1), 1991, pp. 89–102.
69. The term 'Austric' was suggested a hundred years ago as the common ancestor of Austronesian and Austro-Asiatic language groups – see Chapter 5.
70. Bellwood, 1985, op. cit., pp. 152–6.
71. Rong Guanqiong, 'A study of the Historical Records on the Cultural Relationship Between the Ancient Yue People in Lingan Area and the People in Southeast Asia', in *Collected Essays on the Culture of the Ancient Yue People in South China*, The Urban Council, Hong Kong, 1993, p. 167 ff., and Jett, op. cit., pp. 662–88.
72. Bellwood, 1985, op. cit., pp. 149–56.
73. Meacham, 1996 op. cit., p. 99.
74. Bellwood, 1995, op. cit., p. 102.

75. Woolley, op. cit., pp. 8–14.
76. See Bellwood, 1985, op. cit., pp. 219–22; Li Guo, op. cit., pp. 211–18, and Chang, op. cit., p. 50.
77. Woolley, op. cit., p. 12.
78. See also the striking photographs of these figurines in, for example, André Parrot, *Sumer*, Thames and Hudson, France, 1960, p. 55.
79. Bellwood, 1985, op. cit., p. 256.
80. Ibid., p. 152.
81. Anyone wishing to read a detailed personal account of this excruciatingly painful initiation in a Sepik village should read Benedict Allen, *Into the Crocodile's Nest*, Paladin, London, 1989.
82. A. S. Dyke and V. K. Prest, 'Late Wisconsinan and Holocene History of the Laurentide Ice Sheet', in *Geographie Physique et Quaternaire*, 1987, vol. 41, pp. 237–64.

Chapter 3: Wet Feet

1. I will discuss the linguistic arguments in Chapter 5.
2. William Meacham (concerning South China and Southeast Asia), Wilhelm Solheim (East and Southeast Asia), Pamela Swadling (Melanesia).
3. Wilhelm G. Solheim, 'The Nusantao and North-South Dispersals', in *Indo-Pacific Prehistory Association Bulletin 15*, 1996 (*Chiang Mai Papers*), vol. 2, pp. 101–9.
4. See Matthew Spriggs, 'The Dating of the Island Southeast Asian Neolithic: An Attempt at Chronometric Hygiene and Linguistic Correlation', in *Antiquity*, vol. 63, 1989, pp. 587–613.
5. Geyh reported a figure of 7600 BP – before present – (corrected) for the Malacca Strait: M. A. Geyh, 'Sea-level Changes during the Late Pleistocene and Holocene in the Strait of Malacca', in *Nature*, vol. 278, 1979, pp. 441–3. A similar figure has been obtained for Thailand: see Surin Pookajorn, 'Human Activities and Environmental Changes During the Late Pleistocene to the Middle Holocene in Southern Thailand and Southeast Asia', in L. G. Straus *et al.* (ed.), *Humans and the End of the Ice Age: The Archaeology of the Pleistocene-Holocene Transition*, Plenum, New York, 1996, pp. 208–10.
6. Pookajorn, op. cit., p. 210.
7. Joyce C. White, 'A Brief Note on New Dates for the Ban Chiang Cultural Tradition', in *Indo-Pacific Prehistory Association Bulletin 15*, 1996 (*The Chiang Mai Papers*), vol. 3, 1997, p. 103.
8. Peter Bellwood, *Prehistory of the Indo-Malaysian Archipelago*, Academic Press, Australia, 1985, pp. 258–70 (revised edition, 1997, University of Hawaii Press, not available at the time of writing). I will come back to

the arguments supporting the antiquity of the original Austro-Asiatic speakers in Southeast Asia in Chapters 4 and 7.

9. See M. Swanston (ed.), *Past Worlds: The Times Atlas of Archaeology*, Times Books, London, 1995, p. 89.
10. Himanshu Prabha Ray, 'The Emergence of Urban Centres in Bengal: Implications for the Late Prehistory of Southeast Asia', in *Indo-Pacific Prehistory Association Bulletin 15*, 1996 (*The Chiang Mai Papers*), vol. 1, p. 44.
11. Charles Higham and Rachanie Thosarat, *Khok Phanom Di: Prehistoric Adaptation to the World's Richest Habitat*, Harcourt Brace College, Fort Worth, 1994, p. 140.
12. Higham favours later dates during the third millennium BC for both rice-growing in Indo-China and for its introduction by Austro-Asiatic speakers into India; see Charles Higham, *The Bronze Age of Southeast Asia*, Cambridge University Press, 1996, pp. 294–5 and 337.
13. White, op. cit., pp. 104–5
14. Ibid., p. 104.
15. Bellwood, 1985, op. cit., p. 173.
16. B. K. Maloney and F. G. McCormac, 'Palaeoenvironments of North Sumatra: A 30,000-Year-Old Pollen Record from Pea Bullok', in *Indo-Pacific Prehistory Association Bulletin 15*, 1996 (*The Chiang Mai Papers*), vol. 1, pp. 73–81.
17. Bellwood, 1985, op. cit., p. 187.
18. Bellwood, 1985, op. cit., pp. 256–7.
19. Spriggs, op. cit., pp. 587–613.
20. Some might say Harrison's dig was 'notorious', such was his blunderbuss approach.
21. Spriggs, op. cit., p. 595.
22. See Jean-Michel Chazine, 'New Approach in Kalimantan Rock Art and Prehistory', from *IVth Borneo Research Council*, Brunei, 1996, pp. 1–15.
23. Chazine, op. cit., p. 1.
24. Peter Bellwood, 'Austronesian Prehistory in Southeast Asia: Homeland, Expansion and Transformation', in Peter Bellwood (ed.), *The Austronesians: Historical and Comparative Perspectives*, The Australian National University, Canberra, 1995, pp. 100–102.
25. Douglas Newton, 'Reflection in Bronze: Lapita and Dong-Son Art in the Western Pacific', in Jean-Paul Barbier and Douglas Newton (eds.), *Islands and Ancestors: Indigenous Styles of Southeast Asia*, Thames and Hudson, London, 1988, pp. 10–23.
26. John Coles and Lasse Bengtsson, *Images of the Past: A guide to the rock carvings and other ancient monuments of Northern Bohuslän*, Skrifter utgivna av Bohusläns museum och Bohusläns hembygdsförbund, nr. 32, 1994.

27. A particularly fine example is the Galstadt axe, held in the Archaeological Museum of Göteborg, Sweden.
28. Ian C. Glover *et al.*, 'The Cham, Sa Huynh and Han in Early Vietnam: Excavations at Buu Chau Hill, Tra Kieu, 1993', in *Indo-Pacific Prehistory Association Bulletin, 15*, 1996 (*The Chiang Mai Papers*), vol. 1, p. 167.
29. Robert Blust, 'The Austronesian Homeland: A Linguistic Perspective', in *Asian Perspectives*, vol. XXVI, no. 1, 1985, p. 57.
30. Bellwood, 1985, op. cit., pp 273–6.
31. Higham, op. cit., p. 233.
32. Bellwood, 1985, op. cit., pp. 224, 246, 256–8.
33. Wilhelm G. Solheim, 'The Nusantao and North-South Dispersals', in *Indo-Pacific Prehistory Association Bulletin, 15*, 1996 (*Chiang Mai Papers*), vol. 2, pp. 101–7.
34. Geoffrey Irwin, *The Prehistoric Exploration and Colonisation of the Pacific*, Cambridge University Press, 1994, p. 18; also, Thomas H. Loy *et al.*, 'Direct Evidence for human use of plants 28,000 years ago: starch residues on stone artefacts from the northern Solomon Islands', in *Antiquity*, vol. 66. 1992, pp. 898–912.
35. Ibid., p. 35.
36. Jim Allen, 'The Pre-Austronesian Settlement of Island Melanesia: Implications from Lapita Archaeology', in Ward H. Goodenough (ed.), *Prehistoric Settlement of the Pacific*, The American Philosophical Society, 1996, p. 22.
37. J. P. White *et al.*, 'The Balof Shelters, New Ireland', pp. 46–58, quoted in Gosden, 1995, op. cit. p. 814.
38. Chris Gosden, 'Arboriculture and Agriculture in Coastal Papua New Guinea', in *Antiquity*, vol. 69, 1995, p. 816.
39. Irwin, op. cit., p. 35.
40. Ibid., p. 35.
41. Robert F. Service, 'Rock Chemistry Traces Ancient Islanders', in *Science*, vol. 274, 1996, pp. 2012–13.
42. John Terrell, quoted in Service, ibid., pp. 2012–13.
43. P. V. Kirch, *The Lapita Peoples: Ancestors of the Oceanic World*, Blackwell, Oxford, 1997, p. 43.
44. Allen, op. cit., p. 22.
45. Ibid., p. 22.
46. Ibid., p. 23–5.
47. Pamela Swadling, 'Changing Shorelines and Cultural Orientations in the Sepik-Ramu, Papua New Guinea: Implications for Pacific Prehistory', in *World Archaeology*, vol. 29(1), 1997, pp. 1–14.
48. Ibid., p. 9.
49. Ibid., p. 5.

50. Armbands of trochus shell and adzes made from tridacna shell found in the foothills and dating to 6000–5000 years ago, in addition to many Austronesian loan-words in the Enga language of the highlands: ibid., p. 11.
51. Ibid., p. 12.
52. See Chapter 1 for further details.
53. Harry Allen, 'The Time of the Mangroves: Changes in Mid-Holocene Estuarine Environments and Subsistence in Australia and Southeast Asia', in *Indo-Pacific Prehistory Association Bulletin 15*, 1996 (*The Chiang Mai Papers*), vol 2., pp. 193–205.
54. Ibid., p. 202.
55. See Chapter 11.
56. H. Allen, op. cit., p. 198.
57. Technology, animals and, presumably, people, were recently well reviewed by an Australian archaeologist: see Josephine Flood, *Archaeology of the Dreamtime*, Collins, Australia, 1995, pp. 221–36.
58. The dingo could not apparently have arrived earlier than 7500 years ago, although later dates have been suggested (4000–3500 BP – before present – in ibid., Chapter 15).
59. Ibid., pp. 230–33.
60. Ibid., pp. 226–230.
61. Ibid., p. 235.
62. Nichols's work is explored in much more depth in Chapter 4.
63. Flood, op. cit., p. 236.
64. All seven stimuli are from Peter Bellwood, 'Austronesian Prehistory in Southeast Asia: Homeland Expansion and Transformation', in Peter Bellwood (ed.), *The Austronesians*, Australian National University, Canberra, 1995, pp. 101–3.
65. Ibid., p. 103.
66. See Colin Renfrew, *Archaeology and Language*, Penguin, London, 1989, p. 279.
67. Kwang Chih-Chang and Ward H. Goodenough, 'Archaeology of Southeastern Coastal China and its Bearing on the Austronesian Homeland', in Goodenough (ed.), *Prehistoric Settlement of the Pacific*, in *American Philosophical Society*, vol. 86(5), 1996, p. 50.
68. See Chapter 5 for more details of the Bellwood and Blust model of the Austronesian dispersal.
69. Richard J. Huggett, *Cataclysms and Earth History: The Development of Diluvialism,* Clarendon Press, Oxford, 1989, p. 187.
70. Arch C. Johnson, 'A Wave in the Earth', in *Science*, vol. 274, November 1996, p. 735.
71. A. G. Dawson, *Ice Age Earth*, Routledge, London, 1992, pp. 100–101.

72. R. J. Morley and J. R. Flenley, 'Late Cainozoic Vegetational and Environmental Changes in the Malay Archipelago', in T. C. Whitmore (ed.), *Biogeographical Evolution of the Malay Archipelago,* Clarendon Press, Oxford, 1987, p. 55.
73. B. K. Maloney and F. G. McCormac, 'Palaeoenvironments of North Sumatra: A 30,000 Year Old Pollen Record From Pea Bullok', in *Indo-Pacific Prehistory Association Bulletin 15,* 1996 (*The Chiang Mai Papers*), vol. 1, pp. 73–81.
74. Clifford Sather, 'Sea Nomads and Rainforest Hunter-Gathers: Foraging Adaptations in the Indo-Malaysian Archipelago', in Bellwood (ed.), *The Austronesians,* op. cit., p. 232.
75. See Sumet Jumsai, *Naga,* Oxford University Press, 1988.
76. See Chapter 2, and Wilhelm G. Solheim, 'The Nusantao and North-South Dispersals', in *Indo-Pacific Prehistory Association Bulletin 15,* 1996 (*Chiang Mai Papers*), vol. 2, pp. 105–6.
77. Joyce C. White, 'A Brief Note on New Dates for the Ban Chiang Cultural Tradition', in *Indo-Pacific Prehistory Association Bulletin 15,* 1996 (*The Chiang Mai Papers*), vol. 3, p. 106.
78. For recent review on Chanka/Mancala, see Alexander J. de Voogt, *Mancala: Board Games,* British Museum Press, 1997.

Chapter 4: Babel

1. Literally, scholars studying old languages or historical linguistics.
2. Literally, 'with a common birth'.
3. Jeff Marck, 'A Revision to Polynesian Linguistic Subgrouping and its Culture History Implications', in Roger Blench and Matthew Spriggs (eds.), *Archaeology and Language,* vol. 2, Routledge, New York, in press.
4. See Colin Renfrew, *Archaeology and Language: The Puzzle of Indo-European Origins,* Penguin, London, 1989, for further details.
5. Johanna Nichols, 'The Epicentre of the Indo-European Linguistic Spread', in Roger Blench and Matthew Spriggs (eds.), *Archaeology and Language 1: Theoretical and Methodological Orientations,* Routledge, London, 1997, pp. 122–48.
6. E.g. 'suffix': addition at the end of a word; 'prefix': addition at the beginning of a word; 'infix': addition in the middle of a word.
7. S. N. Kramer, *The Sumerians: Their History, Culture and Character,* University of Chicago Press, 1963, pp. 306–7.
8. Marcel Otte, 'The Differentiation of Modern Languages in Prehistoric Eurasia', in Roger Blench and Matthew Spriggs (eds.), *Archaeology and Language 1: Theoretical and Methodological Orientations,* Routledge, London, 1997, pp. 74–81.
9. Johanna Nichols, *Linguistic Diversity in Space and Time,* University of

Chicago Press, 1992.

10. Ibid., p. 185.
11. Ibid., p. 275.
12. Johanna Nichols, *Linguistic Diversity in Space and Time,* Chicago University Press, 1992, pp. 228 and 230.
13. For further explanation see ibid., p. 212.
14. W. Neves and H. Pucciarelli, 'The Zhoukoudian Upper Cave Skull 101 as Seen from the Americas', *Journal of Human Evolution,* 1998, pp. 219–22.
15. James Matisoff, 'On Megalocomparison', in *Language,* vol. 66, no. 1, 1990, pp. 106–119, and 113.
16. James Matisoff, 'Linguistic Diversity and Language Contact', in J. McKinnon *et al.* (eds.), *Highlanders of Thailand,* Oxford University Press, Kuala Lumpur, 1983, p. 65–7.
17. See Charles Higham and Rachanie Thosarat, *Khok Phanom Di: Prehistoric Adaptation to the World's Richest Habitat,* Harcourt Brace College, Fort Worth, 1994, p. 144, and Matisoff, op. cit., 1983, pp. 65–7. In addition to the physical differences the genetic divisions between the so-called 'northern Mongoloid' and 'southern Mongoloid' populations both speaking Sino-Tibetan tongues is emphasized by L. Luca Cavalli-Sforza and colleagues in their authoritative '*The History and Geography of Human Genes*' (abridged paperback 1996, Princeton University Press; p. 233).
18. See Matisoff, op. cit., 1983, pp. 65–6, and Robert Blust, 'Beyond the Austronesian Homeland: The Austric Hypothesis and its Implications for Archaeology', in Ward H. Goodenough (ed.), *Prehistoric Settlement of the Pacific,* in *Transactions of the American Philosophical Society,* 1996, vol. 86 (5), pp. 117–40.
19. Sumet Jumsai, *Naga: Cultural Origins in Siam and the West Pacific,* Oxford University Press, 1989.
20. Robert Blust, 1996, op. cit, pp. 117–40.
21. Ibid., pp. 117–40.
22. See Donn Bayard, 'Linguistics, Archaeologists and Austronesian Origins: Comparative and Sociolinguistic Aspects of the Meacham-Bellwood Debate', and William Meacham, 'Defining the Hundred Yue', in *Bulletin of the Indo-Pacific Prehistory Association 15 (The Chiang Mai Papers),* vol. 2, 1996, pp. 76 and 93–100.
23. Higham and Thosarat, op. cit., p. 141.
24. Wilhelm G. Solheim, 'Southeast Asia and Korea: from the Beginnings of Food Production to the First States', in *History of Humanity: Scientific and Cultural Development,* vol. 1: *Prehistory and the Beginnings of Civilisation,* UNESCO/Routledge, 1994, Chapter 45, pp. 468–80.

25. Surin Pookajorn, *The Phi Tong Luang (Mlabri): A Hunter-Gatherer Group of Northern Thailand*, Prasith Santiwattana, Bangkok, 1992.
26. Clifford Sather, 'Sea Nomads and Rainforest Hunter-Gatherers: Foraging Adaptations in the Indo-Malaysian Archipelago', in Peter Bellwood (ed.), *The Austronesians*, Australian National University, Canberra, 1995, pp. 229–68.
27. Solheim, op, cit., p. 477.
28. David Bradley, 'East and Southeast Asia', in C. Moseley and R. E. Asher (eds.), *Atlas of the World's Languages*, Routledge, London, 1994, p. 159.
29. Malay, the national language, belongs to the Austronesian phylum and is generally regarded as a much more recent introduction than Austro-Asiatic.
30. Iskander Carey in his classic monograph (*Orang Asli: the Aboriginal Tribes of Peninsula Malaysia*, Oxford University Press, 1976, p. 19) notes that the Senoi, or the central linguistic group, have been compared to Mon-Khmer mountain tribes in Cambodia and Vietnam. See also Chapter 3 and Chapter 6 for further discussion.
31. See Jumsai, op. cit.
32. This technique is based on the assumption of a constant rate of vocabulary replacement of a standard hundred word list, in different languages. Nichols (op. cit., pp. 268–9) has pointed out a consistent bias that may be introduced as a result of different language structure.
33. See 'Austro-Asiatic', Britannica CD, Version 97, Encyclopaedia Britannica, Inc., 1997.
34. Miao is also known as Hmong, while Yao is often referred to as Mien.
35. See Peter Bellwood, 'The Austronesian Dispersal and the Origin of Languages', in *Scientific American*, July 1991, pp. 72–3.
36. See Blust, op. cit., p. 122–123.
37. Blust, op. cit., p. 136.
38. See Robert Blust, 'The Austronesian Homeland: A Linguistic Perspective', in *Asian Perspectives,* vol. 26, no. 1, 1984–5, p. 47.
39. Paul Benedict, quoted in Blust, 1996, op. cit., p. 118. In the 1942 paper Benedict referred to today's Austronesian phylum as 'Indonesian'.

Chapter 5: Homeland of the Argonauts

1. See Andrew Pawley, 'Austronesian Languages' Britannica CD, Version 97, Encyclopaedia Britannica, Inc., 1997.
2. K. Alexander Adelaar, 'Borneo as a Crossroads for Comparative Austronesian Linguistics', in Peter Bellwood (ed.), *The Austronesians*, Australian National University, Canberra, 1995, pp. 75–95.
3. Lawrence Reid, 'The Current State of Linguistic Research on the Relatedness of the Language Families of East and Southeast Asia', in

Bulletin of the Indo-Pacific Prehistory Association 15: (The Chiang Mai Papers), vol. 2, 1996, pp. 87–91.

4. Wilhelm Solheim, 'The Nusantao and North-South Dispersals', in *Bulletin of the Indo-Pacific Prehistory Association 15*: (*The Chiang Mai Papers*), vol. 2, 1996, pp. 101–9; see also Chapter 2.
5. Robert Blust, in Darrell Tryon, 'Proto-Austronesian and the Major Austronesian Subgroups', in Peter Bellwood (ed.), *The Austronesians*, Australian National University, Canberra, 1995, p. 20.
6. Kwang-Chih Chang and W. H. Goodenough, 'Archaeology of South-eastern Coastal China and its Bearing on the Austronesian Homeland', in Goodenough (ed.), *Prehistoric Settlement of the Pacific, Transactions of the American Philosophical Society*, vol. 86(5), 1996, pp. 36–56, especially p. 38 and p. 52.
7. Reid, op. cit., p. 88.
8. Ibid., p. 89.
9. In this discussion, for convenience, I am using 'Aslian' to indicate Austro-Asiatic Aboriginal tongues. This is not strictly correct. 'Asli' in Malay simply means 'original'; and colloquially the 'Orang Asli' also includes people speaking Malayic or Austronesian Aboriginal tongues.
10. Adelaar, op. cit., p. 91.
11. Ibid., p. 91.
12. See, for example, Clyde Winters, 'Tamil, Sumerian, Manding and the Genetic Model', in *International Journal of Dravidian Linguistics*, vol. 18, no. 1, 1988, pp. 67–91; also J. Gonda, *Sanskrit in Indonesia*, International Academy of Indian Culture, New Delhi, 1973.
13. Irén Hegedus, 'Principles for Palaeolithic Reconstruction', in Roger Blench and Matthew Spriggs (eds.), *Archaeology and Language I: Theoretical and Methodological Orientations*, Routledge, London, 1997, pp. 65–73.
14. Much of this work by Paul Kekai Manansala is as yet unpublished or unavailable, but can be found on his internet web page: Polmansl@ix.netcom.com.
15. Waruno Mahdi, *Some Linguistic and Philological Data Towards a Chronology of Austronesian Activity in India and Sri Lanka*, paper to the World Archaeological Congress, no. 3, Routledge, London, 4–11 December 1994, New Delhi.
16. See, for example, Terrell in P. V. Kirch, *The Lapita Peoples: Ancestors of the Oceanic World*, Blackwell, Oxford, 1997, p. 95.
17. 'Austronesian Languages', Britannica CD, Version 97, Encyclopaedia Britannica, Inc., 1997.
18. P. V. Kirch, op. cit., p. 95, and Peter Bellwood, *Prehistory of the Indo-Malaysian Archipelago*, Academic Press, Australia, 1985, pp. 110–111.
19. Peter Bellwood, *Prehistory of the Indo-Malaysian Archipelago*, Academic

Press, Australia, 1985, p. 110. Interestingly, one bovid, the mountain anoa (*Bubalus quarlesi*), a type of buffalo, has made it to Sulawesi, thus reaching a point to the east of both lines.

20. 'The Biosphere and concepts of ecology', Britannica CD, Version 97, Encyclopaedia Britannica, Inc., 1997.
21. Geoffrey Irwin, *The Prehistoric Exploration and Colonisation of the Pacific*, Cambridge University Press, 1994, pp. 18–22.
22. Reviewed recently by anthropologist/linguist Donn Bayard from New Zealand: see Donn Bayard, 'Linguistics, Archaeologists and Austronesian Origins: Comparative and Sociolinguistic Aspects of the Meacham-Bellwood Debate', in *Bulletin of the Indo-Pacific Prehistory Association 15 (The Chiang Mai Papers)*, vol. 2, 1996, pp. 71–85.
23. Ibid., pp. 74, 80, and William Meacham, 'On the Improbability of Austronesian Origins in South China', in *Asian Perspectives*, vol. 26, no. 1, 1984–5, pp. 89–106.
24. Solheim, op. cit., p. 101.
25. See Andrew Pawley's section on 'Proto-Austronesian/chronology', Britannica CD, Version 97, Encyclopaedia Britiannica Inc., 1997. This section was contributed in 1976 and reflects views at that time.
26. See K. Alexander Adelaar, 'Borneo as a Crossroads for Comparative Austronesian Linguistics', in *The Austronesians*, op. cit., pp. 75–95.
27. See map in Bellwood, 1995, op. cit., p. 32.
28. See Chapter 2 for further details on the 'Out-of-Taiwan' hypothesis.
29. See Tryon, op. cit. (note 8), p. 26.
30. See Peter Metcalf, *A Borneo Journey into Death*, S. Abdul Majeed & Co., Kuala Lumpur, 1991, Part 5, for further details; see also Chapter 3.
31. Ibid., pp. 233–9.
32. Adelaar, op. cit., pp. 86–7.
33. Blust recognises these tongues as a subgroup of western Malayo-Polynesian in Blust, 1984, op. cit., p. 57.
34. Bernd Nothofer, 'The Relationship Between the Languages of the Barrier Islands and the Sulawesi-Philippine Languages', in Tom Dutton and Darrel Tryon (eds.), *Contact-Induced Change in Austronesian Languages*, Mouton de Gruyter, Berlin, 1994, pp. 389–409.
35. Such as Embaloh and Kayan.
36. See J. King and J. W. King (eds.), *Languages of Sabah, a Survey Report*, Pacific Linguistics, 1984. Also, see Beatrice Clayre, *A Preliminary Typology of the Languages of North Borneo*, Borneo Research Council, Brunei, June 1996.
37. Solheim, op. cit., p. 101.
38. Clifford Sather, 'Sea Nomads and Rainforest Hunter-Gatherers: Foraging Adaptations in the Indo-Malaysian Archipelago', in Peter

Bellwood (ed.), *The Austronesians*, Australian National University, Canberra, 1995, p. 246.

39. Ibid., pp. 247–8.
40. See, for example, Christopher Moseley and R. E. Asher (eds.), *Atlas of World Languages*, Routledge, New York, 1994, p. 159 ff.
41. Bellwood, 1995, op. cit., p. 102.
42. See P. V. Kirch, *The Lapita Peoples: Ancestors of the Oceanic World*, Blackwell, Oxford, 1997, especially Chapter 4.
43. Otherwise referred to as 'Northern Indonesian'.
44. Blust, 1984–5, op. cit.; see also Darrell Tryon, 'Proto-Austronesian and the Major Austronesian Sub-Groups', in Peter Bellwood (ed.), *The Austronesians*, Australian National University, Canberra, 1995, p. 34.
45. These dates are Bellwood's and are meant to reflect his archaeological evidence; Blust's dates, based on linguistic evidence, are 1000–2000 years earlier.
46. Kirch, op. cit., pp. 58–62.
47. Matthew Phelan, 'Fashionably Late: A Re-Examination of Radiocarbon Dates Associated with Dentate-Stamped Lapita Pottery', paper presented to the Vanuatu National Museum ANU Conference: *The Western Pacific, 5000–2000 BP* [before present]; *Colonisations and Transformations*, at Vanuatu National Museum, Port Vila, August 1996.
48. Kirch, op. cit., pp. 44, 62, 66, 77.
49. Kirch, op. cit., p. 59.
50. Kirch, op. cit., p. 92, and Andrew Pawley and Malcolm Ross, *The Prehistory of Oceanic Languages: A Current View*, in Peter Bellwood (ed.), *The Austronesians*, Australian National University, Canberra, 1995, pp. 51–2.
51. From Kirch, op. cit., p. 50.
52. Andrew Pawley, 'Proto-Austronesian/Chronology', Britannica CD, Version 97, Encyclopaedia Britannica Inc., 1997.
53. 'Oceanic Languages', Britannica CD, Version 97, Encyclopaedia Britannica Inc., 1997.
54. I. Dyen, 'A lexicostatistical classification of the Austronesian languages', *International Journal of American Linguistics Memoir*, 19, 1965.
55. A. Pawley and R. Green, 'Dating the Dispersal of the Oceanic Languages', in *Oceanic Linguistics*, 12, 1973, pp. 1–67.
56. W. Howells, *The Pacific Islanders*, Scribner's, New York, 1973.
57. I. Lilley, 'Lapita as Politics'. Paper presented to the Vanuatu National Museum-ANU-ORSTOM Lapita conference, Port Vila, 1996.
58. Ward H. Goodenough (ed.), *The Prehistoric Settlement of the Pacific*, in *Transactions of the American Philosophical Society*, 1996, vol. 86(5), Introduction, pp. 7–8.

59. The geographic exceptions of the Whiteman languages have no Lapita sites.
60. Goodenough, op. cit., pp. 7–8.
61. See Geoffrey Irwin, *The Prehistoric Exploration and Colonisation of the Pacific*, Cambridge University Press, 1994.
62. See Kirch, op. cit., p. 55.
63. In Goodenough, op. cit., Introduction.
64. Stephen C. Jett, 'The Development and Distribution of the Blowgun', in *Annals of the Association of American Geographers*, vol. 60, 1970, p. 670.
65. Kirch, op. cit., p. 53.
66. Peter J. Sheppard and Matthew Felgate, *A Ceramic Sequence From Roviana Lagoon (New Georgia, Solomon Islands)*, paper presented at Lapita Workshop, Vila, Vanuatu, in press.
67. Andrew Pawley and Malcolm Ross, 'The Prehistory of the Oceanic Languages: A Current View', in Bellwood (ed.), *The Austronesians*, op. cit., 1995, pp. 51–2; this group is innovation-*linked* rather than innovation-*defined*. There is no single innovation that all share relative to Proto-Oceanic.
68 S. A. Wurm, Australian National University: Pacific Linguistics Series D., no. 27, 1975.
69. Christian Kaufmann, 'Research on Sepik Pottery and its Implications for Melanesian Prehistory', paper presented at International Conference: *The Western Pacific 5000–2000 BP* [before present]: *Colonisations and Transformations*, at Vila, Vanuatu, July 31–August 6 1996, p. 7, in print.
70. See Chapter 1 for further details of this flood.

Chapter 6: Eve's Genes

1. The Polynesian dispersal arrived at the same time as the Lapita culture; for details of Lapita, see Chapters 3 and 5.
2. The reader may wish to refer to general genetics texts such as: E. J. Mange and A. P. Mange, *Basic Human Genetics*, Sinauer, Sunderland MA, 1994; and G. A. Harrison *et al*, *Human Biology: An Introduction to Human Evolution, Variation, Growth, and Adaptability*, Oxford University Press, Oxford, 1988.
3. Human beings make more than one type of haemoglobin; in newborns the predominant type is called foetal haemoglobin, although small amounts of adult haemoglobin A are also present. These haemoglobins can be easily separated by putting them in a strong electric field on a suitable medium such as starch gel. In normal human babies one will see a thick band due to foetal haemoglobin and, close to it, a thinner band due to the small amount of adult haemoglobin present.
4. Some $-\alpha^{3.7}$-deletions may be missed even at birth; see D. K. Bowden, A.

V. S. Hill, D. R. Higgs, S. J. Oppenheimer, D. J. Weatherall, and J. B. Clegg, 'Different Haematological Phenotypes are associated with the Leftward ($-\alpha^{4.2}$) and Rightward ($-\alpha^{3.7}$) α^{+} Thalassaemia Deletions', in *J. Clin, Invest.*, vol. 79, 1987, pp. 39–43.

5. Stephen J. Oppenheimer *et al.*, 'Prevalence and Distribution of Thalassaemia in Papua New Guinea,' in *Lancet*, 1, 1984, pp. 424–6.
6. See Chapter 16 for more details.
7. See J. B. S. Haldane, *Proc. 8th Int. Congr. Genet.* 267–73 (*Hereditas* Suppl. 35), 1949.
8. Heterozygous in this context meant that a single deletion had been acquired from one parent, while homozygous meant that both parents had contributed a single deletion, leaving their child with two out of four thalassaemia genes working.
9. Oppenheimer *et al.*, op. cit. pp. 424–6.
10. J. Flint, A. V. S. Hill, D. K. Bowden, S. J. Oppenheimer *et al.*, 'High Frequencies of Alpha-Thalassaemia are the Result of Natural Selection by Malaria,' in *Nature*, vol. 321 (6072), 1986, pp. 744–9.
11. All figures are combined heterozygotes and homozygotes expressed as a percentage of the total.
12. This is obviously beyond the scope of this book; however, those interested should see A. C. Senok, K. Li., E. Nelson, L. Yu, L. Tian, S. J. Oppenheimer, 'Invasion and Growth of *Plasmodium falciparum* is Inhibited in Fractionated Thalassaemic Erythrocytes', in *Trans. Roy. Soc. Trop. Med. Hyg.*, vol. 91, 1997, pp. 138–43; and A. C. Senok, E. A. S. Nelson, K. Li and S. J. Oppenheimer, 'Thalassaemia Trait, Red Blood Cell Age and Oxidant Stress: Effects on *Plasmodium falciparum* Growth and Sensitivity to Artemisinin', in *Trans. Roy. Soc. Trop. Med. Hyg.*, vol. 91, 1997, pp. 585–9.
13. Flint, op. cit., pp. 744–9.
14. See Chapter 16 for further information on Kulabob and Manup.
15. Flint *et al.*, *Nature*, op. cit., pp. 744–9.
16. See J. M. Old *et al.*, 'Hb J Tongariki is Associated with α Thalassaemia', in *Nature*, vol. 273, 1980, pp. 319–20. See also A. V. S. Hill *et al.*, 'Haemoglobin and globin gene variants in the Pacific', in A. V. S. Hill and Susan W. Serjeantson (eds.), *The Colonisation of the Pacific: A Genetic Trail*, Clarendon Press, Oxford, 1989, p. 246.
17. M. Pietrusewsky, 'Multivariate Analysis of New Guinea and Melanesian Skulls: A Review', in *Journal of Human Evolution*, vol. 12, 1983, pp. 61–73.
18. See S. W. Serjeantson and X. Gao, 'Homo Sapiens is an Evolving Species: Origins of the Austronesians', in Peter Bellwood (ed.), *The Austronesians*, Australian National University, Canberra, 1995, pp. 165–80; also S. W.

Serjeantson *et al.*, 'Linguistic and Genetic Differentiation in New Guinea', in *Journal of Human Evolution*, vol. 12, 1983, pp. 77–92; and S. W. Serjeantson *et al.*, 'Population Genetics in Papua New Guinea: A Perspective on Human Evolution', in R. D. Attenborough and M. P. Alpers (eds.), *Human Biology in Papua New Guinea: The Small Cosmos*, Clarendon Press, Oxford, 1992, pp. 199–233.

19. G. T. Nurse *et al.*, 'The Elliptocytoses, Ovalocytosis, and Related Disorders', in *Baillière's Clinical Haematology*, vol. 5, no. 1, January 1992, pp. 194–5.
20. A. Baer *et al.*, 'Genetic Factors and Malaria in the Temuan', in *American Journal of Human Genetics*, vol. 28, 1976, pp. 179–88; also A. S. Baer, 'Human Genes and Biocultural History in Southeast Asia', in *Asian Perspectives*, vol. 34, no. 1, 1995, pp. 21–35.
21. S. W. Serjeantson and X. Gao, 'Homo Sapiens is an Evolving Species: Origins of the Austronesians', in Peter Bellwood (ed.), *The Austronesians*, Australian National University, Canberra, 1995, pp. 165–81.
22. Nurse, op. cit., pp. 187–206.
23. Serjeantson, 1995, op. cit., p. 167.
24. Four from the Sunda shelf and three from Wallacea; see Baer, 1995, op. cit., pp. 21–35.
25. Dr Baer excludes Oceanic Austronesian speakers from this analysis.
26. The definition of a clan here is: 'a group of related mtDNA types from one geographic region whose nearest relative comes from a different geographic region.' (Mark Stoneking *et al.*, 'Geographic Variation in Human Mitochondrial DNA from Papua New Guinea', in *Genetics*, vol. 124, 1990, p. 723.)
27. Martin Richards's personal communication.
28. See Clans 1–7, Figure 3, in Mark Stoneking, op. cit., pp. 717–33; also S. W. Ballinger *et al.*, 'Southeast Asian Mitochondrial DNA Analysis Reveals Genetic Continuity of Ancient Mongoloid Migrations', in *Genetics*, vol. 130, 1992, pp. 139–52.
29. Group II in Table 2, in Bryan Sykes *et al.*, 'The Origins of the Polynesians: An Interpretation From Mitochondrial Lineage Analysis', in *American Journal of Human Genetics*, vol. 57, 1995, pp. 1463–75.
30. Type 62 in S. W. Ballinger *et al.*, 'Southeast Asian Mitochondrial DNA Analysis Reveals Genetic Continuity of Ancient Mongoloid Migrations', in *Genetics*, vol. 130, 1992, pp. 143, 145.
31. MtDNA type 10 in Stoneking, op. cit., pp. 717–33.
32. MtDNA types 90 and 76 in Ballinger, op. cit., pp. 139–52.
33. MtDNA type 152 in ibid., pp. 139–52.
34. MtDNA type P150 and AS 71, respectively, in ibid., p. 141.
35. MtDNA type 83 in ibid., pp. 139–52.

36. MtDNA type 89, 94, 106, 109, and 119, respectively, in ibid., p. 146.
37. *[DdeI] – 10394c-* in ibid., p. 146.
38. See Antonio Torroni *et al.*, 'Native American Mitochondrial DNA Analysis Indicates that the Amerind and the Nadene Populations Were Founded by Two Independent Migrations', in *Genetics*, vol. 130, January 1992, pp. 153–62.
39. See Gerald F. Shields *et al.*, 'mtDNA Sequences Suggest a Recent Evolutionary Divergence for Beringian and Northern North American Populations', in *American Journal of Human Genetics*, vol. 53, 1993, pp. 549–62.
40. See Sandro Bonatto *et al.*, 'Lack of Ancient Polynesian-Amerindian Contact', letter in *American Journal of Human Genetics*, vol. 59, 1996, pp. 253–6; also see R. L. Cann and J. K. Lum, 'Mitochondrial Myopia: reply to Bonatto *et al.*', letter in *American Journal of Human Genetics*, vol. 59, 1996, pp. 256–8.
41. See Peter Bellwood, 'The Colonisation of the Pacific: Some Current Hypotheses,' in Hill and Serjeantson (eds.), op. cit., pp. 1–59.
42. MtDNA type 13 in Torroni *et al.*, 1992, op. cit., pp. 153–62, and types 54 and P119 in Ballinger *et al.*, 1992, op. cit., pp. 139–52.
43. Maternal clan 11 in Stoneking, op. cit., pp. 717–33.
44. MtDNA types 12–16 in ibid., pp. 717–33.
45. Ballinger, op. cit., p. 141.
46. Alan Redd *et al.*, 'Evolutionary History of the COII/tRNA lys Intergenic 9 Base Pair Deletion in Human Mitochondrial DNAs From the Pacific', in *Mol. Biol. Evol.*, vol. 12, no. 4, 1995, pp. 604–15; see also Cann and Lum, op. cit., pp. 256–8.
47. It is sometimes called '16217-16247-16261' after the position of the three relevant substitutions.
48. Terry Melton *et al.*, 'Polynesian Genetic Affinities with Southeast Asian Populations as Identified by mtDNA Analysis', in *American Journal of Human Genetics*, vol. 57, 1995, pp. 403–14; also Stoneking *et al.*, op. cit., pp. 717–33.
49. See ibid. (Melton); also Bryan Sykes *et al.*, 'The Origins of the Polynesians: An Interpretation from Mitochondrial Lineage Analysis', in *American Journal of Human Genetics*, vol. 57, 1995, pp. 1463–75; also Alan Redd *et al.*, 1995, op. cit. pp. 604–15.
50. Ninety-five per cent range 5500–34,500, see M. Richards, S. J. Oppenheimer, and B. Sykes, 'MtDNA suggests Polynesian Origins in Eastern Indonesia', in *American Journal of Human Genetics*, in press; Redd and colleagues have obtained an average coalescent of the Polynesian motif of 12,000 years ago. See Redd *et al.*, op. cit., p. 611.
51. Melton., op. cit., pp. 407–11.

52. Except Madagascar, where it is possible that it was introduced from eastern Indonesia. See Richards, op. cit.
53. Ninety-five per cent range 1500–10,000, see Richards *et al.*, op. cit.
54. Ninety-five per cent range 1000–6000, see Richards *et al.*, ibid.
55. Michael Pietrusewsky, 'The People of Ban Chiang: An Early Bronze Site in Northeast Thailand', in *Indo-Pacific Prehistory Association Bulletin 15 (The Chiang Mai Papers),* vol. 2, 1996, pp. 119–47. There is also independent support for local *in situ* development of present day Southeast Asians from dental and other cranial studies. In his revised edition of *'Prehistory of the Indo-Malaysian Archipelago'* (1997, University of Hawai'i Press pp. 89–92 – only just available in UK) Peter Bellwood discusses the evidence under the heading 'Indo-Malaysian continuity model' with particular reference to the work of Turner, Bulbeck and Kingdon.
56. Alpha globin haplotypes Ia and IIa, the triplicated ζ globin gene and certain HLA types characterise Southeast Asian and Polynesian populations, yet are rare in Melanesia; see A. V. S. Hill *et al.*, 'Haemoglobin and Globin Gene Variants in the Pacific', in A. V. S. Hill, Susan Serjeantson (eds.), *The Colonisation of the Pacific: A Genetic Trail,* Clarendon Press, Oxford, 1989, pp. 259–67.
57. 'C' on control region site 16217.
58. Melton, op. cit., p. 411.
59. Corresponding with a 'T' substitution on control region site 16261.
60. Melton, op. cit., p. 411.
61. Redd and colleagues put a date of 27,000 years on the expansion of what they call the Indonesian sequences with 9-bp deletions (lower confidence limit: 17,000 years); see Redd *et al.*, op. cit., pp. 604–15.
62. Hill *et al.*, op. cit., pp. 291–2; also Susan Serjeantson, 'HLA Genes and Antigens', in Hill and Serjeantson (eds.) op. cit., pp. 125–9.
63. An $\alpha^{3.71}$ deletion on a Southeast Asian alpha globin frame.
64. A. S. Tsintoff *et al.*, 'α-Globin Gene Markers Identify Genetic Differences Between Australian Aborigines and Melanesians', in *Am. J. Hum. Gen.*, vol. 46, 1990, pp. 138–43; and June Roberts-Thomson *et al.*' 'An ancient Common Origin of Aboriginal Australians and New Guinea Highlanders is Supported by α-Globin Haplotype Analysis', in *Am. J. Hum. Gen.*, vol. 58, pp. 1017–24.
65. See Hill *et al.*, op. cit., pp. 259–67 and 286–9.

Chapter 7: Orang Asli: Originals

1. 'Orang' in Malay means man, while 'Asli' means original.
2. Iskander Carey, *Orang Asli: The Aboriginal Tribes of Peninsular Malaysia,* Oxford University Press, 1976.

3. The five mtDNA types 62, 71, 72, 54 and 118 at the bases of clusters F, A, D, D* and E, respectively, in Figures 2 and 3, in S. W. Ballinger *et al.*, 'Southeast Asian Mitochondrial DNA Analysis Reveals Genetic Continuity of Ancient Mongolian Migrations', in *Genetics*, vol. 130, 1992, pp. 139–52. Haplogroups F, A, D, D* and E correspond with New Guinean matriclans 1–7, 17, (17), 11 and 9 respectively, in Mark Stoneking *et al.*, 'Geographic Variation in Human Mitochondrial DNA from Papua New Guinea', in *Genetics*, vol. 124, 1990, pp. 717–33. Close links also exist between Southeast Asian haplogroup G and New Guinean coastal matriclaan 9; see Ballinger *et al.*, ibid.
4. Antonio Torroni *et al.*, 'Mitochondrial DNA Analysis in Tibet: Implications for the Origins of the Tibetan Population and its Adaptation to High Altitude', in *American Journal of Physical Anthropology*, vol. 93, 1994, pp. 189–99. The broad division between mainland Southeast Asians including the Senoi and island Southeast Asians including Borneans, corresponds with groups A and B in a similar division based on nuclear genetic markers obtained by L. Luca Cavalli-Sforza and colleagues in their authoritative *The History and Geography of Human Genes* (abridged paperback 1996, Princeton University Press; pp. 234–238). Group C corresponded with negritos.
5. Ballinger, op. cit., pp. 139–52.
6. Torroni *et al.*, pp. 189–99.
7. Haplogroups B and F, in Ibid., p. 196.
8. Type 54 in Ballinger, op. cit., p. 141.
9. Type 13 in group B in Torroni *et al.*, 'Native American Mitochondrial DNA Analysis Indicates that the Amerind and the Nadene Populations were Founded by two Independent Migrations', in *Genetics*, vol. 130, 1992, op. cit., pp. 153–62.
10. Type P119 in Mark Stoneking *et al.*, 'Geographic Variation in Human Mitochondrial DNA From Papua New Guinea', in *Genetics*, vol. 124, 1990, pp. 717–33.
11. Type AS79 from Ballinger, op. cit., pp. 139–52.
12. Table AI in Terry Melton *et al.*, 'Polynesian Genetic Affinities with Southeast Asian Populations as Identified by mtDNA Analysis', in *Am. J. Hum. Gen.*, vol. 57, 1995, pp. 412–13.
13. Table AI in ibid., pp. 412–13.
14. As defined in Torroni *et al.*, op. cit., p. 196.
15. Types AS72 and AS71 in Torroni, ibid., p. 195.
16. See Chapter 5 for further details.
17. Type AS72 in Torroni *et al.*, op. cit., p. 195.
18. S. Barnabas *et al.*, 'Human Evolution: The Study of Indian Mitochondrial DNA', in *Naturwissenschaften*, vol. 83, 1996, pp. 28–9.

19. Torroni *et al.*, op. cit., p. 196.
20. Type 108 in Torroni *et al.*, 'MtDNA and the origin of Caucasians: Identification of Ancient Caucasian-specific Haplogroups, One of Which is Prone to a Recurrent Somatic Duplication in the D-Loop Region', *American Journal of Human Genetics* vol. 55, 1994, pp. 760–76, and type 21, haplogroup T, in Torroni *et al.*, 'Classification of European mtDNAs from an Analysis of Three European Populations', in *Genetics*, vol. 144, 1996, pp. 1835–50.
21. 'Asian' haplotype M, in Antonio Torroni *et al.*, 'Classification of European mtDNAs from Analysis of Three European Populations', in *Genetics*, vol. 144, 1996, pp. 1835–50.
22. The 'C' allele in Tatiana Zergal *et al.*, 'Genetic Relationships of Asians and Northern Europeans, Revealed by Y-Chromosomal DNA Analysis,' in *Am. J. Hum. Gen.*, vol. 60, 1997, pp. 1174–83.
23. Inger Zachrisson, 'Oral Traditions, Archaeology and Linguistics: the Early History of the Saami in Scandinavia', in Roger Blench and Matthew Spriggs (eds.), *Archaeology and Language 1: Theoretical and Methodological Orientations,* Routledge, London, 1997, pp. 371–6.
24. See Chapter 12 for further details.
25. In Bryan Sykes *et al.*, 'The Origins of the Polynesians: An Interpretation from Mitochondrial Lineage Analysis', in *American Journal of Human Genetics*, vol. 57, 1995, pp. 1463–75. See also: Group 3A in M. Richards *et al.*, 'Paleolithic and Neolithic Lineages in the European Mitochondrial Gene Pool', in *American Journal of Human Genetics*, vol. 59, 1996, pp. 185–203.
26. Adrian V. Hill, 'Molecular Epidemiology of the Thalassaemias (including Haemoglobin E)', in *Baillière's Clinical Haematology*, vol. 5, no. 1, January 1992, p. 219.
27. Lie-Injo L. E. *et al.*, 'Distribution of Red Cell Genetic Defects in Southeast Asia' in *Trans. Roy. Soc. Trop. Med. Hyg.*, vol. 63, 1969, pp. 664–73.
28. W. A. Abdullah *et al.*, 'The Spectrum of Beta-Thalassaemia Mutations in Malays in Singapore and Kelantan', in *Southeast Asian J. Trop. Med. Public Health*, vol. 27, 1996, 164–8.
29. See Chapter 3 for further details on the Sakai Cave.
30. Hill, op. cit., pp. 218–21.
31. Ibid., pp. 218–21.
32. Saha, N. 'Distribution of hemoglobin E in several Mongoloid populations of northeast India', *Hum.Biol.* vol. 62, 1990, pp. 535–44.
33. See Chapter 10 for more discussion of the flood myths in the East.
34. A. R. Choudhury *et al.*, 'Haemoglobin E and A2 in Agricultural and Migratory Populations of West Bengal: A Preliminary Report, in *J. Assoc. Physicians, India*, vol. 37, 1989, pp. 588–9.

35. A. Roychoudhury *et al.*, 'The Blood Group and Haemoglobin Types of the Santals', in *J. Indian Med. Assoc.*, vol. 90, 1992, pp. 240–41.
36. K. Ghosh *et al.*, 'Haemoglobinopathies in a Large Hospital in Kuwait', in *Haematologia Budap.*, vol. 25, 1993, pp. 185–90.
37. K. Indrak *et al.*, 'A Czechoslovakian Teenager with Hb E-beta zero Thalassaemia complicated by the Presence of an Alpha-globin Gene Triplication', in *Ann. Hematol.*, vol. 63, 1991, pp. 42–4.
38. H. H. Kazazian *et al.*, 'Hemoglobin E in Europeans: Further Evidence for Multiple Origins of the β e-globin Gene', in *American Journal of Human Genetics*, vol. 36, 1984, pp. 212–17.
39. Tables 3 and 4 in J. Flint *et al.*, 'Why are Some Genetic Diseases Common?' *Human Genetics*, vol. 91, 1993, pp. 91–117.
40. Type IVS 1:5 G>C on beta haplotype − + − + +, in A. V. S. Hill *et al.*, β-Thalassaemia in Melanesia: Association with Malaria and Characterisation of a Common Variant', in *Blood*, vol. 72, 1988, pp. 9–14.
41. Type IVS 1:5 G>C, see: R. Quaife *et al.*, 'The Spectrum of β-Thalassaemia Mutations in the UAE National Population', in *Journal of Medical Genetics*, vol. 31, pp. 59–61.
42. Jonathan Flint *et al.*, 'The Population Genetics of the Haemoglobinopathies', in *Baillière's Clinical Haematology*, vol. 6, no. 1, March 1993, pp. 215–61.
43. R. Fodde *et al.*, 'Multiple recombination events are responsible for the heterogeneity of a^{+}-thalassaemia haplotypes among the forest tribes of Andhra Pradesh, India', in *American Journal of Human Genetics*, vol. 55, 1991, pp. 43–50.

Chapter 8: Five Hundred Cataclysms?

1. See D. S. Allan and J. B. Delair, *When the Earth Nearly Died*, Gateway Books, Bath, 1995, Chapter 9 and 10.
2. See Chapter 1 for more information on the Black Sea views.
3. A. G. Dawson, *Ice Age Earth*, Routledge, London, 1992, pp. 100, 101, 108.
4. See Chapter 13 for more information on the clay-man myths.
5. See Sir James Frazer, *Folklore in the Old Testament*, Macmillan, London, 1918, p. 106, and, in general pp. 104–361.
6. Ibid., p. 338–61.
7. Ibid., p. 343.
8. Ibid., pp. 329–31.
9. See Allan and Delair, op. cit., pp. 241–326.
10. See ibid., especially Part 4.
11. See Chapter 1 for further evidence and details.
12. Tsunamis have been known to travel at an incredible 800km/h (500

mph), and have been recorded as terrifyingly high as 65m (210ft) or more. The estimated 37,000 deaths that resulted from the gigantic explosion of Krakatoa in August 1883 were not caused by volcanic fallout (such as at Pompeii and Herculaneum in AD 79), but by vast tsunamis which obliterated whole settlements in seconds. Note that a tsunami, a word of Japanese origin, in fact has nothing to do with tides.

13. Thera is now known as Santorini, and is found between Crete and the Greek mainland. Whilst the 'Thera was Atlantis' theory has enjoyed a lot of popularity over the last couple of decades, it is still fundamentally flawed. An interesting analysis of it, and other theories, can be found in Francis Hitching, *World Atlas of Mysteries*, Book Club Associates, London, 1980, pp. 132–43, although the location that the author himself prefers, Bimini in the Bahamas, seems equally illogical. This is not least because of its size: both Thera and Bimini are small islands, as opposed to Plato's Atlantis (described in *Timaeus* and *Criteas*) which talks of an area larger than Libya and Asia Minor (Turkey) combined.
14. See Allan and Delair, op. cit., pp. 169–326.
15. See Chapter 1 for more detail on the 'wobbly top' theory.
16. See Chapter 1 for more detail on the flooding of the Black Sea.
17. This particular comparative estimate is from Rosie Mestel, 'Noah's Flood', in *New Scientist*, 4 October 1997, pp. 24–7.
18. See Chapter 1 for more information on the Lake Tyrrell Collapse.
19. Richard Huggett, *Cataclysms and Earth History: The Development of Diluvialism*, Clarendon Press, Oxford, 1989, Chapter 9.
20. See review on 'The Deluge', in Hitching, op. cit., pp. 163–7.
21. Frazer, op. cit., p. 328.
22. See Emmi Kahler-Meyer, 'Myth Motifs in Flood Stories from the Grassland of Cameroon', in Alan Dundes (ed.), *The Flood Myth*, University of California Press, 1988, pp. 249–61.
23. These include: Sir James Frazer's chapter in *Folklore in the Old Testament*, Macmillan, London, 1918; Alan Dundes (ed.), *The Flood Myth*, University of California Press, 1988; G. B. Walker, 'The Great Flood and its Diffusion', in *Diffusion: Five Studies in Early History*, London, Research Publishing Co., 1976, pp. 43–63.
24. Frazer, op. cit., pp. 25 and 44.
25. Ibid., pp. 16 and 27.
26. This conclusion has a scientific basis in the statistical, chronological and geographic analysis of the 'rainbow serpent' in rock art appearing from 6000–4000 years ago in Arnhemland. See Leigh Dayton, 'Flood Gave Birth to World's Oldest Religion', *New Scientist*, 1996, vol. 152, p. 6. See also Josephine Flood, *Archaeology of the Dreamtime*, Angus & Robertson, Sydney, 1995, p. 171.

27. These are described in Chapter 1.
28. See Allan and Delair, op. cit., pp. 25–31.
29. See ibid., especially Parts 4 and 5.
30. See Stith Thompson, *Motif Index of Folk Literature*, Indiana University Studies, vols. 19–23, 1932–6, for more information.
31. Allan and Delair, op. cit.

Chapter 9: Floods in the West

1. See Norman C. Habel, 'The Two Flood Stories of Genesis', in Alan Dundes (ed.), *The Flood Myth*, University of California Press, 1988, pp. 13–29.
2. Sir James Frazer, *Folklore in the Old Testament,* Macmillan, London, 1918, pp. 137–9.
3. For further details about Mallowan, see Chapter 2.
4. From Alexander Heidel, *The Babylonian Genesis*, University of Chicago Press, 1951, pp. 242–5.
5. Principal among these is D. S. Allen and J. B. Delair, *When the Earth Nearly Died*, Gateway Books, Bath, 1995.
6. See Chapter 2 for further discussion.
7. Frazer, op. cit., p. 145.
8. Ibid., pp. 275–6.
9. Ibid., p. 280.
10. Stephanie Dalley (trans.), *Myths from Mesopotamia: Creation, The Flood, Gilgamesh and Others,* Oxford University Press, 1991, p. 6.
11. See Frazer, op. cit., pp. 107–10.
12. George Smith, 'The Chaldean Account of the Deluge', in Alan Dundes (ed.), *The Flood Myth*, University of California Press, 1988, p. 30.
13. Ibid., p. 30.
14. S. N. Kramer, *The Sumerians: Their History, Culture and Character*, University of Chicago Press, 1963, pp. 163–4.
15. Dalley, op. cit., p. 44.
16. See Kramer, op. cit, pp. 328–31.
17. Frazer was the most famous of these.
18. Daniel Hammerly-Dupuy, 'Some Observations on the Assyro-Babylonian and Sumerian Flood Stories', in Dundes (ed.), op. cit., p. 58.
19. Dalley, op. cit., pp. 5–6.
20. See ibid., pp. 9–38.
21. See Chapter 13 for more details.
22. See Dalley, op. cit., p. 22.
23. See Dalley, ibid., p. 31.
24. See Dalley, ibid., p. 33.
25. From Dalley, ibid., p. 33.
26. Dalley, ibid., p. 38.

27. Ibid., p. 5.
28. Hammerly-Dupuy, op. cit., p. 51.
29. See Chapter 1 for more details.
30. Dalley, op. cit., pp. 39–49.
31. S. N. Kramer, *The Sumerians*, University of Chicago Press, 1963, p. 293.
32. Dalley, op. cit., p. 48.
33. Ibid., p. 132, Note 112.
34. Both versions of the entire Gilgamesh epic are in ibid., pp. 39–153.
35. Frazer, op. cit., pp. 146–74, refers to the following Greek flood myths.
36. See footnote 2, ibid., pp. 173–4.
37. Ibid., p. 174.
38. Edward B. Tylor, *Researches into the Early History of Mankind*, London, 1878, pp. 306 ff.
39. See next chapter for more details.
40. W. M. Calder, 'New Light on Ovid's Story of Philemon and Baucis', in Dundes, op. cit., pp. 101–2.
41. Ibid., pp. 101–12.
42. See Rosie Mestel, 'Noah's Flood,' in *New Scientist*, 4 October 1997, pp. 24–7.
43. Frazer, op. cit., pp. 167–71, refers to following Greek myths of the Dardanelles.
44. See Chapter 1 for more details.
45. Frazer, op. cit., p. 180.
46. Ibid., pp. 180–82.
47. Ibid., p. 175.
48. Ibid., pp. 174–5.
49. Ibid., pp. 174–5.
50. Ibid., p. 176.
51. Ibid., p. 178.
52. Dalley op. cit., pp. 11–16.
53. See Chapter 4 for more details.
54. Frazer, op. cit., pp. 338–61.

Chapter 10: Floods in the East

1. Sir James Frazer, *Folklore in the Old Testament,* Macmillan, London, 1918, p. 183.
2. The text of Manu's Flood is paraphrased here from Frazer, ibid., pp. 183–5.
3. Ibid., pp. 185–7.
4. Frazer, op. cit., p. 177.
5. Malabar here presumably refers to the west coast of India rather than Mount Malabar in Java.

6. Frazer, op. cit., pp. 188–9.
7. Ibid., p. 195.
8. Ibid., p. 196.
9. Ibid., p. 196.
10. Ibid., p. 194.
11. Wilhelm Koppers, *The Deluge Myth of the Bhils of Central India*, in Alan Dundes (ed.), *The Flood Myth*, University of California Press, 1988, pp. 283–4.
12. Frazer, op. cit., p. 194.
13. Ibid., pp. 209–10.
14. See K. Lindell, J.-O. Swahn and D, Tayanin, *The Flood: Three Northern Kammu Versions of the Story of Creation*, in Dundes, op. cit, pp. 265–80: they speak the Khmuic branch of the northern Mon-Khmer language family.
15. See Somsonge Burusphat, 'Surface indicators in the Kam origin myth,' in *Mon-Khmer Studies*, vol. 26, 1995, pp. 339–55.
16. Frazer, op. cit., p. 195.
17. Ibid., pp. 199–203.
18. Ibid., pp. 198–213.
19. See David Shulman, *The Tamil Flood Myths and the Cankam Legend*, in Dundes (ed.), op. cit., pp. 293–317.
20. Schulman, op. cit., p. 314.
21. S. N. Kramer, *The Sumerians: Their History, Culture and Character*, University of Chicago Press, 1963, pp. 151–3.
22. See Chapter 15 for further information on the Gardens of Adonis.
23. See Chapter 11 for further details.
24. See Pieter Middelkoop, *Headhunting in Timor and its Historical Implications*, University of Sydney, 1963, for more details; also Pieter Middelkoop, *Amarasisch Timoreesche teksten, Verhandelingen van het Bataviaasch Genootschap LXXIV* (Part 2), Bandoeng, A. C. Nix & Co., 1939.
25. Duarte, Jorge Barros, *Timor: ritos e mitos atauros*, Ministerio da Educacao, Lisbon, 1984.
26. Aone van Engelenhoven (ed.), 'Lord Sailfish: Preliminaries on Storytelling in Southwest Maluku,' to be submitted to Semaian, Dept. of Languages and Cultures in SE Asia and Oceania, Leiden University (given as personal communication).
27. Personal communication from Aone van Engelenhoven.
28. See Chapter 16 for further details.
29. Susan McKinnon, 'Tanimbar Boats', in Jean-Paul Barbier and Douglas Newton (eds.), *Islands and Ancestors: Indigenous Styles of Southeast Asia*, Thames and Hudson, London, 1988, pp. 152–69.

30. Hans Straver, *De zee van verhalen, de wereld van Molukse vertellers,* Steunpunt Edukatie Molukkers, Utrecht, 1993, pp. 93–6.
31. John Baily *et al., Gods and Men: Myths and Legends From the World's Religions,* Oxford University Press, 1991, pp. 12–15. See also Leigh Dayton, 'Flood Gave Birth to World's Oldest Religion,' New Scientist, 1996, vol. 152, p. 6. See also Josephine Flood, *Archaeology of the Dreamtime,* Angus & Robertson, Sydney, 1995, p. 264.
32. That is, unless Amerind is regarded as one phylum.
33. Frazer, op. cit., p. 226.
34. Ibid., p. 227.
35. Ibid., pp. 232–3.
36. Ibid., pp. 233–4.
37. Ibid., pp. 242–3.
38. Francisco Demetrio, *The Flood Motif and the Symbolism of Rebirth in Filipino Mythology,* in Dundes, op. cit., p. 262.
39. Frazer op. cit., p. 225.
40. Ibid., p. 225.
41. Ibid., p. 225.
42. Demetrio, op. cit., pp. 263–4.
43. Ibid., p. 264.
44. Unexplained connections between Meso-American and Eurasian/Oceanic myths tend to crop up frequently. Whilst fascinating, they are outside the remit of this book.
45. See Chapter 15 for further details.
46. Frazer, op. cit., p. 223.
47. Ibid., pp. 223–4.
48. Ibid., pp. 222–3; all myths in this WMP mountain section are from Frazer, pp. 209–24.
49. See Chapter 15 for more information.
50. Frazer, op. cit., pp. 217–18.
51. Ibid., pp. 220–1.
52. See Helen Dennett, *Mak Bilong Sepik,* Wirui Press, Wewak, Papua New Guinea, 1975, p. 116.
53. H. Ling Roth, *The Natives of Sarawak and British North Borneo,* Truslove and Hanson, London, 1896, pp. 300–301.
54. Frazer, op. cit., p. 211.
55. Ibid., p. 224.

Chapter 11: Watery Chaos with Dragons

1. All biblical quotations and references follow the Authorised King James Version unless stated otherwise.
2. Raymond Van Over, *Sun Songs,* Mentor, New York, 1980, p. 8, footnote 8.

3. Colin Renfrew, *Before Civilisation*, Penguin, London, 1990, pp. 16 and 236–71.
4. For the fullest account, see Robert Bauval and Adrian Gilbert, *The Orion Mystery*, Mandarin, London, 1994.
5. Graham Hancock, *Fingerprints of the Gods*, Heinemann, London, 1995, pp. 488–9.
6. Dr Alexander Thom, from Francis Hitching, *The World Atlas Of Mysteries*, Book Club Associates, London, 1980, p.61.
7. For reviews of the subject see Hitching, op. cit., section 3.
8. See Chapter 12 for more information on the Pleiades.
9. See H. R. Hays, *In The Beginnings*, Putnam's, New York, 1963.
10. Jan De Vries, 'Ginnungagap', in *Acta Philologica Scandinavica*, vol. 5, 1930–34, pp. 41 ff.
11. See Stith Thompson, *Motif Index of Folk Literature*, Indiana University Studies, vols. 19–23, 1932–6.
12. See Alexander Heidel, *The Babylonian Genesis*, University of Chicago Press, 1951, Chapter 3. Heidel's biblical translation is given here, for clarity; the Authorised Version translates '*tannîn*' as 'sea dragon'.
13. For the entire Babylonian Epic of Creation, see Stephanie Dalley (trans.) *Myths from Mesopotamia: Creation, the Flood, Gilgamesh and Others*, Oxford University Press, 1991, pp. 233–76.
14. Alexander S. Murray, *Who's Who in Mythology*, Bracken Books, London, 1995, pp. 145–6.
15. John Bailey *et al.*, *Gods and Men: Myths and Legends from the World's Religions*, Oxford University Press, 1992, pp. 34–8.
16. Dalley, op. cit., pp. 39–153.
17. Michael Jordan, *Myths of the World*, Kyle Cathie Ltd, London, 1995, pp. 158–9.
18. Murray, op. cit., pp. 249–50.
19. Heidel, op. cit., pp. 86–7, and 137–8.
20. Murray, op. cit., pp. 216–7.
21. Bailey *et al.*, op. cit., pp. 112–13.
22. See R. K. Gordan (trans.), *The Song of Beowulf*, Dent & Sons, London.
23. Bailey *et al.*, op. cit., pp. 60–63.
24. Ke Wen-li and Hou Mei-Xue (trans.), *Stories from Chinese Mythology*, Nankai University Press, 1991, pp. 19–23.
25. Ibid., pp. 395–9.
26. Raymond Van Over, *Sun Songs*, Mentor, New York, 1980, pp. 337–9.
27. Bailey *et al.*, op. cit., pp. 45–8.
28. H. R. Ellis Davidson, *Gods and Myths of Northern Europe*, Penguin, London, 1990, p. 89.
29. See Chapter 15 for further details.

30. Jan Knappert, *Pacific Mythology*, Aquarian, London, 1992, pp. 59–60.
31. See Chapter 12 for further details.
32. Bailey *et al.*, op. cit., pp. 12–15. See also Leigh Dayton, 'Flood Gave Birth to World's Oldest Religion', *New Scientist*, 1996, vol. 152, p. 6.
33. Raymond Van Over, *Sun Songs*, Mentor, New York, 1980, p. 374.
34. Bailey *et al.* op. cit., pp. 27–31.
35. Van Over, op. cit., p. 91.
36. Ibid., pp. 70–73.
37. Michael Jordan, *Myths of the World*, Kyle Cathie Ltd, London, 1995, p. 39.
38. See Chapter 1 for more details.
39. Heidel, op. cit., pp. 105–7.
40. For more details, see Sumet Jumsai, *Naga: Cultural Origins in Siam and the West Pacific*, Oxford University Press, 1989.
41. Jordan, op. cit., pp. 32–3.
42. Ignatia Olim Marsh, *Tales and Traditions From Sabah*, Sabah Society, Kota Kinabalu, 1988, pp. 9–11.
43. Knappert, op. cit., pp. 185–6.
44. Raymond Van Over, *Sun Songs*, Mentor, New York, 1980, p. 381.
45. Morea Pekoro (trans. Elton Brash), *Orokolo Genesis*, Niugini Press, Port Moresby, 1973, p. 3.
46. Knappert, op. cit., p. 146.
47. Ibid., p. 32.
48. Jordan, op. cit., pp. 50–51.
49. Van Over, op. cit., p. 255.
50. Ibid., p. 127.
51. Ibid., p. 128.
52. Ibid., p. 126.
53. See Chapter 8.
54. Ibid., pp. 48–50.
55. Ibid., pp. 70–71.
56. Ibid., p. 86.
57. The most comprehensive study of the land-diver myths comes in Sir James Frazer, *Folklore in the Old Testament*, Macmillan, London, 1918, Chapter IV.
58. See Gerald F. Shields *et al.*, 'MtDNA Sequences Suggest a Recent Evolutionary Divergence for Beringian and Northern North American Populations', in *American Journal of Human Genetics*, vol. 53, 1993, pp. 549–62.
59. Van Over, op. cit., Part 6.

Chapter 12: Heaven and Earth

1. R. T. Rundle Clark, *Myth and Symbol in Ancient Egypt*, Thames and Hudson, London, 1959, p. 21.
2. Ke Wen-Li and Hou Mei-Xue (trans.), *Stories from Chinese Mythology*, Nankai University Press, 1991, pp. 14–27.
3. See Maribeth Erb, 'Flores: Cosmology, Art and Ritual', in Jean-Paul Barbier and Douglas Newton (eds.), *Islands and Ancestors; Indigenous Styles of Southeast Asia*, Thames and Hudson, London, 1988, pp. 106–19.
4. Jan Knappert, *Pacific Mythology*, Aquarian Press, London, 1992, p. 242.
5. Kal Muller, *East of Bali, From Lombok to Timor*, Periplus Editions (Eric Oey), Basingstoke, 1995, p. 102.
6. Erb, op. cit., p. 111.
7. Muller, op. cit., p 39. See also David Hicks, 'Art and Religion on Timor', in Jean-Paul Barbier and Douglas Newton (eds.), *Islands and Ancestors; Indigenous Styles of Southeast Asia*, Thames and Hudson, London, 1988, pp. 134–51.
8. Muller, op. cit., p. 39.
9. Knappert, op. cit., pp. 267–8.
10. Raymond Van Over, *Sun Songs*, Mentor, New York, 1980, p. 254.
11. Stephanie Dalley, *Myths From Mesopotamia: Creation, the Flood, Gilgamesh and Others*, Oxford University Press, 1991, p. 233.
12. See Alexander Heidel, *The Babylonian Genesis*, University of Chicago Press, 1951, Chapter III.
13. See Dalley, op. cit., for further details.
14. Heidel, op. cit., p. 101.
15. Van Over, op. cit., p. 198.
16. Ibid., pp. 187–92.
17. Ibid., pp. 386–7.
18. Ibid., pp. 187–91.
19. For a translation of relevant parts of Hesiod, see Van Over, ibid., pp. 198–213.
20. Jan Knappert, *Pacific Mythology*, Aquarian, London, 1992, p. 48.
21. Van Over, op. cit., pp. 380–81.
22. For full details see ibid., pp. 198–213.
23. Knappert, op. cit., p. 291.
24. Ibid., p. 48.
25. Van Over, op. cit., pp. 187–91.
26. Knappert, op. cit., p. 148.
27. Van Over, op. cit., p. 381.
28. Ibid., p. 382–5.
29. Michael Jordan, *Myths of the World*, Kyle Cathie Ltd, London, 1995, pp. 64–5.

30. Van Over, op. cit., p. 371.
31. Ibid., pp. 353–61.
32. See Knappert, op. cit., p. 291 for greater detail.
33. Van Over, op. cit., p. 187.
34. Ibid., p. 137.
35. See Susan McKinnon, 'Tanimbar Boats' in Jean-Paul Barbier and Douglas Newton (eds.), *Islands and Ancestors; Indigenous Styles of Southeast Asia*, Thames and Hudson, London 1988, pp. 152–69. As discussed earlier, this last point of island-splitting, along with the other catastrophe myths of these people, seems to place the myth back to the Early Holocene Period.
36. John Bailey *et al.*, *Gods and Men: Myths and Legends from the World's Religions*, Oxford University Press, 1991, pp. 45–8.
37. Van Over, op. cit., p. 299.
38. Ibid., Part 1.
39. Jordan, op. cit., p. 69.
40. Van Over, op. cit., pp. 379–80.
41. Composite of Jordan, op. cit., p. 69 and Van Over, op. cit., pp. 379–80.
42. Ibid., pp. 198–214.
43. Muller, op. cit., pp. 103–4.
44. Van Over, op. cit., pp. 187–91.
45. Ibid., p. 204.
46. From Alexander S. Murray, *Who's Who in Mythology*, Bracken Books, London, 1995, pp. 310–12.
47. Van Over, op cit., pp. 132–40.
48. Knappert, op. cit., p. 48.
49. Ibid., p. 379.
50. Heidel, op. cit., Chapter III.
51. For complete Epic, see Dalley, op. cit., pp. 233–74.
52. Ibid., p. 235.
53. Ibid., pp. 114–15.
54. Heidel, op. cit., p. 115.
55. Van Over, op. cit., pp. 187–8.
56. See Chapters 1 and 8 for further discussion.
57. John Bailey *et al.*, *Gods and Men: Myths and Legends from the World's Religions*, Oxford University Press, 1991, p. 14.
58. Dalley, op. cit., p. 255.
59. Heidel, op. cit., Chapter III: 'Old Testament Parallels'.
60. Van Over, op. cit., pp. 198–209.
61. H. G. Wells, *The Outline of History*, Cassell, London, 1925, p. 80.
62. For a discussion of this controversy, see Colin Renfrew, *Before Civilisation*, Penguin, London, 1973, pp. 34–8.

63. Michael Jordan, *Myths of the World*, Kyle Cathie Ltd, London, 1995, pp. 24–5.
64. Jan Knappert, *Pacific Mythology*, Aquarian Press, London, 1992, p. 115.
65. Alexander Murray, *Who's Who in Mythology*, Bracken Books, London, 1994, pp. 110–11.
66. After Knappert, op. cit., p. 62.
67. Murray, op. cit., pp. 170–71.
68. H. Ling Roth, *The Natives of Sarawak and British North Borneo*, Truslove and Hanson, London, 1896, p. 303.
69. Ibid., pp. CLXX–CLXXI, Appendix 2.
70. John A. Z'Graggen, *And Thus Became Man and World*, Pentland Press, Durham, 1992, pp. 47–51.
71. Knappert, op. cit., pp. 286–7.
72. A. W. Reed, *Aboriginal Stories of Australia*, Heinemann Australia, New South Wales, 1980, pp. 77–83.
73. Knappert, op. cit., pp. 194–5.
74. I have used the abridged and more accessible version of this landmark work.
75. Kal Muller, *East of Bali, From Lombok to Timor*, Periplus Books, Hong Kong, 1995, pp. 184–5.
76. See Jan Knappert, *Pacific Mythology*, Aquarian Press, London, 1992.
77. Stephanie Dalley, *Myths from Mesopotamia: Creation, the Flood, Gilgamesh and Others*, Oxford University Press, 1991, p. 256.
78. Other similar instances can be found in Isaiah 66:22–3, Ezekiel 46:1 and Colossians 2:16.
79. PH. O. L. Tobing, *The Structure of the Toba-Batak Belief in the High God*, Celebes Institute for Culture, 1956, pp. 120–27.
80. Tobing, op. cit., pp. 120–27.
81. M. Leach (ed.), *Funk and Wagnall's Standard Dictionary of Folklore, Mythology and Legend*, HarperCollins, San Francisco, 1984, p. 875.
82. Murray, op. cit., p. 111.
83. Leach (ed.), op. cit., p. 92.
84. Ibid., pp. 874–5.
85. Dalley, op. cit., pp. 233–74.
86. For further information about the Dogon, see R. K. G. Temple, *The Sirius Mystery*, Sidgwick and Jackson, London, 1981; also see Francis Hitching, *The World Atlas of Mysteries*, Book Club Associates, London, 1980, p. 151.
87. Note the use of six here, which is also found in Hindu references to the Pleiades since one of the seven stars is dim. For further reference, see Leach (ed.), op. cit., p. 874.
88. Knappert, op. cit., p. 93.

89. W. W. Gill, *Cook Islands Custom*, Fiji Times and Herald, Suva, 1979, p. 23.
90. Jordan, op. cit., pp. 49–50.
91. Murray, op. cit., p. 329.
92. From Wells, op. cit., p. 81.
93. Glenys Köhnke, *Time Belong Tumbuna*, Robert Brown Assoc., Port Moresby, Papua New Guinea, 1973, p. 54.
94. From Publication of the Office of Tourism of Sumba Barat, entitled *Indonesia: History and Legend of Tourists' Objects in Sumba Barat*, Dinas Pariswata, 1994, p. 31.
95. A notable gap is seen in mainland Southeast Asia. As we shall see in Chapter 13, another creation more like the second or Jehovistic account in Genesis is found in this region.
96. Chi-squared analysis was perfomed to determine whether the observed distribution could have occurred by chance. The null hypothesis was random distribution.
97. The chances of finding two themes together in the same story can be expressed as an 'odds ratio'. This is somewhat analogous to the odds of a favourite horse winning a race. An odds ratio of one or less means no association, while an odds ratio greater than two together with one or more asterisks in Table 9 means a significant association (significance test using 2 x 2 Chi-squared test). The higher the odds ratio, the more likely the two themes are to be found in the same story. The results of this analysis are shown in Table 9 as a matrix of associations between individual themes. It can thus be seen that the group of themes identified in Table 8 as being distributed in Eurasia and Oceania are also individually associated with each other in the same stories.
98. Odds ratio 15; $p<0.001$.

Chapter 13: The Creation of Man

1. Inevitably the sacred texts use man both to refer to a male progenitor and humanity as a whole. Where possible throughout this chapter I have attempted to distinguish these two in discussion.
2. For example, see Alexander Heidel, *The Babylonian Genesis*, University of Chicago Press, 1951, Chapter 3, and Raymond Van Over, *Sun Songs*, Mentor, New York, 1980, pp. 232–3.
3. See Sir James Frazer, *Folklore in the Old Testament*, Macmillan, London, 1918, Chapter 1, especially pp. 3–5.
4. Ibid., p. 10.
5. Ibid., p. 8 ff.
6. Michael Jordan, *Myths of the World*, Kyle Cathie Ltd, London, 1995, pp. 33–4.

7. From Frazer, op. cit., p. 34.
8. Chas. Hose and W. McDougall, *The Pagan Tribes of Borneo*, London, 1912, vol. 2, p. 138, quoted in ibid., p. 34, footnote 3.
9. Jan Knappert, *Pacific Mythology*, Aquarian Press, London, 1992, p. 51.
10. N. Graafland, *De Minahassa*, Rotterdam, 1869, Chapter 1, p. 8 ff., quoted from Frazer, *Folklore in the Old Testament*, Macmillan, London, 1918, pp. 35–6.
11. Ibid., p. 33.
12. See Chapter 5 for more discussion on the ethno-linguistic origins of these minorities.
13. F. M. Schnitger, *Forgotten Kingdoms of Sumatra*, Oxford University Press, 1991, Chapter 12, pp. 126–54.
14. See discussions in Chapters 2–7.
15. See Chapter 4 and 5 for more linguistics details.
16. See Chapters 11 and 15 for more details.
17. Heidel, op. cit., p. 118.
18. See Chapter 12 for more details on *Enuma Elish*.
19. Stephanie Dalley, *Myths from Mesopotamia: Creation, The Flood, Gilgamesh and Others*, Oxford University Press, 1991, pp. 228–76.
20. Heidel, op. cit., pp. 118–19.
21. Ibid., p. 118.
22. Jordan, op. cit., p. 68.
23. Ibid., pp. 66–7.
24. H. Ling Roth, *The Natives of Sarawak and British North Borneo*, Truslove and Hanson, London, 1896, vol. II, clxx–clxxii.
25. Ibid., vol. I pp. 299–300.
26. Knappert, op. cit., p. 15.
27. Frazer, op. cit., p. 9.
28. Ibid., all of Chapter 1.
29. Ibid., pp. 9–10.
30. Ibid., p. 12.
31. Ibid., p. 29. See also M. Leach (ed.), *Funk and Wagnall's Standard Dictionary of Folklore, Mythology and Legend*, HarperCollins, San Francisco, 1984, p. 9.
32. Frazer, op. cit., p. 9.
33. S. N. Kramer, *The Sumerians: Their History, Culture and Character*, University of Chicago Press, 1963, p. 149.
34. Frazer, op. cit., pp. 9–10.
35. William Ellis, *Polynesian Researches*, London, 1832–6, I, p. 110 ff., quoted in ibid., pp. 9–10.
36. George Turner, *Samoa: a Hundred Years Ago and Long Before*, London, 1884, pp. 267 ff., quoted in Frazer, ibid., p. 10.

37. Ibid., p .10.
38. Ibid., p. 11, footnote 4.
39. John Z'Graggen, *And Thus Became Man and World*, Pentland Press, Durham, 1992, pp. 1–3.
40. Ibid., pp. 1–3.
41. For further reference, see Peter Lawrence, *Road Belong Cargo*, Melbourne Universtiy Press, 1967.
42. Z'Graggen, op. cit., pp. 7–8.
43. Frazer, op. cit., p. 10.
44. Ibid., p. 11.
45. W. Radloff, *Aus Sibirien*, Leipzig, 1884, i, p. 360, quoted in Frazer, ibid., p. 11.
46. Ibid., pp. 25–6.
47. The statistical proof of association is based on a simple 2 x 2 Chi-squared test (Table 10 in the text shows the high degree of association between the five motifs).
48. See Chapter 10. See also Charles Higham and Rachanie Thosarat, *Khok Phanom Di: Prehistoric Adaptation to the World's Richest Habitat*, Harcourt Brace College, Fort Worth, 1994, pp. 131–41.
49. The statistical proof of association is based on a simple 2 x 2 Chi-squared test (Table 11 in the text shows the high degree of association between the motifs).
50. Sir James Frazer, *Folklore in the Old Testament*, Macmillan, London, 1918, p. 19 ff.
51. Frazer, ibid., pp. 17–19 and also the following stories.
52. Van Over, op. cit., pp. 61–2.
53. Found in the island of Sulawesi (Celebes) in Indonesia.

Chapter 14: The Quest for Immortality

1. In contrast to most of Frazer's diffusional constructs, this section of his classic *Folklore in the Old Testament* is still quoted in folklore literature: see M. Leach (ed.), *Funk and Wagnall's Standard Dictionary of Folklore, Mythology, and Legend*, HarperCollins, San Francisco, 1984, p. 404.
2. See Sir James Frazer, *Folklore in the Old Testament*, Macmillan, London, 1918, p. 20, for further discussion.
3. Sir James Frazer, *Folklore in the Old Testament*, Macmillan, London, 1918, p. 51. Much of this chapter refers to Frazer's analysis of the Fall myth in his Chapter II (pp. 45–77) of the foregoing book. To avoid repetition and taking up space in the endnotes, I have reduced the references to his text.
4. Stephanie Dalley, *Myths from Mesopotamia: Creation, The Flood, Gilgamesh and Others*, Oxford University Press, 1991, pp. 47–8.

5. Frazer, op. cit., pp. 66–74.
6. Ibid., p. 50.
7. Ibid., p. 53.
8. Ibid., p. 53.
9. Ibid., p. 73.
10. Adapted from Dalley, op. cit., pp. 182–7.
11. See section under 'Adonis/Attis/Osiris' further on in this chapter.
12. Dalley, op. cit., p. 187.
13. Ibid., p. 328.
14. Ibid., p. 187.
15. Ibid., pp. 154–62.
16. Leach (ed.), op. cit., pp. 9–10.
17. Frazer, op. cit., pp. 68–74.
18. Frazer, op. cit., p. 66.
19. Ibid., p. 67.
20. As in 'Cush a son of Ham', in Genesis 10:6; see also Chapter 4.
21. Frazer, op. cit., p. 74.
22. Ibid., p. 75.
23. Ibid., p. 75.
24. Ibid., pp. 73–4.
25. Ibid., p. 72.
26. Dalley, op. cit., pp. 40–41.
27. Ibid., p. 183.
28. See Chapter 4 for more discussion.
29. Leach (ed.), op. cit., p. 844.
30. Ibid., p. 879.
31. Jan Knappert, *Pacific Mythology*, Aquarian, London, 1992, p. 321.
32. There is an assumption by ethnographers that this part of the story was Christianised. See Frazer, op. cit., p. 14.
33. Knappert, op. cit., p. 108.
34. Ibid., pp., 219 and 236.
35. Ibid., pp. 219–20.
36. Ibid., p. 319.
37. S. N. Kramer, *The Sumerians: Their History, Culture and Character*, University of Chicago Press, 1963, pp. 147–8.
38. Dalley, op. cit., p. 187.
39. Kramer, op, cit., p. 154.
40. See Dalley, op. cit., pp. 2–3, 47–9.
41. Kramer, op. cit., pp. 155–60.
42. See Dalley, op. cit., pp. 120–25, 47–9.
43. Kramer, op. cit., pp. 281–4.
44. Leach (ed.), op. cit., p. 495.

45. Ibid., p. 343.
46. Ibid., p. 343.
47. See Alexander Heidel, *The Babylonian Genesis,* University of Chicago Press, 1951, Chapter III, and Frazer op. cit., Chapter 1.
48. Kramer, op. cit., p. 293.
49. Ibid., p. 148.
50. Ibid., p. 148.
51. Ibid., p. 281.
52. Ibid., p. 282.
53. Dalley, op. cit., p. 119.
54. Ibid., p. 105.
55. Kramer, op. cit., p. 281.
56. Ibid., p. 281.
57. Heidel, op. cit., Chapter III.

Chapter 15: The Dying and Rising Tree God

1. See Chapters 6 and 7 for more discussion on genetics.
2. Waruno Mahdi, *Some Linguistic and Philological Data Towards a Chronology of Austronesian Activity in India and Sri Lanka*, Paper to the World Archaeological Congress – 3, New Delhi, 4–11 December, 1994. Proceedings in press (Routledge).
3. John Z'Graggen, *And Thus Became Man and World*, Pentland Press, Durham, 1992, pp. 86–7.
4. Z'Graggen, ibid., pp. 98–9.
5. See ibid., pp. 69–88.
6. Sir James Frazer, *Folklore in the Old Testament,* Macmillan, London 1918, p. 36.
7. See Dominique Collon, *Mesopotamian Cylinder Seals in the British Museum,* vol. 2, British Museum Press, London, 1986, in particular plate XX, no. 148, and plate XXI, no. 151, representing, respectively, a man growing from the roots of a tree, and Etana King of Kish being taken on the back of an eagle to the Heavens.
8. Helen Dennett (ed.), *Mak Bilong Sepik,* Wirui Press, Wewak, Papua New Guinea, 1975, p. 34.
9. Jan Knappert, *Pacific Mythology,* Aquarian Press, London, 1992, p. 50.
10. Ibid., p. 195.
11. This fertility rite is related to the worship of Attis; see also David Attenborough, *The First Eden*, Collins, London, 1987, pp. 105–6.
12. Z'Graggen, op. cit., pp. 23–6.
13. Ibid., p. 92.
14. Michael Jordan, *Myths of the World,* Kyle Cathie Ltd, London, 1995, pp. 224–5.

15. Knappert, op. cit., pp. 195–6.
16. The kind/unkind motif is classified as 'Q2' in Stith Thompson, *Motif Index of Folk Literature*, Indiana University Studies, vols 19–23, 1932–6.
17. The latter names were regarded by the ethnographer as a recent interpolation. See Frazer, op. cit., p. 13.
18. See Chapter 16 for more discussion on Kulabob and Manup and other warring brothers.
19. Glenys Köhnke, *Time Belong Tumbuna*, Robert Brown Assoc., Papua New Guinea, 1973, pp. 20–26.
20. Sir James Frazer, *The Golden Bough*, Macmillan, London, 1949, p. 96.
21. Z'Graggen, op. cit., pp. 26–9.
22. Ibid., pp. 29–32.
23. Personal communication with Dr Adrian Clynes.
24. Knappert, op. cit., pp. 44–5.
25. Stith Thompson was of the belief that the narrative of myths, as opposed to folklore as a whole, was specifically concerned with creation, and what happened 'in the beginning.'
26. See Chapter 16 for further details.
27. Jordan, op. cit., pp. 272–3.
28. Ibid., p. 235.
29. Ibid., pp. 235–7.
30. See previous chapter for more details.
31. S. N. Kramer, *The Sumerians*, University of Chicago Press, 1963, pp. 154–5.
32. Stephanie Dalley, *Myths from Mesopotamia: Creation, The Flood, Gilgamesh and Others*, Oxford University Press, 1991, p. 320.
33. Ibid., p. 154.
34. Frazer, *The Golden Bough*, op. cit., p. 326.
35. Jordan, op. cit., p. 82.
36. Leach (ed.), op., cit., p. 13.
37. Jordan, op. cit., pp. 241–2.
38. Knappert, op. cit., p. 194.
39. This is one of the main conclusions of Frazer's *The Golden Bough*.
40. Ibid., pp. 341–7.
41. Ibid., pp. 399–412.
42. Ibid., p. 342.
43. Personal observation.
44. Frazer, *The Golden Bough*, op. cit., pp. 320, 343.
45. See Jordan, op. cit., pp. 224–5.
46. See Dalley, op. cit., pp 39–153.
47. Frazer, *The Golden Bough*, op. cit., pp. 296–320.
48. See P. V. Glob, *The Bog People*, Paladin, London, 1972 for more information on this cult, especially plates between p. 80 and p. 81.

49. Personal observation.
50. Frazer, *The Golden Bough*, op. cit., pp. 354–5.
51. Ibid., p. 355.
52. Ibid., p. 224.
53. See previous chapter, and Sir James Frazer, *Folklore in the Old Testament*, Macmillan, London, 1918, p. 74.
54. Gittinger, Mattiebelle, 'A Study of the Ship Cloths of South Sumatra: Their Design and Usage', Thesis, Columbia Univ., New York, 1972, unpublished.
55. Nicole Revel-Macdonald, 'The Dayak of Borneo: On the Ancestors, the Living and the Dead', in Jean-Paul Barbier and Douglas Newton (eds.), *Islands and Ancestors: Indigenous Styles of Southeast Asia*, Thames and Hudson, London, 1988, pp. 70–73.
56. Ibid., p. 73.
57. See Raleigh Ferrell, *Taiwan Aboriginal Groups: Problems in Cultural and Linguistic Classification*, Institute of Ethnology Academia Sinica Monograph 17, Taipei, 1969.
58. Waruno Mahdi, *Some Linguistic and Philological Data Towards a Chronology of Austronesian Activity in India and Sri Lanka*, paper to the World Archaeology Congress – 3, New Delhi, 4–11 December 1994, p. 38. Proceedings in press (Routledge).
59. See A. W. Reed and Inez Hames, *Myths and Legends of Fiji and Rotuma Island*, Cambridge University Press, 1967, for further information.
60. *Ficus benjamina*, not to be confused with the Indian Banyan tree *Ficus benghalensis* or Bo tree *Ficus Religiosa*.
61. Mahdi, op. cit., pp. 36–40.
62. Josef Meier, 'Mythem und Sagen der Admiralitätsinsulaner', in Anthropos 2, 1907, pp. 646–67, 933–41.
63. For further discussion see Chapter 7.
64. Mahdi, op. cit., p. 44.
65. Ibid., p. 33.
66. In Jessica Rawson (ed.), *Mysteries of Ancient China: New Discoveries from the Early Dynasties*, British Museum Press, 1996, pp. 11–20, 60–84, 232–9.
67. Ibid., pp. 60–69.
68. Ibid.: illustration on pp. 19 and 75.
69. Ibid., p. 177.
70. Charles Higham, *The Bronze Age of Southeast Asia*, Cambridge University Press, 1996, pp. 148–59.
71. H. Ling Roth, *The Natives of Sarawak and British North Borneo*, Truslove and Hanson, London, 1896, p. 300.
72. Schärer (trans.), 'The Creation of the World According to the Ngaju', quoted in Revel-Macdonald, op. cit., p. 72.

73. Bernard Sellato, *Hornbill and Dragon – Naga dan Burung Enggang: Kalimantan – Sarawak – Sabah – Brunei,* Elf Aquitaine Indone'sie, Jakarta/Kuala Lumpur: Elf Aquitaine Malaysia, 1989.
74. Ph. O. L. Tobing, *The Structure of the Toba-Batak Belief in the High God,* South and Southeast Celebes Institute For Culture, Jakarta, 1994, pp. 21–5.
75. For all Toba-Batak references, see ibid.
76. As in the diver myths; for further discussion, see Chapter 11.
77. Tobing, op. cit., pp. 71–2.
78. Jordan, op. cit., pp. 70–1.
79. For example, see Revel-Macdonald, op. cit., pp. 66–85.
80. Augury is the reading of omens from a bird's intestines or flight.
81. Tobing, op. cit., pp. 167–9.
82. Jordan, op. cit., p. 290; Davidson op. cit., p. 27
83. Dalley, op. cit., p. 189.
84. Ibid., op. cit., p 189.
85. Samuel N. Kramer, *The Sumerians: Their History, Culture and Character,* Chicago University Press, 1963, p. 197; see also previous chapter.
86. See Chapter 12 for further details.
87. Kramer, op. cit., p. 200.
88. Ibid., pp. 198–205.
89. M. Leach (ed.), *Funk and Wagnall's Standard Dictionary of Folklore, Mythology and Legend,* HarperCollins, San Francisco, 1984, p. 500; see also Chapter 12.
90. Kramer, op. cit., p. 153.
91. Alexander Murray, *Who's Who in Mythology,* Bracken Books, London, 1994, p 210.
92. Leach (ed.), op. cit., p. 84.

Chapter 16: Cain and Abel

1. The 'express train to Polynesia' hypothesis was discussed in Chapters 3–7.
2. Sir James Frazer, *Folklore in The Old Testament,* Macmillan, London, 1918, pp. 78–9.
3. Genesis 4:3–5.
4. Personal communication with John Z'Graggen.
5. M. Leach (ed.), *Funk and Wagnall's Standard Dictionary of Folklore, Mythology and Legend,* HarperCollins, San Francisco, 1984, p. 180.
6. Ibid., p. 180.
7. Ibid., p. 993.
8. Michael Jordan, *Myths f the World,* Kyle Cathie Ltd, London, 1995, pp. 225–6.

9. Leach (ed.), op. cit., p. 993.
10. Jordan, op. cit., pp. 172–5
11. Genesis 25:19–34.
12. Samuel N. Kramer, *The Sumerians*, University of Chicago Press, 1963, pp. 218–20.
13. Ibid., pp. 218–22.
14. Ibid., p. 153.
15. See Chapter 10 and Chapter 15 for further details.
16. David Shulman, 'The Tamil Flood Myths and the Canam Legend', in Alan Dundes (ed.), *The Flood Myth,* University of California Press, 1988, p. 301.
17. Waruno Mahdi, *Some Linguistic and Philological Data Towards a Chronology of Austronesian Activity in India and Sri Lanka*, paper to the World Archaeology Congress – 3, New Delhi, 4–11 December 1994, p. 38. Proceedings in press (Routledge, London).
18. Jan Knappert, *Pacific Mythology*, The Aquarian Press, London, 1992, pp. 195–6; see also Chapter 15.
19. Glenys Köhnke, *Time Belong Tumbuna*, Robert Brown & Associates, Port Moresby, Papua New Guinea, 1973, p. 10.
20. S. J. Oppenheimer, D. R. Higgs, D. J. Weatherall, J. Barker, R. Spark, 'Preliminary Communication: α-Thalassaemia in Papua New Guinea', in *Lancet,* no. 1, 1984, pp. 424–6. For further discussion see Chapter 6.
21. Ibid., pp. 424–6; also S. J. Oppenheimer, F. D. Gibson, S. B. Macfarlane, J. B. Moody, C. Harrison, A. Spencer, O. Bunari, 'Iron Supplementation Increases Prevalence and Effects of Malaria: Report on Clinical Studies in Papua New Guinea', in *Trans. Roy. Soc. Trop. Med. Hyg.*, vol. 80, 1986, pp. 603–12; and J. Flint, A. V. S. Hill, D. K. Bowden, S. J. Oppenheimer *et al.*, 'High Frequencies of Alpha-Thalassaemia are the Result of Natural Selection by Malaria', in *Nature*, vol. 321 (6072), 1986, pp. 744–9. For further discussion see Chapter 6.
22. Non-Austronesian villages in Papua New Guinea tend not to have hereditary chieftains, but rather self-proposed elders/orators known as bigmen. Village decisions are made by a consensus of these bigmen.
23. Tok Pisin is Melanesian Pidgin; see Chapter 4 for more information.
24. See Peter Lawrence, *Road Belong Cargo*, Melbourne University Press, 1967, for the definitive work on the Madang Cargo Cults.
25. See ibid.
26. J. A. Z'Graggen (ed. S. A. Wurm), *The Languages of the Madang District, Papua New Guinea*, in *Pacific Linguistics*, series B, no. 41, Australia National University, 1975.
27. See Chapter 6 and 7 for further details.
28. Flint, op. cit., pp. 744–9.

29. See Thor Heyerdahl's enthralling account of his raft voyage in *The Kon Tiki Expedition*, George Allen and Unwin, London, first translated from the Norwegian in 1950.
30. John A. Z'Graggen, *And Thus Became Man and World*, Pentland Press, Durham, 1992, p. 2.
31. Romola McSwain, 'Kulbob and Manub: Past and Future Creator Deities of Karkar Island', in Alice Pomponio (ed.), *Children of Kilibob: Creation, Cosmos and Culture in North-East New Guinea*, in *Pacific Studies*, Special Issue, vol. 17, no. 4, Institute of Polynesian Studies, Laie, Hawai'i, 1994, p. 14.
32. Lawrence, op. cit., pp. 21–3; Z'Graggen, *And Thus Became Man and World*, op. cit., p. 2.
33. Z'Graggen, ibid., p. 2.
34. Ibid., pp. 10–11.
35. Lawrence, op. cit., pp. 21–3.
36. McSwain, op. cit., p. 15.
37. Lawrence, op. cit., p. 22.
38. McSwain, op. cit., p. 22.
39. Alice Pomponio, 'Namor's Odyssey: Mythical Metaphors and History in Siassi', in Pomponio (ed.), op. cit., *Pacific Studies*, vol. 17, no 4, Laie, Hawai'i, December 1994, p. 62.
40. Publication of Madang Province Museum, Papua New Guinea, Kranket version of story.
41. McSwain, op. cit., p. 16.
42. Ibid., p. 16.
43. Ibid., p. 16.
44. Ibid., p. 16.
45. Ibid, p. 17.
46. Lawrence, op. cit., p. 22.
47. Glenys Köhnke, op. cit., p. 60.
48. Ibid, p. 10.
49. McSwain op. cit., pp. 11–28.
50. Lawrence, op cit., p.22.
51. See Mikloucho-Maclay (trans. C. L. Sentinella), *New Guinea Diaries*, Kristen Pres, Madang, Papua New Guinea 1975, for further information.
52. Ibid, pp. 307–26.
53. See Lawrence, op. cit., pp. 222–74.
54. Alice Pomponio (ed.), *Children of Kilibob: Creation, Cosmos, and Culture in North-East New Guinea*, op. cit.
55. Thomas G. Harding and Stephen A. Clark, 'The Sio Story of Male', in Pomponio (ed.), op. cit., p. 33.
56. All six stages from Pomponio, op. cit., pp. 53–88.

57. See Chapters 11–15 for greater detail.
58. See Chapter 15 for more details.
59. See Chapter 5 for greater explanation.
60. W. R. Thurston, 'The Legend of Titikolo: An Anem Genesis', in Pomponio (ed.), op. cit., pp. 183–204.
61. See Naomi M. McPherson, 'The Legacy of Moro the Snake Man in Bariai', in Pomponio (ed.), pp. 153–82.
62. See Bronislaw Malinowski, *Magic, Science and Religion and Other Essays*, Souvenir Press, London, 1974, for further details.
63. See Pomponio, op. cit., pp. 75–80.
64. Ibid. pp. 53–91.
65. Ibid., pp. 53–91.
66. Ibid., p. 84.
67. Alice Pomponio *et al.* (eds.) 'Children of Kilibob; Creation, Cosmos and Culture in North-East New Guinea', in *Pacific Studies*, Special Issue vol, no. 4, Laie, Hawai'i, December 1994. (Note: some of the preceding tales are taken from this volume.)
68. Harding and Clark, op. cit., pp. 5–6.
69. The arguments for this are given in the first half of the book, from Chapters 2–7.
70. Sir James Frazer, *The Golden Bough*, MacMillan, London, 1949, p. 380.
71. McSwain, op. cit., p. 17.
72. See Chapter 5 for more discussion.
73. See Pamela Swadling, 'Changing Shorelines and Cultural Orientations in the Sepik-Ramu, Papua New Guinea: Implications for Pacific Prehistory', in *World Archaeology*, vol. 29, no. 1, 1997, pp. 1–14.
74. Helen Dennett, *Mak Bilong Sepik*, Wirui Press, Wewak, Papua New Guinea, 1975, pp. 76–7.
75. Swadling, op. cit., pp. 1–14.
76. Harding and Clark, op. cit., p. 7.
77. The genetics and physical anthropology of this region were discussed in detail in Chapter 6 and 7.
78. See John Martin, *Tonga Islands: William Mariner's Account*, Vava'u Press, Tonga, 1991.
79. Ibid., p. 306.
80. Ibid., p. 307.
81. See Chapters 8 and 11.
82. Martin, op. cit., pp. 306–7
83. Ibid., p. 300.
84. Ibid., p. 307.
85. Arthur Grimble, *A Pattern of Islands*, John Murray, London, 1960, pp. 32–46, 118 and 151.

86. Thomas G. Harding, David R. Counts and Alice Pomponio, in the *Introduction to Pomponio* (ed.), op. cit., p. 7; see also Chapter 15.
87. See Swadling, op. cit., pp. 1–14.

INDEX

Page numbers in bold indicate maps, tables and diagrams